THE
IMPERIAL
FAMILIES OF
ANCIENT
ROME

THE IMPERIAL FAMILIES OF ANCIENT ROME

MAXWELL CRAVEN

FONTHILL

Michael Grousinski
(1942–1977)

Front cover left: Marble bust of Domitian after the antique. (Bamfords Ltd)
Front cover right: Marble bust of Decius after the antique. (Bamfords Ltd)
Front cover centre: Obverse and reverse of gold solidus of Carausius I found in Derbyshire. (Derby Museum Trust)
Front cover bottom: Part of a view of the arch of Constantine, Rome, photographed in 1858 by Richard Keene. (M. Craven)

www.fonthillmedia.com
office@fonthillmedia.com

First published in the United Kingdom
and the United States of America 2020

British Library Cataloguing in Publication Data:
A catalogue record for this book is available from the British Library

Typeset in Minion Pro 10pt on 14pt
Printed and bound in England

CONTENTS

*

LIST OF GENEALOGICAL TABLES

Note: The tables do not always appear in the text in the order in which they are listed here.

A NOTE ON THE TABLES

An equal (=) sign indicates a marriage, differentiated by numbers where necessary, the marriage number pertaining to the person nearest to it.

Unbroken lines indicate certain or reasonably certain descent.

A broken line indicates that the connection is less certain or speculative.

A wiggly line from a heart symbol ♥ indicates that the parents were not married

A curving line either side of an (a) indicates an adoption.

A vertical line ending in an arrow indicates continuing descent, and where it is picked up in a later chart, the table number is given.

Square [brackets] indicate a missing name or element of one.

The chief element of a person's career follows the name in round (brackets) for identification.

Children are given in order of birth, males preceding females where known, except where clarity dictates otherwise.

All of the tables are followed by brief lives of the principal persons mentioned, arranged alphabetically by *nomen* (where one exists), or by first name.

TEXT CONVENTIONS

The more traditional BC/AD abbreviations for the eras before and after Christ are used throughout. Those emperors traditionally referred to as 'usurpers' are throughout termed 'imperial claimants'

*Emperors are recorded in **BOLD CAPITALS** of the appropriate colour: **BLACK** for acknowledged emperors and GREY for unsuccessful imperial claimants.*

Their names are given in their Latin form, with the form more commonly used in English following in brackets preceded by the words 'Known to history as…'.

The inclusion of so many imperial clasimants has induced me to allocate numbers of emperors who are not normally so accorded, but is seemed logical and helpful to clarity.

*Notes are at the bottom of the relevant page except in the **Brief Lives** sections of each **Table**, where the references are gathered together after each entry in square brackets.*

Brief Lives: *people with many names have their diacritical (usual) names <u>underlined</u> (where known).*

The present location and names of ancient places named in the text is given in brackets after their first mention where possible.

TIMELINE OF IMPERIAL SUCCESSION

Recognised emperors in **bold**; usurpers (imperial claimants) in *italic*.

Julian Dynasty 27BC-41

[Julius Caesar	49-44BC
Interregnum	44-27BC]
Augustus	27BC-14
Tiberius I	14-37
Caius (Caligula)	37-41

Claudian Dynasty 41-69

Claudius I	41-54
Camillus I	42
Britannicus	54
Nero	54-68
Macer	68
Galba I	68-69
[Piso/Galba II]	69
Otho	69
Vitellius	69

Flavian Dynasty 69-96

Vespasianus	69-79
Titus	79-81
Domitianus I	81-96
Saturninus I	89

Antonine Dynasty 96-192

Nerva	96-98
Traianus	98-117
Hadrianus	117-138
Antoninus I Pius	138-161
Titianus	145
Verus I	161-168
Marcus Aurelius	161-180
Avidius Cassius	175
Commodus	180-192
Pertinax	193
Julianus I	193
Niger	193-194
Albinus	195-197

Severan dynasty 192-234

Severus I	193-211
Geta	210-211
Antoninus II (Caracalla)	198-217
Macrinus	217-218
Diadumenianus	218
Antoninus III (Elagabalus)	218-222
Verus II	218-219
Maximus I	218-219
Alexander I	222-235
Taurinus	231
Seleucus	?231
Camillus II ?	233-234

Military Anarchy 234-268

Maximinus I Thrax	235-238
Magnus	235
Quartinus	?235/236
Gordianus I	238
Gordianus II	238
Pupienus Maximus II	238
Balbinus	238
Gordianus III	238-244
Sabinianus	240
Philippus I	244-249
Philippus II	247-249
Sponsianus	248
Silbannacus	?248
Pacatianus	248
Iotapianus	248-249
[Marcus I]	?249
Decius	249-251
Etruscus	251
Priscus	250
Valens I	251
Hostilianus	251
Gallus	251-253
Volusianus	251-253
Aemilianus I	253
Valerianus	253-260

Antoninus IV	253-254
Ingenuus	259
Gallienus	253-268
Saloninus	260
Regalianus	260-261
Macrianus	260-261
Quietus	260-261
Aemilianus II	261-262
Valens II	261-262
Memor	?262
[Antoninus V]	262
Aureolus	268

First Gallic Empire

Postumus 260-269	
Laelianus	269
Marius	269
Victorinus	269-271
Tetricus	271-274
Faustinus	274

Palmyrene Empire

[Maeonius]	267
Zenobia	271-272
Vaballathus	271-272
Antiochus	273

The Soldier Emperors 268-284

Claudius II Gothicus	268-270
Quintillus	270
Aurelianus	270-275
Domitianus II	271
Septimius	271
Urbanus	c.271
Tacitus	275-276
Florianus	276
Probus	276-282
Bonosus	280
Proculus	280
Saturninus II	280-281
Carus	282-283
Carinus	282-285
Numerianus	283-284
Julianus II	283-285
Julianus III	284

The Tetrarchy 284-363

Diocletianus	285-305
Carausius I	285-293
Amandus	286
Maximianus I	286-305, 308, 310
Allectus	293-296
Domtianus III	296-297
Achilleus	297-298
Eugenius I	303
Galerius Maximianus II	305-311

The House of Constantine

Constantius I	305-306
Constantinus I	306-337
Maxentius	306-312
Alexander II	308-310
Severus II	306-307
Licinius	308-324
Maximinus II	310-313
Valens III	316-317
Martinianus	324
Constantinus II	337-340
Constans I	337-350
Constantius II	337-361
Magnentius	350-353
Vetranio	350
Nepotianus	350
Decentius	353
Carausius II	c. 354-358
Silvanus	355
Genceris	358
Julianus IV	360-363

Vantentinian/Theodosian dynasty 363-95

Jovian	363-364
Valentinianus I 364-375	
Valens IV	364-378
Valentinus	368
Procopius	365-366
Marcellus I	366
Gratianus I	367-383
Firmus	c. 372-375
Valentinianus II	375-392
Theodosius I	379-395
Magnus Maximus III	383-388
Victor	384-388
Eugenius II	392-394

The West 395-423

Honorius	393-423

Second Gallic Empire 406-417

Marcus II	406-407
Gratianus II	407
Constantinus III	407-411
Constans II	410-411
Maximus IV	409-411, 419-421
Iovinus	411-413
Sebastianus	412-413

The West 423-465

Attalus	409-410, 414-415
Heraclianus	412-413
Constantius III	421
Johannes I	423-425
Valentinianus III	425-455
Petronius Maximus	455
Avitus	455-456
Marcellus II	457
Maiorianus	456-461
Severus III	461-465

Third Gallic Empire 461-486

Aegidius	461-465
Syagrius	465-486

The West 465-516

Interregnum I	465-467
Anthemius	467-472
Romanus I	470
Olybrius	472
Interregnum II	472-473

Glycerius	473-474
Julius Nepos	473-480
Masties	c. 477-516
Ovida	480-482
Romulus	475-476

The East 395-602

Arcadius	383-408
Theodosius II	402-450
Marcianus I	450-457
Leo I	457-474
Leo II	473-474
Zeno	474-491
Basiliscus	476-477
Marcus III	476-477
Marcianus II	479-480, 484
Leontius	484-488
Anastasius I	491-518
Burdunelus	496-497
Petrus	506
Iustinus I	518-527
Iustinianus I	527-565
Hypatius	532
Maximinus III	539
Stotzas I	541-545
Stotzas II	545-546
Guntharis	545-546
Iustinus II	565-578
Tiberius II	578-582
Mauricius	582-602
Theodosius III	590-602

115 Recognised emperors
 80 Imperial claimants
  4 Dubious

Total: 199

Map: The Roman Empire at its greatest extent: under Augustus (**black line**) under Trajan (**broken line**).

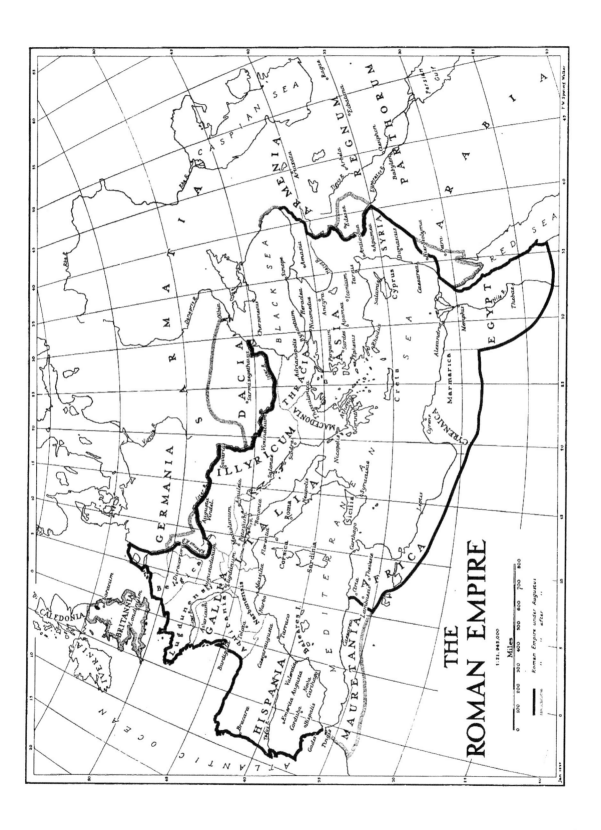

THE
ROMAN EMPIRE

1:21,043,000

Miles

0   100   200   300   400   500   600   700   800

Roman Empire under Augustus
   "   "   after   "

ACKNOWLEDGEMENTS

The author is extremely grateful to the many people who have helped with this book. It was originally inspired by a reading of Syme's *Roman Revolution* in my teens, in research, especially in the later Eastern Empire, by my late kinsman and friend HSH Prince Michael Grousinski, by John Rich and Peter Wiseman (then of the Universities of Nottingham and Leicester respectively) who helped me in the last stages of my higher education. My old friend Terry Westgate, latterly of the University of Westminster, helped me laboriously put much of the known senate onto Fourtran-four in 1970 to be processed at UCL in the hope that it would aid analysis, although the author shamefacedly has to admit that he did not, in the event, become anything like fully computer-literate, until about thirty years later.

Since then, much aid has been rendered by the staff of the libraries of the Universities of Nottingham and Leicester, by the librarians of both the Society for the Promotion of Roman Studies (who photocopied reams of learned articles over the years) and the Society of Antiquaries, and conversations with many friends whose knowledge and experience have been helpful and much valued. Also gratitude is owned to Colin Ridler of Thames & Hudson for initially encouraging the project and most importantly to Alan Sutton of Fonthill Media for agreeing to take it over. To my daughter Cornelia's predilection for doing her student work best in company, I can thank for keeping my nose to the grindstone during several stages of the book's compilation, as she strove to revise for GCSEs, A-levels, her degree and higher degree; to both Robert Innes-Smith and to my wife thanks go for endless proof-reading and much helpful criticism.

*

PREFACE

There have been innumerable books about the rulers of the Roman Empire, men who have exercised an almost unfathomable fascination for people of all eras since they first took power. Yet their families only loom large when they played an overt role in the conduct of affairs, in the raising and dispatch of rulers, as would-be contenders for the purple or, more commonly than is perhaps realised, as recipients a notable career boost on finding themselves related to a new emperor.

All emperors, of course, had families, and many had reasonably well documented ones, too. Furthermore, the last century and a half has seen an increase in the study of the careers of individual members of the various Roman elites from all possible sources (prosopography) with the result that it has become possible to reconstruct many imperial families much more accurately, comprehensively and comprehensibly than had been the case before. Nevertheless, any study of these imperial kin is often neglected as being peripheral to the grand sweep of imperial events, although close inspection of the evidence available rather suggests that they were perhaps rather more important than is sometimes assumed, even if such individuals were overshadowed by the more prominent participants in the dramas that constituted imperial history.

Imperial families were without doubt hotbeds of jealousy, faction and discontent, none more so than amongst the extended family of Augustus as chronicled by Suetonius, Dio, Tacitus and popularized by the late Rober Graves's *I Claudius*, which transferred so memorably onto television some decades ago. As this book attempts to show, even a remote connection with a previous dynasty or emperor could raise unwarranted expectations or provide the spur for a tilt at supreme power. Furthermore, the interconnection between imperial families can be seen to have been a great deal closer than has previously been widely appreciated; succession was very rarely a successful series of transitions from father to son, but was frequently one from kinsman to another, a phenomenon that was commoner than might at first appear.

Because the succession to supreme power in Rome was frequently achieved by assassination or *coup d'état*, the family of the dead or departing incumbent usually found it expedient to efface themselves in short order, however prominent. Yet in many cases, such families more often than not gradually re-established themselves, and one or more members having worn the purple was often the spur to the ambitions of surviving members or descendants. After all, the whole political *raison d'être* of a Roman politician was to accumulate *gravitas,* the honour embodied in a successful career, and the renown brought by the achievement of high or supreme office was ever an irresistible goal, both in the later Republic as later, throughout the Empire. That a pitch at supreme power, successful or otherwise, was likely to be perilous in the extreme did not matter. Not to take one's chance could be perceived as positively shaming by one's peers and family, and potential loss of face, then as now, can be a powerful incentive.

Thus there are several reasons that justify the reconstruction of Imperial families. Until the present era, nepotism was by no means a dirty word. It was universally accepted that by appointing friends or relations to important posts, one got people with whom one was familiar, in whom one had confidence, whose capabilities and limits one knew and, most importantly, people upon whose loyalty one could, with luck, rely. Only ancient China was sufficiently advanced at the same general period to recruit by competitive examination.

Another natural human instinct for those in supreme power, was a desire to retain it within the family. More, the most natural desire is to enable son to succeed father. Yet the Roman Empire did not admit of male primogeniture in a sovereign context, although Roman society certainly functioned along those lines in virtually every other field. This failure to establish a principle of primogeniture was down to the failure of the emperors of the first dynasty to produce any surviving male heirs. Both Caesar and Augustus died without legitimate male issue; in both cases only a daughter. Succession from the dictator to Augustus was by testamentary adoption which, although an acknowledged stratagem for maintaining the family line, was a less legally robust way of doing so compared with an adoption formalised during the lifetime of both parties. Thus Augustus' likely successor was always going to be someone from his wider family circle - M. Claudius Marcellus, or the sons of Agrippa, and ultimately Tiberius: multiple adoptive successions.

This trend continued throughout the duration of the first dynasty, thanks in part to the removal of potential male heirs through assassination; one thinks of poor Britannicus, Claudius' son, who managed to outlive his father, only to be eliminated too promptly to even be acclaimed emperor. It was not until the second dynasty and the death of Vespasian, that two sons successively succeeded their father. Thereafter it was not until the death of Marcus Aurelius 84 years later that another son succeeded, although, like Vespasian's younger son, that son was hardly a satisfactory ruler and his elimination led, inevitably, to a messy change of dynasty. The pattern repeated again in 212 when Septimius Severus died: two sons succeeded, but an unsatisfactory one survived, whose elimination led yet again to upheavals .

Yet when a successor was identified by a childless ruler and formally adopted: Hadrian by Trajan, Antoninus Pius by Hadrian, Marcus Aurelius and Lucius Verus by Antoninus Pius, the succession was often assured. In these, as in the selection of successors by Augustus, the role of the wider family was paramount. These wider kinsfolk were exactly what one would expect whilst emperors continued to be drawn from the senatorial class, for that echelon of Roman society was thoroughly inter-married at any epoch. One thing that the current study seems to establish is that there were connections between dynasties that are not at first apparent and which may well have played a positive part in deciding a man to sieze power. Galba was distantly connected by marriage to the Julio-Claudian dynasty and

Otho more immediately by marriage; the Flavians were connected to them, too, through Corbulo's wife Cassia Longina, and the ephemeral Didius Julianus – the man who 'bought' the empire – was almost certainly descended from Vespasian's elder brother Sabinus (see **Tables XVI & XXVII**), a fact he could not fail to have known and which may well have played a part in stoking his ambitions. Furthermore, despite Domitian's slaughter of Flavian kin, a male line from his nephew Clemens seems to have survived, and a descendant appears to have married Vibia Sabina, a daughter of Marcus Aurelius.

This pattern seems to have endured, too. Despite the dubious *Scriptores Historia Augusta* (HA, see below) claiming that there were descendants of the Emperor Probus living in its author's time – an assertion that normally would be firmly challenged if not entirely discarded – it has been plausibly argued that the aristocratic succession of Probi in the Anician family of the late Empire may well reflect just this.[1] Indeed, this family thereafter produced at least two emperors, Petronius Maximus and Olybrius, along with the ephemeral and reluctant imperial claimant Hypatius, not to mention marital links to all the emperors from Leo I to Maurice (died AD602). The *coup* of Maximus could well, once again, have been encouraged by the knowledge of an imperial lineage - indeed, in his case, a double imperial lineage, for it has also been argued that he was descended from Magnus Maximus, too.[2]

The close inter-relationship of the senatorial aristocracy, as reflected in the complex familial inter-relationships of successive imperial houses, ceased in the third century to have had much effect, once a succession of non-senatorial military strong men had taken supreme power. Yet after a few generations, even this coterie began to be ever more closely knitted together, so that the post-Constantinian emperors form a continuous loosely inter-related sequence, interspersed in the fifth century with senatorial candidates whose links, against all the odds, still harked back to the Antonine era. In other words, the rulers of the Roman Empire were a lot more dynastic than is usually appreciated. An understanding of their families helps us to appreciate this, as well as to explain the motives of the participants in a variety of events. As Anthony Birley has most pertinently written,

> 'The notion of hereditary succession was deeply embedded. Only the adoption of Trajan by Nerva had broken the pattern. Thereafter, kinship counted a great deal – hence Septimius Severus' adoption of the Antonine name for himself (as "son of the deified Marcus" and "brother of the deified Commodus") and for his elder son.'[3]

Hence, this work constitutes an attempt at a fairly exhaustive account, as accurate as possible, of the kin, descendants and wider families of the Emperors of Rome.[4] Ephemeral emperors – usurpers in common parlance, *tyranni* to Roman aurthors but here called

---

1. Drinkwater & Elton (1992) 111-121.
2. *Ibid*. See further below Tables 45, 47 & 58(a).
3. Birley (1987) 224.
4. Recent attempts to reconstruct imperial and other families relying on the succession of nomenclature (in the absence of any other evidence) have been taken into account and acknowledged, but have not been relied upon.

imperial claimants – are also included, because they too are part of the pattern, depite their lack of success. It is to be hoped that this might also point towards further investigation which, in the hands of experienced researchers, could identify new data and provide further answers to the causes of numerous unresolved chains of events and 'what ifs' with which imperial history abounds. The motives of those who stake all on power are often complex; confirming cases where such a bid was impelled by family piety may explain at least an aspect of such a motive.

To understand how this might work in the context of the emperors of Rome from the triumph of Julius Caesar in 49BC to the death (say) of Mauricius (commonly Maurice) in 602, it is necessary to provide, in the form of an introduction, how the system arose and how it worked.

*

INTRODUCTION

From Republic to Empire

The Roman Empire lasted an astonishingly long time, in the west five centuries, with almost a further millennium in the east, falling after two centuries of terminal decline to the Moslem Ottoman Turks in 1453. Only the Empires of China and Japan have matched it, and both its astonishing cohesion and its collapse in the west have been the subject of debate for a very long time and will continue to do so.

Anyone with even a routine knowledge of Roman history might, however, wonder how a monarchy could arise after the passage of more than five hundred years in which a republican form of government was informed by a belief that monarchy, specifically kingship, was in perpetuity politically unacceptable. The key, of course, was to disguise the new, imperial, monarchy of Julius Caesar and his heirs, as but an evolved form of republican government. Indeed the common people of Rome, by the first century BC were thoroughly disenchanted with the ruling oligarchy of the Republic in any case and tended to attach themselves with thoroughly un-republican enthusiasm to the dynasts who bestrode that last era: without them, men like Sulla, Pompey and Caesar would not have been able to sustain the success they had. Likewise, the foiling in 63 of a desperate bid for power by L. Sergius Catilina, an ambitious but compromised aristocrat, turned Cicero into something of a pariah not only with his peers, for ordering the execution of the senatorial malefactor and his immediate followers, but amongst the people as well, for nipping in the bud a movement that seemed to promise them much. Thus although a large proportion of the hereditary nobility – essentially the senate and those families entitled to run for senatorial office – deplored the rise of Caesar, and then Octavian (Augustus), there was no reluctance on the part of the people generally to welcome them and their programme to transform the state into a crowned republic.[5]

Yet, as time went on, the new institution matured gradually into a *bona fide* monarchy with absolute power. Imperceptibly the fictions of a continuing republic and its forms were cast aside or allowed to degenerate into honorifics in favour of a naked despotism. After the Year of the Four Emperors (AD 68), the succession of a new first citizen, the *princeps,*

---

5. As set out with brevity and clarity in Wiseman (2008) 204-205.

endowed with extensive and enduring powers,[6] was no longer prefaced by pro-republican murmurings amongst the grandees in the senate. After the next bloody concatenation, of six emperors in quick succession (AD 193-198), the formal lip service given to republican conventions began to be discarded more overtly; the chaos of the middle and later third century allowed Diocletian and his successors to bring about the emergence of the new autocracy, in which few of those conventions survived in any meaningful form, and from which new ones quickly arose.

I

Monarchy in Ancient Rome

Thus the Romans had an ambivalent relationship with monarchy. According to legend, Rome had been founded by descendants of Aeneas, Prince of Troy, who had initially settled at Alba Longa 20 miles south east of Rome in the Alban Hills, where he had founded a dynasty descending from his second marriage to Lavinia and where a succession of kings had reigned.[7] Traditionally this polity lasted from somewhere around 1160 until crushed by Roman King Tullus Hostilius around 650BC, when the city was largely levelled and the population (and especially its aristocracy) was absorbed by Rome itself. Recently, however, David Rohl, deploying the revised chronology he has established so pertinently for the early history of Egypt (dramatically confirmed by a variety of scientific tests on the fruits of the archaeology of that country), revised the beginning of the Alba saga to around 862 for Aeneas's arrival in Italy.[8] Indeed, some of the earliest versions of the foundation legend make Romulus the grandson of Aeneas, which would make such an hypothesis chronologically rather more convincing.[9]

Most of the ensuing dynasty of Alba Longa, the Silvii, would be elided in consequence: 19 kings to c. 753, some of them with repetitive and unlikely names, suggesting later gap-filling by early annalists. Thus the contention of both Naevius and Ennius that Romulus, Rome's first king, was a grandson or great-grandson of Aeneas, becomes somewhat more convincing than the filling by Livy of a three hundred year chronological chasm created by Eratosthenes' re-dating of the fall of Troy.[10] As Dr. Rohl's book attempts, not unconvincingly, to make clear, the characters made so memorable by Homer almost certainly lived a great deal closer to the time of the first chronicles, and their actual existence as players in early history becomes so much more likely, emphasising a recent revisionist trend in

---

6. The emperors were endowed by the senate with the power of tribunes of the people (which gave them a veto over any acts of the senate) and they numbered the years of their reigns by the number of times they had held this *tribunicia potestas*.
7. Aeneas' first wife Creusa is said to have borne him Illus, alleged ancestor of Julius Caesar's family.
8. Rohl (2007) Ch. XVIII. In the face of scholarly convention he was prepared to accept the reality of Aeneas.
9. Eratosthenes of Cyrene, quoted in Wiseman (2008) 49; Ennius in *ibid.* 240.
10. Livy, i. 3

the re-evaluation of oral and dark age history which currently seems to be tending the same way. Rohl's 'new chronology', because it begins with re-dating Egypt and thus goes onto re-adjust biblical time-frames, has met much academic resistance, both from fellow academics where were unwilling to accept such an all-embracing revision of accepted chronologies, and from others who, because the Bible is also a religious text, tend to treat what it tells us about history with far more cynicism than comparable texts.

Nevertheless, the net result of all this is to re-calibrate Roman history before Rome, as it were, but for Rome itself, its seven kings also span a much larger time-frame than seven ancient adult lives would reasonably be expected to do. Not one king reigned less than 24 years (Ancus Martius), two exceeded 40 and three 30: a most unlikely happenstance, especially in the ancient world. Other characters, probably outsiders such as Lars Porsenna who attacked Rome a year or two after the fall of the Tarquins and on their behalf but ended up making a chivalrous withdrawal, may actually have been part of the original regal sequence. Porsenna may not have been as chivalrous as Livy, for instance, makes him out to be.[11] Pliny the Elder quotes an ancient tradition that he imposed a treaty on the Romans banning the use of iron except for agriculture, which sounds like an imposed treaty of disarmament.[12]

Furthermore, some of the kings in the accepted canon have names which reflect families of much later origin whose prominence arose in various eras of the Republic. The exceptions, to whom we have little option but to attribute historicity, are Romulus, Titus Tatius and the Tarquins. But Ancus Martius (Marcii), Numa Pompilius, Tullus Hostilius and Servius Tullius all bear names prominent in the Republic. One branch of the Marcii, in the republic an *arriviste* plebeian dynasty, actually bore the additional name (*cognomen*) Rex, 'king', probably because in the third century BC one M. Marcius had been elected to the exclusively patrician priesthood of *Rex Sacrorum*; their ascendancy lasted from 357BC to the age of Augustus. The Hostilii were prominent from the late third century BC according to a tribune who, Cicero tells us, only made the connection with the king in 43. The Tullii (new man Cicero aside) were less prominent, but certainly held office in the second century BC and managed three consulships in the last century of the Republic.[13] The poets and historians who first recorded the Kings' names together were all Republican era writers: Q. Ennius, Cn. Naevius and Q. Fabius Pictor, men hardly unfamiliar with the illustrious careers of various contemporary Marcii and Hostilii. The other interesting point is that none of these families under the Republic were of patrician stock – descendants of the ancient nobility of Rome, and on which more anon – but plebeians, only let into the charmed circle of high public office after a revolutionary upheaval in 367BC. Detested though the institution of kingship was under the Republic, we can hardly reconstruct their Royal families; after all, some at least may not even have existed under the names by which we now know them!

---

11. Livy, ii. 10 ff.
12. Pliny, *Nat. Hist.* xxxiv. 139.
13. Wiseman (2008) 314-315.

II

The Republic

There is unlikely to have been a completely clean break between monarchy and republic in 509; life is just not like that. One only has to think of the post-Imperial French Third Republic, the constitution of which was framed around the expected restoration of a constitutional monarchy under Henri V, which operated until 1945 as a republic, but hampered by essentially monarchical institutions. The early 20th century German scholar Friedrich Münzer reflected this when he wrote:

> "The transition from the monarchy to the aristocratic state obviously took place more slowly and cautiously than roman tradition describes."[14]

The polity which gradually emerged was initially dominated by a compact group of ancient families effectively of princely status, the patricians, and amongst them the inclination to monarchy remained potent. Münzer, again, said of them:

> "A seat in the senate was claimed for a clan by its head for as long as he lived, and whoever held the first place, although no longer a king, was a prince; the real nature of his position, its indivisibility and tenure for life, was in sharp contrast to the [republican] principles of magistracy, those of collegiality and annual tenure....the *pontifex maximus* was also held by a single person and for life...and there was a strong hereditary bias in the succesion of *pontifices maximi* (leading priesthoods) of the republic."[15]

An hundred of these patricians were allegedly selected and summoned as a sort of perpetual council (*consilium*) by Romulus, and referred to themselves as conscript fathers (*patres conscripti*), a term used thereafter by members of this group, later the senate, to address their fellows.[16]

The Republic which gradually emerged from the ending of the monarchy was constantly evolving, expediency in the face of external threats and internal turbulence framing the institution as it was in its classic period. Some later existential threats, like the second Punic War, endowed the Roman state with a cohesion that carried it through the next generation or two. Yet the collapse of the Carthaginian attempt to subjugate Rome also endowed the Romans with the beginnings of an overseas empire, which required the prolongation of what had formerly been yearly magistrates' appointments and the need for permanent armed forces, instead of raising troops when necessity demanded, both straws in the wind foretelling future problems. Furthermore, these new territories – the provinces of

---

14. Münzer (1920) 345
15. Münzer *op.cit.* 346, 350, 351.
16. See Livy, 1, 8.7; Dionysius of Halicarnassus 2, 5 & 12; Tac. *Ann.* 2, 25.3.

Africa and Spain – gave the ruling oligarchy a taste for further expansion, which turned the acquisitions of successful self-defence into the prizes of more aggressive relationships with neighbouring peoples and polities. Philip of Macedon's support for Hannibal in 215 had drawn the Greek sphere into the orbit of Roman strategic thinking too, and alliances were sought with a coalition of Greek states to put a curb on Macedonia.

The result, over the following century was the taming of Philip of Macedon and Antiochus the Great of Syria, the sacking of Corinth and the acquisition of more new provinces: abroad, like Macedonia, and in Italy itself: Etruria, Picenum, Campania, Lucania and Bruttium. The peoples of Italy had generally been loyal to Rome in the conflict with Hannibal, but in 187 some 12,000 Latins (non-Roman Italians) were expelled from Rome and more were excluded through loss of civil rights a decade later. The resentments thus stirred up were to fester for decades, fuelled by later perceived slights, before breaking out into the conflict known as the Social War. Nevertheless a century after P. Cornelius Scipio Africanus defeated Hannibal at Zama in 202, Rome had become the supreme power in the Mediterranean.

The wealth accumulated from booty, the influx of defeated enemy personnel as slaves and the acquisition of large tracts of land all began to enrich the Roman citizenry, the senatorial ruling class in particular, and opened up further fissures in the cohesion of Roman society. There were retired soldiers competing for land with grand families seeking to expand their holdings and merchants keen to invest in land the wealth generated by the opportunities for the expansion of trade thus opened up.

Several Roman authors attributed the end of the harmonious relationship between the orders of Roman society to the murder of the reforming tribune Caius Sempronius Gracchus in 122. He sought to take any possible prejudicial interest in court cases away from the judges by giving them to the equestrian order to preside over. As it turned out, this was less than a good idea in practice, but, later Roman authors saw it as the single act that divided Roman Society, and ended a centuries-long era wherein differences were invariably settled by discussion and compromise. This is summed up by M. Terentius Varro who wrote:

> '[Gracchus] encouraged them to hope that they would pay no more than they wanted; he
> unfairly handed the jury-courts over to the equestrian order and made the citizen body two
> headed – the origin of the civil discords.'[17]

Like the murder of his brother Tiberius Gracchus eleven years before in not unrelated circumstances, C. Gracchus paid for his reforms with his life, and indeed other commentators, like Velleius or Appian, considered that first political assassination to be the tipping point after which Roman politics became increasingly polarised and violent.

Be that as it may, the obligations of kinship and more importantly of clientship – of patron and those dependent upon him – further increased the potential for the leaders

---

17. Quoted by T. P. Wiseman, *The Two Headed State: How Romans Explained Civil War* in Breed, Damon & Rossi (2010) 26

of the oligarchy which ruled the Republic from within the senate to exercise influence. There had always been men who achieved a form of primacy, in the war against Hannibal, Q. Fabius Maximus and P. Cornelius Scipio Africanus and two generations later Scipio Aemilianus and L. Aemilius Paullus.

> 'The idea that within the aristocracy one man, because he was the best and greatest, should lead the state was not...foreign to the Romans...it constituted on the contrary, the secret of power (*arcana imperii*) of the aristocracy, which the new man had either the courage or the naivety to reveal...'[18]

This belief, as the system of the republic's governance began to creak under the weight of conquest and expansion, began to find increasing expression in the wake of the upheavals consequent upon the attempt at reform by the two Sempronii Gracchi. They were, after all, members of a family positioned right at the powerful centre of the oligarchy. Yet the first man to put the aspiration to be greatest and best into practical expression was not an aristocrat at all: Caius Marius. The rise of this *arriviste* general to a decade of supreme power and the chaos of the Social War of 90-89 exacerbated the fault lines in the Roman polity to breaking point and ushered in the era of the dynasts, men who, like Marius, but also bolstered by familial connections and an inner circle of supporters, aspired to wield absolute power. They realised that unless the arcane structures of the republic were stretched and re-moulded, the cohesion of the state would be at risk, and each saw himself as the man to do it. It was from this series of attempts that the idea of a return to monarchy began to evolve.

The End of the Republic
This final era of the republic saw grandees like Sulla, Pompey, Crassus and finally Caesar vie for power, backed by enormous resources: soldiers, land for distribution, kinship alliances, dependent clients and the prestige of family and office. Amongst them lay the seeds of a return to monarchy but, given the Romans' visceral detestation of the concept, it was always going to be difficult and risky to make the transition. Yet the ordinary people generally seem to have despised the venality and dominance of the senate too, and the near century of violent upheavals and civil wars only helped to confirm such attitudes. What simpler folk have really wanted throughout the ages has been stability and order. This, the senatorial oligarchy looked to be increasingly unable to deliver, but a single strong man, given the right circumstances, could.

The complicating factor was that it was not always apparent to which of the senatorial strong men to hitch one's wagon: Caius Marius, Sulla, Catilina, Pompey, Crassus and Caesar. Some of these (and their associates) seemed obvious paladins for the cause of those outside the charmed circle of the aristocracy. Marius, a newcomer but a *protégé* of

---

18. Ronald T. Ridley in Münzer (1920) xxvi.

the powerful family of the Caecilii Metelli and consul for the first time in 107, reformed the army, enlisting landless citizens, in order to cure a manpower shortage. He also managed to pull off a string of military victories, ending a long war in Africa and later defeating an incursion of German tribes in the north of Italy, in the process of which he managed to be elected to five further consulships. This did not endear him to more than one powerful senatorial faction, which meant that when his landless legionaries were ready to return to civilian life, the provision of the usual plot of land for their continued support became an urgent problem. Marius at first relied upon various political firebrands, elected as tribunes of the people, to harass his senatorial enemies in to co-operating with his ideas for land-distribution. Then, as disorder spread, his vanity led him to accept an invitation of the senate to assert their authority and suppress, amidst much bloodshed, those to whom he had only shortly before been lending his support. Yet he got little thanks for his pains, and ended up an isolated figure.

When the Social War broke out in 90, against an alliance of Italian groupings, seeking to obtain a fair crack of the whip from Rome for unstinting support going back to the time of Hannibal, Marius was recalled as a commander, and once again proved his prowess in the field, but was bitterly disappointed when he was passed over for a prestigious command against King Mithridates of Pontus, turning once again to the reformist faction he had previously deserted to obtain redress. However, he was outmanoeuvred by his conservative rival, L. Cornelius Sulla, and despite cowing the senate into giving him a seventh consulship, died in office, leaving his cause in tatters and his supporters under threat of a proscription – a very drastic method of eliminating dissent through the publishing of a list of people deemed enemies of the state, with a bounty available to those who could claim to have liquidated them.

Competing Dynasts

From this point until the end of the republic, political life was dominated by a sequence of strong, ruthless politicians backed by plentiful funds to oil the wheels of faction, loyal elements of the military and complex networks of kin, clients (obligated supporters) and allies. Furthermore, they represented a small clique and although not all natural allies by any means, ended up being inter-related partly through happenstance and partly as a result of cementing political alliances by marriage. By the time Augustus had consolidated his rule in 27 BC, the dynastic grouping which had evolved from these three generations of machinations virtually amounted to a new rival faction to that welded together by Augustus himself. The interplay between the descendants of the dynasts and of Augustus and his family was to become a *leitmotiv* throughout the period of the Julio-Claudian dynasty, with fatal consequences for both. Yet it was the blood of these late republican strong men, not of Augustus or his kin, which could be found coursing through the veins of the family of Antoninus Pius and Marcus Aurelius.

Lucius Cornelius Sulla was a patrician of impeccable lineage, ruthless ambition, but of an obscure branch of his wider family (*gens*) with few resources. Yet in seeking to uphold the traditional values of the senatorial aristocracy, he inadvertently engineered a substantial advance towards the collapse of the Republic. He began his career as an officer under Marius, had a considerable diplomatic success with Parthia, and emerged from the Social War as the most successful commander, at the head of a loyal army. He was duly elected to the consulship for 88 and won the subsequent ballot to take up the command against king Mithridates in the east so coveted by his rival Marius, who got the tribunes to veto the appointment in his own interest.

Amid the violence which followed, Sulla was obliged to leave the City. He thereupon gathered the army that he had commanded in the Social War and marched on Rome, the lure of loot in any Mithridatic campaign and subsequent land allotments being his soldiers' spur. His subsequent capture of Rome, the driving out and death of Marius and the subsequent passage through the senate of a number of reactionary laws, was followed by success against Mithridates. But when his allotted period in office expired, he truculently refused to co-operate with his successors and then settled affairs in the east off his own bat, amassing large sums of money and concluding a treaty with Mithridates that let the King off the hook and stored up trouble for the future.

In his absence, control of the senate had lapsed into the hands of the opposition, leading to a second march on Rome by Sulla as soon as he landed back in Italy from the East, on this occasion supported by the young Cn. Pompeius and an opulent young senator called M. Licinius Crassus. This time he had to deal with some opposition, but by 82 he was back in power and persuaded the senate to revive in his favour the near-obsolete emergency magistracy called the dictatorship, anciently held for six months only, but which on this occasion was renewed until he assumed his second consulship in 80. He used the period finally to root out further opposition, to reform the republican constitution in favour of the vested interests of the members of the senatorial order and to improve the efficiency of the processes of government. This included suppressing the power of the peoples' tribunes to veto legislation. Whilst all this certainly strengthened the senate's hold on government, his unconstitutional methods set a pattern which was taken up with alacrity by those who sought to emulate his dominance. In 79 he unexpectedly retired and died the following year, leaving a serious power vacuum.

Cnaeus Pompeius (106-48BC), known as **Magnus** and more colloquially to us as Pompey, was from a newly ennobled family, and inherited huge personal influence and a substantial fortune from his father, who had been a successful commander and consul during the Social War. In 83 he raised an army from his father's troops and joined Sulla's second march on Rome, later purging Sicily and Africa for Sulla, receiving a triumph and acquiring his grandiose additional name (*cognomen*), Magnus. He went on to take commands to suppress rebels: Sulla's former associate Lepidus who, as consul in 78 tried to dismantle Sulla's settlement, and another, rather less eminent man, Quintus Sertorius, a follower of Marius who formed a break-away polity in Spain. This lasted until 73-72, when Pompeius returned, still backed by his faithful forces, having expanded his influence enormously by making extensive grants of citizenship in the wake of his victories in Spain. He received a triumph in 71 and the consulship in 70, despite not actually having entered the senate by holding a junior magistracy, as the conventional career path (*cursus honorum*) demanded. With his colleague Crassus, he pushed through alterations to the constitution, dismantling enough of Sulla's reforms to keep their popular base but not doing it drastically enough to alienate the conservative elements in the senate. Thereafter, and in defiance of the senate, he cleared the Mediterranean of pirates in 67, and the following year took command of an army against King Mithridates, who had become troublesome again, overthrowing the tiresome potentate and making a comprehensive settlement of the eastern provinces, entirely on his own initiative. He returned even richer than Crassus and with huge loyal followings in Italy, Spain and the east. He disbanded his army on his return, celebrated a third triumph but found his demand for land settlements for his troops refused by the senate, forcing him into an unholy alliance with Crassus and the ascendant Julius Caesar, then consul, forming the First Triumvirate (rule of three men) in 59, renewed in 56. He married Caesar's daughter Julia, but when she died in 54 and Crassus was killed in action against the Parthians at Carrhae in Syria the following year, the alliance fell apart. His differences with Caesar were exacerbated by the conservative faction in the senate in order to drive a wedge between them. The final straw was Caesar's extended command in Gaul, the success of which turned him into a real threat to Pompey's dominance. Pompey was thereby projected back into the arms of the conservative faction and, as the (highly irregular) sole consul, posed as the restorer of constitutional orthodoxy. On Caesar's return to Rome, backed by his victorious army in 49, Pompey was charged to oppose him, but made the fatal error of vacating Italy, thinking he could blockade Caesar into submission. He did not allow, however, for Caesar's strategic flair. Caesar crossed the Adriatic without delay and defeated Pompey at Pharsalus the following year. The dynast fled to Egypt where he was promptly murdered.

Marcus Licinius Crassus was an aristocratic senator of an old plebeian family which rose to prominence in the mid fourth century BC. His father having been killed in the massacres ordered by Marius in 87, he fled to Spain, raised a large force from his family's dependants there and in 83 returned to support Sulla's second march on Rome, and it was Sulla's subsequent proscriptions that enabled him vastly to increase his fortune from confiscated property. He differed from Pompey though in that his rise came about by going through the conventional hierarchy of magistracies, his praetorship being followed by the command of six legions against the rebel slave Spartacus, who had already defeated two consuls. In this he was notably successful, but had his thunder stolen by Pompey who, retuning triumphant from Spain, was able to round up and eliminate the defeated rump of the slave army before Crassus could mop up, and claimed far more credit for it than he deserved. The remainder of his career was one of continual rivalry with the influence of Pompey, from their uneasy joint consulship in 70 via several hiccoughs to their partnership in the First Triumvirate with Caesar. He secured a second consulship in 55 and as proconsul was entrusted with a command against the Parthian empire, an essential last throw of the dice to ensure glory, booty and much enhanced influence at the expense of Pompey.

His death in battle at Carrhae in Syria seems so inevitable and the battle so cut-and-dried in favour of the Parthians that one can only wonder if Pompey had not cynically tipped the Parthians off about Crassus's precise plans in case the millionaire dynast really *did* pull off a successful invasion of Parthia!

Caius Julius Caesar, the junior partner in the triumvirate, ultimately emerged dominant, defeating Pompey in 48 and establishing his own pre-eminence, albeit that it was cut short by the celebrated conspiracy of the Ides of March 44. Like Sulla, his was a patrician of a family long in obscurity. His path to power was well planned and as so often with men of destiny, was aided by a good measure of luck. He manoeuvred his way into being elected *pontifex maximus* (chief priest) in 63, the year he miraculously escaped being linked to the failed bid for power of a man of very similar background, Lucius Sergius Catilina. But Caesar's luck held, and Catiline's didn't. Caesar went on to enter the triumvirate and secure the special command in Gaul. His success there propelled him to make a successful bid for supreme power.

Yet, having secured power and defeated Pompey and his allies, it seemed as though he had trouble groping towards a more permanent formula by which to wield the power he had acquired. Like Sulla, he took the consulship and dictatorship, the latter eventually for life. Yet a perpetual dictatorship lacked subtlety and looked to ride roughshod over the sensitivities of those who aspired to retain the framework, at least, of the republic. Mark Antony's famous offer of a crown may have been an attempt to test the water for a move to revive the kingship, disguised as a light hearted charade played out during a festival. Light hearted or not, Caesar, sensing the mood on the occasion, was astute enough to make an elaborate show of rejecting the offer. Following which, a planned expedition to Parthia failed to prevent the execution of the republican plot which resulted in his assassination. Whether one can see Caesar as the first of the Emperors or last of the dynasts has been a moot point for very many years. The late Sir Ronald Syme was certain that the latter was the case, writing:

> "Victorious in the wars, Caesar proved unable to conciliate the upper order; and prominent members of his own party joined in the conspiracy of Cassius and Brutus. Isolated in an autocracy that had not been the goal of his political career, Caesar had ended as a splendid failure. Not the first of the Emperors but the last of the *nobiles*."[19]

As the first of a dynasty which lasted over a century from Caesar's coming to power, however, there is some logic in viewing him as the first true wielder of imperial power.

The Last Dynasts: the Second Triumvirate

Caesar's death left **Marcus Antonius** (known to history as Mark Antony) as incumbent consul, and the dictator's teenaged nephew, **Caius Octavius**, as his testamentarily adopted son and heir. In this work, Caesar is treated as effectively the first Emperor, but in truth,

---

19. Syme, *RP VI 330*; by *nobiles* was meant descendants of a family which had previously held the consulship.

as Syme said, the Republic lingered on in parallel with Caesar and his successors, because the political settlement established by Caesar was still evolving when he died. Thus the Republic nominally continued in the view of most commentators until the Dictator's adopted son finally evolved his own formula for exercising power in 27, although Syme reckoned Octavius's death in AD14 as the real end of the Republic.

These turbulent years, from 44 to 27, were years which were mainly occupied with civil strife and were dominated by new set of ambitious dynasts acting in an approximation of agreement. They were, once again, men in the mould of Marius, Sulla, and Caesar: Caesar's nephew and heir Octavius (testamentorily adopted, and thence styling himself **Caius Julius Caesar Octavianus**, for the time being referred to as Octavian), **Marcus Aemilius Lepidus** and Mark Antony, with a long-running sideshow orchestrated by Pompey's surviving son Sextus, self-restyled Magnus Pompeius Pius. As with the first triumvirate, they were all closely related. Indeed, the six men and Sex. Pompey, involved with the two triumvirates, were all locked together by bonds of marriage and kinship (see **Table I**). It is, in microcosm, the way Roman politics had worked for centuries and, indeed, always would.

These men, less Sextus Pompey, came together in 43 to form the Second Triumviate: Mark Antony, Caesar's colleague as consul in 44 and the man best positioned to take on Caesar's mantle, Octavianus as Caesar's teenaged heir, and Caesar's influential supporter Marcus Aemilius Lepidus. They soundly defeated Caesar's assassins - the upholders of the Republic - at the Battle of Philippi (Filippoi, Edonis, Eastern Macedonia) in 42.

Sextus Pompeius was the only element they had been unable to bring within their alliance. Although his father had been dead for six years, Sextus had inherited his extensive personal following, wealth, dependent clients and some of his mystique. In 44 he put himself at the head of an anti-Caesarian alliance in Spain, but the senate, still trying to act independently of the emerging power-brokers, appointed him to a far-reaching naval command. Once the Second Triumvirate had been formed, a proscription list was issued, as a result of which the distinguished career of the orator Cicero was summarily ended, amongst many others. Sextus Pompey was also on the list but, being in command of a considerable naval force, this was probably a mistake, as he remained a thorn in everyone's side for some time, establishing a base in Sicily and using his continuing support in Rome to force the three dynasts to make a treaty with him in 39. A year later, Octavian took it upon himself to repudiate this and begin an attempt to eliminate Pompeius, whom he characterised as a pirate, but in the event suffered several fairly humiliating setbacks before finally defeating him at Naulochus (Nauloco, Sicily) in 36.

The Triumvirate began to fall apart due to the shortcomings of its weakest element. This was Lepidus. He was stupendously rich, well-connected, like Caesar a patrician, and had managed to get himself elected to succeed Caesar as *Pontifex Maximus,* which endowed him with considerable additional prestige as well as the power to manipulate certain religious observances. His influence was enhanced by control of one Gallic and one Spanish province, assigned to him by Caesar, and boosted by inherited influence in a second Gallic province.

Lepidus received a second consulship in 42 (his first was in 46) but, after Philippi, with Antony and Octavian in control of all the eastern provinces previously controlled by the dictator's assassins, his influence was overshadowed. Later he was deprived of his provinces and assigned to Africa, leaving him bereft of armed forces. Yet he still managed to come to Octavian's aid against Sextus Pompey in 36 with 14 legions, and played a sufficiently pivotal a role in the 'pirate's' downfall to challenge Caesar's heir, but his troops promptly deserted to Octavian, leaving him all washed up, stripped of his powers and the Triumvirate at an end. Yet as *pontifex maximus* his person was sacrosanct, hence Octavian spared his life, and he remained in office until his death in 12BC, much to the irritation of his nemesis, who desperately wished to assume this prestigious office himself, especially as his adoptive father had held it for nearly 20 years.

TABLE I   SULLA & THE TWO TRIUMVIRATES

In this table all dates are BC unless indictated. Triumvirs in lower case bold and emperors in upper case bold.

TABLE I BRIEF LIVES

M'. Aemilius Lepidus
Not a notable figure, although he was proconsul of Africa in 21-22 [Syme AA 129-130].

M. Aemilus Lepidus
Patrician, consul 46, 42, triumvir 43-37 & 37-36, when stripped of his powers and obliged to retire from active politics; last non-imperial *Pontifex Maximus*, as which he succeeded **CAESAR** in 44. He died 12 having married Junia, the half-sister of Caesar's assassin, Q. Servilius Caepio Brutus (previously M. Junius Brutus).

Q. Aemilius Lepidus
Patrician assumed to have married Cornelia, daughter of Faustus Sulla and Pompey's daughter [Syme AA 112, 262/5; cf. PIR² A363].

M. Aemilius Scaurus,
Patrician consul 115, as a *protégé* of the Caecilii Metelli, whose conservative faction he eventually led; he celebrated a triumph as consul for victories in Liguria, later appointed leader of the senate (*princeps senatus*) died c. 91 [Syme (1939) 20, 31f.].

Antonia
The elder see **TABLE VI**

Antonia
The younger see **TABLE VI**

Iullus Antonius
See below, **TABLE VI Brief Lives**

M. Antonius (Mark Antony)
Raised to patrician rank by Caesar, of whom he was a close adherent, fighting under him in Gaul and in the first civil war. Grandson of an orator of the same name (consul in 99), he was tribune of the people in 49, consul in 44, triumvir 43-37 & 37-33. [See above].

L. Caecilius Metellus Delmaticus
Member of an old and grand plebeian family, consul in 119.

Faustus Cornelius Sulla
Patrician, quaestor in 54; an adherent of the 'brutal and vicious' demagogue T. Annius Milo Papianus. He joined Pompey in the first civil war in 49, and was killed as a prisoner three years later. [Gruen (1974) 192; Syme (1939) 39]

L. Cornelius Sulla Felix
See main text above

Julia (the elder)
Daughter and only surviving child of **AUGUSTUS** by Scribonia (usually known as Julia the elder), born 39BC, she married (i) in 25BC M. Claudius Marcellus [see **Table V**] but he died in 23BC leaving no issue. She married (ii) the next heir, Augustus's boyhood friend and chief support, M. Vipsanius Agrippa who died in. 12BC. She was involved in a scandal (or plot) in 2 which resulted in her conviction for adultery and exile to Pandateria (Ventotene, Pontic Is., Tyrrhenian Sea), where she died in AD27.

C. Julius CAESAR
See paragraph in main text, above. Although it was not possible to include the connection on **TABLE I**, Caesar's aunt was the wife of the missing dynast, **C. Marius**. M. Antonius was also descended from another branch of the family.

C. Julius Caesar Octavianus
Formerly C. Octavius and subsequently **Imperator Caesar Divi f. AUGUSTUS** [see below].

M. Licinius Crassus

See introduction. He lost his younger son, P. Licinius Crassus, acting as one of his commanders at Carrhae (Harran, Turkey). The issue of his elder son continued to flourish.

C. Octavius

The first senator of his family, from Velitrae (Velletri), the father of Augustus married Julia, sister of **CAESAR**; he was praetor in 61 and died 58. Augustus's mother was his second wife. He had another daughter by his first Ancharia [Syme (1939) 35, 36].

Pompeia

Daughter of Pompey, who re-married the patrician L. Cornelius Cinna (praetor 44) or more probably his namesake who was quaestor that year [Syme AA 30 & n. 124].

Cn. Pompeius Magnus (Pompey)

See introduction. He was a scion of a family which came to prominence in the mid- 2nd century BC and was born in 106. After his first marriage (to Antistia) his four subsequent marriages were entirely dictated by political and fiscal advantage. His second wife was to the patrician Aemilia, daughter of M. Aemilius Scaurus by Caecilia Metella which bound him firmly into the high nobility of the Republic; his next wife was Mucia, mother of his two sons; his fourth marriage was Julia the daughter of Caesar and his fifth wife was Cornelia, widow of Publius, the unfortunate son of Crassus the triumvir, and daughter of P. Cornelius Scipio, who was adopted into the Caecilii Metelli.

Sex. Pompeius, later Magnus Pompeius Pius

He was the younger son of Pompey by Mucia, and was born c. 70, see introduction above. He was presumably quaestor about 48, but after the death of his father went on the run. He was consul designate for 33 [Syme (1939).157, 231-2].

Scribonia

Wife of Sextus Pompey and sister of **AUGUSTUS'** second wife.

Scribonia

Married as his second wife, **AUGUSTUS** and mother of his only child, Julia. Sister of L. Scribonius Libo (below).

L. Scribonius Libo

Father-in-law of Sex. Pompeius, he was of a minor branch of a distinguished family, and was a partisan of his son-in-law. He eventually deserted him for the faction of Mark Antony, being rewarded with the consulship (in 34), after which he seems, very wisely, to have retired [Syme, AA 255f].

Ser. Sulpicius Galba

Otherwise **GALBA AUGUSTUS**, See **Section B Part II(a)** below

With Lepidus effectively neutralised, the Roman world was divided between Octavian and Antony. With both ambitious to complete the job of succeeding Caesar (who cast an inordinately long shadow) there was never going to be a permanent settlement and the tensions between the two gradually escalated. Like Caesar, Antony's hegemony of the eastern provinces brought him into contact – in both cases intimate – with the Queen of Egypt, Cleopatra VII.

But the marriage lost Antony much goodwill at Rome for he dumped his wife – crucially, Octavian's sister – for the exotic Egyptian. Fortunately, before the fall of Sextus Pompey and Lepidus, the Triumvirate had given itself another five-year term which enabled the two to rub along after a fashion, with Antony increasing his hold in the east – despite yet another unsuccessful attempt to invade Parthia. What with his position in the east becoming increasingly monarchical, and his three children by Cleopatra being assigned regal dominion over some his territorial acquisitions (or nominal ones), his powerbase in Rome was, by the end of the second five year triumviral agreement, looking decidedly uncertain.

Thus in 31, Octavianus moved against him, narrowly winning the naval battle of Actium, and six months later managing to conquer Egypt, precipitating the celebrated suicide of Antony and Cleopatra in 30. The young dynast promptly killed his adoptive half-brother Ptolemy IX Caesarion (Caesar's natural son by the Queen) whilst the queen's children by Antony he swept aside - at least one survived to have descendants – leaving him in unchallenged power over the entire Roman world. The stage was set at last for Empire.

III

Monarchy Revived: The Principate

Octavian in 30BC was, at 32, essentially an all-powerful private citizen, but in reality there was no one to challenge his supremacy. The question was how to establish himself in unchallenged supreme power on a basis of apparent legitimacy, and avoiding the mistakes of his predecessor, Caesar. He maintained power at first by being elected consul every year from 31 to 23, but in 27 he adopted a new style by which he wished to be known: Imperator Caesar Divi f[ili] Augustus - literally meaning 'Commander Caesar, son of the God (i.e. Caesar, deified by the senate in 42), the Revered One' - and handed all the powers that he had accumulated during the previous 16 years back to the senate, which, by carefully worked out and perfectly choreographed stage management, were duly returned to him, including the control of all the militarily important provinces for a period of ten years, and which was subsequently bestowed for life. These he controlled by choosing governors from the ranks of the senators who had already been consul or praetor (depending on the importance of the province) and leaving the senate to appoint governors to all the remaining ones. Egypt was a special case; the legacy of Antonius was that no senator was to enter it without his personal consent, and it was to be governed by a man of Equestrian rank – a member of the élite who was not a senator. Henceforth the Equestrian Order was to form the chief recruiting ground for the bureaucracy; it was not until 218 that a member of it was to become emperor.

Augustus henceforth styled himself *princeps* (from which we derive our word, prince). An absence whilst campaigning and a serious illness four years later modified this arrangement, and he thereafter doffed the consulship in favour of the grant of the power of veto of a tribune of the people (*tribunicia potestas*) for life. Further problems with this arrangement, led him to accept a further offer of consular power (*potestas*) – but not the office itself – in 19. Together these two gave him the authority to over-ride provincial governors where necessary and to veto legislation of which he did not approve. This set the pattern for the following two centuries. Gibbon said that Augustus established 'an absolute monarchy under the disguise of a commonwealth', which sums the matter up most succinctly.

Augustus also ensured that he treated the senate with respect, his personal prestige and ability to handle people with relative tact meaning that the settlement worked remarkably well. One inherent flaw was that without Augustus' sure-footed ability and authority to handle the Empire's ruling class – which was essential for the smooth running of what was now the greatest polity since the time of Alexander the Great – there were no guarantees of stability; another was the succession. About the former there was no mechanism that could effectively be devised, except the goodwill of senior advisors and senior ex-consuls, as members of the élite with the greatest prestige and experience. Concerning the latter, Augustus was set on keeping the principate (as we can henceforth for the time being call it) within his own family on the basis that it represented continuity from Caesar himself as the man who (notionally) initiated the new order, although there was still a belief, especially after his death in AD14, that any senator with the right connections, wealth and outstanding character could be regarded as *capax imperii*: qualified (or worthy) to rule. In practice, such men tended to live very precarious lives.

Sir Ronald Syme has convincingly argued that the true end of the Republic came with Augustus's death in AD14, for following that event elections were transferred from the peoples' assemblies to the senate in the September; power was henceforth contained within an aristocratic closed shop dominated by one person with, effectively, absolute power.[20] Augustus managed the delicate balancing act of appearing to allow the senate to govern whilst remaining in personal control to the general satisfaction of most participants. His successors rarely found that balance and, in failing to do so, exposed the true nature of the new monarchy, often with bloody consequences. Yet even tyrants need administrators and generals, so some kind of *modus vivendi* with the senate and non-senatorial élite had to be found, but this relationship tended to evolve patchily over succeeding reigns.

The successors of Augustus did not necessarily fill his shoes worthily. His family managed to succeed to the imperial purple four times, although that of Claudius (41-54) was not in any way planned, but the result of a rather muddled *coup,* whilst the succession of the latter's stepson Nero was manipulated to exclude Claudius' son Britannicus. Unfortunately, Nero was eventually deposed in a *coup* engineered by a distinguished senator and ex-consul, Galba, at the head of an army, causing the events that followed, wherein three more emperors succeeded each other in rapid succession, each as the result of an armed *coup*. It emerged that the family of Caesar and Augustus had lost its mystique; henceforth the gift of power clearly lay with the armed forces.

Yet the dynastic urge continued, and the upset of AD68-69 was followed by the Flavian dynasty, three emperors to 96, and then, after another succession hiccough, by Traianus (Trajan) whose successors form a coherent, but not father-to-son succession until the

---

20. Syme AA 51.

murder of Commodus, the only eldest son to succeed in the entire era, in 192. This also led to a vicious civil war between three contenders before one (Septimius Severus) emerged to stabilise the situation and ensure continuity. This pattern of a dynastic succession ending in an unsatisfactory *princeps,* deposed as the prelude to a civil war, began to gather momentum from the beginning of the third century, which in turn brought about another fundamental change in the governance of the Empire.

IV

Power Corrupts: The Dominate

This acceleration in disputed successions which began in the third century was not solely the result of a succession of unsatisfactory *principes.* After all, there had been a succession of holders of supreme power who could be singled out as entirely unsatisfactory – Caligula, Nero, Domitian, Commodus – but despite the massacres, dereliction of duty and other gross shortcomings, the empire continued to be efficiently administered, its armies competently led and its provinces adequately governed.

This situation began to break down in the third century. Not only were further unsatisfactory emperors followed by rivals, mainly unsuccessful usurpers (here called imperial claimants) to replace them, but these upheavals began to feed on themselves and become the norm, which bled the Empire of resources, manpower and had unfortunate effects on the smooth administration of the state. In 217-218, 238, 244, 249, 251, 260 and especially in 268-70, bouts of uncertainty, brought about by rival imperial claimants contesting power backed by armed might, led to general uncertainty. This poisonous breakdown coincided with a period of economic uncertainty (which it exacerbated considerably), leading to serious inflation and the progressive debasement of the currency. This happened against a background of outbreaks of insecurity on the borders of the Empire. Armies which were supposed to be defending vulnerable borders, like the Danube, or the Rhine, were all too frequently being withdrawn to pursue the personal ambitions of commanders, raised, sometimes without even their own connivance, to the purple, leaving the empire in peril of incursions of barbarians; a particularly nasty one occurred in Gaul in the 260s which coincided with the rule there of an imperial claimant to the Empire, forging from 260 a completely separate polity in north west Europe which endured with reasonable success for fourteen years.

At first, these imperial claimants were like the emperors they aimed to replace, generally senators, generals or provincial governors and, on succeeding in their endeavours, would hasten to the senate for recognition and the grant of the proconsular and tribunician power that would bestow legitimacy upon them. In this work, the successful ones are highlighted in **BOLD** and upper case. Those that failed to obtain recognition, either from an emperor already holding power as colleague, or from the senate, are here called imperial claimants and are set out below in GREY and upper case. Sometimes, rival imperial claimants would put the senators in a quandary, not knowing who to favour and sure that the man they did not favour, if ultimately successful, would ensure that examples were made of the leading backers of the rival. Yet there were other men, not in the senate, who were prepared to bid for power. Macrinus, who successfully took power on the murder of Caracalla in 217 was a senior military officer of equestrian rank, ideally placed to assume the purple, backed by loyal troops, but was not a senator. Although his rule failed to endure, it established a second principle of empire: that it was essential to be a senior, competent and successful military commander to make a bid for the purple, but it was no longer essential to be a senator. Suddenly the complexion of power looked as if it might change.

This change was accelerated after the death of the Emperor Gallienus – a member, as will be demonstrated below, of a long established senatorial family – in 268. Entrusted by his father and predecessor, Valerianus, with the defence of the west, he had responded to lightning cross-border raids on the part of various barbarian tribes by the creation of a mobile mounted field army, commanded by equestrian career soldiers. This excluded senators from their traditional role as military commanders, which caused deep resentment, for it interrupted at a stroke the normal career path of a member of a senatorial family from junior magistrate to consul via an accepted succession of military posts and commands, through provincial governorships and commissions. Gallienus's idea was also to make it much more difficult for such men to become imperial claimants. To this end, the Severan dynasty had already sub-divided military provinces to make them smaller, in turn to ensure that each governor had far fewer troops at his disposal, again in a bid to make a bid for power more difficult.

This new order of military men was also favoured for provincial governorships – certainly those reserved to the patronage of the Emperor, which mainly kept the senators out of even this aspect of their traditional career path. Even junior officer posts – the military tribunate – were suddenly closed to senators and restricted to equestrians. Yet even that order of Roman Society was undergoing fundamental changes, initiated by the decree of the Emperor Caracalla extending Roman citizenship to all free-born citizens of the Empire. Instead of a property qualification, the rank could be attained merely through a commission in the army, for instance, so that the make-up of the equestrian order quickly became intermixed with soldiers and ex-soldiers from all corners of the Roman world.

Suddenly therefore, the traditional élite which had run Rome since the Kings, the senatorial aristocracy, found themselves side-lined by a rival élite who were acquiring power by throwing back invaders and helping to break the vicious circle of decline. Consequently, by the time Gallienus was finally murdered by a group of these new professional equestrian senior commanders outside Milan, it was one of them, Marcus Aurelius Claudius, who succeeded him as Claudius II. Apart from a few fairly ephemeral exceptions, it was to be more than a century before another senator was to take power as emperor after that.

It was these non-senatorial Emperors, almost all from emergent families mainly of non-Roman stock, whose scant regard for the niceties of respect for the *amour propre* of the senate and military imperatives, led to a much greater concentration of power in imperial hands.

Power was exercised as situations demanded, whether proactively or reactively, and the last vestiges of republican conventions faded. Some magistracies fell into desuetude, the patrician élite became virtually obsolete (although as we have noted, descendants of a few patrician families continued to sit in the senate) and a number of religious traditions and groupings seem to sink without trace. This, then was the 'dominate' where the emperor became a true monarch.

V

The New Empire: Naked Autocracy

The new class of professional soldiers from amongst whose ranks most emperors subsequent to Gallienus came stopped the rot to some extent. Aurelian ended two break-away empires: that of Palmyra in 272 and the Gallic one in 274, before falling victim to the inevitable *coup*. After a brief pause, he was succeeded by Probus, who built on Aurelian's good work and secured the boundaries of the state before falling victim to yet another *coup*, which resulted in the condemnation of his memory by a cowed senate although, in the longer term, his name lived on and his reputation amongst the senatorial nobility rapidly recovered. Under his short-lived successors however, the ills which had manifested themselves so dramatically in the reign of Gallienus recurred, and the successful usurpation of another successful soldier, Diocletian, in 284 marked a turning point, although at the time this was unlikely to have been apparent.

Diocletian swiftly abolished the Praetorian Prefecture, the holders of which post had been effectively kingmakers in the years of chaos (and to some extent before). This was done as part of a far-reaching military re-organisation, wherein other powerful posts came into being instead and to which the sort of officer who had become praetorian prefect could aspire. He was also was able to consolidate his rule by taking a colleague, Maximianus, in 286. Following that, each emperor, responsible for the eastern and western halves of the empire respectively, in 293 appointed a deputy each, thus making perfectly clear that not only was the empire being ruled by partners in harmony (making them much less vulnerable to assassination), but there were designated heirs waiting in the wings. This system of a rule by four is called the Tetrarchy. Furthermore, Diocletian decreed that after 20 years, the two senior emperors would retire in favour of their deputies who would in turn appoint two assistants of their own.

Thereafter, a concerted attempt was made to stabilise the economy by re-valuing the coinage and fixing prices. The flight from the land and the difficulty of getting people to run town councils, caused by the complete collapse of the currency, was misguidedly tackled by making the post in which one found oneself at the time the necessary decree was promulgated thenceforth hereditary. The number of the provinces was increased and their sizes further reduced, again to deter *coups*; they were further grouped into dioceses under a governor general initially called a *vicarius* but who by the fifth century had become styled praetorian prefect, although the responsibilities in no way resembled those of the old prefects.

None of this could be achieved by the adherence to quasi republican niceties nor by garnering consent. It was imposed top-down, and the reign of Diocletian marks the final shift from overt monarchy to naked autocracy.

The system Diocletian evolved collapsed, like the Soviet Empire, for failing to take account of the competitive side of human nature. Diolcletian retired in 305 after just over 20 years sure enough, but his colleague Maximian resented forced retirement and staged a come-back through his son, whom Constantine the Great – himself the son of a deputy emperor, who had succeeded his father by acclamation (in York) in defiance of the tetrarchic system – defeated in 312 at the Battle of the Milvian Bridge. It took Constantine until 324 to eliminate finally the last remnants of the tetrarchy and re-establish sole personal rule. His triumph in this respect cemented the autocracy which the Roman Imperial system had by this time most assuredly had become.

Constantine also reformed the currency again, much more effectively than had Diocletian, restoring the money economy as a fully functional system, although he extended the compulsory hereditary principle from agriculture to trade. He reformed the civil administration, opening, after three generations, most posts to senators once again and re-defined the troublesome and over-powerful post of Praetorian Prefect. He centralised the élite core of the mobile army created by Gallienus to act as a 'fire-fighting' unit of considerable potency to be deployed as required to re-inforce border units (*limitanei*) when trouble broke out on the frontiers. He also divided the position of supreme army commander, called master of the soldiers (*magister militum*), into two, one for the increasingly important cavalry and another to command the infantry. Finally, Constantine converted to and recognised Christianity as having parity with the state paganism which had pertained since the days of the Kings, laying the ground for another change in the tenor of Imperial government.

It was this system, the Constantinian settlement, increasingly tempered by the ever-increasing influence of the Christian Church, which endured throughout the remainder of the period under review. It worked tolerably well for nearly a century - usurpations were generally fewer and rarely successful, prosperity returned and the empire became again proactive. Unfortunately, as the period of barbarian migrations began, the idea of dividing the empire as adumbrated by Diocletian and the Tetrarchy was again brought to the fore, and with the death of Theodosius I in 395, the east and west were divided between his two sons, neither of whom were truly fit to rule in the hands-on way their father and his predecessors had practised. In the east, this led to an increase in instability, but in the west it began a long process of dissolution. In both parts of the empire, the emperor henceforth would create laws (by decree or confirmation) and give advice to senior office holders through rulings (collected together by both Theodosius II and Justinianus I to form the basis for the law of the Empire), to take advice and make appointments. This led to the formation of a distinct permanent court around the person of the emperor, very few of whom were ever again to take the field in person.

Once the dynasty of Theodosius had ended in 455, the last few western emperors were again selected from the senatorial aristocracy. But the power vacuum created by the inadequacy of Honorius, the son of Theodosius I, led to the gradual development of a series of highly capable and determined Masters of the Soldiers, whose power and influence can only be described almost as surrogate emperors, who actually governed, leaving the emperor, isolated in his glittering and introspective court. These men, like Stilicho, Aëtius and Ricimer in the west, were all of barbarian descent to some degree, and in due course decided upon the emperor in whose name they were prepared to govern, very much in the mould of the Tokugawa Shoguns in Japan after 1603, over a thousand years later. But whereas the Tokugawa never moved to end the imperial succession (indeed, surviving through fourteen successions to resign their authority to a re-invigorated emperor in 1868), these western imperial warlords eventually took over, but as kings of their own peoples, not as emperors. In doing so, they governed technically as viceroys in the name of the remaining emperor in Constantinople, who was sufficiently far away to cause them few problems – at least, that is, until one, Justinianus I, decided to turn back the clock. In his name Vandal Africa, part of Spain and all of Italy were reconquered, but the latter at a terrible material cost. After decades of warfare, the towns were deserted, the fields untilled, the aristocracy decimated and the senate, after a century of existence under alien Kings, finally went into eclipse.

The broad sweep of the decline and fall of empire is complex, bloody and in many ways fascinating. The chronicling of the imperial families and their members can only a be sideshow, but a sideshow with its own relevance, momentum and fascination.

VI

Institutions and Élites
To record the members of Imperial families is necessarily to be moderately *au fait* with the ramifications of the ruling elements of Imperial Rome which evolved as part of a continuing process.

Patricians and Plebeians
Originally the common Roman people were the *plebs* – the plebeians – separate from which was an elite group called the patricians. This élite was said to have been derived from a select group (some said an hundred men), which included elements of the nobility of the Trojan-founded city of Alba Longa, selected by Romulus to provide him with advice, support and companionship. Amongst these were the ancestors of Julius Caesar, the Julii, claiming descent from Iullus son of Aenaeas and his Latin wife, Lavinia, who had allegedly founded Alba Longa.[21] Virgil, of course, worked the whole saga into the incomparable *Aeneid* as a celebration of the princely status of the family of the new ruler, Augustus.

---

21. Wiseman (2004) 19-20

Something of the early history of this group can be discerned in the administrative divisions that made up the extra-urban territory of Rome. This land was divided up into geographical districts each called *tribus*, a word which gives us one with (for us) a quite different meaning: 'tribe', which we understand as a cohesive group of families, probably allied by kinship. Here it means a topographical unit, but with its own kind of internal cohesion, for each and every Roman citizen was enrolled in one and included it in his formal nomenclature. The city itself contained four of these 'tribes' and the surrounding countryside sixteen, making a total of 20. The four urban tribes were all named from topographical features: Collina, Esquilina, Palatina and Quirina, whereas the rustic tribes all bore the family names, thought to have been those of the dominant landowner in that part in the days of the Kings, when the system evolved (supposedly under Servius Tullius). The rural tribes' names, in alphabetical order, were: Aemilia, Camilia, Claudia, Cornelia, Fabia, Galeria, Horatia, Lemonia, Menenia, Papiria, Pollia, Pupinia, Romilia, Sergia, Voltinia and Voturia. Not all of the family names endured as leading patricians under the republic, like the Galerii and the Camilii, others vanished without a trace, like the Lemonii, Pollii and Voltinii whilst the Horatii, Menenii and Romulii fade out fairly early in the history of the republic, and in any case, their names are only known from lists of magistrates whose antiquity is now regarded as suspect. Nevertheless, their existence as *tribus* names confirms their whilom existence and all boasted legendary ancestors reaching back into the mists of time. Nevertheless, an abbreviated version of the name of the tribe persisted as an official element of a Roman citizen's nomenclature until the third century AD and longer amongst the aristocracy.

The continuity of an élite from the earliest times, whether patricians or merely a dominant clique, has to some extent been confirmed by archaeology. John R. Patterson has written:

> On the slopes of the Palatine [Hill] Carandini excavated a series of aristocratic houses....four of which, each laid out around a central atrium, [which] dated back to the late sixth century BC, themselves built on top of a line of a wall which has been identified with that of Romulus' first city. The longevity of these regal period houses (associated by the excavators with the kings themselves, and with the aristocratic families close to them) is very striking and suggestive of continuity within the leading families of Rome.[22]

The people were thus governed by this aristocratic clique, members of which were eligible to sit in the senate. Those who were not members of senatorial families, but still of superior status were the *equites* and this rank was also that held by members of senatorial families before they entered the senate. An *eques* (pural *equites*) was a mounted soldier, usually called a knight in English, but latterly a generic term referring to the business class from which were drawn administrators and, under the earlier Empire, middle ranking soldiers and

---

22. Patterson (2010) 222. Count Andrea Carandini is perhaps the doyen of Archaeologist working on the origins of the City.

some governors of minor provinces. The commercial dominance of the *equites* stemmed from a law of 218BC preventing senators from engaging in business. Given sufficient accumulated wealth, members of this equestrian order had the opportunity to enter the senate by offering their sons as candidates for minor magistracies. Their numbers were swollen as the empire expanded by the granting of citizenship to the leading citizens of the provincial towns of the Empire by the conquerors or governors of their provinces. By the end of the third century AD, they were the dominant class of the Empire both administratively and militarily, although in the fourth century, the *equites* had ceased to exist in practical terms. By that era, officials were granted titles of rank, those applicable to those whose status would in former years have been equestrian, bore those of *vir perfectissimus, vir egregius* and *vir eminentissimus*. In contrast, senators, from the second century styled *vir clarissimus*, by the fifth century were styled *vir illustris* (or *inlustris* – the two were interchangeable).[23]

The Senate

Originally the patricians formed a select group, a proto-assembly, from which the kings and later the early republic drew magistrates, and who were advised by it. The number of senators rose to 300 with the early republic, and the patricians, who are then supposed to have comprised it, eventually formed two distinct groups. One – a sort of super-élite – consisted of five clans: the Aemilii, Claudii, Cornelii, Fabii and Valerii, called the *gentes maiores* (greater clans). The remaining identifiable family groupings, the *gentes minores* (minor clans) numbered around 45 or 50. The primacy of the *gentes maiores* however, persisted long after the plebeian families were admitted into the senate and the various magistracies. This was especially true of a small number of religious offices, and there was of course a strong hereditary bias throughout the entire system of republican government.

Sulla doubled the senate's membership in 80BC. Not to be outdone, Caesar put the number up to 900, at which level it remained, rising *ad hoc* during the two decades following Caesar's assassination to about 1000, until Augustus purged it and reduced the number once again to 600.[24] He added a property qualification of 1,000,000 sesterces (HS); birth would no longer be quite enough. Strangely, as the power and influence of the senate diminished, its numbers again crept up. By the time Constantine the Great had established Constantinople, he endowed it with another, separate, senate, at which time both it and the original one in Rome, had numbers approaching 2,000. Some exceedingly opulent families had members in both senates but the vast bulk of senators by this time and certainly later were senior civil and military officials upon whose retirement senatorial rank had been bestowed by the Emperor, or which had become an automatic perquisite of having held office.

Once the republic had come into existence, the *plebs* began to demand access to the senate and a share in power via the various magistracies. They felt that they were second class citizens, especially as they were prohibited to inter-marry with patricians until 445.

---

23. Both spellings are used where applicable below, depending on contemporary usage.
24. Wiseman (1971) 6-8.

Yet four years before, they had managed to obtain recognition for the creation of a board of ten 'tribunes of the people' with the power of veto over senatorial laws, responsible to the *concilium plebis,* to protect the plebeians from the patricians, who alone then held public office. Nevertheless, it took the *plebs,* through numerous upheavals and false starts – well documented by later historians, but probably largely lacking authenticity – until 367 until members of plebeian families were finally allowed to enter the senate and share in the holding of magistracies.

Even then, the patricians reserved a number of important privileges, chief of which was that one of the two consuls in any given year was to be a patrician, The system that worked tolerably well until the last era of the republic. Yet, once power had been shared with the plebeians, the patricians thereafter exercised an ever-decreasing influence, at least until the first century BC, when the dynasts, who included the patricians Sulla, Caesar, Octavianus and Lepidus, allowed this élite within an élite to flourish once again. Indeed, both Caesar and Augustus favoured the old patrician families, even the most obscure, promoting them and guaranteeing their loyalty. Both also raised plebeian families (some newly emerged, if high-achieving) to patrician status to replace the extinctions and losses caused by the civil wars and proscriptions. This adlection of new families into the ranks of the patricians was something which a number of the Emperors also favoured, and the first emperor who was not a member of a patrician family (whether an ancient one or one of more recent creation) was Pertinax in 193. The entire system was eclipsed in the later 3rd century and abolished by Diocletian. When the rank of patrician finally re-appeared under Constantine, it had become an honorific granted for life only to extremely eminent generals, administrators and courtiers. It was granted relatively sparingly, so it still acquired its own cachet, but as a term it thereafter had a completely different meaning from its preceding incarnation. Furthermore, although a number of senatorial families in the 4th and 5th centuries were demonstrably descended from family made patrician before the end of the second century AD, there is never any mention in the sources of the time of this formerly exalted status.

In the last era of the Western Empire, the senate had again become something much closer to its origins, with responsibility of Rome itself, but still full of members of very distinguished families who had estates scattered across the empire and who wielded enormous influence both at court and elsewhere. With the diminishing authority of the emperors in the West, their influence increased and they once again supplied provincial governors and army commanders. With the diminution of the non-Imperial consulship and its extinction under Justianian I, the rank of *exconsul* was nevertheless preserved and granted to distinguished members of the élite.[25] One important aspect of recent studies is that an unexpectedly extensive degree of continuity in the senatorial aristocracy between the Principate and the later empire, although some of the most recent work has been perhaps a shade too speculative to have become widely accepted.[26]

---

25. Brown (1984) 131, 137.
26. Arnheim (1972) *passim*. Settipani (2001) *passim*.

Career Opportunities

Political progress in the Republic and early Empire involved holding a series of magistracies of ascending importance, and a senator, whether patrician or plebeian, strove to stay the course until he reached the supreme office of consul. This progression through the magistracies of ascending importance was held crucial to the establishment of a man's standing (*dignitas*) and position in relation to his peers.

Anciently, the **consulship** (abbreviated cos. + relevant year), a collegiate institution of two men elected annually and holding supreme power, was believed to have been instituted on the fall of the monarchy, the first two being Lucius Junius Brutus and Lucius Tarquinius Collatinus. However, modern scholarship considers much of the consular and related lists (*fasti*) prior to 366 to be something which evolved in the last decades of the Republic, being refined in the early years of the Emperor Augustus and which included a good number of probably genuine people, few of whom were likely to have been consuls. This has led recent scholars to believe that the consulship as we have come to understand it dates from the Licinian-Sextian law of 367 and not before. It has been credibly postulated that previously there had been a single (patrician) supreme official called the *praetor maximus,* which office is in fact attested in a passage of Livy relating to events in 363 and elsewhere.[27]

However, from the middle and later republic, the career path or *cursus honorum* began with the holding of a very junior extra-senatorial post of which there were 26, later lumped together as the vigintisexvirate (*XXVIviri*), reduced in number by Augustus to 20, becoming the **vigintivirate** (*XXviri*). One of the most prominent of these posts for instance was a group called the *IIIviri monetales*, a board of three responsible for issuing coin, upon which they regularly added their names and various symbols pertaining to their families. A member of a noble family would seek election as a *XXvir* in his early twenties after a stint as a junior officer (*tribunus militum*) in the army. After that, one sought the **quaestorship**, to which one would be elected by the *comitia tributa* for a year once one had reached 27 (in the late republic this was increased to 30). This was a financial and administrative post, one at first appointed for each consul, and plebeians seem to have been quaestors from a much earlier period than they became eligible for the senate in 367. Usually they were drawn from the senatorial class and went on to become higher magistrates. Sulla increased their number to 20 and gave them automatic right to sit in the senate on laying down office, and as the empire increased, so did the number of quaestors, although their financial responsibilities were reduced. The office survived the upheavals of the later third century and mutated into a much more senior administrative post.

As seen above, one result of the strife in the early republic between the plebeians and the patricians was the creation of **tribunes of the people** (*tribunus plebis*), entitled to veto legislation passed by the senate as a salutary brake on the predisposition to tyranny seemingly then innate in the patriciate. By the second century BC the post also guaranteed entry to the senate, and was thus an excellent way of replenishing the stock of senatorial

---

27. Livy, 6.2, 2; 7.3, 5-7.

families, as well as taming the political stance of some of the more radical. Once the post became integrated into the senatorial *cursus honorum,* members of distinguished senatorial families (but not patricians who were by definition barred) with a political programme to promote would seek election to the tribunate, classic examples being the ill-fated siblings Tiberius and Caius Sempronius Gracchus in 133 and 121 respectively.

Another plebeian office that came into being in the early republic was that of **plebeian aedile**, two of whom were elected annually by the *comitia tributa* annually to oversee public buildings and archives. Once the consulship had been introduced in 367, the aedileship acquired a sort of patricians-only *doppelgänger* called the **curule aedile**, two further magistrates being elected annually by the senate, adding trading standards, road repairs, bread rations and running public festivals to the duties of both.

With the supersession of the *praetor maximus* by the consulship in 367, the word **praetor** was appropriated for the office of *praetor urbanus*, the supreme civil judge, but later merely a legal officer, to which in 241 a *praetor peregrinus* was added with responsibility for disputes involving non-Roman citizens. Again, as Roman hegemony expanded, so did the number of praetors, Sulla settling on eight, and the emperors adding more per year, although their duties changed over the years, and once they had ended their office they could be granted *imperium* (right of independent command) and sent out to govern provinces as **propraetors**.

The consuls presided over the meetings of the senate and were the supreme military commanders and under the republic their names were put forward by the senate for election by the *comitia centuriata*. The minimum age was at first 36, raised to 42 in the first century BC, although patricians had accelerated promotion and were eligible two years earlier than plebeian candidates. The consuls, like most of the other magistrates, entered office at the beginning of the year and gave their names to the year, a system which endured into the sixth century, when consuls failed to be appointed for some years, and the system broke down, to be replaced by the AD/BC system of Dionysius Exiguus.[28] If a consul died in office - as in the early years of the Second Punic War, when Hannibal had the upper hand – a replacement called a **suffect consul** was elected and, from the period of the Triumvirs and consistently from the time of Augustus, the pair of consuls who gave their names to the year - *consules ordinarii* or **ordinary consuls** – retired after a few months to be replaced by one or more pairs of suffect ones (*consules suffecti*). This met the increased the demand for men of consular rank (and experience) fit to govern important provinces and command armies as the empire continued to expand. Consuls went on to govern provinces as **proconsuls**, the idea of extending a magistracy going back to 326, so that a commander in the field did not have to lay down office in mid-campaign when his year of office ended. Later it was accepted that any magistracy carrying *imperium* - the authority to command - could be thus extended.

---

28. The last consul held office in 541, Flavius Anicius Faustus Albinus Basilius Junior. Thereafter a titular consulship was held by the emperor on his accession up toi the 7th century..

Holding the consulship - which made a man a *consularis* (consular) - was the pinnacle of a most men's career, and also conferred *nobilitas* - noble status - upon the family. There has been much debate over whether this extended to the descendants of the first consul in the family only, or whether it extended to his siblings' or even cousins' posterity. Furthermore, a similar debate has raged as to whether holding lesser curule (higher) magistracies, especially the praetorship, also conferred a lesser *nobilitas*. Thus it is often felt reasonable to describe anyone descended in the male line from a consul – suffect or ordinary – as 'noble' and anyone descended from a man who had held the praetorship as a 'praetorian noble'. 'Republican nobles' are usually taken to refer to people descended in the male line from men who held the consulship in the republic, a status which, under the Empire, began to enjoy a cachet all its own, as did membership of ancient patrician families, rather than one raised to patrician status by Caesar or one of his successors.

Every five years under the republic, the senate would elect two men of consular rank for eighteen months as **censors** to keep a register of property, private citizens and to assigning people to a *tribus*. They were also responsible for holding a *lustrum*: ensuring the senate was up to strength and that its members were actually qualified to their positions. They had a moral oversight, too, and could purge (relegate) senators who were considered morally lax. Censor was the highest office to which one could aspire in the republic, but its powers were diminished by Sulla, and Augustus took over the powers previously wielded by the censors and all his successors continued to exercise this authority, too, enabling them to adlect (select and appoint) new senators at various levels of seniority, including into the patriciate, or to purge that body, too, if it suited him.

There were also extraordinary magistracies. In the republic, if both consuls were killed, the senate appointed an ex-consul to arrange elections of a suffect one. This person had similar temporary power and was called the ***interrex*** literally 'between kings', suggesting the convention went back to pre-republican days. Likewise, in times of dire emergency, the consuls could appoint a ***dictator*** who held office with over-riding authority for six months only and would appoint an assistant called the ***magister equitum*** (master of horse). The abuse of the former post by Sulla (by which time it had long fallen into desuetude) and then by Caesar, led to its subsequent abolition.

There were also a series of high offices connected with the state religion. They seem to have evolved from the religious functions of the kings, and indeed the title of one, the *rex sacrorum* ('king of sacred things') clearly indicated; this and most others were life appointments. The influence of these was all-pervasive, at least until the third century AD. Chief of these religious offices were the members of the college of priests (***pontifices***) headed by the *pontifex maximus*, which office carried considerable influence. That is why Caesar felt it was so important to try to obtain the post in 63BC, and why Augustus merged it in the person of the Emperor on the death of Lepidus, Caesar's successor in the office, in 12BC.[29]

---

29. The title was dropped by the Emperor Gratian in 381.

The *rex sacrorum* and the *pontifex maximus*, were probably two separate offices created from one regal function. Both were originally was held for life by patricians, but after the admission of a plebeian as *pontifex maximus,* only the *rex* remained restricted to patricians and theoretically outranked the *pontifex maximus* but had far less authority.[30] There were also colleges of **Augurs, haruspices, flamines** (flamens) and **fetiales** of which the latter two were reserved for senators (the major *flamines* had to be patricians). The oldest religious college in Rome was the **Arval Brethren** (*arvales*) and consisted of twelve men chosen for life from the highest nobility. Under the empire, groups of priests had to be appointed to organise the worship of any emperor who had been deified, starting with the cult of Caesar himself and were, at least at first, supposed to be patricians, as were the **Salii** two groups of 12 priests dedicated to the worship of Mars. The **Epulones,** the organisers of sacred feasts on appropriate festivals for senators, consisted of a board of senators, the numbers of which rose from three to ten from the republic to the empire. The **Luperci** were two colleges of priests, the *Luperci Quinctilii* and the *Luperci Fabii,* the names of which again consist of those of patrician families. Finally there were the **Vestal Virgins**, who watched and tended the sacred fire in the state hearth within the Temple of Vesta in Rome and guarded a number of other sacred objects. They were originally four but later six, chosen between the ages of 6 and 10 by the *pontifex maximus* from girls of noble family to serve for 30 years but in practice usually for life. They could be buried alive for unchastity, but were influential in many other ways and, unlike any other Roman women, independent.

Most of these magistracies, priesthoods and posts made the transition from republic to empire, albeit in some cases changed, and tend to crop up in abundance in the annals of imperial families, which makes a knowledge of their functions and their holders' status fairly important. After the period of Diocletian and Constantine, the entire structure changed radically, and senators were for a time restricted to largely honorary positions, like consul, and praetor (the latter merely responsible for giving punishingly expensive games), the proconsulships of Africa, Asia and Achaia (with more junior legates under them), and the governorships of a number of small but prestigious provinces in Italy styled correctors, proconsuls or merely consulars. The most prestigious posts in the later empire to which senators could aspire was that of Prefect of the City of Rome (*praefectus urbis Romae* or PUR for short), but senators seem on occasion to have held a number of the new posts, Masters of the Soldiers (*magister militum*), governors of groups of provinces called Dioceses (*vicarii*) and a number of prestigious administrative and court positions. Non-senators served as senior military officers, provincial governors - *praesides* – and a variety of other posts of considerable influence.

Amongst these was **Praetorian Prefect**. The holders of this office loom large throughout the saga of the successive Imperial families up to the end of the third century AD. Originally equestrian guard commanders charged with ensuring the safety of the Emperor, his family

---

30. The first plebeian *pontifex maximus* was T. Coruncanius appointed in 253.

and entourage, they swiftly assumed enormous influence, backed by a substantial number of crack troops, stationed, uniquely, in the City of Rome itself, from which by tradition, all other troops were barred. From the time of Tiberius, whose reign was dominated by the praetorian prefects Sejanus (L. Aelius Seianus) and Macro (Q. Naevius Sertorius Macro), these men became king-makers and, by the third century, were successively not only the most powerful men in the Empire, but were responsible for the majority of instances of *régime* change. Diocletian, recognising this, abolished the post in his far-reaching and complex reforms, but in due course the Masters of the Soldiers took over a similarly influential rôle and, as the power of the emperors waned in the fifth century, men like Stilicho, Aëtius and Ricimer wielded enormous power in the West at least.

Other equestrian prefectorial posts were also very influential, like those of Egypt and of the Corn Supply (*anonae*), and prefects served in all provinces as financial officers under the senatorial governors until the third century, when provinces were drastically reduced in size and placed in charge of equestrian *praesides*. Many senior ex-prefects were adlected into the senate on laying down office and often went on to hold senior magistracies. Thereafter the sub-senatorial élite were dominant in the wielding of power on behalf of the rulers. It took until 217 for the first man of equestrian rank to become emperor (Macrinus), but after the death of Gallienus, most of his successors were not senators.

VII

Roman Names and Conventions
As with many societies, personal names evolved from a single name, or names with a second qualifying element, into more complex ones as populations expanded and élites sought to mark their descent from distant ancestors.

Names
The earliest Roman names in literature are, of course, those of Romulus and Remus, single names, but recorded only by tradition and fable yet not by anything so convenient as an inscription. Indeed, the earliest name about which we can be positive is that of a patrician. An incomplete inscription discovered at Satricum, a Latin town some 40 miles south of Rome, reads

'...the companions of Poplios Valesios'

and it is agreed that it dates from the very end of the sixth or beginning of the fifth century BC.[31] The more conventional rendering of the archaic spelling would be Publius Valerius. This could, therefore, refer to one of the five men who are said to have served as consuls

---

31. Wiseman (2008) 311.

in year one of the republic, 509BC, a man who is said to have served three further times as consul and who merited attention from Livy and an entire comparative biography from Plutarch.[32] In the Roman *fasti* he is styled Publius Valerius Publicola, the son of Volesus Valerius, a style by which he was probably not called in his lifetime, although Publicola ('man of the people') is a style he merited, even if he did court unpopularity by building himself a new house on the Velian Hill. Whether the man in the Satricum inscription is one and the same is not known, but he certainly could have been.

Thus the majority of Roman names of all classes of people throughout much of the republic consisted of two elements, of which the second (the *gentilicium or nomen*) was the name of the family grouping or clan – the nearest equivalent to our surname – and established the male line ancestry. Women did not adopt their husbands' names on marriage but retained their *gentilicium/nomen* throughout their lives, but for more precise identification their husband's name in the genitive could be added, eg. Cornelia Metelli (Cornelia wife of Caecilius Metellus). This reflected the importance of *patria potestas* - the father's primacy - which defined membership of the *gens* or clan. Some families with a number of daughters needing more precise identification added Secunda, Tertia or Quarta, or with two *maior* and *minor*, as with the two daughters of Mark Antony by Augustus's sister Octavia: Antonia Maior and Antonia Minor.

The first element (*praenomen*) was the given name, thus Publius Valerius and his father Volesus Valerius. Roman names, at least in their most formal manifestations, also invariably included the patronymic and the *tribus*, both almost always abbreviated:

Sex. Geganius Sex. f. Col.[33]

(*Sextus Geganius, son of Sextus, of the Collina tribe*).

This man, from his urban tribe, the Collina, must be a late 2nd century BC descendant of the Geganii of the very early republic, of which family not one is recorded as a magistrate after 367; like Sulla and Caesar, the scion of an ancient minor patrician clan but unlike them with no subsequent time in the political spotlight. The *nomen* normally ended in '*-ius*' (female '*-ia*') although there were rarer ones ending '-eius', '-anus' or even '-a'. The *praenomen* became highly formalised quite early on, and although in Italy generally there was a wide variety of them, the Roman **élite** stuck to a rather limited number which were invariably abbreviated in a standard form for formal purposes, although frequently used in full for conversation, in correspondence and literature. As they will be all-pervasive in the nomenclature of the family members of the emperors up until the 4th century, it is worth listing them:

---

32. Livy, 2, vii. 6-7; Plutarch *Publicola* 10.3.

33. CIL VI.1308

A. = Aulus	N. = Numerius
Ap.= Appius	P. = Publius
C. = Caius	Q. = Quintus
Cn.= Gnaeus	Ser. = Servius
D. = Decimus	Sex.= Sextus
K. = Kaeso	Sp. = Spurius
L. = Lucius	T. = Titus
M'. = Manius	Ti. = Tiberius
M. = Marcus	V. = Vibius

In the later empire, the Imperial name adopted by the House of Constantine, Flavius became a sort of *praenomen*, abbreviated as Fl. Some of these names fell into disuse at various times and especially in the period of transition from republic to empire; others were always rare, although some of these persisted amongst the lesser folk of provincial Italy. There was a very strong tendency throughout the republic and earlier empire for the eldest son to be given the same *praenomen* as his father. Women did not normally have *praenomina* and bore only the family *gentilicium*.

One thing that our example of Sex. Geganius lacked was a third name, the *cognomen*, which evolved from the late fourth century BC as a means of distinguishing different branches of the same clan bearing the same *nomen*. Although the *fasti* accord consuls and other magistrates with *cognomina* right back to 509BC (frequently indeed with more than one), it is generally agreed that these are mostly retrospective, and the earliest certain evidence is the epitaph of the patrician L. Cornelius Scipio, consul in 298 and censor in 290BC:

L. Cornelius Cn. f. Scipio[34]
(*Lucius Cornelius Scipio son of Cnaeus*).

This Scipio would have been born and thus named around 342BC, pushing the use of authentic *cognomina* back to the mid-fourth century BC at least. Thus probably we may accept the full names as given of those on the official *fasti* from 367/6 at least as authentic. The Scipio inscription is by no means complete, however, as it omits the tribe, but another early one provides us with this as well:

Q. Marcius P. f. Ser. Rex[35]
(*Quintus Marcius Rex son of Publius of the Sergian tribe*)

---

34. CIL. I² 6.
35. CIL I² 2172; from Patavium.

Marcius, although his clan claimed descent from the King Ancus Martius (a claim made overtly on the coins of his kinsman C. Marcius Censorinus of 86BC[36]) gained his *cognomen* from his forebear M. Marcius having being appointed, although not a patrician, as *rex sacrorum*. Indeed, some senators were keen to preserve more than their father's name in their formal style, putting in as well their grandfather, great-grandfather and indeed even their great-great-grandfather. One,

L. Nonius L. f. Sex. n. C. Sosi Cos. pron. Vel. Quinctilianus[37]

(*Lucius Nonius, son of Lucius, grandson of Sextus, great-grandson of Caius Sosius consul [and triumphator], of the Velian tribe*).

This man, living in the mid-1st century, but of no particular distinction, named his father and grandfather, then added his grandmother's father, C. Sosius, consul in 32, who had previously earned a triumph fighting in the east under the auspices of M. Antonius; clearly he was inordinately proud of him.

The three elements of a name: *praenomen, nomen* and *cognomen* became the classic *tria nomina* (three names), the mark of a Roman citizen in the late republic and the first two and a half centuries of Empire. Non-citizens tended to have two names, a given name and a patronymic, and slaves only one. Liberated slaves – freedmen – bore the *tria nomina* consisting of a *praenomen,* the *nomen* of the man who gave him his freedom with his original given name as a *cognomen*. A similar convention prevailed with foreigners granted citizenship; even St. Paul would have had the *tria nomina*, although we do not know which governor enfranchised the Jewish Saul, who became Paul, so we cannot guess at his *praenomen* and *cognomen*.[38]

Adoptions

These conventions of naming, especially on inscriptions (to which the Roman upper classes were much addicted, such manifestations of their ancestry being a means of enhancing their *dignitas*) are most helpful in working out family relationships, and can fill in gaps in contemporary accounts and other sources. One complicating factor, however, is adoption. Adoption of a son from one family into another was a remarkably common way in which one could secure the continuity of one's line. It was taken very seriously, and once adopted, there was no going back; the adopted son becoming a *bona fide* and inalienable member of the family into which he was transferred. At first, patricians were forbidden to adopt plebeians, and *vice versa*, for a plebeian adopted by a patrician would automatically become a patrician too (and the other way round). Yet as the depredations of civil war

---

36. Sydenham (1952) p. 111-122, No. 713; the obverse bears the heads of Martius and Numa Pompilius. The daughter of the latter was supposed to have been mother of the former. How they lost their patrician status is unknown.
37. CIL IX. 4855.
38. Ironically, it could have been Pontius Pilatus himself.

and proscription took their toll, these conventions became relaxed. Survival of the line was paramount, although to release a son to be adopted was always a risk, as the case of L. Aemilius Paullus, consul in 182 and 168, censor and augur. He allowed the son of Scipio Africanus to adopt one son, and the grandson of the famous Q. Fabius Maximus to adopt another. Yet before he died, his surviving sons had also both died without leaving children, ending his line in strictly legal terms, although his male blood-line continued amongst the Fabii until the mid-1ˢᵗ century AD. Thus an adoption secured the line, although one occasionally reads of descendants of adoptees as being considered by modern scholars as not quite *kosher*, a sentiment no Roman would have accepted. Unrecorded adoptions in the early Imperial period may for instance account for the survival of the names of a number of grand republican noble families.

Adoption usually required the person being adopted to take the name, status and tribe of the person adopting him, with his original *nomen* as an added name - an extra *cognomen* or *agnomen* - in adjectival form. Thus the son of Aemilius Paullus adopted by the younger Scipio became P. Cornelius Scipio *Aemilianus*. Adoptions were usually arranged between one head of family (paterfamilias) and another, but it was possible for one paterfamilias to place himself under adoption, as happened c. 55BC with the radical patrician P. Claudius Pulcher, who had himself adopted by one Fonteius Capito, giving him plebeian status (he dumbed his *nomen* down to Clodius instead of Claudius) enabling him to stand for election as a tribune of the people for purely political purposes. The process here was called *adrogatio* (literally, 'calling forward').

Furthermore, there were two general forms of adoption, one undertaken when both parties were alive and consenting, and a testamentary form, done under a request in a will. In the first, the person adopted changed both name and tribe. Thus, when it is noticed in the course of research that the tribe changed in a family but not the name, an adoption is the most likely interpretation, even if the names involved do not necessarily reflect this. However, an adoption could also be done through a man's will, called testamentary adoption. In this case, the adopted son changed his name in precisely the same way, but preserved his original tribe, filiation (the indication of his father's *praenomen*) and status. As Sir Ronald Syme noted,

'No private action such as a testamentary adoption can change the tribe.'[39]

Thus in the most classic example, Julius Caesar's youthful nephew C. Octavius C. f. Scapt., on being adopted under the terms of the dictator's will, became C. Julius C. f. Scapt. Caesar Octavianus, his adoptive father's family being in the Fabia tribe.

In this case, though, no sooner had Caesar's young heir become Octavian, the purged senate deified the late dictator, thus enabling Octavian to re-style himself - uniquely at the time - C. Julius Caesar Divi f. Octavianus ('Caius Julius Caesar Octavianus son of the God').

---

39. Syme, RP VI 426-427, cf. AA 52-53.

Here we can see conventions of Imperial naming emerging. This took a step forward in 27 when Octavian re-styled himself Imp. Caesar Divi f. Augustus (see section III above).

Henceforth, every emperor, without serious exception, adopted the names of Augustus and Caesar both becoming part of the future baggage of imperial nomenclature but, as the centuries passed, both ultimately became, effectively, titles; indeed, Caesar in the later Eastern Empire eventually became a relatively lesser imperial style, bestowed on more distant kin.

Multiple names
The cavalier use of *cognomina* by Augustus merits a slight divergence on the subject of their origins. Most of the earliest (and indeed, most commonly met with) derived from personal characteristics, like *Rufus* ('red headed'), *Strabo* ('squinting') or *Crassus* ('thick, dense or solid' – probably of body rather than mind). Others, as with Marcius Censorinus and Marcius Rex, derived from notable offices held by the founder of a new branch of a family. A third derivation was from notable achievement: *Africanus* for Scipio in recognition of his final defeat of Hannibal at the battle of Zama in 202, bestowed in perpetuity by the senate. Others included *Macedonicus* (for victory in Macedonia) for Q. Caecilius Metellus, consul in 143, but that of his contemporary L. Mummius Achaicus (for victory at Corinth) seems to have been retrospectively self-adopted by his grandson. Others, like M. Antonius Creticus, (Mark Antony's father, praetor in 74), for achieving very little against pirates in Crete, seems to have been applied by detractors and dropped by his son.[40]

These territorial *cognomina* used as names with the addition (normally) of '-icus' were officially bestowed by the senate very sparingly, but once the principate had become established, they were revived by the imperial family. Augustus earned several, but instead of bearing them himself, bestowed them on his heirs. Victory against the Germans allowed Tiberius's nephew to be named Germanicus Claudius Nero, becoming, on adoption by Augustus, Germanicus Julius Caesar. The emperor Claudius named his son Britannicus Claudius Nero to commemorate his conquest of Britain, for which he received a triumph. Non-members of the Imperial family aspiring to such honorific cognomina, like Cn. Cornelius Lentulus Gaetulicus consul in 23, were actively discouraged. Indeed, Gaetulicus was the last.[41] The Emperor Nero was adopted by Claudius with the *cognomen* Germanicus, and Vitellius bore it, too. In the third century, adding such names – often undeservedly – became the norm, some rulers bearing a number of them. Thereafter, conquest being at a premium, the practice diminished noticeably.

From the last decades BC, too, senatorial families began to take *cognomina* or *agnomina* (additional *cognomina*) that reflected the ancestry of their mothers, which tendency began to muddy the genealogical waters when it comes to using the hitherto rigid Roman naming conventions to discern likely forebears or collateral kinsmen. Hence when Quinctilia - sister

---

40. Macedonicus: van Ooteghem (1967) 61; Mummius: Syme (1986) 75; Creticus: Southern (1998) 14.
41. PIR² C1390. The Gaetuli were a turbulent Libyan people.

of the patrician consul annihilated in the *Teutoberger Wald* in Germany by Arminius in 9AD - married L. Nonius Asprenas, the elder son took his father's name as convention expected, and the younger was called Sex. Nonius Quinctilianus – thus bearing his maternal grandfather's *praenomen* and adjectival *nomen* to commemorate a socially much more illustrious descent than that of his father.

In 212 the Emperor Caracalla decreed that all free people who lived within the Empire would henceforth become Roman citizens. The consequences were that most of the people so enfranchised added the forenames Marcus Aurelius to their existing given names and could officially insert their patronymic in the usual place. The entire operation ignored the distribution of these millions of new citizens into tribes, so that element of the old style of naming began to wither. In practice, the *tria nomina* itself began to break down too. Many of these new citizens ignored their *praenomina* and just added Aurelius - often abbreviated on inscriptions and documents to 'Aur.' - to their given names. Only the senatorial aristocracy and some provincial élites clung onto the old system, but it was not universal. Men like Q. Aurelius Symmachus, consul in 391 and the Gallic *littérateur* C. Sollius Sidonius Apollinaris, prefect of the City of Rome in 468-69, persisted with them; even Symmachus' great-grandson, consul in 485 and the penultimate consul using the old Roman naming system, still bore such a name.[42] The last holder of the *tria nomina* recorded had an epitaph raised over his mortal remains in Muslim North Africa in the earlier part of the eighth century. Yet what seems to have happened is that the decree of 212 created a second system of naming and for a while, the two continued side by side.[43]

As regards the élite, the water was muddied by multiple naming (polyonymy). As the late republican grandees struggled to preserve their exclusivity they revived family names from the distant past and either used them as *praenomina*, or *cognomina* or added them as extra ones. As ancient stock began to diminish further in the early empire, the tally of names men wished to hold on to, acquired either through the marriage of heiresses or adoption, rose until we find men from the later 1st century with several names. This process reached its apogee with Q. Pompeius Sosius Priscus, consul in 169, whose formal style boasted no less than 38 names none of which, interestingly, specifically relates to a senatorial family of the Republic:

Q. Pompeius Q. f. Q. n. Senecio Roscius Murena Coelius Sex. Julius Frontinus Silius Decianus C. Julius Eurycles Herrculanus L. Vibullius Pius Augustanus Alpinus Bellicius Sollers Julius Aper Ducenius Proculus Rutilianus Rufinus Silius Valens Valerius Niger Claudius Fuscus Saxa Amyntianus Sosius Priscus.

---

42. Symmachus: PLRE I. 4; Q. Aurelius Memmius Symmachus, cos. 485, PLRE II.9; Sidonius Apollinaris, *ibid.* Apollinaris 6.

43. Salway, B., *What's in a Name? A Survey of Roman Onomastic Practice from c. 700BC to AD700* in JRS LXXXIV (1994) 124-145.

From this genealogist's nightmare, things could only go downhill. It is necessary to find a cross reference from Roman writing or a less formal inscription to work out Senecio's informal style and thus find a clue to his male line from his *gentilicium* although this man is an extreme example. One advantage of polyonymus or multiply named people is that there are plenty of clues as to their ancestry and family connections, although making the precise connections is more of a challenge. Syme, however, comes to our rescue with a rule of thumb, saying,

> 'When the nomenclature of polyonymous senators is abbreviated on consular *fasti*, what there stands is normally the man's real name: that is the paternal.'[44]

We can tell from the few examples of full names being given in the 6th century that this habit died hard amongst the high aristocracy.

Later naming styles

Besides this continuing upper-class system of names, the second style of naming that evolved amongst the Roman élite continued until well beyond the collapse of the West, although the *praenomen*, which had begun to flag as an element of nomenclature from the 1st century began to fall out of use across the board from the mid-3rd century.

The new generation of non-senatorial military men tended to originate from obscure provinces or from 'barbarian' areas beyond the frontiers recruited into the army. Their names thus differed from the *tria nomina* of previous era and also from the polyonymous assemblages of the old governing class. The diacritical name – the name by which a man was called - tended to be the *cognomen* rather than the *praenomen* (henceforth dropped), but the *nomen* remained.[45] This was usually an Imperial one, reflecting the reign of the emperor under which the person attained his citizenship – from 168 to 212 invariably Aurelius.

Yet the dynasty which arose following the revival of the Empire under Diocletian adopted a number of *gentilicia* and *praenomina* – mainly from reasons of prestige – which ended up being adopted by lesser men. Of these, Flavius (abbreviated Fl.) effectively became a new *praenomen*, but was used also as an honorific, prefixed to the remainder of a person's name, just like the old *praenomen*. Thus the person's true name was invariably that following the perfunctory honorific of Flavius. As the fourth century faded into the fifth, too, we find that, particularly the senior barbarian-born generals, were actually men with a single name, prefixed by Flavius, as with Flavius Stilicho (consul, 400, 405), or Flavius Bauto (consul, 385). Except among the aristocracy, names were shrinking, simplifying, after almost 800 years of increasing complexity.

Also from this time, names of all sorts began to be used singly, usually with '-ius', to Latinise them. Sometimes this was done to form a *signum*, or nickname added to an

---

44. Syme RP VI 465; thus one recovers the diacritical name – the one by which a man was normally known.
45. Salway (1994) 140-141; The last examples of senatorial use of a praenomen were Q. Aurleius Memmius Symmachus (consul 485) and C. Rufius Acilius Sividius (consul 488).

existing name, especially amongst the senatorial class, but eventually *signa* ended up as diacritical names, usually used singly. The last known example of a name consisting of a *nomen* and *cognomen* was Julia Rogatiane, buried at Volubilis, in newly Islamicised Africa Proconsularis in 655.[46]

Roman Genealogy

Genealogy was '...valued at the time [i.e. that of Augustus] in high society and [is] never to be neglected in the study of Roman social and political history.'[47] Thus it is worth saying a word about the methods we are obliged to rely on in the absence of most of the sources available to the Augustan upper class.

We can identify the descent of Roman people from a variety of sources: monumental inscriptions, papyri (mainly preserved in the sands of northern Egypt), poetry, imperial rescripts or edicts, laws, lists of officials (*fasti*), histories, letters and literature. None are wholly unequivocal. The filiations on *fasti* and inscriptions are generally reliable, but open to interpretation. Literary references can be misleading, especially, as allusions to particular people are rarely given with full names and require interpretation. Worst of all are histories, for historians and annalists tended to have axes to grind. Furthermore, in any written source, transmission over two thousand years leads to copying errors, gaps in manuscripts (*lacunae*), and inventive re-interpretations on the part of Medieval copyists. As we have seen, Roman aristocrats tended to muddy the waters by taking names from the distaff side of their ancestry, like Cornelius Cinna *Magnus* (cos. 5), P. Clodius Thrasea *Paetus*, suffect consul (*cos. suf*) in 56, not to mention *C. Ummidius Quadratus* suffect consul in 118 whose entire name was taken from his grandmother's father.[48]

In Roman times, the sources were still complete, and Roman authors were interested in genealogy. Cicero, as a 'new man' (*novus homo*), the first of his family to enter the senate and rise to the consulship, was acutely conscious of the origins of his coevals, as well as being himself the victim of snobbery. His friend Pomponius Atticus actually indulged in genealogical research, enabling Cicero to astonish Papirius Paetus by informing him that his family were of the ancient patriciate.[49] Likewise, he had an eye for plebeian families falsely claiming ancient patrician origins, and Atticus was actually commissioned to research the pedigrees of the Junii Bruti, the Fabii, Aemilii and the Claudii Marcelli.[50] The revival of ancient names by surviving patrician grandees in the later republic and early empire excited the suspicion of some. The ex-consul Valerius Messalla Rufus (cos. 53) apparently scrutinised the claims of Caesar's stooge Scipio in the run-up to the Battle of Thapsus, the 'contemptible' Cornelius Scipio Pomponianus Salvitto, considering him suspect, and

---

46. *Ibid.*, 135 n. 67; Africa was the last Latin speaking province; pocket of the language were still in existence in the 12th century (Conant (2012) 363 & n. 3).
47. Syme, RP VI 254.
48. Syme (1989) 75.
49. Syme, *loc.cit*; Paetus: Cicero, *Ad fam.* ix. 21.2.
50. Syme, *op.cit.* 76, citing Cornelius Nepos, *Vita Attici* 18.3.

later denied that the distinguished patrician family of the Valeriii Laevini of his day were in any way related to him.[51]

The case of Salvitto highlights some interesting aspects of this thorny problem of Roman pedigrees. Unfortunately, we do not know for sure how genuine a Scipio this Salvitto was, but the most likely explanation is that he was the testamentarily adopted son of a junior officer in the entourage of Cn. Pompeius Stabo (Pompey the Great's father) in the so-called Social War, whose name has come down to us in a contemporary list as Cn. Cornelius Cn. f. Pal.[52] The urban tribe - into which in the main only patricians and freed slaves were enrolled – suggests a Scipio not otherwise recorded; perhaps a son of the Cn. Scipio who was praetor in c. 109BC. Salvitto's natural father was presumably someone called Pomponius Salvitto. Indeed, he may have been the commander of a unit of auxiliary horsemen commanded by Pompeius Strabo, for another list of his forces includes the *Turma Salvittana*, 'Salvitto's troop'. This was a Spanish unit commanded, no doubt by one Salvitto, who was probably a Spaniard who had obtained his citizenship under a Pomponius as proconsul in his home province.[53] Yet the fact was, that Roman senatorial historians looked down their noses at him in a way they did not look down on other adoptees. Clearly it was all a matter of snobbery, as Sulla, Caesar and Catilina – all members of Patrician families long sunk into obscurity – found out at the outset of their careers. Salvitto's adoption may well have been genuine, and by a real member of the Scipionic family, but both adopter and adoptee were perceived as hopelessly outside the charmed circle of those entrenched in power.

There are other dangers for the researcher. A family of Caecilli in Pompeii, once the great plebeian house of the Caecilii Metelli had died out in the reign of Augustus, assumed the cognomen Metellus without any possibility of the two families being related.[54] Likewise an ex-praetor called L. Pinarius Natta – on the face of it a member of an obscure patrician family, probably extinct in the Triumviral Wars – prosecuted the senatorial historian A. Cremutius Cordus on behalf of the menacing Praetorian Prefect Sejanus in 25. Yet it emerges that he was from Abellinum in Italy, and had risen to the senate via the military tribunate and an army prefecture.[55] Whilst it is possible that his family had been dispersed in poverty to the provinces as a result of the Civil Wars, his humble origin more likely suggests a case of a non-patrician family called Pinarius usurping an obscure but suitably distinguished name. He must have left at least one grandson, for a former suffect consul from Vespasian's reign called C. Scoedius Natta Pinarianus would appear to have been an adopted grandson.

In the first century, it may well be that people knew very well the difference in origin between Natta the friend of Sejanus and L. Pinarius Natta, a young pontifex from the 50s BC; there were undoubtedly records from which such things could be verified, and clusters of ancestral busts of suitable antiquity thronged the domestic shrines of the great and good.

---

51. Syme, *op. Cit.*, 77. On Salvitto: Pliny, *Nat. Hist.* 35. 8 & Suetonius, *Caesar* 59.

52. ILS 8888.

53. CIL. I².706. A trooper in this unit included a Cn. Cornelius Nesilla.

54. CIL. IV. 5788.

55. Tac. Ann. 4..34.

Unfortunately most such records failed to survive the following millennia, meaning that we have to be cautious.

Furthermore, this habit of hitching oneself to a distinguished family - part of the human condition in any era – reaches epidemic proportions when it comes to the antecedents and families of emperors, and cases occur throughout this book. Constantine's claim to have been descended from Claudius II is the best known, but the obscure Emperor Tacitus is claimed by the notorious *Scriptores Historia Augusta* (henceforth HA) to have been a descendant of Cornelius Tacitus, the author of the *Annals, Histories* and *On Britain and Germany,* whilst a descent from the Sempronii Gracchi was claimed for Gordianus II, whilst his successor Balbinus was a supposed descendant from Caesar's friend Cornelius Balbus.[56] Theodosius I was said by the panegyricist Pacatus to have been a descendant of the (childless) emperor Trajan.[57] Occasionally there may have been a grain of truth in these claims, but we have no means of checking. Other, later, non-Imperial claims occur. The letters of Sidonius Apollinaris reveal that it was then accepted that the Gallic Praetorian Prefect of Gaul, the senator Polemius, was also descended from Cornelius Tacitus, and that Leo, a man of senatorial family living near Narbo (Narbonne) was descended from the second century jurist M. Cornelius Fronto.[58] Sir Ronald Syme, whilst admitting the possibility, points out that there had been "a great breach in continuity in the third century" from which few records survived, making it impossible for us to check the likelihood of such assertions, then or now.[59] Yet these descents and others were by no means impossible. After all, despite the vicissitudes of the past millennium, some of the old aristocracies and princely houses of Europe can trace antecedents back to the time of Charlemagne.

Through all the ages of the Empire, there undoubtedly was a continuity of bloodlines, even though we can largely only piece them together by inference and circumstantial evidence. Thus claims by various Imperial groupings that they might have this or that connection are not to be dismissed too lightly, yet any judgement we might make has to be based on the sources of the evidence, and sometimes that evidence can be very dubious. In consequence, here are quite a few pecked lines in the pedigrees that follow!

VIII

The Main Sources

Some sources can be taken as generally very reliable. Inscriptions, especially those in stone, frequently to give a man's descent - a filiation going back one, two of more generations – his voting tribe, which can say something about the place his family came from, his *origo*, and

---

56. Syme (1968) 162 ff. Gracchi & the Gordians: Syme (1971)169.
57. Quoted in Syme (1968) 113-114.
58. Sid. Ap. Epp. Iv. 14.1 & viii. 3. 3.
59. Syme (1958) II. 798.

details of his career, in which one may deduce much about his status, including whether he was a patrician or not. Even the inscriptions of household slaves and freedmen can through light on the family to which they belonged. Only where an inscription is damaged and substantial portions are missing does the imprecise art of trying to decide what has been lost from the gaps come into play, and often there is more than one possible interpretation of the missing portion.

Hundreds of thousands of papyri have been uncovered in the Nile delta area of Egypt, principally centred on Oxyrynchus. Most of these records, some extremely full concern the families and lives of mainly quite humble people, but they have also thrown light on the Imperial styles of various obscure emperors even helping to firm up the dates that some of these more ephemeral rulers actually held power. Others have added flesh to the careers and kin of high officials, especially of the eastern half of the later Empire.[60]

Also from the late period Emperors and high officials had ivory diptychs made, exquisitely carved, bearing their formal image, usually full names and other details, and many have survived, which also aid us in understanding them and their families., whilst at the other end of the spectrum, coins are vitally important in understanding imperial styles, reigns, and often kin. A Roman coin was almost like a newspaper in that each issue of coins brought its recipients a message, usually in the design of the reverse. Indeed, the emperor's image on the obverse was also as important, for on the edges of the Empire, it was helpful to know who was in power, and with whom, especially at times of flux. The difference between a well-attested imperial claimant and an ephemeral one was whether they managed to mint an issue of coin. Some did not, and of these men, many defy supporting identification or attestation from any other source.

Imperial decrees and pronouncements on legal matters also comntain useful information. Principal amongst these is the Emperor Justinian's *Digest*, which incorporates portions of the second century *Digest* of Salvius Julianus (consul 148) and the third century legal collections of Domitius Ulpianus (died 223). Other official documents also survive archaeologically or quoted in historical writings.

From the time of Constantine, too, men with roles akin to the modern poets laureate called panegyricists proclaimed lengthy laudatory declarations of the splendour, achievements, lineage and other qualities of the emperor. Many of these survive, and although highly partisan and full of hyperbole, can throw helpful light on the emperor and his circle. The most eminent of the authors of these, Claudius Claudianus also composed panegyrics on other prominent grandees of the court as well, which included the part Vandal *generalissimo* Flavius Stilicho, revealing his links to the Imperial family. The Emperor Augustus, of course, composed his own panegyric, as it were, which was carved in stone and set up in public and which has survived: the *Index Rerum a se Gestarum* (A Record of his Endeavours) normally referred to as the *Res Gestae*. Needless to say, this is a document

---

60. For instance the Areobindi, who flourished 366-600 and became connected by marriage with the Emperors Anastasius, Olybrius and the Empress Theodora.

packed with pro-*régime* 'spin', although it is still helpful. The writers of surviving letters can also help us, for incidental references to imperial kinsmen and others crop up and can add connections not apparent in other sources. Pliny the younger (C. Plinius Caecilius Secundus, c. 62-113), a senator and ex-consul, wrote 10 surviving books of letters, which throw much light on his contemporaries, some of whom were forebears of the Antonine Emperors. The last book of the ten includes his correspondence with Traianus. Literature and poetry too can provide clues, although the genealogical snippets in, say, Juvenal's *Satires* are in the main too enigmatic to be of that much use.

The trickiest of all the sources, but the most seductive are the historical narratives that have come down to us. There are very many, but there are portions of imperial history which none adequately cover, whereas other portions are covered by two of more, providing us with a comparative yardstick by which to judge their reliability. A large part of the reign of Augustus is not adequately covered, important parts of the mid-second century, vast acreages of the third and from the early fifth century the sources become irritatingly patchy and provincial.

Because no new original MSS concerning Roman history have emerged for over half a millennium,[61] those we do possess have been gone over with a fine tooth combs by modern historians, their evidence weighed and assessed and their relative reliability determined.

Cassius Dio Cocceianus (150-235, consul 216 and 229) was a senatorial historian who also wrote a history of Rome (*Historiae Romanae*) in 80 volumes, although being originally from Nicaea in Bithynia, he wrote in Greek. His history is remarkably full, but not all books survive, leaving us with only a summary of those covering 9 BC to AD 46 and the last couple of books are also incomplete. Later, Eastern Empire historians summarized much of his work, so some gaps can be filled. C. Velleius Paterculus wrote a two-book History of Rome (*Historiae Romanae*) to AD30 which goes some way to filling in the gaps in surviving accounts of the reign of Augustus in authors such as Cassius Dio. Flavius Josephus (c. 37-c. 96) was a Jewish aristocrat who defected to Rome during the Jewish Revolt, a conflict he chronicled in the seven books of the *Bellum Judaicum*. That and his later *Antiquitates Judaicae* of 20 books, both throw light on Imperial history, the latter an important source for Caligula's reign.

Cornelius Tacitus was of Gallic origin and entered the senate, rising to a suffect consulship in 97. He was the son-in-law of Cn. Julius Agricola, the most famous of the governors of Britain, prompting him to write his life, an important source for the early history of Britain along with a further volume on Germany both appearing in 98. From the point of view of reconstructing Imperial genealogies, though, two of his works enjoy pre-eminence: *The Annals* (*Annales*) and *The Histories* (*Historiae*) which together originally gave a detailed history of the events from 14 to 96. Unfortunately, only one incomplete MS survived the so-called Dark Ages, with the result that we are missing the years AD37 to 47, 66 to 68

---

61. Since Petrarch unearthed 29 of Livy's 142 books of his *Ab Urbe Conditur* (*History of Roman from its Foundation*) c. 1365, of which only 35 in all survive, and the bulk of Plutarch's *Lives* re-appeared two generations later.

from *The Annals* (with other, lesser gaps) and everything from 70 to 96 of *The Histories*, but fortunately, the surviving portion of the latter describes in detail the 'Year of the four Emperors' (AD69).

Suetonius (C. Suetonius Tranquillus, c. 70-c. 140) was a senior civil servant of equestrian rank who wrote, possibly after having been dismissed by Hadrian in 122, biographies of Caesar and his eleven successors to Domitian (*De Vita Caesarum*, usually called *The Twelve Caesars*). There is much of the character of the emperors along with anecdotal material, genealogical information and much else, although each life is reasonably compact but much which might assist us is missing. Suetonius seems to have inspired others in the writing of Imperial biographies, too, of which some, like those of the third century Marius Maximus, do not survive, but of those that do, we have entire those of Eutropius and Sex. Aurelius Victor. Eutropius was consul in AD387 wrote a ten volume brief Roman history called the *Breviarum ab Urbe Condita* which is valuable in giving – albeit in very terse form – an account of the chaotic events of the third century from 238. Aurelius Victor also wrote a sequence of rather brief imperial biographies, from Augustus to Julian the Apostate, but which have been interpolated by further, anonymously contributed, material.

Eusebius (c. AD260-340), who was later Bishop of Caesarea, wrote the *Historia Ecclesiastica*, an account of the Church from the earliest times to the time of Constantine, whose life (*vita*) he also wrote, which gives us a reasonably reliable account of the first third of the fourth century. His valuable *Chronikon* (a two book universal history) survives in a Latin version by St. Jerome. For an account of the middle part of the fourth century we rely on Ammianus Marcellinus (c. AD328-395), the last great Roman historian to write in Latin. He wrote a Roman history (*Rerum Gestarum*) in 31 books starting at the demise of Domitianus and continuing to 378, but unfortunately, only the last 18 books survive. Once his narrative comes to an end we are thrown onto a reliance on Zosimus, a late 5th century writer who produced a *New History* (*Historia Nova*) in four books from Augustus to the sack of Rome in 410, which is of great importance for the late period, filling in the gaps from the end of Ammianus Marcellinus to 410.[62]

After 410, there is no single reliable work for a century, until the sixth century historian Procopius (c. 500-565). He was secretary of the Emperor Justinian's marshal Belisarius' and wrote what was effectively a first-hand history of the wars of Justinian, followed by the *Historia Arcana*, or *Anecdota* (Secret History) which virulently attacked Justinian on almost every aspect of his rule, whilst at the same time revealing much scandalous and defamatory information about his court yet providing valuable information about his family. It was not published for about 400 years after being written, which was probably what the author intended.

Other historians and writers either covered poorly recorded eras, like Herodianus (c. 180-250) who wrote a valuable Greek account of all the Emperors from 180 to 238,

---

62. The work of church historian Sozomenus also contributes a little for the decade or so following this date as does that of Orosius..

or wrote accounts which throw light on imperial families rather more incidentally. For instance Plutarch (L. Mestrius Plutarchus), the early second century author of 50 parallel lives of eminent Greek and Roman men, managed to include Galba and Otho, usefully supplementing Tacitus' *Histories*.

The third century from 238 to the beginning of the Tetrarchy is the most poorly recorded period, which is particularly irritating because it was a time of great turmoil, a dizzying succession of short-lived and ephemeral Emperors and, had we a detailed contemporary account of it, we might be much better able to understand it. There does exist, however, the *Scriptores Historia Augusta* (HA). This is a series of imperial biographies, collected together as a single work but purporting to have been written by six authors, none of whose names appear in any other context. The surviving work runs from 118 to 284, but originally probably took up where Suetonius left off in 96. The problem with the HA is that it is largely fictitious, and many of the third century names mentioned therein especially are thought to be entirely figments of the author's imagination. One says 'author's' because it has been established beyond reasonable doubt that, instead of being a work of six contributing authors put together in Diocletian's reign, it was actually written by an unknown senatorial author writing (tongue, it would seem, in cheek) in the middle of the last decade of the fourth century.[63] Strangely, the HA more or less behaves itself down to the reign of Caracalla (211-217), being at least a passable record generally in accord with what we know from other sources, but thereafter goes off the rails completely, each new reign being the spur to various flights of fancy, the true events of history forming an infinitely flexible framework through which a variety of fictional characters (often bearing names with distinct resonances of the late fourth century) flit in and out. Even with the biographies from 118 to 217, the names of the lesser characters - about whom we would be very glad to know more – are almost as suspect as those of the following century. The genealogies of men like Pescennius Niger, and Clodius Albinus are particularly misleading.

Today it is thought that the basic source for these early parts of HA, as well as Aurelius Victor and Eutropius (see above), is a lost but very complete and heavily factual source called *Kaisergeschicte*, or KG for short, which was too long for the compiler of HA and certainly for both of the others, and they all abridged it in different ways.[64] Thereafter the compiler was short of an obvious source to hand, bar the extremely curt entries in Victor and Eutropius, and decided to elaborate using his imagination and perhaps, half-remembered stories heard, perhaps in his student days. From the point of view of the recording of families of emperors of the third century, however, the HA is completely useless.[65] The author simply invents family members for these emperors, which is doubly frustrating because we know that the proceedings of the senate and a great deal of administrative records were then in existence and no doubt available to a diligent historian, yet the author

---

63. Syme (1968) 211-220.
64. Syme (1971) 71
65. Syme (1968) 162 f.

was happy to invent. Sometimes, as when he asserts that Gordian I was descended from the Sempronii Gracchi, his fiction is coincidental with a degree of truth, for Gordian bore the name Sempronianus, which no doubt gave him the idea, although perhaps the notion came to the author from one of his senatorial near-contemporaries, the interestingly named Furius Maecius Gracchus, recorded as a provincial governor in 350.[66]

*

66. Syme (1971) 169. PLRE I Gracchus 3; NB his kinsmen Arrius Maecius Gracchus (late fourth century) and Gracchus (Prefect of the City 376-377) : *Ibid.* Gracchus 2 & 1 respectively.

PROLOGUE: JULIUS CAESAR

Accounts of the emperors of Rome invariably begin with either Julius Caesar or his nephew and adopted son Octavian, later called Augustus. Both had emphatically made themselves sole ruler by a vote of the senate and manipulating republican magistracies by distorting them to suit their purposes (see Introduction II).

Ancestry

Caius Julius Caesar belonged to a patrician family, but to a lesser branch of a relatively obscure one.[67] Nevertheless in the first century BC being a patrician still counted. They still strove to fill their share of magistracies and priesthoods and as a group, they still retained a distinct but difficult to define *cachet*. Furthermore, Sulla's settlement had gone some way to re-entrench their privileges.

Casear's family, the Julii, like several patrician clans (*gentes*), claimed descent from mythological forebears who may well have been real people – Professor Wiseman's analysis of the mythology of Rome points to the weight of evidence, much of it circumstantial, in favour of a basis of truth.[68] In this case, the Julii claimed descent from Aeneas, Prince of Troy and the founder of a Trojan colony on the Italian mainland. Furthermore, through Aeneas' first marriage to Creusa, the daughter of Helen of Troy and King Priam, they could trance a descent from Dardanus son of Jupiter and Batea, grand-daughter of Scamander. Rohl's hotly-debated chronological revision of the ancient world would, if accepted, actually endow the myths with a plausibility that would justify the comment of Professor Cornell when he says that

> "It is likely enough that many of the stories preserved in the literary tradition were handed down by word of mouth in the fifth and fourth centuries, and that at least some of them were celebrated in drama and song. This is altogether much more probable than the alternative: that the stories were consciously invented after the practice of historical writing had been introduced at the end of the third century. As for the authenticity of the stories…they should not be dismissed out of hand. There existed more than one means of oral transmission, and there can be no objection in principle to the suggestion that the traditional stories might be based on fact."[69]

---

67. See Introduction pp. 24-25 on patricians.
68. Wiseman (2004) *passim*.
69. Rohl (2007) 303-343, 463-487 (asnd see introduction *supra*); Cornell (1995) 12.

Naturally all this is completely unprovable in absolute terms, especially as there are three unbridgeable gaps. From Aeneas' son Illus there would appear to have been some twelve generations[70], representing their period as members of the princely élite of the proto-Roman Italian kingdom of Alba Longa, until we reach Iullus Julius to whose son, Proculus Julius, the recently dead Romulus allegedly appeared in the guise of the god Quirinus in 716 – assuming we accept the received chronology.[71]

Notwithstanding, we have to remember that Livy, in relating all this - which conveniently placed the Julii amongst the most ancient of patrician families - was writing under the sway of their descendants, something that might be construed as likely to influence the strict impartiality of the author in presenting his facts.

From Proculus Julius there are still a further five generations in the Julii missing before one reaches N. Julius, whose existence is inferred from the filiation given by later generations (on what basis is not clear) to his grandson, C. Julius Iullus, said to have been one of the consuls for 489BC.

In fact the consul of 489 left no identifiable issue, for the next Julius was his nephew, Vopiscus Julius Iullus in 473, whose filiation establishes that he was the grandson of the previous Julian consul's father Lucius.[72] Note, too that the *praenomen* Vopiscus (and the earlier one, Proculus) lies well outside the usual canon of sixteen or so common ones (introcution VII above): it was a habit of ancient patrician families to cling to such unfamiliar *praenomina,* culled from the lost recesses of their family history, in the first century or so of the republic, bearing in mind the caveat that there is little proof that the *fasti* from 509 to 367 bear much resemblance to what actually went on. Yet in Caesar's day, the revival of these arcane names again became fashionable amongst the survivors.

One might think that having recorded the first family consul (and thus provided at least a name from two centuries earlier) it might be possible to trace Caesar's descent thenceforth without too much trouble. In fact there are further gaps, the first coming in the mid-fourth century BC – as with a number of otherwise well-attested patrician families – just about the very the time, as it happens, that the patricians had been obliged to share their power with plebeian families.[73]

Thus, after C. Julius Iullus, who was appointed *dictator* in 352BC, the continuity of the family undergoes a gap of about a century – to L. Julius Libo, consul in 267, although thanks to his filiation (likely to be perfectly authentic at this date), we can be sure of the existence of his grandfather, another Lucius, presumably living a generation after the *dictator* of 352. The fact that the consul's colleague was a plebeian, confirms his patrician status, meaning that Libo was accepted as a descendant of the consul of 473. The change of last name (*cognomen*) was common enough at this period, although later, when the patricians became

---

70. Representing approximately 250-300 years in temporal terms.
71. Livy, I.16
72. All the dates in this section are BC dates
73. Munzer (1999) 27, 413.

thinner on the ground, the historic nomenclature was clung on to, rather than changed.

In the table that follows, the most senior branch of the family is omitted for clarity. Apart from the fact that they are assumed to descend from L. Julius Libo, the precise descent of their first consul, in 157BC is uncertain. There followed consuls in 90 and 64.

Yet two more gaps occur before we can be positive about Caesar's ancestry for Libo's children are nowhere definitely attested. The next consul of the Julian clan on the official *fasti* is Sex. Julius Caesar in 157BC. The filiation gives his father as a Sextus, without a doubt the Sex. Julius Caesar who served as praetor – the next rank in the republican magistracy down from consul – in 208, when Hannibal was still rampaging through Italy. He was also the first of the family to bear the *cognomen* Caesar; the consul's grandfather was a Lucius. Now, as L. Julius Libo was consul 110 years *before* Sex. Caesar, the likelihood is that Sextus's grandfather was someone else. Perhaps Lucius, Sextus' grandfather, was a son of Libo, but we cannot be certain. The only positive thing is that the consul of 157 shared office with a plebeian and, as a patrician was a *bona fide* member of the patrician Julian clan: irritatingly, we can be sure of his ancestry, but not of the detail.

But that is not the end of it, for while we know from filiations on the *fasti* and elsewhere that Sex. Julius Caesar was grandfather of Lucius the consul of 90 and great-grandfather of another Lucius, the consul of 64, we still cannot confirm the precise detail of the Dictator's descent. We know his grandfather must have been a Lucius – probably the man who was praetor in 166 – but the use of the *cognomen* only serves to tell us that this Lucius was either a younger son of Sextus, the praetor of 208, or a grandson of the latter's father, assuming it was he and not his attested son, who assumed the Caesar *cognomen* in lieu of Libo. The consul of 64 was proscribed in 43 and no more is heard of him. Very possibly he succumbed in the proscription. His sister was M. Antonius's mother (see **Table VI**).[74]

Julius Caesar's poverty and obscurity, despite his patrician status was, therefore, because he was descended from a junior branch of a family of only middling political attainments.[75] As will be seen from **Table II**, the dictator was the only known son of a younger son of a younger son so, even within his own branch of the family, he was about as junior as one could get.

But all that was to change, rather dramatically, with obscurity and the desire to restore *dignitas* to the family name as the driving force behind a fierce ambition coupled with outstanding military and political talents.

---

74. Syme, RR 64, 164, 192, 197.
75. Syme (1939) 25.

TABLE II: JULIUS CAESAR'S ANCESTRY

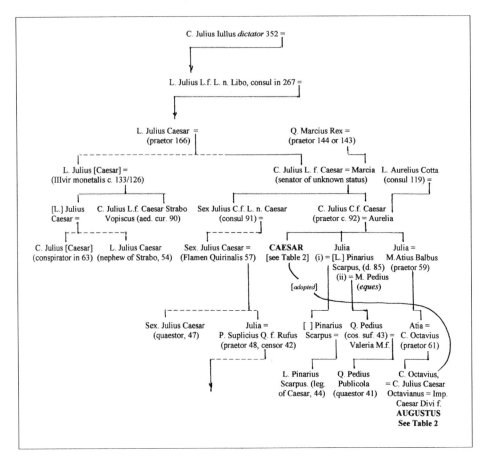

TABLE II: BRIEF LIVES

Atia

Second wife of **AUGUSTUS**' father C. Octavius (Praetor 61BC); she was the daughter of M. Atius Balbus, a rich ancestor-minded senator from Aricia, who served as praetor in 59.

Aurelia

Mother of Julius **CAESAR**, daughter of plebeian noble L. Aurelius Cotta, consul in 119BC.

C. Julius [Caesar]

Joined the conspiracy of L. Sergius Catilina (Catiline) in 63BC and was active on Catiline's

behalf in Apulia. His identity is by no means certain, however [Gruen (1995) 421 & n. 65].

C. Julius Caesar

Patrician & praetor in 92BC, reviver of the fortunes of his family and father of **CAESAR**. His sister married the *arriviste* military demagogue C. Marius, consul 107 and six times more.

C. Julius CAESAR

The dictator, see below & **Tables I & III**

C. Julius Caesar Strabo Vopiscus

Patrician and curule aedile in 90BC

L. Julius Caesar

Patrician and great nephew of Strabo Vopiscus who prosecuted a fellow senator in 54BC [Cicero, *Ad Atticus* iv. 17.5].

L. Julius [Caesar]

Patrician and recorded only as an entry level senator as *Triumvir monetalis* (mint master) between 133 and 126BC. The symbolism on his coins are sufficient to establish his Caesarian antecedents [Sydenham (1952) No. 442].

L. Julius Caesar

Patrician and praetor 166BC. His presumed elder brother, Sex. Julius Caesar, consul in 157, was great-grandfather of Lucius consul in 64, whose son was killed fighting **CAESAR** in 46.

Sex. Julius Caesar

Patrician consul in 91BC; the coins attributed to him at the start of his career show Venus Genetrix being crowned by Cupid, reflecting the origin of the family from Iullus, grandson of Venus and Anchises [Sydenham (1952) no. 476 & n.]

Sex. Julius Caesar

Patrician, *flamen Quirinalis,* an ancient minor priesthood, in 57BC [FS No. 2009]

Sex. Julius Caesar

Patrician, *quaestor* in 47BC, partisan of **CAESAR** in 49, his fate is unknown [Syme RR 64].

C. Julius Iullus

Patrician, *dictator* 352BC; the first of the family recorded as holding office was C. Julius Iullus, consul in 489, although the dictator of 352 was descended probably in the fifth generation from his nephew, Vopiscus Julius Iullus, consul 473.

L. Julius Libo

Patrican consul in 267BC. His descent from the foregoing is by no means clear. Either he or C Julius, an augur attested in 251 (possibly his brother), is the ancestor of **CAESAR** [FS no. 1983]

C. Octavius

see **Table IV**

C. Octavius

Subsequently **C. Julius Caesar Octavianus** finally **AUGUSTUS** - see introduction & **TABLES III-VII(b).**

Q. Pedius

Suffect consul in 43BC; he was the first of his family in the senate and had been a key commander of **CAESAR** in Gaul and in the Civil Wars. His equestrian father Marcus had married Julia, widow of Pinarius Scarpus and elder sister of **CAESAR**. His wife was a patrician Valeria, hence the cognomen of his son, Q. Pedius Publicola, *quaestor* 41 [ILS 3102; Gruen (1995) 119]

L. Pinarius Scarpus

Member of a patrician family long in eclipse, whose grandfather of the same name had married Caesar's elder sister and died in 85BC. Naturally enough therefore, he was a commander of the Caesarian faction in 44 and inherited under **CAESAR'S** will, which he is said to have passed on to **Octavianus.** Later he was a supporter of Mark Antony, for whom he was governing Cyrene in 31 when he surrendered to **Octavian** into whose service he passed [Gruen, *loc.cit.*]

P. Sulpicius Rufus

Patrician, legate of **CAESAR** in Gaul and the Civil wars, rewarded with a praetorship (in 48BC) and censor 42. There may well have been descendants for Valerius Maximus names two brothers, both former consuls (in AD54 & c. 55), who were forced to commit suicide by NERO in 66: P. Sulpicius Scribonius Proculus & [ ]. Sulpicius Scribonius Rufus, whose names suggest that they could well have been sons of the [. Scriboni]us

Proculus who was praetor in AD16 by a [?grand-] daughter of the censor of 42BC. If they carried the blood of the Julii, their deaths should occasion no surprise. [Gruen (1995) 382; Syme RR 65 & n. 4; Valerius Maximus vi.7, 3]

Valeria

Patrician wife of Q. Pedius and thought to be a daughter of M. Valerius Messalla Niger (consul 61) by a second marriage.

*

JULIUS CAESAR
(1st January 48-15th March 44)

Background

Caesar's full style was **C. Julius C. f. C. n. Fab. Caesar.** He was in power from 49BC to 44, but was born in 100 and was famously assassinated on 15th March 44. He served as dictator from 49 to 44, at first, with reasonable conformity with the republican constitution, for sixth month periods, but for a ten year term in 46 and in perpetuity from January 44. He was consul in 59 (as one of three *de facto* triumvirs with Pompey and Crassus) and again in 48, 46, 45 and 44. His earliest office was quaestor in 68 followed by service in Hispania Citerior (Further Spain) and then by election as curule aedile in 65. He wangled election to the prestigious religious office (reserved for Patricians) of pontifex maximus from 63, was praetor in 62, followed by a successful military command in his old province in Spain, which entitled him to a triumph, which he waived in order to stand for the consulship. After his term of office, he obtained a five year term as commander of a large army in Gaul and Illyricum, renewed in 55. His conquest of Gaul (with two expeditions to Britain) and the immense booty therefrom, ensured his popularity and primacy, and he returned to Rome with his army – entering Italy at the head of it illegally – effectively seizing power in 49. Pompey's alliance with Caesar, always shaky, had evaporated on the death of Crassus at the hands of the Parthians at the Battle of Carrhae in 53, and on Caesar's approach to Rome he rashly left the City and was defeated at Pharsalus in 48. Caesar's famous reform of the calendar was introduced from 1st January 45.

Despite three marriages, he died without surviving legitimate children, his only daughter, Julia, having died in childbirth, probably in 54, and her son by Pompey lived for only a short time. He did, however, leave a natural son, called Ptolemaeus Caesarion, by Queen Cleopatra of Egypt, with whom he enjoyed a dalliance in 48-47, and quite probably when the Queen and her entourage came to Rome in 46, and where they stayed until Caesar's death in 44. There is some uncertainty about poor Caesarion, for there is no mention of him in Caesar's will, and all subsequent accounts of him indeed are later, which means there must remain some uncertainty that he really was Caesar's child.[76] Yet the sources all seem to accept that he was Caesar's natural son and, indeed, the fact that he was liquidated by Octavian in 30, after his mother's suicide, goes a long way towards confirming it.

Caesar nevertheless seems to have been spurred on by the apparent barren-ness of Calpurnia to resort to mistresses, meaning that the first century AD claim of an upper-class Gaul to be descended from him could conceivably have had some substance. Unfortunately for him, being a Gaul rather negated any effect that this lofty descent might have endowed. There were also rumours that Brutus was his natural son, his mother Servilia having been prominent amongst the dictator's paramours and at about the right time. His descendants, however, failed to survive the Civil Wars, unlike those of P. Cornelius Dolabella, born either in 76/75 or 71BC, suffect consul in 44, also alleged to have been Caesar's son.[77]

TABLE III: JULIUS CAESAR'S FAMILY

Continued from Table II (above) NB: all dates are BC in this pedigree unless otherwise stated.

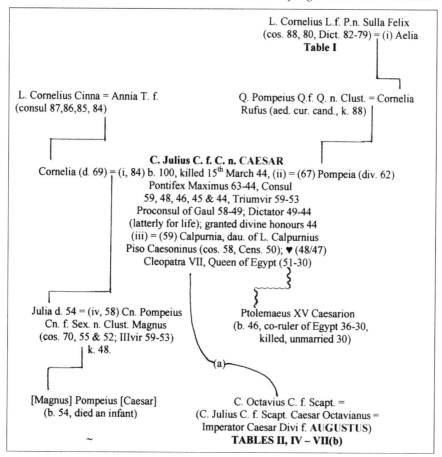

L. Cornelius L.f. P.n. Sulla Felix
(cos. 88, 80, Dict. 82-79) = (i) Aelia
Table I

L. Cornelius Cinna = Annia T. f.
(consul 87,86,85, 84)

Q. Pompeius Q.f. Q. n. Clust. = Cornelia
Rufus (aed. cur. cand., k. 88)

C. Julius C. f. C. n. CAESAR
Cornelia (d. 69) = (i, 84) b. 100, killed 15th March 44, (ii) = (67) Pompeia (div. 62)
Pontifex Maximus 63-44, Consul
59, 48, 46, 45 & 44, Triumvir 59-53
Proconsul of Gaul 58-49; Dictator 49-44
(latterly for life); granted divine honours 44
(iii) = (59) Calpurnia, dau. of L. Calpurnius
Piso Caesoninus (cos. 58, Cens. 50); ♥ (48/47)
Cleopatra VII, Queen of Egypt (51-30)

Julia d. 54 = (iv, 58) Cn. Pompeius
Cn. f. Sex. n. Clust. Magnus
(cos. 70, 55 & 52; IIIvir 59-53)
k. 48.

Ptolemaeus XV Caesarion
(b. 46, co-ruler of Egypt 36-30,
killed, unmarried 30)

(a)

[Magnus] Pompeius [Caesar]
(b. 54, died an infant)

C. Octavius C. f. Scapt. =
(C. Julius C. f. Scapt. Caesar Octavianus =
Imperator Caesar Divi f. **AUGUSTUS**)
TABLES II, IV – VII(b)

76. Suetonius *Caes.* 52.2; Plutarch, *Caesar*, 49; most recently discussed in Goldsworthy (2006) 496-497.
77. Syme RP III (1984) 1236-1250; if true of Brutus, an additional (and very personal) motive for tyrannicide.

TABLE III: BRIEF LIVES

Annia T. f.

Daughter of the consul of 128, T. Annius Rufus; on Cinna's death in 84 she re-married M. Pupius Piso Frugi, consul in 61 and an adherent of Pompey.

Cleopatra VII

Cleopatra was the last ruler of Egypt of the Macedonian dynasty, descended from Ptolemaeus, a general of Alexander the Great. She succeeded her father Ptolemaeus XII Auletes (80-51) jointly with her brother Ptolemeus XIII, who predeceased her. Her liaison with **CAESAR** 48-47 strengthened her position, but that with Mark Antony from 41 and after 37 and their marriage in the longer term weakened it. **Octavianus** defeated them both at the Battle of Actium in 31 and both committed suicide the following year. She also bore four children by Antonius: Alexander Helios and Selene (both b. 41), followed after **Mark Antony's** return to the East by Ptolemaeus (b. 37) and Cleopatra. Alexander was made King of Armenia in 34 and Ptolemaeus was proclaimed joint ruler with his mother as Ptolemaeus XVI Helios in 30 aged 6. The sons were killed in 30, as was Selene who had at the last moment been proclaimed Cleopatra VIII Queen of Egypt, whilst Cleopatra survived to become the wife of the Numidian prince, C. Julius Juba, whom Augustus made king of Mauretania and who left descendants cf **Table LVI**.

Cornelia

Patrician lady, second wife of **CAESAR**, and mother of his only surviving legitimate child, Julia (qv below). In 81 her husband refused to divorce her when ordered to do so by Sulla, his deceased father-in-law's chief political enemy. She died in 69. Her brother, L. Cornelius Cinna was praetor in 44 and one of **CAESAR's** assassins [Syme RR 65 & n.].

Cornelia

Cornelia was a daughter of the dictator L. Cornelius Sulla who married a distant cousin of Pompey, Q. Pompeius Rufus (who was killed by the followers of Marius and Cinna in 88 whilst a candidate for the curule aedileship) [Syme RR 25, 279]

L. Cornelius Cinna

Cinna was a member of a minor branch of the patrician *gens Cornelia* and the chief supporter of the popularist general C. Marius in his later efforts to retain power. As consul in 87, he disregarded an oath to observe the conservative legislation imposed by Sulla by force and proposed reforming legislation. After further perturbations he was consul again in the three years following (when he ruled conciliatorily and with moderation) before being killed at Ancona by resentful recently levied troops [Syme RR 65]

L. Cornelius Sulla Felix

See **Table I Brief Lives**

Julia

Patrician, daughter and only surviving legitimate child of **CAESAR.** By the formation of the first triumvirate she became, inevitably, a political pawn. She was first betrothed to a patrician called Servilius Caepio (possibly Caesar's future assassin M. Junius Brutus, who was adopted into that family, becoming Q. Servilius Caepio Brutus), but was instead married in 59 to **Pompey** as his fourth wife. She reportedly had a strong personality and great personal magnetism, which preserved the fragile political alliance between her father and husband. Her death in childbirth in 54 leaving a short-lived son, did much to dilute the adhesion of the triumvirate. She was buried in the Campus Martius 'with the honours of a princess' [Syme RR 100].

C. Julius Caesar
See **Table II Brief Lives**

C. Julius Caesar Octavianus
Otherwise **AUGUSTUS**
See **Introduction, Tables IV to VII(b).**

[Magnus] Pompeius [Caesar]
The name of this unfortunate child (b. & d. 54) is not known for sure.

Q. Pompieus Rufus
Candidate for the post of *curule aedile* when assassinated in 88, and son of the like-named consul for 88, whom Pompey had killed despite being his second cousin [Syme RR 24, 28, 279]

Ptolemaeus XV Caesarion
Proclaimed the true son of **CAESAR** at Alexandria by **Mark Antony** and **Cleopatra** in 34. Captured at the fall of Alexandria in 30 when his parents killed themselves, and was later killed by **Octavianus** after having been paraded in his triumph at Rome [Syme, RP III (1984) 1248].

I (a)
THE JULIANS

The Imperial Succession
Augustus
Tiberius I
Caius (Caligula)

Beginnings
C. Julius Caesar Octavianus from 12th August 30BC had finally emerged the single most powerful person in Rome, although it took another three years for him to successfully formulate the way he intended to govern the huge empire, so much expanded by both himself and his adoptive father (see above Introduction III)

Maintaining supremacy
In 27, he adopted a revised nomenclature – a new style, as it were – calling himself **Imperator Caesar Divi f. Augustus** taking the full propaganda value from the deification of his adoptive father by his faction in the senate in the wake of his assassination. Sir Ronald Syme makes a telling distinction here regarding the legacy of Caesar:

> "That was all he [Augustus] affected to inherit from Caesar, the halo. The god was useful, but not the dictator: Augustus was careful sharply to discriminate between *Dictator* and *Princeps*. Under his rule Caesar the Dictator was either suppressed outright or called up from time to time to enhance the contrast between the unscrupulous adventurer who destroyed the Free State in his ambition and the modest magistrate who restored the republic."[78]

Thereafter he ruled essentially with his bosom pal M. Vipsanius Agrippa, until the latter's death in 12BC.[79] The problems he faced thereafter included a longing amongst the senators, despite fairly radical reform of the membership of that body, for a return to true republican government; the persistence of various factions inimical to him, the network of familial and political alliances that he forged and the problem of succession.

The first manifested itself from time to time in plots, beginning with one led by the elder son of Augustus' triumviral colleague, M. Aemilius Lepidus, in 30BC followed by others led by Varro Murena and Egnatius Rufus. The factions set up tensions which tended to come to the fore at times of crisis, as when Augustus' daughter, Julia, was found to be the

---

78. Syme (1939) 53-54
79. Freudenberg (2014) 105-107

epicentre of a circle of adultery and treason in 2BC. They also coalesced around the men chosen by Augustus to succeed him.

Thus the question of who should succeed Augustus (like his adoptive father he had only managed to produce a daughter) was seen as crucial and became increasingly so, as each designated heir – all bound to his family by blood or marriage, strengthened by adoption – predeceased Augustus. Nor did anyone really question that hereditary nature of this succession, such was the prestige of Caesar, despite frequent discussion amongst the senior senators concerning the qualities of men they adjudged to be *capax imperii* – having the capacity to grasp and hold power, to be "up for it" in modern terminology.

The complex structure of the dynasty, therefore, was dictated by the lack of male heirs and by the repeated attempts to bind to itself various individuals, singled out by the *Princeps* as the Favoured One. That he had, in the end, to fall back on the stepson, Tiberius, whom he never really liked, dictated the Claudian element in the dynastic designation. After Tiberius' succession, the problem of lack of heirs was exacerbated by the continued loss of likely candidates within the family by murder.

Yet public opinion was found to be insistent on the continuation of the principate at times of transition, when substantial groupings in the senate were seriously minded to try to restore republican forms, as was especially apparent in 7 and 41AD, the latter after the murder of Caligula. The choice of the obscure and physically handicapped Claudius also reminded the senate that the family of the *princeps* still commanded prestige and mystique too powerful to ignore, despite the perceived shortcomings of the surviving candidate. It took the vain incompetence of Nero to alienate them completely.

After that, the fat was really in the fire.

Succession problems

The emperor Augustus came from a family newly risen into the senate from provincial opulence, although it was claimed, no doubt on the instigation of the first *Princeps* himself, that they were a branch of the ancient plebeian senatorial house of the Octavii. Either way it was sufficiently current for Suetonius to transmit it as truth.[80] He relates that they were admitted into the senate and made patricians under the kings, although the record shows that the first member of the family on record is the plebeian tyro Cn. Octavius Rufus who was *quaestor* in 230. His son Caius was praetor in 205BC, father of the first of a succession of three consuls, the last, Cn. Octavius (in 87BC). Cn. Octavius, a supposed brother of the praetor of 205 served as a military tribune at about the same time (the war against Hannibal was still being fought), and was the claimed ancestor of Augustus. M. Octavius, an admiral who fought under M. Antonius at the battle of Actium in 31 appears to have been the last recorded member of this plebeian noble family.[81] What makes the connection

---

80. *Divus Augustus* 2
81. On his membership of this family, see Syme (1939) 296. Thanks to this his existence would have been precarious had he survived.

unlikely was that the senatorial Octavii were in the Aemilian tribe, whereas Augustus' forebears were in the Scaptia.[82]

Setting the members of the Julio-Claudian dynasty out in tables is a challenge to tax the most ingenious. The main problem is that, although we lack a good continuous narrative of Augustus' reign, that period was nevertheless one of a rich literary legacy, plentiful lapidiary inscriptions, and other sources. We have unprecendentedly plentiful information. Furthermore, Augustus's choices of possible successors tended to die on him. For the ancient world, his reign of 31 years was unusually long, which generated its own problems. Thus, the adoption of a succession of heirs, all of whom came from well documented families replete with kinsfolk, who through each adoption took a step or two nearer the seat of power, saw the Imperial family expand with dizzying rapidity.

Augustus's heirs (all but No. 5 died of natural causes) are best tabulated:

1. M. Claudius Marcellus (nephew & son-in-law), designated 27BC, died without issue in 23BC.
2. M. Vipsanius Agrippa (son-in-law), designated 21BC, died 12BC, leaving sons formally adopted by Augustus:
3. C. Julius Caesar (grandson & adopted son), designated 17BC, died AD4, without issue.
4. L. Julius Caesar (grandson & adopted son), designated 2BC died AD2 without issue.
5. Agrippa [Julius Caesar] Postumus (grandson & adopted son), designated 4AD, sidelined by relegation in 7 and killed in 14 without issue.
6. Ti[berius] Claudius Nero/Ti. Julius Caesar (stepson, son-in-law & adopted son), designated AD4; finally succeeded Augustus in AD14.

Proximity to the *princeps* was one thing, but sharing his blood was another again, and it has been important to try and record the descendants of Augustus' sisters because these people were seen as part of the coterie of kinsfolk who surrounded him. Thus the descendants of Augustus' elder half-sister Octavia, married to Sex. Appuleius, and those of his twice married younger sister formed an outer layer of the Imperial circle. They were, of course, like those actually carrying the emperor's blood in their veins, drastically thinned out by Augustus' immediate successors, ever insecure when it came to possible rivals. Some seem to have become safely obscure, yet the evidence of names and other clues suggest that their posterity lasted in some cases a century or two, and in one case quite possibly a lot longer. The obscurity of some of these Imperial kinsfolk was because they left no mark on events nor left a surviving inscription. This would have been down either to poverty, relatively early death (before a career could be forged) or exile, whether voluntary or, like Iullus Antonius's son(s), obligatory. Yet they remain an interesting group, which have here been divided amongst three tables: **IV, V** & **VI**.

82. Taylor (1960) 271, 275.

TABLE IV: THE FAMILY OF AUGUSTUS 1

C. Octavius C. f. of Velitrae =
(living c. 120)

C. Julius Caesar = Aurelia
(praetor c. 92)

Q. Ancharius =
(pr. before 88)

C. Octavius of Velitrae, banker =
at Velitrae

M. Atius Balbus = Julia
(praetor 59)

Ancharia = (i) C. Octavius (Praetor 61, d.59). (ii) = Atia

Sex Appuleius = Octavia
(pr. before 30)

C. Octavius C.f. (b. 61, d. AD14)
[C. Julius Caesar Octavianus,
Imperator Caesar Divi f.
AUGUSTUS (27-AD14)]
See Table VII

Octavia
(i) = M. Claudius
Marcellus (consul 50)
(ii) = (iv) M. Antonius
(cos. 44; triumvir, d. 30)

***

Sex Appuleius Sex f.
(cos. 29) = Quinctilia,
dau. of Sex. Quinctilius
Varus (quaestor 49)

M. Appuleius Sex. f.
(qu. 45, consul 20) =

C. Fonteius Capito
(cos. 33) =

See Table V

See Table VI

Sex. Appuleius
(consul AD14) =
Fabia Numantina
dau. of Paullus
Fabius Maximus

P. Appuleius
Varus (senator)

Appuleia
Varilla =
M. Aemilius
Lepidus
(senator AD17)

Appuleia = (?)
Sex. Pompeius
(senator)

M. Appulieus = Fonteia
(senator)

~

Sex. Appuleius
(d. after AD17)

Appuleia
Varilla ♥ [ ]
Manlius [ ]

M. [Aemilius] Lepidus
(senator in AD37) =

Sex. Pompeius Sex.f. =
(consul AD14, d. AD38/39)

[child]

Sex. Pompeius Magnus
(Arval brother & Salius
Palatinus k. AD40)

M. Aimilius [?Lepidus]
(pontifex & flamen AD101)

TABLE IV: BRIEF LIVES

M. Aemilius Lepidus

Patrician senator living AD17, who died from grief when divorced by his wife, Appuleia [Pliny, *Natural History* VII. 122, 186]

M. [Aemilius] Lepidus patrician, born 12 or just after, married Julia Drusilla (sister of **CALIGULA**) – see **Tables VII(b) & IX** – received accelerated promotion in the senate (probably at least to the praetorship) but was killed on the order of his Imperial brother-in-law AD39 for alleged involvement in the obscure conspiracy of Cn. Cornelius Lentulus Gaetulicus. [Syme AA 136. 283. 298]

M. Aimilius [?Lepidus] senator, holder of a priesthood at the very beginning of the second century AD; the archaic spelling of his *nomen* suggests that he might well have been an Aemilius Lepidus sunk into relative obscurity, although if so, his descent can only be a matter of conjecture. The historic *cognomen* can be traced through two emergent families in the early empire, suggesting that **CALIGULA'S** slaughter might not have been as comprehensive as is generally supposed. [CIL VI 998]

Ancharia

A lady of an emergent senatorial family who was the first wife of the father of **AUGUSTUS**. Her father was Q. Ancharius who was praetor before 88BC; her brother of the same name (also a praetor) was an early opponent of **CAESAR.**

M. Antonius (Mark Antony)

See introduction and **Tables I & VII(b) Brief Lives**

Appuleia Varilla

Senior grand-niece of **AUGUSTUS** wife of M. Lepidus (qv), who divorced him before AD17 when prosecuted for adultery with a senator called Manlius, who was duly banished. Whether this man was a last gasp of the ancient patrician Torquati or of an emergent family is unkown [Tacitus, *Annals* ii.50.1]

M. Appuleius Sex. f.

A second generation senator, legate of **AUGUSTUS** at Tridentum 22BC and consul in 20. He had a son M. Appuleius, about whom nothing is known, and a daughter (qv. Sex. Pompeius) [ILS 86; Syme AA 42f].

Sex. Appuleius

Husband of the elder half sister of **AUGUSTUS** as a result of which he was appointed *Flamen Julialis* and a man of obscure origin from Luna. Probably his background much resembled that of his father-in-law [Syme AA 30, 37, 43].

Sex. Appuleius

Consul in 29BC, an arval brother, governor of Spain in 28 for which he was awarded a triumph, then proconsul of Asia and finally of Illyricum in 8. Married to the daughter of the ill-fated patrician governor of Germany, P. Quinctilius Varus [Syme AA 315f]

Sex. Appuleius

Consul AD14, husband of Fabia Numantina, a patrician lady of impressive antecedents, daughter of Paullus Fabius Maximus (Consul 11BC), who set up a gravestone to her young son, whom, she describes as the last of the Appuleii [ILS 935]

Atia

She was later married L. Marcius Philippus (consul 56), whilst her younger sister married her step-son Lucius Philippus (suffect consul 38). This alliance brought in M. Porcius Cato (praetor 50) who had married Philippus's sister Marcia [Syme AA 403-404]. See also **Table II Brief Lives.**

M. Atius Balbus

See **Table II Brief Lives**

Aurelia

See **Table II brief lives**

C. Claudius Marcellus

A member of the distinguished plebeian branch of the Claudian clan, consul 50BC, a supporter of Pompey, died 41 or 40; two brothers, his cousins M. Claudius Marcellus and another Caius, were consuls in 51 and 49 respectively. He married Octavia (minor) as her first husband. [Syme AA 141-143]

C. Fonteius C. f. Capito
A member of an old family of praetorian rank who was a personal friend of **Mark Antony** (acting as his negotiator with **Octavianus**) and who nominated him as suffect consul in 33 [Syme AA 37]

Julia
See **Table II Brief Lives**

C. JULIUS CAESAR
See Prologue and **Tables II & III**.

C. Octavius
A successful banker at Velitrae in the earlier part of the first century BC, son and grandson of men of the same name. He was wealthy enough to be able to encourage his son (the father of **AUGUSTUS**) to buy his way into a senatorial career, aided by his marriage to **CAESAR'S** niece Atia (qv).[Syme AA 37, 40, 418]

C. Octavius C. f. C. n.
Natural father of **AUGUSTUS** he was praetor in 61, but any hope he may have had of attaining the consulship (he had Caesar's support) – not at all easy nevertheless for a man of emergent family, a *novus homo* (new man), at that time – was frustrated by his death in 59 [Gruen (1995) 175 & n.49]

C. Octavius
See **C. Julius Caesar Octavianus**

Sex. Pompeius Sex. f. opulent senator, owner of vast estates in Campania, Sicily and Macedonia, whose father is but a name, although believed to be married to an Appuleia, as this man, consul in AD14, was a relative of **AUGUSTUS**. His grandfather, also Sextus (consul 35), 'an aged non-entity' was raised to the rank of Patrician by **AUGUSTUS** in 27 and was a half-nephew or half-brother of POMPEY[83] - hence the name of his son (qv) [Dio, LVI.29, 5; Syme AA, 97, 99, 197, 263, 317, 327].

Sex. Pompeius Magnus
Son of the preceding, killed by **CALIGULA**, partly to engross his enormous estates and partly because of the resonance of his name and his propinquity to **AUGUSTUS**. No known issue [Syme AA 132, 414]

Quinctilia
A daughter of Sex. Quinictilius Sex. f. Varus a young senator, again of obscure patrician family, who was quaestor in 49 but was killed the following year in defence of the republic at the Battle of Philippi. She was sister of the patrician consul of 13 P. Quinctilius Varus, who was killed with most of his army in AD9 whilst governor of Germany by Arminius (Hermann) in the Teutoberger Forest. He was the first consul in his family since 453! [PIR² Q31; Syme AA 313, 316]

---

83. As the consul of 35 was 'aged' when consul, he may be identifiable with the Sex. Pompeius who appears as a boy in 82, in Plutarch's account of Cato the younger, in which case he was the half-brother of the dynast.

Table V is of interest, not only because it provides a genealogical link between Augustus' sister, **CLAUDIUS I** and the Emperor **COMMODUS,** who reigned two centuries later, but also because, from L. Bruttius Quinctius Crispinus (consul AD187), a likely descent can be traced down to the later fourth century AD (and, possibly beyond). A C. Bruttius Praesens was consul in AD 217 and another – his presumed son - in 246, another was a *pontifex* under the Tetrarchy in the late 3rd century and a fourth governed Lucania and Bruttium (S. Italy) under the dynasty of Constantine a generation or two later. Indeed the latter's son may have been the Bruttius Praetextatus Argentius who governed Byzacena in the later fourth century.[84] That it was this line of the Bruttian family, with its Quinctian connection, is confirmed by the Bruttius Crispinus who was a provincial governor in AD352.[85] In the late fifth century, indeed, the remains of a senator's name reading [   ] Quin[c]tius [   ] appears carved on one of the seats reserved for senators in the Flavian Amphitheatre in Rome; not necessarily a descendant but conceivably one and, if so, the last possible descendant of a *relation* of **AUGUSTUS**.

If all this can be accepted, we are looking at a family who remained in the governing elite of Rome from the fifth century BC, for the Quinctii Crispini claimed descent from the legendary L. Quinctius Cincinnatus, twice consul and twice *dictator*; the man who was called from his plough to rescue the state from a military crisis in 458BC. His supposed descendant, upon whose reality we can rely, was K. Quinctius Claudus, consul in 271, grandfather of the first member of the family to bear the *cognomen* Crispinus (curly haired), serving as consul in the war against Hannibal in 208. The male line, however, appears to have failed during the proscription ordered by the Second Triumvirate in 43, resulting in the formal adoption of a younger son of the equally patrician Ser. Sulpicius Rufus (another casualty of the proscription), who became, in classic Republican style, T. Qunictius Crispinus Volcanus Sulpicianus and was consul in 9BC. Unfortunately, he too turned out to be childless, and so in turn adopted a younger son of the patrician suffect (additional) consul of 29BC, Potitus Valerius Maximus, who in his turn became T. Qunictius Crispinus Valerianus, consul in AD2. He died in 27, and is thought to have been the father of one Quinctius Cinncinnatus, the nomenclature of whose likely posterity strongly suggests he married a daughter of Paulus Aemilius Regillus (or very a close relation). Thus the adoptive line went back to the original Cincinnatus and the actual one to the first Valerius, P. Valerius Publicola, first consul of the Republic, in 509.[86] The Bruttii and Laberii, however, go back only as far as the Flavian period.

---

84. PIR² B160, 163, 166, 167 & 169, PLRE I. Praetextatus 2, cf. Mennen (2011) 89-91, Settipni (2000) 341.
85. PLRE I Crispinus 4
86. See above, Introduction VII.

TABLE V: THE FAMILY OF AUGUSTUS 2

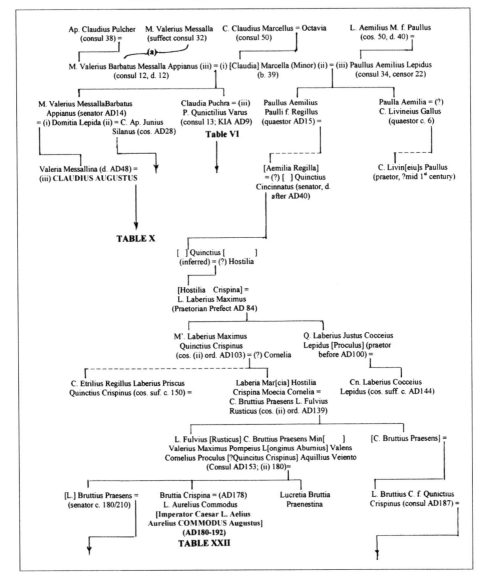

Ap. Claudius Pulcher (consul 38) =	M. Valerius Messalla (suffect consul 32)	C. Claudius Marcellus = Octavia (consul 50)	L. Aemilius M. f. Paullus (cos. 50, d. 40) =

(a)

M. Valerius Barbatus Messalla Appianus (iii) = (i) [Claudia] Marcella (Minor) (ii) = (iii) Paullus Aemilius Lepidus
(consul 12, d. 12)　　　　　　　　　　　(b. 39)　　　　　　　　　(consul 34, censor 22)

M. Valerius MessallaBarbatus Appianus (senator AD14) = (i) Domitia Lepida (ii) = C. Ap. Junius Silanus (cos. AD28)

Claudia Puchra = (iii) P. Qunictilius Varus (consul 13; KIA AD9)
Table VI

Paullus Aemilius Paulli f. Regillus (quaestor AD15) =

Paulla Aemilia = (?) C. Livineius Gallus (quaestor c. 6)

Valeria Messallina (d. AD48) = (iii) CLAUDIUS AUGUSTUS

[Aemilia Regilla] = (?) [　] Quinctius Cincinnatus (senator, d. after AD40)

C. Livin[eiu]s Paullus (praetor, ?mid 1st century)

TABLE X

[　] Quinctius [　　　] (inferred) = (?) Hostilia

[Hostilia Crispina] = L. Laberius Maximus (Praetorian Prefect AD 84)

M'. Laberius Maximus Quinctius Crispinus (cos. (ii) ord. AD103) = (?) Cornelia

Q. Laberius Justus Cocceius Lepidus [Proculus] (praetor before AD100) =

C. Etrilius Regillus Laberius Priscus Quinctius Crispinus (cos. suf. c. 150) =

Laberia Mar[cia] Hostilia Crispina Moecia Cornelia = C. Bruttius Praesens L. Fulvius Rusticus (cos. (ii) ord. AD139)

Cn. Laberius Cocceius Lepidus (cos. suff. c. AD144)

L. Fulvius [Rusticus] C. Bruttius Praesens Min[　] Valerius Maximus Pompeius L[onginus Aburnius] Valens Cornelius Proculus [?Quincitus Crispinus] Aquillius Veiento (Consul AD153; (ii) 180)=

[C. Bruttius Praesens] =

[L.] Bruttius Praesens = (senator c. 180/210)

Bruttia Crispina = (AD178) L. Aurelius Commodus [Imperator Caesar L. Aelius Aurelius COMMODUS Augustus] (AD180-192)
TABLE XXII

Lucretia Bruttia Praenestina

L. Bruttius C. f. Qunictius Crispinus (consul AD187) =

TABLE V: BRIEF LIVES

[Aemilia Regilla]

Putative patrician daughter of Paullus Aemilius Regillus (qv). An alliance between Regillus' family and Cincinnatus is the only convincing way to explain the persistence of the names Quinctius Crispinus, Lepidus and Regillus amongst the descendants of L. Laberius Maximus.

Paullus Aemilius Lepidus

Patrician, born c. 70BC, suffect consul 34, last non-Imperial censor 22. Elder brother of the Triumvir M. Lepidus. His *praenomen* was 'borrowed' from the *cognomen* of a more distinguished but long extinct branch of the family. [Claudia] Marcella (minor) was his third wife whom he married c. 16; he had previously been married to Sempronia and Cornelia, who died in 16, having children by both. [Propertius IV.ii.37; PIR² A373; FS 512; Syme AA 10-112, 150f].

L. Aemilius Paullus

Patrician, son of M. Lepidus, consul in 78BC and the daughter of a Cornelius Scipio, born c. 83BC; *triumvir monetalis* 63; quaestor 59; consul 50, d. 40 [Syme AA 105-106].

Paullus Aemilius Regillus

Patrician, son of Paullus Aemilius Lepidus, b. to Paullus Lepidus and his third wife Marcella, perhaps posthumously 13BC; quaestor of tthe Emperor in AD15 and a *XVvir sacris faciundis*. He should have reached his consulship in 23, leading Syme to conclude he may have died in the plague of AD 21/22, yet he was alive in AD47 when he took part in **CLAUDIUS'S** *ludi saeculares* (Jubilee games). It is possible he held a suffect consulship, record of which has been lost (there were a few) or was considered in some way unsuitable, either by his proximity to the purple or some defect of character. The machinations of Messallina may have finally accounted for him. Again, he bore a *cognomen* revived from one in use in the early history of the family [PIR² A396; FS 526; Syme AA 149-150]

Bruttia Crispina

Empress of **COMMODUS AUGUSTUS**, she was the daughter of L. Fulvius....Aquillius Veiento (qv) and married in AD178 to the future Emperor.

C. Bruttius L. f. Pompt. Praesens L. Fulvius Rusticus

Like his son, twice consul, suffect in AD119 & ordinary consul in AD139. The family were raised to patrician status around AD138/140

by **ANTONINUS PIUS**. Laberia was probably his second wife, his first seemingly having been [Aburnia] Campana by whom he had another son. [PIR² B164]

[L.] Bruttius Praesens

Patrician family by creation, and attested as a member of the senate in the period c. AD180/210 and the C. Bruttius Praesens who was consul in AD246 was almost certainly his son as was, in all probability, L. Bruttius Crispinus (consul AD 224) [PIR² B167, 160].

L. Bruttius C. f. Quinctius Crispinus

Patrician by creation, first cousin of the Empress **BRUTTIA CRISPINA** and consul in AD187. Nothing is known of his father, who was probably called C. Bruttius Praesens would have been another son of the consul of AD139 and Laberia. It is possible, bearing in mind the complexity of the names of the consul (ii) 180, that he was actually a brother of the empress. His bloodline (and thus that of Augustus's sister) would appear to have endured until the later fourth century (see above p. 65) [ILS 8265; PIR² B169].

[Claudia] Marcella minor

Younger sister of Marcella (major), and a niece therefore of **AUGUSTUS,** she married twice: to M. Valerius Messalla Barbatus Appianus (consul 12BC) as his third wife and then to Paullus Aemilius Lepidus, suffect consul in 34BC (also as his third wife) [Syme AA 59, 147f]

Claudia Pulchra

A patrician and daughter of M. Valerius Messalla Barbatus Appianus, consul in 12BC, who was, prior to his adoption, a Claudius Pulcher, hence his daughter's style. She became the third wife of P. Quinctilius Varus, the ill-fated consul in 13BC. Much later, in AD26 she was prosecuted and condemned for adultery. For her issue by Varus, see **Table VI** [Syme AA 315; Tac. Ann. iv. 52,1]

CLAUDIUS I AUGUSTUS
See Table X and main text.

C. Claudius Marcellus
See above **Table IV Brif Lives**

Ap. Claudius C. f. Pulcher
A member of the senior brnach of the ancient patrician house of the Claudii, he was consul in 38BC, despite having been proscribed, with his brother Caius, by the triumvirs in 43. He later enjoyed a triumph, and was a member of the first revived college of Arval Brethren in 29. Father *inter alia* of M. Valerius Messalla Barbatus Appianus (qv) and a daughter who is thought to have married C. Junius Silanus [Syme AA 46, 91, 149,197].

L. Cornelius L. f. Regillus
Senator, mid-1st century AD. His *cognomen* clearly implies a descent from the Aemilii Regilli, and it is suggested here that his filiation clearly implies that he may have been the son of a second marriage of Aemilia Regilla and a L. Cornelius, probably a Lentulus – perhaps a son of L. Cornelius Lentulus consul in 3BC - as suggested here [ILS 1917E].

Domitia Lepida
Daughter of L. Domitius Ahenobarbus, consul in 16 and the elder of Mark Antony's two daughters by Octavia (see **Table VI**). She married as her first husband M. Valerius Messalla Barbatus Appianus, junior, who died when still a young man, leaving her with a daughter, the notorious Messallina, first wife of **CLAUDIUS I (Table X)**. She went on to marry twice more, to Faustus Cornelius Sulla (a descendant of the dynast Sulla)

and C. Ap. Junius Silanus, consul in AD28 (on whom see **Table VIII**). She was also the aunt of **NERO AUGUSTUS** who was born a Domitius Ahenobarbus [Syme AA 151-166].

C. Etrilius Regillus Laberius Priscus [Quinctius Crispinus]
On balance this man must be a son of M'. Laberius Maximus Quinctius Crispinus (qv); he was suffect consul c. AD150. The inscription which names him omits part of his name, which it seems logical to restore as [Qunictius Crispinus] for which there appears to be space, on the precedent of the name of his putative father and sister (qv) He may have been adopted by an Etrilius, perhaps Cn. Etrilius [   ], a suffect consul in the previous generation, and probably a descendant of M. Etrilius Lupercus, the ex-praetor responsible for paving the streets of Lepcis Magna, in Africa, whilst legate there in AD29 and thus of senatorial descent.

L. Fulvius Rusticus
See above, **C. Bruttius Praesens L. Fulvius Rusticus**

C. Ap. Junius Silanus
The Junii Silani were a junior branch of the more famous Junii Bruti, emerging with a praetor in 212, but becoming prolific thereafter. The father, C. Junius Silanus, attested as a senator in 18BC, married as a first wife, Atia, the aunt of **AUGUSTUS** but C. Ap. Junius Silanus is thought to have been the offspring of a second marriage, to a Claudia, a daughter of Ap. Claudius Pulcher, consul in 38BC, and thus sister of M. Valerius Messalla Barbatus Appianus (qv) – hence his unusual addition of the distinctive extra *praenomen* Appius, used (then) exclusively by the family of Pulcher. He was consul AD28, governed Tarraconensis in Spain, was one of the Arval Brethren from AD23 but was murdered at the instigation of the Empress Messallina in AD42. The family were given patrician rank c.

27BC. He was the third husband of Domitia Lepida (qv) by whom he had a daughter, Junia Torquata [ILS4923; PIR² J822; Lewis (1955) 124; Syme (1949) 9 & AA 193]

[Lab]eria Mar[cia] Hostilia Crispina Moecia Cornelia

Daughter of M'. Laberius Maximus (qv) and wife of C. Bruttius Praesens L. Fulvius Rusticus the consul (ii) of AD139. Whilst the pedigree attempts to explain the Hostilia and Cornelia elements in her name, the rare *nomen* of Moecia could have come from anywhere [PIR² H228 & L15].

Cn. Laberius Cocceius Lepidus

Suffect consul c. AD143/145 and presumed to be a son of the following. A son may have been [?Cn. Laberius] Silanus [Cocceius] Justus An[   ] Cn. Lepidi f., a 2nd century ex-praetor His filiation Lepidus seems to make his descent clear.[CIL II. 2838].

Q. Laberius L. f. Aem. Justus Cocceius Lepidus

A son of L. Laberius Maximus, and a man of praetorian rank in AD100 when he was proconsul of Cyprus. Probably he shared a common ancestor with L. Cocceius Justus, a senator and contemporary of similar rank, both probably kin to M. Cocceius Proculus, a military tribune during the 'Year of the Four Emperors' [PIR² C1220, L7].

L. Laberius Maximus

Laberius Maximus was the son of a magistrate of the same name from Lanuvium and quite probably a descendant of L. Laberius Lepidus, a junior military officer who died at Interamna Nahars (Terni) c. AD1. He was one of the great equestrian officers of the Flavian era serving as Procurator of Judea in the wake of the sack of Jerusalem by the future emperor **TITUS,** Prefect of Egypt 82-84 and finally Praetorian Prefect, before being adlected into the senate, probably with praetorian rank. His wife was perhaps Hostilia Crispina, here postulated as a grand-daughter of Aemilia [Regilla] and Qunctius Cincinnatus. Cincinnatus or perhaps his heirs may have been relegated from the senate for poverty or exiled (or worse) through court intrigue, making a match with a distinguished equestrian official perfectly credible [PIR² L8]

M'. Laberius Maximus Quinctius Crispinus

Manius served as suffect consul in AD89, ordinary consul in 103, but was one of four senior ex-consuls disgraced and executed by Hadrian within months of his accession in 118; no-one quite knows what lay behind it. His daughter (not shown) Laberia Crispina, married Servilius Pudens, whose son Q. Servilius Pudens was consul (ii) 166 and brother-in-law of **LUCIUS VERUS**, see **Table XXI Brief Lives** [PIR² L9].

C. Livineius Gallus

Probably a son of L. Livineius L.f. Gal. Regulus, himself offspring of an ex-praetor exiled in 58BC. He was quaestor c. 7, is thought to have married Paulla Aemilia, dau. of Paullus Aemilius Lepidus, consul 50BC and from his probable son's name the likely parent of C. Liveneius Paullus (qv) [PIR² L288; Wiseman (1971) 228]

C. Livineius Paullus

The *cognomen* of this man, a senator at some unknown stage in the mid-1st century AD, suggests that it is likely that he may have been the son of the above and Aemilia, for Aemilian names seem to proliferate amongst a notable coterie of mid to late 1st century senators as this table attempts to demonstrate [PIR² L289].

P. Quinctilius Varus

A member of an old patrician family, long sunk into obscurity and brother-in-law of

Sex. Appuleius (Consul 29BC: **Table IV**). His father was quaestor in 49BC, but was killed in action in the final stages of the Civil War, in 46.Of amiable temperament, he was Consul in 13BC Varus was killed by the German leader Arminus (Herrmann) in the *Teutoberger Wald* (near modern Osnabrück) with most of his three legions in AD9, causing Augustus to rave 'Quinctilius Varus, give me back my legions!' The name of his first wife is unknown, but he married as his second M. Agrippa's daughter Vipsania; his third wife was Claudia Pulchra (qv) [PIR² Q29; Appian. BC iv.28; Syme AA 54-58, 313-318].

[T. Quinctius] Cincinnatus

Senator, humiliated for taking excessive pride in his ancestry by Caligula AD40. He subsequently failed to reach the consulship and may have been bumped off. The family were old patricians who effectively ended in the male line (after a century and a half without a consulship), with the death of T. Quinctius Crispinus, quaestor in 69BC. His son – not actually on record anywhere - adopted a Sulpicius – probably a younger son of Ser. Sulpicius Rufus who was proscribed in 43 – who, as T. Quinctius Cripinus Volcanus Sulpicianus, was consul in 9BC. He in his turn adopted a Valerius Messalla, possibly a son of Potitus Messalla (suffect consul in 29BC) who was consul in AD2; Syme suggests, however, that they were adoptive brothers. It is presumed that Cinncinatus was the son of the consul of AD 2, who died in AD27. A son of Cincinnatus who married a Hostilia is postulated who would have been the parent of Hostilia Crispina (qv). [ILS5939; Cic. *Pro Fonteio*; Suet. Calig. 35,1; PIR² Q43; Barrett (1989) 238 & n. 96 Syme AA 157-158].

Valeria Messallina

Daughter of M. Valerius Messalla Barbatus Appianus (thus an imperious Claudius Pulcher by descent) Messallina was the third wife of **CLAUDIUS I AUGUSTUS** (qv **TABLE X**) whom she married around AD39. She, it turned out, was an amoral murderous virago and came spectacularly unstuck in AD48, but not before she had brought about the death of numerous members of various distinguished families, being fearful of any possible competition for imperial honours that might emperil the chances of her son and Claudius's official heir **BRITANNICUS** [Syme AA 147].

M. Valerius Messalla

Patrician, but a relative nonentity, although suffect consul in 32, he was the younger son of M. Valerius Messalla Rufus, consul in 53 but, being childless was obliged to adopt the younger son of Ap. Claudius Pulcher (consul 38) [Syme AA 228, 247].

M. Valerius Messalla [Barbatus] Appianus

A member of one of the major ancient patrician families, and by birth a Claudius Pulcher and adopted by M. Valerius Messalla, consul in 32BC. He is given the name Barbartus in only one late source. He was consul in 12BC, and died soon after taking office. His third wife was [Claudia] Marcella (minor) [Syme, AA 147 n. 38].

M. Valerius Messalla Barbatus Appianus

Senator AD14, son of the consul of 12BC and [Claudia] Marcella (minor), Octavia's daughter. He was the first husband of Domitia Lepida (see Brief Lives, **Table VI**) but died before he could hold the consulship in AD20 (unusually for a kinsman of the emperor, of natural causes) [Syme AA 148-150, 164f].

Table VI belongs with the preceding table as it gives the descendants of the other daughter of Octavia, sister of **AUGUSTUS,** Marcella (major) and provides, through the family of Cornelius Cethegus, the possibility of descendants of Octavia surviving identifiably into the fourth century or even beyond; only probable, that is, for whilst we can be fairly sure of the general outline of the descent, the actual generation-to-generation detail is lost.

TABLE VI: THE FAMILY OF AUGUSTUS 3

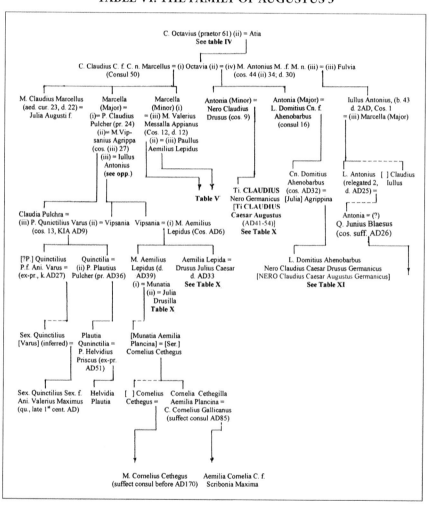

TABLE VI: BRIEF LIVES

Aemilia Cornelia C.f. Scribonia Maxima
Recorded as a *c[larissima] p[uella]* - a 'most distinguished girl' (i. e. of senatorial family) at an uncertain date, probably early third century, although Morris suggested second century. M.

Gavius Cornelius Cethegus, a patrician, probably of recent elevation and a fairly certain descendant of C. Cornelius Gallicanus (qv), was consul in AD 170 and left two sons, both *Salii Palatini* (Palatine Priests): M.[?Cornelius] Cethegus (died AD189) and [?C.] Cornelius Cethegus, recorded in AD183, of whom the latter is a strong candidate for Aemilia's parent. The Scribonia element in her name also suggests kinship with Augustus, seemingly derived via a different genealogical route, perhaps through Ser. Cornelius Cethegus. [Morris (1965) 88f.].

M. Aemilius Lepidus

Member of an ancient patrician family, second son of Paullus Aemilius Lepidus (consul 34BC, qv). He was consul in AD6 proconsul of Asia 26-28 and died in 33; Agrippa's daughter Vipsania was his first wife. A man of capability, integrity and wisdom, he was said to be *capax imperii* ('fit to rule'). His son was a victim of **CALIGULA** (see **Table IV Brief Lives**) [Syme (1970) 30-49]

Paullus Aemilius Lepidus

See **Table V Brief Lives**

Antonia

Elder sister of the above born 39 and wife of L. Domitius Cn. f. Ahenobarbus, consul in 16BC, and thus grandmother of the Emperor **NERO** [PIR² A884]

Antonia

Younger of the two daughters of the Triumvir **Mark Antony** by Octavia, born 36 and married to Nero Claudius Drusus (consul 9), step-son of **AUGUSTUS** and younger brother of the Emperor **TIBERIUS I**. She died in AD37 [PIR² 885]

Antonia

Daughter or sister of the exiled L. Antonius (the latter attested indirectly by CIL VI.11959). Possibly the wife of either Q. Junius Blaesus or his brother, suffect consuls in AD26 and c. 28 respectively, and both of whom committed suicide at the prompting of **TIBERIUS** in AD36, having been mixed up in court intrigue. Her son would have been the Junius Blaesus who died probably by poison at the instigation of **VITELLIUS** in AD69 [Syme AA 144, n. 19, 163].

Iullus Antonius

Second son of **Mark Antony** (qv) by his third wife Fulvia, born before 40, and third husband of Marcella (major), whom he married in 21BC. A new patrician, he was consul in 10, going on to be proconsul of Asia. Although valued by the Emperor, he was implicated in a great scandal concerning his daughter Julia in 2BC and Augustus' disillusionment led to his execution or obligatory suicide. He is thought to have left two sons (one died young) and a daughter [PUR² A800/801; Syme AA 58-59, 9].

L. Antonius

The son of Iullus Antonius by the elder [Claudia] Marcella and thus a new patrician, he was relegated from the senate on the fall of his father and sent with his siblings into exile to Massilia (Marseilles). We only know his name because Tacitus recorded his death there in AD25. We are not told if he was married or had issue, but we might well suppose so, for we find that Junius Blaesus (see **Antonia** above), the senator of praetorian rank who died in the Civil War of 69 was labelled by the detestable emperor **VITELLIUS** as 'a traitor who boasted that he was descended from the Junii and the Antonii'. Unfortunately we have no means (bar this enigmatic clue) of telling for sure. Syme considers that Blaesus' mother might have been Domitia, an aunt of **NERO** [Tac. *Ann.* iv. 44, 3; *Hist.* iii. 38, 31; PIR² A802, I737; Syme AA 59, 118, 163].

M. Antonius [Mark Antony]

See also **Introduction** on his role on Caesar's murder Of a plebeian family of only recent nobility, despite the supposed existence of a trio of patrician magistrates bearing this *gentilicium* in the later 5th century. It was however, possible that he was descended from the M. Antonius who was Master of Horse (the dictator's number two, the *magister equitum*) in 333BC but whose son Lucius was relegated from the senate in 307. The family of Antonius was raised to patrician status by Julius Caesar in 45. The illustrious supporter of Julius Caesar and lover of Cleopatra VII of Egypt was consul 44 and 34; triumvir 43-35, defeated by Octavian's fleet off Actium in 31, committed suicide 30. He married (i) Fadia (by whom he seems to have had no issue), (ii) his cousin Antonia (by whom a daughter), (iii) Fulvia (by whom his two sons), (iv) Octavia and of course, finally, (v) Queen Cleopatra, by whom he had two sons and two daughters.

[Claudia] Marcella [major]

Born c. 53, married three times (i) to P. Claudius Pulcher (praetor in c. 24BC, qv); (ii) to M. Vispanius Agrippa, **AUGUSTUS**' great friend and chief minister (qv), and (iii) to Iullus Antonius (qv) [Syme AA 149].

[Claudia] Marcella [minor]
See **Table V Brief Lives**

Claudia Pulchra
See **Table V Brief Lives**

CLAUDIUS I AUGUSTUS
See **Table X** and main text.

Nero Claudius Caesar
See **NERO AUGUSTUS & Table X**

Nero Claudius Drusus
Patrician husband of the elder Antonia, he was younger brother of Emperor **TIBERIUS** and thus also a step-son of **AUGUSTUS**, who married

their mother Livia (daughter of M. Livius Drusus, hence this man's *cognomen*) and Ti. Claudius Nero, a patrician of ancient family, but of the junior patrician branch of the Claudian House. His birth having occurred after Livia had deserted Nero for **Octavianus** (as he then was) there was always a slight question over his parentage, causing **AUGUSTUS** to dote on the lad to the exclusion of his elder brother, the dour future Emperor **TIBERIUS.** Drusus wielded increasing influence after the death of Agrippa in 12 until his own death during his consulship (and on campaign on the Elbe in Germany) in 9.

[?M.] Claudius Iullus
Conceivably the younger son of the unfortunate Iullus Antonius. He perhaps was exiled in 2BC very young. The inscription from which the name comes is unlikely to be to a person of more humble station: the combination of names is against it, bearing in mind Iullus Antonius's Claudian wife. It is otherwise very difficult to explain such a combination of names, although it is possible that more than the *praenomen* is missing from the inscription [PIR[2] C903].

C. Claudius Marcellus
See **Table V Brief Lives**.

M. Claudius Marcellus
Member of the plebeian branch of the Claudian family and son of the above, he was born 42, elected curule aedile in 23BC, but died within months. Married 25 as her first husband, **AUGUSTUS'** daughter Julia, whereupon he became, albeit briefly, the Princeps' first official heir presumptive [PIR[2] C925].

P. Claudius Pulcher
Plebeian member of an ancient patrician family, being son of the notorious tribune P. Claudius

Pulcher (later P. Clodius [Capito Fonteianus]) who got himself formally adopted by the plebeian *monetalis* P. Fonteius Capito in order to become a plebeian himself in 58BC. He was killed in 52 leaving his widow Fulvia, later third wife of **Mark Antony** (qv); the son was b. c. 54, praetor in c 24BC and an augur and also probably had a son, Ap. Claudius Pulcher (not shown) who was a junior senator when exiled in 2BC [ILS 882; PIR² C985/7; Wiseman (1970) 207-221].

Cornelia Cethegilla Aemilia Plancina

Daughter of a Cornelius Cethegus, of an ancient patrician family going back to the third century. Her father's name is lost but he was probably a son of Ser. Cornelius Cethegus, consul AD24 and is thought to have married Aemilia Plancina. She was wife of C. Cornelius Gallicanus, suffect consul in AD85 (qv). [ILS 6675; PIR ² 1485; Wagner (1975) 178, ped. 20]

M. Cornelius Cethegus

Patrician from a junior branch of the ancient Cornelian family revived in the late Republic, either by the Cornelii Lentuli (much given to resurrecting long-forgotten names from their distinguished ancestry) or by marriage alliance with that family. A descendant of a probable brother or other close relative of Cornelia Cethegilla (qv) Marcus was suffect consul not long before AD170. He seems to have adopted M. Gavius Squilla Gallicanus, a descendant of Cornelia Cethegilla (qv), who duly became M. Gavius Cornelius Cethegus and ordinary consul in AD170 [CIL VI 1978].

Cn. Domitius Ahenobarbus

Member of an old and distinguished noble plebeian family, he was consul in AD32. Later in 37 Suetonius claims he was accused of committing incest with his sister, Domitia Lepida, the third wife of C. Ap. Junius Silanus (see **Table V**). He died in AD40, possibly of natural causes, although at this juncture in the reign of **CALIGULA** one cannot be sure; the emperor certainly relieved the son of the marriage – the future emperor **NERO** – of his father's legacy, but he was inclined to grab legacies in any case. Ahenobarbus married the treacherous Julia Agrippina, a grand-daughter of Emperor **AUGUSTUS** and had an elder brother, Lucius, who died fairly young [Syme, AA 142, 159, 179].

L. Domitius Ahenobarbus

Father of the preceding and consul in 16, he later served as proconsul of Africa. He was son of Cn. Domitius Ahenobarbus, consul in 32BC (d. 31) a close associate of **Mark Antony's** and of Aemilia, sister of Paullus Aemilius Lepidus, hence the name of his daughter, Domitia Lepida. He was, apparently, detestable and arrogant, although he celebrated a triumph after service in Illyricum and Germany, so was without doubt a good general. He died in AD25 [Syme AA 157-159, 311].

L. Domitius Ahenobarbus
see **NERO AUGUSTUS**

Fulvia

Fulvia was the daughter of a senator who flourished at the time of the formation of the First Triumvirate, M. Fulvius Bambalio ('stutterer', so named from a personal trait) said to have been the grandson of a *nobilis* – a man descended from consuls – and thus probably a Fulvius Flaccus, a powerful dynasty in the second century BC. Before dying in Greece in 40BC she managed to marry the tribune P. Clodius (P. Claudius Pulcher, qv), followed by a noble non-entity, C. Scribonius Curio, and finally **Mark Antony** [Syme AA 26, 56, 149, 198, 264, 398]

P. Helvidius C. f. Arn. Priscus

Husband of Plautia Quinctilia (qv), and an ex-praetor by AD51. He was a new man, the son of C. Helvidius Priscus from Cluvium, a legionary *primus pilus* (senior warrant officer). His brother Caius, praetor in AD70, fell foul of the Emperor **VESPASIAN** in AD75 [ILS994].

Julia

Julia, was the only surviving child of **AUGUSTUS** and is usually known as Julia (the elder). She was born 39BC, married (i) in 25, M. Claudius Marcellus [see **Table V Brief Lives**] but he died in 23 leaving no issue. She married (ii) the next heir, the Princeps' boyhood friend and chief support, the *novus homo* M. Vipsanius Agrippa, who served as consul in 37BC, 28 and 27 & died in 12. She was involved in a scandal (or plot) in 2BC which resulted in her conviction for adultery with a plethora of exceedingly distinguished people (most of whom might have been viewed as potential challengers for supreme power in due course) including Iullus Antonius (qv) and she was exiled to the island of Pandatera, where she died in AD27 [Syme (1974) *passim.*]

Julia Drusilla

Daughter of Germanicus (see **Brief Lives Tables VII (a) and X**) and married L. Cassius Longinus (consul AD30). She was later the second wife of M. Aemilius Lepidus (died AD40), but had no issue by him. Cassius' daughter is thought to have been (on grounds of chronology if nothing else) the product of an earlier marriage [Syme AA 171-175, 179].

[ ] Junius Blaesus

Praised by Tacitus, praetor late in the reign of **NERO** and in AD69 governor of Gallia Lugdunensis, but poisoned at the instigation of the Emperor **VITELLIUS,** mainly, it would seem, that he was 'a traitor who boasted that he was descended from the Junii and Antonii'. Had it been an empty boast **VITELLIUS** would probably have resorted to a different excuse for killing him, hence the assumption that his father

was probably married to a sister of L. Antonius. [Tacitus, *Histories* iii.38,3; PIR² I737; Syme AA 144, 163, 310].

Q. Junius Q.f. Blaesus

Born in 18 or 17, into a junior senatorial family, Blaesus' father was married to a Junia Silana and was suffect consul in AD10, late in life, whilst he himself held the same office in AD26. His wife, and mother of his son (qv), killed by **VITELLIUS** because of her ancestry, was surely the daughter of Iullus Antonius. He died by his own hand, anticipating condemnation by **TIBERIUS** in AD36 [PIR² I739 Syme AA 144, 163, 304, 310]

Munatia

This marriage is postulated on the basis of Morris (1965) 89f.; Settipani would move the marriage back one generation and make Munatia a second wife of of the consul of 6 [*op.cit.* (2000) 88]

Octavia C.f.

One of the sisters of **AUGUSTUS,** married first to C. Claudius Marcellus and secondly, purely for political reasons, to **Mark Antony,** who swiftly dumped her for Cleopatra VII. She died in 10BC (see **Table III Brief Lives**)

P. Plautius Pulcher

Presumed to be a younger son of M. Plautius Silvanus consul in 2BC and a member of a senatorial family. He was praetor in AD36, the family being given patrician status by **CLAUDIUS** in AD47, but dead by AD54. The fact that he seems not to have held the consulship might suggest that his death occurred very soon after his praetorship, c. AD 37 – perhaps one of the last victims of **TIBERIUS**. The reason for his bearing the Claudian *cognomen* is far from clear; possibly his father had an unrecorded wife before Lartia, the only one recorded for him. His first wife was a

Vibia, his second Quinctilia, a daughter of Varus (below). His sister was the first wife of the Emperor **CLAUDIUS** [ILS 921P; ILS964; Syme AA 87f., 418, 430].

P. Quinctilius Sex. f. Varus
See **Table V Brief Lives**

[?P.] Quinctilius P.f. Ani. Varus
Betrothed, when still a lad, to a daughter of Germanicus, probably Julia Livilla, born in AD18, although in the event, she married M. Vinicius. He seems later to have married a Servilia, although Arnheim attributes him with a Valeria Messallina as a wife, too, although that would not be necessary to explain the Valerian names of his putative grandson, bearing in mind that his mother was Claudia Pulchra, but a Valeria by her father's adoption (see **Table V Brief Lives**). He was praetor before AD27 in which year he was prosecuted, although any verdict on the case was deferred and the outcome is unknown. In keeping with the murderous tendencies of the times - thanks to Praetorian Prefect, L. Aelius Seianus (otherwise Sejanus) - Seager suspects that, as we hear no more of him, he was probably killed or committed suicide, although bearing in mind the crucial gaps in Tacitus, it might conceivably not have been so, although had he lived much longer he would have surely enjoyed the consulship. A son existed but did not apparently flourish, possibly therefore the father of the next entry [ILS 2681; Tac. *Ann.* iv.66; PIR2 Q19, 30; Arnheim (1972) No. 138; Seager (1972) 205; Syme AA 149, 314].

Sex. Quinctilius Sex. f. Ani. Valerius Maximus
Quaestor of Pontus and Bitrhynia c. 100 and probably Pliny's friend Maximus. At first glance is voting tribe clearly suggests descent from Varus the consul of 13, whilst the two *cognomina* may reflect the fact that the latter's third wife, Claudia

Pulchra (from whom this man must descend) was by adoption a Valerius Messalla, which family also used Maximus as an additional cognomen. Whilst his father is only on record solely in his filiation, his grandfather was surely the early-1st century praetor [?P].Quinctilius P.f.Ani. Varus (qv). Again, in him the blood of the Octavii seems to have surived to the end of the 1st century - but probably no longer as, again, this man seems not to have made it to a consulship and there are no obvious candidates to suggest the survival of any posterity. Against this suggestion is the fact that he was commemorated at Alexandria Troas, and may have been a native of that place and that his tribe and names are co-incidental, often a hazard when there is little other evidence. In either case, PIR^2 Vol. V tells us that he was grandfather of the twin consuls for 151 Sex. Quni[c]tilius Valerius Maximus and Sex. Quin[c]tilius Condianus. Both of the two ex-consuls in the next generation were killed on the orders of **COMMODUS** [ILS 1018; Pliny, letter 8, 24; PIR^2 Q21, 22, 24, 25, 26 & 27,].

M. Vipsanius L.f. Agrippa
The close friend, chief minister and son-in-law of **AUGUSTUS,** Agrippa (who, out of sensitivity for his obscure origins did not use his *nomen*) was Consul three times, in 37, 28 and 27. His origin was not elucidated in any ancient source, except from his filiation his father was a Lucius, and the name suggests that the family originated in Venetia or Istria. Nearly everything the Princeps did between the triumvirate and Agrippa's death in 12 was aided and abetted by his friend. His first wife was Caecilia Attica, daughter of Cicero's close friend T. Pomponius Atticus; indeed, they probably shared a similar background. His second wife was [Claudia] Marcella (minor qv) but he was obliged by the Princeps to divorce her and marry his daughter Julia, by whom he had three sons and two daughters. [Syme AA 44]

*

Having looked at **AUGUSTUS'** wider family, all of whom were closely involved with the events of the dynasty to AD68, the man himself now follows as first emperor (princeps in the terminology of the era), along with his descendants, split, for convenience into two separate tables, **VII (a) & (b).**

⋆

AUGUSTUS
16 January 27BC – 19 August AD14

Reign

Imperator Caesar Divi f. Augustus better known as the emperor **AUGUSTUS,** a patrician by adoption and prior to that by creation, was in sole power in the Roman world from 31BC and reigned as Princeps under the style of **AUGUSTUS** from 27 until his death at Nola on 19th August AD14. He was born at Rome 23 September 63BC as **C. Octavius C. f. C. n. Scapt.,** but was testamentarily adopted on 8th May 44 by **Julius Caesar** as **C. Julius C. f. C. n. Caesar Octavianus** the adjectival form of his original name being added to that bestowed by the adoptor in the usual way. He was granted propraetorian *imperium* in January 43 by the senate. After the formation of the Second Triumvirate and the deification of his adoptive father in January 42 he changed his style to **C. Julius Caesar Divi f. Imperator** having been hailed as *imperator* (*generalissimo*) for the first time by his troops the year before. In 40, purely for propaganda reasons, he further modified it - this time in a totally innovative way with no precedent, legal or otherwise – to **Imperator Caesar Divi f.,** which effectively set the standard of address for most subsequent rulers of the Roman world until the fourth century AD.

At the time of the first constitutional re-ordering of 27BC, designed to confirm him totally in power but to give the illusion of a return to normal (republican) government, he assumed the style – granted by the senate on 16th Janaury - by which he was known from then on until his death (above). At the second re-ordering he was granted the power of a tribune of the people for one year – effectively making him a supernumerary tribune – 26th June 23, renewable yearly thereafter – the basis of his effective power and that of his successors.

He was consul thirteen times, starting with a suffect consulship in 43, then ordinary consulships in 33, 31, 30, 29, 28, 27, 26, 25, 24, 23, 5 and 2; he assumed the role of *pontifex maximus* on the death of Lepidus in 12.[87] He was hailed as *imperator* a further twenty times and in 2BC the senate conferred the title *Pater Patriae* ('father of his country') upon him.

The achievements of the first Emperor's reign are such as to challenge the most artful paraphraser. It is possible to apply a whole variety of adjectives to sum up his talents and elusive personality, but he always seems to escape easy categorisation. Sir Ronald Syme

---

87. PIR² I215

comes across as something less than an admirer, although others accord him praise. He was certainly a far more astute politician than his uncle but a much less able commander. His achievement was to weld the empire together, to make sense of all its parts and endow it with a cohesion which lasted almost longer than its parts.

His mastery of propaganda and his elevation of Rome into a worthy imperial capital lent focus. Early consolidation in Spain and the East, were followed by dramatic conquests in the Balkans and on the Danube, although a clear objective in extending Imperial rule from the Rhine to the Elbe received a fatal set-back - despite ringing successes before and afterwards - through the defeat and virtual annihilation of three legions under P. Qunctilius Varus in the *Teutoberger Wald* in AD9.

He married firstly, in late 44BC, Clodia (divorced 40), daughter of P. Clodius and Fulvia, who had re-married **Mark Antony** but they had had no issue (the marriage was probably not consummated) before Augustus made a second political marriage in 40 to Scribonia (divorced 39), daughter of L. Scribonius Libo, an equestrian banker who, unlike Augustus's grandfather was a genuine descendant of a second century *praetor* of the same name. Her brother, however, had entered the senate, rising to consul in 34BC, despite a politically perilous early alliance with Pompey and then with his freebooter second son, Sextus.

Scribonia had been married twice before, her descendants constituting a body of imperial 'connections' – people not close enough to be regarded as part of what we have to begin to call the Imperial family, but close enough to have imperial domestic and political issues affect them. These husbands were first, Cn. Cornelius Lentulus Marcellinus, one of the consuls for 56 and the son of a Claudius Marcellus adopted into the patrician house of the Lentuli and secondly P. Cornelius [Scipio] almost certainly the obscure member of the once great patrician clan of the Scipiones, who was suffect consul in 35BC. The posterity of the issue of both marriages survived well into the mid-first century AD, and in some cases further. We encounter one line in the ancestry of **ANTONINUS PIUS** (**Table XX** below).

In January 38BC Augustus had married for the third time, to Livia Drusilla, wife of the patrician Ti. Claudius Nero, *praetor* in 42BC, a supporter of the Republic who had ended up siding with Antonius before returning to Rome in 39. It was, apparently, a love match, but was politically advantageous as well. Livia was born in 58, daughter of M. Livius Drusus Claudianus, *praetor* in 50 and born the son of C. Claudius Pulcher (consul 92) but adopted by the popularist tribune of 91, M. Livius Drusus, a member of an old plebeian family boasting their first magistracy as far back as 323.[88]

Although absent from most accounts, Livia would seem to have had a brother, and thus yet another connection to trouble **AUGUSTUS'** suspicious advisers, like Maecenas and Agrippa. His existence is only implied by the scattered inscriptions of daughters, but C. Livius Drusus must have been a senator under the triumvirate, unless proscribed or killed in battle immediately after Caesar's assassination. His daughters were: Livia C. f. Pulchra

---

88. M. Livius (C. f. Drusus), *magister equitum* that year; cognomen possibly applied retrospectively, see *Fasti Hydatii* & CIL.I²/130; on Livia herself, see PIR2. L 301

– her cognomen clearly emphasising her descent from Claudius Pulcher the consul of 92BC – and Livia C. f. Livilla.[89]

Livia Drusilla was pregnant with their second son, Drusus Claudius Nero when Augustus married her, yet the marriage was long lasting and successful. A defining element in Livia's life was to line her elder son up as **AUGUSTUS'** chosen successor, to which end her hand was discerned by the cynical in the early demise of M. Claudius Marcellus, Caius and Lucius Caesar and the exile of Agrippa Postumus. Whether or not the scheming master of intrigue she is often portrayed – the evidence is equivocal – she was a constant support for **AUGUSTUS** and the source of much advice, sound or otherwise. She died without having further issue in AD29 aged 86.

Apart from various conspiracies and scandals already alluded to, the Emperor's last years were marred by shadowy conspiracies, largely hushed up and inadequately disinterred by contemporary chroniclers. The most significant took place in 6/7AD and centered around L. Aemilius Paulus. This co-incided with the relegation from public life and exile of an obvious heir, Agrippa Postumus, the youngest brother of C. and L. Caesar, both already dead. He was accused of being an unstable character and generally irresponsible, but was clearly the focus of a move to thrust him forward as the true successor at the expense of **TIBERIUS**. Furthermore, he was not the only person exiled, for Paullus's wife Julia the younger, the grand-daughter of **AUGUSTUS** was also packed off to an island, allegedly for immorality and adultery, just as her mother had nine years before. She is supposed to have had a child by D. Junius Silanus the year before, and may even have married, suggesting, if true, that Paullus was dead, which he was not.[90] The result was that **TIBERIUS** was brought back into the mainstream in 12AD, commended to the senate as senior senator (*princeps senatus*), given full powers by the senate and people and generally made subject of a declaration of succession.[91] By the time the old Emperor died on 19th August 14, his position was apparently unassailable, but underneath, less so than might have been supposed.

The descendants of Augustus himself are here split into two tables, **VII(a)** dealing with the descendants of **AUGUSTUS'** grand-daughter Vipsania and L. Aemilius Paullus, and **VII(b)** dealing with the posterity of Vipsania's younger sister and the dashing young general Germanicus. This presents problems of its own, for the blood of Augustus was spread very widely in the Julio-Claudian era. Whether we can be sure it survived thereafter is much less secure. Having the blood of so illustrious a forebear in one's veins would hardly be likely to guarantee survival under a different dynasty, and there may have been efforts made to obfuscate such connections, however proud a family might be of them in private, by deploying nomenclature imaginatively or merely censoring it. Yet even having the images of illustrious ancestors in one's house - an essential element of upper class Roman family life - could prove fatal under insecure and unstable princes like **CALIGULA, NERO** or **DOMTIAN**.

---

89. AE (1969/70) 118, from Formiae and CIL.XIV. 3796 from Tibur

90. Pettinger (2012) 129-132: the child was probably covertly killed. Julia had even been adopted as his daughter by **AUGUSTUS**, *ibid*. 132 n. 36.

91. *Ibid.*, 145, 151.

Further reading:

Barrett, A. A., *Caligula: the Corruption of Power* (London 1989)

Goldsworthy, A., *Caesar* (London 2006)

Kokkinos, N., *Antonia Augusta* (London, 1992)

Seager, R., *Tiberius* (London 1972)

Southern, P., *Augustus* (London 1998)

Southern, P., *Mark Antony* (Stroud 1998)

Suetonius Tranquillus: *The Twelve Caesars* trans. Graves, R., (London 1957)

Syme, Sir R., *The Augustan Aristocracy* (Oxford 1989)   **AA**

Syme, Sir R., *The Roman Revolution* (Oxford 1939)   **RR**

Tacitus, Cornelius, *Annals of Imperial Rome* (London 1966)

Weigel, R. D., *Lepidus, The Tarnished Triumvir* (London 1992)

TABLE VII (a): THE POSTERITY OF AUGUSTUS 1

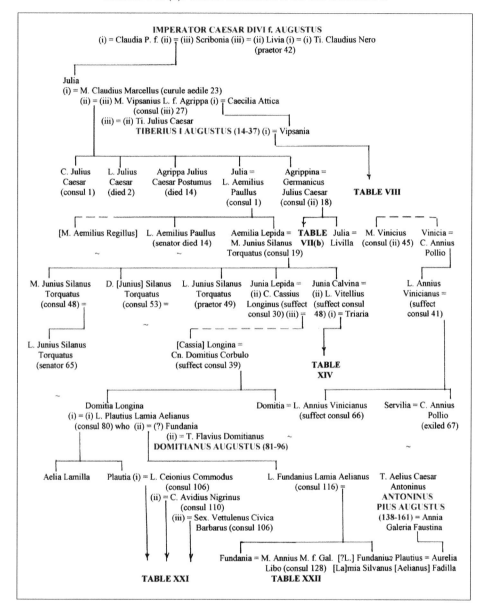

TABLE VII (a) BRIEF LIVES

Aemilia Lepida

Patrician lady, daughter of L. Aemilius Paullus (see **Table VII (b) Brief Lives**) married M. Junius Silanus [Torquatus] consul in AD 19. Prior to her marriage, she was betrothed to Ti. Claudius Nero, the younger brother of Germanicus (and later the emperor **CLAUDIUS**) but this was called off on the fall of her father in AD7, when her intended husband was barely 17 [PIR[2] J 839; Syme AA 174, 188, 191-192].

[M. Aemilius L. f. Regillus]

Thought to be a younger son of L. Aemilius Paullus (see below), but only known from an inscription to family slaves and thought to be distinct from Paullus Aemilius Regillus (see **TABLE V Brief Lives**) [CIL VI 4422 etc.]

L. Aemilius Paullus

Patrician son of Paullus Aemilius Lepidus (consul in 34BC) and his father's first wife Cornelia, daughter of P. Cornelius Scipio (suffect consul in 35BC). He was also nephew of the Triumvir **M. Aemilius Lepidus**. He was consul in AD1 and was probably born c. 28BC - calculated on the date of his consulship which *should* have fallen, as a patrician, when he was 34, but probably came to him five years earlier, as a reward for marrying a princess - Julia, grand-daughter of **AUGUSTUS**. The marriage was in 5 or 4BC. As it turned out, Julia, like her mother, seemed to have a penchant for seeking solace in others' arms and was at the centre of a conspiracy and in AD7 was convicted and condemned for adultery whilst pregnant, with the result that she, too, was banished to an island, her house demolished, her alleged child, once born, exposed, and debarred from burial in the Imperial mausoleum. He was probably killed in 8 [PIR² A391; Pettinger (2012) 124 n 7, 139, Syme AA 118-127].

L. Aemilius Paullus

Patrician, son of the preceding but probably died early in AD14 whilst still only 17 [PIR² A392].

C. Annius Pollio

Brother of the younger Annius Vinicianus he was a senator who was exiled by **NERO** in AD67. His wife Marcia Servilia was a daughter of Q. Marcius Barea Soranus (suffect consul 55) by a daughter of the stoic patrician M. Servilius Nonianus (consul 35). A late first century suffect consul who is recorded only as [ ] Pollionis f[ilius   ] may be

a son, adopted into another family. His uncle, Q. Marcius Barea Sura, was the father of Marcia Furnilla, wife of the future emperor **TITUS** whom she divorced in c.AD 67. It is likely that she had a sister who was the mother of another future emperor **TRAIANUS** see **Tables XV and XVIII Brief Lives** [PIR² A678, B55, M218, S590; Birley (1987) 242; Jones (1992) 11, 59, 201; Levick (1999) 23; Syme (1958) II. 560]

L. Annius Vinicianus

Son of a senator called C. Annius Pollio, he married a lady who is generally thought to have been a sister of M. Vinicius, see **Table VII (b) Brief Lives**. A prime mover in the assassination of **CALIGULA** in January AD41, probably as a result of the death of his friend M. Aemilius Lepidus, he was implicated in the attempted coup against **CLAUDIUS** by *CAMILLUS* and paid with his life for it [FS626; PIR² A677; Syme AA 181, 278].

L. Annius Vinicianus

Son of the preceding, he was a supporter of the Stoics, military tribune in the east under his father-in-law and later suffect consul in AD66 the year he was put to death, it is believed for planning to assassinate **NERO** in the plot of C. Calpurnius Piso [PIR² A701-702; Holland (2000) 207-207]

Aurelia Fadilla

Died c. AD134, presumably without issue, see also **Table XX Brief Lives** [Birley (1987) 242]

C. Avidius Nigrinus

See below **Table XXI Brief Lives**

[Cassia] Longina

Attested by inscriptions (which omit her *nomen*) as the wife of the general Cn. Domitius Corbulo, she is assumed to be the daughter of Cassius Longinus (below). Sir Ronald Syme suggested that

Longinus had been previously married, and that Cassia Longina would have been a daughter of this earlier alliance, not Junia Lepida, mainly on the grounds that Junia Lepida's *presumed* age militating against her being Domitia Longina's mother and the lack of any reference to Augustan descent in the sources that mention her [Syme (1970) 34-39].

C. Cassius Longinus

A distinguished jurist and descendant of one of the assassins of **CAESAR,** he was suffect consul in AD30. He was exiled by **NERO** but survived to be recalled by **VESPASIAN** [Tac. *Ann*. xvi. 9;PIR² C501; Jones (1992) 43].

L. Ceionius Commodus

See beow **Table XXI Brief Lives**

Domitia Longina

Daughter of Nero's ill-fated marshal Cn. Domitus Corbulo and Cassia Longina, daughter of C. Cassius Longinus, she would have ben born c. AD50/51. However, as her mother was known just as Longina, her membership of the famous family of one of Caesar's assassins is far more probable than any other, eg. C. Pompeius Longinus Gallus, an obscure consul. She married L. Plautius Lamia Aelianus whom she left (probably under duress) to become the consort of the future Emperor **DOMITIAN** in 70. She was still alive in 126.[CIL.IX 3426; Suet. *Divus Titus* 10; Syme (1958) I. 300 & II. 560n; PIR² D181].

Cn. Domitius Corbulo

Son of a similarly named senator who came to prominence, presumably from a new family, in the reign of **AUGUSTUS** becoming praetor in AD17. The son had a much married lady called Vistilia for a mother (his father's second wife, his first being a trelative of **VITELLIUS** (qv), and was suffect consul in AD39 before going on to become one of the empire's great generals. He spent many

years under Nero securing the Eastern frontier, but ultimately lost his life through his own success, **NERO** seeing him as a threat and securing his suicide which might well strengthen the case for her Augustan descent. By Cassia Longina he had in addition to his two daughters, almost certainly a son, Cn. Domitius [Corbulo] Ponticus, who rose to a praetorship under **VESPASIANUS,** but who probably died before he could advance to a consulship, thereafter, no further traces of the family [FS 1484; ILS 9518; Syme (1970) 30-99.].

T. Flavius Domitianus

DOMITIANUS I AUGUSTUS see Part B, II(b) below.

Fundania

Married to an uncle of **MARCUS AURELIUS,** see below **Table XXII Brief Lives**

L. Fundanius Lamia [Plautius] Aelianus

Assuming he became consul *suo anno* (the first allowable year) he would have been born c.AD 83, which would fit well with a re-marriage of Lamia Aelianus [PIR² A204; Birley (1987) 34, 238, 246].

[L.] Fundanius Plautius [La]mia Silvanus

A patrician youth, who presumably died young [PIR² A206; Birley, *op.cit*. 246].

Julia

See below **Table VII(b) Brief Lives**

Junia Calvina

Accused of incest with her brother by **CALIGULA**, almost certainly a baseless charge. She was later exiled in the wake of the Messallina affair, recalled in 59 and lived on to a distinguished old age, finally dying in 79. She married L. Vitellius, suffect consul in AD 48 and a victim of the fall of his brother the Emperor **VITELLIUS** [ILS 6239; PIR² I856].

Junia Lepida

Accused of incest with her nephew L. Junius Silanus Torquatus (qv) by **CALIGULA**, almost certainly also a baseless charge. In AD33 or 34 she had married (as his second wife) C. Cassius Longinus, consul in AD30 and presumably became thereby the (step-)mother of Longina. It is not known what became of her [PIR² I861].

D. Junius Silanus Torquatus

The Silani were a distinguished family of the ancient plebeian nobles thought to be a cadet branch of the Junii Bruti; they first come to notice in a praetor during the war against Hannibal. The posterity of his elder son became extinct in the late Republic, but his younger son adopted a younger son of the patrician T. Manlius Torquatus (consul 165BC) and all the numerous Silani of the early Empire were descendants of this match, hence the extra name (*agnomen*) of this man and his sons. Three brothers, sons of M. Junius Silanus (praetor in 77BC) were raised to patrician rank by Augustus in 27. This man and those which follow are descendants of one of these brothers and are thus patrician by creation. Decimus was the second son of M. Junius Silanus and Aemilia (qv), he was b. c. AD21, was consul in AD53 and was obliged to commit suicide AD 64 [FS 2137; ILS 9339; PIR² I837]

L. Junius Silanus Torquatus (elder)

Third son of M. Junius Silanus and Aemilia (qv), he was born AD26 and had the honour of being a companion of the Emperor **CLAUDIUS** on his invasion of Britain aged 15, being afterwards betrothed to Octavia his infant daughter. He became praetor in AD49 but died that year through the machinations of the new Empress, Agrippina [FS 2130; PIR² I829; Syme AA 192]

L. Junius Silanus Torquatus (younger)

Alleged by **CALIGULA** to have committed incest with his aunt, Junia Lepida, by AD60 L. Silanus had become a *Salius Palatinus* (Palatine priest, an office normally reserved for patricians) but was caught up, whether innocently or complicitly is not clear, in the conspiracty of C. Calpurnius Piso against **NERO** in AD65 and was sent into exile, being dispatched by a centurion on arrival, apparently unmarried [ILS 9339; PIR² I838]

M. Junius M. f. Silanus [Torquatus]

M. Silanus was married to Aemilia Lepida (qv) and was consul AD19. He was alive in AD35 & may even have died in his bed [PIR² I839].

M. Junius Silanus Torquatus

Born 14 and consul in 48 aged 34. He was the eldest son and heir of the preceding but died by poisoning in 55 [PIR² I833].

L. Plautius Lamia Aelianus

Although they claimed descent from the plebeian Plautii who enjoyed their first consulship in 358, the Plautii Silvani, to which family Lamia belonged in the male line, first enjoyed the consulship in 2BC, although they had been of senatorial stock since at least 90. A member of the family had been the first wife of **CLAUDIUS I**, and he elevated them to patrician rank in AD47. Lamia's father, Ti. Plautius Silvanus was thus **CLAUDIUS'** nephew by marriage, but had been adopted by Aelius Lamia, a senator recorded in AD37, and had married his daughter. He was born c. 45, was suffect consul in 80 and first husband of Domitia Longina (qv). He seems to have acquiesced in his wife deserting him in 70 for **DOMITIAN**, with whom she remained until she fell for an actor and dancer, when she was repudiated. Lamia was not so lucky, being killed on the orders of **DOMITIAN** sometime around 93, but not before, seemingly, re-marrying a Fundania, judging from the name of his son. Settipani suggests that his second wife was a daughter of Q. Fabius Barbarus Antonius Macer, suffect consul in 64 [PIR² A205;Syme AA 187; Jones (1992) 184-185; Settipani (2000) 282, 305].

Sex. Vettulenus Civica Barbarus
See below **Table XXI Brief Lives**

L. Vitellius L. f. L. n.
A patrician by the elevation to that status of his father, L. Vitellius P. f., the trusted counsellor of **CLAUDIUS I,** who was consul for the second time in AD47 and shared the office of censor with the Emperor in 48, the year patrician status was bestowed. The father was the fourth of the five sons of a senior equestrian officer under **AUGUSTUS,** all of whom became senators. L. Vitellius's younger brother was the venal senator A. Vitellius (later briefly the Emperor **VITELLIUS** in AD69) who served as ordinary consul the year Lucius was suffect, AD48. Junia Calvina was his second wife, whom he divorced in AD47 or 48; his first, Triaria, being mother of his only child, a daughter. He lost his life in the downfall of his brother in AD69 [PIR¹ V501; Syme AA 17]

TABLE VII(b):THE POSTERITY OF AUGUSTUS 2

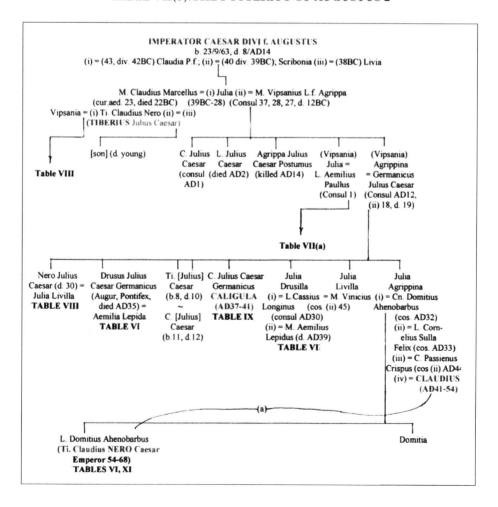

TABLE VII(b) BRIEF LIVES

M. Aemilius Lepidus
See **Table VI Brief Lives**

L. Aemilius Paullus
Consul 1AD, see **Table VII (a) Brief Lives**

CALIGULA
See **CAIUS AUGUSTUS** below .

L. Cassius Longinus
A descendant of a family of the ancient plebe-ian nobility and a descendant of the assassin of **CAESAR**. Born around 4, he was allegedly easy-going, and was consul in AD30; around the time he married Germanicus' daughter (and sister of **CALIGULA**) Julia Drusilla in AD33, before divorcing her to allow her to marry M. Aemilius Lepidus, in whose fall she was fatally implicated. Longinus' fate is not known; he may even have died in his bed.
[Syme AA 97-100]

M. Claudius Marcellus
Son of C. Claudius Marcellus (consul 50BC, see **Brief Lives Table V**), he was born 42BC, curule aedile in 23, died of natural causes shortly after-wards. He married 25 as her first husband, Julia (the elder) daughter of **AUGUSTUS**, whereupon he became Augustus' first official heir presump-tive, for which his family were raised to the patriciate. There were no children [PIR² C925].

Ti. Claudius Nero
Otherwise **TIBERIUS I AUGUSTUS** see below and **Table VIII**.

Ti. Claudius Nero
Otherwise **NERO AUGUSTUS**, see below.

L. Cornelius Sulla Felix
Member of an old patrician family and a descen-dant of the son of the Dictator **Sulla** who had married **Pompey's** daughter (see above **Table I Brief Lives**), hence an embodiment of the dynasts of the late Republic, a dangerous political legacy in a polity where memories were long. He was consul in AD33 and was the stepfather of the Emperor **NERO.** His wife, Germanicus' daughter Julia Agrippina, was a masterful and ambitious woman [PIR² C1462/5]

Cn. Domitius Ahenobarbus
See **Table VI Brief Lives.**

L. Domitius Ahenobarbus
Otherwise **NERO AUGUSTUS**, see below **Part I(b).**

Julia (the elder)
See **Table VI Brief lives**

Julia
Born 19 or 18BC, married L. Aemilius Paullus c. 4BC. Adopted as his daughter by **AUGUSTUS** in 4, but had an adulterous relationship with D. Junius Silanus and possibly had a child by him, subsequently murdered. Exiled with Paullus in AD7 and died after a very long exile on Trimeus (kept alive, so it was said, by the intervention of the Empress Liva) in 28 [Pettinger (2012) 129-132; Syme AA 103].

Julia Agrippina
Normally known as Agrippina the Younger. Eldest daughter of Germanicus and born in AD15, she seems to have been an inordinately ambitious, scheming and ruthless woman, who died as she lived. Like her sisters, she was accused

of incest with her brother **CALIGULA** (case not proven). Nevertheless, her first husband (whom she married in 28) died in AD40, possibly (but not certainly) as a result of a conspiracy against the Emperor but she herself was also involved and was exiled to the island of Pontica. She returned the following year, and married L. Cornelius Sulla Felix who seems to have died not long afterwards and she then wooed but failed to ensnare the aristocratic future emperor **GALBA** before settling c. 40 on C. Sallustius Crispus Passienus (qv). He became consul for the second time (probably as a result of marrying a princess) in AD44 in which year he suddenly died, leaving his fortune to Agrippina's son, L. Domitius Ahenobarbus, born AD37. One source tells us she poisoned him. Two years later, she married the Emperor **CLAUDIUS I,** managed to persuade him to adopt her son (as Ti. Claudius Nero Germanicus) whom she ultimately manoeuvred into succeeding to the purple in AD54 (she is alleged in another source to have poisoned her husband, the emperor). She got her cone-uppance, however, in March AD59, when her son had her murdered. [PIR² I641]

Julia Drusilla

Second daughter of Germanicus, b. 16 or 17; like her sisters, she was accused of incest with her brother **CALIGULA** (case not proven). She was then (35) married L. Cassius Longinus (consul AD30) and two years later became the second wife of M. Aemilius Lepidus (died AD40), but had no issue by either, it seems. Died in AD38 and deified by her brother **CALIGULA** (see **Tables VII(a) & VIII Brief Lives**) [PIR² I664]

Julia Livilla

Born 16 or 17, apparently a great beauty, like her sisters, she was accused of incest with her brother **CALIGULA** and adultery with that emperor's friend (and victim) M. Aermilius Lepidus

(see **Table IV Brief Lives)**, which resulted her being sent into exile on Pontica with her sister Agrippina (qv). On her return in AD41 she aroused the jealousy of the Empress Messalina (see **Table X Brief Lives**) and was again exiled (this time to Pandatera) and shortly afterwards killed (c. 42). Her nephew, L. Annius Vinicianus later went on to fall foul of **CLAUDIUS I.** [PIR² I674]

Agrippa [Julius Caesar] Postumus

He was born shortly after Agrippa's death in 12. He was the youngest son of M. Vipsanius Agrippa (qv) and Julia, the daughter of **AUGUSTUS,** by whom he was adopted after the deaths of his two elder brothers, in AD4, as next heir. However, he appears to have had personality difficulties, being truculent, uncouth and indifferent, which caused the Princeps to prefer **TIBERIUS** over him as a potential successor, especially as the Empress Livia preferred her own son over Postumus, who was only as her step-grandson. He was exiled in AD7 to Sorrento and then the island of Planasia where, in the days after the accession of **TIBERIUS,** the great Imperial minister Sallustius Crispus had him killed, allegedly without the new Emperor's knowledge, aged just 26 [Pettinger (2012) *passim.*, PIR² 214].

C. Julius Caesar

Eldest son of M. Agrippa and Julia, born in 20BC and adopted formally in 17 as his heir by **AUGUSTUS,** symbolically taking the name of Caesar the Dictator. As a patrician (by creation and adoption) his consulship should have fallen in or about AD13 and even with the sort of five year remission granted to members of the Imperial family it would have fallen not earlier than AD7 or 8, but Augustus was desperate to get him into position as heir in every sense, especially as he was very popular with the people. He was sent to the East with the army at 19, and was still there, in Syria, when nominated as Consul in AD1. The expedition he nominally led was a success, but he was wounded fighting the Parthians and died in Lycia en route to Rome in AD4.

C. Julius Caesar Germanicus

Youngest son of Germanicus and, by AD37 when he succeeded as Emperor, the only survivor. [PIR² I217]. See below, **CALIGULA AUGUSTUS.**

Drusus Julius Caesar Germanicus

Second son of Germanicus Julius Caesar. His formal style was Drusus Julius Germ[anici] f. Aug[usti] pron. Caesar, he was born AD7 or 8, quaestor in AD28 in which year he married Aemilia Lepida (qv); a pontifex and augur; arrested by Sejanus in AD30, died in prison, probably murdered, AD35, leaving no children [PIR² I220]

Germanicus Julius Caesar

The gifted and personable son of Nero Claudius Drusus, the favourite stepson of **AUGUSTUS** by one of the daughters of **Mark Antony** (qv **Introduction**), Ti. Claudius Nero Germanicus was born in 15BC and turned out to be intellectually gifted and a good orator. When Agrippa's two eldest sons died, **TIBERIUS** was formally adopted by the Princeps, as Ti. Julius Caesar, and in AD4 he in turn adopted his nephew Germanicus as his heir (becoming Germanicus Julius Ti. f. Augusti n. Divi pron[epos] Caesar), thus securing the succession. He was consul in AD12 and again in AD18. For most of these years he was serving in the armed forces, displaying considerable military gifts and quelling a serious mutiny on the Rhine in AD14. He was sent to the East in AD17 but fell ill at Antioch and died in AD19, the distinguished governor there, Cn. Calpurnius Piso (who did not like him) being

condemned, probably wrongly, for poisoning him. He married [Vispania] Agrippina, probably in AD5. He is attributed by most authors with unique gifts of handsomeness, leadership and affability to which the character and demeanour of those of his children who reached maturity hardly testified; they included the unstable tyrant, **CALIGULA.** [Full style, ILS 107; PIR² I221]

L. Julius Caesar

Born 17BC the second son of Agrippa and Julia, he was formally adopted in the year of his birth simultaneously with his elder brother Caius by Augustus. Quaestor in AD1, he died AD2 en route to join the forces in Spain, unmarried, although at the time betrothed to Aemilia Lepida, sister of M'. Aemilius Lepidus (consul AD11) who went on to marry first, a much older man, the *novus homo* P. Sulpicius Quirinius, who had been consul in 11BC and on his death Mamercus Aemilius Scaurus (suffect consul in AD21) [PIR² I222]

Nero Julius Caesar

Eldest son of Germanicus, born probably in AD6, he was first of all betrothed to Junia Metella, daughter of the last of the illustrious Caecilii Metelli, being daughter of Q. Caecilius Metelus Creticus Silanus (consul in AD7) and a Junius Silanus by birth, but she died before they could marry. His full formal style was Nero Julius Germ[anici] f. Ti. Augusti n. [Divi] Aug. pron. Caesar. He became quaestor in AD 24, years in advance of the usual age (the privilege of a prince of the Imperial family) He had married Julia, the daughter of Drusus Julius Caesar and Livia Julia, the widow of Caius Caesar (qv **Table VIII Brief Lives**) in 20. He had risen to a praetorship when in AD29 he was indicted for treason through the machinations of the scheming praetorian prefect Seianus, exiled and was killed in 31 [Formal style ILS107; PIR² I223; Wiseman (1974) 190-191].

Ti. [Julius] Caesar

A son of Germanicus, b. c. AD8, like his brother Caius Caesar, he died an infant probably in AD10. [PIR² I225, 218]

Ti. Julius Caesar Augustus

Otherwise **TIBERIUS AUGUSTUS see Part I(b).**

C. Sallustius Crispus Passienus

Of an emergent family, he was the son of C. Passienus Rufus (consul in AD4) but was adopted by C. Sallustius Crispus, the last great equestrian minister of **AUGUSTUS.** He married first Domitia, aunt of **NERO** and secondly, that Emperor's widowed mother, the scheming Agrippina, (qv). Crispus was a brilliant forensic orator and wit, but rich and obsequious; he was consul in AD27 & 44, but died in unexplained circumstances in the latter year. That his widow and thus his step son, **NERO** inherited his considerable fortune seems instructive [Syme, AA 159-163, 180,182].

M. Vinicius P.f. M. n. L. pron. Pob.

The family came from Cales, in Campania, south of Rome, and were of junior senatorial stock. Both his father Publius and great-grandfather Lucius (one of the great marshals of **AUGUSTUS)** had held the consulship, whilst he himself held it twice, in AD30 (with Cassius Longinus, qv) and again in AD45. He was apparently an elegant orator and a man of gentle disposition. He married Germanicus' daughter Julia Livilla (qv) and seems to have emerged unscathed from the dangers that beset his wife, despite being proposed as emperor after his Imperial brother-in-law's assassination. He survived until AD46 when, inevitably, Messallina, whom he spurned, encompassed his demise, by poison. [PIR¹ V445; Syme AA 181].

[Vipsania] Agrippina

The wife of Germanicus (qv) and youngest of the daughters of Agrippa. She was a great support of her husband and single minded in her efforts to avenge his death (as she saw it), to the detriment of Cn. Piso, who was accused of encompassing it. Subsequently she showed herself feisty and not to be browbeaten by **TIBERIUS** and his sinister minister, Seianus. The inevitable consequence was that she was condemned and exiled in AD29 to the Mediterranean island of Pandateria and later starved herself to death [Syme, AA, 93f.,132-133, 428f.].

[Vipsania] Julia

Born 19 or 18BC, marr. L. Aemilius Paullus consul AD1, c. 4BC. She and Paullus were banished for adultery in AD7; he seems to have died in late 13 or early 14; she died on an island off the coast of Apulia in 28 [Syme (1986) 123-125].

M. Vipsanius L.f. Agrippa

See above **Table VI Brief Lives.**

*

TIBERIUS I
19 August AD14 – 16 March 37

Background

Ti. [Julius] Caesar Augusti f. Divi n. is the style employed on adoption in AD4 by the old patrician senator Ti. Claudius Nero, son of the *praetor* of 42BC and Livia, who re-married the emperor **AUGUSTUS**.[92] **TIBERIUS** was born in the year of his father's praetorship and was *quaestor Augusti*, that is, in personal attendance as quaestor on **AUGUSTUS** himself, in 23, the start of his senatorial career. He inherited the estate of a childless well-wisher – who could indeed have been distantly related – M. Gallius (one of the praetors in the fateful year of Caesar's assassination), on condition of a testamentary adoption. Suetonius tells us he soon dropped the name **M. Gallius Nero Claudianus** and reverted to his own. This would not have affected his patrician status.[93]

He was *praetor* in 16BC and thereafter had a distinguished military career in the east Gaul, Pannonia (12-9) and Germany (9-7), proving himself to be a general of more than ordinary competence. Yet things began to go sour for him in 12 when Agrippa died and he became the 'long-stop' heir to Augustus, with only Agrippa's three very young sons to keep him from the cauldron of power, something he did not enjoy. Furthermore, his younger brother Drusus was long favoured over him, which no doubt rankled. Both, however, were given the proconsular power late in 11BC for five years.

Also in 12, Augustus, no doubt at the prodding of Tiberius' mother, the empress Livia, obliged him to divorce his wife of many years, Agrippa's daughter Vipsania (they were betrothed in her infancy) in order to marry his own mother-in-law and step-sister, Julia, with whom he did *not* get on, leading to their parting at an early date. It is said that he could never even catch sight of Vipsania thereafter without being moved to tears, although she seems to have re-married C. Asinius Gallus, consul in 8BC, without further trauma.

Tiberius was consul in 13BC and in 7 (when he was again granted the proconsular power)[94] and in many ways was the obvious successor in terms of effectiveness, prestige and authority, yet was very much overshadowed in the longer term by C. and L. Caesar and it seems to have grated along with the failure of his marriage to Julia. Consequently, he withdrew from public life and to Rhodes in 6BC, the year Augustus, who doesn't emerge from the ancient sources as really liking Tiberius, granted him the tribunician power. Four years later Julia was implicated in the shadowy conspiracy, news of which cannot have helped. Yet with the death of Caius Caesar in AD4 he had to be recalled, bearing in mind that

---

92. ILS107; PIR2, C 941. He was, however, occasionally (eg. AD7) styled Ti Julius Caesar Augusti f. Claudianus, cf. CIL vi. 40339, cf. Dio 55.27.3-4.].

93. Suetonius *Tiberius* 6.3; a testamentary adoption strictly speaking did not affect the adoptee's status – patrician or plebeian – or tribe – except with Octavian/Augustus, of course! See Syme (1986) 53-54

94. Dio, LIV, 33,5 & 34, 4

Agrippa Postumus, who was adopted by the Princeps at the same time, was quietly sidelined three years later, either because he was the focus of a faction which had previously supported Caius Caesar or because he was considered temperamentally unsuitable. **TIBERIUS** was adopted (on 26th June) by **AUGUSTUS** and in his turn ordered to adopt his brother's eldest son, Germanicus, who thus got precedence over his own surviving son, Drusus, which rankled even further. In 12 he was made *princeps senatus,* given the proconsular *imperium,* earned putting down the Pannonian revolt and repairing the damage in Germany of the disaster of Varus' defeat in the *Teutoberger Wald* in AD9, and designated heir.[95]

He was first hailed as *imperator* in 9BC then again a year later, followed by AD6, 8, 9, 11, 13 and16. He assumed the office of *Pontifex Maximus* on the death of Augustus, and was granted tribunician power 26th June, 6BC for five years and then again 26th June, AD4, renewed annually. He adopted, at the same time as he himself was adopted by **AUGUSTUS**, 27th June AD4, Nero Claudius Drusus, elder son of his brother Drusus (see below) who became his official heir.

Reign

Having succeeded, leading to a slight adjustment in nomenclature (to **Ti. Caesar Divi Aug[usti] f. Divi n.**), it was apparent that he was damaged goods. Always rather aloof, with few real friends, his long disengagements from the political front line either in exile or at war, put him at a disadvantage. The disappointments and humiliations of the preceding reign seem to have left an indelible mark on his psyche, compounding an inherent failure properly to communicate his feelings either to his family, advisors or the senate. Furthermore, he did not really want the job; Augustus was something of a hard act to follow anyway and he was at heart a republican, unable or unwilling to risk any restoration which could easily plunge the Empire back into factional warfare.

Nor was the succession a foregone conclusion. Andrew Pettinger has recently suggested that the transition was really quite fragile and identified M. Scribonius Drusus Libo as the leader of a serious plot to push the new Princeps aside and either restore the Republic or take power himself.[96] A descendant of Pompey and great-nephew of Scribonia, the second wife of **AUGUSTUS,** Libo was at the time a praetor along with his probable half brother Scribonius Proculus, whilst his elder brother of the whole blood, Lucius, was one of thee consuls for the year. His machinations were not aided by the attempt of one of Agrippa Postumus's slaves, Clemens, to impersonate his former master and promote himself as *Princeps.* This ultimately failed, and **TIBERIUS,** through the medium of his first great equestrian minister, Sallustius Crispus (who had caused Postumus to be killed in the first place, probably on his own initiative), played down the entire matter and once apprehended, Clemens was quietly disposed of. With Libo, a very prominent member of the ruling élite, a trial for treason (*maiestas*) had to be staged, and the offending challenger for power neutralised of in as

---

95. Pettinger (2012) 143-145
96. Pettinger (2012) *passim.*

near legal a manner as possible. It was not to be the last time a member of Libo's family was to be destroyed by the lure of supreme power, for *CAMILLUS* Scribonianus, leader of an attempted *coup* in AD42 and Piso, the designated heir of **GALBA,** were both close kinsmen. Ironically though, the Scribonian blood-line was also a notable element in the distinguished ancestry of **MARCUS AURELIUS** 150 years later (see **Table XXII Brief Lives**).

As a result, **TIBERIUS** treated the senate at first with kid gloves, but as time went on and his position seemed increasingly secure, we find hostile prosecutions being launched in the senate almost out of the blue, with senators getting killed or persuaded to suicide for ridiculous reasons. Simultaneously, the emperor's close advisors acquired increasing amounts of power. Thus by the time he had retired permanently to Capreae (Capri) in AD29, his affairs were in the hands of an increasingly confident praetorian prefect with powerful familial links to a number of senatorial families called L. Aelius Seianus, known to history as Sejanus. By the time he was finally toppled in AD31, much permanent damage had been done, many distinguished lives lost and more in his bloody downfall. In spite of this, his successor, Q. Naevius Sutorius Macro, was hardly an improvement.

These events and the gradual attrition of the Imperial family by death and misadventure, tend to disguise the fact that administratively **TIBERIUS** reign was predominantly peaceful and prosperous. At his death at Circeii on 16th March 37, he left a healthy realm to an exceedingly unhealthy survivor of the holocaust he had made of his immediate family: the emperor **CAIUS (CALIGULA).**

Further reading:
Pettinger A., *The Republic in Danger* Oxford 2012
Seager, R., *Tiberius,* London 1972
Syme, Sir R., *The Augustan Aristocracy* Oxford 1986

TABLE VIII: THE POSTERITY OF TIBERIUS

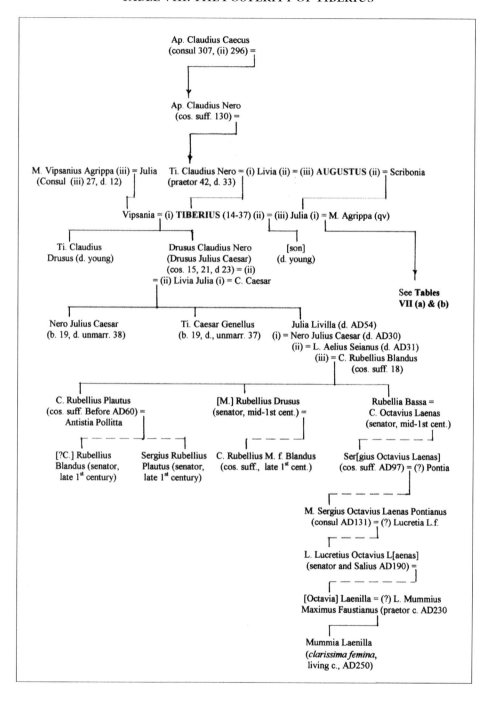

Ap. Claudius Caecus
(consul 307, (ii) 296) =

Ap. Claudius Nero
(cos. suff. 130) =

M. Vipsanius Agrippa (iii) = Julia   Ti. Claudius Nero = (i) Livia (ii) = (iii) **AUGUSTUS** (ii) = Scribonia
(Consul (iii) 27, d. 12)   (praetor 42, d. 33)

Vipsania = (i) **TIBERIUS** (14-37) (ii) = (iii) Julia (i) = M. Agrippa (qv)

Ti. Claudius   Drusus Claudius Nero   [son]
Drusus (d. young)   (Drusus Julius Caesar)   (d. young)
                            (cos. 15, 21, d 23) = (ii)
                            = (ii) Livia Julia (i) = C. Caesar

See **Tables
VII (a) & (b)**

Nero Julius Caesar   Ti. Caesar Genellus   Julia Livilla (d. AD54)
(b. 19, d. unmarr. 38)   (b. 19, d., unmarr. 37)   (i) = Nero Julius Caesar (d. AD30)
                                                         (ii) = L. Aelius Seianus (d. AD31)
                                                         (iii) = C. Rubellius Blandus
                                                         (cos. suff. 18)

C. Rubellius Plautus   [M.] Rubellius Drusus   Rubellia Bassa =
(cos. suff. Before AD60) = (senator, mid-1st cent.) =   C. Octavius Laenas
Antistia Pollitta   (senator, mid-1st cent.)

[?C.] Rubellius   Sergius Rubellius   C. Rubellius M. f. Blandus   Ser[gius Octavius Laenas]
Blandus (senator,   Plautus (senator,   (cos. suff., late 1st cent.)   (cos. suff. AD97) = (?) Pontia
late 1st century)   late 1st century)

M. Sergius Octavius Laenas Pontianus
(consul AD131) = (?) Lucretia L.f.

L. Lucretius Octavius L[aenas]
(senator and Salius AD190) =

[Octavia] Laenilla = (?) L. Mummius
Maximus Faustianus (praetor c. AD230

Mummia Laenilla
(*clarissima femina*,
living c., AD250)

TABLE VIII: BRIEF LIVES

L. Aelius Seianus (Sejanus)

Praetorian prefect and chief adviser to **TIBERIUS**, becoming *his eminence grise* after the Emperor withdrew to Capri. He was the son of L. Seius Strabo (prefect of Egypt AD14-16) but allied to senatorial families and adopted by L. Aelius Gallus, who had been Prerfect of Egypt early in the reign of **AUGUSTUS**. He was Praetorian Prefect in succession to his father in AD14 and remained so until his death. His long-game plan was to replace **TIBERIUS** with Ti. Gemellus (qv) whom he then hoped to control totally. To achieve this he had to eliminate all other heirs, a task which he set about with gusto. The final temptation was to secure an ordinary consulship (despite not being a senator) which he achieved in AD31 and at the same time to procure an alliance himself with a princess of ther Imperial house, hence his marriage with Julia Livilla (whose husband he had just derstroyed), both acts which comfortably overstepped the mark (he was, after all, an equestrian, called by Tacitus *municipalis adulter* – 'small-town adulterer') and precipitated his fall and execution that same year. All in all, a nasty piece of work. [Syme AA 302-303]

CALIGULA
See below and **Table VII (b)**

Claudia Livilla
See **Julia Livilla**

Ap. Claudius Caecus
One of the outstanding men of the middle Republic, the patrician Caecus was fifth in descent from Ap. Claudius Sabinus, the founder of the dynasty and consul in 495BC. He was twice consul, defeated the Samnites when praetor in 295, and censor in 312. He was responsible for the building of the Appian Way and Rome's first aqueduct, the Aqua Appia.His younger son, Tiberius was the first to use the name Nero.

Ap. Claudius Nero
Patrician great-great-great-grandson of Caecus, he is noted only for having served the year out as suffect consul following the death in office of L. Cornelius Lentulus in 130BC; grandfather of the praetor of 42 [Badian (1990) 402, n. 10].

Drusus Claudius Nero
Later styled **Nero Claudius Drusus** and, after Tiberius's adoption by **AUGUSTUS** in AD4, **Drusus Julius Ti. f. Aug. n. Divi pron. Caesar**. The eldest surviving son of **TIBERIUS** he was a patrician, born after his parents' divorce in 12BC, consul in AD15 and again in 21; he married c. AD8 his cousin [Claudia] Livilla (later Livia Julia), herself born 14BC, the widow of Augustus's heir, C. Caesar. He received the tribunician power in AD22. He died, probably poisoned, in September AD23, his widow, mixed up in Sejanus's downfall, died by suicide in 31 [ILS107]

Ti. Claudius Nero
Patrician and Caesarian partisan, quaestor in 48BC. After Caesar's death, however, as praetor in 42 he supported the Republicans, then Mark Antony after Caesar's death and had the humiliation of losing his wife Livia Drusilla to the young Octavianus in 37; they married in January the following year. Nero seems to have retired thereafter [Syme, AA 94, 99f].

Julia Agrippina
See **Table VII(b) Brief Lives**

Julia Drusilla
See **Table VII(b) Brief Lives**

Julia Livilla
Patrician, born AD6 as Claudia Livilla but changed her name on her grandfather's adoption in AD4 to Julia Livilla, sometimes rendered as Livia Julia. She married first her cousin, Nero Julius Caesar (the elder), the eldest son of Germanicus but had no issue by him, who was exiled by Sejanus in 29 and put to death. Sejanus is known to have married, shortly before his fall, a princess of the family, and Syme convincingly suggests Julia Livilla was the one obliged to ally herself with the scheming minister. However, he was killed within a month or two of the marriage, and she again re-married in AD33 the relatively obscure senator C. Rubellius C. f. Blandus When a widow, she was twice exiled, the second time, through the machinations of the empress Messallina, to Pandateria where she was put to death in 54 [PIR². I303; Syme AA 170-171].

Drusus Julius Caesar Germanicus
See **Brief Lives Table VII (b)**

Germanicus Julius Ti.f. Divi Aug. n. Divi pron. Caesar
See **Table VII(b) Brief Lives Table**

Nero Julius Caesar (the elder)
See **Table VII(b) Brief Lives**

Nero [Julius] Caesar (the younger)
Patrician, eldest surviving son of Drusus (qv), born AD19, made one of the Arval brethren in 26/29 and died, a victim of **CALIGULA** in 38, unmarried. [Lewis, (1955) 147].

Ti. Germanicus [Julius] Caesar Gemellus Born in 19, twin with his brother Nero (qv), named

with **CALIGULA** by **TIBERIUS** as his co-heir in 35 and in 37 given, *inter alia*, the title *princeps juventutis* – 'Prince of Youth' – and adopted as his son by the former. He was forced to suicide later the same year, suspected of involvement in a plot against **CALIGULA**, unmarried [Syme AA 311f]

Livia Drusilla
Daughter of M. Livius Drusus Claudianus, praetor in 50BC, who was born a younger son of the patrician consul for 92, C. Claudius Pulcher, but was the adopted son of M. Livius Drusus, ambitious member of a distinguished plebeian noble family, killed as a revolutionary tribune of the people in 91. Livia was born 58 married in 43 to a distant kinsman, Ti. Claudius Nero, giving him two sons, but left him in 38 for **Octavianus (AUGUSTUS)** becoming Rome's first Empress. She is usually pictured as her husband's closest advisor, and constantly manoeuvred to get her elder son **TIBERIUS** into the succession, to which end the deaths of Marcellus, C. & L. Caesar and the exile of Agrippa Postumus might well be attributable. She survived everyone but her elder son, dying in AD29, and earning deification from **CLAUDIUS** in AD42.

L. Lucretius Octavius L[aenas?]
A patrician by creation, as he was co-opted a member of a priestly college open only to patricians, the *Salii Palatini* in 190. Thought to be a son of M. Segius Pontianus (qv) [PIR² L409]

Mummia Laenilla
Mummia is probably the last person traceable possibly to have the blood of **TIBERIUS I** in her veins, assuming her descent can be accepted. Her mother, [**Octavia**] Laenilla probably married L. Mummius Maximus Faustianus who held the praetorship in the 2nd quarter of the 3rd century, but not descended from the republican Mummii [PIR² M708, 713].

C. Octavius Laenas

Senator who flourished c. AD33/70; his father, an ex-consul, was possibly adlected into the patriciate in 48. He was a first cousin through the marriage of his aunt, Sergia Plautilla, to the emperor **NERVA** [see below, **part III(a) Table XVII Brief Lives**] He married Rubellia Bassa, daughter of Julia Livilla and Rubellius Blandus. (qv) [ILS952; Syme (1958) II. 627-628]

Ser[gius Octavius Laenas?]

Assuming the reconstruction of the name from the fragmentary inscription (the *praenomen* could be Servius, although no candidates of the period suggest themselves), he was a patrician by creation, presumably son of the preceding. Either way he was suffect consul 97, perhaps married to a Pontia [Syme, *loc.cit.*].

C. Rubellius C. f. Blandus

Suffect consul in 18, whose father was a praetor and proconsul of Crete under **AUGUSTUS** and whose great-uncle was a rhetor mentioned by Cicero in 43. From the evidence of names, the father may have married a sister of L. Sergius Plautus, praetor in AD2. [Cicero, *ad Fam.* iii.26.1; PIR² R110; Syme (1982) 66]

[C?] Rubellius Blandus

Possibly the younger son of C. Rubellius Plautus and a degenerate noble living in the late 1ˢᵗ century, assuming we can take Juvenal at face value. [Juvenal, *Satire* viii. 39f., PIR² R106]

C. Rubellius M. f. Blandus

Suffect consul late 1ˢᵗ century; honoured at Marruvium and presumably the son of Rubellius Drusus (qv below) [JRS LXVI (1976) 185 & n. 136]

[M.] Rubellius Drusus

Senator, known only as [ ] *Blandi f. Drusus*, mid 1ˢᵗ century, presumably younger brother of Rubellius Plautus [PIR² R112]

[C.] Rubellius Plautus

Suffect consul between AD38-60, he was advised in the latter year in a letter by Nero to put himself beyond the reach of conspiracy and retire to his estates in Asia, where he was put to death two years later by a centurion sent by the emperor. His *praenomen* is not certain. By his wfe Antistia Pollitta he had one, perhaps two sons [PIR² R115; Syme, AA 160, 182, 281f]

Sergius Rubellius Plautus

Presumed elder son of C. Rubelius Plautus (qv), a senator in the later 1ˢᵗ century, assuming he escaped the slaughter of his family in 65; otherwise perhaps to be identified with the preceding. Settipani places him as a third son of the sufferct consul of 18. [ILS 281; Settipani (2000) 268-273].

M. Sergius Sergi f. C. n. Octavius Laenas Pontianus

Patrician, consul AD131, perhaps husband of a Lucretia L. f. His filiation helps to confirm the identification of his putative father Sergius Octavius Laenas (qv). [ILS952; Syme (1958) II. 627-628]

CAIUS
(Known to history as Caligula)
16th March AD37- 17th January 41

——————

Background

C. [Julius] Caesar is better known as **CALIGULA,** a name meaning 'little boots' given to him by the soldiers when he accompanied his father Germanicus on campaign.[97] He was born a patrician by descent and adoption on 31st August, AD12; *quaestor* in 34, he was designated Tiberius's heir in 35 along with Tiberius Gemellus (see above), whom he had killed after his accession in March 37. He was brought up by the women in his family, surrounded by the sons of various foreign client kings, notably M. Julius [Herod] Agrippa, the future King of Judaea, but enjoyed immense popularity as his father's son. He was given absolutely no responsibility by Tiberius, whose last Praetorian Prefect, Q. Naevius Cordus <u>Sutorius Macro</u>, seeing which way the wind was blowing, attached himself to his cause (aided by his wife, Ennia Thrasylla, who connived at his adultery with her) only to be disposed of after **CALIGULA'S** succession.

Reign

As emperor, he took the style **C. [Julius] Caesar Germanicus Augustus** and was acknowledged as Pontifex Maximus. He entered upon a suffect consulship, and held further consulships in 39, 40 and 41, the latter two as sole (ordinary) consul. He was also granted the tribunician and proconsular power by the senate on accession and (rather improbably for someone so divorced from military affairs) hailed as *imperator*, an embarrassment not repeated. His lack of public office distanced him from the constitutional niceties observed by Augustus and Tiberius, and his personality, wayward and possibly manic, inclined him increasingly towards the sort of autocratic behaviour expected of his friend Herod Agrippa. Added to which, he scandalised the governing class by allegations of incest, murder, and the threat (or joke) to make his horse, Inchitatus, ordinary consul with him for 40. In foreign relations – especially with the Jews – his policies were disastrous, his profligacy extraordinary and his behaviour outrageous. A planned invasion of Britain in 40 failed to materialise and ended in a lot of expensive posturing. Nevertheless, he is only accused of having brought about the deaths of 27 leading people, 14 being senators, although over only four years this may be regarded as pretty deleterious. Caligula became seriously ill in October 37 and was *hors de combat* until the year's end; only after this episode did his behaviour become seemingly deranged and unstable; scholarly attempts to identify the cause have yet to agree on its nature.[98]

———————————————————————————————————————

97. Tacitus, *Annales* 1.41.2; PIR² I 217
98. Suet. *Caius Caligula* xiv.2, 24, 51, discussed in Barrett (1989) 71, 73-74.

The first serious plot against him, that of Lentulus Gaetulicus (the details of which are obscure, but which involved Caligula's brother-in-law Lepidus in some way), failed and ended in the conspirators' deaths; it was the second, put into action on 17th January 41, which succeeded.

CALIGULA'S immediate ancestry and adoptive ancestry is to be found in the previous section **Table VII(a)**. His Claudian – male line – ancestry will be found under **CLAUDIUS Table X**. During his brief reign, he managed to marry four times – one per year seeming a high turnover by any reckoning.

The *first* marriage was in 33 to Junia Claudi[ll]a, daughter of M. Junius Silanus, suffect consul in AD15 whose unknown wife may well have been a relative of Tiberius's, bearing in mind Junia's second name, a feminine diminutive of Claudius.[99] A member of a different branch of the family to Aemilia Lepida's husband [see above, **Table VI**], she had died in childbirth prior to Caligula's accession.

His *second* wife was Livia Orestilla (according to Suetonius[100]) or Cornelia Orestina (according to Dio[101]), whom he married before the end of 37, but had put aside either after a few days (or again, according to Dio, after two months), after which he divorced her, apparently for showing no signs of pregnancy. She was in fact probably called Cornelia Livia Orestilla and was the daughter of a senator called Scipio Orestinus, descended not only from a branch of the the Cornelii Lentuli (Scipios by adoption), but also from obscure kinsmen of the Empress Livia, the Livii Ocellae, and the grand republican house of the Mucii.[102] Her ultimate fate is unknown.

In September 38, Caligula married as his *third* wife Lollia Paulina, the grand-daughter of the consul of 21BC, M. Lollius. Lollia's sister, Lollia Saturnina, married D. Valerius Asiaticus, whose descendants can be traced well into the second century, if not beyond. Lollia was formerly the wife of P. Memmius Regulus, suffect consul in 31; Caligula divorced her around March 39. She was banished and put to death in exile in 48 through the machinations of Empress Messallina (qv).

Not long after his divorce, Caligula married as his *fourth* wife, Milonia Caesonia, born around AD5, the daughter of the sixth and last marriage of a much married matron of modest extraction called Vistilia, who had had three daughters by a previous marriage, although her husband's name is lost to us. Nevertheless, she was, as a result, a half-sister of **NERO'S** marshal, Corbulo, father of the Empress Domitia Longina (see **Table IV Brief Lives**). They had a daughter, Julia Drusilla, born within about a month of their wedding.

CALIGULA had numerous other *affaires* with members of both sex. He was said on occasion to have pleasured the wives of guests at private dinners and then returned to the table to regale the party with an account of the occasion. He was accused of incest, allegedly with all three of his his sisters, especially Julia Drusilla; also of having affairs with Ennia, the

---

99. Syme (1986) 195
100. *Caligula* 25.1
101. *Op. cit.* 59.8.2
102. PIR² C1492, C1441. Conceivably related to the adoptive mother of GALBA (see below **Part B II(a)**.)

wife of his predecessor's Praetorian Prefect, Macro, and Pyrallis, a concubine. The only one alleged to have produced recorded named offspring was with Nymphidia, daughter of C. Julius Callistus, a freedman of the emperor who became a trusted member of the his staff, and was later a senior civil servant (*a libellis*) under Claudius.[103] She was married to a man called Asiaticus – not the consular married to empress Lollia Paulina's sister, however – but by **CALIGULA** had, so it was later claimed, a son C. Nymphidius Sabinus, who, after service as a junior equestrian officer, was appointed praetorian prefect by the emperor **NERO** in 65 but on the emperor's fall in 68, persuaded the Guard to support the emperor **GALBA** but was eventually killed making a failed and futile attempt - based on his claimed ancestry – to claim the imperial purple himself, presumably unmarried and childless.[104] Strangely, all his promiscuity seems to have stopped once he had married Caesonia and fathered Drusilla.

Further reading:

Barrett, A. A., *Caligula, The Corruption of Power* London, 1989.

Winterling, A., *Caligula, a Biography* California, 2011

Wiseman, T. P. (ed. & Trans.) Flavius Josephus *Death of an Emperor* Exeter, 1991.

TABLE IX: CALIGULA'S WOMEN

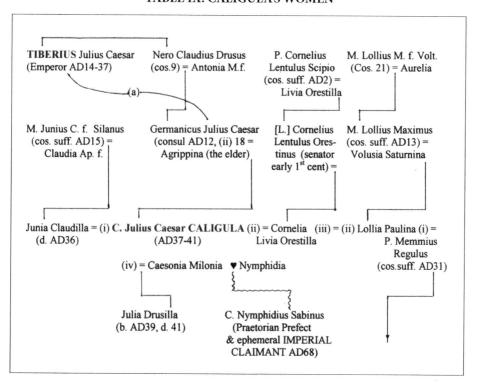

---

103. PIR² I229
104. Plutarch, *Galba* ix.1.

TABLE IX BRIEF LIVES

Caesonia Milonia

Daughter of the much married matron Vistilia, daughter of Sex. Vistilius, by her sixth (and last) husband, whose name was Caesonius, but who has completely escaped record. She was older than the Emperor, having been born c. AD5, and without doubt must have been divorced or a widow. She is said to have been rather a loose-living woman, but seems to have made a success of her marriage to the Emperor, which took place in July AD39, when she was about eight months pregnant. She and her daughter died at the hands of the conspirators soon after her husband's assassination, January AD41 [Syme, AA 145, 271].

CAIUS (CALIGULA) AUGUSTUS

See above.

Cornelia Livia Orestilla

Second wife of the Emperor, married and divorced within weeks in AD37, little is known about her either before or after her brief period as Empress.[Dio lix.8, 7-8; Suetonius *Gaius Caligula* xxv.1; PIR² C1492]

[L.] Cornelius Lentulus Orestinus

Patrician; a younger son and recorded only as a senator early in the first century AD.

P. Cornelius Cn. f. Lentulus Scipio

Patrician, suffect consul in AD2, and a member of the junior branch of the Cornelian family, the Lentuli, he acquired his extra name (*agnomen*) Sir Ronald Syme thought by having been testamentarily adopted by P. Cornelius Scipio (consul 16BC) the last of his line. [PIR² C1397; Syme AA 252, 296-297]

Julia Drusilla

CALIGULA'S daughter, born summer AD39, killed with her mother January 41.

[Julia] Nymphidia

Probably the Emperor's concubine very early in the reign, bearing in mind the likely age of their son (if indeed he was their son) when he was NERO's praetorian prefect.

C. Julius Callistus

Former slave enfranchised by the Emperor, probably before his succession. Originally called just Callistus, he took his former master's *praenomen* and *nomen* in the traditional way on gaining his liberty. By AD40 he was chief secretary (*ab epistulis*) in which role he continued uinto the next reign [PIR² I229]

Junia Claudilla

Not directly connected with the Imperial family, married in AD33 on the recommendation of TIBERIUS. Died in childbirth c. AD36.

M. Junius C. f. Silanus

A member of a distinguished noble family, patrician by creation, his wife seems to have been a Claudius Pulcher (hence his daughter's *cognomen*). He was suffect consul in AD15 and the eloquent chief toady of TIBERIUS, who allowed him the privilege of casting the first vote in senatorial ballots (effectively leader of the senate - *princeps senatus*) above more senior men. Brother of C. Ap. Junius Silanus, he lost his pre-eminence, and was driven to suicide in spring AD37, having been prosecuted on the orders of his former son-in-law by the father of Agricola (later the conqueror of most of Scotland). [Syme AA 192-196].

Lollia Paulina

After having been cast aside by the Emperor, she was later touted (by Callistus, qv) as a candidate for the hand of **CLAUDIUS I** after the death of Messallina, but ended up being banished by him at the prompting of Agrippina (the younger), by that time Empress, for dabbling in magic and astrology. She was later killed by an officer of the guard [Syme AA 176-178, 184].

M. Lollius M. f. Volt.

A man from an emergent family probably from Ferentinum who was a loyal supporter of **AUGUSTUS** accorded the quality of integrity by the poet Horace, but of corruption and craftiness by the historian Velleius. He was the first governor of Galatia in 24BC, of Thrace in 19 and squired C. Caesar in Syria, but suffered a serious defeat in Gaul in 17. Either way, he fell out with **TIBERIUS** at an early stage in his career and fell from grace and died in AD2 [PIR^2 L311]

M. Lollius Maximus

His consulship was doubted by Syme, but his subsequently been confirmed. He married a Volusia Saturnina.[PIR^2 L312]

P. Memmius P.f. Gal. Regulus

Senator from a family of praetorian rank in the late Republic who came to the rescue of **TIBERIUS** in helping to encompass the fall of Sejanus when suffect consul in AD31. He was governor of Moesia under **CALIGULA** and found himself obliged to give his second wife Lollia Paulina up to him. By a previous marriage he had a son, C. Memmius Regulus (consul in AD63). [PIR^2 M468, 467.]

C. Nymphidius Sabinus

Alleged (by himself more than any) to have been a natural son of the Emperor. Plutarch however, avers that he was the son of a gladiator called Marcianus and in any case was born *after* his mother's dalliance with **CALIGULA.** He must have embarked on an equestrian career, and was selected, late in his reign, by **NERO** as one of the new praetorian prefects. On the Emperor's deposition and suicide (which he encompassed) he promised his regiment that the new Emperor would pay them a bounty of 30,000HS, but the newly proclaimed but preternaturally tight-fisted **GALBA** refused to 'buy' his soldiers and sacked Nymphidius, who thereupon proceded to the Praetorian camp and proposed himself for the supreme office (playing on his real or supposed paternity), but was quickly killed by his own men, keen to get on the right side of **GALBA** and with luck to receive a bounty in any case. [Holland (2000) 228-229, 231, 233; Morgan (2006) 40-41].

TIBERIUS AUGUSTUS

See above, and **TABLE VIII**

The Imperial Succession
Claudius I
Britannicus
Nero

Imperial Claimants
Camillus
Clodius Macer

Although the next emperor, **CLAUDIUS**, shared the same ancestry as **TIBERIUS** and **CALIGULA**, the difference was that neither he nor his father, Drusus, were ever adopted into the dynasty of **JULIUS CAESAR** and **AUGUSTUS**, thus retaining their Claudian name, the family being an ancient republican patrician one and said to have been of Sabine origin. A story of Callimachus from the 3rd century BC tells of a Roman, chafing at the disability caused by a battle wound in the thigh, was told by his mother to be proud of his lameness. The Latin *claudus* meaning "lame" in this story, told of someone referred to only as Caius, is thought to be a foundation tale of the dynasty. Another story has them settling in Rome in the late regal period under their Sabine leader, Attus Clausus.[105] Thereafter they continued in their conservative ways, producing an astonishing number of prominent republican leaders and fragmenting into several branches, of which the Nerones, from which the Imperial family sprang, were in some ways the least distinguished – until Tiberius became *princeps*, that is.

CLAUDIUS I
17th January AD41- 13th October 54

CLAUDIUS, born an old patrician in 10, led a completely sheltered life, mainly amongst the women of his family, an existence he latterly shared with his nephew Caius (**CALIGULA**. He was kept out of public life because of his perceived disabilities: a severe stammer, slight malformation of the body, bouts of illness, often apparently serious and (so it was thought) mental torpor. In fact he was intellectually gifted and a keen antiquarian, especially concerning the early history of Rome. He continued Livy, and wrote histories of Etruria and Carthage.

He was brought out of the obscurity which had no doubt preserved his life, by **CALIGULA**, who made him (suffect) consul for 37 and kept him in the court, although he seems to have been denied any role in the senate. It is said that he was literrerally stumbled across

---

105. Wiseman (2004) 56-57, 66-67.

by the rampaging praetorians after Caligula's murder and, as the last surviving prince of the Julio-Claudian house, he was set up by them as the next *princeps*. Modern historians are not wholly convinced of his innocence of the plot that removed his predecessor; there are grounds for thinking he was wholly or partly complicit.[106]

Background

As a youth, the new emperor was betrothed to **Aemilia Lepida** (see above **Table VII(a) Brief Lives**) but this was broken off when her mother Julia was disgraced in AD7. He was then due to marry **Livia Medullina Camilla**[107], daughter of the very grand patrician protégé of **TIBERIUS**, M. Furius Camillus, consul in AD8 (and sister of the imperial claimant *CAMILLUS*). Tragically, she died on their wedding day. He eventually married Plautia Urgulanilla, a friend of the Empress Livia, whom he divorced not so long afterwards in AD24 through allegations of adultery. His next essay in matrimonty (by AD 28) was Aelia Paetina[108] daughter of a jurist of noble descent, Q. Aelius Tubero, and a relation of **TIBERIUS'** poisonous praetorian prefect, L. Aelius Seianus (Sejanus). The union survived the fall of Sejanus, but foundered in the wake of the accession of **CALIGULA,** and they appear to have divorced in AD37. He then married c. AD38 a woman with much closer links to the Imperial house (she was cousin once removed of **CLAUDIUS**) and splendidly well connected, Valeria Messallina. She was great-grand-daughter of **AUGUSTUS'** sister Octavia twice over. After his accession, to strengthen her position and to secure the succession of her infant son **BRITANNICUS,** she resorted to a murderous regime of eliminating perceived threats; which thinned the Imperial House out alarmingly before she lost control completely, took a lover, C. Silius, and went through a form of marriage with him as part of a sort of rolling orgy in AD48 which promptly resulted in her demise. She was replaced the following year by Agrippina, who proved just as effective an attritional factor in the family, being determined to secure the succession for *her* son Lucius by Cn. Domitius Ahenobarbus, whom she ultimately persuaded the Emperor to adopt as his joint heir with **BRITANNICUS,** laying the ground for further blood-letting.

Reign

Ti. Claudius Drusi German[ici] f. Nero Germanicus[109] succeeded to the Empire in January 41 and was granted the tribunician power (to be renewed yearly on the anniversary) by the senate and hailed as *imperator* on accession and on twenty six further occasions. He was also acknowledged as pontifex maximus and *pater patriae*. Thereafter re-styled himself **Ti. Claudius Caesar Augustus** during the census he held under his own auspices when, for antiquarian reasons, he had himself transferred to the Quirinian voting tribe. This was the

---

106. Levick (1990) 35

107. PIR² L304; her connection with the Livii defies identification - perhaps through her mother.

108. PIR² A305

109. PIR² C942

first time the name Caesar had been assumed for no genealogical reason and without an official adoption; **CLAUDIUS** was the first of many emperors to do this. From this point on 'Caesar' like 'Augustus' effectively became a title. On this occasion, too, he also raised a number of families to patrician status, the first time this had ben done since the early part of Augustus's reign. Seven families – *gentes* – were certainly so elevated, with another eight probables, including the families of the future emperors **OTHO** and **VITELLIUS**. He held the consulship in 37 and 41 (both as suffect consul), in 42, 43, 47and 51 and was intending to hold it in 55, crucially the year his sons, natural and adopted, would attain the age of manhood – 14, the *toga virilis* – and could be formally designated his heirs as they were, indeed, in his will, which was (naturally) not made public by **NERO** in case people would realise that he was technically supposed to share power with **BRITANNICUS.**

CLAUDIUS'S first task on succeeding to the purple was to put down – rather heavy handedly – a group of prime movers in the assassinastion of Caligula and other idealistic – or arch-conservative – senators who were planning to govern without a *princeps* at all. A further revolt by a descendant of the family of Augustus's second wife, Scribonia, L. Arruntius *CAMILLUS* Scribonianus, governor of Dalmatia (qv below) - had to be put down as well.

Relations with the senate were difficult and fraught with uncertainties, the emperor's inexperience, insecurity and the unreliability of certain senatorial elements combining to make dealing with the governing elite difficult. He had no faction of supporters in the senate, which forced him to rely on a very few senatorial toadies like L. Vitellius, but more upon powerful freedmen and equestrian advisers, further putting the senate's nose out of joint and building up resentment.

Nevertheless, the governance of the empire remained stable and military success was again achieved, in Germany, Mauretania and, of course, setting in train the final conquest and annexation of Britain. Claudius was a strange mixture both in himself and as revealed in his surviving edicts; 'pedantic and idiosyncratic' and a 'donnish buffoon' are both valid comments, alongside the cruelty found in most members of his family. Furthermore, relations with the elite were additionally compromised by his two empresses, the last of whom allegedly had him poisoned through the agency of a crone called Lucusta and a plate of poisoned mushrooms, which acted with fatal effect on 13th October 54. Murder cannot be proved, but almost everyone at the time assumed it was true and the circumstantial evidence is overwhelming. Power and self-interest once again supervened over the legal niceties of contstitutional politics. As Barbara Levick so aptly says, legality in the early principate was '…stretched to breaking point by the very existence of the emperor.' Indeed, she makes the point that it was in Claudius's reign the head of state progressed from *princeps* to emperor.[110]

Further reading:
Griffin, M. T, *Seneca: A Philosopher in Politics* (Oxford 1976)
Levick, B., *Claudius* London, 1990.

---

110. Levick (1990) 76-77, 78

TABLE X: CLAUDIUS AND HIS FAMILY

Continued from Table VIII

M. Livius Drusus Claudianus   Ti. Claudius Nero
(praetor 50) =   (praetor before 63) =

AUGUSTUS (iii) = (ii) Livia   (i) = Ti. Claudius Nero   Claudia = Q. Volusius [L.f.] Vel.
M. Gallius Q. f.   (praetor 42)   (senator 50)
(praetor 44)

(a)

Ti. Claudius Nero   Nero Claudius Drusus Germanicus
(M. Gallius Nero Claudianus;   (consul 9, d. 9) = Antonia M.f.
Ti. Julius Divi f. Caesar Augustus)
TIBERIUS I (AD14-37)
= (ii) Julia; (i) = (div. 12) Vipsania

(a)

Drusus Julius Caesar (ii) = (ii) Claudia   Nero Claudius Germanicus   Ti. Claudius Nero Germanicus
(cos. AD15, 21, d. 23)   Livilla   (Germanicus Julius Caesar) =   **CLAUDIUS I (AD41-54)**
                   (Livia Julia)   (Vipsania) Agrippina   (i) = Plautia Urgulanilla
                                             (ii) = Aelia Paetina
                                                (iii) = Valeria Messallina
                                                     (iv) = (iv) Julia
                                                Agrippina (i) = Cn.
                                              Domitius Ahenobarbus
                                                (cos. AD32)

[see Table VIII]   **[see Table VII (b)]**

[Ti. Claudius] Drusus   Claudia
(d. AD20)

                     Claudia Antonia
                 (i) = Cn. Pompeius Magnus   (a)
                 (ii) = Faustus Cornelius
                 Sulla Felix (cos. AD52)

Ti. Claudius Caesar **BRITANNICUS**   Claudia Octavia = (i) L. Domitius Ahenobarbus
(nominally **AUGUSTUS AD54-55**)   (Nero Claudius Caesar Drusus
                                          Germanicus) **NERO**
    M. Salvius **OTHO** (i) = (ii) Poppaea Sabina (iii) = (ii) **AUGUSTUS (AD54-68)**
       AUGUSTUS (AD69)   (iii) = (v) Statilia Messalina
       (See Part II, section(a))

Claudia (2-4/AD63)

NB. The adoption of Tiberius by Augustus has been omitted from Table X for clarity.

TABLE X BRIEF LIVES

Aelia Paetina

The second wife of **CLAUDIUS** was daughter of Q. Aelius Tubero, and a close relation of **TIBERIUS'** poisonous praetorian prefect, L. Aelius Seianus (Sejanus). The union, which was solemnised by AD28 survived the fall of Sejanus, but foundered in the wake of the accession of **CALIGULA,** and they appear to have divorced in AD37 [Syme AA 181, 277, 306].

Antonia M. f.

Younger daughter of Mark Antony and Octavia, sister of **AUGUSTUS** and married to **TIBERIUS'** younger brother Drusus. She lived a long life and was granted the style and title of Augusta by her grandson, **CALIGULA** in AD37 shortly before her death that year.[PIR² A885]

Claudia

Elder daughter of **CLAUDIUS** and his second child, she was born c. AD23/24, but disowned by her father in the wake of his divorce from her mother, who was accused of adultery. [PIR² C1060; Suetonius, *Claudius* 27. 1]

[Claudia] Antonia

CLAUDIUS' second daughter (by Aelia Paetina) was born in AD 27 or 28 and married Pompeius Magnus in AD41. She re-married Sulla Felix in AD46 or 47 and after he in turn had fallen victim to the murderous propensities of the Emperor, **NERO** himself considered her as a matrimonial prospect in AD65, but the fact that C. Calpurnius Piso, prime mover in a serious attempt to overthrow him that year, was also wooing her, rather put him off. Thereafter, she fades from history [Syme AA 277-279; PIR² A886].

Claudia Livilla (Livia Julia)

Claudia Livilla was born about 12 and changed her name on **TIBERIUS'** adoption by **AUGUSTUS** in AD4. She married C. Caesar in AD1 (Dio says a year earlier) but he died without having had any issue. She was later put in an invidious position when her daughter by Drusus, Julia Livilla, was obliged to marry **TIBERIUS'** scheming Praetorian prefect, Sejanus. She was accused by Sejanus' divorced wife of conspiring with him to poison Drusus in AD23 and the allegation was re-inforced by the torture of staff. She took her own life days after Sejanus's fall [Syme, AA 171]

Claudia Octavia

Born AD39 or 40 and married **NERO** in 53, She was exiled in 62 and died the same year [PIR² C1110]

CLAUDIUS I AUGUSTUS

See above.

Ti. Claudius Caesar BRITANNICUS

See below, main text.

Nero Claudius <u>Drusus</u> Germanicus

Patrician and younger brother of **TIBERIUS,** he was born 38BC after his mother's re-marriage and was consequently favoured by **AUGUSTUS** over his elder brother. A gifted military commander, he campaigned successfully against the Rhaetians in 15BC. He took up arms against the Germans in 13-11 during which a series of victories brought him to the west bank of the Elbe, as a result of which he was granted the additional name (*agnomen*) of Germanicus (possibly afterhis death) He was consul in 9BC, during which year he died unexpectedly from a fall from his horse. Around 16 he married Antonia, younger daughter of **Mark Antony** by Octavia, sister of **AUGUSTUS** [PIR² C857]

Nero Claudius Germanicus
See **Germanicus Julius Caesar**

Ti. Claudius Drusus

Elder son and eldest child of **CLAUDIUS** he was born c. AD11 but died in 20 as a result of choking on a pear, which he had thrown into the air and caught in his mouth. At the time he was betrothed to Aelia Junilla, the daughter of Sejanus, so perhaps it was a blessed relief. [PIR² C856]

Ti. Claudius Nero

Patrician and praetor before 63BC, he served on the staff of **Pompey** in his campaign against Mediterranean piracy in 67.

Ti. Claudius Nero

See **Table VIII Brief Lives**

Faustus Cornelius Sulla Felix

Patrician Faustus was the son of Faustus Cornelius Sulla and the second marriage of Domitia Lepida, an aunt of **NERO**; he was a descendant of **Sulla** and **Pompey** and his uncle was L. Cornelius Sulla (see **Table VII(b) Brief Lives**) with all the political baggage that implied. He was also step-brother to Messallina, which is why he found himself in AD47 obliged to marry Cn. Pompeius Magnus' widow Antonia, by whom he had a son who died young. He was rewarded with a consulship for AD52, but was sent into exile by **NERO** as a 'crafty dissembler' in AD60 and was killed in AD62, the last of his line [PIR² C1464; Syme, AA 164,181, 183].

Cn. Domitius Ahenobarbus

See **Table VI Brief Lives**

M. Gallius Q.f.

Gallius's father seems to have entered the senate in 80 under Sulla, but he and his brother Quintus conducted a celebrated feud with consular aspirant M. Calidius. Why Ti. Nero was willing to allow his son to be adopted by Gallius is unkown; he was wealthy, and Nero's family considerably impoverished by the civil wars, so the future emperor took the inheritance and rapidly dropped the name. [Suetonius *Tiberius* 6.3]

Julia

Daughter and sole heiress of **AUGUSTUS** See **Table VI Brief Lives.**

Julia Agrippina

See **Table VII(b) Brief Lives**

Drusus Julius Caesar

See **Table VIII Brief Lives**

Livia

See **Table VIII Brief Lives**

Livia Julia

See **Claudia Livilla**

M. Livius Drusus Claudianus

A Claudius Pulcher adopted by the revolutionary peoples' tribune M. Livius Drusus (killed 91BC) He was praetor 50, a supporter of the Republic who committed suicide after the Battle of Philippi in 49. M. Livius Drusus Libo (consul 15BC) was his adopted son, a Scribonius by birth [Syme AA 257].

NERO AUGUSTUS

See below

OTHO AUGUSTUS

See **Section B part II(a)**

Plautia Urgulanilla

Plautia was the daughter of a close associate of **TIBERIUS,** M. Plautius Silvanus, a member of an old senatorial family, recently ennobled. The Urgulanius whom her *cognomen* attests is unknown. She was a friend of the Empress Livia, but **CLAUDIUS** divorced her not so long afterwards through allegations of adultery and the suspicion of connivance at murder [Levick (1990) 24]

Cn. Pompeius Magnus

Cn. [Licinius] Pompeius Magnus was a younger son of M. Licinius Crassus Frugi (consul in AD27) who married a Scribonia and whose paternal grandfather had been a Calpurnius Piso by birth. He was so named because of his descent from the Triumvir **Pompeius** whose great great grandson he was (via three female lines). He was also descended from L Cornelius Cinna and by adoption from the triumvir **Crassus**, so carried a great deal of ideological baggage in Roman terms. One of his brothers was adopted as his heir by **GALBA** (qv). By his marriage to the daughter of the Emperor, he was an impediment to the prospects (as she saw them) of his son by Messallina, **BRITANNICUS.** Consequently, he was accused of conspiracy and killed, along with his parents. All were undoubtedly blameless. [Dio, 60-.27, 5 & 31,7]

Poppaea Sabina

The Poppaei were originally from Picenum and entered the senate in the Second Triumvirate, a pair of brothers achieving consulships in AD9. The daughter of the elder, apparently a great beauty, married a senator called T. Ollius (probably the grandson of an acquaintance of Cicero's) and had a daughter who bore her mother's name rather than her rather less distinguished paternal one. She too was outstandingly good looking and both women were adept schemers. Her first husband was **CLAUDIUS'** first Guard Prefect, Rufrius Crispinus, but she swiftly moved on to M. Salvius **OTHO,** later briefly Emperor, and from whom **NERO** snatched her, first as mistress and then as wife. Tacitus said of her that 'she had everything she could want – except goodness.' She died in pregnancy after being kicked by her petulant husband in AD65. The remorse of **NERO** resulted in her subsequent deification [Cicero, *ad Att.* 13.37, 3 & 48, 2; Tacitus, *Annals* 13.45].

Statilia Messallina

Statilia Messallina was, like Poppaea, another lady who took the name of her mother rather than that of her father. The Statilii were recent Patricians, the general T. Statilius Taurus having been so elevated by **AUGUSTUS** in 27. Statilia's mother was the daughter of a similarly named man, consul in AD11 and a patrician Valeria Messallina, but only distantly related to the murderous wife of **CLAUDIUS.** The father was a descendant of the poet, L. Valerius Catullus (of an equestrian

family, unrelated to his mother-in-law) but who had entered the senate and been suffect consul in AD31. **NERO** was Statilia's fifth husband and like, Poppaea, she had been his lover previously and, like Caesonia, was undoubtedly somewhat older than the Emperor. Her first husband's name is not known, but her second an Annius (their son, inevitably, took the name Messalla), her third was D. Valerius Asiaticus, and her fourth spouse was one of the consuls for AD65, M. [Julius] Vestinus Atticus, also of an emergent family. She had sons by both Asiaticus and Atticus. She also managed to long outlive **NERO**. [Syme AA 240-241]

TIBERIUS AUGUSTUS

See above.

Valeria Messallina

Splendidly well connected, Valeria Messallina was great-grand-daughter of **AUGUSTUS's** sister Octavia twice over. She married the Emperor in AD38 and, in order to strengthen her position and to secure the succession of her infant son **BRITANNICUS,** she resorted to a murderous regime of eliminating perceived threats; it thinned the Imperial House out alarmingly before she lost control completely, took a lover, C. Silius and went through a highly erotic form of marriage with him in AD48 which resulted in their deaths and those of their supporters [Syme AA 147, 165-166, 178-182]

Q. Volusius [L.f.] Vel.

A member of an old praetorian family and brother-in-law of the praetor of 42, he was recorded as a senator in 50BC. Their son was suffect consul in 12BC and their posterity acquired patrician status before AD87 and continued in the senate, enjoying consulships well into the 2nd century AD [Cicero, *Ad Atticus* 5.2,6; FS 3573; Tacitus, *Annals* III. 30]

CAMILLUS
AD42

At the juncture of change from **CALIGULA** to **CLAUDIUS I** there was an attempted military *coup* led by a grandee whose full name was L. Arruntius L. f. Ani. Camillus Scribonianus, who had been consul in AD32 and who was then governing Dalmatia. It seems to have been precipitated by the execution of C. Ap. Junius Silanus in Rome shortly before. That *CAMILLUS* was put up to it by M. Annius Vinicianus, the man who instigated the plot against **CALIGULA** seems likely, and there is some doubt as to whether the idea was to march on Rome and re-establish the Republic or the declare himself *princeps*. The *pronunciamento* seems to have had the latter effect, however, but at the religious ceremony to inauguarate the attempt, the omens were very poor and that, with other unfavourable portents, persuaded the soldiers in his legions to change their minds, and declare themselves loyal to the dynasty after all. *CAMILLUS* fled to the island of Issa and was there killed by a soldier called Volaginius. The entire affair lasted but five days, although the actual dates are lost to us. The result at Rome was a series of savage prosecutions and executions of those connected with the matter.

CAMILLUS himself was a younger son, born into the ancient patrician family of the Furii, his father being M. Furius Camillus, consul in AD8, who defeated Tacfarinas in Africa and was a friend of **TIBERIUS.** The family's first consulship was in 488BC but the last before Scribonianus' father had been in 136. His mother was the daughter of M. Livius Drusus Libo, consul in 15BC (qv **Table X Brief Lives**) and a nephew of Scribonia, ex-wife of **AUGUSTUS**, who had been adopted by **TIBERIUS'S** grandfather M. Livius Drusus (praetor in 50BC). *CAMILLUS SCRIBONIANUS* had been testamentarily adopted by L. Arruntius (consul AD6) whose mother brought descent from Pompey and Sulla. Finally he had married Vinicianus's cousin, making him highly eligible for power and marking him out for treason. Neverthless, his sons were spared and there is evidence for the long survival of his stock, albeit in the distaff.[111]

*

---

111. ILS 5032; FS 1789; PIR² A1140; Rutledge (2002) 164-165

BRITANNICUS
13 Oct. AD54- 11 Feb. 55

BRITANNICUS was born into the purple on 12th February AD41, was named, a little later from his father's triumph as conqueror of Britain, and was only 7 when his mother was executed for her insane fling with C. Silius. Once **NERO** was formally adopted by **CLAUDIUS** in AD54, his name was changed to **Britannicus Claudius Caesar.** He was never granted the usual popwers by the senate, being under age, unlike **NERO,** who was nearly 17 on accession and thus technically of age. Named in the Emperor's supressed will as joint heir with **NERO,** he was only nominally therefore in power until he died at the dinner table, allegedly of an epileptic fit on 11th February AD55. Needless to say, nobody failed to see his imperial colleague's hand in the matter.

*

NERO
13th October AD54-9th June 68

Background

L. Domitius Cn. f. L. n. Ahenobarbus was born at Antium 15th December AD37, a plebeian noble by descent, but adopted by the Emperor **CLAUDIUS** in AD49 as **Nero Claudius Caesar Drusus Germanicus**, making him a patrician. Before his mother married **CLAUDIUS** the year before, the young son of the ex-consul Cn. Domitius Ahenobarbus can at least have expected a life of leisure interrupted by absurdly early elevation to consular rank and possibly the governance of a senatorial province in middle life. As the grandson of Germanicus, there would be the added ingredient of personal danger as a minor member of the imperial circle. Like both his imperial predecessors – both to some extent social misfits, as **NERO**, too, turned out to be – he was brought up from the age of three by women, chief amongst them his ruthlessly ambitious mother Agrippina (junior). He was eleven when he suddenly found himself in the Imperial family and barely twelve before he was adopted by his step-father, with all the pressures, both covert and public, his new poisition inevitably attracted: no chance of a normal childhood, then.

Reign

On his accession as (joint) successor in 54 he was styled **Nero Claudius Caesar Augustus Germanicus,** adding the office of *Pontifex Maximus* and the title *Pater Patriae* ('father of his country') after **BRITANNICUS'** death in February 55. He was the first emperor never to have been a senator prior to his accession, and although granted the tribunician power by the senate on 4th December following his accession, he did not hold a consulship until 55, following it with others in 57, 58, 60 and 68. He was hailed as *Imperator* on his accession – now a formality, having nothing to do with success on the battlefield – and thirteen times subsequently. Despite the highly suspicious demise of **CLAUDIUS**, followed by the appallingly public and still highly questionable death of his half-brother, his reign started well. Holland even goes as far as to remove from **NERO** the motive for conniving or acquiescing in the death of **BRITANNICUS**.[112] He maintains that he was a young aesthete with literary, thespian, poetic and sporting pretensions, with no particular desire to become the hag-ridden ruler of most of the known world - he just wanted to be free. This argument fails, however, to take into account the social obloquy likely to be attracted by a senator of patrician rank indulging such tastes publicly, not to mention the obligations and expectations that bound Roman aristocrats to the straight and narrow. As it turned out, only by wielding supreme power was the young emperor able to indulge his exhibitionist love of the performing arts. It may be doubted that his reputation would have stood up to scrutiny had he occupied a private station in life.

Nevertheless, **NERO'S** predilections, especially as he got older, were much appreciated in the Hellenised east. Furthermore, under the guidance of his tutor, L. Annaeus Seneca the younger and the praetorian prefect appointed in 51, Sex. Afranius Burrus, the first few years were tranquil and successful ones, although **NERO** did tend to make unsuitable political decisions against advice. Yet the tensions with the senate experienced under Claudius were largely avoided and, even after the untidy killing of Agrippina in 59, Nero was still able to rule fairly sensibly.

Yet from AD60/61 he began to show signs of instability, grossness, appalling self-indulgence – the behaviour of a spoiled truculent brat suddenly freed from control. In this case, the controls were taken off through the execution of his mother (in 59), the poisoning of Burrus (in 62) and the retirement not long afterwards of Seneca who, in 65 pre-empitvely took his own life over alleged implication in Piso's conspiracy.

Despite acceptance in the eastern provices, aided by the triumphant progress of the brilliant general Corbulo, there was much discontent, especially in the west. Provincial government underwent a number of hiccoughs caused by maladministration or complacency, culminating in Boudicca's British revolt in 61[113] and various other perturbations. The excessively bloody reaction of Piso's conspiracy, the fire at Rome and the public extravagance and boorishness of the Emperor all conspired eventually to spark revolt. This manifested itself in Gaul in 68, under the local aristocrat C. Julius Vindex, who tried to involve the support of the long-serving governor of Hispania Tarraconensis, Ser. Sulpicius **GALBA**. The latter hung back until Vindex had been dealt with by neighbouring governor, Verginius Rufus but, with the unexpected backing of the praetorians under Nymphidius Sabinus, he raised the standard of revolt and eventually, seeing that his position was hopeless, the Emperor took his own life outside Rome 9th June 68, allegedly uttering the *bon mot* 'qualis artifex me decessit!' – 'what an artist dies in me!'

He left behind him no obvious heir – he had had most of his surviving relatives, even quite distant ones, murdered – and the universal realisation that the army, not the senate,

---

112. *Op. cit.* (2000) 81-82
113. The more Celticised version of the queen's name, Boudicca is more favoured these days, but Boadicaea is what the Romans called her.

would in future be the final arbiter of the succession. Unfortunately, to reach that conclusion, three more emperors were to die and thousands killed in civil conflict: a heavy price to pay to learn what to us, with hindsight, seems like the obvious.

NERO married *firstly* in 53 **Claudia Octavia** daughter of Claudius and Messallina (see **Table X Brief Lives**) whom he divorced for barren-ness in 62 and who was killed in exile on Pandateria later that year on the bizarre charge of being adulterously pregnant! His *second* wife, who had been his mistress for some time previously and whom he married twelve days after divorcing Octavia, was **Poppaea Sabina** (see **Table X Brief Lives**). NERO forced her compliant second husband - his contemporary and drinking partner M. Salvius Otho, later the Emperor **OTHO** (qv) – to agree to a divorce. She was already pregnant by **NERO** at the time with their daughter, Claudia who, however, lived only three and a half months; he took her death very badly indeed. Poppaea miscarried in 65 and died of internal haemorrhaging, although malicious rumour put it about that he had kicked her to death after she scolded him for coming home late from chariot racing. This seems unlikely, however, and she was later deified by a compliant senate. He took in AD66 and as his third wife, **Statilia Messallina** by whom he had no further issue – but who survived him to be wooed by **OTHO** in AD69.

Further reading:

Barrett. A. A., *Agrippina: Mother of Nero* London, 1996

Griffin, M. T., *Nero: the End of a Dynasty* London, 1984

Griffin, M. T., *Seneca: a Philosopher in Politics* Oxford, 1992

Holland, R., *Nero: the Man Behind the Myth* Sutton, Stroud, 2000.

*

THE ANCESTRY OF NERO

The great repuiblican house of the Domitii was one of those plebeian families which came into power through the reforms of the mid-4th century BC which probably helped form the senate and consulship as it has come down to us. They claimed descent from Lucius Domitius who in the early 2nd century was alleged to have encountered Castor and Pollux on the road, who turned his beard red, a tale which was later projected back to the 5th century battle of Lake Regillus in order to endow the family with a spurious antiquity.[114] The first branch of the family to rise to real prominence was called Calvinus – a diminutive of *calvus*: bald – in the person of Cn. Domitius Calvinus consul in 332BC. It is impossible to reconstruct the descent of this family, for there was no member of it in office between the son of the consul of 332 and Marcus, the father of a couple of brothers active in the senate of Marius and Sulla. Their use of first names – *praenomina* – like Marcus and Publius, not found amongst the Ahenobarbi, allied to different voting tribes (Menenia for the Calvini and Fabia for the Ahenobarbi)

---

114. Wiseman (2004) 185, 188

make it doubtful if the latter were really a cadet branch of the Calvini at all. The sister and heiress of the last Calvinus, a legate of Caesar[115] married M. Junius Silanus whose issue we have encountered marrying into the posterity of Augustus - see **Table VII (a) Brief Lives.**

TABLE XI: NERO'S FAMILY

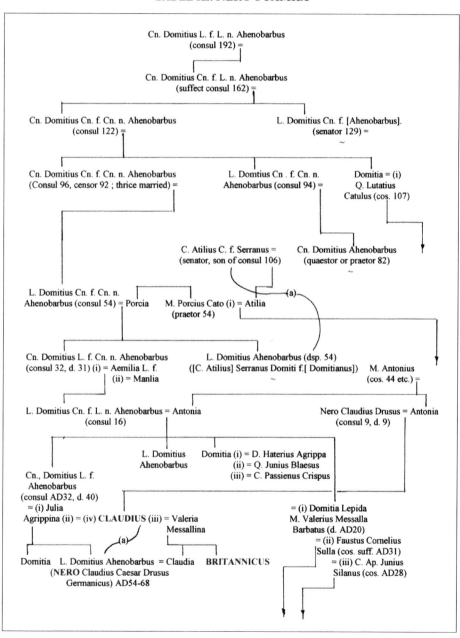

---

115. Gruen (1995) 342 & n.

TABLE XI BRIEF LIVES

C. Atilius C. f. Serranus

Serranus, still alive in 54BC, was a man largely un-noticed by the history of this turbulent period, although his father Caius, a member of the ancient plebeian nobility, had been consul in 106BC. His daughter married Cato and he later adopted her nephew by marriage; probably he had a son or sons who died young about that time. In fact he appears to have adopted two sons, as witness Sex. Atilius Serranus Gavianus (born a Gavius) a tribune of the people in 57. His Domitian adopted son outlived him, but not, it would seem, by long.

Nero Claudius Drusus
See **Table X Brief Lives**

Faustus Cornelius Sulla

Patrician, suffect consul in AD31 in place of Sejanus, his father was L. Cornelius Sulla Felix, a great grandson of both Sulla and Pompey, who died in AD21. Faustus was the father of the Faustus Sulla who married the daughter of **CLAUDIUS** [PIR² C1459;Syme, AA 164, 311].

Cn. Domitius L. f. L. n. Ahenobarbus

Consul in 192BC, the son of the man who had his beard turned red.

Cn. Domitius Ahenobarbus

Suffect consul in 162BC elected to replace one of the original pair of consuls, whose election had been vitiated by irregularities and who had been obliged to abdicate [FS 1476].

Cn. Domitius Cn. f. Cn. n. Ahenobarbus

Conqueror of Cisalpine Gaul, where his family long had great influence; he was consul in 122BC and celebrated a triumph over the Averni. He caused the building of a road that led from Italy to Spain, the Via Domitia [FS 1474].

Cn. Domitius Cn. f. Cn. n. Ahenobarbus

Pontifex Maximus in 103BC, consul in 96, censor in 92, and like his descendant, **NERO,** pontifex maximus. Ahenobarbus had three wives, none of whose names are known and all of whom had died before his censorship. He notably championed a wronged Gaul from the province his father conquered and organised [FS 1475].

Cn. Domitius Ahenobarbus

A partisan of Marius, he was killed by Pompey whilst serving in Africa either as quaestor or praetor in 82BC .

Cn. Domitius L. f. Cn. n. Ahenobarbus

Born c. 70BC, and consul in 32, remembered as a naval commander and as a supporter of Mark Antony who deserted him before the Battle of Actium and died shortly afterwards. His first wife (and mother of his children) was Aemilia Lepida, dau. of L. Aemilius Paullus, brother of the Triumvir, **M. Aemilius Lepidus** and (ii) Manlia, thought to be the daughter of L. Manlius Torquatus, consul in 65. See also **Table VI Brief Lives** [CIL VI 31735; FS1477]

Cn. Domitius Ahenobarbus

A younger son, born 2 or 1BC, consul in AD32 died 40 [see above, **Table VI Brief Lives**].

L. Domitius Cn. f. Fab. [Ahenobarbus]

Only known from an inscription showing him to have served on a senatorial commission in 129BC, but useful in giving us his voting tribe

L. Domitius Ahenobarbus

Praetor of Sicily in 96 and consul in 94 he was a supporter of Sulla and was killed for it c. 88

L. Domitius Cn. f. Cn. Ahenobarbus

Born 99 or 98BC, consul in 54, opposed to Pompey and then to the triumvirs and finally Caesar, and as a result joined the Republicans in the Civil War, being killed in action at Pharsalus in 48, commanding Pompey's left wing. He was married to Porcia, sister of the conservative politician, M. Porcius Cato Uticensis, *praetor* in the same year [FS1478].

L. Domitius Ahenobarbus

A senator died young and without issue in 54BC after having been adopted by C. Atilius Serranus. Recorded as **Serranus Domiti f.,** his full style was likely to have been **C. Atilius Serranus Domitianus.**

L. Domitius Ahenobarbus

Consul in 16BC who married **Marcus Antonius'** daughter Antonia (they had been betrothed in 37) (see above, **Tables IV & VI Brief Lives**). He later governed Africa, Illyricum and Germany. He was cruel, arrogant and extravagant and a skilled charioteer to boot. He seems to have kept clear of politics and court intrigue, however and died in AD25. [FS1479; Syme, RR, 421ff.]

L. Domitius Ahenobarbus

Elder son of the consul of 16BC, he accompanied C. Caesar to the East and behaved rather badly there, killing one of his freedmen and being expelled from his circle of friends. He is not heard of much thereafter. [Syme AA 155-156, 167]

L. Domitius Ahenobarbus

Later the Emperor **NERO** on whom see above.

D. Haterius Agrippa

The Haterii were, according to Tacitus of an old senatorial family, Agrippa's grandfather having been a jurist who was proscribed by the triumvirs in 43. The father, Q. Haterius who had been a tribune of the people in 30, had to wait until he was about 58 before receiving a suffect consulship (in 5BC). His second wife was a daughter of Agrippa, hence the *cognomen* of his allegedly libidinous youngest son Decimus, who was also a tribune of the people (in AD15). He married Domitia about a year later and rose to a consulship in AD22. His spendthrift son, Q. Haterius Antoninus' *cognomen* celebrated his mother's descent from Mark Antony. After AD32 we hear no more of Agrippa; possibly he became a victim of **TIBERIUS** [Syme AA 162-163; Tacitus, *Annals*, iv.61; Wiseman (1971) no. 200].

Q. Junius Blaesus

See **Table VI Brief Lives**

C. Ap. Junius Silanus

A member of the junior branch of the Junii Silani (for those of the elder branch, see **Table VII(a) Brief Lives**). His grandfather, C. Junius M.f. Silanus married a daughter of the patrician Ap. Claudius Pulcher, and he was given his praenomen additionally to mark this. He was consul in AD28, so was probably born c. 6BC. He governed Hispania Tarraconensis, married Domitia in AD41 and fell victim to Messallina the following year, leaving by a previous marriage, an only child, a son who reached a suffect consulship in AD 54. His uncle, M. Junius Silanus (suffect consul in AD14) was briefly father-in-law of **CALIGULA,** see **Table IX Brief Lives.**

Q. Lutatius Catulus

Marius's colleague in the consulship of 102BC, he celebrated a joint triumph with Marius in 101, more politically symbolic an event than martial. He was noted for his cultural interest and literary patronage. He later fell out with Marius and in 87 was a victim of the old general's brief reign of terror.

M. Porcius Cato

A member of a plebeian noble family and a descendant of the celebrated orator of the same name who was consul in 195BC, Cato was a Stoic and a man who held the traditions of the constitution of Rome in great reverence. Despite youth and (later) only praetorian rank, he led the defenders of the Republic against the First Triumvirate. He was a candidate for the consulship in 51, but failed to get elected. After the death of Pompey in 48, he rallied the Republican cause and died at Utica, which African city he defended against Caesar, once the latter had obtained victory at Thapsus in 46. He bore posthumously the *agnomen* Uticensis – 'of Utica' [Plutarch, *Cato junior*].

C. [Sallustius] Passienus Crispus
See **Table VII(b) Brief Lives.**

M. Valerius Messalla Barbatus
See **Table V Brief Lives.**

Imperial Claimant under Nero

MACER
April – October 68

Background

Lucius Clodius Macer was praetorian legate (colonel) of the one legion stationed in Africa in the time of **NERO**. He revolted in April or May 68, cutting off the food supply of Rome, possibly at the instigation of Calvia Crispinilla, which cannot have done much for the equanimity of **NERO**. Although probably at first encouraged by **GALBA**, *MACER* raised a legion, the *Legio I Macriana Liberatrix* in addition to the *Legio III Augusta* that he already commanded, presumably raising suspicion that he also harboured imperial ambitions, and, once installed at Rome in October 68, **GALBA** had him killed by the procurator Trebonius Garutianus, probably aided by Papirus, a senior centurion.[116]

Although *MACER* did not directly assume an Imperial style, he minted *denarii* at Carthage bearing his portrait and name along with the legend S[enatus] C[onsultum], suggesting senatorial approval for his actions, which he is unlikely to have received; certainly there is no attestation for such a thing. Indeed it harks back to a republican tradition and style dormant since the Second Triumvirate. He also styled himself *librerator* and *propraetor Africae,* which suggests he was putting down markers as to his ambitions.[117]

As a legionary legate, Clodius was relatively junior, having only held the praetorship, nor is he known to have had any discernable family connections, least of all to the Imperial house. Unless he was a scion of the family of L. Clodius Rufius (suffect consul in 7BC) and, say, a woman from the praetorian Mytilenian family of Pompeius Macer, he was probably the first of his family to enter the senate, which would leave him with even less leverage in the events unfolding around him. Indeed, Tacitus called him a 'small-time tyrant', the term *tyrannus* being established short-hand for a usurper or imperial claimant, in his time at any rate. He cannot be seen as an overt imperial claimant, as evidenced by the lack of a laurel wrerath on his coin portrait yet, by issuing a coinage, raising troops and acting independently, he was everything but. Certainly he was seen by **GALBA** as such or he would not have gone to the trouble of having him liquidated. It may be that the SC on his coinage suggests that he aspired to restore the republic in some way.

*

---

116. Tacitus, *Histories,* i. 7, i.73 & ii. 37; cf. Morgan (2006) 40, 43, 96, 258.
117. RIC I. Clodius Macer 6, 15, 35 var. & 36.

The Imperial Succession
Galba I
[Galba II]
Otho
Vitellius

GALBA
9th June 68 – 15th Jan. 69

Historical background

GALBA was the first emperor from outside the Julio-Claudian dynasty, created by the army of which, as governor of Hispania Tarraconensis (Southern Spain), he was a relatively senior commander. Yet, although from outside the charmed – and very deadly – circle of the Imperial dynasty, **GALBA** was in fact distantly related, although this was no doubt one element behind his decision to put himself forward for, at that time, such a connection would still have meant a lot; not for nothing was the name of Caesar endlessly adopted by his successors. Furthermore, we know that **GALBA** was very proud of his ancient lineage, which he no doubt saw as a qualifying element. He had also been adopted into a junior branch[118] of the family of **AUGUSTUS'** Empress, Livia (who thought highly of him), which would no doubt have acted as a re-inforcing factor.[119]

GALBA'S wife was a daughter of M.' Aemilius Lepidus, consul in AD11, himself a grandson of **Lepidus** the Triumvir, and through his mother, grandson of both **Sulla** and **Pompey**, therefore combining in her ancestry the blood of a triumvir from each of the First Triumvirate.

Galba seems always to have been stuffy and an aloof but rigorous soldier and disciplinarian. He was the perfect military tool of the dynasty, an excellent subordinate but, when it came to the crux, not really fitted for supreme power, being too severe, rather petty and tight-fisted. Worse, he lacked charisma.

Ser. Sulpicius C. f. C n. Ani. Galba was born into the old patrician family of the Sulpicii (see below **Table XII**) on 24th December 3BC (other evidence suggests two years earlier) near Tarracina, son of C. Sulpicius Galba and Mummia Achaica, a lady of distinguished consular ancestry but whose family had, subsequent to the two triumphs of L. Mummius

---

118. Suetonius, *Galba* 4, 1. Table XII attempts to demonstrate the connection, albeit on slender evidence.
119. *Ibid.* 3, 4;

as a result of victories in Spain (153BC) and against the Achaean League (146), gone into obscurity.[120] As a youth Galba was adopted as her son by his stepmother, Livia Ocellina, becoming **L. Livius Ocella <u>Ser. Sulpicius Galba</u>,** the first recorded example of an increasing fashion, especially in the second century AD, of combining two entire names in one rather than the more usual formula of L. Livius Ocella Sulpicianus. Probably he wished to keep the more presitigous name to the fore.[121] He married Aemilia Lepida in AD20.[122] His career in the senate was combined with a military life, which was consistently successful, aided by the patronage of the Empress Livia, along with **TIBERIUS, CALIGULA** and **CLAUDIUS.** He was consul in AD33 and went on to hold provincial commands in Upper Germany, where he enforced discipline after the revolt against **CALIGULA** by Lentulus Gaetulicus, in Africa and in southern Spain, where he was in charge from 60.

Reign

The revolt of the Gallic aristocrat C. Julius Vindex at Vesontio (Besançon) in Gaul in May 68 gave him his cue and, although Vindex was crushed at Lugdunum by Verginius Rufus, the governor of Germany, who subsequently declined his soldiers' offer of the purple (and lived), **GALBA** had quietly gathered support of his opposite numbers in five provinces, making the whole declaration look rather more carefully planned in advance than first appeared. His attempt was greatly facilitated by the declaration in his favour by the Praetorian Prefect C. Nymphidius Sabinus, a man who, after all (were his claims of Imperial birth in fact true), was Galba's nephew by marriage.

GALBA was actually proclaimed Emperor by his troops at Carthago Nova (Cartagena), Spain, on 3rd April, but until 9th June, when **NERO** died, he has to be viewed only as an imperial claimant. Thereafter he assumed the imperial style **Ser. [Sulpicius] Galba Imperator Caesar Augustus.** Once again, like Claudius, he assumed the Julio-Claudian names of Imperator, Caesar and Augustus and indeed from this time on they were to become a *sine qua non* of Imperial titulature. He was consul for the second time, suffect, in succession to Nero, in the same year and consul (for the third time) at the start of 69. Galba finally arrived in Rome in October, where the senate had voted him tribunician and proconsular powers and acknowledged him as pontifex maximus.

He thereupon set about being old fashioned and a disciplinarian. This included a certain amount of gratuitous killing but opinion was poisoned against him by his haughty demeanour and the poor quality of his advisors, one an odious ex-slave, Icelus, granted equestrian status by the new emperor. The public purse being virtually bankrupt through **NERO**'s profligacy, his first task was to claw back enough money to ease the burdens of government. Hence his calling in of all gifts made by **NERO** and hence his refusal of a

---

120. DNP 11. 8

121. She was beautiful and wealthy too: Suetonius, *Galba*, 3, 4. It would seem that the adoption was testamentary and that he retained his patrician status. The table shows another possible style adopted; neither is sure.

122. Syme (1986) 130

donative to the Praetorians: 'I levy soldiers, not buy them', he declared. Furthermore, some of his supporters whom he had been obliged to reward with positions in the government turned out to be incompetent, greedy and unpopular.

Nor was he devoid of rivals, apart from Vindex, who had hardly risen above the status of rebel, for *MACER* had risen in rebellion in April 68. He was apparently encouraged, by a rather louche *femme fatale* and former lover of **NERO'S** called Calvia Crispinilla, to reject **GALBA** and use the corn supply to the capital as a lever to promote his own interests.[123] **GALBA** reacted quickly, instructing the local procurator – the senior equestrian officer in a province – to kill the presumptuous legate. This the procurator, Trebonius Garutianus, did in October.[124]

GALBA'S coup had not gone down well in Germany, for a variety of reasons, however. Therefore on 2nd of January AD69, Aulus **VITELLIUS** was acclaimed emperor there, suddenly impressing upon **GALBA** that his position was by no means secure. On 10th January, under the threat of this mobilisation against him, the Emperor felt it wise to adopt as heir a younger, more charismatic man (and also, being **GALBA**, a very noble one) chosing L. Calpurnius Piso Frugi Licinianus, whom he consequently adopted as his son and successor, not only passing over his perfectly eligible nephew, Cornelius Dolabella – as it turned out fortuitously, for he survived the upheavals and went on to a consulship under the Enperor **DOMITIANUS** – but also **OTHO** who, as governor of Lusitania when **GALBA** was acclaimed, had supported him from the outset, and had built up debt on the promise (widely believed) that he would be the old man's successor.

Like the Emperor's late wife, Aemilia Lepida, Piso was a descendant of the triumvirs **Crassus** and **Pompeius** - the former's grandson having been adopted by M. [Calpurnius] Piso Frugi. **GALBA'S** heir was the son of the triumvir's great-grandson, the distinguished consular M. Licinus Crassus Frugi, consul in AD27, whose familiy were raised to patrician status by Claudius in 47. As the Emperor's legal son, Piso seems from a fragmentary inscription, to have taken the style **[Ser. Sulpicius Gal]ba C[aesar Licinianus]** presumnably becoming Galba instead of Piso, and so nominally **GALBA II**. Both were assassinated at the instigation of **OTHO** five days later on 15th January, **GALBA** an hour or two before his heir..

*

---

123. Tacitus. *Histories,* 7, 3.1
124. *Op. cit.,* 7.1

TABLE XII: GALBA'S FAMILY

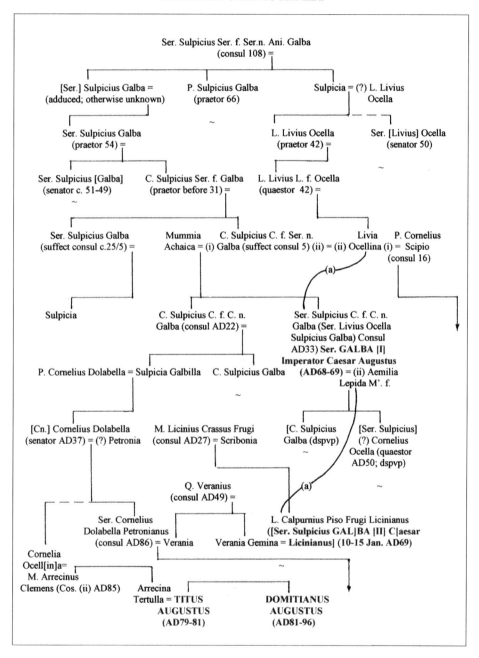

The Sulpicii, of whom **GALBA** was virtually the last recorded male member, were extremely ancient members of the patriciate and their pedigree went back to the time of the kings – all obfuscated by a mythical origin, whereby Minos, King of Crete by Pasiphäe had a son Glaukos who accompanied Kastor and Polydeukes (later achieving Roman divine status as Castor and Pollux) to Italy, where he became the first King of the Labici, in northern Latium.

Glaucus, therefore, was the claimed ancestor of the family.[125] The first Sulpicius on record was Ser. Sulpicius P. f. Camerinus supposedly consul in 500BC (and brother of Q. Sulpicius Camerinus, consul a decade later). There is much uncertainty about the precise pattern of his posterity, the family producing branches bearing *cognomina* Saverrio, Longus, Paterculus, Galus, Galba, Rufus and Peticus, almost all of which names were from time to time revived by members of the two surviving branches in the later Republic, the Galbae and the Rufi. Nor is it clear whether the family were a *gens maior* or a *gens minor*; Münzer thought them 'borderline'. Galba's first known ancestor with this name was P. Sulpicius Galba, consul in 211 and again in 200. Contemporary with him were Servius and Caius Galba, respectively curule aedile and a minor pontifex, quite possibly his brothers. The consul was succeeded by a son, Servius, praetor in 187 and he by his son of the same name, consul in 144. The pedigree set out above, begins with *his* son, Ser. Sulpicius Galba, who was consul in 108.

TABLE XII BRIEF LIVES

L. Calpurnius Piso Frugi Licinianus

Adopted as his son and heir by **GALBA**, becoming [Ser. Sulpicius Gal]ba C[aesar Licinianus]. He was born AD38, a younger son of M. Licinius Crassus Frugi (consul in AD27) whose father had been in turn adopted by M. Licinius Crassus (the grandson of the unfortunate Triumvir) out of the Calpurnii Pisones, hence the revival of the name. The family were ancient senatorial nobility in both lines, raised to patrician status in AD48. He had only reached the rank of praetor, been nominated a XVvir s. f. and become one of the Arval Brethren when he was exiled by **NERO** in or before AD65; his recall was to be a poisoned chalice. [Style on adoption: CIL.VI.2054; ILS 240]

Cornelia Ocell[in]a

Cornelia's parentage is nowhere given; yet the conjunction of the *nomen* Cornelia with Ocella, strongly suggests descent from someone with an association with the stepmother of **GALBA**. She married to M. Arrecinus Clemens (see further **Table XVI Brief Lives**) [PIR2 C. 1491]

Cn. Cornelius Dolabella

A *sacerdos* (official priest) in AD40, he was killed in 69 merely for being Galba's great-nephew, despite not being selected as his heir. His wife was probably a Petronia [PIR² C. 1347; Syme AA 280, 299]

P. Cornelius Dolabella

Patrician, competent general (in Dalmatia) and consul in 10AD. He was a friend of **TIBERIUS** although considered obsequious by some [Syme AA 97, 316, 327, 424]

Ser. Cornelius Dolabella Petronianus

Patrician, and consul in AD86 [ILS 3673; PIR2 C. 1351]

P. Cornelius Scipio,

Parician and consul, 16BC, Syme considers that he had no natural children but testamentarily adopted P. Cornelius Lentulus (suffect consul in AD2), who therefore retained his original filiation of Cn. f. Cn. n. and merely added Scipio to his

---

125. Wiseman (2004) 24. Suetonius further informs us that on the distaff side he claimed descent from Pasiphäe and King Minos and that he had his pedigree set up outside the Imperial residence on his accession.

existing name. From him there appears to have been a line of Scipios down to at least the time of **DIOCLETIANUS.**

GALBA AUGUSTUS
See main text above.

Livia L. f. Ocellina
Daughter of L. Livius L. f. Ocella, praetor in 42 under the triumvirate and a legate in the civil war that followed. Beautiful and rich member of an ancient senatorial family; second wife of C. Sulpicius Galba.[PIR² L305 & p. 8; Suetonius *Galba*, 4.1]

L. Livius L. f. Ocella
Praetor in 42BC, and a legate in the civil war that followed, thought to have been son of L. Livius Salinator, a moneyer in 84. [ILS 936; PIR² p. 81]

L. Livius Ocella
The quaestor in 42BC, the son of the predecessor, whose career may well have been held up in the Civil Wars and other upheavals. [cf. PIR² L305]

Ser. [Livius] Ocella
Noted as a senator in 50BC and probably the brother of the praetor of 42; the *praenomen* (forename) Servius being unknown amongst the Livii, that his mother might be a Sulpicius seems highly plausible. Note also the connection between the two families forged by the future Emperor's father's marriage to Livia Ocella (qv): it might well have been one of long standing [Cicero *ad Att.* 201.4, 205.3].

Sulpicia
Parrician, assumed to be the sister of the Catalinarian praetor and who seems to have married a Livius Ocella.

C. Sulpicius Ser. f. Galba
Parician and praetor between 42 and 31BC; noted as a much-quoted historian whose work is now lost, but according to a story in Suetonius, was still living when the future Emperor was a young boy, so must have died c. AD1/2. [DNP I. 6; Suetonius 4; Syme, AA, 71, 75].

C. Sulpicius C. f. Ser. n. Galba
Patrican and suffect consul in 5BC. He was supposedly short and very ugly (or, possibly, deformed). Nevertheless, after the death of Mummia, his first wife, the reputedly beautiful Livia Ocellina was pleased enough to marry him. [DNP II.6; Syme AA 77, 94, 194, 229].

C. Sulpicius Galba
The future Emperor's older brother, born c.14BC, was consul in AD22, but denied a subsequent provincial governorship through the conniving of the Emperor **TIBERIUS.** He apparently frittered away his inheritance and committed suicide in AD36 [DNP II.7; ILS 202, 7228]

P. Sulpicius Galba
He was *praetor* in c. 66BC and a consular candidate in the year of Catilina's revolt, 63, when he was condemned for complicity. It is possible that he and the praetor of 54 were brothers, although both seem to have held office more than a generation after the consul of 108.

[?Ser. Sulpicius] Cornelius Ocella
GALBA had two sons, and we know the name of neither for certain. The elder was born c., AD24/25 and in AD48 was betrothed to be married but died shortly afterwards. The younger was born c. AD27/28 and was quaestor in AD58, but seems to have died not so long afterwards, perhaps in AD60. A senator recorded as Cornelius Ocella might be one of these sons; he was quaestor

in AD50 (so could have been the elder), but is not heard of subsequently. Alternatively, he may be a descendant of Livia Ocellina's first husband, P. Cornelius Scipio's adopted son.

Ser. Sulpicius Galba

Consul in 108BC, his place in **GALBA's** ancestry is denied by Syme but accepted, as here, by Münzer. [AA 75]

Ser. Sulpicius Galba

Suffect consul at an unknown date between 25BC and 5 and the elder brother of the Emperor's father. [CIL.VI.9319]

Verania Gemina

As her name implies, Verania was the twin sister of the wife of Ser. Cornelius Dolabella Petronianus; both women were the daughters of Q. Veranius, a consul (in AD49) from an emergent family, who was sent to govern Britain by Nero in AD58 and died within months of arrival [ILS 240]

*

[GALBA II]
10-15th January 69

Not normally acknowledged, but *de jure* Emperor if only for a few hours
See above, *sub* GALBA

*

OTHO
15th January – 16th April 69

Background

M. Salvius OTHO was born on 28th April 32, the younger son of L. Salvius Otho Titianus, who was the first consul of what was previously a relatively obscure senatorial family.[126] The father was raised to the patriciate in AD48 by **CLAUDIUS**. The future Emperor entered the senate with a quaestorship in 58, having already become a member of the priestly Arval Brethren, probably through the especial favour of **NERO**. He was sent to govern Lusitania from whence he returned to Rome with **GALBA**. He married c. AD56, as her second husband, Poppaea Sabina, by whom he had no children by the time he was sent to Lusitania by **NERO**, whose mistress she already was and whose wife she promptly became (see **Part I (b)** above). Although he was actively seeking a second wife after his accession, he never had a chance to re-marry and died just short of his 37th birthday - without issue.

126. FS 2975; PIR² S43

Reign

Although **GALBA** appointed **VITELLIUS** to govern Lower Germany in December AD68, the latter was already intriguing to replace the aged martinet. Meanwhile, **NERO'S** former chum **OTHO** had been a keen supporter, and was another appointee of **GALBA'S** during his bid for the purple. Moreover, **OTHO** was on the spot later when it became clear that the Praetorian Guard were sufficiently disaffected as to be prepared to depose **GALBA**. Furthermore, by that time, the younger man felt that he had been passed over in favour of Piso/**GALBA II** as heir to the empire and his unnecessarily violent *coup* was entirely separate from anything **VITELLIUS** was hatching in Germany.

Having been acclaimed emperor 15th January 69, he held a suffect consulship. He adopted the Imperial style **Imperator M. Otho Caesar Augustus** and was probably invested with the tribunician power following his announcement to the senate on the evening of 15th that he had accepted the purple; if not it would have followed within days. He became Pontifex Maximus from 9th March, the date of his departure from Rome to face **VITELLIUS.**

Thus, although he obtained the extremely reluctant support of the senate and most of the provinces, he never really consolidated his position, for **VITELLIUS** had begun to move against him almost from day one of his principate. His restoration of **NERO'S** statues – ordered to be pulled down by **GALBA** – was no doubt a bid to win the support of all those who never lost their affection for the last of the Julio-Claudians. He also attempted to ally himself with **VITELLIUS**, dangling before him the prospect of joint power, even proposing marriage to the governor of Germany's daughter, although in the process he was obliged to soft-pedal the overtures he had been making to **NERO'S** dowager Empress, Statilia Messallina.

Despite deploying what limited forces he had to prevent **VITELLIUS** crossing the Po, aid from the Balkans was too slow in reaching him, and he was defeated at the first battle of Cremona on 14th April. He dithered for a day or so and then, to spare the empire further civil strife – or so he thought – took his own life on the 16th at nearby Brixellum (Brescello). **VITELLIUS** thus succeeded to the empire by a third successive violent *coup*. Tacitus, usually a harsh critic, notes that **OTHO'S** personal conduct as Emperor – unlike his profligate days as **NERO'S** soul-mate – was both exemplary and praiseworthy. He was popular in death in a way he could only have dreamt of in life.

TABLE XIII: THE FAMILY OF OTHO

OTHO was of recent senatorial family, Suetonius telling us that his grandfather was the first member in the senate and whose own father had been an equestrian married to a 'peasant' girl, conceivably of un-free stock.[127] However, the M. Otho, a peoples' tribune in the tumultuoius year of 43, must have been a very close kinsman if not the future Emperor's

---

127. Suetonius *Otho* 1, 1-2.

great-grandfather himself, as suggested here. The senate was heavily purged after the inauguration of the Second Triumvirate, and M. Otho could well have been one of those, recently ennobled (or even of more ancient, if obscure stock) but sent packing back into the ranks of the equestrian order. If so, to retire during the Civil Wars to the family's native Ferentium (Ferento) would have been a logical, even a prudent move. **OTHO** himself was a patrician – by elevation of his father by **CLAUDIUS** in AD48 – but not of consular rank, having governed Lusitania as an ex-quaestor. The family appear to have originated in Ferentum, although there were senatorial Salvii under the later republic: a *prefectus Sociorum* in 168 and a *praetor* of 74; they might well have been kin.

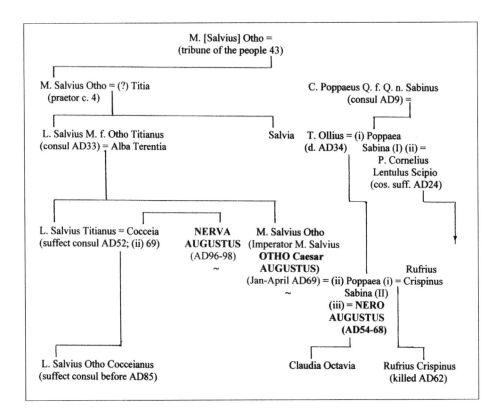

TABLE XIII BRIEF LIVES

Cocceia

Daughter of M. Cocceius M. f. Pap. Nerva, suffect consul in AD40, of a family which had emerged in the Triumviral era, and sister of the future emperor **NERVA AUGUSTUS,** see further **Section C part III(a) & Table XVII.**

P. Cornelius Lentulus Scipio

Praetor in AD16, then a legionary commander, consul suffect in 24, and proconsul of Asia. He was the son of the similarly named suffect consul of AD2, himself the testamentarily adopted son of that P. Scipio who had been the first husband of **GALBA'S** step-mother. His mother may have been an Aurelius Orestes, as several descendants bore Orestinus/Orestilla as a *cognomen,* including his brother and a sister. His son by Poppaea served as suffect consul in AD68, probably on the strength of his kinship with **GALBA** who made the appointment. [PIR² C1376/1393; Syme, AA 178, 296-299].

OTHO AUGUSTUS

See above.

Poppaea Sabina (I)

Like her daughter, (qv) the mother was a great beauty, although as her first husband she only managed to catch T. Ollius, an equestrian who died after having beren caught up in the fall of Sejanus. She went on to marry the patrician P. Cornelius Lentulus Scipio, adoptive grandson of the P. Cornelius Scipio who had been the first husband of **GALBA'S** step-mother, Livia Ocellina (see **Table XII Brief Lives**) [ILS 5459; Syme, AA 178, 184].

Poppaea Sabina (II)

See **Table X Brief Lives**

C. Poppaeus Q. f. Q. n. Sabinus

Probably the second generation of his family in the senate; the family (of 'modest origins') came from Picenum (Marche). He was consul in AD9 – so born c 41BC – and died in AD36. He also had a younger brother, Q. Poppaeus Secundus, suffect consul also in AD9. [Wiseman (1971) 340; Tacitus, *Annals* vi. 59]

Rufrius Crispinus

Equestrian, appointed praetorian prefect under **CLAUDIUS** in AD47.

Rufrius Crispinus

Probably equestrian, he was killed in a Neronian purge in AD62, probably unmarried.

Salvia

She was briefly betrothed to Drusus Julius Caesar, brother of **CALIGULA.** Any subsequent marriage she may have made is not known.

M [Salvius] Otho

Peoples' tribune in the crucial year of 43BC; quite possibly the father of the praetor of c. 4BC but subsequently relegated from the senate. [Badian, E., *Historia* XII (1963) 143; cf. Wiseman (1971) 258 no. 375]

L. Salvius Otho Cocceianus

He had been **a**ppointed a *salius* in or by AD63, and he served as suffect consul under the Flavians – he held consular rank by AD85 – and was killed by the Emperor **DOMITIAN** in 93, for rather tactlessly celebrating the anniversary of his uncle's accession, without known issue [Jones (1992) 185; PIR² S144].

L. Salvius M. f. Otho Titianus

Born c. 1BC but said to be the bastard son of

Tiberius "whom he closely resembled" according to Suetonius, but such resemblances can demonstrably found quite frequently without resort to ties of close kinship to explain it; in this case it looks like contemporary tittle-tattle. His second *agnomen* is likely to have been assumed to commemorate his maternal family. He rose to be consul in AD33 and was promoted to the patriciate by Claudius in 48 allegedly for informing on an incipient plot against him. He married to Alba Terentia – her family connections are unclearbut she was perhaps a sister of Q. Terentius Culleo, consul in AD40 and thus of an ancient family previously of praetorian rank in the senate. He died about AD55. [PIR² S141; Suetonius *Otho, 1, 2*]

L. Salvius [Otho] Titianus The fact that Titianus served as consul in AD52 suggests that he was some 15 years older than the future emperor and was therefore born c. AD17; he may, therefore, have been the son of an earlier marriage of his father's although the gap is not impossible for one marriage. He married Cocceia, daughter of M. Cocceius Nerva, suffect consul in 40, making the future emperor **OTHO** brother-in-law to the

Emperor **NERVA**. His brother appointed him consul for a second time to open the year 69, and he was allowed to complete his term by an unexpectedly clement **VITELLIUS** [PIR² S45; Relationship to **NERVA**: Jones (1992) 185 & n.].

M. Salvius Otho

Triumvir in charge of the money supply in c. 7BC and praetor around 3BC [ILS 5937; Suetonius *Otho* 1, 2; Wiseman (1971) p. 259 No. 376].

Titia

It is possible to speculate that this was the name of the future emperor's grandmother, for it has only been preserved in the *cognomen* of his father and elder brother – or at least such is the clear inference. She was probably the daughter of L. Titius – of an old senatorial family that had not previously risen above the praetorship – whose brother was suffect consul in 31, whilst he himself is only kjnown as having served as a junior officer in Caesar's Civil Wars. and who married a patrician Fabia Paullina, for Suetonius tells us his marriage was a grand one [PIR² T274; Syme RR 498; Suetonius, *Otho* 1]

VITELLIUS
16th April – 20th December 69

Background

Aulus Vitellius was born on 7th (or possibly the 24th) September AD14[128] and is credited by Suetonius with having been one of the youths Tiberius gathered around him on Capri in his declining years. He thus acquired the unsavory *cognomen* of **Spintria** (rent-boy), which rather set the tone for the rest of his career as a somewhat louche character, although had his accession to the principate been successful in the long term, the reportage of his life might have been rather different. Nevertheless, he managed to keep on the right side of **CALIGULA, CLAUDIUS** and **NERO**, which was something of an achievement, although

---

128. Suetonius gives both birth dates, and the year, but says he was 56 at his death, which would make the year 13: *Vitellius* 3

one accomplished in the shadow of his powerful father, Lucius. He was consul in AD48 (his brother Lucius succeeding him as suffect the same year) and governed Africa 55-57 with every sign of probity and success. Nevertheless, he walked with a limp acquired in a youthful chariot wreck whilst racing with **CALIGULA.** He was very tall, but his gluttony led to his becoming heavily paunched.

He married firstly his cousin Petronia, daughter of P. Petronius, the suffect consul of AD19 and Plautia, daughter of A. Plautius by his aunt.[129] They divorced in AD62 having had a son who died in uncertain circumstances before the couple parted. In the same year, Vitellius re-married; his bride was Galeria Fundana, daughter of a man who had been praetor before 54 and who was probably called – if her daughter's name is anything to go by – Galerius Fundanus. Her grandfather was probably the Prefect of Egypt from AD16 to 31, C. Galerius who was married to the author Seneca's maternal aunt Helvia.[130]

Reign

VITELLIUS became an imperial claimant by acclamation on 2nd January 69, a day after the army in Germany had refused to take the oath to **GALBA,** and acceded fully to the purple on the death of **OTHO** on 16th April, following his victory in the first battle of Cremona. Not that the gluttonous, venal and un-soldierly Vitellius was present; he remained in comfort in Gaul and stayed there until his two generals, A. Caecina Alienus and Fabius Valens had captured Rome, before - fatally – slowly moving to the capital and enlivening the journey with unpalatable displays of triumphalism, drunken-ness, venality and indiscipline, both amongst his forces and his entourage. They arrived to celebrate a totally inappropriate triumph in late June, although the transition of power went unexpectedly smoothly.

VITELLIUS' bid for supreme power was without doubt based on his own hyper-inflated view of his abilities, leavened with a dash of vanity. Furthermore, he had a link with the Julio-Claudian dynasty through his brother Lucius' second marriage to Junia Calvina, Augustus's great-great-grand-daughter, being the offspring of M. Junius Silanus (consul in AD19) and Aemilia Lepida, daughter of the younger Julia and L. Aemilius Paullus (see above, **Table VI Brief Lives**). Although this link had by 69 been broken through divorce (Junia Calvina survived to die in AD79), it without doubt played a part in Vitellius's thinking. But, even arrived in Rome, Vitellius's hold on power was clearly becoming tenuous.

He persuaded the senate to ratify his succession, to grant him the tribunician and proconsular power and bestowed upon him the office of Pontifex Maximus, along with four major priesthoods that went with it in all legitimised successions. He took the style of **A. Vitellius Germanicus Imperator Augustus** tactfully eschewing the name Caesar, which reflects creditably on him, suggesting a diplomatic element of tact and modesty his biographers entirely fail to mention. On the other hand, he had hardly earned the

---

129. Tac. *Ann*. iii. 49.1; Levick (1999) 15.
130. Griffin (1992) 453-454; **VITELLIUS'S** new sister-in-law married C. Calpurnius Piso, the leader of the plot against **NERO** of 65, *op. cit.* 96 & n. 2

'Germanicus' by successfully campaigning against the Germans; he had merely been a rather re-active governor there.

On 1ˢᵗ July T. Flavius **VESPASIANUS**, fresh from quashing the Jewish revolt, was unexpectedly acclaimed Emperor in Judaea and within a week or two **VITELLIUS** was made aware of this. Yet before **VESPASIAN'S** friend and supporter C. Licinius Mucianus could really get going *en route* to the west to face down **VITELLIUS**, Antonius Primus, a legionary commander in Pannonia – much closer to Italy – and Fuscus, the powerful procurator of neighbouring Illyricum, had also declared for Vespasian, and had already started for the Po.

VITELLIUS found himself defending more or less the same ground as had **OTHO** in April and, on October 24-25ᵗʰ was soundly defeated at the second battle of Cremona, which was followed by an appalling four-day sack of the city. He made a less than effective strategic withdrawal southward but met his Waterloo, as it were, when part of his army, sent against the Flavians at Narnia (Narni) on 17ᵗʰ December, went over to the enemy. The game was up. **VITELLIUS** retreated to Rome, which fell on 20ᵗʰ. He was killed on the same day, having fled to his mother's house whence he was eventually flushed out and crudely butchered. Only his mother, widow and daughter survived the carnage.

*

TABLE XIV: THE FAMILY OF VITELLIUS

The origins of the third short-lived emperor of 69, who briefly held power in the hiatus between the reigns of **NERO** and **VESPASIAN** are rather similar to that of **OTHO**: a member of a local family in Italy making good and sending a son to the senate. Suetonius, however, gives space to a tale of Elogius's that Faunus, legendary King of Latium, married a demi-goddess called Vitelia and that their posterity later became regal patricians, one being the wife of L. Junius Brutus the regicide; to counteract this, he also points out stories of more humble – but equally suspect – origins. Yet in the case of the Vitellii, the founder of the dynasty from Nursia (Norcia) sent four possibly even five sons into the senate – quite an achievement. The marriage of the Emperor's daughter allowed his blood line to survive into the 3rd century. An entirely alternative suggested table has been put forward as a chronologically more cohesive alternative, making Libo [Rupilius] Frugi's wife **VITELLIUS'** daughter and their grand-daughter being married to L. Fundanius Lamia Aelianus (**see Table VII(a)**.) It seems somehow less convincing, however.[131]

---

131. It contains fewer asttested relationships, chronology notwithstanding: Settipani (2000) 279, 2ⁿᵈ table.

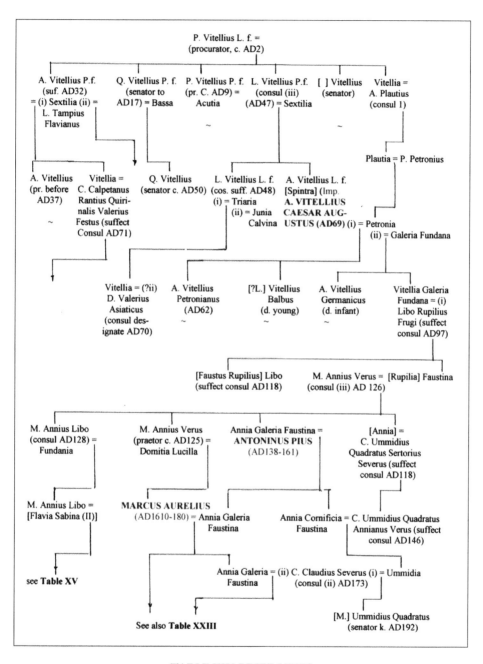

TABLE XIV BRIEF LIVES

Annia Cornificia Faustina

Only sister of **MARCUS AURELIUS** died fairly young in AD152. **See Tables XXII & XXIII(b)** [PIR² A708]

M. Annius M. f. Gal. Libo

The consul of AD128 inherited his maternal grand-father's name, representing a continuation of the blood of the family of Scribonius Libo. On his like-named son see **Table XV Brief Lives** [PIR² A667]

M. Annius M. f. Gal. Verus

Patrician by creation (of the Flavians). There remains little explanation as to how this man rose to three consulships, unless, being of an emergent family from Ucubi (Espejo) he may have had links, now lost to us, with the family of **HADRIANUS**, the Aelii of Italica (both in Spain). He was suffect consul in AD97, consul in 121 and again in 126, and in addition held the prestigious office of Prefect of the City of Rome (PUR) from 118. [PIR² A895]

M. Annius M. f. Gal. Verus

The father of **MARCUS AURELIUS** only rose to a praetorship, probably in AD124 or 125, and died in office. His wife was the daughter of P. Calvisius Tullus Ruso (consul AD109) a nephew of **HADRIANUS**. [PIR² A696, C357, D183]

ANTONINUS I PIUS AUGUSTUS

See below & **Table XX**

MARCUS AURELIUS AUGUSTUS

See below and **Tables XXII & XXIII**

<u>C.</u> Calpetanus Rantius Quirinalis <u>Valerius P. f. Pompt. Festus</u>

Known to history as Valerius Festus, he was a leading supporter of **VESPASIANUS** who made him suffect consul in AD71 and may well have been ancestor of a late 2ⁿᵈ century ex-consul also called Valerius Festus [ILS 5833, 5927]

Cn. Claudius Severus

A man whose father held the consulship as a member oif an emergent family, he was a close friend of **MARCUS AURELIUS**, who rewarded him with a second consulship and raised him to the patriciate – se also **Table XXIII Brief Lives.**

Galeria Fundana,

Daughter of a man who had been *praetor* before AD54 and who was probably called – if her daughter's name is anything to go by – [C.] Galerius Fundanus. Her grandfather was probably the Prefect of Egypt from AD16 to 31, C. Galerius, who was married to the author Seneca's maternal aunt Helvia; Vitellius's new sister-in-law married C. Calpurnius Piso, the leader of the plot against Nero of 65 [Griffin (1992) 453-454 & 96 & n. 2].

P. Petronius,

Suffect consul in AD19, augur and long the proconsul of Asia. Some would insert a son, also P. Petronius between him and **VITELLIUS'S** wife. [CIL VI. 6866; Tac. *Ann.*, iii. 49.1; Settipani (2000) 280; Syme AA 237, 329]

A. Plautius

Suffect consul in 1BC as father of, amongst others, A. Plautius, suffect consul in AD29, the conqueror and first governor of Britain, 43-47 [Tacitus, *Annals* 3, 49.1; Levick (1999) 15]

Libo [Rupilius] Frugi

Patrician by creation, suffect consul in AD97, living AD 101, he (re-)married, as her first husband, Matidia Salonina, later the mother-in-law of **HADRIANUS**. His identity is slightly spedculative, but it may be presumed that an unidentified Rupilius (probably of ancient noble senatorial stock, but long in obscurity, rather than an emergent senator) married the sister of **GALBA'S** heir, Piso (son of M. Licinius Crassus Frugi and Scribonia, see **TABLE XII Brief Lives**), hence the *praenomen* and *cognomen*. The daughter's *cognomen* suggests also a descent from the family of Sulla; perhaps Libo Frugi's mother. [Birley (1966) 249f. amplified in Birley (1987) 244; cf. SHA *Marcus*, 1, 4]

[Faustus Rupilius] Libo

All we have for this presumed son of Libo Frugi is his *cognomen* and consular date. As only Libo appears on the inscription, comparison with his (presumed) sister would suggest the above restoration of his name, although he may have had other names too, as was then becoming the fashion. [CIL VI. 207]

Sextilia

Suetonius said that the Sextilia married to L. Vitellius was '…a noble-hearted woman of distinguished family'. Whilst it is by no means certain who this lady was, the remark rather suggests that she belonged to the senatorial Sextilii, which family rather fades away at the beginning of Augustus's reign, the latest on record being M. Sextilius Q.f., a triumvir monetalis (moneyer) in c. 25BC, who could conceivably have been their father. On record for nearly three centuries, they never made higher office than the praetorship. [Badian (1965) 113-115].

L. Tampius Flavianus

A member of an emergent family, Flavianus was suffect consul before AD47. His son (presumably by Sextilia) held the same office c 54/68 and again in 75, despite his kinship with the Emperor **VITELLIUS** having placed him in a delicate position in 69 when he was the immediate superior, as governor of Pannonia, of Vespesian's champion, Antonius Primus. If the younger Flavianus's mother *was* Sextilia re-married, this would satisfactorily explain his attested 'kinship' with the future Emperor [Syme (1958) II. 593].

C. Ummidius Quadratus Sertorius Severus

Patrician by creation (by **CLAUDIUS**) in favour of his great grandfather, suffect consul in AD40. He himself was born c. AD83/4 and assumed by Birley to have been adopted by a Sertorius Severus, but it is perhaps more likely that his father's second wife (of which he was a son) was a Sertoria and that the name was tacked onto his patronymic, as happened with his son, too; suffect

consul in AD118, following which he was governor of Moesia Inferior. [Birley (1986) 244-245]

C. Ummidius Quadratus Annianus Verus

Suffect consul in AD146 [Birley *loc.cit.*; Syme (1958) 478-480 7 n.].

[M.] Ummidius Quadratus

Son of Claudius Severus by Ummidia, and adopted by his maternal uncle, M. Ummidius Quadratus Annianus (consul AD167). He himself fell victim to his cousin the Emperor **COMMODUS** in AD193, apparently young and unmarried [Birley, *op..cit.,* 247].

D. Valerius Asiaticus

Son and namesake of the first senator from Gaul who had been twice consul, in AD35 (suffect) and again in 46, but who fell victim to the machinations of Messallina. Despite this milestone in senatorial history, one notes M. Valerius Asiaticus, an ex-quaestor, relegated from the senate (probably by the Triumvirs after 43BC), who must surely have been a forebear. Possibly he subsequently settled quietly in Vienne (Gaul) as an equestrian businessman. The son of the Gallic ground-breaker was designated suffect consul for AD70 by (perhaps surprisingly) **GALBA** who also made him governor of Gallia Belgica. In the table he is shown as marrying Vitellia; we know Vitellius caused them to be betrothed, but whether they had the opportunity to tie the knot prior to the overthrow of the Emperor is not known. Although both appear to have survived that event. Asiaticus did have children, but by a previous marriage, possibly to **NERO'S** widow, Statilia Messallina, he had two sons and possibly a daughter, too [Syme, RR 79 & n. 5].

Vitellia

It has been suggested that she was the sister of the procurator, not a daughter [Settipani (200) 280].

Vitellia Galeria Fundana

Probably the first born of the marriage, spared when captured by Antonius Primus in AD69 and given a dowry by Vespasian the following year. Such generosity suggests that she might have been astonishingly good looking with character to match [Suetonius *Vespasian* 14; PIR² G33].

A. Vitellius P. f.

Entered the senate and rose to a suffect consulship in AD32, during which he died. He married Sextilia, whose sister married his brother Lucius (see below).

A. Vitellius A. f.

Appears to have held a praetorship before AD37 but of whom nothing further is heard – perhaps one of **CALIGULA'S** un-named victims.

A. Vitellius L. f.

See above **VITELLIUS AUGUSTUS**

A. Vitellius Germanicus

Reputedly he had a serious stammer.

[A.] Vitellius Petronianus

He had one eye and was allegedly killed by his father in his youth, before AD62.

L. Vitellius P. f.

The notorious chief minister of **CLAUDIUS**. He was suffect consul in AD34, 43 and ordinary consul (a signal honour) in 47. He held the censorship with **CLAUDIUS**, the following year, in which role he adlected himself into the patriciate. He died in AD52 of a heart attack a day after having been accused of treason, having married Sextilia (still living when her son became emperor), almost certainly the sister of his brother Aulus' wife [Suetonius, *Vitellius* 3].

L. Vitellius L. f.

Elder son, suffect consul in AD48. He married Junia Calvina, a descendant of Augustus (see above, **Table VI Brief Lives**) but whom he divorced also in 48 or shortly before; she re-married C. Cassius Longinus. He re-married Triaria - conceivably a member of the republican senatorial house of the Valerii Triarii - who was with him in the defence of Italy but who may have survived him. Lucius was killed following surrendering his forces at discretion to the Flavians outside Rome a day or two after the death of his brother leaving issue by Triaria [Junia: Tac. *Ann.* 12, 4.1; Triaria: Wiseman (1971) no. 459].

[A?] Vitellius Germanicus

He was born between AD63 and 68, but his *cognomen* was only added after 1st January 69 so he did not enjoy it long, being killed by order of **VESPASIANUS'** supporters Mucianus and Primus shortly after his father, around 21st December 69.

P. Vitellius L. f.

Of equestrian rank but rose to hold an important procurator's post as **AUGUSTUS'S** financial agent. The order, of his sons' births (there was a fifth, un-named one too), according to Suetonius was: Aulus, Qunitus, Publius and Lucius, although on career evidence, the order Publius, Aulus, Qunitus and Lucius would appear more likely [Suetonius, *Vitellius* 2].

P. Vitellius P. f.

Praetor c. AD9, a friend of Germanicus and a *sacerdos* 20, he was implicated in Sejanus's fall and committed suicide in 32. He married Acutia (who died in 37) [FS 3552; ILS 6445; Wiseman (1971) 502]

Q. Vitellius P. f.

A senator of unknown seniority – possibly quite junior – when relegated for venality in AD17, after which we hear nothing further of him except that his wife was called Bassa [ILS 3104].

Q. Vitellius Q. f.

A senator in the mid-1st century AD [ILS3104].

The Imperial Succession
Vespasianus
Titus
Domitianus I

Imperial Claimant
Saturninus I

Historical Background

The victory of **VESPASIAN** and the establishment of the Flavian dynasty – the name deriving from the family's *nomen* or family name of Flavius – marked the end of some eighteen months of civil war, upheaval and uncertainty.

Once established, **VESPASIAN,** ably assisted by his elder son **TITUS,** ruled moderately and with a sure touch. The senate was replenished with loyal supporters of the dynasty, other senatorial families were raised to the prestigious status of patrician (giving a fast-track to the highest offices); a *modus vivendi* with the traditional governing *elite* was established which satisfied both sides, and in due course a series of military victories, like those of Cn. Julius Agricola - the father-in-law of the senatorial historian Cornelius Tacitus - in Britain, consolidated the empire.

Even the descent into paranoia of **DOMITIAN, VESPASIAN'S** younger son and **TITUS'S** successor, with the resulting cull of senior members of the senatorial elite, had little lasting impact on the smooth running of the empire.

The only discernable hiccough seems to have been the attempted usurpation of L. Antonius *SATURNINUS* at the beginning of 89 in Germany, with which some commentators have linked the shadowy affair of the execution of the governor of Britain, Sallustius Lucullus – floated rather daringly but perhaps unconvincingly, as the son of the British (Catuvellaunian) prince Adminius by Miles Russell[1].

Lucullus was put to death for daring to name a new type of spear after himself and not the Emperor. Was the real reason resentment on Lucullus' part (or on the part of his officers) in having to withdraw from the successful part-conquest of Scotland achieved by Agricola, himself later disgraced? And was *SATURNINUS*' bid related? These are murky waters and, as so often with unsuccessful imperial claimants, little light seems to penetrate to allow the true course of events and real underlying motives to be discerned with our present state of knowledge.

---

[1] *Current Archaeology* 204 (5/2006) 630-635; author's argument against, letter, *op.cit.* 205 (7/2006).

The Dynasty and its links

The Imperial family itself descended from a family of middling sort from Reate (Rieti), the first family to hold the purple not of ancient patrician stock of the republic, bar the relatively ephemeral **OTHO** and **VITELLIUS,** although as we have seen, even they were patrician by creation. Yet even compared to them, the Flavian dynasty's origins were, to put it kindly, unassuming. Furthermore, **VESPASIAN** was the first Emperor to be a *novus homo* – a new man – without even a senatorial father.

The first member of whom we know anything concrete had served as a centurion – an *elite* one, nevertheless, a *primus pilus* – who had fought under **Pompey** at the Battle of Pharsalus in 49BC. There was also a story going around at the time of Vespasian's bid for power that this man, his grandfather, was the son of a Gaul, who had settled in Reate and was an agent for hiring labour from his native land to gather in the Italian harvest. Levick points out that his grandfather's *cognomen* – Petro – is indeed of Gallic origin, so there may indeed have been at least a grain of truth in what was clearly intended at the time as a slur.[132]

The family, despite burgeoning wealth, never quite managed at this stage to aspire to equestrian rank and both **VESPASIANUS'S** mother and grandmother were higher up the social scale than the Flavii themselves. The former, Vespasia, was a senator's sister and equestrian's daughter and the latter, Tertulla, was of also of equestrian stock.[133] Once established, links were forged with the previous dynasty by the marriage in AD70 of **DOMITIANUS** – albeit in predicably disreputable circumstances – with Domitia Longina [see **Part A**, **Table VI** above].

Prior to that, however, **TITUS** seems to have become the brother-in-law to the future Emperor **TRAJAN'S** father. This link to the following, Antonine, dynasty was later strengthened by two further marriages amongst the descendants of **VESPASIAN'S** elder brother. His daughter Flavia Sabina, married twice and her descendants from both alliances – the Pedanii Fusci and the Caesennii Paeti - made Antonine connections including a marriage with the sister of **HADRIAN. Table XV** sets out the male line of the dynasty; that following one (**XVI**) charts their descendants in the female line.

*

132. Levick, B., *Vespasian* (London, 1999) 6-7
133. Suetonius, *Vespasian*, 2, 1; 5, 2.

VESPASIANUS
(known to history as Vespasian)
20th December 69 – 23rd June 79

Background

T. Flavius [T. f. T. n. Quir.] Vespasianus, was born 17th November 9AD at Falacrinae (Falacrine), near Reate. In 39 he married Flavia Domitilla [I], probably his second cousin[134], whose own status had to be regularised before the marriage could take place. After her death she was retrospectively accorded the rank of Augusta.

Although a late-starting senator of good reputation, the new emperor was of the first generation of his family to enter the senate and the first not to have been a patrician, either of ancient standing or of recent creation. His career, which began under **TIBERIUS**, owed something to flattery of **CALIGULA** and much to his successor's freedman Narcissus. It was, nevertheless, one of unchecked military competence and success, starting with a junior command during the invasion of Britain in which he covered himself with glory. The only set-back was that Agrippina did not like anyone connected with Narcissus, yet Vespasian was chosen to accompany **NERO** on his tour of Greece, when he famously caused displeasure by dropping off during one of the Emperor's recitations; miraculously, he and his reputation survived.

It is well known that **VESPASIAN**[135], aided by his elder son **TITUS** as legate, was engaged in putting down the Jewish revolt at the time that **NERO** died. Between then and the accession of **VITELLIUS**, he had crushed most resistance, taken Jerusalem and destroyed the temple. The events of AD68-69 were not lost on the general in Palestine: the power base had swung from a senatorial and familial one to one firmly rooted in the military, although family ties still played a part, bearing in mind that both **GALBA, OTHO** and **VITELLIUS** had fairly close links to the Julio-Claudian dynasty. Nevertheless, military competence and a good reputation throughout the legions looked to be an excellent start.

The success of the Jewish War, as the author Josephus called it, put **VESPASIAN** in a position pre-eminent to avenge **GALBA**, spurred on by the accession of the venal **VITELLIUS**, whom **VESPASIAN** would have known personally perfectly well, for it is worth bearing in mind that all the protagonists were drawn from the same *elite* and were acquainted as well as being, in some cases, related.

Reign

What exactly **VESPASIAN** had in mind, when he was acclaimed, as his *modus operandi* for securing power, does not in the event seem apparent, for as we have seen, the impetuous Antonius Primus (see above, *sub* **VITELLIUS**) got the show on the road before anyone had

---

134. Jones (1984) 3
135. The modern usage will be employed henceforth.

realized it. By 20th December 69, Vespasian was in control, albeit at the cost of the life of his valued and wise elder brother, T. Flavius Sabinus, killed out-of-hand by **VITELLIUS'S** supporters on 18th December in the run-up to the fall of the City.

His first style on succession (December AD69) was **Imperator T. Flavius Vespasianus Caesar** but within two months it was changed to **Imperator Caesar Vespasianus Augustus.** He also received the tribunician power renewable on 10th December yearly, to which were added later that year (AD70) *Pater Patriae* and *Pontifex Maximus* – all *in absentia.*

Although there was a year's mopping up to be done in the Holy Land – like the reduction of Masada - **VESPASIAN** had sufficient confidence in **TITUS** to finish the job well, and appointed him as his replacement, before heading first for Alexandria and then Rome where he arrived two months short of the first anniversary of the fall of his predecessor.

He seems to have found that the empire had run perfectly well throughout all the upheavals, run by the less glamorous 'B' list members of the *élite*, not necessarily connected to the former dynasty nor the ancient aristocracy. These men Vespasian promoted, attempting through a combination of shrewdness, ruthlessness and administrative adroitness in forging a new *élite* out of the best elements of the old, especially as he found himself distrusting the survivors of the clique that had been behind the ousting of **NERO,** like Helvidius Priscus, an early casualty of the new regime. The new Emperor was, in a sense, the first since **AUGUSTUS** to understand the delicate balancing act that had to be maintained between the ruler and the senate, and managed it rather well. A good sense of humour seemed to have helped.

Modelling himself on **CLAUDIUS**, he had the senate elect him censor for 73/74 and not only replenished the ranks of the senate from the more senior and provenly competent members of the equestrian order – especially those whose services to himself and his family had commended them – but also nominated a group of prominent and loyal senators for adlection into the patriciate, almost all from new emergent families. He reformed aspects of the administration, especially the fiscal side, for he had taken over a desperately depleted treasury. This only served to enhance his reputation for mean-ness with money, for tax rises, new taxes and other, less straightforward means of replenishing the fisc, were resorted to.

He died in his bed at his villa at Aquae Cutiliae (near Cittaducale) 23rd June 79, thus being the first to do so without hint of foul play since **AUGUSTUS** 65 years before, quipping on his death-bed, 'Methinks I am becoming a God'. He was succeeded by his son **TITUS** – rather than an adopted heir – the first such father-to-son succession ever, leaving aside the unfortunate **BRITANNICUS**. He was subsequently deified by the senate.

*

TITUS
23 June 79 – 13 Sept. 81

Background

TITUS Flavius Vespasianus was born 30th December AD39 at Rome and whose uncontested claim was that he was brought up at court with **CLAUDIUS'S** ill-fated son, **BRITANNICUS**, whom he befriended and on the occasion of whose death he was present.[136] He had a very successful career as a military tribune in Britain and Germany, thereafter opting for jurisprudence. He was elected to a quaestorship for 64, later accompanying his father to Palestine as his legate, in which role he proved himself uncommonly competent.

On his father's accession his style changed to **T. Caesar Aug. f. Vespasianus** and he was granted the tribunician and proconsular power on 1st July 71, the former renewable yearly in 10th December. After the fall of Jerusalem in September 70 he had been hailed as *imperator* by his troops, and consequently by 72/73 he had added to his name as **Imperator Titus Caesar Augusti f. Vespasianus.**[137] He was consul for the first time with his father to open 70, holding office again in 72, 74, 75, 76, 77 and 79. **VESPASIAN** also appointed him – irregularly, since he was a senator and not an equestrian – Prefect of the Praetorian Guard, hitherto one of the two most senior equestrian positions in the empire, no doubt feeling that a totally reliable person in charge of that turbulent unit was essential after the excesses of the previous twelve months. **TITUS,** in this position, was able to do a great deal of his father's dirty work. Indeed, his role under his father was to act as his executive assistant, whilst Vespasian made the decisions.

TITUS'S love life was a trifle tangled. He married for the first time c. 63, Arrecina Tertulla, younger daughter of M. Arrecinus Clemens, Praetorian Guard commander from AD40 until he was executed in the over-reaction to the murder of **CALIGULA** for complicity. The family, as we have seen, was probably already related to the Flavii, probably through Vespasian's grandmother Tertulla. Arrecina died c. 65. He re-married, before 66, the socially much more distinguished Marcia Furnilla, probably the daughter of Q. Marcius Barea Sura, a relatively undistinguished senator, of a family which appears to have entered the senate early in Augustus's reign. Her grandfather, Q. Marcius Barea Soranus had come late to a (suffect) consulship in AD52. She derived her second name from her mother, Antonia Furnilla.[138] Antonia in her turn was the daughter of an otherwise unknown A. Antonius and, in all probability a descendant of C. Furnius, consul in 17BC, a member of an obscure senatorial family, whose father had been a triumviral *praetor*.[139] It sems highly liklely that a sister – another Marcia – was the mother of the future emperor

---

136. Suetonius, *Titus,* 2
137. Syme, RP III (Oxford 1984) 1071
138. ILS 953
139. Dio, lii. 42,4

TRAJAN (see **Section C part III(a)**), which could explain why that emperor's father, M. Ulpius Traianus was first appointed to command one of his legions against the Jews (with **TITUS** in charge of another), made suffect consul on Vespasian's accession and later (in 74) raised to the patriciate.[140]

However, **TITUS** divorced Marcia shortly after the birth of their daughter, having fallen for Julia Berenice, a daughter of M. Julius Agrippa I, Tetrarch, later King of Judaea, who had died in AD44. She had had three distinguished husbands, the last of whom, who had died in 63, was none other than Polemo II, king of Pontus and Cilicia, a great-grandson of **Mark Antony** through his daughter, who had married Pythodorus of Tralles. She came to Rome with him, but was immensely unpopular – the example of Cleopatra should have served as a warning – and was ordered home to Judaea on **VESPASIAN'S** instructions in 75, after which **TITUS** seems to have rapidly got over her.

Reign

During 79 – on 23rd June - he succeeded his father, when he added **Augustus** to his style and succeeded as *Pontifex Maximus*. He was consul again - with his younger brother – in 80, and by the time of his death had been acclaimed *imperator* 16 times. Several Roman emperors, on succession, gave every appearance of being likely to make a good fist of the job, but turned out to be monsters – **CALIGULA, NERO, DOMITIAN** and so on. Yet **TITUS** came to the throne with a louche reputation and as hated for his effectiveness as praetorian commander as for his predilection for the Jewish Queen Berenice, but somehow transformed himself almost on the instant into a good natured and benevolent ruler, greatly lamented on his premature demise – like his father, at Aquae Cutiliae – 13th September 81 after a reign of 2 years and 2 months. He was deified by the senate almost immediately after his death.

DOMITIANUS I
(Known to history as Domitian)
13th Sept. 81 – 18th Sept. 96

Background

T. Flavius **DOMITIANUS** was born 24th October AD51 at Rome and brought up separately from **TITUS**, probably with his uncle T. Flavius Sabinus, with whom he most certainly was on 18th December AD69 when the forces of **VITELLIUS** had them surrounded on the Capitol; he was fortunate to escape unscathed, probably aided by his youth. On his father's accession he was re-styled simply **Caesar Domitianus** later adding *Princeps Iuventutis*.[141] His first consulship came in 71 before he was twenty – strictly against convention, but not the first example – and he followed with further consulships in AD73, 75, 76, 77, 79, 80 and after his accession every year from 82 to 88, then in 90, 92 and 95, seventeen in all.

---

140. Jones (1992) 11, 59, 201; Birley (1987) 242.
141. ILS 246

Reign

DOMITIAN is not seriously suspected of having either killed his brother or have hastened his end, despite little evidence of any particular warmth between them. Nevertheless, when it became clear that **TITUS** was dying, **DOMITIAN** repaired immediately to the praetorian guard camp to promise donatives and exact oaths of fidelity. He was duly acclaimed on 14th September AD81 took the style **Imperator Caesar Divi f. Domitianus Augustus** became *pontifex maximus*, was invested with the tribunician and proconsular power, to be renewed on 10th December each year following, and was hailed as *imperator*, being so hailed a further twenty two times during his reign. Domitia Longina was hailed as Augusta at the end of September 81 and their infant son, who had died some time before, was deified. Later on he was elected consul for ten years in succession and censor for life, albeit that he subsequently declined to enter into many of the consulships.[142]

Like so many tyrants, he started well and instituted a number of governmental reforms, which were generally welcomed. Indeed, even after the first few years, when the worst side of his nature had begun to take hold, he was a competent and reliable administrator. Yet he never warmed to the partnership **AUGUSTUS** had tried to maintain between *princeps* and senate, holding that body in contempt – after all, like **NERO** he had never been a member of it as a private citizen – and although he chose some pretty competent senators to do the work of governing the empire and fighting its wars, they were more like courtiers, setting a trend for the future.

He waged a successful war against some German tribes in 82-83, awarding himself a triumph and the additional name **Germanicus,** despite having remained in his litter throughout most of the campaign. More serious was a revolt in 85 of the Dacians in the Balkans who crossed the Danube and killed the local governor. It took two years hard fighting to restore order and three more to secure the region, although a negotiated peace had to be settled in 89 in order to switch forces to deal with an incursion of two other warlike tribes in the area of the upper Danube. In the end, troubles along much of the Danube led to a series of campaigns right up to the time of Domitian's death.

Unfortunately, as time went on, it also meant that such men became more than a little nervous at their call to serve, since the casualty rate of senators condemned to death was Neronically high, including, by the time of his death, all the surviving males in his own family, probably excepting one of the children of T. Flavius Clemens, the consul of 95 who was executed not long afterwards for 'atheism'[143], who is proposed in **Table XV** (below) as the likely forebear of M. Annius Sabinus Libo, a cousin of **COMMODUS**.

As time went on, paranoia seems to have taken a grip, leading him to style himself in correspondence as *dominus et deus* (Lord and God), to rename September and October

---

142. Dio 67, 4.3.
143. A term taken by Eusebius (in reference to his wife) as indictating a conversion to Christianity, a happenstance not these days given much credence: Eusebius *Hist. Eccl.* III.18.4

'Germanicus' and 'Domitianus' after himself[144] and instituting a regime of spies and inform-
ers with a reliance upon torture, some particularly unpleasant. He also declared himself
perpetual censor, giving himself a free hand in manipulating the lives of his *élite*. He was
solitary, humourless, timorous and insecure which led to a cycle of plots, the supression of
which culminated in the killing of his 'atheistical' nephew Clemens (and probably his sons,
whom the emperor had adopted as potential heirs) and the exile of his widow, a tragedy
which appears to have triggered the conspiracy which resulted in his assassination on 18th
September AD96 after a reign of fifteen years and four days.

DOMITIAN'S worst scare was on the twentieth anniversary of the acclamation of
VITELLIUS, 1st January 89, when L. Antonius *SATURNINUS*, suffect consul probably
in 82 and at the time governor of Upper Germany, headed a military uprising which, in
the event, was quickly put down by *SATURNINUS'* opposite number in Lower Germany,
supported by the future emperor **TRAJAN** whose consulship the following year is unlikely
to have been a co-incidence.

Yet the effect on **DOMITIAN'S** insecure and suspicious mind was doubtless salutary,
although the casualty rate amongst the senate, court and administrators, only began to
accelerate, becoming almost a 'terror', from 93 until his death. Once dead, he was not
deified, but suffered a *damnatio memoriae* (erasure of memory) in the senate, in which
his statues – only in gold or silver according to his own edict – were melted down and his
inscriptions erased.

DOMITIAN was said to have been a voluptuary and a seducer of women, although the
alleged affair with his niece Julia, widow of his cousin Sabinus - killed as the result of a
ceremonial solecism in AD82 or 83 – is largely discounted by modern scholarship. Despite
this, he was only once married, although that came about discreditably, for in AD70 he
enticed the aristocratic Domitia Longina from the distinguished patrician (by creation)
L. Aelius Lamia Plautius Aelianus, a man whom he later had killed, in 87 or 88, allegedly
for making Domitian the butt of witticisms. Yet Lamia had the last laugh, for his posterity
included the Emperor **LUCIUS VERUS** and thus close kin to the later Antonine Emperors.
Neither of his two sons by Domitia survived infancy, although the younger was styled Caesar.

Further reading:

Levick, B., *Vespasian* (London 1999).
Jones, B. W., *The Emperor Titus* (London 1984)
Jones, B. W., *The Emperor Domitian* (London 1992)
Suetonius, *The Twelve Caesars*: Vespasian, Titus and Domitian.
Syme, R., *Antonius Saturninus,* in *Roman Papers* III (Oxford, 1984

---

144. ILS 268 & 269 on the additional honorific.

TABLE XV: THE FLAVIAN DYNASTY

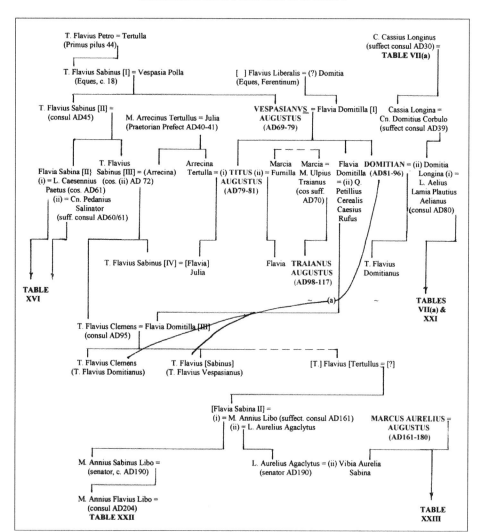

TABLE XV BRIEF LIVES

M. Annius M. f. Gal. Libo

First cousin of Emperor **MARCUS AURELIUS** and a member of a family from Ucubi (Espejo, Spain). A fourth generation senator and a third generation patrician, his grandfather had been adlected into the patriciate by **VESPASIANUS** in 73/74. Born 128, quaestor 158/9 and suffect consul in 161. His wife, it can be confidently deduced, was Flavia Sabina [II]. [ILS 7190; PIR[2] A668]

M. Annius M. f. Gal. Flavius Libo

Son of Sabinus Libo he was consul in 204, the year of the saecular games, suggesting the favour of the Emperor **SEPTIMIUS SEVERUS** who had by this time declared himself an adopted son of **MARCUS AURELIUS** and would presumably have looked on Libo as a cousin. Nothing more is heard of him and he may have fallen victim to **CARACALLA** in 211 or 213. [PIR[2] A648].

M. Annius Sabinianus

Suffect consul c. 225 and probably the imperial claimant *SABINIANUS* in Africa in 240 - assuming his name can be read as 'Annius' and not 'Asinius'. If the former, he may have been a son of Sabinus Libo, in which case his claim would have been impelled, whatever the necessities of his actual *coup*, by his impeccable imperial connections. See **Part IV(b), XXXVIII** for the alternative suggestion that he was in fact an Asinius. Either is possible [SHA, *Tres Gordiani* XXIII, 4]

M. Annius Sabinus Libo

Only known son of Libo and [Flavia Sabina], he was a late second century senator who failed to rise – as far as is known – to the consulship. He may have become a victim of **COMMODUS,** who was well known for his penchant for eliminating possible rivals and a man whose veins contained the blood of **VESPASIAN'S** family would have provided an irresistible potential victim. [ILS 6183; PIR^2 A688]

Arrencina Tertulla

Daughter of M. Arrecinus Clemens and first wife of **TITUS**. Married 60/61, died, probably in childbirth in 63.

M. Arrecinus Tertullus

Praetorian Prefect AD40-41, and killed *pour encourager les autres* on the orders of **CLAUDIUS** for his part in the assassination of **CALIGULA** along with his brother-in-law, Julius Lupus, who had served under his command as a praetorian tribune. His *cognomen* might have been Clemens; the sources are contradictory. Lupus' adoptive grandson, L. Julius Ursus Servianus (consul (iii) 134) married the sister of the emperor **HADRIANUS**. Their daughter married Cn. Pedanius Fuscus Salinator, a descendant of Vespasian's brother Sabinus [Jones (1992) 40-42 & n]

L. Aurelius Agaclytus

Greek born freedman of the emperor **LUCIUS VERUS** and obliged by him to marry between 162 and 167, the widow of his cousin, Libo, herself nowhere named in the sources but clearly a Flavian princess and probably called, judging by her descendants' names, Flavia Sabina**.**

L. Aurelius L. f. Agaclytus

Son of **LUCIUS VERUS'** freedman of the same name, presumably by the widow of M. Annius Libo**,** Flavia Sabina II. Permitted without doubt, thanks to his connectons, to enter the senate. Married as her second husband, a daughter of **MARCUS AURELIUS,** thus allying the blood of the Flavian and Antonine dynasties but unfortunately, no children are known. If there were any, no doubt **COMMODUS** soon sealed their fate.

Domitia Longina
See **Table VII(a) Brief Lives.**

DOMITIANUS AUGUSTUS
See **above.**

Cn. Domitius Corbulo
Suffect consul AD39; great Neronian marshal forced to commit suicide in 67. Wife of Cassia Longina, see **Table VII(a) Brief Lives** [Syme (1970) 27-39, esp. 37].

[Flavia]
Daughter of **TITUS** by **Marcia Furnilla;** died young.

Flavia Domitilla [I]
Daughter of **Flavius Liberalis**, for whom her father eventually established her right to full citizenship. She was formerly the mistress of another man of equestrian status, Statilius Capella, from Sabratha (in Libya). She married her kinsman,

the future Emperor **VESPASIANUS** in 39 and died sometime after 51 and before her husband's accession. Posthumously accorded the style of **Augusta** [Jones (1984) 199, n. 8]

Flavia Domitilla [II]

Born c. 45, probably the member of the family who married c. 67 as his second wife, Q. Petillius Cerealis Caesius Rufus, suffect consul in 70 and consul (ii) in 74, although this is doubted by Levick who thinks she was born c. 53/54 and would thus be too young for the match, but supported by Brian Jones. Cerealis was a long-attested friend of **VESPASIANUS** and a leading supporter in his bid for power. She died, probably in childbirth, just before the accession of her father, leaving an only daughter [Levick (1999) 23; Jones (1992) 48, 55].

Flavia Domitilla [III]

Born c. 64, married c. 86/88 to her first cousin T. Flavius Clemens [II] consul in 95 but killed on the orders of **DOMITIANUS,** that same year on grounds of 'atheism', but of Judaism according to Dio and Christianity according to Eusebius. She was, at the same time, exiled to the island of Pandateria and later killed, but not before the couple had produced seven children, none of whose original names are known. It is thought that there were at least three daughters and another son. No hint of his name survives, but a princess of the Flavian dynasty can be shown, from the names of her son and grandson, to have married M. Annius Libo consul in 161 and first cousin to **MARCUS AURELIUS**, see **part III(b)** [Dio, LXVII, 4, 1-2; Eusebius, *Hist. Eccl.* 18, 4.]

[Flavia] Julia

Daughter of **TITUS**, born 10th August 63, probable first cousin of the future emperor **TRAjAN** and wife of her first cousin, T. Flavius Sabinus [III], marrying him after having been turned down by **DOMITIAN** himself; widowed by 83. Allegedly

Domitian's lover after her husband died. She was accorded the rank of Augusta c. 80 and died before 3rd January 91, following which she was deified [Suetonius, *Domitian* 22 ; Levick (1999) 199]

Flavia Sabina [I]

Born c. AD27; thought to have married twice. First to L. Caesennius Paetus consul in 61and thereafter to Cn. Pedanius Salinator suffect consul in 60 or 61, the order of the marriages being based solely on the ages of the children based on their consulships.

[Flavia Sabina II]

Almost certainly the name of the daughter of the surviving son – whose name and career are unknown – of T. Flavius Clemens and Flavia Domitilla [III]. From the name of her son and grandson, it can be shown that her first husband was M. Annius Libo cousin of **MARCUS AURELIUS**, see **part III(b)** She re-married (as the un-named "widow of Libo") and at the emperor **LUCIUS VERUS'** bidding, his freedman, L. Aurelius Agaclytus [Birley(1987) 243]

T. Flavius Clemens

Born 60, husband of Flavia Domitilla [III] consul 95, in which year he was killed for "Atheism" and his wife sent into exile. Farther of seven children, two sons being adopted by **DOMITIAN** and later killed on his orders. A third son may well have been the parent of [Flavia Sabina II] [PIR[2] F240].

T. Flavius Domitianus [I]

Elder son of **DOMITIANUS I** b. 73, who died in childhood, see above; his brother (name unrecorded) but styled Caesar after 81, is omitted from the table. [Suet, *Domitianus* 3, 1].

T. Flavius Domitianus [II]

Born AD81, adopted as son and heir by **DOMITIANUS I** in 95, but killed in 96

unmarried. His original name was prtobably
Clemens [PIR² F257].

[T.] Flavius Liberalis

From Ferulium; an *optio* (clerk) to a quaestor
there but thought to be kin to Vespasian. He may
have married a Domitia, possibly not herself a
Roman citizen, as their daughter did not hold full
citizenship either [Jones (1984) 3, cf. Suetonius,
Vespasian 3].

.

T. Flavius Petro

Served as a centurion in the army, riising to
primus pilus (literally 'first lance' or chief centurion). He married **Tertulla** from Cosa, possibly
related to the family's later kin, the Arrecini.

T. Flavius T. f. Quir. Sabinus [I]

A wealthy tradesman of equestrian status who
married **Vespasia Polla** – from whom the future
emperor derived his *cognomen* - the daughter of
an equestrian, Vespasius Pollio. Her brother was a
new senator who, by AD30 had reached the rank
of praetor [PIR² F351; Wiseman (1971) No. 480].

T. Flavius T. f. Sabinus [II]

Born c. AD3, entered the senate on the qualifying basis of his father's fortune. Consul in 45,
but killed by **VITELLIUS'S** supporters in Rome
whilst trying to oust the Emperor, 18th December
69. Wife's name unknown. [PIR² F352].

T. Flavius T. f. Sabinus [III]

Born 30, suffect consul in the dying days of 69,
ordinary consul in 72 but he had died between 79
and 81, Married [Arrecina Clementina], herself b. c.
35, daughter of M. Arrecinus Clemens, praetorian
Prefect under **CALIGULA** and probably related to
Tertulla. Settipani suggests he was instead married
to a Cocceia, probably a sister of **NERVA** [PIR²
F353/354; Settipani (2000) 273, 2nd table].

T. Flavius Sabinus [IV]

Born 53, consul in 82 and married to [**Flavia**]
Julia daughter of the emperor **TITUS,** and thus
a first cousin by marriage of the (future) emperor
TRAJAN. He was killed at the instigation of
DOMITIANUS in 83. His children seem not to
have survived infancy [PIR² F355]

T. Flavius Vespasianus

Born 82, adopted as his son by **DOMITIANUS I**
in 95, but killed in 96, unmarried. His name was
originally probably Sabinus [PIR² F397].

L. Junius Caesennius Paetus

Born 43, consul in 79 with his cousin, **TITUS.**
His wife was probably Arria, sister of C. Arrius
Antoninus, grandfather of **ANTONINUS PIUS,**
see **part III(b)** [PIR² C174].

Marcia

There is little doubt that she was the sister of
TITUS' wife **Marcia** Furnilla. She married
M. Ulpius Traianus, father of the Emperor
TRAIANUS and a comrade-in-arms of
VESPASIAN [Jones (1992) 201, n. 53].

Marcia Furnilla

Daughter of the senator Q. Marcius Barea Sura
and Antonia Furnilla. The latter was the daughter
of an A. Antonius (otherwise unknown but not
related to the Triumvir) and a Furnia. The latter is
likely to have been a daughter or grand-daughter
of C. Furnius, consul in 17BC, a member of an
obscure senatorial family whose father had been
praetor under the triumvirs. [ILS 953; Levick
(1999) 23 ; Dio, LII, 42, 4].

[Cn.] Pedanius Fuscus Salinator

Suffect consul in 84 and originally from Barcino
(Barcelona) [Jones (1992) 207 n. 122].

Q. Petilius Cerealis Caesius Rufus

Suffect consul 70 and again (ii) in 74. Husband of **VESPASIAN'S** daughter, although previously married and with two sons when he married her. Son of L. Caesius Cordus, praetor 21 and adopted son of [Q.] Petillius Rufus, also a praetor in the early years of **TIBERIUS,** possibly of an old senatorial family going back into the Republic [Jones (1992) 47 & n. 113; Syme (1958) 595n]

TITUS AUGUSTUS

See above

M. Ulpius Traianus

Father of the emperor of the same name, known to history as **TRAJAN.** A former comrade-in-arms of **VESPASIAN,** praetor before 66, consul 70, adlected into the patriciate in 74 and posthumously deified by his son in 105/106. From Italica (Spain) of a family which migrated thence from Tuder, in Umbria (see **part IV**, table **XIX**).

*

TABLE XVI: FLAVIAN COUSINS

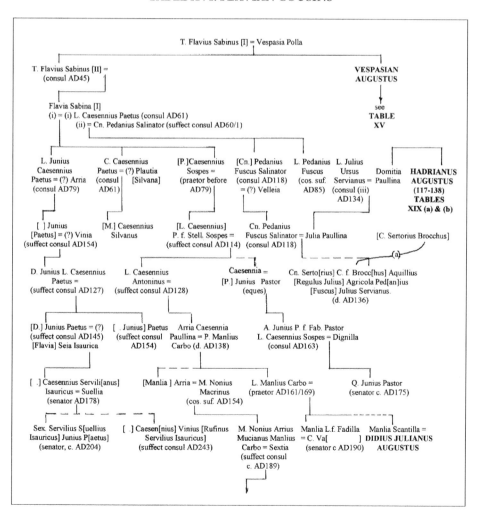

TABLE XVI BRIEF LIVES

Arria Caesennis Paulina

A lady of senatorial rank (*clarissima femina*) in the mid-2nd century; probably Caesennius Antoninus's daughter.

L. Caesennius Antoninus

Suffect consul in 128, his *cognomen* derived from the grandfather of **ANTONINUS PIUS** through his mother, that emperor's great aunt.

C. Caesennius Paetus

Serving as a military tribune (junior army officer) in 63, a senator by 75. From the name of his presumed son, he probably married an otherwise unrecorded Plautia Silvana. It is by no means impossible that she could have been a former sister-in-law of Empress Domitia Longina (below), for her first husband was a member of that family (see **Table VII(b) Brief Lives**).

L. [Junius] Caesennius Paetus

Born c. AD18, consul in 61 and first husband of **Flavia Sabina [I]**. The Paetus element of his name may have derived from his mother, perhaps called [Junia Paetina] and postulated as a possible daughter of L. Seius Tubero (suffect consul in AD18), a cousin and adoptive half brother of Tiberius' murderous favourite Sejanus. Tubero was by descent an Aelius Tubero, a branch of the ancient and distinguished Republican family the Aelii Paeti. The 'Junia' would appear to reflect the name of Tubero's second wife, sister of Q. Junius Blaesus, suffect consul in AD10. One inscription gives this man the additional name of Junius. The family was raised to the patriciate by **VESPASIANUS** in 74. [ILS 995; PIR² C173; Jones (1992) 57 & n. 122; Syme (1986) 200-312]

[.] Caesennius Servili[anus] Isauricus

A young patrician elected a *Salius Palatinus* in 178 and of praetorian rank by 204. A Caesennius Isauricus is recorded as the husband of a Suellia, surely the same man.

[M.] Caesennius Silvanus

A junior army officer, recorded in 101/103, his *cognomen* suggesting the family of his mother.

[L. Caesennius] P. f. Stell. Sospes

Suffect consul 114. The name of his grandson suggests that he left only a daughter, probably married to the equestrian [P.] Junius Pastor [ILS 1017; Jones (1992) 49 n 123 & 114 n 46]

[P.] Caesennius [L.] f. Stell. Sospes

Curule aedile and praetor before 79. His wife was probably Arria, sister of C. Arrius Antoninus grandfather of Emperor **ANTONINUS PIUS** - see **part III(b)**, as suggested by Syme [Syme (1984) 1057].

[L(?)] Caesen[nius] Vinius [Rufinus Servilius Isauricus]

Suffect consul in 243 and either the brother or son of Sex. Servilius S[uellius] etc.

DIDIUS JULIANUS AUGUSTUS

See below. **Section IV(a) & Table XXVII.**

L. Julius Ursus Servianus

He was born AD 47 as Ser. Julius Servianus of an emergent family, but had been adopted by the kinsman of **VESPASIAN** (see above **Table XIV Brief Lives**), L. Julius Ursus, consul (iii) in 100 (nephew of Julia who marr. M. Arrecinus Clemens) and was himself suffect consul in 90, again in 102 and for a prestigious third time in 134. He governed

Germania Inferior, Pannonia and then took a leading role in **TRAJAN'S** Dacian wars. He was also a correspondent, friend and patron of Pliny the Younger. His natural son [L. Julius] Africanus seems to have died young, hence his adoption of his grandson by his daughter Julia. He was forced to commit suicide in 137 aged ninety [FS. 2090; PIR² I122, 630. 631; Syme (1958) II. 598-604].

L. Junius Caesennius Paetus

Born 43, consul in 79 with his cousin, **TITUS**. His wife was probably Arria, sister of C. Arrius Antoninus, grandfather of **ANTONINUS PIUS** see **Part III(b)**. [PIR² C174; Jones (1992) 48 & n123]

D. Junius L. Caesennius Paetus

Suffect consul in 127. He was more likely the son rather than the grandson of the consul of 79, who appears to have held the magistracy at the earliest possible age, whilst his own term of office may have been delayed. [PIR² J790]

[?L. Junius] Paetus

Only known as a suffect consul in 154; the likelihood that he was a brother of the suffect consul of 145 is strong. He (or, less probably on grounds of chronology, his brother) seems to have married [Flavia] Seia Isaurica**,** the last element of whose name strongly suggests a descent from Caesar's upper class adherent, P. Servilius Isauricus, as the *nomen* Servilius also emerges in their posterity.

[D.] Junius Paetus

Ex-praetor and legate of Lycia-Pamphilia in 142-143, probably to be identified with the D. Junius [ ] who held a suffect consulship in 145 [PIR² J792].

A. Junius P. f. Fab. Pastor L. Caesennius Sospes

Consul 163, married to Dignilla. Syme considers him to be a "genuine" adoption by Junius Pastor rather than an actual son. If so, there is no need to postulate a marriage between his adoptive father and a member of this family, although it is not unlikely. If this is accepted, it is likely he was a son of Caesennius Antoninus (qv). [ILS 1095; PIR² J796 ; Jones (1992) 49; Syme (1984) 1056]

[P.] Junius Pastor

an equestrian, perhaps married to a daughter of Sospes (suffect consaul in 114) and certainly the adoptive father of the preceding.

Q. Junius Pastor

A senator of the mid to late 2nd century, known only from a tile-stamp. [PIR² I795].

Manlia L. f. Fadilla

Her *cognomen* would suggest a descent from the Antonine dynasty. Her husband was an *augur* and *rex sacrorum* in the late 2nd century, suggesting a person of some eminence in familial terms, at least, see also below, **Part IV(a)** [FS 2340 & 3354; PIR² M164].

L. Manlius Carbo

Praetor during the joint reigns of **LUCIUS VERUS** and **MARCUS AURELIUS.**

P. Manlius Carbo

Senator, probably from an emergent family, died AD138.

M. Nonius Arrius Mucianus Manlius Carbo

Also the holder of important religious offices. His wife's full name was Sextia Asinia Polla, a member of an old senatorial family from the republic and also a descendant of Asinius Pollio, a friend of **CAESAR** who was consul in 40BC [PIR² M115; FS 2520]

M. Nonius Arrius Paulins

Urban praetor in AD224. There were clearly descendants of this family (thus carrying the Flavian bloodline) but there is insufficient evidence to reconstruct a secure descent.

M. Nonius M. f. Fab. Macrinus

Consul in AD154; the marriage is adduced from the name of his son [PIR² M140; FS 2532]

[Cn.] Pedanius Fuscus Salinator

See above, **Table XV Brief Lives.**

Cn. Pedanius Fuscus Salinator

Consul in 118, he married in 106 **Julia Paullina** daughter of Ser. Julius Servianus (who after adoption became L. Julius Ursus Servianus), consul (iii) 134, by Domitia Paullina, sister of Emperor **HADRIANUS** [CIL. III. 13826; FS.2639; Syme (1958) 247].

L. Pedanius Fuscus

Suffect consul in 85; the likely ancestor of [.] Pedanius [   ], sufferct consul in 167.

Cn. Pedanius Salinator

Second husband of **Flavia Sabina [I]** and suffect consul in 60 or 61, a member of a family from Narbo in Gaul.

[C. Sertorius Brocchus]

His existence can be confidently adduced from his adoptive son's name, but he is nowhere independently attested.

Cn. Serto[rius] C. f. Brocc[hus] Aquillius [Regulus Julius] Agricola Ped[an]ius [Fuscus] Julius Servianus

Young senator, probably an ex-quaestor, despite his patrician status (by creation in 74). His names suggest that he was the adopted son of C. Sertorius Brocchus, suffect consul in 137. He was said by Dio to have been 18 when, as heir presumptive and Servianus's grandson, **HADRIAN** considered both such a threat to his plans for the succession that he was forced to commit suicide along with his grandfather in AD137. Syme, preferring to identify the hapless prince with another young senator with many names, several in common with this man, considers 25 to have been the victim's age - see below, **Part III(b)**. Interestingly, these names may include those pertaining to Sallustius Lucullus – suspected of being the same as the suffect consul Sallustius Blaesus – **DOMITIAN'S** victim whose death may be linked to the rebellion of *SATURNINUS*, in which respect both men include the names of Lucullus' illustrious predecessor as governor of Britain, Cn. Julius Agricola. Syme (*loc.cit.*) pooh-poohs any relationship, but there is, nevertheless, likely to have been some common kinship link with Tacitus' father-in-law; Settipani coinsiders them probably cousins once removed and direct descendants. [Dio, LXIX, 17, 1; Settipani (2000) 307; Syme (1984) 1166-1169].

Sex. Servilius S[uellius Isauricus] Junius P[aetus]

A senator living in the early 3rd century, with a memorial at Brixia

*

Imperial claimant under Domitian

SATURNINUS I
1ˢᵗ – 25ᵗʰ Jan. AD89

The imperial claimant **L. Antonius** *SATURNINUS* was probably of a knightly family of Roman origin long settled in Tarraco (Tarragona) in the province of Further Spain. Little is known of his antecedents, nor the name of his wife. His family were presumably permitted to live by Domitian, or else we would have heard of their elimination. Syme suggests his father is probably to be identified with a cultic high priest and retired magistrate of Tarraco (Tarragona, Spain), L. Antonius L. f. Gal. Saturninus. He was adlected into the senate by Vespasian, either in AD69 or in his censorship in 74, with praetorian rank, going on immediately to govern Macedonia 74/76 followed by Judaea in 78/81, after which he was suffect consul in about 82.

He was appointed governor of Upper Germany either in 87 or 88 and was acclaimed at Moguntiacum (now Mainz), Lower Germany, on 1ˢᵗ January 89 at the head of a military revolt (see above) being defeated in battle 25 days later by A. Bucius Lappius Maximus, the neighbouring governor; the mopping up was done by the future emperor **TRAJAN**. *SATURNINUS* was either killed in the fighting or took his own life subsequently. He seems to have issued no coins.

The reasons behind the revolt are extremely difficult to fathom, nor does there seem to be much evidence that *SATURNINUS* was actually acclaimed Emperor; he had few qualifications for the purple – no kinsman of a triumvir he. He was a man with no following in the circles likely to matter, had he been successful, although it is worth noting that Sir Ronald Syme did consider him a proper imperial claimant.[145] It is impossible to even hazard a guess as to whether he jumped, was pushed or the victim of circumstance.

One source claims that he was a 'disgusting and scandalous fellow' and not to be trusted with money, lending some credence by his seizure of his legions' pay chest, although that might be taken as a sensible precaution by anyone attempting a military *coup* in the provinces.

An Antonia L. f. Saturnina recorded in the late-2ⁿᵈ century AD married to the senator C. Arrius Pacatus might conceivably have been a descendant of the family, but both names were hardly rare..

Further reading::
Syme, R., *Antonius Saturninus* in *Roman Papers* III (Oxford, 1984) 1070-84

145. Syme (1958) I. xi

The murder of **DOMITIAN** might well have ushered in a period of chaos, as happened following the death of **NERO**, especially as in the outcome an elderly contemporary (and relative) of **OTHO** ended up holding supreme power: **NERVA**. Yet he was no **GALBA**; he did not make the same mistakes, there was a reasonable amount of support for him, both the emperor and the senate knowing that the arrangement was only a holding operation. The unspoken successor was M. Ulpius Traianus, known to history as **TRAJAN**, then serving in Germany. That he managed to return and take over on **NERVA'S** death was a measure of his *potentia*. There was no one of the right background, ability and charisma to challenge him. Thereafter, succession was by adoption until the death of **MARCUS AURELIUS**, but the succession of his son **COMMODUS** in 180 marked another dark period, with a ruler who was insecure and only interested in the trappings of power. That he was such a flawed person led to his eventual murder, but the person selected for the **NERVA** role, **PERTINAX**, failed to hold the ring and paid the price. The succession thereafter of **IULIANUS I,** the man who was prepared to give the Praetorians the most generous donative, was the signal for a repeat of the catastrophic events of AD69: a series of civil conflicts with three imperial claimants, **NIGER, ALBINUS** and **SEVERUS I,** all of whom were at one time or other recognised by the senate. But this time, the conflict was more drawn out, more bloody, with consequences that would cast a long shadow over the following hundred years.

⋆

III(a) NERVA TO HADRIAN

The Imperial Succession
Nerva
Traianus
Hadrianus

NERVA
(18 September 96- 27 Jaurary 98)

Background

The Emperor **NERVA** is, in historical terms, something of an appendage to the Flavian era, being an acknowledged stop-gap emperor to ensure that the political vacuum created by the assassination of **DOMITIAN** was filled, if only temporarily, whilst the true inheritor of the Flavian position, **TRAJAN** marshalled his forces and in due time effected a smooth take-over, ushering in the next era, wherein once again, there was something of a partner-ship – however illusory in reality – between *princeps* and senate, between the ruler and the ruling class. **NERVA**, therefore, acted as a bridge between the two.[146]

The choice by those privy to the assassination of **DOMITIANUS** – not their first, however - of the elderly senator **NERVA** is not necessarily an obvious one to modern eyes, except insofar as the old fellow (he was actually only 61, albeit in indifferent health) was childless and his family virtually extinct, thus being unlikely to produce any claimant to his position on his death, although Dio says he had relatives then living, perhaps, as Syme surmises, Se[rgius] Octavius Laenas suffect consul in the significant year of 97[147]. There indeed *were* other cousins then alive, one degree further removed, [see below, **Table XVII**]. The new ruler himself appears to have been without enemies, which helped. The choice, moreover, was the senate's, which was good news as far as the ruling *elite* were concerned, but less so for the army and general populace, who had less gripe with **DOMITIAN** – after all, neither element was likely to lose any sleep over the regular executions by the emperor of kinsmen or senators.

Genealogically, **NERVA** belonged to the previous era, in that he was the brother-in-law of the Emperor **OTHO** and that his maternal aunt was the daughter of **TIBERIUS'** grand-daughter Julia by Rubellius Blandus (see **Table VI**). As, however, he adopted **TRAJAN** in his own lifetime, rather than by testamentary bequest, he stands at the beginning of this fresh sequence of rulers, which show a regular uninterrupted succession down to 192. Furthermore, with hindsight, it can be seen as an era of continued and fruitful co-operation between emperor and senate in governing the empire; it is also generally considered to have been the high point of the empire. By the end of the following dynasty, the Severans, the cracks were beginning to show.

M. Cocceius [M.f. M. n. Pap.] Nerva was born a patrician on 8th November AD35 at Narnia (Narni), north of Rome. He entered the senate with election as quaestor about 62 and was rewarded by **NERO**, extraordinarily, with triumphal ornaments and two statues - for his aid in exposing the plot of C. Piso in 65,[148] suggesting that he was inclined to cultivate the ruler of the day, to put it mildly. He served as praetor in 66 but missed a consulship in his earliest qualifiying year (*suo anno*) in 68; perhaps **NERO** had gone cold on him by then. Nevertheless, he was accorded the honour of being **VESPASIAN'S** colleague as consul in AD71, going on to a second consulship in 90; he was also a respected figure with **DOMITIAN**, as with **NERO**, which might suggest that the story that he had once seduced the young **DOMITIAN** was spurious. There is no record of him as provincial administrator, general or even, like his father and grandfather, jurist, only a reputation as a minor poet and intellectual. He was also cautious, self-effacing when things got tricky, and safe.

---

146. Syme (1958) 1-12; Syme AA, 220, 223.
147. Dio LXXVIII. 4. 1; Syme (1958) II. 627, see above **Table VIII**
148. Tacitus, *Annals* 15, 71

Reign

On being acclaimed emperor, as soon as **DOMITIAN'S** demise was announced, 18th September AD96, he was hailed as *imperator* and took the style **Imperator Nerva Caesar Augustus** to which a relieved senate added, within a few days, *Pater Patriae*, Pontifex Maximus the proconsular *imperium* and the tribunician power, renewable, as was usual, annually. He served his third consulship in 97 and another in 98, receiving a second imperial acclamation in October 97 when the name **Germanicus** was added to his imperial style, no doubt reflecting an unrecorded success of Roman arms in that theatre of empire, the upper province of which was then, significantly, under the governorship of M. Ulpius Traianus.

NERVA'S reign was touch-and-go when it came to stability during its first year, however, culminating in a mutiny of the praetorian guard in the early autumn of 97, a happenstance which usually betokened the immediate demise of the incumbent emperor. The prefect, Casperius Aelianus, at the head of a strong detachment of his men, locked Nerva in the palace and demanded the release into their custody of two of the six men responsible for the murder of **DOMITIANUS**, the only emperor to have upped their pay since **CLAUDIUS**. **NERVA** stood up to them, but the men were seized and summarily killed anyway. That the elderly emperor was in none-too-good health and was childless probably saved his life. Nonetheless, his authority was entirely vitiated, a fact he appreciated well enough to realize that the designation of an heir likely to be effective and popular with the army was required with immediate effect.

He chose the man who had been involved in the suppression of the insurrection of L. Antonius *SATURNINUS* in 89, M. Ulpius Traianus, a highly competent general and almost certainly a nephew by marriage of the popular and well-remembered emperor **TITUS,** a factor which without doubt contributed much to the selection of a man of a family relatively new to senatorial rank. At the end of October 97, then, **NERVA** formally adopted **TRAJAN** who thenceforth became styled **Caesar Nervae f. [M. n. Pap.] Nerva Traianus Germanicus.**

The question remains as to what extent **TRAJAN** manipulated the adoption himself, how much the running was made by his allies in Rome and how much was due to unbiased good advice offered to **NERVA**. As **TRAJAN** was away in Upper Germany throughout the reign, it is difficult to see his involvement being particularly direct. The opportunity to mount a subtle *coup* following the praetorian mutiny was something Trajan could hardly control either immediately or directly at a distance, unless the mutiny was itself a carefully planned element of the plot. Either way, **TRAJAN'S** involvement, either directly or otherwise, seems today to lie well beyond proof.

In the event, **NERVA** died three months or so after **TRAJAN'S** adoption, on 27th January 98, and the latter succeeded with what appears to have been a complete lack of problems, despite not being in the capital

Further reading:
Syme, Sir R., *Tacitus* 2 vols. (Oxford 1958) I. 1-29; II. 627-628.

*

TABLE XVII: THE FAMILY OF NERVA

The Cocceii were from Narnia (Narni) in Umbria and seem not to have been of senatorial rank until the triumvirate, although the brothers Lucius (a legate in 41 and 37BC) and M. Cocceius Nerva, consul in 36BC, were probably adlected into the senate by Julius Caesar.[149] That the suffect consul of 39, C. Cocceius Balbus – also doubtless a Caesarian appointment - was a relative is not in much doubt[150] but whether he was a half-brother, cousin or more distant kinsman is unclear. What is clear, however, is that Balbus was made a patrician by Octavian in 30 and that enhancement in status appears to have also applied to the Cocceii Nervae suggesting that they were possibly three brothers. Unfortunately, the surviving *fasti* (consular lists) fail to endow either M. Nerva or C. Balbus - both supporters of **Mark Antony** - with a filiation, depriving us of the chance of drawing any further conclusions about their ancestry. Both M. Nerva and Balbus were hailed as *imperator* following feats of military prowess. The suggestion that another (unrecorded) sister of NERVA married Vespasian's elder brother Sabinus (qv) is speculative.[151]

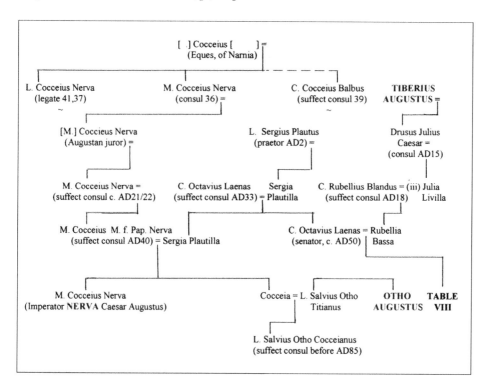

149. Wiseman (1971) Nos. 125 & n 126; PIR² C1223-1224 ; Syme (1986) 48 & n. 106, 221 f., cf. Syme (1939) 200, 267

150. Wiseman, *op. cit.* no. 124; PIR² C1214

151. Settipani (2000) 273. Settipani also suggests (*loc.cit*) that Sergia Plautilla actually must have married the father of the consul of 33

TABLE XVII BRIEF LIVES

Cocceia

Married L. Salvius Otho Titianus, elder brother of the emperor **OTHO**, suffect consul in 52 and again by his brother's appointment, in 69 [Jones (1992) 185].

C. Cocceius Balbus

Possibly proconsul of Macedonia and hailed as *imperator* at Athens in the triumvrial period [Syme AA 48 & n, 273]

L. Cocceius Nerva

'Earned credit on diplomatic missions' in the triumviral period [Syme AA 48 & n].

M. Cocceius Nerva

Senator from at least 48BC, so quaestor in or by 41, praetor before 38, originally a supporter of Antonius, hailed as *imperator* and was consul for 36, a *quindecimvir sacri faciundis* in 31 and a new patrician in 27 [Syme AA 48, 223]

[M.] Cocceius Nerva

Probably died too young to have held recorded office, unless with PIR one can believe that the suffect consul of AD21/22 was his son, rather than grandson, which the chronology rather suits; Sir Ronald Syme preferred the version given here. Nerva may have been, like his own son, a jurist. His birth would have fallen about the time of his father's consulship [PIR² C1225; Syme (1958) II. 627].

M. Cocceius Nerva

He was also a jurist and suffect consul in AD21 or 22 he would have been born c.15/12BC. He was made *curator aquarum* (overseer of the aqueducts of the city) in AD24 and retired to Capri with Tiberius, dying there in AD33 [PIR2, C.1225; Tacitus, *Ann.* vi. 26.1 & 58, 1]

M. Cocceius M. f. Pap. Nerva

Suffect consul in AD40; probably born about AD6 or 7, who married c. AD33/34, Sergia Plautilla the younger, daughter of C. Octavius Laenas , see **Table VIII** [Barrett (1989) 30, 196]

M. Cocceius NERVA

See above

Drusus Julius Caesar
See **Table VIII Brief Lives**

C. Octavius Laenas

Suffect consul in AD33. The family originated in Paelignum and Peter Wiseman comments that M. Octavius Marsus, a legate in the upheavals following Caesar's death, was 'doubtless an ancestor' of this man, in which case he was of at least the third generation of his family in the senate, if the first to hold a consulship. The change of *cognomen* could conceivably have arisen through a marriage of Marsus with a lady of the ancient noble Popillii Laenates, the last member of which distinguished family seems to have been relegated from the senate in 73. Laenas was elevated to the patriciate in AD48 by **CLAUDIUS**. For their descendants, see **Table VIII Brief Lives** [Wiseman (1971) No. 292 & p. 247; ILS952].

C. Rubellius Blandus
See **Table VIII Brief Lives**

L. Salvius Otho Cocceianus
See **Table XIII Brief Lives**

L. Salvius Otho Titianus
See **Table XIII Brief Lives**

Sergia Plautilla

She is here proposed as wife of Laenas, the suffect consul of 33 rather than the mother of C. Rubellius Blandus, as the Sergian names in that family seem to come later than allowed by PIR [cf. PIR² R109; Syme RP IV 177f.]

L. Sergius Regis f. Arn. Plautus

By adoption a patrician Sergius Plautus, a family long in eclipse, having last enjoyed high office in 200BC when C. Sergius Plautus was praetor. The filiation suggests that he was born a Marcius Rex, a family of ancient plebeian nobility, perhaps the Marcius Rex who was a ward of Ap. Claudius Pulcher, consul in 54BC. His adoptive father may have been the [?L. Sergius] Plautus recorded by Wiseman as an emergent triumviral senator in 35, likely to be a Sergius. His patrician status is confirmed by the fact that he was a *salius* by 12BC; he was also a stoic author. He may have had a son, too, M. Sergius [?Plautus], suffect consul early to mid-1st century AD. [ILS 281, 2922; PIR² S378; Badian (1963) 1401; Wiseman (1971) No. 54]

*

TRAIANUS
(Known to history as Trajan)
27 Jan. 98 - 9 August 117

TRAJAN was effectively emperor from the moment of his adoption in the autumn of AD97, although it was not until three months after the death of **NERVA** that he deigned to visit the imperial capital. He was always the soldiers' emperor – himself a soldier but of a sufficiently senatorial background to understand the subtleties of government by carrying the senate with him. He was one of the greatest and most memorable of emperors and under him the empire reached perhaps its greatest extent. Apart from his undoubted military genius, he was also endowed with good sense, tact and restraint – perhaps better expressed as patience. This enabled the reign to be remembered as a golden age of expansion – and hence prosperity – and civil tranquillity. It was only in old age, towards the end of his reign that the Emperor's relations with the senate began a sharp deterioration. Even so, compared with the well-remembered excesses of **DOMITIAN'S** last years, it was only a relatively minor perturbation.

It took **TRAJAN** well over a year to return to Rome, setting a precedent for a trend much more noticeable in the later third and fourth centuries, when it became clear that Rome's importance to the Empire's governance was of considerably less importance than might be supposed. The intervening period had been profitably spent, however, with the new Emperor embarking upon a tour of inspection of his northern and eastern frontiers. He must have felt extremely confident in the loyalty of the senate and praetorians, far away in Rome, for as events in later eras demonstrated, the first few months were the most dangerous ones in a new reign, before a new regime could be properly established.

His conduct thereafter was largely exemplary, although we are somewhat influenced by the younger Pliny's laudatory *Panegyricus* delivered before the senate when its author assumed the suffect consulship in September 100. Trajan himself was a master of tact in his dealings with the governing classes, despite exercising power more directly than most of his predecessors. His success was down to his compliance with convention, his appreciation of the delicate balancing act between princeps and senate and his emollience.

Background

M. Ulpius M. f. TRAIANUS was born on 18th September AD53 and served as military tribune under his father in Syria 73/76, reached the quaestorship in c. 78 and, as a patrician, missing out on the next stage in the promotional ladder, the aedileship or tribunate of the people, proceeding to a praetorship in c. 84, following which he was a legionary legate in Hispania Tarraconsensis, from whence he became involved in the measures taken by **DOMITIAN** to put down the rebellion of *SATURNINUS*. He was suffect consul in 91, after which we hear almost nothing of him (bar his being sent to govern Germany), until his accession. He either went into hibernation in Domtian's last, dangerous, period or else served loyally and with the necessary low profile. He was adopted by the Emperor **NERVA** in October 97, becoming **Caesar Nervae f. Nerva Traianus Germanicus,** but remained in Upper Germany, where he was provincial governor, as appointed on the Emperor's accession.

Reign

The new emperor acceded to the principate, was elected pontifex maximus, acclaimed *imperator* for the first time and was granted the tribunician and annually renewable pro-consular powers on 28th January 98. On the deification of his predecessor a short time later, he took the style of **Imperator Caesar Divi Nervae f. Nerva Traianus Germanicus Augustus**[152] rapidly adding *Pater Patriae* after and *Optimus*[153] before 'Augustus'. He was then already ordinary consul (for the second time) at this juncture, holding the consular *fasces* again in AD100, 101, 103 and 112.

He was, indeed, a soldier to his core, and a capable one at that. Even when not campaigning he appears to have been more at home in pastimes like hunting, in which he could express his *machismo*. He was nevertheless, almost certainly bisexual and, if Dio is to be believed, with paedophilic predilections when it came to relations with his own sex. Despite that he appears to have been basically a kind man, a more than competent administrator, a fine general and superb tactician.

His next opportunity to flex his military muscles was in 101 when he set out to subdue the Dacians, a Balkan people who occasionally caused serious trouble on the Danubian frontier of the Empire, who managed to hold off a major offensive by **DOMITIAN** in the later 80s. A partial annexation in that year was followed by another campaign in 105 and within 18 months Dacia had become a new Roman province, the struggles between the parties being immortalised in bas relief on **TRAJAN'S** column in Rome. He added the name

---

152. ILS 282
153. ILS 305

Dacicus in 102 and **Parthicus** in 114[154] receiving further imperial acclamations in 101-102 (three altogether), 105, 106, and a further seven in 113-117, mainly on the field of battle.

A final campaign was against Parthia, after the latter had interfered in the client kingdom of Armenia in 114. **TRAJAN** annexed Armenia and then Mesopotamia ending with the capture of the Parthian capital at Ctesiphon a year later. Thereafter the eastern campaign began to go awry with a Mesopotamian revolt and Trajan's failure to capture the crucial stronghold of Hatra. Perhaps a whiff of defeat reached north Africa, for almost simultaneously, the Jewish populations in Cyrenaica, then Cyprus and Egypt rose up in a particularly bloody revolt. There was also news of further trouble in Germany, causing Trajan to break off his campaign in the east and hurry back to Rome, despite a circulatory complaint which he is said, in some sources, to have attributed to poison. He was forced by a worsening of his condition to pause at Selinus in Cilicia (subsequently Traianopolis), apparently wrote out a declaration of adoption of his successor and expired on 9th August 117.

During his reign, he arranged for the deification of his father M. Ulpius Traianus and the elevation to the rank of Augusta of both his sister and wife in AD105. The latter, whom he married in c. 75, was a lady from Nemausus (Nîmes) in Gaul, called Pompeia L. f Plotina, about whose family nothing is known, although Syme suggests that she might have been a kinswoman of her husband.[155] As the son of an established senator, the young Trajan's wife might perhaps have been connected to another rising senatorial family; perhaps she was the daughter of the Gallic senator L. Pompeius Vopiscus, whom the Emperor **OTHO** had nominated to a suffect consulship in AD69, although there is not enough information about him to be at all sure, except that he came from the province in which Nemausus lay. Either way, there were no children, and the succession passed, probably through the astute machinations of the Empress, who died in AD123, to his closest male relative, P. Aelius **HADRIANUS**, already serving alongside her husband, virtually as his deputy in Mesopotamia. Theoretically, **TRAJAN** lived long enough to adopt him, but the genuine-ness of this adoption is widely doubted by modern scholarship.[156] Anthony Birley says, 'the adoption was, at best, by a dying man and stage managed by the Empress.'[157] He died aged 64 after a reign of 19 and a half years and was later deified by the senate.

*

Further reading:

Birley, A. R., *Hadrian, The Restless Emperor* (London 1997)

Grant, M., *The Antonines: The Roman Empire in Transition* (London 1994)

Syme, Sir R., *Tacitus* 2 Vols., (Oxford 1958)

---

154. ILS 286, 304

155. Syme (1958) II. 604, 794 & see below.

156. Syme, *op. cit.* I. 239-241

157. Birley (1997) 77

TABLE XVIII: THE FAMILY OF TRAJAN

The Ulpii claimed to have originated at Tuder, in Umbria, but migrated in the republic to Italica, in Baetica, one of the Spanish provinces, where Scipio Africanus had settled the veterans of his army during the second Punic war.[158] Unfortunately, we do not know the full name of Trajan's great grandfather (his *praenomen* might possibly have been Lucius), but he had at least two attested offspring, a son and a daughter.

A note of caution needs to be entered here, however. Trajan's family develops a whole new existence in the *Scriptores Historiae Augustae* (HA, see introduction) which attributes the Emperor **AURELIAN** with a senatorial mentor and adoptive father called Ulpius Crinitus, 'who used to assert that he was of the House of **TRAJAN**'.[159] This man was the supposed son of Ulpius Crinitus, suffect consul in AD238. Crinitus himself we are told was suffect consul before 255, (ii) in 257 and (iii) in 270, according to the HA, which further avers that he had 'had consular descendants.' The HA also claims Crinitus as the parent of Ulpia Severina, wife of L. Domitius Aurelianus, allegedly suffect consul in 258, and Augustus as the Emperor **AURELIAN** (270-274).[160] Roman law would, in reality exclude the possibility of an adopted son marrying his (natural) sister. The entire matter is unconfirmed anywhere else and may confidently taken to be fiction.

---

158. see *ibid.* I. 30; II. 604, 605, 785-786
159. HA *V. Aureliani* 10.3f., 11. 1-8, 12.1, cf. Syme (1971) 4, 100-101.
160. PIR² D135

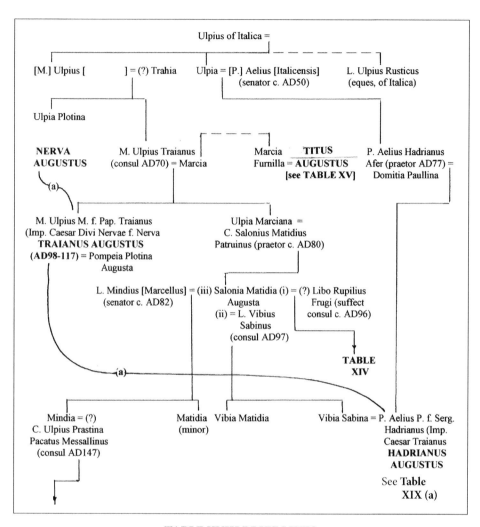

TABLE XVIII BRIEF LIVES

P. Aelius Hadrianus Afer

Born AD46, praetor in 85, d. 86; married Domitia Paullina [Syme (1958) II 603]

P. Aelius P. f. Serg. Hadrianus

See below **HADRIANUS AUGUSTUS**

Domitia Paulina

See below, **Table XVIII(a) Brief Lives**

Marcia

See **Table XV Brief Lives**

Salonia Matidia.

She is thought to have married (i) (as his second wife) Libo Rupilius Frugi, suffect consul before 97, by whom she is thought to have had no issue. She then appears to have married L. Vibius Sabinus. Matidia's third husband appears to have been Mindius. Later she was made Augusta and deified when she died December 119 [ILS327; PIR² M367; Birley (1997) 64, 107 Syme (1958) II. 795 nn].

Mindia

Possibly the mother of C. Ulpius Prastina Pacatus Messallinus (qv)

L. Mindius [?Marcellus]

Another Flavian senator, in connection with whom note the Claudian ex-praetors L. Mindius Pollio and L. Mindius Bolanus, one of whom might be the parent or close relation.

Pompeia L. f. Plotina

Daughter of an L. Pompeius, probably from Nemausus (Nîmes), where a basilica was built in the Empress's honour. A consul's wife, Pompeia Marullina honoured at this period at Nimes bore names suggesting kinship with both Plotina and **HADRIANUS** (qv) [Syme (1958) II. 603]

Libo Rupilius Frugi,

Suffect consul before AD97. His daughter Rupilia Faustina was the grandmother of **MARCUS AURELIUS** (qv) See **Tables XIV & XXIV Brief Lives** and below.

C. Salonius Matidius Patruinus

He was praetor prior to AD83 and probably died around AD106. He came from Vicetia (Vicenza) [Birley (1997) 308, 310; Syme (1958) 603 & n.]

Ulpia Marciana

Declared Augusta in AD105, died 106 and deified [Birley (1997) 64, 107, 308, 310].

Ulpia M. f. Plotina

Living, possibly, unmarried in AD70 [as surmised by Syme (1958) II. 604].

L. Ulpius L. f. Rusticus,

Eques of Italica; it is possible that he or another close kinsman may have had senatorial

descendants which might account for the origin of the Ulpii Prastinae.

C. Ulp[ius P]rastina Pacatus Messallinus

Consul in 147 whose wife may have been **TRAJAN'S** great neice Mindia [Marcella] the elder. His *agnomen* suggests a descent – however obscure – from the Valerii Messallae, but through his mother, whose name is recorded as Petillia Messalina (his father's name is lost from the inscription). She may have been a daughter of Q. Petillius Rufus, son of Q, Petillius Cerealis, consul in 70, (on whom see above, **Table XVI Brief Lives**) perhaps through a daughter of the brother of **NERO's** last wife, Statilia Messallina, L. Valerius Catullus Messallinus, consul (ii) in 85. He was the father of C. Ulpius C. f. Prastina [Messallinus] suffect consul in the mid to late 2nd century, perhaps to be identified with the Ulpius recorded as a priest of the prestigious cult of the deified Augustus in 184 and thus probably a patrician. The Ulpii Prastinae do seem to have continued, witness M. Ulpius [Pr]asti[na], praetor in 186 and an Arval Brother, Prastina, an Arval Brother in the period 222/235 and Prast[ina] Messallinus, suffect consul c. 244/247 (the last two possibly one and the same man); no certain blood relations of **TRAJAN** however. [AE (1959) 347; ILS5594]

[M.] Ulpius [   ]

An *eques* of Italica whose wife, if the *cognomina* of his son and grandson are to be taken as their first use within the family, may have been called Trahia Note, in this connection, that Italica certainly had a leading citizen at a somewhat earlier period called M. Trahius C. f.; this man's *praenomen* probably Marcus if one can accept Syme's speculation regarding his possible daughter Ulpia M.f. Plotina. Settipani suggests that P. Coelius Apollinaris (cos. suff. 111) was, through his mother, a grandson of an unnattested brother of M. Traianus, consul 70 [Rufino (1990) 309; Settipani (2000) 225; Syme (1958) II. 794 & n. 9].

M. Ulpius Traianus

Entered the senate under **NERO**, and had served as *praetor* by 66 after which he served as legate of Legion X *Fretensis* under **VESPASIAN** in Palestine and was suffect consul probably in 70 on Vespasian's recommendation. He was later adlected, again at the recommendation of **VESPASIAN** in his capacity as censor, to the Patriciate. He governed Syria in 73/4-76/77 and went on to be proconsul of Asia 79/80 [ILS 8797] earning triumphal ornaments on his return for averting a war with Parthia, probably through a pre-emptive strike. The date of his death is unknown but probably fell in 105, in which year he was deified by the senate at the prompting of his son. He married, probably in 51/2, Marcia almost certainly the sister of Marcia Furnilla, wife of his colleague-in-arms the future emperor **TITUS,** see also above, **part II(b).** They were possibly daughters of the Claudian senator Q. Marcius Barea Sura. [ILS 8797; *JRS* XLIII (1953) 154 & (1958) I. 30-33, 66n, 233; Jones (1992) 11, 59 & n; Syme (1958) II. 595, 603, 604 & n. 8].

Vibia Matidia

A lady of senatorial rank living in the early to mid 2nd century, possibly unmarried [PIR^2 M368]

Vibia Sabina

Married in 100 P. Aelius P f. Hadrianus, later the emperor **HADRIAN** and who was later adopted as his son by Vibia's great-unlce **TRAJAN** [Birley (1997) 16, 42]

L. Vibius C. f. Sabinus

Consul AD97. A possible sister is the Vibia who was third wife of P. Julius Ti. f. Lupus (suffect consul AD97/98), whose first wife was Arria Fadilla, mother of **ANTONINUS PIUS.** Because her son by Lupus enjoyed the names C. Julius Lupus T. Vibius Varus Laevillus, it might be reasonable to assume that this man's father was a C. Vibius Varus, and thus a member of a family going back to an Augustan senator, L. Vibius L.f. Rom. Varus Appianus, patron of Heira Caesarea. His agnomen suggests an adoption, in which case the Romilia may not have been his originasl voting tribe, in which case the family may have been senarorial for two or three generations longer. Indeed, his nomenclature might suggest very grand connections in that era. [IGR IV. 1353; Birley (1997) 16. 45. 308, 310]]

*

HADRIANUS
(known to history as Hadrian)
7th August 117 – 10th July 138

Background

Whilst **TRAJAN** may be portrayed as a paragon of manly virtue and an ideal soldier-emperor, **HADRIAN** was a much more complex man. Although he enjoyed a successful military career fostered by his predecessor and cousin once removed, he also had a strong predilection for intellectual pursuits and the liberal arts, despite a keen appreciation of the chase. He also fancied himself as a Helenophile – his contemporaries referred to him as

Graecinus (Greekling) – and also dabbled actively in poetry and architecture, even to the extent of persecuting Apollodorus of Damascus, **TRAJAN'S** architect, when he presumed a little professional criticism of the Emperor's lavish new self-designed villa complex at Tivoli.

Furthermore, there was once again a slightly suspect succession. Whereas **TRAJAN** might be legitimately suspected of having engineered - albeit at a distance - his adoption by **NERVA,** the matter was at least done and dusted in public. When **TRAJAN** died, however, there was some considerable doubt as to whether **HADRIAN** had been adopted by his predecessor at all, so rapid was his demise, this despite **HADRIAN'S** relative proximity, as his kinsman's right-hand-man in his capacity of governor of Syria at the time. Not only that, but when he finally returned to Rome – having divested the empire of **TRAJAN'S** two new Eastern provinces on equivocal terms and diverted to the Balkans to quell the revolt there *en route* – four senior senators of consular rank had been put to death, allegedly for conspiracy.

The lengths to which **HADRIAN** went to deny involvement in these unfortunate events suggested his guilt with greater clarity to many, which burdened his reputation ever after. He laid the blame squarely on the senate, for that body's acquiescence was a *sine qua non* of such proceedings, which were invariably brought under one of a group of existing laws. Under such as **TIBERIUS, NERO** or **DOMITIANUS,** however, the senators were cowed by threats – subtly expressed or otherwise – into voting for a motion to have someone exiled or killed. However, in this case, the Emperor was absent and unable to threaten, unless he covertly contacted one of his allies in the senate.

Unfortunately, too few details have come down to us for a half-reliable judgement to be made. Worse, the real motive for the removal of this powerful and well-connected group, remains obscure. Were it obvious, we could draw reliable conclusions. The most obvious explanation is that they opposed **HADRIAN'S** accession, either because they thought him not the right man for the job or saw though the fraudulent adoption masterminded by the Empress and took a high minded (and risky) stance in favour of senatorial election of a successor.

That aside, **HADRIAN** subsequently undertook to execute no senator without fair hearing and, like his predecessor, ruled effectively whilst paying elaborate lip-service to the constitutional niceties preserved by **AUGUSTUS** to maintain the illusion that the Republic still endured.

P. Aelius P. f. Serg. Hadrianus[161] was born Rome 24th January AD76; on his father's death he became the ward of **TRAJAN** and of the *eques* Acilius Attianus. In 94 he became *decemvir stlitibus iudicandis* (one of a board of ten to adjudicate on minor lawsuits) along with two prestigious quasi-religious appointments, as *praefectus feriarum Latinarum* (a temporary stand-in for a magistrate – usually a consul – obliged to leave the City to attend an age old festival of the Latin League) and *sevir turmae equitum* - leader of a squadron of horsemen at the annual ride-past of the members of the Equestrian Order. He was Military tribune of II Legion *Adiutrix* in 95-96 and then with V Legion *Macedonicus* 96-97; he entered the senate in AD101 as quaestor and a member of **TRAJAN'S** personal staff and, probably

---

161. ILS 308

the year before, a priest of the most junior of the four great priestly colleges, a *Septemvir (VIIvir) Epulonum.* He is also recorded as having been a priest of the cult of the Deified Augustus – one of the *Sodales Augusti* – but it is not clear when. As these were generally patricians it may have occurred later and certainly implies that **TRAJAN** raised his family to patrician rank; this must have been after his tribunate, however, which he held in 102 after he had returned from the Emperor's Dacian HQ. He is also recorded as *curator actae senati* – keeper of the senate's records. He held the praetorship in 105 - exceptionally about 18 months earlier than the rules allowed, probably through his newly bestowed patrician standing - after which he governed Pannonia Inferior (107) and held a suffect consulship in 108. He was appointed governor of the pivotal province (in the context of **TRAJAN'S** Parthian war) of Syria, and was still *en post* when the emperor died. His adoption papers arrived on 9th August 117 and he heard of **TRAJAN'S** death two days later (and four days after the actual event), when he was duly acclaimed.

Reign

On accession **HADRIAN** was styled **Imperator Caesar Traianus Hadrianus Augustus**,[162] hailed as imperator for the first time, appointed *pontifex maximus* and voted the tribunician and proconsular power by the senate, renewed on 10th December each following year. Unusually, he was only acclaimed *imperator* once more in his life, in 135, after the suppression of the Jewish revolt. He took a second consulship – an ordinary one this time – in 118 and a third (and final one) in 119, the sparing use of such titles being a potent sign of his confidence in the security of his position, despite the rocky beginning. He took the additional title of *pater patriae* as late as 128. He married Vibia Sabina in 100[163], but she died in 136, and they had no issue.

Although by no means disposed towards warfare, despite twenty years close association with **TRAJAN, HADRIAN** managed to visit every province in the Empire to acquaint himself with them, their officials, people and idiosyncrasies. These visits included the one to Britain, which led to the construction of the famous wall which bears his name. This created much good will and also made it easier for him to formulate policy and appoint administrators appropriately. Indeed, the day-to-day administration of the Empire, which was radically improved by **TRAJAN**, was further streamlined and perfected by his successor.

Having spent fifteen years avoiding armed conflict, **HADRIAN** ended up by provoking it, when he decided to re-found Jerusalem, sacked and largely abandoned by **TITUS** in 70, as Aelia Capitolina. This involved building what was effectively a new city, but included the highly provocative erection of a new temple, to Jupiter Capitolinus, on the site of the temple built by Herod. This triggered a catastrophic revolt under Simon bar Kochbar which lasted more than three years, required the military presence of the emperor himself and cost over half a million lives.

---

162. ILS 310
163. ILS 323

His reign ended as it had begun, with the un-necessary deaths of two distinguished senators, Hadrian's brother-in-law L. Julius Ursus Servianus and the latter's grandson, a promising young senator rejoicing in no less than ten names but known as Cn. Pedanius Fuscus [see **Table XVI**]. The latter, who, after his grandfather, was **HADRIAN'S** nearest heir male and thus had been raised in the expectation of succeeding to the principate, was at the centre of what appears to have been a none-too-well organised plot in AD137 which was quickly identified and dealt with. Both were forced to commit suicide.

Once again, the problem revolved around the succession, for **HADRIAN** was the fifth emperor in a row to die without a male heir or childless. In 136, with what appeared to be a serious debilitating illness developing, he adopted L. Ceionius Commodus, consul in that year. His nomination caused surprise, for his qualifications were and are difficult to discern. No relative, he was the stepson of C. Avidius Nigrinus, the consul of AD110[164] who was one of the four senior men executed whilst **HADRIAN** was *en route* for Rome at his accession; was he trying to make amends? Commodus was also married to Nigrinus's daughter. No other explanation, except for the supposition – supported only by artfully assembled circumstantial evidence – that Commodus was Hadrian's illegitimate son, seems to be convincing.[165]

The problem was that Ceionius turned out to be more desparately ill than his adoptive father and, having been assumed cured from a disease which involved coughing up blood, was given tribunician and proconsular power and sent to the Danubian provinces with special powers. He returned at the end of 137 but died suddenly on New Year's Eve. By this time, **HADRIAN'S** wife was dying (she was dead by March) and he himself was very ill, too. He thus hastily adopted, on 25th February 138, a new heir: the fifty one year old senator T. Aurelius Fulvus Boionius Antoninus, whose consulship had been back in AD120, but whose military experience was also extremely limited. This was the future Emperor **ANTONINUS PIUS**.

To complicate matters, but to keep the succession settled for the following generation too, he obliged Antoninus, who had no son, to adopt in his turn the five year old son of Ceionius Commodus, along with the intended husband of Antoninus' daughter, a man called M. Annius Verus - later respectively the emperors **LUCIUS VERUS** and **MARCUS AURELIUS**. Some Roman and most modern commentators have assumed with hindsight that **MARCUS** was the intended long-term heir, but T. D. Barnes has argued convincingly that it was, in fact, **LUCIUS**.[166]

This settled the succession, as it turned out, until **MARCUS'S** death in 180: a remarkable happenstance, given the volatility imparted by the prospect of total power and the general dislike in which **HADRIAN** was held in his declining years, fuelled by his initial choice of heir and by the fate of Servianus and Fuscus – and others hinted at but not named by one

---

164. PIR² A1407
165. Syme (1958) 601 & n. 4
166. Barnes (1967) 65-79

source.[167] He died after a painful illness – allegedly wished upon him by the dying curse of Servianus – at Baiae (Baia) on 10th July. He was subsequently deified by a (reluctant) vote of the senate on a motion of his successor.

Further reading:
Birley, A. R. *Hadrian the Restless Emperor* London 1997
Opper, T., *Hadrian: Empire and Conflict* London 2008

*

TABLE XIX(a): THE FAMILY OF HADRIAN

Hadrian claimed in his autobiography, which is preserved fragmentarily both in the *Historia Augusta* account of his reign and that of the much more reliable Cassius Dio, that his family hailed originally from Hadria (Atri, Abruzzo), hence his *cognomen*.[168] Nevertheless, the family had been settled at Italica in Spain since an ancestor was settled there with many other ex-soldiers, by P Cornelius Scipio in 206. That, by the end of the republic, the Aelii of Italica had become one of the leading families of the province of Baetica, is emphasised by the fact that the first named member of the family, Marullinus, was a senator under the triumvirate, if not earlier; the census to qualify was, after all a million sesterces, although in the triumviral interlude, odd promotions were not uncommon, as with Marullinus' fellow Baetican, L. Cornelius Balbus, adlected to the senate after Caesar's death and the first ever non-Italian consul, holding office in 40BC. Birley suggests that Marullinus was a prominent supporter of Caesar in a largely Pompeian province, and was made a senator as a reward in 48.[169] There is a certain reliance - in the two pedigrees required to lay **HADRIAN'S** connections out with any clarity - on the HA life of Hadrian. Despite the strictures made about this work in the introduction, it is generally accepted that the material relating to the Antonine emperors is largely reasonably sound.

---

167. Birley (1997) 289-295, 300.
168. SHA I, 1
169. Birley (1997) 13

TABLE XIX (a): HADRIAN

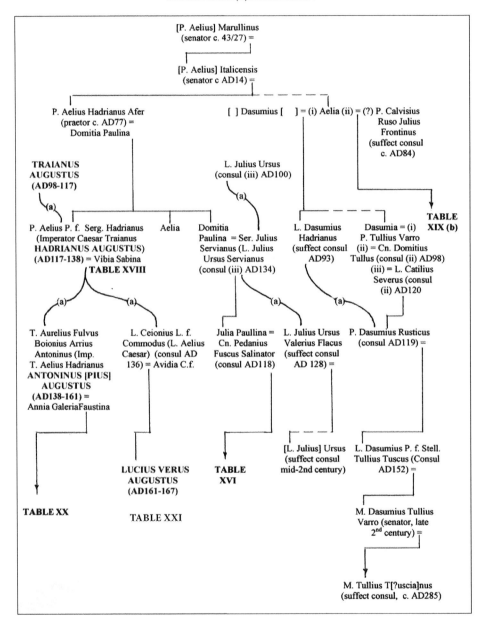

TABLE XIX(a) BRIEF LIVES

Aelia

Settipani suggests a second sister of Aelia, as putative mother of M. Annius Verus (consul (iii) 126) (see **Table XIV**) [Settipani (2000) 289, 294]

L. Aelius Caesar

See L. Ceionius Commodus, below.

P. Aelius P. f. Serg. Hadrianus
See above **HADRIANUS AUGUSTUS**

P. Aelius Hadrianus Afer
Hadian's father was born c. AD45/46 praetor c. 84 died 85, certainly by January 86 [Birley (1997) 16]

[P. Aelius] Italicensis,
Probably a senator, b. c. AD20, perhaps married to a Dasumia, or to an Ulpia Plotina, thus kin to **TRAJAN** [Settipani (2000) 285; Syme (1958) II 603]

[P?] Aelius Marullinus
Senator c. 49/31BC [HA *Hadr.* I.2; cf. Syme (1958) II. 603; PIR² M219; Wiseman (1971) 209, No. 5]

P. Calvisus Ruso Julius Frontinus,
See **Table XIX (b) Brief Lives.**

L. Catilius Cn. f. Claud. Severus Julianus Claudius Reginus
His family came from Apamea in Bithynia, and his father, Cn. Catilius Longus (adlected into the senate with the rank of praetor by **VESPASIAN** in AD74) had married the daughter of T. Claudius Faustus Reginus, an equestrian from the Chersonese, hence his full name. He commanded a legion in Germany, was suffect consul 110, governor of Cappadocia and Armenia, proconsul of Africa, consul for the second time in 120 and PUR in 138. When the father of **MARCUS AURELIUS** died, Severus played a leading part in the youth's upbringing along with his grandfather, Verus. He was disgraced in 136 by the Emperor, probably for presuming too much about himself for the succession and later removed from office as PUR. He did however, have descendants who appear to have flourished down to the mid-third century. [FS 1120; ILS 1014, 5082, PIR² C558]

L. Ceionius Commodus
Patrician by creation, on adoption by **HADRIAN** he was styled L. Aelius Caesar. He was born c.103, praetor in 133/4, consul in 136, he was sent to Pannonia by the Emperor, returning, ill, in December 137 and dying of tuberculosis on New Years Eve [Birley (1997) 198, 290-295].

L. Dasumius Hadrianus
Suffect consul, 93, his family were also from Italica, like Hadrian's, but via Corduba (Cordoba) in Spain. The family were said to descend from Dassumus, king of the Italian tribe of the Messapii whose grandson, Dasumius son of Sallentinus Malemmius, was granted Roman Citizenship. His father may have borne the *cognomen* Pollio, if his sister's names are any guide (see below **Table XIX(b) Brief Lives**) [SHA *Marcus* I, 6; Syme (1958) 603-4]

P. Dasumius L. f. Stell. Rusticus
Consul in 119, and son of Dasumia by her first husband. His original name prior to his testamentary adoption by Dasumius Hadrianus would have been L. Tullius Varro [Syme (12958) II. 600; Birl;ey (1997) 102. 124]

L. Dasumius P. f. L. n. Stell. Tullius Tuscus
Born c. 110, quaestor c. 140, suffect consul in 152, governor in the 160s of Upper Germany and Pannonia, also an augur and *sodalis Antoninianus* [FS 1434; PIR² D16]

M. Dasumius Tullius Varro
Senator living in the late 2nd century [PIR² D17]

Domitia Paullina
The elder, she of a family from Gades (Cadiz), in Baetica, Spain.

Domitia Paullina

The younger, married L. Julius Ursus (Ser. Julius Servianus, see **Table XVI Brief Lives**) c. AD89, probably as his second wife, but died c. AD132 without having been created Augusta [Birley (1997) 19, 20 & n. 20; ILS 325; Syme (1958) II. 600]

Cn. Domitius Tullus
See below **Table XIX(b) Brief Lives**

[L. Julius] Ursus

Suffect consul c. AD155/162. Only his *cognomen* survives, and it is only a presumption he was the son of the suffect consul for AD128. However, there are no other obvious candidates.

L. Julius Ursus Servianus
See above **Table XVI Brief Lives**

L. Julius Ursus Valerius Flaccus

The adopted son of Servianus, but the actual son of C. Valerius Flaccus Setinus Balbus, a senatorial poet and ex-praetor who flourished in the Flavian period, who must have been a member of the ancient patrician Valerii Flacci, probably through the adoption by C. Valerius Flaccus Tanur[ianus], probably a praetor from c. AD14/37, of one Setinus Balbus, allegedly a Neapolitan schoolmaster. Even this last must have been, from his name, an adopted son, but the last Valerii Flacci of the late Republic and early Augustan age are presumed to have been the offspring of C. Valerius Flaccus who died at Pharsalus in 48BC. The first consul of the name was master of horse in 321BC, a descendant of Rome's first consul. The adoption may have been part of Servianus's arrangements prior to his suicide, bearing in mind that he was aware that his grandson and heir was also to die. It was either testamentary (in which case Lucius would have retained his patrician status, or formal; we lack the data to be sure. He was suffect consul in AD128 [CIL.VI.2123-4; FS. 3398; ILS 6123, 6388, 6392PIR² part IV p. 298.]

LUCIUS VERUS AUGUSTUS
See below.

Cn. Pedanius Fuscus Salinator,
See above **Table XVI Brief Lives**

M. Tullius T[uscia]nus

Suffect consul c. AD285. And proconsul of Africa c. 300-301, thus being in the van of senators at last permitted to re-enter the administration of the Empire. His descent from the Dasumii and Tullii Varrones is by no means certain but, from his names, quite plausible [PLRE I T....nus]

P. Tullius Varro
See **Table XIX (b) Brief Lives.**

*

TABLE XIX (b): HADRIAN'S COUSINS

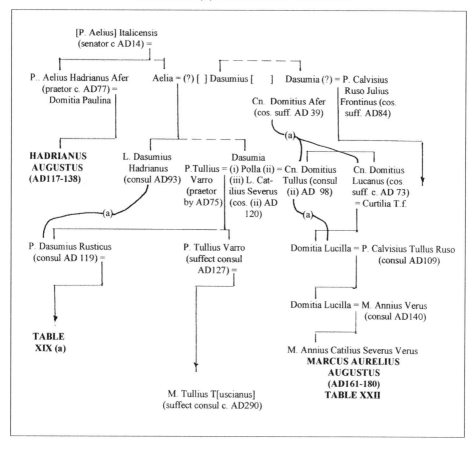

TABLE XIX (b) BRIEF LIVES

M. Annius Verus

See **Table XIV Brief Lives**

P. Calvisus Ruso Julius Frontinus,

Suffect consul c. AD84 and rex sacrorum in the 90s, having been made a patrician c. 84, he was the natural son of Julius Frontinus an *eques* from Narbo (Narbonne). He became the adoptive son of P. Calvisius Ruso, suffect consul in 79, himself son of P. Calvisius Sabinus Pomponius Secundus, suffect consul in AD44, who in his turn was probably born a Pomponius Secundus (a son of the much married Vistilia and adopted into the family of C. Calvisius Sabinus consul in

AD26). He thus had good Julio-Claudian connections including a double one to the family of **AUGUSTUS'S** first heir Claudius Marcellus. His second wife (not shown) was Eggia, widow of L. Maecius Postumus (suffect consul 98) who testamentarily adopted one of Eggia's brothers [FS1065; Syme, PR IV, 1f. & (1970) 31-32; for an alternative view: Settipani (2000) 289].

P. Calvisius Tullus Ruso

Consul AD109, he added *cognomen* Tullus 107 under the terms of his father-in-law's will [FS 1068].

Dasumia Polla

Her *cognomen* may reflect that of her father (whose name is not known); her relationships were sorted out by Sir Ronald Syme [Syme RP V 523].

Domitia P. f. Luculla

The elder [ILS 8652]

Domitia P. f. Luculla

The younger [ILS 8653A]

Cn. Domitius Sex. f. Vel. Lucanus

Consul c. AD73; probably the elder of the two brothers who were sons of Sex. Curvius Tullus, an emergent senator. Both were subsequently testsmentarily adopted (as witnessed by their retention of Survius' *praenomen* and voting tribe) by the greatest orator of his day and suffect consul of AD39, Cn. Domitius Afer, who came from Nemausus (Nîmes) and was quite possibly a kinsman of Corbulo and died in AD59 (see **Table VII (a) Brief Lives**). Lucanus married the daughter of T. Curtilius Mancia (suffect consul AD55) and died c. AD93 [PIR² C1623, D126, 152, 167].

Cn. Domitius Sex. f. Vel. Tullus

Suffect consul in c AD77 and again in AD98, died 107, leaving his son-in-law his heir.

P. Tullius Varro

He was a probably a descendant of the Caesarian senator, C. Tullius Rufus (from Tarquinii) whose son was in the Stellatina voting tribe as was this man's son (qv). The *cognomen* may have come from a marriage in the Augustuan period with a lady of the family of the Terentii Varrones. His sister was a Vestal Virgin in AD83 and he entered the senate as a quaestor in the fateful year AD69 and was an ex-praetor in AD75 [CIL.VI.27739; ILS 1002, 5771; PIR² T392].

P. Tullius Varronis f. Stell. Varro

Suffect consul in 127; a descendant may have been M. Tullius T[?uscia]nus, suffect consul late 3rd century, and proconsul of Africa c. AD300/301 [ILS 1002, 1047; PIR² 394; PLRE I. 872].

*

The Imperial Succession
Antoninus
Marcus Aurelius
Commdus

Imperial Claimants
Titianus
Avidius Cassius

ANTONINUS I
(known to history as Antoninus Pius)
10th July 138 – 7th March 161

Backgorund

With **ANTONINUS PIUS** we enter the zenith of the Roman Empire at a time when it was ruled by a man generally regarded, through the following millennium at least, as a paragon amongst Roman emperors, as the ideal of the enlightened ruler. Indeed, even in his own time he was sufficiently admired, alongside his successor **MARCUS AURELIUS**, to be held up as a yardstick against which all who followed him were compared. That they all, to some degree, failed to measure up perhaps shapes our perception of the empire as a whole.

Out of the somewhat chaotic and contradictory measures taken by **HADRIAN** to secure an appropriate successor suitably poised to take over, came **ANTONINUS PIUS**, chosen, it would appear to hold the stage pending the majority of the men who would become **MARCUS AURELIUS** and **LUCIUS VERUS**. Such a role would have adversely affected many men, coloured his decisions or even inspired him to alter **HADRIAN'S** intentions altogether, but **ANTONINUS** was not that man. For almost a quarter of a century he reigned self effacingly, with admirable restraint and enormous dedication. His period wearing the purple was perhaps a favourable one in any case, being relatively free of threats within or from outside the empire and it could be argued that he flourished in the afterglow of the brilliant military achievements of his two eminent predecessors. The internal threats were probably mitigated by his adoption, on **HADRIAN'S** wish, of his two successors, L Ceionius Commodus's son L. Ceionius Commodus, later **LUCIUS VERUS** and **HADRIAN'S** true *protégé* and **TRAJAN'S** great-great-great nephew, M. Annius Verus, the future **MARCUS AURELIUS**, allied to the fact that all **ANTONINUS'S** children had died young except for his daughter Faustina, whom he married off to his successor at the earliest opportunity.

As regards external threats, there was plenty of warfare to be fought. Southern Scotland was won, probably on the back of a revolt suppressed, wars were fought in Mauretania, Germany and Dacia. Not only that but revolts of varying seriousness erupted in Egypt, Greece and even in recently pacified Judaea. Nevertheless, such was Roman prestige after generations of military success, that diplomacy, often as not, was all that was required to achieve a favourable outcome in any crisis.

The only fly in the ointment regarding the succession sprang from the senate's extreme reluctance to vote divine honours for **HADRIAN** which, out of filial piety, **ANTONINUS** was insistent about, if only to maintain the legitimacy of his own position and the respect he felt was essential to the office of *princeps*. A perceptive and moving speech from the emperor, a fine orator in any case, swayed the chamber and the vote was passed.

T. Aurelius Fulvus Boionius Arrius **Antoninus** was born at Lanuvium on 19th September, AD86, the year of his grandfather's second consulship, and inherited an Etruscan estate, at Lorium, where he spent as much time as he could throughout his life.[170] There is no evidence of service in the army as a junior officer, and he entered the senate with a quaestorship, as a patrician jumped the aedileship or tribunate, and after a praetorship was made ordinary consul in 120 confirming that, even then, Hadrian must have held him in high esteem. He governed Asia in 135-136, but by that time – before 120 to fit her elder daughter's wedding date[171] - he had married **Annia Galeria Faustina** ('the elder'), daughter of M. Annius Verus (consul (iii) in 126), by Rupilia, daughter of Libo Rupilius Frugi and Vitellius's daughter Galeria Fundana [see above, **part III (c), Table XIV**]. She died in autumn 140 and was deified. He was adopted by Hadrian 25th February 136, and the same day himself adopted his nephew M. Annius Verus and L. Ceionius Commodus. He thus became **Imperator T. Aelius Caesar Antoninus**[172] and succeeded **HADRIAN** 10th July 138, when he added **Augustus** to this style.

Reign

At this juncture, he assumed the role of *pontifex maximus* was acclaimed *imperator* for the first time and was granted the tribunician and proconsular power, to be renewed annually thereafter on 10th December. He also added, as we have seen, the name **Pius** and the following year, in which he served his second consulship, added *pater patriae*. A third consulate followed in 140 and a fourth and final one in 145, eighteen months after his second imperial acclamation, in recognition of the end of the successful campaign in Britain. In 150-151 he briefly added the name **Hadrianus** after 'Aelius' in his style, moving 'Caesar' to precede his *praenomen* as illustrated on various coin issues of ther period.

ANTONINUS attempted to rule by consent, reformed further aspects of Roman law and even in the reign's two treason trials, made sure that the proceedings were unbiased and beyond criticism; nor on either occasion, did he encourage a witch hunt for co-conspirators, real or imagined. Nevertheless, the reasons for his addition, within months of his accession, of the soubriquet 'Pius' to his official nomenclature remain unclear; the HA fields five suggestions in short order! Probably it was through his insistence on having his predecessor deified.

---

170. PIR² A1513
171. Birley (1987) 243
172. ILS 331

The Aurelii Fulvi came, on the authority of the HA, supported by other evidence, from Nemausus (Nîmes), in the province of Gallia Narbonensis. They will have been descended from Roman or enfranchised Latin traders – *negotiatores* – who first settled there, keen for a quick profit in the years following. Conceivably, the 'Pius' name was already in the family, for there was an ex-quaestor called Aurelius Pius recorded near the start of **TIBERIUS'** reign who could easily have been an ancestor.[173] There is no reason why the Tiberian ex-quaestor could not have been from Nemausus too; he would have been a near contemporary of D. Valerius Asiaticus (suffect consul in AD35 and ordinary consul in 46), generally regarded as having been the first well-attested Gallic consul, although senators from the province of Narbonensis first appeared under Caesar.[174] Against that, and unlike the unprovable case of **HADRIAN**, there is no reference to so long a pedigree in the *Historia Augusta*, although that somewhat unreliable work says nothing to exclude it.[175] All one can say is that it appears – bearing in mind its meaning: 'dutiful' or 'respectful' – highly appropriate bearing in mind the Emperor's qualities.

The empire was ruled in quite the opposite way to the peripatetic and restless fashion adopted by **HADRIAN,** for **ANTONINUS** remained in or near Rome throughout his long reign. He was, in short, the ultimate delegator of authority, a sign of supreme confidence in any ruler in any era.

ANTONINUS PIUS died at Lorium 7th March AD161, untroubled by any successor problem. His predecessor's scheme of things moved well-oiled into its second phase and he was succeeded by his two adopted sons, having formally delegated power to **MARCUS** during his brief last illness, thus ensuring the primacy of the more competent of the pair without wounding Lucius' *amour propre*.

*

Further reading:

Birley, A. R., *Marcus Aurelius; a Biography,* London, 1987

Birley A. R. (ed.) *Lives of ther Later Caesars:* London, 1976

Grant, M. *The Antonines: The Roman Empire in Transition* London, 1994

*

---

173. Tacitus, *Annals.* i. 75

174. Wiseman (1971) 22-23, nos. 104 (T. Carisius), 107 (Cassius Barba) and 131 (Cominius Longinus).

175. SHA *v. Antonini,* i. 1

TABLE XX: THE FAMILY OF ANTONINUS PIUS

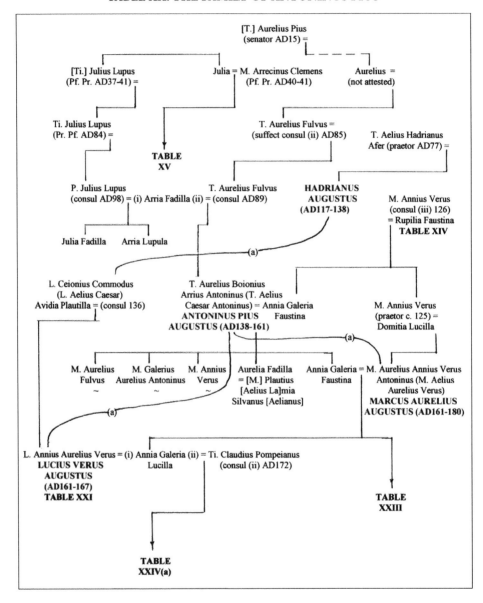

TABLE XX BRIEF LIVES

M. Aelius Aurelius Verus

See **MARCUS AURELIUS** below & **Table XXII**

T. Aelius Caesar Antoninus

See above, **ANTONINUS PIUS AUGUSTUS**

L. Annius Aurelius Verus

Formerly L. Ceionius Commodus (the younger), see below **LUCIUS VERUS AUGUSTUS**

M. Annius Verus

See **Tables XIV, XIX (b) Brief Lives**

M. Annius Verus

Son of **ANTONINUS PIUS**, died young before AD138.[Birley (1987) 243-244]

M. Arrecinus Clemens

Praetorian prefect. AD40-41, see **Table XIV Brief Lives**

Arria Fadilla

Daughter of C. Arrius Antoninus, a new man as far as is known, from Nemausus (Nîmes) in Gaul, suffect consul 69 and (ii) 97, by his second wife, Fadia. Arrius' first wife was Boionia Procilla, hence **ANTONINUS PIUS** having that element in his (original) nomenclature. Her descendants by Arrius Antoninus appear to be traceable down to the end of the third century [Birley (1987) 242].

Arria Lupula

Possibly married to one Caepionianus, a senator living in the 130s, as suggested by a brick stamp [JRS LXI (1991) 141].

M. Aurelius Annius Verus Antoninus

See **MARCUS AURELIUS AUGUSTUS** below & **Tables XXII & XXIII**

M. Aurelius Fulvus Antoninus

Died young before 138 [Birley 9987) 235, 242]

T. Aurelius Boionius Arrius Antoninus

See **ANTONINUS I PIUS AUGUSTUS**

T. Aurelius Fulvus

Suffect consul in 70 and (ii) 85 and PUR. The family were also from Nemausus in Gaul [Birley (1987) 235, 242; Syme (1958) II 605].

T. Aurelius T. f. Fulvus

Consul AD89 [Birley (1987) 235, 242; Syme (1958) 605]

[T.] Aurelius Pius

A junior senator AD15. Possibly the founder of the senatorial branch of the family of **ANTONINUS PIUS** [Birley (1987) 55]

L. Ceionius Commodus

Consul 136, adopted by **ANTONINUS PIUS** that year as L. Aelius Caesar, see above and **Table XIX (a) Brief Lives**.

L. Ceionius Commodus

See above L. Annnius Aurelius Verus.

Ti. Claudius Pompeianus

Consul (ii) AD172. For his descendants, see **Table XXII Brief Lives.**

M. Galerius Aurelius Antoninus

Died young before AD138 [Birley (1987) 235, 242f.]

HADRIANUS AUGUSTUS

See above

Julia Fadilla

She possibly married a Cn. Julius [ ] and had issue: Cn. Julius Cn. f. Verus praetor c.143 suffect consul 150/4 and (ii) 180 a supposition based mainly on the consul's *cognomen* [PIR^2 667]

Julia Lupula

She possibly married Claudius Orestes, suffect consul in the mid-second century, grand father of a Julia Fadilla if she really existed out- outside the pages of the HA, which informs us that she married a man called Toxotius, which latter bore a name which fails to appear on record (outside the HA) before the 4th century [PIR^2 I618, 667, 668, 676].

P. Julius Lupus

Consul AD98 [PIR^2 389]

[Ti.] Julius Lupus

It has been suggested by Jones that the Julii Lupi and Julii Ursi were close kin, connected by marriage with the Arrecini and hence closely linked to the Flavian dynasty (see also **Table XIV Brief Lives**). Lupus was praetorian prefect AD37-41 and his sons are thought to have been Ti. Julius Lupus (qv) and L. Julius Ursus (consul AD84), ancestor of Servianus [PIR² 388; Jones 1992) 40-42].

Ti. Julius Lupus

Prefect of Egypt AD84 [PIR² 390]

[M.] Plautius L. [f. Ani. Aelius La]mia Silvanus [Aelianus]

Son of L. Fundanius L. f. Lamia Aelianus and from his voting tribe, likely to be a male line descendant of the Plautii Aeliani and thus a patrician by creation. He was a *salius* before 138 and held a suffect consulship in 145. One of his aunts, [Plautia] Fundania married the uncle of **MARCUS AURELIUS**, M. Annius Libo (consul 128), see **Table XIV Brief Lives**. His princess wife died shortly after their marriage in 135, perhaps in childbirth; there were no known descendants [FS2723]

Imperial claimant under Antoninus I Pius

TITIANUS
AD145

The *Historia Augusta* (HA) tells us that a senator was tried before the senate for 'attempted usurpation' in 145.[176] He was subsequently condemned and suffered a *damnatio memoriae* - his name being erased from monuments and the consular lists (*fasti*). From other sources we know he had an accomplice and that both committed suicide of their own accord.

The senators in question were Atilius *TITIANUS* and Priscianus, identifiable as **T. Atilius Rufus Titianus**, consul in 127 and **M. Cornelius Priscianus**, also an ex-consul. The latter was condemned for 'hostile action disturbing the peace' – from which it seems reasonable to conclude that Atilius was proably the imperial claimant and 'beneficiary'.[177] The acclamation seems to have occurred in Hispania Tarraconensis and the motivation is completely lost to us. The likelihood is that they were brothers-in-law, quite probably united by *TITIANUS* being married to a sister of Priscianus, their father probably being L. Cornelius Priscus, suffect consul in 104. Atilius's second *cognomen* may also link him, albeit not particularly closely but perhaps enough to enhance his motivation, to the imperial family of the time. The name suggests that his mother may have been a Titia as was the mother of L. Epidius Titius Aquilinus, brother–in–law of L. Ceionius Commodus, Hadrian's short-lived first choice as heir. The identity of the two postulated Titias is more problematic, however.

---

176. HA *V. Pii* VII, 3-6.

177. PIR² A130; Syme (1958) II. 596 n. & (1971) 38

> Atilius was presumably the grandson of T. Atilius Rufus, a suffect consul of c. AD75, who died in 84, a man probably of North Italian origin. We are told that **ANTONINUS** spared and supported his son – whose full name has not survived – and Corneliuis Priscianus, a senator of praetorian rank by 166 may well be a son of Atilius's co-conspirator, similarly spared. The entire episode is shrouded in mystery and, like *SATURNINUS,* the acclamation was not accompanied by an issue of coinage.
>
> *

VERUS I
(known to history as Lucius Verus)
7 March 161 – c. 1 Feb. 168

Background

VERUS, as the son of **HADRIAN'S** original choice as successor, was given an assured place in his stead, allowing for his adoptive father **ANTONINUS PIUS** to reign in the interim. Yet, as he and **MARCUS AURELIUS** grew closer and formed a genuine partnership, **LUCIUS** ended up very much the junior element and this may have formed his character, for he turned out a lightweight, a bit of a voluptuary and not noted for any particularly sterling qualities.

Yet, as events following his accession in 161 were to show, neither did he betray any particularly evil tendencies either and any inclination he might have had to plough a furrow that might have cut across any of **MARCUS'** was probably headed off by the consideration – and on occasion, patience - which the latter constantly showed him.

The Ceionii, from which family Lucius Verus descended, were of Etruscan stock perhaps from the colony of Bononia (Bologna). The only Ceionius – an exceedingly rare name - to come to the notice of history (rather than on a purely provincial inscription) prior to the man with whom **VERUS'** pedigree begins is the otherwise anonymous Ceionius who was a *praefectus fabrum* (prefect of the camp, an equestrian WO2) in AD9[178]; his relationship to those that follow is thus possible but un-proven.

The name reappeared in the early 4th century (setting aside the entirely fictional father of Clodius **ALBINUS** alleged by the HA[179]) in [M.] Nummius Ceionius Albinus (consul (ii) 263), who was probably descended from M. Ceionius Silvanus through the unrecorded marriage of a female descendant.[180] From them stemmed an extensive dynasty of Ceionii traceable into the 5th century.[181]

---

178. Stech (1912) no. 241.
179. Ceionius Postumus, HA *V. Albini* 4, 5-6, also suggesting descent from the patrician Postumii Albini of the Republic.
180. PLRE I Albinus 9 & stemma 21 (p. 1141)
181. PLRE I stemma 13 (p. 1138),

L. Ceionius Commodus was born 15[182] December AD130 at Rome.[182] His name changed on his father's adoption 136, probably to **L. Aelius Commodus** but he was again adopted 25th February 138 by **ANTONINUS PIUS**, simultaneously with the latter's adoption by **HADRIAN**, becoming **L. Annius Aurelius Commodus**.[183] The family had been raised to patrician rank by creation in AD74. He was given the *toga virilis* in 146, was *quaestor* 152 and consul in 154.

Reign

On accession, **MARCUS** caused the senate to vote **LUCIUS** the titles Caesar and Augustus, and having himself taken the additional surname of Antoninus in considerartion for his adoptive father, Pius, bestowed that of Verus upon **LUCIUS** and the pair were jointly acclaimed *imperator*. He was thenceforward given the formal style **Imperator Caesar L. Aurelius Verus Augustus** and served his second consulship in 161.[184] He was voted the tribunician power and proconsular *imperium* 7th March 161 (renewable every year thereafter on 10th December, as was customary). The office of pontifex maximus was, however, deemed to be indivisible, and was granted to **MARCUS AURELIUS** rather than **VERUS** – whether by agreement or by *fiat* is impossible to say. In 163 he married **MARCUS AURELIUS'** daughter Annia Aurelia Galeria Lucilla (see below **table XXI**), later granted the style of Augusta, and they had a daughter and son, both of whom died young and the names of neither of whom are known.[185] Lucilla was later exiled to Capri by **COMMODUS** for allegedly inspiring a conspiracy against him and was later killed.

VERUS was nominated to lead an expedition in 162 to quell a potential conflict with Parthia over a client state in the buffer zone between the two empires: Armenia. The following year Armenia was re-taken and one of the commanders, Avidius Cassius, went on to invade Parthia and capture the capital, Ctesiphon. The key to the entire campaign was that whilst **VERUS** appears to have lolled around in Antioch enjoying himself (and a rather unsuitable courtesan called Panthea), he was being excellently served by his generals, who turned out to be notable able and loyal.

Thus little real credit was accorded to **VERUS** for winning the war, which was celebrated by a triumphal return to Rome in 166, although this view has been recently challenged.[186] Nevertheless, the emperor's right was to celebrate a triumph, even if he had not been leading from the front. One is almost inclined to give **VERUS** the credit for leaving the campaign to the professionals who amply justified his faith in them. The only foolish thing was to be perceived to be living it up in the oriental fleshpots whilst the fighting was actually going on - either that or **VERUS** just might have been lucky. Yet he demonstrated another positive

---

182. PIR[2] C606; JRS LVII (1967) 65-79

183. ILS 357

184. ILS 366

185. Settipani allows the daughter to live until 16 (182) marry the senator [Ti] Claudius Pompeianus Quintianus and have a son., L. Aurelius Commodus Pompeianus (consul 209): *op.cit.* 302.but cf. **Table XXIV (a)**

186. Bishop (2018) *passim.*

side to his character by inviting **MARCUS**, his co-ruler to share his triumph with him – as well he might. He was given the additional styles of **Armeniacus** in 164 and **Parthicus Maximus** in 165, both a year before **MARCUS**[187]; he added **Medicus** in the year of his triumph, which was held on 12th October 166, to celebrate suppression of a revolt amongst the Medes. By 167, too, *Pater Patriae* had been added to his titles and a third consulship followed that year too, with imperial acclamations in 163, 165, 166 & 167.

No sooner had these festivities been concluded than an attack was manifest on the Danube frontier, followed by a full-scale assault on the empire in this quarter. Thus in 168 both emperors set off to deal with the situation, although they were not far along the way when news reached them that the trouble had been dealt with. Nevertheless, they pressed on, oversaw a re-ordering of the defences in the sector and then set off back to Rome, but on the way back, **VERUS** suffered a stroke, was carried on to Altinum (Altino near Venice) and died three days later, very late in January or early February AD168. He was subsequently deified by the senate.

Later, **MARCUS AURELIUS** wrote of him in his *Meditations* that he was a brother

'...whose natural qualities were a standing challenge to my own self- discipline, at the same time as his deferential affection warmed my heart.'

*

---

187. Barnes (1967) 71

TABLE XXI: THE FAMILY OF LUCIUS VERUS

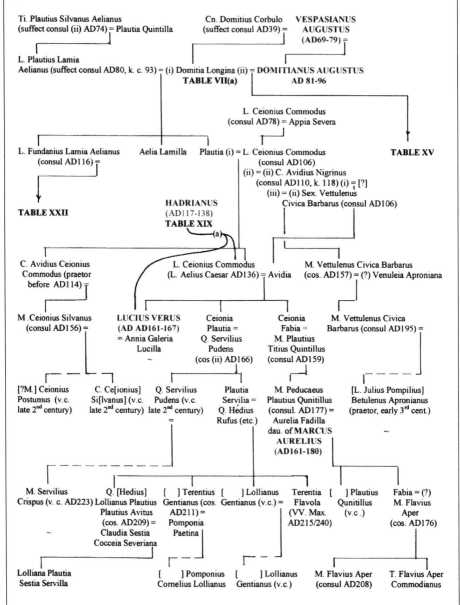

TABLE XXI: BRIEF LIVES

L Aelius Lamia Plautius Aelianus
Consul AD80, killed on the orders of **DOMITIANUS** (to whom he had long before surrendered his wife) AD93. He was a descendant of the Plautii Silvani and the Aelii Lamiae, both minor families under the Republic but of high standing under **AUGUSTUS** and his successors, see **Table X Brief Lives** [PIR² A205].

C. Avidius C[eioni]us [Comm]odu[s]

Praetor before AD114, about which time he died. From his name, he may have been adopted by Avidius Nigrinus. Settipani suggests he was son of Avidius (or his brother T. Avidius Quietus) by Ceioniuis Commodus' aunt [Settipani (2000) 283 n. 3]

C. Avidius Nigrinus

A second generation senator, the nephew of Plutarch's friend, T. Avidius Quietus, (suffect consul in 93), he was consul 110, the whilom heir of emperor **HADRIAN** until involved in a conspiracy and killed 118. He was twice married. By his first wife (whose name is unknown) he had two daughters, one of whom married L. Ceionius Commodus, his step-son by his second wife, Plautia (by whom he had a daughter, Avidia Plautia). He may have adopted his younger stepson, C.Avidius Ceionius Commodus (qv) [ILS 8217; PIR² 1408]

L. Ceionius Commodus

He was consul in 78, having previously been pro-praetor in Palestine and probably before that a commander under Vespasian in the Jewish War, and was subsequently accorded the status of a patrician by **VESPASIAN** suggesting that he stood in high favour with that emperor. He was governor of Syria under **TITUS**. He married Appia Severa, daughter of Sex. Appius Severus, a Narbonensian of equestrian standing. ILS 1003; PIR² C603]

L. Ceionius Commodus

Consul in 106 who married Plautia, daughter of L. Aelius Lamia Plautius Aelianus and Domitia Longina, see above **Table VI Brief Lives**. [PIR² C604]

L. Ceionius Commodus

Was chosen as **HADRIAN'S** successor was adopted by that Emperor and became **T. Aelius**

Caesar, acquiring at the same time the tribunician *potestas* and proconsular *imperium*. He however died shortly afterwards on 31ˢᵗ December 137. See above and **Table XIX(b) Brief Lives.**

L. Ceionius Commodus (L. Aelius Caesar)

See **Table XIX (b) Brief Lives**

[M.] Ceionius Postumus

Grandson of C. Avidius Ceonius Commodus, probably son of M. Ceionius Silvanus. senator c. AD190, but only attested in HA and claimed as the father of **CLODIUS ALBINUS,** universally thought to be unlikely in the extreme (see note above). Nevertheless there is no reason why he should not have a separate existence. His wife is alleged in the HA to bear the distinguished name of Aurelia Messallina, who is less likely to have existed; her name seems to have been taken from the elite of **TIBERIUS'S** reign [HA *V Clodii Albini*, 4, 5]

C. Ce[ionius] Si[lvanus]

Unlike the preceding, apparently an attested son of the consul of 156; he was also a senator, c. AD190 [CIL. VI. 9354]

M. Ceionius Silvanus

Consul AD156 he perhaps married an Annia Albinia; Syme had other ideas about his parentage [PIR² C610; cf Syme (1957) 314]

DOMITIANUS AUGUSTUS

See above and **Table XV**

M. Flavius Aper

Consul 176. on his family and sons, see **Table XXIII(b) Brief Lives**

L. Fundanius Lamia Aelianus

Consul 116, he was born a Plautius Silvanus but whose grandfather was adopted into the Aelii

Lamiae in **CLAUDIUS'S** reign. It is assumed he was adopted by a Fundanius, but the individual has not been positively identified. Alternatively he may have married an heiress of this family, for the ancient plebeian Fundanii had held a solitary consulship in 243, but fade from record in the late Republic. It may be they survived as junior senators, or outside the senate, and their name was revived for the sake of its antiquity. A daughter was probably the wife of M. Annius Libo (consul 128), see below Table XXII [PIR² A204].

[. Hedius] Lollianus Gentianus
A junior senator, he was dead by 209 [ILS 4947; PIR² H34].

[. Hedius] Lollianus Gentianus
A senator c. 235 he is presumed to have been the son of the preceding, but could just as easily be a nephew [PIR² H35].

Q. [Hedius] Lollianus Q. f. Pol. Plautius Avitus
The eldest son, he was consul 209 and married Claudia Sestia Cocceia Severiana. The position of his filiation in his name suggests that he was setting what later became an increasing trend in dispensing with his *nomen* [FS 1869; PIR² H34]

Q. Hedius L. f. Pol. Rufus Lollianus Gentianus
Suffect consul before 201, he was grandson of L. [Hedius Rufus] Lollianus Avitus, suffect consul in 114 and apparently the first senator of his family, which came from Umbria or Liguria. They were made patricians in the early or mid second century [FS 1871; ILS1145, 4927, 5024; PIR² H39, 40 & 42]

[Hedius] Terentius Gentianus
Second son of the preceding, like his brothers he may also have eschewed official use of his *nomen*. He was *Flamen Dialis* (high priest of Jupiter) 204/15 and consul in 211. His wife was

Pomponia Paetina[FS 3228; ILS4927]

[L. Julius Pompilius] Betulenus Apronianus
Son of the consul AD195 he seems to have been adopted by A. Julius Pompilius Piso, who had been suffect consul in 180. The change in the initial letter his *nomen* is a common corruption of B for V. He was praetor c. AD220 [PIR¹ V. 477]

LUCIUS VERUS
See above

M. Peducaeus Plautius Quintillus
Consul AD177, see **Table XXIII Brief Lives**

Ti. Plautius Silvanus Aelianus
Suffect consul (ii) AD74, adopted son of M. Plautius Silvanus (praetor 24) he was suffect consul AD45 and ordinary consul in 74. It is by no means clear who adopted whom, and although his names suggest he was born an Aelius Lamia adopted by Silvanus, some commentators are in favour of the reverse, see also **Table VII(a) Brief Lives**

Pomponius Cornelius Lollianus Hedianus
M. Servilius Crispus
Senator AD223, whose kinship rests solely on the suggestion that his great-grandmother was Laberia Crispina, daughter of the consul for 103, M'. Laberius Crispinus, giving him a descent from the Quinctii Crispini of the republic and making him a cousin of the Empress Crispina.. See **Table V Brief Lives**. [ILS 3621]

Q. Servilius Q. f. Q. n. Hor. Pudens
His family descend from Q. Servilius Pudens a suffect consul of the last years of **NERO** or the few years following. The son married Laberia Crispina, this man's mother. He was suffect consul c. AD150. Being the brother-in-law of **VERUS** probably ensured this otherwise unremarkable ex-consul was rerwarded with the honour of a

second (ordinary) consulship im 166. Little is known of his wife, Ceionia Plautia, see **Table V Brief Lives** [ILS 330, 1084; PIR² C614, S.595 & stemma; Birley (1988) 238 n. 2]

Q. Servilius Pudens

Senator, c.190. He may have had a sister, Servilia Pudentilla, for the names of Q. Rutilius Pudens Crispinus, suffect consul before AD238 strongly suggest his mother was of this family [PIR² S596].

Terentia Flavola

Chief Vestal Virgin AD215/240

M. Vettulenus Sex. f. Quir. Civica Barbarus

Consul AD157; he probably married Venuleia Aproniana

Sex. Vettulenus C. f. Civica Barbarus

The first known senator of this Sabine family was T. Vettulenus P. f. Quir. Quadratus who was tribune of the people or praetor under **AUGUSTUS**. Barbarus's father and uncle were both Flavian suffect consuls and were given patrician rank, although this man;'s father was a victim of **DOMITIANUS** and he himself was consul in AD106. Plautia was his econd wife; his first was called Pompeia M.f., and he had a son by her, too, who left descendants [Syme (1957) 309, 311]

*

MARCUS AURELIUS
7 March 161 – 17 March 180

First successful joint rule

The Emperor **MARCUS AURELIUS** was, as we have seen, groomed for eventual succession from a very tender age, when he was adopted by **ANTONINUS PIUS** as part of **HADRIAN'S** somewhat convoluted heir and a spare succession settlement. That he could go through the entire lengthy reign of his adoptive father without taking violent measures to hasten his accession speaks much for the relationship between the two men and for **MARCUS'S** temperament. Yet all the sources agree that the relationship was harmonious, making an instructive contrast with the truculence, resentment and mistrust which existed between Tiberius and Augustus during the only earlier comparably lengthy imperial apprenticeship.

The other aggravation with which **MARCUS** was saddled and which must have become provocatively manifest on his accession, was his younger adoptive brother, **LUCIUS VERUS** whose character was, as we have seen, rather the antithesis of that of the tolerant, philosophical, sport-loving **MARCUS**, being venal, louche and indolent. Again **MARCUS'** astonishing capacity for tact, restraint and tolerance therefore continued to be tested – without doubt to the hilt – for the seven and a half years of their joint rule. Furthermore, it was the first occasion in Roman history on which two *Augusti* of equal rank had successfully taken and retained power. This very fact set a precedent for numerous further occasions from the 3rd century; the fact that it was not a complete failure doubtless encouraged imitators, although more often than not with predictably chaotic and often bloody results.

The success of the arrangement was in that **ANTONINUS** always ensured that **MARCUS** had primacy over his brother, which suited their temperaments, it would appear, of all three. Furthermore, **MARCUS** may have succeded to the arrangement in the hope – soon proved a vain one – that by sharing power and responsibility, he might have time to pursue his study of philosophy.

Background

The new ruler was born **M. Annius Verus,** a patrician, at Rome on 26th April AD121, adopted as a son by his paternal grandfather on the death of his father in 124/125 and in 127 was enrolled in the Equestrian Order by **HADRIAN,** who apparently held him in high esteem, even in childhood, punningly calling him 'Verissimus'.[188] According to the HA he was 'named after his step-[great]-grandfather on his mother's side' which would suggest that his full name at birth was **L. Catilius Severus [M.] Annius Verus** or similar.[189] This Severus, consul for the second time in AD120, was called, in full: L. Catilius Severus Julianus Claudius Reginus.[190] The adoption by his grandfather may have led to the dropping of Catilus Severus's name. In 136 **HADRIAN** betrothed him to Ceionia Fabia, daughter of the man about to be the Emperor's chosen successor, L. Ceionius Commodus, and when that development occurred shortly afterwards, he clearly became the heir presumptive in waiting. This arrangement, of course, failed to survive Commodus's death on 1st January 138, but on 25th February 138 he was for a third time adopted, on this occasion by Hadrian's adopted successor, **ANTONINUS PIUS,** taking the full style of **M. Aelius Imp. Titi Aeli Hadriani Antonini f. Pap. Aurelius Verus** but the much simpler **M. Aelius Aurelius Verus** was commonly used.[191]

He was appointed quaestor under age, also in 138, and in the year following was granted the name – or title, as it was rapidly establishing itself – of Caesar, changing his style to **Aurelius Caesar Augusti Pii** f. This would appear to be the first occasion on which an emperor or future emperor bore a style of nomenclature which had no *praenomen*, even the honorific 'Imperator' first so used by **AUGUSTUS.**

The following year he held his first consulship, holding a second in 145, two years before receiving the tribunician power on 10th December 147, which was renewed annually throughout his life on that day and month. After **ANTONINUS'** accession, the betrothal to Ceionia Fabia was broken off and he was instead betrothed in 139 and married in April or May 145 to **ANTONINUS'S** only daughter **Annia Galeria Faustina** (II), who was raised to the rank of Augusta in 147 on the birth of her first child.[192]

---

188. Dio LXI. 29.2. Thus, Verus = true; Verissimus = truest.

189. *V. Marci Aurelii* 2.3 see **Table XIX(a) Brief Lives** where M. Annius Catlius Severus Verus is suggested.

190. PIR², C558, see above, **Table XIX(a) Brief Lives**.

191. CIL.III.7060; ILS 354

192. PIR² A716

Reign

On his accession, 7th March 161, **MARCUS AURELIUS** was hailed as *imperator* for the first time, made *pontifex maximus*, granted proconsular power and was styled: **Imperator Caesar Marcus Aurelius Antoninus Augustus** to which he added – reluctantly but at the insistence of the senate in 166 – *Pater Patriae*. Various additional honorific names to mark triumphal campaigns were added to the **Armeniacus** of 165 thereafter: **Medicus** and **Parthicus Maximus** also in 166[193] **Germanicus** in 172 and **Sarmaticus** ion 175. He also enjoyed further Imperial acclamations in 163, 165, 166, 167, 171, 174, 175, 177 and 179 – ten in all.

Calamities at home and a crisis on the eastern frontier left both new emperors with their hands full, **MARCUS** dealing with the former whilst despatching **LUCIUS** off the the east, to deal with the question of Armenia. One suspects that **MARCUS** thought that to be in charge of so important a venture would afford **LUCIUS** the opportunity to prove himself a capable ruler and soldier. A magnificent triumph was celebrated, shared by both emperors. Unfortunately, their return in 166 was accompanied not only by abundant booty, but with a serious plague, which played havoc with the City's population, not sparing the ruling élite and over the succeeding years, decimated the potential manpower of the Empire with the result that it was ever after on the back foot and short of home-grown recruits for the army. It may well have been the plague which impelled a group of Teutonic tribes to threaten the northern frontier in 167. A first irruption was successfully dealt with, but a second in 168 alarmingly reached northern Italy and both emperors set out to deal with the situation. Once again, order was eventually restored. The emperors settled the dispositions and appointments on the frontier before returning, on which journey **VERUS** unexpectedly died.

Thereafter, **MARCUS** was able to govern alone until the time in 177 when he felt obliged to associate his surviving son, **COMMODUS,** in power. This must have been an even bigger disppointment than having to cope with **LUCIUS,** for it was obvious from a very young age that the lad was deranged to some extent, showing signs of extreme cruelty, mood-swings, fantasising and extreme self-indulgence: all **LUCIUS'** faults with some of **NERO'S** and **CALIGULA'S** thrown in.

In between times, though, **MARCUS** reigned in as exemplary a fashion as had his adoptive father, although he was obliged to return to the German and Danubian frontiers for over four years to campaign against further rebellious tribes, the Marcomanni and Quadi. This was eventually entirely successful, and had he not died when he did, plans were afoot to create a new province to the north east to encompass Germany between Rhine and Elbe, a scheme unfortunately abandoned by his un-martial successor. All this was despite the most successful general of **LUCIUS'** eastern campaign and governor of Syria, C. *AVIDIUS CASSIUS*, mounting, in 175, a full-scale usurpation, which was, in the event, put down without too much disruption. Again, great clemency was shown to the usurper's surviving family, and **MARCUS'S** relations with the senate were entirely deferential and designed to work as a partnership.

---

193. ILS 366

The last part of the reign was taken up with further campaigns on the north eastern frontier before **MARCUS**, who had long been in declining health, died near Sirmium (Sremska Mitrovica, Serbia) whilst on campaign on 17th March 180, leaving a large family, a desperately unstable son and heir and his *Meditations,* a work of Stoic philosophy relecting on the contradictions between the ideal and the realities of humane governance. He was immediately voted divine honours by the senate.

MARCUS AURELIUS and **ANTONINUS PIUS** were the two emperors held up to posterity as ideal rulers. The contrast between them was that whilst the latter's reign was attended by almost universal good fortune, the former was beset by calamities. That the latter survived them all with reputation intact surely singles him out as the ultimate paragon, let down only by the random nature of the hereditary system, for had the decade long plague begun in AD167 carried off **COMMODUS** instead of his other sons, subsequent events might have been very different. Even if all had died, most of **MARCUS'S** sons-in-law were highly capable, respected men, and not merely decorative patricians; any would have proved competent, one or two might have been outstanding.

*

TABLE XXII: THE ANCESTRY OF MARCUS AURELIUS

The Annii of Marcus's line came from Ucubi (Espejo), in the Spanish province of Baetica and it has been suggested by Sir Ronald Syme that prior to their migration, Lanuvium (Lanuvio) might have been their town of origin.[194] In 48 BC, Annius Scapula, an equestrian of undoubted Italian ancestry and 'of the highest rank and influence in that province' was executed for being involved in a pro-Pompeian plot to murder Caesar's governor of the province, Q. Cassius Longinus, a cousin of the conspirator. If not a direct ancestor, he was quite probably related to the Veri.

There are also three other possible kinsfolk difficult to include in any stemma through lack of evidence. One was M. Annius Afrinus, suffect consul c. 67, in the era of **NERO**; the family increasingly used 'Marcus' as a *praenomen* even when there was more than one brother, preferring to change the *cognomen* of each instead, so Afrinus could even have been a brother of the first Verus, and a kinsman of **HADRIAN**, his exceedingly unusual *cognomen* being closely cognate with Afer, **HADRIAN'S** father's name.[195] Such a connection[196] would explain a great deal about Hadrian's second and final succession settlement. The name Cornificia, which emerges in the family with Marcus's sister, may further suggest that the lost generations of this provincial family were closer to events in the capital than the surviving evidence might suppose, for it suggests marriage with a

---

194. *Ancient Society* 13/14 (1982-83) 260 f.

195. Syme (1958) II. 792

196. Attested, but without specific details in Dio LXIX. 21.2

grand-daughter of L. Cornificius, consul in 33BC, also from Lanuvium, although he had otherwise no recorded descendants.[197]

Finally, another first century possible kinsman, also of equestrian rank, could have been Annius Faustus an unpleasant delator in the last years of **NERO** who was condemned by the senate in the reign of **GALBA**. His name recurs in that of the suffect consul of 121, suggested by Settipani as a possible brother of M. Annius Verus, consul (iii) 126.[198] Both would therefore pre-date the alliance with Rupilia Faustina, whose extra name indicates a descent from **Sulla** and was passed on to two empresses. Thus if the two Annii Fausti were indeed kinsmen, the occurrence of the *cognomen* is more likely to have been a co-incidence rather than an indication of an even earlier alliance with the posterity of the triumvirs.

TABLE XXII BRIEF LIVES

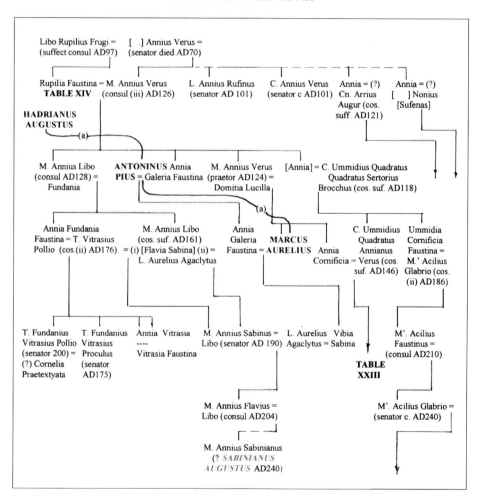

197. PIR² C1503; Wiseman (1971) 139
198. Settipani (2000) 299

M.' Acilius Glabrio

The family was an ancient Republican noble one, going back to M.' Acilius C. f. L. n. Glabrio, consul in 191BC. The male line changed in the Augustan period when M.' Glabrio (suffect consul in 33) adopted the son of C. Memmius L. f. Gal., the latter voting tribe being that of all subsequent Glabriones. The family were made patricians by **CLAUDIUS** in 48. Consul in 240. His son was M.' Acilius Glabrio consul 256 with his cousin, [L.] Valerius [Claudius] Acilius Priscillianus Maximus, whose father [Ti.] Claudius Cleoboles married Glabrio's aunt, Acilia M.' f. Manliola (qv). In his turn, Cleoboles' father (of the same name) married Acilia Frestana, a sister of Glabrio, consul 210 [PIR² A72]

M.' Acilius M. f. Gal. Glabrio Cn. Cornelius Severus

Suffect consul c. AD173 and consul in 186. The marriage is conjectural, but explains the importation of the name Faust[in]us into this family from this point. He was offered the purple by **PERTINAX** but wisely declined the honour. His father, (consul 152) married Arria L. f. Plaria Vera Priscilla which introduced the latter name into the family [CIL VI. 1331; Münzer (1999) 88; Syme, RP III (1984) 1329-1333]

M.' Acilius [Glabrio] Faustinus

He was consul in 210 and may have married a Manlia, as his daughter was called Acilia M.' f. Manliola. He had brothers (both by Ummidia): M. Acilius Vibius Faustinus, [M.' Acilius] Glabrio Cn. Cornelius Severus who died aged 13 and possibly Acilius Severus, an Arval Brother 183/876 along with two, possibly three sisters. His son, M.' Acilius Glabrio seems to have produced descendants identifiable down into the late 5th century. [FS 434; ILS. 1133-34, 5024; PIR² A57, 69, 80, 86, 709, C73/140]

Annia Cornificia Faustina

Born 122/123, married c. 136 C. Ummidius Quadratus Annianus Verus (see below) and died 152 [PIR² A708]

Annia Galeria Faustina ('the elder')

Died in 140 married T. Aurelius Fulvus Boionius Antoninus, otherwise **ANTONINUS PIUS** (see above **Table XXII**) and had issue [PIR2, A715].

Annia Galeria Faustina ('the younger')

She married her cousin **MARCUS AURELIUS** (*qv* above) [PIR² A716]

M. Annius Afrinus

Suffect consul c. 67, thought to be a kinsman of the first Annius Verus [PIR² 630; Birley (1987) 244]

M. Annius M. f. Gal. Flavius Libo

Patrician by creation and of Flavian descent, he was consul in 204 and a Salius Palatinus [FS.607]

M. Annius M. f. Gal. Libo

Patrician by creation. He was probably the elder son, taking his *cognomen* from his maternal grandfather. He was consul in 128 and must have married Fundania daughter of L. Fundanius Lamia Aelianus, see **Table XXI** above. [ILS 7190; Birley (1987) 244; PIR² A667].

M. Annius M. f. Gal. Libo

Patrician by creation. Born AD128, Suffect consul AD160. The names of his son and grandson suggest thsat his wife was a Flavian princess, on whom see **Table XIV Brief Lives**. According to the HA, his widow married the Imperial freedman L. Aurelius L. Veri lib. Agaclytus (qv) [FS p. 530; ILS7190; PIR² A668; Birley (1987) 243]

L. Annius Rufinus

Senator c. AD101, 'C. Anni Veri frat[er]' who had estates at Veleia. There are several Annii Rufini (both common names) in the following centuries who may or may not be descendants [FS619; ILS 5777, 6675]

[.] Annius Verus I

Adlected into the senate with the rank of ex-praetor either under the influence of **NERO'S** Corduban minister, Seneca or by **VESPASIAN** in 70. He would appear to have been dead by 73/74. [PIR² A694; Birley (1987) 243].

M. Annius Sabinianus

Suffect consul before AD239, possibly the same man as the imperial claimant SABINIANUS in AD240 (see below page 298).

C. Annius Verus

Senator, late 1st or early 2nd century [ILS6675].

M. Annius Verus

He was born in 58 and his family adlected into the Patriciate by Vespasian in 73/74, presumably on the reputation of his father or friendship with the Emperor. If his father was not dead, the wonder is that he never made consul in the first three or four years of the reign. If he was, his services to Vespasian must have been considerable to have merited the teenage son's being made a patrician. Furthermore, he went on to hold three consul-ships: a suffect one in 97 and ordinary ones in 121 and 126 as well as the prefecture of the city (PUR) in 118, yet at no time stands out as a notable general or for any other achievement likely to merit such honours. Kinship to **HADRIAN** no doubt helped, though. The date of his death is not clear. He married Rupilia Faustina, daughter of Libo Rupilius Frugi, suffect consul in 97, bringing to her husband's family an incomparable array of distinguished republican antecedents as well

as the rather less elevated blood of the Emperor **VITELLIUS**. He may have had two sisters, one married to Arrius Augur (suffect consul AD121) and the other to a Nonius Sufenas (see below) [PIR2, A. 695; Syme (1958) II. 790-792].

M. Annius M. f. Gal. Verus

Patrician by creation. Praetor AD124 or 125, and died in office. He married, before Domitia Lucilla ('the younger'), daughter and heiress of P. Calvisius Tullus Ruso, consul in 109 and his second wife, Domitia Lucilla ('the elder') (see **Table XIX (b) Brief Lives**) [PIR2, A. 696; ILS 7190; Birley, *op. cit.* 244]

M. Annius Catilius Severus Verus Known to history as **MARCUS AURELIUS** see above.

ANTONINUS PIUS

See above **and Table XX**

Cn. Arrius Augur

Suffect consul 121. His marriage is postulated on the strength of the name of one of his sons, L. Ar[rius] Verus; the others were Cn. Arrius Augur, and C. Arrius Cornelius Proculus (suffect consuls in c. AD150 and 145 respectively). It has been sug-gested that this family were a branch of that of C. Arrius Antoninus, ancestor of **ANTONINUS PIUS**, see **Table XX Brief Lives** [Birley (1987) 242]

L. Aurelius L. f. Agaclytus

Son of the like-named Imperial freedman of **VERUS** (allegedly too loyal and efficient to be much liked) and the widow of M. Annius Libo (but whose on the face of it unlikely alliance is attested only in the HA, and thus cannot be entirely relied upon even in this more reliable part of that work). He was a senator in the late 2nd century, when he was the first husband of Vibia Aurelia Sabina, one of the daughters of **MARCUS AURELIUS.** From his names, it is just possible that C. Aurelius Appius Sabinus (consul 240) was a son or grandson [Birley (1987) 239; Grant 1994) 29].

Cn. Claudius Severus,
Ordinary consul (ii) in 173 (see also the Posterity of Marcus Aurelius, below) and father of [.] **Claudius [Severus]** adopted by cousin once removed (or uncle, if the identity here proposed of his mother is correct) as **[M.] Ummidius Quadratus [?Claudianus Severus],** see above.

T. Fundanius T. f. Vitrasius Polio
He was adlected into the *Salii Palatini* 170 and was still living in 235 (unless he had a son of the same name). He may have married a lady by the name of Cornelia [Sextia] Praetextata, and if so, the *Promagister* of the priests of Vesta c. AD300, Vitrasius Praetextatus, may have been a grandson or great-grandson, with a daughter, Vitrasia, who, by M. Maecius Memmius Furius Baburius Caecilianus Placidus (consul 343), was the parent of Symmachus' father-in-law Memmius Vitrasius Orfitus. [FS1775, 2433, 3556; ILS 5024; PLRE I Orfitus 3, Placidus 2, Praetextatus 3]

MARCUS AURELIUS
See above.

[Nonius Sufenas]
The Nonii Sufenates were a minor late Republican senatorial family, the latest recorded member of which was M. Nonius Sex. f. Ani. Sufenas, *praetor* in 55BC It is perfectly possible that they could have continued to hold minor magistracies only and escaped mention until the 2nd century; alternatively, the *cognomen* Sufenas may have passed known through female lines, to be revived in the Trajanic era, as was then the fashion, and which might explain the son's reluctance to record his *nomen*. This man's marriage with an Annia is postulated on the strength of the *agnomen*, of

his presumed son P [?Nonius] Sufenas Verus, suffect consul c. 132. A conceivable descendant might have been L. Nonius Verus, suffect consul c. 311 [CIL XVI 714; DNP 1087; PLRE I. Verus 4; Wiseman (1971) no. 277].

Ummidia Cornificia Faustina
Married a husband whose name is not known (M.' Acilius Glabrio (qv above) is a suggestion) and had an attested daughter: **Annia Faustina.** If the suggested marriage is correct, then the son would be M.' Acilius Faustinus, as shown [Birley (1987) 243 (for the pros and cons of the alliance)]

M. Ummidius Annianus Quadratianus
Consul in 167, who probably died of plague at about that time having adopted a son of Cn. Claudius Severus [Syme, *op.cit.,* 100].

C. Ummidius Quadratus Annianus Verus
Suffect consul in 146 married his cousin, Marcus Aurelius's sister Annia Cornificia Faustina (see above) [Syme, R. in *Historia* 17 (1968) 98f., cf. RP III (1984) 1158-1178]

M.] Ummidius Quadratus [Claudianus Severus]
Whom **COMMODUS** had killed for alleged conspiracy c. 192.

C. Ummidius Quadratus Sertorius Severus,
Suffect consul in 118 a descendant of a distinguished family which first came to prominence under Augustus and himself probably a Sertorius (and thus a kinsman of the Pedanii – see **Table XXI** above) prior ro an adoption into the Ummidii [Birley (1987) 244-245]

Vibia Aurelia Sabina
Apart from the surprising alliance with a freedman's son (albeit a cousin, if the HA is to be believed) she had been previously married to L.

Antistius Burrus, conaul 181 [Birley (1987) 239]

T. Vitrasius Pollio

Full name T. Pomponius Proculus Vitrasius Pollio, he was suffect consul 152, governor of Upper Pannonia, PUR 175 and consul (ii) 176. The first recorded members of this family were successively prefects of Egypt under **TIBERIUS** and **CALIGULA**, then they are lost sight of until this man's grandfather, a senator under Trajan and his father, who was suffect consul in c. 137 and was granted patrician status, probably by **HADRIAN**. He may have been adopted by or married the heiress of a Pomponius Proculus, hence his son's name. [ILS 1112]

*

TABLE XXIII: THE CHILDREN OF MARCUS AURELIUS

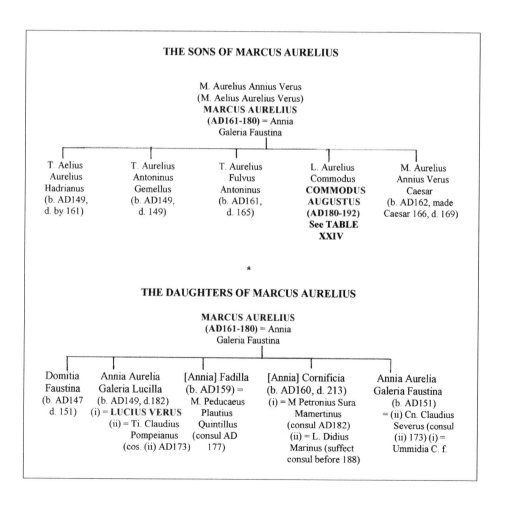

THE SONS OF MARCUS AURELIUS

M. Aurelius Annius Verus
(M. Aelius Aurelius Verus)
MARCUS AURELIUS
(AD161-180) = Annia
Galeria Faustina

| T. Aelius Aurelius Hadrianus (b. AD149, d. by 161) | T. Aurelius Antoninus Gemellus (b. AD149, d. 149) | T. Aurelius Fulvus Antoninus (b. AD161, d. 165) | L. Aurelius Commodus **COMMODUS AUGUSTUS** **(AD180-192)** **See TABLE XXIV** | M. Aurelius Annius Verus Caesar (b. AD162, made Caesar 166, d. 169) |

*

THE DAUGHTERS OF MARCUS AURELIUS

MARCUS AURELIUS
(AD161-180) = Annia
Galeria Faustina

| Domitia Faustina (b. AD147 d. 151) | Annia Aurelia Galeria Lucilla (b. AD149, d.182) (i) = **LUCIUS VERUS** (ii) = Ti. Claudius Pompeianus (cos. (ii) AD173) | [Annia] Fadilla (b. AD159) = M. Peducaeus Plautius Quintillus (consul AD 177) | [Annia] Cornificia (b. AD160, d. 213) (i) = M Petronius Sura Mamertinus (consul AD182) (ii) = L. Didius Marinus (suffect consul before 188) | Annia Aurelia Galeria Faustina (b. AD151) = (ii) Cn. Claudius Severus (consul (ii) 173) (i) = Ummidia C. f. |

The only one of the Emperor's sons to survive childhood was **COMMODUS**, who married but had no children. His next and youngest brother M. Aurelius Annius Verus was made next heir and given the title Caesar in AD166 aged just four, perhaps because **COMMODUS** was then ill, or merely as a precaution. However, he too died young, probably from the plague, in 169. On the other hand, all the daughters bar the eldest lived to maturity and married.

THE DESCENDANTS OF MARCUS AURELIUS

The most striking thing abnout the descendants of **MARCUS AURELIUS** is their propensity for being eliminated, not only by the deranged **COMMODUS**, but by the Severan dynasty, both Septimius **SEVERUS** himself and his successor, **CARACALLA.** As with the Julio-Claudian dynasty and with **DOMITIAN,** being close to the purple in blood was very dangerous, especially if one showed any ability or was in any way prominent. Hence a high proportion of the grand children of **MARCUS AURELIUS** especially were permanently removed from the scene by various expedients. Note: the **Brief Lives** for all the descendants follow **Table XXIV(d).**

TABLE XXIV(a) THE DESCENDANTS OF MARCUS AURELIUS 1

ANNIA GALERIA AURELIA LUCILLA

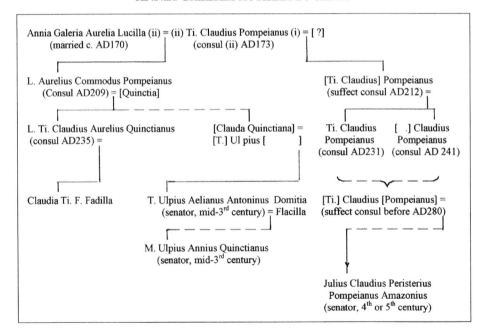

TABLE XXIV(b) THE DESCENDANTS OF MARCUS AURELIUS 2

ANNIA AURELIA GALERIA FAUSTINA

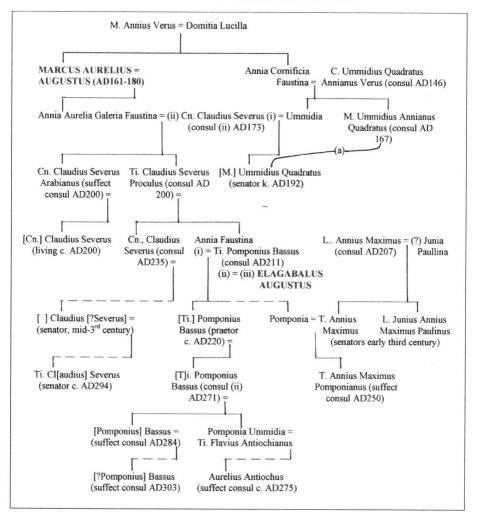

TABLE XXIV(c): THE DESCENDANTS OF MARCUS AURELIUS 3
[ANNIA] FADILLA

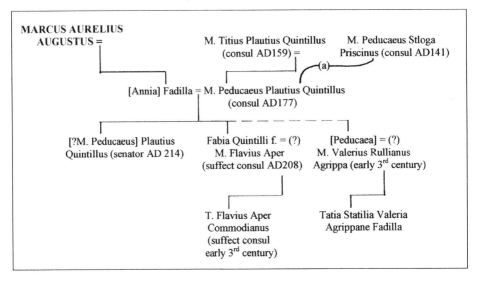

TABLE XXIV(d): THE DESCENDANTS OF MARCUS AURELIUS 4
[ANNIA] CORNIFICIA

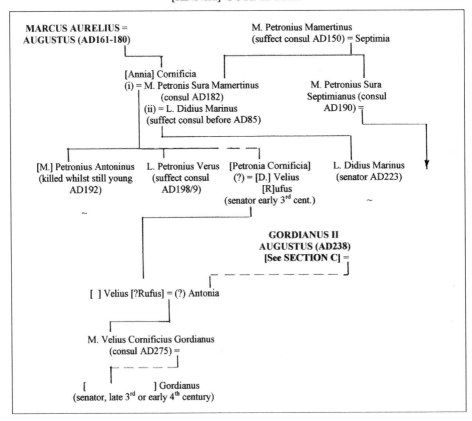

TABLE XXIV (a) – (d) BRIEF LIVES

[Annia] Fadilla

The diminutive *cognomen* Fadilla must derive from an untraced ancestor bearing the rare masculine version, Fadus [PIR² F96]

L. Annius Maximus Paullinus

Senator, early 3ʳᵈ century. His names suggest that his mother may have been called Junia Paullina, otherwise unknown.

T. Annius Maximus

Senator early 3ʳᵈ century, son of L. Annius Maximus, consul 207 who was a patrician by creation (perhaps of **ANTONINUS PIUS** in 161). The family were probably related to the contemporary consular houses of L. Annius Fabianus and L. Annius Italicus, suffect consuls before 161 and 194 respectively and all in the Quirinia voting tribe. Their origin may have been from Puteoli (Pozzuoli) [ILS 8080; PIR² A671, 672].

T. Annius T.f. Quir. Maximus Pomponianus

Suffect consul 250. Bassus, who was consul in the Gallic Empire 262 and (ii) 266, may have been a possible younger brother. [?ILS 2725; CIL V 5266; PLRE I. Bassus 1]

Aur[elius Antiochi]ani f. Antiochus

Suffect consul before 285, proconsul of Africa between 285 and 290 [PLRE I. Antiochus 13]

L. Aurelius Commodus Pompeianus

Born 176, consul 209 and killed at the behest of **CARACALLA** 213. It may be presumed, on the reconstruction proposed here, that his wife was a Quinctia and perhaps a relative of the Quinctii Crispini, eg. L. Bruttius Quinctius Crispinus consul 187, see **Table V Brief Lives** Note Settipani's suggestion that he might be a son

of a Ceionia and Avidius Quitus, see **Table XXI Brief Lives**. [FS 892; PIR² C568; Settipani 302.].

Claudia Ti. f. Fadilla

Her *cognomen* and filiation attach her securely to this family. She was recordced as *c[larissima] p[uella]* (a girl of senatorial rank) in the mid-3ʳᵈ century. [PIR² C1093]

[.] Claudius [?Pompeianus]

He was custodian of the sacred buildings of Rome in 280, and would have been a suffect consul prior to appointment to so prestigious a post; although only his *nomen* survives, this office also links him to the consul of 241.

Cn. Claudius Severus

Grandson of C. Claudius Severus, suffect consul 112, who had been the first man sent to govern **TRAJAN'S** newly conquered province of Arabia and hence his son's name, Cn. Claudius C. f. Severus Arabianus who was consul in AD146. The family came from Pompeiopolis (Taşköprü, Turkey), Greece. The family are thought to have been kin to the Claudii Pompeiani (qv). Severus was a patrician, probably so created when he married Faustina. He was suffect consul in AD163 and served again as ordinary consul a decade later. He seems to have had an (elder) brother called C. Vibius Gallio Claudius Severus, who only seems to have risen to the rank of praetor before AD156. His first wife was an Ummidia, a family already twice married into the Veri [PIR² C1023, 1024].

Jul[ius] Cl[audius] Peristerius Pompeianus Amazonius

A *v[ir] c[larissimus]* and *consularis* (senatorial governor) of Sicily some time in the fourth or fifth centuries. *Clarissimi* were slightly lower in rank by this era, being outranked by *illustres*. The conjuncture of the names Claudius and Pompeianus a century (or even more) later may merely be co-incidence; both are common names, whereas Amazonius is a *signum* – a unique extra distinguishing soubriquet, almost a nickname, which in time became hereditary and *signa* later became indistinguishable from any other personal name [PLRE I. Pompeianus 7].

L. Ti. Claudius [ ]f. Quir. Aurelius Quinctianus
A patrician and consul in 235 [FS 1169; PIR² C 992; ILS1181]

Ti. Claudius Pompeianus
This man's father bore the same name and was an equestrian from Antioch. He was suffect consul in AD162 and ordinary consul 173. He was also made a patrician, probably on his second marriage. His first wife's name is unknown, but he seems to have had a son by her whose posterity survived by far the longest if we can accept Pompeianus Amazonius (qv) as a plausible descendant. He was probably a brother or other close relative of Ti. Claudius Paullinus (also suffect consul AD162). He also had a nephew, executed for being part of Lucilla's conspiracy against **COMMODUS** in AD182 [JRS CII (2012) 211; FS 619; PIR² C973].

[Ti. Claudius] Pompeianus
Known only as suffect consul for AD212, he would seem to be the right age for an eldest son of the consul of AD173 [PIR² C567/569]

Ti. Claudius Pompeianus
Consul AD231 [PIR² C972].

[.] Claudius Pompeianus
Consul AD241, later in 244 appointed curator of the sacred buildings of Rome.

L. Didius Marinus
An unusual marriage (of after 193) for a Princess, even for a second marriage: Marinus was an equestrian, albeit a grand one, having been a junior procurator in Britain c 193-197 going on to several more important procuratorships up until 211. He later attained senatorial rank and had married Cornifica c. 213. Either he or his son was a senator and patron of Canusium (Canosa di Puglia) in 223. It is likely that the son, as he bears no name associated with the Antonine dynasty, was the product of a former marriage. This may also have ensured his survival. He appears to have ended up a senator. The family either came from Mediolanum (Milan) or Syria [ILS 6121; PIR² D71; Birley (1981) 300].

M. Flavius Aper
Suffect consul 208. He was the son and grandson of consuls of the same name (in 176 and 130 respectively) the latter being the son of another M. Flavius Aper, suffect consul in 103 who was possibly the son of, or identical with, the emergent praetorian Gallic senator M. Aper of Tacitus' *Dialogus*. The family had some kind of (poorly understood) connection with the Republican Servilii Vatiae. This man's uncle, L. Flavius Aper married into the family of **SEPTIMIUS SEVERUS** see **Table XXX Brief Lives** [Syme (1958) I. 109, II. 799-800].

T. Flavius Aper Commodianus
Suffect consul, earlier 3rd century [ILS 2350]

Ti. Flavius Antiochianus
Suffect consul at an unknown date, consul (ii) 270 PUR 269-70 & (ii) 272. It is possible that his wife was the sister, not daughter of the consul (ii) of 271. [PIR² F203; PLRE I.203; on Pomponia Ummidiia, PIR² P781]

[G]ordianus

A senator named on a list recording payments made in the late 3rd century or early fourth. If not a separate person, he just could be the same man as (and independent attestation for) M. Velius Cornificius Gordianus (qv below) [PIR² G192; PLRE 1]

M. Peducaeus Plautius Quintillus

Consul in 177, killed by **SEVERUS** after 205. He seems to have been adopted by the consul of 141 M. Peducaeus M. f. Stloga Priscinus - that is, if the order of his names is to be taken at face value; G. Barbieri was of the opinion that the adoption was the other way round. Such an adoption would also imply the excistence of a second son, perhaps the Plautius Quintillus who was a senator in 214. There may have also been another daughter (Peducaea Plautilla) who married the Emperor **ALBINUS**, see below **section IV(a)**. The family of Peducaeus Stloga descended from brothers, Quintus, suffect consul in 89 and Marcus, consul in 93, and possibly from T. Peducaeus, suffect consul in 35BC, a descendant of the emergent senator Sex. Peducaeus, who was tribune of the people in 113BC, although the five generation gap between the Triumviral consul and the brothers arouses doubts [PIR² P474; Barnes (1978) 52; Birley (1987) 238, 239, 247; Wiseman (1971) No. 313].

[?M. Peducaeus Plautius] Quintillus

Senator AD 212/213 and perhaps a victim of **CARACALLA**. The missing first part of his name might have revealed Antonine links [PIR² Q37].

[M.] Petronius [?Sura] Antoninus

Patrician senator killed on the orders of **COMMODUS** 192 along with his nephew, according to the HA, see note on his father (qv) [PIR² P272].

M. Petronius Mamertinus

Son of a procurator of an African family, M. Petronius Sura, he was suffect consul 150 and his family subsequently made patrician. He married Septimia, daughter of the African C. Claudius Septimius Aper. Her brother P. Septimius Aper entered the senate and was consul in AD153. More to the point, he was a kinsman of the Emperor **SEPTIMIUS SEVERUS**. Mamertinus' sister also married a Septimius, this time a direct ancestor of the future Emperor, **see Table XXX Brief Lives** [PIR² P287; Birley (1988) 44, 225].

M. Petronius M. f. Vel. Sura Mamertinus

He was consul in 182 but was killed on the orders of **COMMODUS** in 191, and his elder son (as here, Petronius Antoninus) suffered the same fate not long afterwards. We only have the word of the HA for this, but until the end of the Antonine dynasty it is reasonably reliable, although it still contains some made up names and Antoninus could of course be amongst them, being unattested elsewhere. However, the existence and name of his putative brother lends confidence [HA *V. Comm.* VII, 5; FS p. 833; PIR² P311; Birley (1988) 225].

L. Petronius Verus

Like Antoninus, his *cognomen* would suggest descent from, Cornificia. He was suffect consul in 198 or 199. Conceivably he was father or grandfather of Petronius Faustinus, suffect consul at an unkown date in the 3rd century [PIR² P315].

[Pomponius] Bassus

Suffect consul 284 [PLRE I.2]

[?Pomponius] Bassus

Suffect consul 303, later propraetorian legate in Moesia [PLRE I.3].

Ti. Pomponius Bassus

A member of a family that entered the senate under the Flavian dynasty with T. Pomponius Bassus (suffect consul 94). His grandson seems to have adopted a son of the senator D. Terentius Gentianus who became C. Pomponius Bassus Terentianus suffect consul under **MARCUS AURELIUS** and was the father of the consul 211, later governor of Moesia. C. Pomponius Magnus, suffect consul in AD211, was possibly a brother as was L. Pomponius Bassus, suffect under **CARACALLA** [PIR² P700]

[Ti.] Pomponius Bassus

Praetor c. 220, legionary legate under his father in Moesia [PIR² P701]

[T]i. Pomponius Bassus [?Fa]ustus

Patrician and suffect consul 259, corrector of Italy 268, PUR 270-271, *princeps senatus* 268-270 & ordinary consul (ii) 271. It is not clear quite when this family were raised to patrician status. It was bestowed increasingly rarely as the 3rd century wore on. He married Pomponia Gratidia, a descendant of the suffect consul of AD185, L. Pomponius Gratus. He was latterly *princeps senatus* [FS 274; PIR² P702; PLRE I.17; Mennen 2011) 119-120]

M. Titius Plautius Quintillus

Consul 159, son of L. Epidius Titius Aquilinus (consul 125) whose marriage into the Imperial family is conjectured by Birley following Sir Ronald Syme. If it can be accepted, he would have been brother-in-law to **LUCIUS VERUS** see **Table XXI** [Birley (1987) 247].

M. Ulpius Annius Quinctianus

A third century senator, proconsul of Macedonia, tentatively placed somewhere in mid-century. He could, of course, be a brother of the following,

Antoninus; that they must have been close kin cannot be in doubt. [Thomas (1984) I. 188, 57]

T. Ulpius Aelianus Antoninus

This man's inclusion is a trifle speculative, for he is only known as a senator from Prusias ad Hypium (near Düzce, Turkey) from the early or mid-third century (his dating is not at all certain, nor is that of his possible son), but his names are such as to suggest most strongly descent from **M. AURELIUS** although a more certain son, Papianus, betrays no such name. If he does belong here, he must be the grandson of the consul of AD209, in order to explain the occurrence of the cognomen Quinctianus, itself redolent of the inheritance of the Empress Crispina. He was of a recently emergent family, bearing in mind the use of the *praenoemen* Titus, typical of families granted citizenship under **TRAJAN** [Madsen (2009) 6]

M. Ummidius Annianus Quadratus

Consul 167, name occasionally found as Quadratianus which seems likely to be an error. He adopted his nephew, who was probably originally called C. Claudius Severus. [FS p. 929]

[M. Ummidius] Quadratus

A young senator, the adopted son of M. Ummidius Annianus Quadratus, who was killed in 192. He himself was executed in 182 for involvement with the conspiracy of Lucilla against **COMMODUS** [PIR² Q2; Birley (1988) 61, 82]

C. Ummidius Quadratus Annianus Verus
See **Table XIV Brief Lives**

M. Valerius Rullianus Agrippa

Senator living early 3rd century and about whom little is known. In Republican terms, Rullianus would be thought of as a name of the Fabian family, but at this remove such a descent seems unlikely. Likewise, families like the Haterii advertised their descent from **AUGUSTUS'S** minister Marcus Agrippa by using that name, but it later became popular in any case so once again no conclusions can safely be drawn. His marriage is suggested on the strength of his daughter's use of the name Fadilla which strongly suggests descent from **MARCUS AURELIUS**

[D.] Velius [R]ufus

Only known as a senatorial military tribune (a junior officer attached to a legion), and difficult to date, most commentators opting for the early 3rd century. There is at least one name missing from the inscription. If he is correctly placed here, his father would have been D. Velius Rufus Julianus [?Junianus], consul in 178 and yet another of the victims of **COMMODUS**. The family go back as senators for three generations before that when C. Velius Salvi f. Rufus, an ex-legionary and senior centurion, was procurator of Pannonia and Dalmatia 90/93. The justification for postulating this marriage is the nomenclature of one of the alleged consuls for AD275, M. Velius Cornificius Gordianus (qv) whose name (unfortunately only quoted in the HA and thus quite possibly spurious) also suggests a possible link (shown above)

with the Gordian family, although the name could have derived from another family entirely, as the *cognomen* was not unique to the three emperors of that name. To be sure, the author of the HA is most emphatic in stating that members of the Gordians' family were still alive in his day (in reality the late 4th century) and Syme was of the opinion that such might represent a fact well known to the anonymous author and, unusually, a snippet upon which we may rely. If, on the other hand we assume that, being in the HA, it is all made up, then it must be treated as fiction. [HA *V. Comm* IV. 9; Kennedy (1983) 183-196; Syme (1971) 238]

M. Velius Cornificius Gordianus

The HA calls this man Aurelius Cornificius Gordianus and makes him a suffect consul for 275, but he is nowhere else attested and his existence must therefore be treated with great caution. It seems not unreasonable to correct the reading of his name (if real) to fit a postulated Velian connection – after all, why else did **COMMODUS** kill the consul of 178 if he were not a relation by marriage? Cf. also Rufus (above). Nevertheless, Syme would have us ignore him completely [HA *Vita Aureliani* 41, 3; Syme (1971) 238, n. 5]

*

AVIDIUS CASSIUS
23rd April – 28th July AD175

This Imperial claimant was born c. 128/130 when his equestrian father was **HADRIAN'S** *ab epistulis Graecis,* and brought up in Alexandria – indeed, he could have been born there, for his father Heliodorus had accompanied **HADRIAN** there in 130.[199] He would have entered the senate as *quaestor* c. 153/154, would have gone on to be *aedile* or people's tribune around 155/156 and *praetor* before 163 – possibly about 158/159 - when legate of *Legio III Gallica.* He was consul in 166 and governor of Syria from the same year as well as the holder of special proconsular powers in the East c. 172-175[200] much as Corbulo had been under **NERO** just over a century before.

He was acclaimed emperor in Syria by 23rd April 175, in the belief that **MARCUS** had died. The rapid and peaceful acceptance of his *pronunciamento* rather re-inforces the belief that he was descended from the princes of Commagene, with all the ramifications of kinship and obligation arising therefrom. He continued to believe that **MARCUS AURELIUS** had died and had him deified by what ever legitimising apparatus he had by then established in his sphere of influence. He was assassinated on a visit to Alexandria by 28th July the same year. His wife's name is unknown, but from her younger son's *cognomen* it might be reasonable to assume it may have been Maecia. Further, she may have been dead by 175, for some of the gossip transmitted by the HA suggest that the Empress Faustina was expecting Avidius to marry her once his succession was assured.

If the sources for *AVIDIUS CASSIUS* are right, his usurpation must rank as one of the more unfortunate, for it would appear that this hero of **VERUS'S** pacification of the east bearing in mind he was persuaded to assume the purple by a false report of **MARCUS AURELIUS'** death allegedly encouraged by that Emperor's wife, Faustina the younger, suposedly his lover.[201]

In 175, *CASSIUS* – held in high regard by the Emperor - was still nominally governor of Syria but with extended *imperium,* granted following his suppression of a revolt in Egypt in 172. This included special dispensation, as a senator, to enter Egypt when required, too.[202] The appointment was so that he could hold the east whilst the Emperor campaigned against the troublesome Germans. Because the male heir – **COMMODUS** – was still only 13, the death of **MARCUS** would probably have led to a power struggle between various generals and imperial sons-in-law, especially the

---

199. Birley (1987) 186
200. PIR² A1402
201. Dio LXXI. 22.3 & 23.1 has to be the most reliable account.
202. Birley (1987) 174-75 n. 32

aged but esperienced Ti. Claudius Pompeianus, and clearly, given the misinformation fed to him, *CASSIUS* must have thought he had a good chance (but being unrelated to the Imperial house, the influence of Faustina must have played a crucial role) and acted with resolve.

His troops acclaimed him emperor and his Alexandrian origin stood him in good stead as regards support in the east. By the end of April, the whole eastern sector of the empire, including Egypt, was in his control; a papyrus of 3rd May confirms this, as does another dated from the previous month. That done, he resolved to set out for Rome to secure his rule, despite having being declared a public enemy by the senate and despite his having eventually become aware that the Emperor was not dead at all. On his eventual departure, therefore, he was assassinated on or before 28th July by soldiers loyal to **MARCUS** and aware that he was in fact alive. His reign, we are told, lasted three months and six days.

Ironically, one alleged cause of all the trouble, the Empress Faustina, died only a month or so afterwards, aged 45 (and mother of fourteen)[203] as she and the Emperor moved through the eastern provinces to restore confidence. Unlike most of the imperial claimants who came after him, *CASSIUS* appears to have minted no coins – at least none in his own name.

Whilst *CASSIUS* was not related to the Imperial House, he cannot have been unaware of his genealogical heritage, being of a family of Syrian nobility from Cyrrhus and claiming descent from the Seleucid Kings of Syria.[204]

---

203. Four were of infants who did not live long enough to receive a name, as far as we know; hence only ten offspring on **Table XXIII**.
204. Birley, (1987) 185-186, cf. Syme (1971) 129, n. 3, the details deriving from Greek inscriptions, IGR III 500, OGIS 263 & 766, amplified by Wagner (1974) 168, 172-3, 177 & Astarita (1983) 32. I am also indebted to Prince Kyril Toumanov for further information transmitted via HSH the late Prince Michael Grousinski

TABLE XXV: THE FAMILY OF AVIDIUS CASSIUS

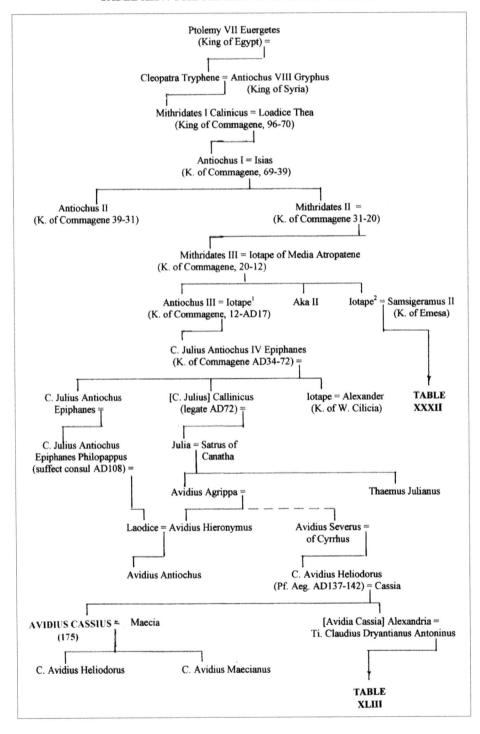

Ptolemy VII Euergetes
(King of Egypt) =

Cleopatra Tryphene = Antiochus VIII Gryphus
(King of Syria)

Mithridates I Calinicus = Loadice Thea
(King of Commagene, 96-70)

Antiochus I = Isias
(K. of Commagene, 69-39)

Antiochus II
(K. of Commagene 39-31)

Mithridates II =
(K. of Commagene 31-20)

Mithridates III = Iotape of Media Atropatene
(K. of Commagene, 20-12)

Antiochus III = Iotape[1]   Aka II   Iotape[2] = Samsigeramus II
(K. of Commagene, 12-AD17)   (K. of Emesa)

C. Julius Antiochus IV Epiphanes
(K. of Commagene AD34-72) =

C. Julius Antiochus   [C. Julius] Callinicus   Iotape = Alexander   **TABLE**
Epiphanes =   (legate AD72) =   (K. of W. Cilicia)   **XXXII**

C. Julius Antiochus   Julia = Satrus of
Epiphanes Philopappus   Canatha
(suffect consul AD108) =

Avidius Agrippa =   Thaemus Julianus

Laodice = Avidius Hieronymus   Avidius Severus =
                                          of Cyrrhus

Avidius Antiochus   C. Avidius Heliodorus
                           (Pf. Aeg. AD137-142) = Cassia

AVIDIUS CASSIUS = Maecia   [Avidia Cassia] Alexandria =
(175)   Ti. Claudius Dryantianus Antoninus

C. Avidius Heliodorus   C. Avidius Maecianus

TABLE
XLIII

TABLE XXV: BRIEF LIVES: AVIDIUS CASSIUS

Antiochus I Theos Dikaios Epiphanes Philomaios Philellen

King of Commagene 69-39

Antiochus II

King of Commagene 39-31 In 29 he was summoned to Rome and executed by **AUGUSTUS,** because he had caused the assassination of an ambassador whom his brother Mithridates had sent to Rome

Antiochus III

King of Commagene 12-AD17 [Stemma, PIR² Pt. I, p. 140]

[Avidia Cassia] Alexandria

Settipani supposes her to be a daughter of the claimant, not the sister. She married the Lycian grandee and senator Ti. Claudius Dryantianus Antoninus, He died in AD178. After the collapse of Cassius' revolt they were "entrusted to the protection of their uncle by marriage" a wealthy Lycian, Claudius Titianus.. It would appear that the family's property was seized by the state after Dryantianus's death. It is thought that she was the great great gandmother of Sulpicia Dryantilla, the Empress of the Imperial Claimant *REGALIANUS*, **see section C.** [PIR² A512 & C859; 1043; HA, V. *Avidii Cassii* X. 1; Birley (1987) 205; Settipani (2000) 460 n. 5].

[T.] Avidius Agrippa

Presumably the first of his family to receive Roman citizenship, probably from T. Avidius Quietus (suffect consul AD 93).

[T.] Avidius Antiochus

He is attested as a kinsmnan of Avidius Cassius [PIR² A1401].

C. AVIDIUS CASSIUS
See above.

C. Avidius Heliodorus

He rose from a senior bureaucratic post (*Ab epistulis Graecis*) to become Prefect of Egypt AD137-142. He was later adlected into the senate before 161 and married a Cassia, claimed by the HA to have been a descendant of the assassin of Caesar. In fact, she was most probably a descendant of a T. Julius [   ] (another descendant of the Kings of Syria) and Cassia Lepida, whose daughter Julia Berenice was living AD116. [ILS 8910; OGIS 263; PIR2, A.1405; V. Avidii Cassii 1, 3]

C. Avidius Heliodorus

After the collapse of Cassisus' revolt, he was exiled by Marcus Aurelius but was later pardonied, but was later executed by Commodus after 180.

[.] Avidius Hieronymus

He was husband, it is surmised, of Laodice, daughter of C Julius Antiochus Epiphanes Philopappus (cf. above).

C. Avidius Maecianus

Killed in the suppression of Cassisus' revolt, July 175 [PIR2, A.1406].

[.] Avidius Severus

A citizen and decurion (local councillor) of Cyrrhus, wrongly said by the HA to have been Cassius' father. [HA V. *Avidii Cassii* 26.2]

Cassia

Settipani suggests that she might be a niece of C. Julius Alexander Berenicianus, suffect consul 116, whose mother was probably Iotape, a Seleucid princess.[Settipani (2000) 461].

Ti. Claudius Dryantius Antoninus

See below, **Table XLIII Brief Lives.**

Iotape (the younger)

Married Alexander, King of Western Cilicia in 72, 6th in descent from Mark Antony through the daughter of his second marriage (to his cousin, daughter of C. Antonius) who married Theodorus of Tralles. For her posterity see **Tables XXXII & XXXIX Brief Lives**

C. Julius Antiochus IV Epiphanes

King of Commagene 34-72 was the last of his line to reign and was deposed by **TITUS** acting on behalf of his father. He married his sister, Iotape Philadelphus.[PIR² I149]

C. Julius C. f. Fab. Antiochus Epiphanes

Married Claudia Capitolina, dau. of Ti. Claudius Balbillus, prefect of Egypt AD55-59, his cousin [PIR² C813, I149]

C. Julius C. f. Fab. Antiochus Epiphanes Philopappus

Suffect consul in 108, by which time raised to the Patriciate by Trajan [ILS 840] whose wife was probably a cousin of the Greek born senator C. Julius Eurycles Herculanus. Their son, C. Julius Philopappus, was a senator in the mid-2nd century whose line can be discerned (with gaps) to the fourth century. [PIR² I151]

[C. Julius] Callinicus

Served as a legate to his father in an attempt to resist the invasion of the Kingdom by Caesennius Paetus (see **Table XVI Brief Lives**) in AD72, but fled to Parthia, but later allowed by **VESPASIANUS** to live in honourable retirement at Rome.[PIR² I228]

Maecia

Settipani suggests she might have been Volusia Maeciana, daughter of L. Volusius Maecianus, prefect of Egypt in 161, and that there was also a daughter, Alexandria [Settipani (2000) 459-460]

Mithridates I Callinicus

King of Commagene 96-70BC 14th in descent from Bagabigna, Satrap of Armenia (and ancestor of the Orontid Kings of Armenia and the Bagratids of Georgia to the present) married Laodice Thea Philadelphus, daughter of Antiochus VIII Gryphus, king of Syria (by Cleopatra Tryphene, daughter of Ptolemy VII Euergetes, King of Egypt, the latter being descended from Ptolemy I, a Macedonian and a general of Alexander the Great). Through the female line he too was descended from the Kings of Pontus, and those of Syria, descended from Spittamenes, King of Bactria

Mithridates III

King of Commagene 20-12 His sister Aka II married the equestrian Ti. Claudius Thrasyllus, one of whose sons, Ti. Claudius Balbillus, was prefect of Egypt AD55-59 and whose daughter married C. Julius C. f. Fab. Antiochus Epiphanies, son of the last King of Commagene (qv)

Satrus	**Thaemus Julianus Satri f.**
A noble of Canatha in Syria was thought to have married to a daughter of Callinicus, who was a member of the house of Commagene [ILS 7529]:	Syrian negotiator (businessman) in the Gallic province of Lugdunensis and a decurion of Athelanum in Syria [ILS 7529]

*

COMMODUS
17 March 180 - 31 Dec. 192

Background

COMMODUS, who ascended the throne so distinguished by his father at eighteen, was the first emperor to have been *porphyrogenitus* – born in the purple, son of an emperor reigning at the time of his birth, bar poor, tragical and ephemeral **BRITANNICUS**. Yet it was the misfortune of Rome that almost all sons succeeding fathers turned out badly, from **DOMITIAN**, through **COMMODUS** to **CARACALLA**. Before the rise of the House of Constantine, most others were merely appallingly short-lived. One reason, it could be argued, was that the fathers, all strong, effective rulers, were such a hard act to follow, but in reality, all three seem to have been cursed with various forms of personality disorder.

L. Aurelius Commodus was born 31ˢᵗ August 161 at Lanuvium and on 12ᵗʰ October 166 was raised to the rank of Casear, which name he added to his own. As early as 15ᵗʰ October 172 he was allowed to add the style **Germanicus**, followed in March/April 175 by **Sarmaticus** as well. He had been received into all the priestly colleges on January 20ᵗʰ the same year. He was hailed *imperator* in 176 and again the following year, when he also held the consulship and was made joint ruler with his father as **Imperator Caesar Lucius Aurelius Commodus Augustus**,[205] being given the title *pater patriae* as well as the tribunician and proconsular powers, to be renewed annually on 10ᵗʰ December. He was consul for the second time in 179 and gained his third imperial acclamation with another (his fourth) in 180, prior to his accession.

His wife was Bruttia Crispina, whom he married before setting out for Germany with his father. She was the daughter of C. Bruttius Praesens - his full name was L.Fulvius C. f. Pompt. [Rusticus] C. Bruttius Praesens Min[   ] Valerius Maximus Pompeius L[onginus Aburnius] Valens Cornelius Proculus [   ] Aquilius Veiento.[206] He had been consul in 153 and again (reflecting this alliance) in 180. On her ancestry see **Table V**.

---

205. ILS 375
206. ILS 8265

Reign

On accession, he was styled **Imperator Caesar L. Aurelius Commodus Antoninus Augustus**[207] becoming Pontifex Maximus seven months later. In October 180 he assumed the *praenomen* **Marcus** in lieu of **Lucius,**[208] adding 'Pius' after 'Antoninus' two years later and, three years on from that, also added 'Felix', more probably as a reflection of the sort of feel-good factor he hoped emanated from himself, than from his descent from Sulla (see **Tables XIV & XXII Brief Lives,** above). Yet despite all this, in 191 he reverted to the simpler style of **Imperator Caesar L. Aelius Aurelius Commodus Augustus**[209] evoking more the nomenclature of his late adoptive uncle, **LUCIUS VERUS** than that of his father, as his previous style had done. In 182, having thrown away all the empire's advantages in Germany, he ironically added **Maximus** to his 'Germanicus' and just over two years later assumed the triumphal *cognomen* of **Britannicus**. His third consulship came in 181, fourth in 183, fifth in 186, sixth in 190 and finally his seventh in 192. His remaining imperial acclamations were: 182 (V), 183 (VI), 184 (VII) and 186 (VIII). Later in his reign he also took the additional names **Hercules Romanus,** reflecting his increasing obsession of himself as a re-born Hercules.

On his father's death, **COMMODUS** made a neat, appropriate speech to the legions in Germany, immediately ended a successful and promising campaign on the frontier which could have left most of modern Germany a Roman province and the borders of empire arguably much more secure. He then returned home to sully his already slightly dubious reputation with acts of astounding cruelty, caprice and perversity that saw his reign begin with his obsession with gladiators becoming apparent and end with his being worshipped as a god, and in particular as the personification of Hercules. The running of the empire was left to a succession of egregious favourites.

Nor had he had any contact with the workings of the senate, and consequently, like **DOMITIAN,** he placed little value on the formal proceedings of that body, that underpinned the delicate balance between the ruler and the governing class. As before, this enabled the extirpation of members of that class the easier for Commodus, who cared little for form and legal niceties, even less for the elite, who kept the huge ramshackle machinery of empire creaking along surprisingly effectively.

Another problem was that the conspiracies that ended the rule of these insane men nearly always led to civil war, even if the replacement emperor was generally agreed upon beforehand, as witness the fate of **GALBA**, of **NERVA** (almost), of **PERTINAX** and many others in the 3rd century. And if not a civil war, a counter-coup, as with **MACRINUS** and **ELAGABALUS,** or the **GORDIANS.**

Nevertheless, the point was made when discussing **DOMITIANUS,** that the governance of the empire hardly faltered at such times, except where conflicting generals were on the

---

207. ILS 376
208. ILS 177
209. ILS 400; PIR² A1482.

march. The impact of a half-mad emperor tended to be on the individuals of the highest level of the governing class: the senior senators and courtiers. And as the historians who recorded these doleful events were usually themselves from that background, the impact of the wayward head of state is inevitably magnified thereby.

Yet if, as appears to have happened between 185 and 195, a substantial portion of the ruling elite suffered savage proscription, then government, which relies on their experience and good will, falters. On the other hand, such events open the way for new blood, in the shape of newly promoted men with plenty of administrative experience.

COMMODUS bothered little with the minutiae of imperial government; indeed, he bothered very little with it at all. He also surrounded himself with rather strange and, to his peers, unacceptable people: charioteers, gladiators, catamites and other oddballs. The atmosphere created of fear, loathing, and unpredictability, led to frequent conspiracies, some imaginary, others perfectly real, as that of **COMMODUS'S** sister Lucilla, using her husband's nephew, Ti. Claudius Pompeianus Quintianus and M. Ummidius Quadratus as catspaws. The attempt was hopelessly bungled and the particiants executed. This was followed by the murder of his first favourite, Saoterus, and led to a bloodbath of possible accomplices, many his kin, and to a complete withdrawal from public life, his contact with reality being maintained by his praetorian prefects Sex. Tigidius Perennis and his successor the freedman's son, M. Aurelius Cleander.

Thereafter **COMMODUS**, clearly a bisexual satyromaniac, revelled in private orgies and was largely protected from all diversions. Plots continued, and in 191 large parts of Rome burned down, giving the emperor the chance to appear bountiful and undertake extensive restoration works, albeit that these were not completed for a decade or so. There was also unrest in the army, and in Britain the garrison attempted to elevate a senior commander called Priscus to the purple, but the selected victim wisely declined, but the Prefct of the Preaetorian Guard, effectively in control of the government, sacked all the British legionary legates as a precaution and sent the future emperor **PERTINAX** out to take control. Later, one Maternus, the leader of some deserters who had been roaming Gaul since the abrupt end of the war in Germany, tried to assasasinate the Emperor in Rome. A successful attempt to eliminate the Emperor was, it seemed, inevitable. It came in 192. Having re-named the months of the calendar after himself (nothing new there, *pace* **DOMITIAN**), **COMMODUS** now re-styled himself Hercules as putative founder of Rome, which itself he intended to re-name Colonia Commodiana at a ceremony in new year 193, an occasion which was to be accompanied by games at which he would emerge as both sole perpetual consul and gladiator, having murdered the consuls elect beforehand.

The conspiracy this time was to kill the Emperor on the night before the planned games, on New Year's Eve 192. Despite a glitch, it succeeded, and **COMMODUS** was finally despatched. The only problem thereafter was to install an agreed replacement and avoid a power-struggle.

There were no children from his marriage to Crispina before he claimed to have caught her in adultery, banished and later had her killed in 182. After his death his memory was erased (*damnatio memoriae*) by the senate. But this was reversed by **SEVERUS** in 196, who also then had him deified within the Antonine cult, mainly because he wanted his own successful bid for power to be read as an act avenging the deposition of the last of the Antonines, in the remembered glory of whose rule he wished to bask.

But in the event, installing an agreed replacement ruler did not prove so simple, and a four year period of upheaval ensued, including two bloody civil wars. The year 193 became the Year of the Five Emperors and made the Year of the Four Emperors 124 years before look like the palest avatar.

Further reading:
Birley, A. R., *Marcus Aurelius – a Biography* 2nd (revised) edition (London 1987).

*

THE SEVERI TO THE GORDIANS[210]

*

IV(a)
THE YEAR OF THE FIVE EMPERORS
AND THE SEVERAN DYNASTY

The Imperial Succession
Pertinax
Iulianus I
Albinus
Severus I
Geta
Antoninus II
Macrinus
Diadumenianus
Antoninus III
Alexander I

Imperial claimants
Niger
Verus II
Maximus I
Taurinus
[Uranius]
Seleucus

The assassination of **COMMODUS** appears to have been well planned and that the perpetrators had either obtained the agreement of the general and ex-consul **PERTINAX** that he should step into the shoes of **COMMODUS** or they had decided they would offer him the throne and were fairly certain that he would accept. The hope was that there would be a transition from a grizzled old war-horse who would stabilize things and sort out the chaos of the previous decade, and then hand over to an entirely suitable and well qualified younger man, perhaps young Pertinax. Yet it did not go as anticipated. **PERTINAX** failed to establish himself and in the aftermath a successor was chosen by the officers of the Praetorian Guard, who had failed to anticipate that news of the fall of **PERTINAX** would result in the best placed military governors making declarations, as in 69. This time there were again three candidates left to fight it out, with the role of **VESPASIAN** falling to the much less emollient **SEPTIMIUS SEVERUS**.

---

210. Note that all dates henceforth will be AD unless specified.

PERTINAX
1ˢᵗ Jan. - 28ᵗʰ March 193

Background

No one could say that the conspirators who seized their chance in murdering **COMMODUS** had really evolved any plan as to what to do if they succeeded. Consequently, the praetorian prefect, Laetus and the Imperial freedman Eclectus, the Emperor's *cubicularius* (chamberlain), having pulled off their *coup* on New Year's night 192, had to act extremely quickly in order to avoid the possibility of civil war.

Quite why they chose the first generation senator, freedman's son and former general Pertinax is quite unclear, except that he had a track record of being steadying influence. Yet there were several kinsmen and sons-in-law of **MARCUS AURELIUS** still then living and in Rome whom they could have chosen, one or two possibly better choices. Indeed, one of them, Claudius Pompeianus (see **Table XXIV(a) & Brief Lives**), actually proposed the 66-year old retired general **PERTINAX** to the assembled senators, supporterd by M.' Acilius Glabrio, another kinsman of the Antonine dynasty (see **Table XXII Brief Lives**). Glabrio, a scion of the republican nobility, had been proposed as Emperor by **PERTINAX** prior to the general's acceptance of the purple, but had wisely demurred. In consequence, he left descendants traceable into the sixth century.

P. Helvius PERTINAX was born 1ˢᵗ August 126 at his mother's villa in the Appenines at Alba Pompeia (Alba). At first, from c. 147 he worked as a teacher but in 161 he became dissatisfied with the low pay – nothing changes – and joined the army. Although an equestrian, he was rapidly commissioned and enjoyed a quite remarkable career which, in view of his lack of powerful patrons, has to reflect exceedingly well on his abilities as both a soldier and an administrator. He was next appointed prefect of a cohort of Gauls in Syria, going on to become tribune of *legio* VI Victrix stationed at York. His natural aptitude and leadership qualities fuelled his rise and he was given a command in Moesia on the Danubian frontier where he quickly covered himself with glory. Thereafter he served as *procurator alimentorum* (quatermaster) and *praefectus classis* (fleet commander) in Germany.

He was made a senator about 170 by being adlected on the emperor's nomination, either amongst the tribunes of the people or the aediles. He served as praetor in 171/172, thereafter commanding a legion in Pannonia Superior, where he achieved a stunning victory beyond the frontier of the province. He was nominated suffect consul in 175, in which office his colleague was, ironically, his successor as emperor, **DIDIUS JULIANUS**, after which he governed, successively, the Moesias, Dacia and Syria being *en post* at the later when **COMMODUS** succeeded. On his return, he was encouraged to retire but was recalled in 185 to be entrusted by Commodus with the suppression of a mutiny in the army of Britain, after which he governed Africa.[211] He was appointed prefect of the City of Rome (PUR) in 189, in which office he was still serving when offered the purple, and had

---

211. PIR² H73; cf. Birley (1981) 377f., where he states that the HA biography is on the whole, truthful.

served as ordinary consul in AD192, an honour that usually accompanied the successful tenure of PUR. He was never given patrician status, and was thus the first fully recognised emperor unquestionably not to have been so.

Reign

PERTINAX was perceived as a safe pair of hands and his house was conveniently placed for the conspirators to reach under cover of darkness. The backing of the praetorian guard was, however, crucial, and their loyalty was quickly bought by a donative of HS12,000 per man, a move wisely endorsed by the new Emperor who, although thought to be strict and prudent, was reluctant to make the same mistake as **GALBA**. This sordid but necessary preliminary over, the newly acclaimed emperor, soldiers and people, marched to the senate house, where he was duly acclaimed.

Thus on 1ˢᵗ January 193, he assumed the consulship (his third) which Commodus had expected to take up, was appointed *Pater Patriae*, given the tribunician and proconsular powers. He was also named *princeps senatus* (president of the senate) and assumed the style **Imperator Caesar P. Helvius Pertinax Augustus**.[212] His wife, Flavia Titiana,[213] was made Augusta on her husband's elevation. She was a daugher of T. Flavius Claudius Sulpicianus, whom he made PUR in his own stead. Sulpicianus was later to make a bid for the purple himself in the famous 'auction' of 28ᵗʰ March 193 (see below) being relived of office in consequence, but spared in the aftermath.

The main problem to be faced was the near-bankruptcy of the treasury, not through poor administration but by the colossal cost of **COMMODUS'S** vanities and in spite of the seizure of the property of numerous liquidated senators. This **PERTINAX** rashly blamed on the Imperial freedmen, rather than on **COMMODUS** himself, the memory of whom, like that of so many tyrants, was still cherished by the Roman mob, isolated by obscurity from his murderous caprice.

The situation was, in fact, much as it had been on the assassination of **NERO**, therefore, and **PERTINAX** began to make all the same mistakes, being too strict and trying to introduce all the reforms that he rightly saw as being urgently needed rather too quickly, thus alienating most elements of the governing élite, especially the praetorian guard, who were the real power-brokers. Indeed, early in March the praetorians tried to stage a *coup* whilst **PERTINAX** was out of town, although quite why they chose the name-rich patrician consular Q. Sosius Pompeius Falco is unclear; possibly they reckoned he was worth a hefty donative should the *coup* succeed. However, it didn't really get off the ground and Falco was pardoned; the matter had not got far enough even to qualify him as an imperial claimant.

They tried again at the end of the month. On 28ᵗʰ March a detachment of some 300 guardsmen burst into the Imperial Palace and, meeting little resistance, burst in on the

212. ILS 407, 408, 409
213. PIR² F444

emperor who, despite being urged to flee, thought he could outface his attackers. Whilst reasoning with them and trying to explain his policies, one hothead, perhaps seeing that the old general was beginning to be heeded, rushed forward and ran him through with his sword shouting, 'the soldiers have sent you this', at which the remainder quite lost their grip and **PERTINAX** died under a welter of blows. He was deified by the senate 1st June 193, confirmed by an elaborate ceremony some ten days later, his cult to be supervised by the *sodales* (priests) of the cult of the Antonine Emperors.

Meanwhile the scramble for power had begun in earnest; the year of the four emperors had returned – in spades.

TABLE XXVI: THE FAMILY OF PERTINAX

It is not known from whence in the empire Pertinax's ancestors came; all that is known is that his father was a slave called Successus who was liberated probably by the Ligurian equestrian M. Helvius Maximus of Alba Pompeia.

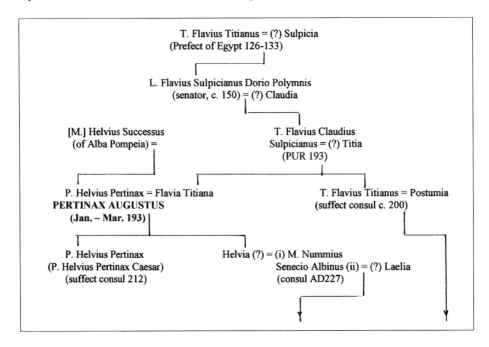

TABLE XXVI: BRIEF LIVES

T. Flavius Claudius Sulpicianus

Born at Hierapytna (Ierapetra, Crete) where his father was no doubt serving, he was suffect consul c. 170, an Arval Brother shortly afterwards, proconsul of Asia in 186 and PUR in 193.

JULIANUS pardoned him after he outbid him for the succession at the Praetorian camp in the wake of the death of **PERTINAX**, but he was killed by **SEVERUS** in 197 probably for supporting **ALBINUS**. He was a member of a complex and powerful dynasty whose influence lasted well into the fourth century [PIR² F373; Birley (1988) 84, 96, 127].

L. Flavius Sulpicianus Dorio Polymnis

A senator who flourished in the mid-2nd century. His son's nomenclature suggests that he married a Claudia.

T. Flavius T. f. Col. Titianus,

Prefect of Egypt 126-133 and from Praeneste (Palestrina) originally. If Dorio Polymnis was indeed his son, he must have married a Greek lady, probably a Sulpiciana.

T. Flavius Titianus

He was of praetorian rank by the time **SEVERUS** had finally esztablished himself and was suffect consul somewhere around 200. He married a Postumia and had two consular sons and grand-sons and the family may have continued into the fourth century [PLRE I. Titianus 8, 9; Varus 2, 3]

Helvia

Her actual name is nowhere directly atrtested, but Helvia is likely. In March AD193 she was betrothed to (and probably later married) a nephew of her father's successor **DIDIUS JULIANUS** - probably M. Nummius M. f. Senecio Albinus, consul in 227 whose mother was Vibia L. f. Salvia Varia - and spared the massacre of 28th March [PIR² H. 81]

[M.] Helvius [M.] lib. Successus

He was a successful freedman, probably given his freedom by M. Helvius Maximus an equestrian of Alba Pompeia who, after liberation made a fortune in the wool trade. He apparently married a lady from a substantial family [PIR² H77].

P. Helvius Pertinax

See above **PERTINAX AUGUSTUS**

P. Helvius [P.f.] Pertinax

After his father's acclamation, he became styled **P. Helvius Pertinax Caesar** and was made *princeps iuventutis* (leader of youth). He was born some-time prior to 175 but was still a youth at the time of his father's elevation. He was brought up in the household of his maternal aunt, Flavia Sulpiciana, in whose house he was at the time of the assassi-nation, which enabled him to escape his father's fate. He was made a member of the college of Arval Brethren in AD185 and in June 193 was appointed *flamen Helvianus* by **SEVERUS** who in 200 granted his family patrician status. He served – belatedly for a patrician – as suffect consul in 212, before being killed on the orders of **CARACALLA** for supporting his brother **GETA**. It is not known if he married or had issue; there are no persons known bearing any name that might suggest that he left descendants [ILS 410; HA, *V. Carac.* IV. 9 ; PIR² H74]

M. Nummius M. f. Senecio Albinus,

He was descended from a grand-daughter of L. Ceoionius Commodus, consul AD106. (**Table XXI Brief Lives**). If the marriage did take place, those involved were lucky to have survived the pogroms of the years leading up to **SEVERUS'S** sole rule in February 197. If they did marry, they may not have had any surviving children, for none of the descendants of Albinus carry a name obviously associated with Pertinax's family, although the consul of 227 certainly did have issue. John Morris postulates his wife as having been a daughter of M. Laelius Firminus Fulvius Maximus Aemilianus. [HA V. Pert. 15.7; ILS 410; PIR² H74; Morris (1965) 88-96 & stemma].

✳

IULIANUS I
(Known to history as DIDIUS JULIANUS)
28th March – 1st June 193

Background

Having killed **PERTINAX,** the Praetorian commanders were on the one hand fearful that the mob might take a hand and attack them but at the same time realised that the Imperial dignity was entirely in their hands. To obviate trouble with the populace, the gates of the praetorian camp were closed and to expedite the latter, word was sent out that the Guards officers were prepared to hear proposals.

In the event, two men came forward and both were essentaially prepared to offer generous donatives for each soldier. Instead of attempting to decide on the candidates' merits, the guard commanders instead decided to see who would offer the most generous donative. It was, in effect, a naked piece of auctioneering and can be seen to have permanently devalued the status of the *princeps*. The two eventual candidates were M. Didius Severus Julianus and the father-in-law of the late lamented emperor, T. Flavius Sulpicianus. Both were distiguished senators well into middle life, but after several hours of negotiations, the praetorian commanders accepted **JULIANUS'S** bid, not only because he was able to offer more money per head, but because he artfully suggested that Sulpicianus, as Pertinax's father-in-law, was likely to seek revenge on certain elements within the guard for their actions.

Although in most ways well qualified for the purple, being the second most senior ex-consul then living and with a highly distinguished career behind him, **JULIANUS'S** every action thenceforward was influenced by his being beholden, in so squalid a way, to the praetorian Guard; he was a prisoner of his own overarching ambition and lust for power. The traditional Roman noble's constant quest to enhance his *virtus* and the *dignitas* of his house was here poisoned at its apogee by the corrupt spirit in which the culmination was brought to fruit.

M. Didius Petronius Severus Julianus[214] was born at Mediolanum (Milan) on 30th January 133, brought up in the household of Domitia Lucilla, **MARCUS AURELIUS'** mother and, with her support, was elected one of the Board of Twenty, c. 153/4, and designated quaestor a year before the legal minimum age, so served in 162. He was aedile in 164, praetor in 166 – all with the Emperor's support, then went off to Germany to become legate of *Legio* XXII *Primigenia*. He then was appointed governor of Belgica, during which longish tenure he defeated a barbarian incursion. This got him an ordinary consulship with the future emperor **PERTINAX** as colleague - once again with the emperor's support - in 175. At some stage after AD180, he was also made a *sodalis Antoniniano* (priest of the cult of Antoninus Pius and Marcus Aurelius). Thereafter he governed Dalmatia followed by Lower Germany. Under **COMMODUS**, he was accused of conspiring against the emperor

---

214. ILS 412; PIR² D77

with a certain Salvius – perhaps his uncle, an ex-consul - but nothing more is heard of the matter. Thereafter he governed Bithynia and followed **PERTINAX** in the proconsulship of Africa, leading the former presciently to call him, on one celebrated occasion, 'My colleague and successor' – thereby creating an omen ripe for fulfilment.

Reign

DIDIUS JULIANUS was acclaimed emperor by the praetorians 28th March 193 and the same day was, by decree of the senate, named emperor, given the tribunician and procon-sular powers (no doubt renewable annually on 10th December) and his family adlected into the patriciate. He was thenceforth styled **Imperator Caesar M. Didius Severus Julianus Augustus.** His wife, Manlia Scantilla, was named Augusta as was his daughter, Didia Clara. He was hailed *imperator* on 9th April and coin evidence confirms that he was also Pontifex Maximus and suffect consul, his second consulship.

Once the news of the death of **PERTINAX** had reached the provinces, others, considering that they had as good a claim as **JULIANUS**, if not better (by being backed by a sizeable military force), immediately made rival bids for the supreme office. This ultimately led to the appearance during April of three imperial claimants: C. Pescennius Niger (governor of Syria), D. Clodius Albinus (governor of Britain) and L. Septimius Severus (governor of Pannonia Superior). Yet **JULIANUS** was thus suddenly faced with an appalling crisis. He found himself faced with three rivals, each backed by an army, and with formidable domestic problems: unpopularity amongst the populace in Rome, a great deal of un-co-operative cynicism amongst his fellow senators and further problems with the praetorians caused by his inability to pay the promised donative in full and on time.

Before the end of April, **JULIANUS** was forced to take defensive measures against **SEVERUS,** who had temporarily neutralised **ALBINUS** by negotiation and had acted more decisively than **NIGER,** whom he had by-passed, and marched on Rome. These prepara-tions were hampered by the reluctance of the praetorians to dirty their hands, especially in the cause of an emperor rapidly looking like a lame duck and who in any case had not fully discharged his fiscal obligations to them. **JULIANUS** therefore turned to the senate to suggest that they appoint **SEVERUS** as joint ruler, but this otherwise prudent move came too late, for **SEVERUS'S** progress was by this stage, in late May, too well advanced for there to be any doubt about the outcome.

On 1st June, the senators, doubtless fearing for themselves in the event of not having been seen to have supported **SEVERUS** from as early on in the proceedings as possible, decided to ditch **JULIANUS.** They thus elected **SEVERUS** as Emperor (with **ALBINUS** as Caesar), deified **PERTINAX** and declared the unfortunate incumbent a public enemy, passing a decree of death on him.

The hapless 'cash-and-carry' emperor was found by the senate's emissary, deserted and alone in the palace. Amid much abject pleading the sentence was pronounced and the unfortunate ruler killed.

Now all that the empire had to do was to watch the bloody contest for power amongst the three marshals unfold, taking the story into the next era of Imperial history. The Year of the Five Emperors was about to move into top gear.

Further reading:
Birley, A. R. (ed. & trans.) *Lives of the Later Caesars* (London 1976) being the first twelve – and most reliable – biographies of the *Historia Augusta*

*

TABLE XXVII: THE FAMILY OF IULIANUS I

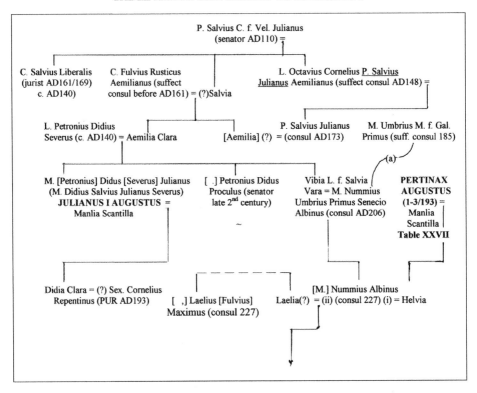

Working out the ramifications of the family of **JULIANUS** presents considerable problems, mainly stemming from the beginning of the emperor's unreliable *Life* in the HA, which reads:

> [He]…had for great-grandfather Salvius Julianus, twice consul, prefect of the City and jurisconsult…his mother was Aemilia Clara, his father Petronius Severus, his brothers Didius Proculus and Nummius Albinus and his maternal uncle Salvius Julianus. His paternal grandfather came from Mediolanum [Milan]…and his maternal grandfather from the *colonia* of Hadrametum [Sousse, Tunisia].[215]

---

215. *V. Did. Jul.* 1.

There seem to be too many people here. The alleged great grandfather presents the first problem. This Salvius Julianus – there are two in the account – was the tutor of **MARCUS AURELIUS** who was promoted at a young age by **HADRIAN**. He held the consulship – as far as we know – only once, an ordinary one later in life, in 148, having been born about 85.[216] His full name was L. Octavius Cornelius P. f. P. Salvius Julianus[217] and he was clearly of a Roman family from Bixia, but if in fact from Hadrumentum, the family were recent migrants to Africa. **DIDUS JULIANUS**, however, was born in 133, which means there can only have been one intervening generation, not two as the HA would have us believe. Another problem lies with his siblings, for Nummius Albinus cannot have been his blood brother, nor his half brother.[218] Fortunately, Nummius's wife's name gives the clue to the solution of the second problem: she was Vibia L. f. Salvia Vara, and most likely sister of the whole blood of the emperor. Her name also tells us the *praenomen* of Julianus's father, Lucius, and suggests a link somewhere back along the blood-line with the Vibii Vari, an old senatorial family which never achieved much eminence; perhaps that was how they managed to survive. Thus Nummius Albinus was **JULIANUS'S** brother-in-law, not brother. He was, of course, probably also the son-in-law of **PERTINAX** (see above, **Table XXVI Brief Lives**).

There is another problem, too. The emperor's *cognomen*, Julianus, echoes that of the eminent Antonine jurist Salvius Julianus, as does the Salvia in his sister's name, establishing the connection with the consul of 148, as alleged by the HA. However, it seems unlikely that the Salvius Julianus claimed as the uncle would have influenced the naming of both niece and nephew alone, and that the HA, a work of almost exactly two centuries later[219], merely became confused. The uncle, Salvius Julianus, must in fact have been intended for the jurist's elder son, P. Salvius Julianus, consul in 173, later one of **COMMODUS'** victims; Birley presumes that he married the sister of the emperor's mother Aemilia Clara, also allegedly Hadrumetine. The most satisfactory answer is that a sister of the jurist married the Emperor's grandfather, C. Fulvius Rusticus Aemilianus and his daughter later married the Milanese *eques* Didius Severus. On the only inscription relating to Julianus[220] his name reads:

M. Didius [Sev]erus Julianus

which unfortunately has a gap, leaving his full appellation unclear. This is probably best filled with his father's additional name, Petronius. Some of the rest can be filled from the *denarii* he issued: Imp. Caes. M. Did[ius] Sever[us] Iulian[us] Aug[ustus].[221]

---

216. Of course, he could have held a suffect consulship earlier which has dropped from record.
217. ILS 2104 – shortened version of his name – & 8973
218. Morris (1965) 91; PIR² N173
219. Syme (1968) *passim.*
220. ILS 412.:
221. *Coins of the Roman Empire in the British Museum* IV. li. 16

TABLE XXVII: BRIEF LIVES

Amelia Clara

An alternative to the Nummius connection set out here, is that this lady married (ii) a postulated Nummius, and had a son, M.Nummius Albinus, married to an Umbria, sister of M. Umbrius Primus, suffect consul 185 [Settipani (2000) 387]

Didia Clara

Augusta from March to June 193, and said to have been exceedingly beautiful. She was betrothed in March 193, to Sex. Cornelius Repentinus, an African senator appointed prefect of the city and suffect consul in 193 by **JULIANUS**. It is not certain that they actually married, but it remains likely. Repentinus was son of a Praetorian Prefect of the same name who had held office early in the reign of **MARCUS AURELIUS**. Both were spared by **SEVERUS** but their issue, if any, has not been identified [PIR² D79]

L. Fulvius Rusticus Aemilianus

Suffect consul from before 161 and probably raised to patrician status around that time. The family originated from Mediolanum (Milan) and had been senators for some three generations, although it is very difficult one to re-construct with any precision. He is thought to have married Numisia Q. f. Procula, but more than one marriage was exceedingly common amongst the Roman élite in any age and a putative marriage with a sister of the eminent Salvius Julianus might help to explain why part of his nomenclature should have descended to **JULIANUS**; the fact that the younger Julianus was his uncle by two marriages seems somehow less likely He was probably also a close relation of M. Laelius C. Fulvius Maximus, thought to have been father of the imperial claimant *IOTAPIANUS*, see **Table XXXIX Brief Lives.**

M. Laelius [Fulvius] Maximus Aemilianus

Consular colleague of M. Nummius Senecio Albinus in 227 [Mennen (2011) 105 & n. 96]

Manlia Scantilla

The Empress's origins have never been satisfactorily pinned down. She was said to have been physically ill-favoured and was given the style of Augusta in March 193 along with her daughter.

M. Nummius Senecio Albinus

Consul in 227. Suggested by Morris as the husband of a daughter of M. Laelius Firminus Fulvius Maximus [Aemilianus] and sister of Albinus's consular colleague in 227. If so, she may have followed Helvia, **PERTINAX'S** daughter (see Table XVVI above). Their posterity continued into the 5th century. [PIR² L162, 194, 198, N235; Mennen (2011) 115; Morris (1965) 88-96 & stemma].

M. Nummius M. f. Gal. Umbrius Primus Albinus

Consul in 206 and adlected into the patriciate by **SEVERUS**; believed to have been the son of M. Nummius Albinus, a senator killed in 197, and now thought to be the adoptive son of M. Umbrius Primus. [HA, *V. Pert.* 15.9; Mennen (2011) 113, n. 128, 114-115.Morris (1965) 88-96; PIR² N238].

L. Octavius Cornelius P. f. [P.] Salvius Julianus Aemilianus

Born 85, consul 148, governor of Africa 168-169; eminent jurist and tutor of **MARCUS AURELIUS** who raised his family to patrician status [FS 2559; ILS 8973 for additional *cognomen*; Birley (1987) 86]

[. Petronius] Didius Proculus

If he existed, presumably a senator [PIR² D74; HA, *V. Did. Jul.* 1]

[L.] Petronius Didius Severus

Recorded only as a *sacerdos* (priest), mid-2nd century. PIR² provides this man with ancestors, going back three generations to Q. Petronius C. f., father of Petronia Vera and Q. Petronius Severus who married Didia Iucunda and were parents of (1) Q. Petronius Severus and (2) a younger son, **JULIANUS'S** grandfather, another [?C.] Petronius Didius Severus [PIR² D77].

P. Salvius C. f. Vel. Julianus

Probably the first in his family to enter the senate in which he apears to have been active c. AD80/110. Syme considered that the family came from Brixia (Brescia) [ILS 8973; Syme RP VI 459-462].

P. Salvius Julianus

Consul 173, killed before 192 married [Aemilia] sister of Aemilia Clara, **JULIANUS'S** mother.

M. Umbrius M.f. Gal. Primus

Suffect consul in 185 or 186, and probably the adoptive father of M. Nummius Umbrius Primus Senecio Albinus. Both were in the Galeria tribe, suggesting a formal adoption; the alternative is that they were father and son, with the Consul of 206 adopted by a Nummius. [PIR² 596; Settipani (2000) 387]

Imperial Claimant under Didius Julianus

NIGER
(Known to history as Pescennius Niger)
April 193 – c. 1st May 194

Background

C. Pescennius *NIGER* really rates as an imperial claimant rather than a 'legitimate' emperor, for his elevation was never recognised by the senate. Yet he issued a fairly prolific coinage and is invariably included in the official canon of Roman emperors.

The episode of **JULIANUS'** coming to power, once news of it had reached the provinces, and more especially the armed provinces, produced outrage amongst their governors and legionary legates. Many of the former were contemporaries and perhaps even friends of the participants, but few can have failed to have been appalled by the events of 28th March 193. In the event, three senatorial governors were, or had themselves, proclaimed emperor, and a repeat of the events of 68-69 seemed about to unfold.

C. Pescennius Niger was born c. 135/140, beginning his career as a centurion in the army and by dint of talent and success, appears to have reached a senior equestrian command, distinguishing himself in Dacia early in the 180s alongside **CLODIUS ALBINUS**. This might suggest that by this time he had been adlected into the senate, but not necessarily; he could have been one of Albinus's prefecturial commanders. Nevertheless, he must have been adlected sometime in that decade, for he rose to a suffect consulship in c. 189/190, going on to govern Syria, where he was still *en post* when he heard of Pertinax's murder.[222]

---

222. This and the command in Dacia are attested by Dio LXXII. 8 & LXXIV. 6

Reign

Both **SEPTIMIUS SEVERUS** and *PESCENNIUS NIGER* were proclaimed at about the same time – immediately news came through to them at the very beginning of April; *NIGER* in Syria and **SEVERUS** in Upper Pannonia.

NIGER was proclaimed by his legions at Antioch (he could command ten overall) but seems to have thereafter made no move. Indeed, he is said to have been a rather negative sort of person, '…remarkable for nothing, good or bad'[223] which is strange, for his proclamation was widely supported by rioting in Rome.

He took the style **Imperator Caesar C. Pescennius Niger Justus Augustus,**[224] the last name, Justus, being a post-acclamatory assumption, presumably in order to set the tone for his rule. He must have achieved some kind of recognition from the senate, to whom he apparently sent numerous messages, for he assumed a second consulship either on acclamation or at the beginning of 194 - he is "co[n]s[ul]. II" on three separate types of coin - but it was, if recognised at Rome at the time, have been a suffect one for the ordinary consuls for that year were **SEVERUS** and **ALBINUS.** Likewise, his coin types understandably make no mention of the pontificate, nor of the proconsular and tribunician power.

By the time **SEVERUS,** whose province was much closer to the capital and who acted with commendable celerity once he had been acclaimed, was in control of the capital, *NIGER'S* proclamations and messages to the senate were being intercepted. By the end of June the claimant's children were being sought to be placed under house arrest, whilst those of Asellius Aemilianus - Niger's chief henchman in Rome, despite being a kinsman of **SEVERUS'** then ally, **CLODIUS ALBINUS** - were seized.

NIGER set up HQ at Byzantium and began to strike coins (albeit from rather crudely engraved dies), but was besieged there by an army under L. Marius Maximus, later a notable historian, to whose aid **SEVERUS** had despatched his ally L. Fabius Chilo, before even having arrived in Rome. However, Chilo had suffered a reverse by July, but nevertheless *NIGER'S* success caused the senate, under pressure from **SEVERUS,** to declare him a public enemy. Undeterred, *NIGER* remained confident and was soon calling himself a 'New Alexander', despite being put on the defensive by the proximity of Marius Maximus and the imminent arrival of **SEVERUS** himself. Not long afterwards, **SEVERUS** having arrived, *NIGER* made an offer to share the Empire with him, which was summarily rejected, although as a counter-offer, **SEVERUS** declared that he was prepared to spare his rival's life if he were to surrender and go into exile. This offer may have been refused on the basis that **SEVERUS** was unlikely to honour it and indeed, his later treatment of opponents rather re-inforces such a view. It may be too, that *NIGER* saw that remaining in control of the east and consolidating his

223. Dio LXXIV
224. Coin evidence

position might be a better medium term policy, rather anticipating in the sort of division of the empire made by **VALERIAN** and **GALLIENUS**, later by the Tetrarchs and permanently by **THEODOSIUS I.**

By October, *NIGER'S* lieutenant Aemilianus had been defeated and killed and, by the beginning of 194, **SEVERUS'** general Ti. Claudius Candidus had won a last minute victory over *NIGER* at Nicaea, news of which caused Egypt to defect to **SEVERUS.** After two further months of cat-and-mouse, a final battle was fought on the river Issus, the site of one of Alexander the Great's most momentous victories, ironically enough, bearing in mind the challenger's propaganda – in which *NIGER'S* forces were routed and he himself fled to Antioch, intending to make for Parthia, but was caught and killed in late April or early May. The last resistance was over by 21st of the latter month.

Thereafter, **SEVERUS'S** only rival was **ALBINUS.**

*

TABLE XXVIII: THE FAMILY OF PESCENNIUS NIGER

The main problem with *NIGER* is the sparseness of information about him. Even the HA, bursting with information, almost all of it extremely unreliable, gives the game away by saying:

> It is unusual and difficult to set down a proper written account of those whom the victory of others made into usurpers (*tyranni*). For this reason not all the facts about these men are fully recorded in the chronicles and annals….Not much care is taken in research into their life and antecedents.[225]

Thus, what follows is the HA's idea of *NIGER'S* family and is not to be relied upon in any way. People whose existence can be checked against other sources are so indicated.

Niger's **grandfather** was allegedly a minor official at Aquinum (Aquino), whence the family came – although the writer of the HA immediately qualifies this information with '…although this fact is even now considered doubtful'.[226] We are not vouchsafed his name. Neither can we be sure of his father's name; in the table below it has been suggested that, if it was correct, it represented a possible adoption, as shown. Alternatively, the father might have been born an Annius but adopted by a Pescennius, possibly even a senatorial one. Everyone else is independently attested, although we have no hint as to the actual names of Niger's wife, sons or daughters-in-law.

SEVERUS returned to Rome and conducted a bloody purge of senators who had been disloyal in various ways. In the HA's list of these unfortunates, some of the names

---

225. HA *Pesc. Niger* 1.1-2
226. A republican *triumvir capitalis* (and thus a potential senator) C. Pescennius in 129 and L.Pescennius T. f. who made a dedication at Firmum at about the same period are recorded; one of them or a kinsman may well have enfranchised Niger's family.

are attested; it includes a whole gaggle of Pescennii.[227] Although the HA does not claim that they were kinsmen of Niger, the implication is pretty clear. Yet, if *NIGER* and his brother were the first senators of their family, as would seem to be the case, there is hardly enough scope to explain the appearance of no less than five senatorial kinsmen, although the ramifications of the family of Septimius **SEVERUS** might suggest that this is not entirely impossible. But if so, why do neither Dio nor Herodian mention it? These men are thus all Pescennii, their *cognomina* being: Festus, Veratianus, Aurelianus, Materianus, Julianus and Albinus.

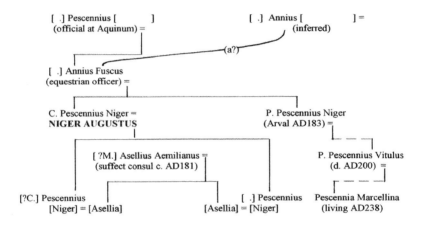

TABLE XXVIII: BRIEF LIVES

Annius Fuscus

Given by the HA as the Emperor's father. Had his name included the additional *nomen,* Annius, it would probably have come down to us, so Fuscus's very existence has to be treated with caution. Adoption by an Annius would clear the anomaly up, but cannot be substantiated.

[?M.] Asellius Aemilianus

Probably of an emergent family, he would have been born c. 138, suffect consul c. 181, legate of Syria 189, proconsul of Asia in 193 (no doubt appointed by **NIGER**),

killed by **SEVERUS** after his rival's defeat. The Asellius Claudianus alleged by the HA as a victim of Severus, would have been a close kinsman, were we able to verify his existence [Dio, 74, 6; Herodian, 3, 2, 2-3; HA *V. Severi* XIII, 1]

Pescennia Marcellina

The rareness of the name amongst the élite suggests that this lady, was a member of this ephemeral Imperial Family. Depending of her age, she would have probably been the daughter or sister of Vitulus. Although only in the HA, the fact that she defrayed the costs of the praetorship – essentially the praetorian games – of the future emperor **PUPIENUS MAXIMUS** c. AD210 is quirky enough to have the ring of truth, although rather less likely, she is said to have 'adopted him as a son' However, Maximus's names are too well attested to admit the possibility of a Pescennius element amongst them. [HA: V. *Max & Balb.* V, 7].

Pescennii

The HA claims **NIGER** had two sons; both of them married daughters of Asellius Aemilianus [PIR² P255, cf. 256].

P. Pescennius Niger

He is attested as a member of the Arval Brotherhood, c. AD160s to after AD183, which was a very prestigious preferment for a wholly new man who was but of praetorian rank. The prospect of the HA being completely wrong and the family having been senatorial after all has to be kept in mind. If indeed a relation, he was probably killed following his elder brother's defeat. PIR² tries to identify him with his brother, but that would necessitate two mason's errors [FS2644; cf. PIR² P253].

P. Pescennius Vitulus

A senator and *Salius Palatinus* who died in AD200. Assuming HA's list of supernumerary Pescinnii is false, then he is likely to have been a son of the preceding, who possibly died in his father's lifetime, but if the five unfortunate Pescennii really existed, he could be the son of any one of them. In either case, as a Palatine Priest, he was probably a patrician, although it is difficult to envisage the occasion of such a conferral of rank [FS2645; PIR² P257].

*

ALBINUS
(Known to history as Clodius Albinus)
c. June 195 – 19th February 197

Background

D. Clodius Albinus must have been born about 147 since he appears to have become a senator c. 175, although his quaestorship might have preceded this date. The outline given in the HA is not to be trusted, as Birley points out.[228] Prior to that, he would have served on one of the various boards of young careerists who made up the viginvirate followed – it would certainly appear – by a period as military tribune. His praetorship would have fallen in the earlier 180s (it is impossible to determine if he held an aedileship or a peoples' tribunate) followed by the command of a legion and/or governorship of a minor province. The HA tells us that his military tribunate was in command of Dacian cavalry, that his minor governorship was Bithynia and that he was governor of Lower Germany, none of which

---

228. Birley (1981) 147.

can be otherwise attested.[229] It is thought by modern scholarship that the Lower Germany appointment is likely and that it would have immediately preceded his certain appointment to Britain in 191, thus falling in 189/190. This would put his suffect first consulship c. 187 or 188. If the German governorship is rejected, the consulship can be safely re-allocated to 190, in which year there were, in addition to the two ordinary consuls, no less than 22 suffect ones, of whom only about eight are known for certain.

He married a wife whose name is not known for certain, although the HA claims **MARCUS AURELIUS'** son-in-law M. Peducaeus Plautius Quintillus as **ALBINUS'S** father-in-law, whioch would make her Peducaea Plautia.[230] Whilst one might have expected so momentous a fact to have been recorded elsewhere, the effectiveness of **ALBINUS'S** subsequent condemnation may have eradicated this 'slur' on the family of the divine **MARCUS**, especially once **SEVERUS** had attached himself to it in 195; the connection is supported indeed, by T. D. Barnes.[231] Perhaps **ALBINUS'S** wife was indeed a daughter of Quintillus but by a previous wife. They are known to have had two sons either killed on 19th February 197 or exiled then and killed later with their mother, when Severus carried out his cull of the senate.[232]

He was not acclaimed *imperator* by his soldiers as far as we know – although such an event is quite possible and had happened (abortively) twice in Britain during the reign of **COMMODUS** – but was appointed Caesar by **SEVERUS** in early April 193 in order to secure his flank against a potent rival. He took the style **D. Clodius Albinus Caesar**[233] and we may assume that the senate ratified this state of affairs after June 1st, and no doubt granted him, with **SEVERUS,** the tribunician and proconsular power, renewable every 10th December in the usual way. He probably acquired an imperial acclamation from his army, too. June 193 probably also marks the change in his style to **D. Clodius Septimius Albinus Caesar**[234] the addition of 'Septimius' being to set out the more clearly his position as notional heir of **SEVERUS**.[235] He was (ordinary) consul (ii) with **SEVERUS** for 194. Through most of his subsequent period in power he was effectively ruling and administering the northern European provinces: the Gauls, Germanies, Britain , Spain, almost as a forerunner of the Gallic Empire which arose under **GALLIENUS**.

Nobody can tell what **CLODIUS ALBINUS'S** true intentions were when he heard about the murder of **PERTINAX** in April 193. Furthermore, his mother was from Hadrumetum (Sousse) in Africa, from whence some of **JULIANUS'S** family also hailed, which might have inclined **SEVERUS** to believe him unreliable. Another consideration was that Asellius

---

229. V. *Albini* 6. 1-6

230. HA, V. *Albini* 10.7. See **Table XXIV Brief Lives**.

231. *The Sources of the Historia Augusta* (Brussels 1978) 52; but peremptorily denied by Birley (1988) 244 n. 26, who is happier going along with an Asellia.

232. Marius Maximus, quoted in HA, V. *Albini* VII. 3, IX. 4

233. Coin evidence

234. ILS 414, 415

235. It is always possible, of course, that he was formally adopted by **SEVERUS** in order to become Caesar.

Aemilianus, who had swung his considerable influence behind *NIGER* was (according to the HA at least) related to **ALBINUS.** To drive a wedge between them might also be prudent; more to the point, it might even open Aemilianus to offers.

Judging by the speed of events, little discussion through messages passing along the *cursus publicus* (postal system) can have taken place. The likelihood is that **SEVERUS** sent a message saying that he had been proclaimed and offering **ALBINUS** the role of junior colleague and eventual successor. This would have been perfectly convincing, bearing in mind that **SEVERUS'** two sons were five and four years old respectively and that infant mortality was high.

On the other hand, there must always have been the fear that **SEVERUS** would eventually dump his fellow African, an eventuality for which there seems no doubt that **ALBINUS** prepared over the years of their partnership. Initially, however, whilst **SEVERUS** advanced rapidly on Rome against **DIDIUS JULIANUS,** and then east to deal with *NIGER* and the Parthians, **ALBINUS** held northern Europe for him

Reign

ALBINUS was apparently regarded as a good-natured man, and seems happy to have remained in Britain as Caesar for the two years following his appointment, although in regular contact with Rome, presumably for administrative purposes; in the capital he was getting quite a bit of support from senators who preferred him to **SEVERUS**. Had he any serious suspicions of his senior colleague he would surely have crossed the channel and marched on Rome himself, a relatively safe option, as **SEVERUS** was for a long time away, following up his victory over **NIGER** followed by a punitive expedition against Parthia.

However, in the middle of this campaign, about May 195, **SEVERUS** announced that he was the 'son of the Divine **MARCUS**' (Aurelius) and at the same time proclaimed as Caesar his elder son Bassianus, renaming him, in accordance with his bizarre self-adoption into the Antonines, **M. Aurelius Antoninus Caesar**. As soon as this news reached **ALBINUS**, his position must suddenly have appeared exceedingly precarious.

Yet **SEVERUS** could not risk a war against **ALBINUS** whilst advancing on Nisibis, the Parthian capital; perhaps he wanted the news that there was another official heir to force **ALBINUS'S** hand so that, by the time he was back in the west, he had a ready made *causus belli* to use against his erstwhile colleague. He had apparently already attempted to have **ALBINUS** assassinated.

ALBINUS could thus either resign, and hope to be allowed to retire, or fight. He chose the latter and, crossing the channel, declared himself Augustus in opposition to **SEVERUS**. This provoked the latter to call upon the senate to declare **ALBINUS** a public enemy, which they did on 15th December 195; this was his 'official' deposition.

SEVERUS arrived back in Rome by the end of August 196, having taken measures to bottle **ALBINUS** up in Northern Europe, although one general, Virius Lupus – ancestor of a long line of senators – was dealt a drubbing by **ALBINUS'** forces. Nevertheless, by autumn, **SEVERUS** had gone north again and was heading a campaign to finish the matter.

When **ALBINUS** assumed the purple on his own account, he styled himself **Imperator Caesar D. Clodius Septimius Albinus Augustus**. Whilst one might have expected him to have dropped the Septimius element pretty quickly, it appears on three versions of his coinage titulature before being dropped. It is possible, in the light of the savagery meted out to over sixty senators after his fall, that the senate may – at least for a time - have recognised him as co-emperor, but this would have ceased before Severus returned to Rome in May 196. He does not appear to have held or claimed the pontificate.

Despite heading a much superior force against **ALBINUS,** however, it took **SEVERUS** until February 197 to bring the matter to a resolution. Yet **SEVERUS** came within an ace of losing the final battle outside Lugdunum (Lyon) in Gaul on the 19th before fortune swung his way, **ALBINUS'** forces were eventually crushed, the city burned, plundered and the corpse of the unfortunate co-emperor brought to him to be humiliatingly mutilated and thrown into the Rhône. The HA claims the Empress and those of his children who were present also died, but there is a suspicion that his wife may have died prior to his elevation, otherwise she would without doubt appeared on coins, nor does either Dio or Herodian mention them.[236]

Family

As with *NIGER*, the family of **ALBINUS** is only recorded in any detail in the pages of the *Historia Augusta* and is thus exceedingly suspect. The only things other sources attest is that his family was noble (that is senatorial and 'patrician born'[237]) came from Africa (Hadrumetum)[238] and that he was married with children. He was also closely related to Asellius Aemilianus, *NIGER'S* chief lieutenant.[239] The remaining reliable facts about **ALBINUS** come from Dio and Herodian, too.[240] The reliable elements in the HA probably came from the lost history by Marius Maximus. The HA claims a descent for him from the Ceionii and Postumii Albini[241], whilst going on directly to explain the name Albinus in the light of the whiteness (Latin *albus* = white) of his skin both as an infant and as an adult. This is thought by Sir Ronald Syme, perfectly reasonably, to be a satirical reference to the pretensions (if any there actually were) of the rather grand Ceionii Albini of the HA's putative author's day.[242] There was no senatorial family of Clodii using the *praenomen* Decimus, however, although it could have been adopted from a marriage alliance with a D. Junius (much commoner) of course. Africa, however, also produced the near contemporary equestrian official D. Clodius Galba, which might serve to confirm the African origin claimed for him. **ALBINUS** also is alleged to have had kinsmen, Aelius Bassianus[243],

236. Eg., Herodian, 2, 15, 2; Dio says he 'excelled in family' LXXXVI.6.2
237. *Ibid.,* 3, 5, 2
238. Coin evidence confirms this
239. Dio LXXIV, 6.2
240. *Ibid.,* LXXIII 14, 3 Herodian, 2, 15; 3, 6, 6, 3 & 7.1.
241. V. *Albini,* 4. 1 - unlikely, and unattested as an alliance at any period.
242. Syme (1968) 163, supported by Settipani (2000) 284 n.
243. HA, V. *Albini* 4. 7

Clodius Celsinus, Baebius Maecianus and Lollius Serenus[244] none of whom are elsewhere attested, although the first looks as if he should be related to the later Severi (see below) and the second name first appears in the later 3rd century as the ancestor of a distinguished 4th century family. The remaining two are expressed on **Table XXIX** as possible brothers-in-law of the emperor. Only those names in Italics represent attested personages. Finally, the link with *NIGER'S* lieutenant Asellius Aemilianus is highly unlikely, and the wife of **ALBINUS** may stand as *possibly* Peducaea Plautilla. As almost everyone on **TABLE XXIX** is probably fictional, Brief Lives have been dispensed with.

TABLE XXIX: THE FAMILY OF CLODIUS ALBINUS

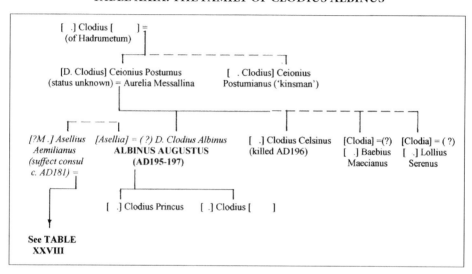

*

SEVERUS I
(Known to history as SEPTIMIUS SEVERUS)
9th April 193 – 4th February 211

Background

L. Septimius SEVERUS was born 11th April 145 of native Punic stock from Lepcis Magna (Khoms, Libya) in Africa, a soldier of exceptional ability and a man apparently utterly convinced in his own destiny.[245] He is thought to have served on the Board of Twenty in 164 and served as quaestor in 169 and again, in Sardinia in 170-1. He served as legionary legate to his cousin C. Septimius Severus during his proconsulship of Africa in 173-74 serving immediately thereafter as peoples' tribune. He married in 173 or 174 a Lepcis lady, Paccia

---

244. HA, *op.cit.* 6, 1
245. FS 3036; PIR² S346

Marciana, who died c. 184/186.[246] There may have been two daughters of the marriage if the HA is to be believed, but they are not attested elsewhere, despite being allegedly provided with husbands and dowries in 193.[247] He was praetor in 177 and thereafter a legionary legate of *Legio IV Scythica* in Syria under the future emperor **PERTINAX** but both were dismissed in 182.

His career went into eclipse until he was recalled to govern Gallia Lugdunensis in 184. In the summer of 187 he re-married, his bride being Julia Domna, daughter of Julius Bassianus, a member of the ruling family of Emesa and high priest of the local cult there, and by her had two sons. He went on to govern Sicily in 189, and in 190 he was one of the unprecedented 24 suffect consuls appointed. In summer 191 he was appointed governor of Upper Pannonia, where he was acclaimed emperor 9th April 193 and received his first imperial acclamation.

It has been suggested that **SEVERUS** was lined up as a sort of imperial long-stop, when **PERTINAX** was elevated to the purple, in case anything went wrong. His appointment to Upper Pannonia in summer 191, effectively by praetorian prefect Aemilius Laetus (also an African), after having been left idle following his consulship, is instructive; his was the nearest army to Italy, too. Was the murder of **COMMODUS** and elevation of **PERTINAX** (or some worthy brother-in-law of the emperor) already being planned by Laetus and his brother Pudens with a medium term maturation date? Did the conspirators forsee **PERTINAX** (or other mature contender) as a holding candidate like **NERVA**, prior to putting in their own man and fellow African?

The fact that **PERTINAX** had to face down two alleged plots prior to his own murder – those of Maternus and Falco, neither of which got far enough even to qualify as imperial acclamations – may, as we have seen, have put **SEVERUS** on the alert. Even if Laetus had *not* told him he was their preferred candidate (it would have been safer not to, after all), his own astrologically propelled ambitions might well have been sufficient for him to be well positioned to sieze the main chance.

Reign

When the crunch came and the news of **PERTINAX'S** murder reached him, it is not clear whether **SEVERUS** proclaimed himself emperor before he heard about the elevation of **NIGER** or not; without doubt, the news soon reached him, and hence his neutralising of **ALBINUS** in Britain by associating him in power as Caesar. He made all the right decisions thereafter, however. He marched swiftly on Rome, stayed aloof once news reached him of the death of **JULIANUS** – psychologically very astute – before neutralising the praetorian guard, taking them by surprise by sacking the entire corps and then entering the City and restoring order with brutal thoroughness, reserving sufficient tact to avoid further rioting by supporters of *NIGER.*

---

246. ILS 440
247. *Op. cit.*, V. *Sev.* 8.1; of course, if they existed, they could have died in infancy.

He then received an imperial acclamation, his second, and contrived an elaborate ceremony of deifying **PERTINAX**, whose name he took, before setting out for the east to deal with *NIGER*, whose entourage and supporters he extirpated ruthlessly: a warning, if any were needed one might think, for those in Rome who might by inclined to switch their allegiance to **ALBINUS**, once he had declared in his own favour. Following this he waged a brilliantly successful campaign deep into Parthia as further retribution for the Parthian king's support of *NIGER,* looting Ctesiphon, restoring the recaptured Trajanic province of Mesopotamia, attempting to capture Hatra and making a visitation of Egypt.

It was during this campaign that he declared himself to be a son of **MARCUS AURELIUS** and made his son Bassianus Caesar, thus throwing down the gauntlet to **ALBINUS**. As **SEVERUS** returned slowly west in 196, **ALBINUS** set about trying to consolidate a power base from which to match **SEVERUS** in the inevitable clash. He should have advanced on Rome as soon as he heard of his rival's dynastic declaration in 195; only that could have given him the advantage he needed, commanding as he did, far fewer legions. Even so, the final battle was an extremely close-run thing.

On his return, **SEVERUS** cowed the senate much as Sulla had done at the end of the Social War, and proscribed 67 senators, of whom 29 were actually killed. The amount of property seized caused him to appoint a new procurator to deal with it all. He debased the coinage to pay the army, their first rise for over a century; even **ALBINUS'S** coinage was of a better standard. This marked the first of many debasements that happened with increasing frequency during the ninety or so years to come. He formed a fresh praetorian guard from provincial soldiers drawn from his loyal legions and permitted soldiers the right to marry for the first time.

As the self-styled avenger of **PERTINAX,** he initially styled himself **Imperator Caesar L. Septimius Severus Pertinax Augustus.** On 9th June 193 he was voted the tribunician and proconsular powers (although as proconsul of an armed province he already had the latter short term), both renewable on 10th December each year, and the pontificate.[248] He also assumed the (suffect) consulship, his second, and before departing to deal with *NIGER* was also voted the style Father of his Country (*pater patriae*). He received two more imperial acclamations the year following, four in 195, another after **ALBINUS'S** defeat in 197 and another two later that year, adding a British one in 207, twelve in all.

In 194 he was ordinary consul (iii) and in the summer of the following year re-styled himself **Imperator Caesar L. Septimius Divi Marci Pii f. Divi Commodi fra[ter] Severus Pius Pertinax Augustus Arabicus Adiabenicus** - the latter pair of honorifics being added to mark his wresting of those provinces back from the Parthians - at the same time re-naming his elder son Bassianus 'Antoninus' and declaring him Caesar. Just as his attempt to link himself to the name of **PERTINAX** was useful in his initial efforts to legitimise his position, now he was keen to associate himself with the preceding dynasty to which he indeed had marital links, via the Petronii Mamertini and the brothers L. and M. Flavius

---

248. ILS 413

Aper. In other words, the link, one that was well known amongst the senatorial élite, was something he clearly felt could be drawn upon, enhance and make concrete in order to give his régime an additional underpinning of legitimacy. So confident was he that he felt able to call himself **COMMODUS'S** adoptive brother, no doubt as a sop to the people, who had much less cause to hate the late tyrant than the senate, whose numbers he had so assiduously diminished. Henceforth **SEVERUS** was another son of the Divine **MARCUS** and his elder son could stand confidently as heir bearing the late and well beloved emperor's name too. In 198, after his second eastern campaign, he added **Parthicus Maximus** to his titles and in 209 or 210 further added **Britannicus Maximus**.

By the time he returned from the East in 202, his elder son Bassianus, now M. Antonius Antoninus but known to history as **CARACALLA**, had been declared co-Augustus, but his arranged marriage to the daughter of Severus' boyhood friend and closest advisor, C. Fulvius Plautianus – commander of the Praetorian Guard with extra powers which he seems to have mis-used extensively – was much resented. In 205, Plautianus was summarily killed, either for plotting to seize the empire for himself, or because Caracalla had 'set him up' in revenge for having had to marry the daughter whom he hated. She herself was sent into exile and was killed as soon as her ex-husband succeeded in his own right.

In 208 **SEVERUS** set out for Britain, taking both his sons – for long irreconcilably at loggerheads – with him. The province had suffered a barbarian insurrection and internal tribal rebellion during the period when **ALBINUS**, the governor, was pursuing his imperial ambitions in Gaul, and the emperor's intention seems to have been to settle the island once and for all – to carry on, as it were, where Cn. Julius Agricola had left off 125 years before. The younger son, **GETA** was left in charge of civil administration whilst **CARACALLA** and his father campaigned north of the wall, meeting with a considerable measure of success, although **SEVERUS'S** increasing frailty combined with **CARACALLA'S** indifference to the aims of the war made them less effective than intended.

They retired to Eburacum (York) for the close season 210-211, where **SEVERUS** finally breathed his last on 4th February in the latter year. He was the last emperor to die in his bed of natural causes until **DIOCLETIAN** a century later. Having decided that he had curried sufficient favour with the army, **CARACALLA** immediately declared that enough had been done in settling the north – an ironic echo of Commodus's breaking off the Marcomannic War in 180 – and the two brothers returned in haste to Rome with their father's ashes. On arrival the senate decreed his deification – a move that no doubt stuck in the craw of many senators, resentful at **SEVERUS'S** brutality and lack of respect for the institution that they represented and which, after all, effectively produced the elite that governed the empire for him.

Whilst he restored stability to the empire, his cruelty and single-mindedness finally ended the deferential diarchy which had existed between princeps/emperor and the senate under the long summer of the Antonines. The disturbances which followed from the assassination of **COMMODUS** were far more prolonged at almost four years than anything that followed the death of **NERO.** Yet it was a mere *apéritif* for the chaotic years to come in the mid-3rd century. Nevertheless, as a war-leader – whether against rivals or foreign enemies – his arms met with an unparalleled success never to be seriously repeated. He had, indeed, left a legacy of stability and good government unaffected by the rivalry and cruelty of the court.

Family

L. Septimius Severus was a scion of a well-to-do family of equestrian rank and native (Punic) descent from Lepcis Magna in the province of Africa, where they appear to have been part of the local aristocracy. They would also appear to have acquired full citizenship in the earlier Flavian era, perhaps through the patronage of a member of the late Republican senatorial family of T. Septimius Sabinus, proscribed by the triumvirs in 43, although the last recorded member of the family was a mere *curule aedile* under Augustus with no obvious African connections.[249] Another possibility is that they were enfranchised by Septimius Flaccus, legate of *Legio III Augusta* stationed at Lepcis in the Flavian period – assuming, that is, the name is not an error for 'Suellius'.[250]

The pedigree is largely based on that of Birley.[251] Interestingly, **SEVERUS** belonged to the junior branch of the family, members of which were still of equestrian status when their cousins were enjoying consulships. The earliest likely ancestor bore a name redolent with the glories of the Barcid dynasty of Carthage, Hanno.

The table that follows is securely based on Anthony Birley's with a few minor adjustments; a somewhat different interpretation of the evidence produced in Settipani's pedigrees.[252] The latter adduces the name Geta amongst the Severan family as being possibly descended via M. Vitorius Marcellus (a friend of L. Septimius Macer c. 100) from C. Hosidius Geta of a prominent Julio-Claudian senatorial family which probably requires too many assumptions.

---

249. ILS 5921, 7856
250. Birley (1988) 219
251. *Op. cit.,* 212-229
252. Settipani (200) 234, where the *praenomen* of the consul (ii) of 207 is given as Caius.

TABLE XXX (a): THE FAMILY OF SEPTIMIUS SEVERUS

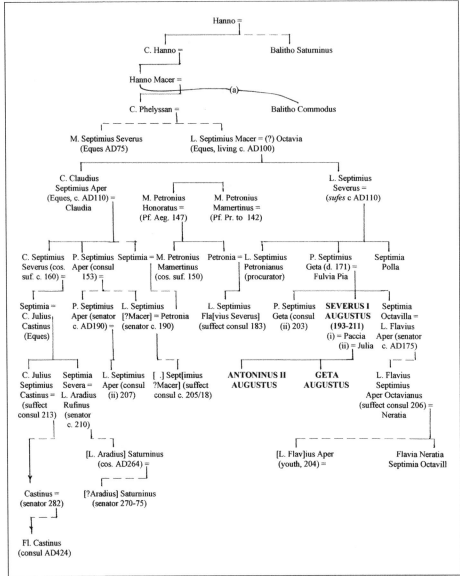

SEVERUS'S mother was a Fulvia Pia from Lepcis and that connection led to her nephew, C. Fulvius Plautianus being appointed one of the Emperor's first praetorian prefects at the beginning of his reign. His daughter subsequently married **CARACALLA**, but was repudiated by him when Plautianus fell in 205. Whilst the putative connection with the emperor **GORDIANUS III** may be pressing the rather patchy sources too hard, it remains as a possibility, re-inforced by the position of a likely nephew of **CARACALLA** as ordinary consul for the fateful year which brought the Gordian family, albeit fleetingly, to power. Again, Settipani adduces a complex nexus of kinship between Plautianus and the Haterii and Plautii of Lepcis Magna, but supported by few solid attested relationships, and resting solely upon nomenclature, where in truth, most of the names are really relatively common ones. It seemed too speculative to be included here.[253] What is slightly speculative is the relationship between Timisitheus and the wife of Fulvius Faustinus

TABLE XXX (b): SEVERAN KIN

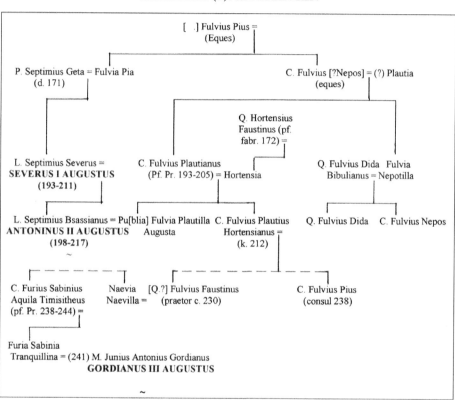

TABLES XXX(a) & (b): BRIEF LIVES

[L.] Aradius [Roscius] Rufinus [Saturninus Tiberianus]

This man is thought to be an early 3rd century junior senator; he was a *IIIvir stlitibus judicandus* and a *curio*. Probably a second generation senator, his father, Aradius Rufinus being apparently the first of the family in the senate; they were from Bulla Regia (near Jendouba, Tunisia) in Africa. This man's elder brother founded a line which is

traceable to the 5th century [FS 704; PIR² A1013]

[L. Aradius] Saturninus

Consul in 264, according to PLRE, possibly to be identified with the imperial claimant *SATURNINUS II* who made an unsuccessful bid for power against **GALLIENUS** between the date of the consulship and the latter's death in 268 – assuming he really existed, despite his three mentions in the HA. [HA *V Gallieni*, 9. 1, *TT*. 23, 1-2, 4 & *Firmi* 2. 1; PLRE I. Saturninus 1,2, p. 805]

[. Aradius] Saturninus

A senator living in the reign of the emperor **AURELIAN** [PLRE I. Saturninus 3].

[C.(?) A]teius Junius Tiberianus

A military tribune in 249 and probably to be identified with the Junius who was consul in 263 [PIR[2] I842; PLRE I Tiberianus 1],

Castinus

Senator in 282 and a possible grandson of C. Julius Septimius Castinus killed 218 (qv) although as he was commemorated as a native of Legio (Asturias, Spain) a note of caution is in order [PIR[2] C535 PLRE I Castinus 1]

C. Cl[audius] Septimius Aper

His mother was probably a Claudius, from one of the local families bearing that *nomen* [Birley (1988) Appendix 2, No. 16]

Flavia Neratia Septimia Octavilla

Unmarried lady of senatorial rank early 3rd century, who set up a dedication to her father [CIL. VI. 1415].

L. Flavius Aper

Senator c. AD175/180, younger brother of M. Flavius Aper who probably married the grand-daughter of **MARCUS AURELIUS, see TABLE XXIV(c).**

[L. Flav]ius Aper

Clarissimus puer (a boy of senatorial rank) in 204. He may have grown up to marry and have descendants, although L. Flavius Aper, suffect consul between 268 and 282 seems to have begun as an

equestrian governor (*praeses*) of Pannonia Inferior, which would suggest that he was unrelated, but note also [? Flavius] Ap[er] who was consul in the Gallic empire between 262 and 266 [PLRE I. Aper 1-3].

L. Flavius Septimius Aper Octavianus

Peoples' tribune under Severus, later suffect consul c. 206 and a priest of the cult of Hadrian. He married Neratia probably daughter or grand-daughter of L. Neratius Proculus, suffect consul 160 [CIL.VI. 1415; FS 1710]

Fulvia Nepotilla

Sister of the praetorian prefect, her husband is thought tto have mbeen a fairly close relative. The status of their offspring is not wholly clear. [Birley (1988) 221]

Pu[blia] Fulvia Plautilla

She married **CARACALLA** in 202 after a two year betrothal, was divorced in 205 and liquidated in 212. She was made Augusta on her marriage [PIR[2] F564; Birley (1988) Appendix 2, No. 29].

[.] Fulvius Pius

Equestrian originating from Lepcis; although only known from HA, his reality generally accepted [HA *V. Sev.* I. 2].

[?Q.] Fulvius Faustinus

Suggested here as a possible brother of C. Fulvius Pius (qv). He was an ex-praetor in the early 3rd century who was married to Naevia Naevilla

C. Fulvius Pius

Ordinary consul in 238, the year in which his future and putative nephew by marriage came to power [PIR[2] F553]

C. Fulvius C. f. Quir. Plautianus

SEVERUS' cousin, comrade-in-arms and

praetorian prefect from his accession. Later granted the style of a senator as *clarissimus vir* (*cv*), obtained consular rank through having been awarded triumphal ornaments and given patrician status. He was consul (ii) 203. He fell from power, was exiled and killed 205, and suffered *damnatio memoriae*. His wife's name is not 100% certain, but generally accepted. There were no Hortensii at Lepcis, so she may have been of an Italian family; Q. Hortensius Q. f. Col. Faustinus, an equestrian officer who served as *praefectus fabrorum* (*pf fabr.*) 172 and was a patron of Tibur (Tivoli), which might explain the probable recurrence of the *cognomen* two generations on [FS 1773; ILS 1328, 8662, 8689 & 9003;PIR² F554 & H208]

C. Fulvius C. f. Quir. Plautius Hortensianus

Son of the praetorian prefect, he was killed in 212. Settipani conjectures that he may married the sister of L. Aurelius Gallus (consul 198 & one of **SEVERUS'** victims) and was ancestor of the later Neratii. [ILS 9004; Settipani (2000) 328]

C. Furius Sabinius Aquila Timisitheus

Eastern-born praetorian prefect to **GORDIAN III** to whom in 241 he married his daughter. He was probably born a Sabinius and it is thought his mother was a Naevia, which would explain the name of his sister, the wife of Fulvius Faustinus (qv); see also **Table XXXIV Brief Live**s. [ILS 1330].

C. [H]anno

Of Lepcis 53/54, dedicated a public building in the names of his son and grandson. His name essentially means Caius son of [H]anno [Birley (1988) 213 No. 2]

[H]anno Macer

Of Lepcis, mid-1st century [Birley (1988) 213 No. 3]

C. [H]anno f. Phelyssam

Of Lepcis young in 53 [Birley (1988) 213 No 6].

C. Julius Septimius Castinus

A trusted friend of **CARACALLA**, suffect consul 213, killed 218 by **ELAGABALUS.** [ILS 1153; PIR² I566; Birley (1988) 215 No. 19].

Paccia Marciana

Of Punic origin, she was the first wife of **SEVERUS,** only possibly the mother of two short-lived daughters who are only mentioned in HA and thus of dubious authenticity. She died 187 at the latest [CIL.VIII. 19494; Birley (1988) 225 No. 56]

M. Petronius Honoratus

Prefect of Egypt in 147. He and his brother (below) were sons of M. Petronius Sura, a procurator from Africa. A possible third brother (or other close relative), Sex. Petronius Mamertinus, seems to have entered the senate directly, being quaestor c. 121 praetor later [FS 2660; PIR² P281]

M. Petronius Mamertinus

Praetorian prefect 139-142 [PIR² P288]

M. Petronius Mamertinus,

Suffect consul 150, adlected by **ANTONINUS** into the patriciate, a kinsman of the orator, M. Cornelius Fronto and son of L. Septimius Severus's brother-in-law, Honoratus. PIR on the other hand, makes him son of Mamertinus. His elder son married Cornificia, daughter of **MARCUS AURELIUS, see Table XXIV(d) Brief Lives.** PIR² P287; Birley (1988) 225 No.57]

Septimia Polla

Unmarried and very rich she was commemorated

by a silver statue at Lepcis. [Birley (1988) 214 No. 10]

Septimia Severina

A Christian lady of senatorial rank who married in 363 Flavius Julius Catervius, a senator of prefectorial rank who died in 379, having been a senior official of the Imperial Treasury (*Comes Sacrae Largitionum*). Whilst the lady's names were both relatively common, the combination (albeit the second one in the diminutive) might have been regarded as a trifle presumptuous without a blood line to support it. Their son was named Bassus, an echo of **CARACALLA'S** original *cognomen*. [PLRE 1.Bassus 7, Severina 1].

[.] Sept[imius   ]

Governor of Pannonia in the period AD211/222 and therefore a former sufferct consul in an unknown year [Birley (1988) 214 No. 12]

[.] Septimius [   ]

Governor of Dalmatia and imperial claimant there as *SEPTIMIUS* in 271, but later killed by his own troops, cf. **Section V(d)** [PLRE I Septimius 1]

L. Septimius P. f. Quir. Aper

Born c. 174, suffect consul c. 200, ordinary consul (ii) 207, but killed by **CARACALLA** in 213 after the death of Geta [HA *V Carac.*III 6-7; Birley (1988) 214, No. 14]

P. Septimius C. f. Aper

Suffect consul in 153, he is the first recorded consul from Lepcis [Birley (1988) 214, No. 15]

P. Septimius P. f. Quir. Aper

Senator, late 2nd century

L. Septimius Bassianus/M. Aurelius Antoninus

See below **CARACALLA AUGUSTUS**.

L. Septimius Fla[vius (?) Severus]

Suffect consul in 183, but possibly a Fla[ccus] although perhaps to be identified with the Septimius Severus in Herodian [Herodian 4, 6.3; Birley (1988) 219, Nos. 23, 24]

P. Septimius L. f. Quir. Geta

Of equestrian status at Lepcis, thought to have served as military tribune and as *advocatus fisci*; died 171 [Birley (1988) 215-218, No. 20]

P. Septimius Geta

Suffect consul before 190, ordinary consul (ii) 203, died 204 [Birley (1988) Appendix 2, Nos. 21, 24; FS 3033; PIR² S453]:

P. (later L.) Septimius Geta

See below **GETA AUGUSTUS**.

L. Septimius [?Macer]

Senator, later 2nd century, who married his cousin, Petronia. It is just possible that he may be identified with Septimius Antipater, a senator recorded in 182 [HA *V. Sev.* I, 2; FS 3026; Birley (1988) 218-219, No. 23].

L. Septimius L. f. Quir. [Severus Petro]nianus

A procurator in 143 but later promoted to the senate. If his *agnomen* if correctly restored, there may have been an earlier connection with the Petronii Mamertini as well. Perhaps a sister of Honoratus married this man's father.

[(?)L.] Sept[imius (?) Petronianus]

An early 3rd century *praetor* and governor Pannonia Inferior 211/222.

C. Septimius C. f. Quir. Severus

He entered the senate and was suffect consul 160;

proconsul of Africa 174-175 where his cousin once removed, the future emperor, was his legate. He died after 177 [FS 3035; Birley (1988) 219, No. 25].

L. Septimius Severus

A *sufes* (annually elected magistrate, one of a pair) and first *duumvir* (councillor) at Lepcis, when it was given the status of a *colonia* early 2nd century; he also served as a prefect from c. 95. He "could have had a senatorial career for the asking" had he bothered, apparently. Probably the man of this name mentioned by thre poet Statius in his *Silvae* [Statius, *op/cit.* 4.5 Birley (1988) 220, No. 26]

L. Septimius Severus

See above **SEVERUS AUGUSTUS**

[P.(?)] Septimius Severus

Senator killed by Caracalla in 213 [Herodian 4.6.3; Birley (1988) 219]

M. Septimius Severus

Duumvir, Baetica AD75; unlikely to be a relative, but conceivably he migrated.

*

GETA
c. 1st November 210 – 26th December 211

Background

GETA was the younger son of **SEVERUS,** born 7th March 189; he was made Caesar on his brother Bassianus' elevation to the rank of (co-)Augustus in 198 as **P. Septimius L.f. Geta Caesar.**[254] He does not appear to have had a formal *cursus honorum* in the senate, becoming a member of that body through his appointment as consul in 205 at 16. He was consul (ii) in 208. His *praenomen* changes from 'Publius' to 'Lucius' a very few years later, his style changing to **L. Septimius Geta Nobilissimus Caear,**[255] but it was changed back again to before he was appointed co-emperor in 210.[256] It may be that as Caracalla had become 'Marcus' in 198, Geta was entitled to his father's *praenomen* in lieu. It has also been suggested that it was to avoid being mixed up with his kinsman P. Septimius Geta, who was consul in 203, but the dates are not really congruent.[257]

Reign

It is thought that **SEVERUS'** intention was only ever to be succeeded by one son, the elder, but the Empress Julia Domna was a powerful and 'pushy' woman who favoured her younger son. In so doing (despite no doubt being mindful of her elder son's character)

---

254. ILS 439
255. ILS 427
256. ILS 433
257. Birley (1988) 218

she undoubtedly signed **GETA'S** death warrant. It was entirely thanks to her, too, that he was eventually appointed co-Augustus at York. His style on appointment as emperor was **P. Septimius Geta Nobilissimus Caesar Pius Augustus** and it is from this period that emperors increasingly adopt 'Pius' into their nomenclature on an entirely formulaic nature, whereas with the Severans, it merely acknowledged their alleged membership of the *familia* of **MARCUS AURELIUS.** Again, from this point, Caesar becomes increasingly qualified by 'most noble' (*nobilissimus*). The fact that his style retained the term Caesar does rather suggest that he was very definitely the junior partner.

GETA was also appointed *princeps iuventutis* (Prince of Youth) and, with his elevation as co-emperor in October or November 210, received the (divided) pontificate, tribunician and proconsular power, renewable on 10th December annually. He was constantly at loggerheads with his elder brother and, despite having become something of a martyr through being killed by **CARACALLA**, there seems every evidence that he would have been little better either as person or as a ruler had the position been reversed; both were in effect, spoilt brats, far too heavily imbued with the values of their eastern potentate ancestors rather than with those sober Roman virtues embodied, at least to some extent, in their father.

After succeeding, the two did everything in opposition, making governance difficult, and causing the palace to be physicially divided into two completely separate establishments. A scheme to divide the empire between them was scotched by their mother, in whose arms **GETA** eventually expired, unmarried, during an official audience on 26th December 211, having been stabbed in front of her by **CARACALLA** – an audience being about the only occasion they could be together and far enough from their bodyguards to enable an assassination to be effectively carried out. He suffered a *damnatio memoriae* after his death, passed *force majeur* by the senate.

*

ANTONINUS II
(Known to history as CARACALLA)
28th January 198 – 8th April 217

Background

L. Septimius Bassianus was born 4th April 188 and named after his maternal grandfather. Although a promising youth, rivalry with his younger brother, his mother's favourite, permeated his every action, caused deep bitterness, all fuelled by the unexpected elevation to the purple of **GETA** in 210. It is assumed, but not attested, that his *praenomen* was Lucius, but this is most likely in the tradition of the Roman *elite* of the time. In 195 he was re-named, to accord with his father's self-appointment as a son of **MARCUS AURELIUS**

as **M. Aurelius Antoninus Caesar**.[258] At the age of only 9, he was, on 28th January 198, made co-emperor with his father as **Imperator Caesar M. Aurelius Antoninus Augustus,** receiving his first imperial acclamation, the proconsular and tribunician powers along with the pontificate – the third time this single office had been divided, although on his younger brother's elevation it was held by three people! Later in the same year he added **Pius** after **Antoninus.** The senate voted him the title of *pater patriae* the following year and in 200 the name **Felix** was added after **Pius,**[259] this combination setting a trend that became increasingly popular in the 3rd century and which survived until the end of the 6th century, for emperors to prefix 'Augustus' with 'Pius Felix' on their accession as a matter of course and usually rendered on coins as P F AVG.

He was consul first in 202, then in 205 and 208, with a further imperial acclamation in 207. As his father's lieutenant in their campaigns in Scotland in 209-210, he assumed, jointly with **SEVERUS**, the additional honorific of **Britannicus Maximus.** In a clear attempt to consolidate an old family alliance, he was betrothed in 200 and in 202 had married (on his father's orders) Publia Fulvia Plautilla, the daughter of his father's henchman, fellow-townsman and cousin, P. Fulvius Plautianus, whom he divorced and exiled in 205, on the fall of her father. Recent analysis of coin evidence suggests that they had a short-lived daughter c. 204 whose demise perhaps lay behind the divorce.[260]

Reign

On succeeding his father in February 211, his style changed to: **Imperator Caesar M. Aurelius Severus Antoninus Pius Augustus Britannicus Maximus.**[261] The assassination of his brother, who had his own faction and supporters in all walks of Roman life, left **CARACALLA** exposed and he felt consequently that it was necessary to bribe the Praetorian Guard and cow the Senate into acquiescence, although he was clearly unconvinced by the effectiveness of either tactic. He therefore had recourse during 212 and 213 to a widespread proscription in which, we are told, 20,000 supporters or suspected supporters of **GETA** were massacred, from all ranks of Roman society. These actions wrecked any hope there might have been for the acceptance, from the senate downwards, of his rule.

On the other hand, as good tyrants do, he quickly made it his business to curry popularity with the army, in which he succeeded brilliantly - at the crushing expense of the treasury – by giving them an immediate pay-rise of getting on for 50%. Setting out for Germany on campaign, he increased that esteem by sharing the soldiers' discomforts and disdaining the luxuries usually enjoyed even by field commanders - hence his universally adopted nickname "Caracalla" the name of a particular type of hooded military cloak that he habitually wore. This German campaign was a success, however, earning him a fourth

---

258. ILS 419
259. ILS 425 which also includes 'L. f.'
260. Bronze As (24mm, 10.26 g, 12h). Rome mint 202-203; rev. shows Plautilla as Pietas standing R. holding sceptre and her daughter RIC IV 581.
261. ILS 448

imperial acclamation and the additional titles of **Germanicus Maximus** the same year, in which he was also consul, for the fourth time.

His most lasting legacy to the empire was his edict of 212 granting full Roman citizenship to all free citizens of the Empire. Although the short-term idea was to increase tax revenues to fund military spending (especially his universal military donative), the long-term effect was to endow all the inhabitants of the Empire with a sense of belonging, thus binding it together. The other long-term effect was to completely change the way names were applied; it spelt the death of the *praenomen* and the *gentilicium*, the bearing of which were no longer a prerequisite of citizenship. Vast numbers of citizens so enfranchised, however, adopted his *praenomen* and *nomen*, 'M. Aurelius', if only to accord with convention; several of the emperors and imperial claimants in the chaotic period following c. 260 were probably examples, although we cannot be absolutely sure of this.

These matters settled, **CARACALLA** set out for the east, but rather spoilt his no-non-sense image by becoming increasingly intoxicated with the mystique of Alexander the Great, culminating in absurd ceremonies performed at the site of Troy and at Alexandria, where in the end it all went very sour, and the emperor on a whim ordered a massacre of thousands of unarmed civilians early in 216. He had a long term physical ailment as well as a serious inferiority complex, fuelled by his clash with and murder of his brother, and had probably reached a stage where his personality was beginning to become completely unbalanced; the disease, bearing in mind his lack of children and the paucity of stories about any promiscuity, may have been of a sexual nature.

From Alexandria, **CARACALLA** carried out a well-planned and successful campaign against Parthia, earning himself the additional style **Parthicus Maximus**. During the run-up to the opening of the campaigning season of 217, however, his efforts to buy the loyalty of thee troops proved to have been in vain and he was assassinated in Osrhoëne, whilst taking a comfort break, *en route* from Edessa to Carrhae on 8th April.

The Empress Plautilla was killed in 212 after **GETA'S** execution. Her brother C. Fulvius Plautius Hortensianus shared her fate.[262] **CARACALLA** was also accused of 'marrying' his mother, or at least committing incest with her, a story which occurs in the HA and several other later sources but which is dismissed by modern scholarship.

CARACALLA was deified by a reluctant senate at the prompting of **MACRINUS.**

Further reading:

Birley, A. R., *The African Emperor* (London 1988)

Birley, A. R (trans. & ed. from the HA) *Lives of the Later Caesars* (London 1992).

Turton, G., *The Syrian Princesses* (London 1974)

*

---

262. Birley (1988) Appendix 2, nos. 29, 33 see **Table XXX Brief Lives** (above)

MACRINUS
11ᵗʰ April 217 – 8ᵗʰ June 218

Background

M. Opellius Macrinus[263] was a Numidian, born at Caesarea (Sharshal/Cherchell) in Mauretania in 164, probably of equestrian parents. The fact that he was called **MACRINUS** and his son **DIADUMENIANUS** (Diadumenus in the HA and some later sources) is a strange co-incidence, bearing in mind that Nero had a freedman called Macrinus, living around 64, whose father had been called Diadumenus, too.[264] Could there have been some remote line of distaff descent from him to the usurper?

He trained as an advocate but his relatively undistinguished bureaucratic equestrian career flourished under the patronage of the African henchman of Severus, C. Fulvius Plautianus, whom he eventually succeeded as joint Commander of the Praetorian Guard around 212, having previously served as a procurator in an unknown capacity.[265]

He is usually credited in the ancient sources with being prime mover of the plot to assassinate **CARACALLA** but the fact that it took three days to acclaim him after the murder suggests that those who encompassed the emperor's death had not decided on a candidate to succeed him. Alternatively, the candidate upon whom they had lit perhaps refused – possibly they had lighted on **MACRINUS**' elderly and respected colleague as Praetorian Prefect, M. Oclatinius Adventus - or the whole thing was very spur-of-the-moment. Furthermore, it seems likely that the proscriptions of both **SEVERUS** and his son had eliminated any credible candidates, any *capaces imperii*, from the ranks of the Severan kin or the governing élite in the senate. As it is, with hindsight, it might appear that **MACRINUS** merely took advantage of a confused situation and had himself acclaimed, assuming the name Severus and bestowing that of Antoninus on his son, whom he associated with his rule by nominating him Caesar.

Reign

On accession, 11ᵗʰ April 217, as the first emperor not to have been of senatorial rank, he styled himself **Imperator M. Opellius Severus Macrinus Augustus**, adding **Pius Felix**[266] when he had been recognised by the senate, adlected into the Patriciate, given the senatorial rank of an ex-consul and declared *pater patriae,* probably in June.[267] They also granted him the tribunician and proconsular powers, nominally from his accession and renewable on 10ᵗʰ December each year. He was also recognised as supreme pontiff. He was ordinary consul for the year following, 218.

---

263. FS 2579; ILS 461; PIR² O108
264. ILS 5798
265. Dio LXXVIII. 11. 1f
266. ILS 462, 463
267. HA, *V. Macr.* 7.1

He married Nonia Celsa according to the HA, but no coins were struck in her name, nor is any wife mentioned in any other source and if she existed at all, she may well have been dead prior to **MACRINUS'** acclamation.[268] The name of her son suggested to Birley that she was in fact a daughter of the Puteolan *eques* Cn. Haius Diadumenianus, who had been procurator of both provinces of the emperor's native Mauretania about 202.[269] Birley speculated that her name therefore may have been Haia, not Nonia, unless her name *is* reported accurately by the HA.[270] The only child of the union of whom we have knowledge is the son, **DIADUMENIANUS.**

The reign began with some minor extirpation of difficult elements and by some administrative changes to bring trusted men into important posts. He allowed the late emperor's mother Julia Domna to remain at Antioch and rather foolishly left her to her own devices, a mistake the brutal **SEVERUS** would never have made. He was aware, however, that she was seriously ill and must have assumed that she was no threat, although in reality she was conspiring actively, only starving herself to death when ordered to leave the Syrian capital when wind of her activities reached him. Even then, the ancient sources may have misunderstood, for she is thought to have had cancer, probably of the breast, and may have reached the stage of her affliction when she could no longer eat anyway. In either case, it suited the Severan party in the province very well to suddenly acquire a second martyr.

All might have gone well but for the fact that the delay in the Parthian campaign caused by **CARACALLA'S** self indulgence in staying too long at Edessa, followed by the further delay caused by the succession, had allowed the Parthians, previously in disarray, to re-group. Thus when the two sides met near Nisibis, the battle apparently ended in stalemate, although the subsequent truce concluded by Macrinus included the payment of a colossal subsidy to the Parthian King, which rather suggests that the emperor was at more of a disadvantage than might at first seem apparent.

In either case, the cost of the 200,000,000 sesterces (HS) settlement and the fact that Roman arms were by no means triumphant, told heavily against **MACRINUS**, as did his removal of some military privileges in the aftermath, probably as a punishment for the soldiers' failure to perform successfully.

A rebellion, without doubt formented by the family of Julia Domna, broke out on 15-16th May 218, when the 14 year old nephew of **CARACALLA**, Varius Avitus, son of Domna's sister Julia Maesa, was brought from his native Emesa and smuggled into the camp of a nearby legion, the officers and men of which promptly acclaimed him, believing, it was said, that he was **CARACALLA'S** natural son.

MACRINUS did not at first take this development too seriously, except that he proclaimed his son, **DIADUMENIANUS**, already recognised as Caesar, as co-Augustus on that very same day, hoping thereby to win the propaganda war. Soon, however, **MACRINUS'S** forces began to suffer a stream of desertions, which a further donative failed to stem. The emperor

---

268. *Ibid., V. Diadumen.* 7.7
269. *Op. cit.* 191; PIR² H8. Her brother was a new senator of the same name, suffect consul by 202.
270. Birley (1988) 191-192.

thereupon fell back on Antioch to re-group. An engagement was fought with the rebels outside the city, in which **MACRINUS** – much to most peoples' surprise – was worsted, whereupon he retreated north in the hope of rallying support in Europe, whilst he sent his son east to Parthia. In the event, neither **MACRINUS** made it across the Bosphorous nor **DIADUMENIANUS** across the Euphrates. **MACRINUS** was caught and killed allegedly on 8th June, although it could have been nearer the end of the month. There is an alternative tradition that has him surviving in hiding until October 218.[271]

⋆

DIADUMENIANUS
16th May – c. 11th June 218

MACRINUS was succeeded - *de jure* and if only for a few days - by his young son and co-ruler, **M. Opellius Diadumenianus**[272] who had been recognised as **M. Opellius Severus Diadumenianus Caesar** by June 217. His name changed again later by the insertion of **Antoninus** in lieu of Severus.[273] He was born in 208 and was thus but 9 years old on his father's accession.. On appointment as Caesar, he was also styled 'prince of youth' as **CARACALLA** had been.[274] However, his style was soon changed and the 'Caesar' qualifed by 'most noble'.[275] After May 16th 218 he was raised to the rank of Augustus – a move never ratified by the senate, but immortalised on his coinage – as **Imperator Caesar M. Opellius Antoninus Diadumenianus Augustus.**

On his father's defeat in battle outside Antioch, he attempted to escape to Parthia, but was caught at Zeugma, on the Euphrates not far from Samosata (Turkey) and killed a few days after his father's demise.

Family

The family are regarded as from the Roman province of Mauretania, but although referred to as a 'Moor' he could have just as easily been of Roman colonising stock as rather than native; the 'Moor' soubriquet seems to have been applied perjoratively in either case.

Whilst the names of the Neronian freedman and his father (above) may be co-incidence, it is worth noting that the only previous Opellius with an élite appointment was a man of this name who served as a legionary legate under **Mark Antony** in Judaea around 35BC. Perhaps this man, having ended up on the losing side, rather than return to Rome and risk proscription by Octavianus after 31, went into exile in the train of the dynast's daughter by Cleopatra, who married Juba II of Numidia, later King of Western Mauretania (see also **Table LVI**).

---

271. Dio, LXXVIII, 39.1, cf. Herodian 5, 3.11 & 5, 5.8.
272. FS 2578 ; ILS 461; PIR[2] O107.
273. ILS 8919
274. ILS 462A
275. ILS 465

TABLE XXXI: MACRINUS' POSSIBLE FAMILY

---

*

ANTONINUS III
(Known to history as Elagabalus)
16th May 218 – 11th March 222

Background

The young man used as the centrepiece of the plot to topple **MACRINUS** was called Varius Bassianus but was acclaimed emperor as **ANTONINUS**, officially the third to bear that name. He was already hereditary high priest of the local cult at Emesa. Like **SEVERUS'** empress Julia Domna, he was of the blood-line of the priest-kings there. The sacred black meteoritic stone which was the centrepiece of worship at Emesa was called, like the god whom it represented, Ela-gabal. The prestige conferred on its high priest made a deep impression on the 14 year old Bassianus, to the extent that he required people to address him by it; hence its subsequent use to identify him **ELAGABALUS** despite his formal throne name of **ANTONINUS**.

He was, prior to his arrival in Rome in the early summer of 219, much under the influence of the women of his family, all powerful, and with their ambitions unfettered by the lack of living male kin, the new emperor's father having died a couple of years previously, his grandfather a year later and his uncle having been killed by **MACRINUS** as a result of the *coup*. This dramatic turn of events had been brought about by his mother and her lover Eutychianus, also known as Gannys, but he was executed before the end of the year, mainly because his increasing influence was too threatening for **ELAGABALUS**; he also clashed with the young man in an attempt to persuade him into leading a temperate lifestyle.

Reign

[**Sex.**] **Varius Avitus Bassianus** was probably born at Emesa in March 204 and had succeeded to the position of High Priest of Emesa by 218, which hereditary succession justifies much of the working out of his descent from the Kings; presumably the senior male line was extinct by 218, probably as a result of **MACRINUS'S** elimination of many of the family as potential rivals. The name Bassianus, derived from the Arabic *basus,* itself a priestly title, helps confirm the descent.

He was acclaimed emperor 16th May 218, taking the name and style **Imperator Caesar M. Aurelius Divi Antonini Magni f. Divi Severi Pii n. Antoninus Pius Felix Augustus**[276] which (less the filiation) was identical to that of **CARACALLA** (or 'Antoninus the Great', as he seems to have become in the same filiation) whose natural son he was claiming to be. On recognition by the senate three months later, when he was granted the tribunician and proconsular power (back-dated to 16th May and renewable on December 10th each year) and recognised – ironically as it turned out – as *Pontifex Maximus*; they also added *Pater Patriae*. In 220, he added the titles: *Sacerdos Amplissimus Dei Invicti Solis Elagabali* – High Priest of the Unconquerable sun god Ela-gabal.[277] He was consul – suffect – in 218, and thereafter ordinary consul in 219, 220 and 222.

He married three (although possibly five) times. Firstly in late summer 219 to **Julia Cornelia Paula**[278] thereafter styled Augusta. She was described by Herodian as 'most noble'[279] but her family connections are difficult to unravel, especially as she was endowed with three rather common names. Her brother or father was probably the jurist Julius Paullus,[280] although the HA claims he served as a senior civil servant under **SEVERUS** and was appointed Praetorian Prefect by **SEVERUS ALEXANDER**, by which most commentators assume HA actually meant **ELAGABALUS**, which would make more sense.[281] This connection would not make Julia 'most noble', however, so perhaps the connection was a descent from Julius Paulus, a praetor exiled under Nero,[282] whose daughter was called Julia Agrippina, honoured at Antioch in Pisidia (by Yalvaç Turkey) and bearing a *cognomen* probably relating to the Judaean ruler M. Julius Agrippa.[283] This might be seen as putting **ELAGABALUS'S** first wife and his own family in the same ancestral circle of eastern potentates and make them distantly related. They had, however, divorced by the end of 220.

---

276. ILS 467 (without filiation) & ILS 469 (with)

277. ILS 473

278. PIR² I660

279. Herodian, *op. cit.,* 5,6.1

280. PIR² I453

281. *V. Pesc. Nigr.* 7, 4

282. PIR² I452

283. Reigned King of N. Judaea 53-92, d. 93; PIR² I132

Secondly and illegally, he married late in 220 (or early in 221) the Vestal Virgin Julia Aquillia Severa[284] thenceforth also Augusta. Again, her family are not explicitly identified in the ancient sources. Probably her father or brother was M. Julius Aquillius Tertullus, an early 3rd century aedile.[285] Whether he was the parent, it is certainly thought her brother was T. Jul[ius] Clatius Severus, suffect consul at about this period or a little later[286]; their descent was almost certainly from C. Julius Severus, suffect consul in 139 and his wife, Claudia Aquillia and thus again a representative of the old client Kings of the east, in this case of Julius Severus, of Attalus, King of Asia.[287] She could, therefore, have been another kinswoman of the boy emperor but, notwithstanding, they were divorced within a very few months.

He married thirdly in July 221 [Claudia] Annia Faustina (again thenceforth Augusta). She was a daughter of Ti. Claudius Severus Proculus consul in 200, himself a son of Cn. Claudius Severus by Annia Aurelia Galeria Faustina, fifth child of **MARCUS AURELIUS, see Table XXIV(b)**. The bride's illustrious descent was clearly intended to bolster the emperor's flagging prestige, but the emperor divorced her before the end of the year too, returning to Aquillia Severa. There was no known issue by any of these.

Acceptance of the new ruler by the senate, sight unseen, and the ratification of his status was swift, despite misgivings engendered by the cruelty of **CARACALLA**. The new emperor's supporters must have been extremely sure of his acceptance throughout the empire, for to dally nearly a year in the east and then to spend an inordinately long time travelling to Rome ceremonially accompanied in state by the black stone might, in any other context, seem a recipe for disaster.

On arrival, the stone was installed in a new Palatine temple, and its high priest's only diversion from self indulgence and cruelty lay in his daily morning devotions and sacrifices to it. The trend was to set Ela-gabal up as the centre of a monotheistic cult at the expense of Rome's traditional pantheon. This, of course, was never going to gain acceptance (if only they could have predicted the events of a century later!) and, almost as bad, involved massive public expenditure. Otherwise, licence ruled virtually unchecked, led by a narcissistic bisexual, transvestite and highly exhibitionistic emperor.

Appointments of men from obscure backgrounds, on whom Julia Maesa - who with her daughter, Julia Soaemias, **ELAGABALUS'S** mother - directed imperial policy could rely, caused much offence and derision. The army was never quite happy, although the Syrian princesses' competence and the sheer youth of the Emperor, kept the inevitable crisis at bay for three and a half years against all the odds. Nevertheless, there had been four attempted rebellions within a year or so of **MACRINUS'S** murder, three in his native Syria, involving the imperial claimants *VERUS II, TAURINUS, GELLIUS MAXIMUS* and *SELEUCUS* (on whom see below).

---

284. PIR² I648
285. PIR² I172
286. PIR² I268
287. PIR² I573

Two policies were tried to give the boy-emperor some respectability. One, as we have seen, was to marry him off suitably. The second, and last-ditch, policy was to adopt an acceptable heir, on the assumption that he would never produce one of his own. The surviving son of Julia Maesa's younger sister, Julia Avita Mammaea, 13-year old Alexianus, was therefore named Caesar late in 221 taking the name **SEVERUS ALEXANDER**. This merely resulted in loss of face for the emperor and repeated attempts to have Alexander killed, reviving still raw memories of the **CARACALLA-GETA** conflicts. In the end, open support for **ALEXANDER** amongst the praetorians resulted in **ELAGABALUS** throwing a tantrum in front of them and the guardsmen summarily killing him on 11th March 222.

ELAGABALUS was the second emperor to follow **CARACALLA** and adopt the style 'Pius Felix Augustus' in his titulature. It was revived again by **GORDIAN III**, although **AEMILIANUS** was the first emperor to use it consistently on coins.

*

ALEXANDER I
(Known to history as SEVERUS ALEXANDER)
11th March 222 – 22nd March 235[288]

Background

The not unexpected demise of **ELAGABALUS** at the hands of the praetorian guard projected his young cousin the Caesar **ALEXANDER** into power. With him came his mother, Julia Mamaea. Unlike her unfortunate sister, Julia Soaemias, Mamaea was able to control her son, and he turned out to be a relatively normal youth, although *perceived* at least, as being inordinately under his mother's thumb. Not only that, but behind Mamaea was her own mother, **SEPTIMIUS SEVERUS'** sister-in-law, Julia Maesa and, for almost two years these two powerful and strong willed matrons ruled the empire as joint Augustae in **ALEXANDER'S** name. He was under their thumb all right, but this was to be expected in one so young. It was only when he reached the age of maturity and failed to free himself from their influence that matters began to drift out of his control.

[M.] **Gessius Alexianus Bassianus**[289] was born 1st October 208, or more probably 209, at Arca Caesaraea (Arqa, Lebanon).[290] He appears to have come to Rome in 219 in the train of **ELAGABALUS** with his mother. Adopted by **ELAGABALUS** in late autumn 221 as his heir, being granted the name and style of Caesar accordingly as **M. Aurelius Alexander Nobilissimus Caesar**[291] adding **Imperi et Sacerdotis Princeps Iuventutis** ('power-endowed and priestly prince of youth'). He was consul for the first time as colleague of his cousin in 222.

---

288. The date is not certain. The HA opts for 22nd March, but modern analyisis of the evidence suggests about ten days earlier.
289. PIR² A1610
290. He was only 12 in 221: Herodian 5, 7, 4
291. ILS 474

Reign

He was acclaimed by the praetorians on 11th March, 222, and took the style **Imperator Caesar M. Aurelius Severus Alexander Pius Felix Augustus.**[292] He was given an imperial acclamation on 13th March and the same day was recognised by the senate and granted the proconsular and tribunician power, to be renewed annually thereafter on 10th December; he was also recognised as pontifex maximus; later he was granted the title of *Pater Patriae* as well. In 226 he was consul again and received a second imperial acclamation; although he was acclaimed *imperator* another eight times between 226 and 235, the precise dates are not clear. He held his third and final consulship in 229. He celebrated a triumph in September 233 on his return from Mesopotamia, the HA claiming that he added **Persicus Maximus** to his name, but as this appears neither on coins nor inscriptions, it must be dismissed as fiction.

He married in October or November 225 **Gneia Seia Herennia Sallustia Barbia Orba Orbiana,**[293] the daughter of the senator L. Seius [(?) Sallustius Herennius Macrinianus]; she was accorded the title Augusta and he was created Caesar as **L. Seius Caesar.** His identity is elusive, although he was probably a descendant of P. Seius Fuscianus consul (ii) in 188, childhood friend of **MARCUS AURELIUS** and a patrician by creation. Yet a note of caution needs to be sounded at this juncture, for Syme urged us 'not to entirely discard' the HA's name for him - Macrinus - and to consider that he might have been a prefect of the Praetorian Guard.[294] The Empress Orbiana must also have been close kin to Q. Sallustius Macrinianus, a contemporary senator, the son or grandson of an eponymous procurator of Mauritania in 194.[295] It is much more difficult to identify a likely Herennius, though, despite there being precious few families of this name in the senate known for the general period; although the Herennius Orbianus who was a member of the Arval Brethren in the mid-2nd century is also likely to have been an ancestor.[296] The HA, inevitably, muddies the water further by naming Alexander's wife in one place as 'Memmia daughter of the ex-consul Sulpicius, grand-daughter of Catulus' and much later on as the daughter of Macrianus.[297] This has led some to speculate that Alexander married three times, but as Fink pointed out[298] Memmia is clearly a straight steal from the family of **GALBA** and his first wife (see **Table XII**)[299] and the second perhaps from the recently deposed emperor **MACRINUS** or even from the future imperial claimant *MACRIANUS*, see below, **part V(a)**. In fact the HA may merely reflect a still-known fact, that members of Seia's family were called Macrinianus.

---

292. ILS 479
293. ILS 486
294. Syme (1971) 157.
295. ILS 3055
296. PIR² H81
297. V. Sev. Alex. 20, 3 & 49, 3-4
298. Fink (1939) 329
299. Suet. Galba 3, 4

It is worth noting too that, according to the HA (with all the reservations that must engender), a relative of Gessius Alexianus Bassianus was Catilius Severus, later his advisor.[300] This is presumably Cn. Catilius Severus, suffect consul in 200 and an Arval Brother 213/221[301] or a son, perhaps the contemporarily attested L. Catilius Severus. Presumably he was descended from or close kin to L. Catilius Severus Julianus Claudius Reginus consul (ii) 120, who briefly adopted **MARCUS AURELIUS** (qv above **Table XXII Brief Lives**). The consul of 200 was son of an Aurelia – perhaps the association was too much for the compiler of the HA. No credible kinship to Severus Alexander can be detected, however.

A tantalising sidelight on Alexander's family history is the HA's tale that he had a pedigree drawn up showing his descent from the Caecilii Metelli of the Republic.[302] Whilst this is most likely fiction, it is so unlikely a tale that there is always the possibility it is *not* made up. If the HA story contains any truth, it is probably a remote element of the Empress's pedigree that was drawn up and not **ALEXANDER'S**.

Julia Maesa died in 224, whereupon the less able Mamaea took over, extending her reach accordingly. Hence the marriage of Alexander to an aristocrat of obscure stock, a clear attempt to bolster the not-wholly-liked Emesan dynasty with an alliance with the metropolitan *elite,* just as Soaemias had attempted to do with the far less tractable Elagabalus.

The ploy failed because the Augusta Orbiana, unsurprisingly, put Mamaea in second place by the very nature of her position. Indeed, if we only knew more about her, we might appreciate that she showed some mettle, and increasingly kept Mamaea out of things. Added to which, making the father-in-law Caesar also placed at least some control of affairs into hands other than her own. In 227 Mamaea banished the young Empress to Libya and had Seius Caesar killed for attempting to use the praetorians against her.[303]

Orbiana's other mistake was a result of her relatively enlightened decision to appoint a council of wise men to advise the emperor, including the jurist Domitius Ulpianus, known to history as Ulpian, whom she appointed one of the Praetorian Prefects with enhanced powers.[304] He introduced some useful reforms and oversaw the reversal of almost all Elagabalus's administrative and religious excesses. Unfortunately, he was not a military man and lost the respect of the guard, one of his measures provoking three days of rioting between the praetorians and the people. As a result of this, he felt obliged to execute two praetorian guard officers, a firm decision too far. A detachment of the praetorian guard promptly killed him in the Imperial Palace.

This seems to have set an unfortunate precedent, for the soldiers perceived the emperor as young, weak and worse, under the control of a woman. Thus there were periodic outbreaks of trouble throughout the reign, not only in the praetorian camp but in the military provinces as well – an ominous sign.

---

300. *V. Sev. Alex.* 68. 1
301. ILS 5039
302. *V. Sev. Alex.,* XL. 3
303. McHugh (2017) 146
304. PIR² D169

Nevertheless, the reign has also been hailed as marking a restoration of the gubernatorial diarchy between emperor and senate, although Dio might suggest that the relationship was mainly window dressing. **ALEXANDER** was still advised by a council of senators and promoted praetorian prefects to senatorial rank, but his mother did not let go of power to the extent that the senate regained much themselves. Nevertheless, they still provided the governing élite and were for a time at least no doubt mollified.

Another problem was that, for all the dynastic instability since **CARACALLA'S** eastern campaign, the empire had been at peace. However, the peace was shattered when the 500 year empire of Parthia was overthrown by Artaxerxes (Ardashir), a noble subject of the last Parthian king, Artabanus V who, by 226, had re-invented his realm in the guise of the ancient Persian Empire. In 230, he took back the province of Mersopotamia, created by **SEVERUS** after his capture of Ctesiphon some thirty years before. The restoration of the situation was essential to the prestige and future safety of the empire. Preparations began in 231, but were bedevilled by an imperial claimant, probably *TAURINUS* (see below). Diplomacy was tried, reverses were experienced, but a successful outcome was obtained and Artaxerxes finally withdrew from the disputed province, giving guarantees to Alexander – or so we are told. What actually happened, though, is not at all clear, but Roman arms, despite setbacks must have eventually triumphed for so ambitious a sovereign as the first of the Sassanids to voluntarily withdraw. This enabled **ALEXANDER** to celebrate a triumph.

Unfortunately, the armies on the German and Danubian frontiers had been reduced in strength to bolster the anti-Persian expeditionary force, and the German tribes seized the opportunity to cause much trouble and destruction. In 234, **ALEXANDER** led the army across the Rhine and restored order, but made the fatal mistake of attempting to reach a negotiated solution to include a substantial grant to the barbarians to keep the peace. Looked at from the perspective of the army, of course, this meant less likelihood of loot and pillage, the spoils of war being a major incentive to discipline and good morale. At the same time, the Emperor was pursuing a policy of financial retrenchment in the military sphere which was already impacting on remuneration.

One of the most senior equestrian officers, a Thracian called Maximinus, is thought to have used this to sow discord and in the resulting mutiny, **MAXIMINUS** was acclaimed by his men on 21st March and the following day **ALEXANDER**, his mother and their entourage were murdered by a detachment of NCOs at Vicus Britannicus (Bretzenheim), near Mogontiacum (Mainz). **ALEXANDER** left no issue and suffered a *damnatio memoriae* from his successor, but was finally deified by the senate in 238.

This rash act on the part of the army plunged the empire into five decades of unrest and turbulence. When order was finally restored, a very different Roman empire had emerged.

Family

Both **ELAGABALUS** and **SEVERUS ALEXANDER** were descended from the priest-kings of Emesa, the first of whom was an Arab Sheikh ruling there in the mid-60s BC when Pompey was consolidating his conquests in the region. He recognised him as a client of the Empire as King of Emesa and Phylarch of the Arabs in 64-63 BC.[305] This first ruler claimed descent from **Menenaeus**, mythical founder of Chalcis in Syria. Later members of the family were reputedly descended from the Achaemenid and Arascid kings via a Median heiress – a claim made by their kinsman, the philosopher Iamblichus, which Birley sees no reason to doubt.[306]

We possess many of the names of the priest-kings of Emesa, but their inter-relationships are far less secure; Table **XXXII,** based on Birley, errs on the side of caution. A more ambitious reconstruction of the family and its kins has been published by Settipani, including a proposed possible descent for **ELAGABALUS'** second wife from the Judaean royal house and C. Julius Alexander of Egypt through the senatorial Plancii.[307]

---

305. The pedigree is based on that of Birley (1988) 219-224 & PIR²
306. *Op. cit.,* 224, no. 48
307. *Op.cit.* 448, 456

TABLE XXXII: THE LATER SEVERANS

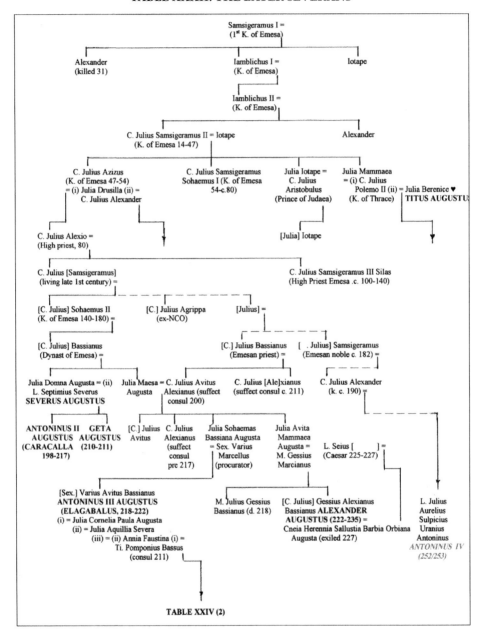

TABLE XXXII: BRIEF LIVES

Alexander

Prince of Emesa, killed in 31BC [Dio 52. 2, 2; PIR² A497]

[.] **Gessius Alexianus Bassianus**

See above **ALEXANDER I AUGUSTUS**

[?M.] Gessius Marcianus,

An equestrian officer from Arca Caesarea, he was an ex-procurator later adlected into the senate and killed during the reign of **MACRINUS** 218. His sister Julia Gessia Bassiana, her consular husband and children shared his fate. [PIR² G171].

Iamblichus I,

King of Emesa c. 52-31BC when he was killed with his brother [PIR² I7]

Iamblichus II

High priest and phylarch of the Arabs, restored as King of Emesa in 20 BC, died 14.

Iamblichus

Whose family was from Chalcis and who lived at Apamaea, c. 250-c.325 was a likely descendant of Sohaemus I [PLRE I. 1].

Julia Avita Mamaea

Created Augusta in 222, killed in the rebellion of 235 The HA would have us believe that she married (i) an unknown ex-consul by whom she had issue, and that on his death she was allowed to retain her rank despite re-marrying Gessius Marcianus, who was an equestrian officer. The couple are alleged in the HA to have had another child, a daughter, [Julia] Theoclia, later said to have been betrothed, or about to be betrothed, to the Caesar C. Julius Verus Maximus, son of the Emperor **MAXIMINUS I.** It is there suggested that she probably ended up married to "Messalla" – possibly intended for the genealogically distinguished L. Valerius L. f. Messalla Apollinaris, consul (ii) 233, but if so, if so it would have been as a second wife, for he had been suffect consul in Caracalla's reign and had a son who was consul in 253 and was thus born c. 222 – all very unlikely [HA, *V. Due Max.* 29, 1-5; ILS 1190-1191; PIR² G171 & I649].

Julia Domna

Later **Augusta** 193-218 married by c. 187, as second wife of the Emperor **SEPTIMIUS SEVERUS** and died at Antioch 218. 'Domna' is from an Arab name meaning black, see above **Table XXX Brief Lives** [PIR2, I 663;. Birley (1988) 222, No. 38].

Julia Maesa

Later **Augusta** 218-224. He name is from Arabic *masa* = 'swinging gait'. Married (her cousin) [C.] Julius Avitus and had issue (see below). Died 223 and deified 224 [PIR² I678; Syme (1971) 147].

Julia Soaemias Bassiana

She was Augusta from 218 until she was killed 222 [PIR² I704]

[C.] Julius Agrippa

A former chief centurion who died childless leaving his neice, Empress Julia Domna as his heir [Birley (1988) 223 no. 43 who accepts identification with the empress as perfectly possible].

[C.] Julius Alexander

Emesan noble, killed on **COMMODUS'S** orders c. 190 because of his prowess at hunting; it is possible that his father was an un-named Emesan and close relation, rather than as here [Dio LXXII. 14; PIR2, J. 135; Birley (1988) p. 223 No. 42].

C. Julius Alexio

High Priest and probably also King of Emesa, late 1ˢᵗ century [PIR² I143]

C. Julius Aristobulus

Prince of Judaea, married Iulia Iotape mid 1ˢᵗ century. Birley suggests that his name derived by descent from the Median princess once betrothed (and presumably subsequently married) to Alexander Helios – the son of **Mark Antony** by Cleopatra [PIR² I45; Birley (1988) 24].

L. Jul[ius] Aur[elius] Sulp[icius] Ura[nius] Antoninus

As *(URANIUS) ANTONINUS IV* imperial claimant at Emesa, acclaimed to help defend the area against Shapur of Persia in 253 see below **part V(a)** [PIR² I195.

C. Julius Av[itus] Alexianus

Began with a brilliant equestrian career, but later adlected into the senate by **SEVERUS** becoming praetor, suffect consul, legate of Dalmatia and proconsul of either Africa or Asia; died of natural causes 218. [Birley (1988) p. 223 No., 45, cf. PIR² I192 & probably to be identified with Julius Avitus, PIR² I190].

C. Julius Azizus

King of Emesa as **Azizus** from AD47 to 54. He married, as her first husband, Julia Drusilla (who later re-married M. Antonius Felix, procurator of Palestine at the time of St. Paul's mission by whom she had issue but which are omitted from **Table XXXII**) and again to C. Julius Alexander (King of Western Cilicia), and sister of Julia Berenice (above), daughter of Herod Agrippa I of Judaea.

[C.] Julius Bassianus

High Priest & dynast of Emesa mid-2nd century [PIR² I202]

M. Julius Gessius Bassianus

Senator and Master of the Arval Brethren in 214, after which we hear no more of him; probably killed by **MACRINUS;** had he lived, or left a son, one or other would surely have been named Augustus in lieu of Alexander in 222 on grounds of age precedence [FS 2039; PIR² I 342]

C. Julius Polemo II

King of Thrace and Prince of Olba, married as his second wife. Julia Mammaea. He was a descendant of **Mark Antony**. The Prince of Olba was previously married to Julia Berenice, daughter of Herod Agrippa I of Judaea, herself mistress of the emperor **TITUS** (see **Table XV**)

C. Julius Samsigeramus II

Granted Roman citizenship, presumably before AD14, as dynast of Emesa, he reigned 14-47, died 54 [PIR² I541]

C. Julius C. Juli Alexionis f. Fab. Samsigeramus *qui et* Silas

High priest and probably also King of Emesa (as **Samsigeramus III?**). Note that Birley points out that there is no specific evidence for the extinction of the Kingdom after 74 [PIR² I542; Birley (1988) 224 No. 47].

C. Julius Samsigerami Regis f. Sohaemus I

King of Emesa 53 and of Sophene from 54; died after 74 (probably c. 85/90); granted consular ornaments before 74 [ILS 8958; PIR² I582]

[C. Julius] Sohaemus

Senator, suffect consul c. 135/140, appointed by **ANTONINUS PIUS** King of Armenia in 140 and, presumably restored to Emesa as **Sohaemus II,** as he "reigned in succession to his ancestors" for forty years with a short interval 161-163. The name is from the Arab *Suhaym* [Birley (1988) 222, no. 41]

Samsigeramus I

Cicero made much sport on this man's name at Pompey's expense. He was dead by 51BC [Cic. *Ad. Att.* 11.16.2; Strabo xvi. 2.10]

L. Seius [   ]

Syme suggests he might have been called in full L. Seius Sallustius Herennius Macrinianus. Settipani agrees and adduces his descent from

Seius Fuscianus, suffect consul (i) 188. [Settipani (2000) 325 n. & 326.Syme (1971) 157

[Sex.] Varius Avitus Bassianus
See above, **ANTONINUS III AUGUSTUS**

Sex. Varius Marcellus,
An equestrian officer and former procurator of Britain during the Emperor **SEVERUS'S** last campaign there, adlected into the senate with rank of praetor c. 212, dying whilst governor of Numidia 213/214 He had at least one other son clearly implied by ILS 478, whose name not known, but perhaps an elder son, who died before 222; another (less likely) possibility is the HA's Varius Macrinus, a general serving in Illyricum under **ALEXANDER SEVERUS** but, if he existed at all, he was more likely a cousin [HA *V. Sev. Alex.* 58, 1; Birley (1988) 224].

*

Imperial claimant under Antoninus III

VERUS II
c. November 218- January 219

VERUS was an imperial claimant at Tyre in Syria in the months that followed the elevation of **ELAGABALUS**, in winter 218-219. He was said to have risen from centurion to the senate (probably through adlection by **CARACALLA** to fill in gaps left by his depredations) and was in 218 legate of IIIrd Legion Gallica in the East. He was probably faced with troops reduced to mutiny by news of the excesses of **ELAGABALUS**, despite his legion having been amongst those who supported him initially. The rising was put down early in 219, *VERUS* presumably killed and the Legion disbanded. Marcius Veracilius Verus, an early 3rd century suffect consul, of whose family little is known is the most likely culprit, but what was he doing serving as a legionary legate if he had been consul?[308] Nothing is known of the family.

*

308. Dio 80. 7

MAXIMUS I
218-219

[L.(?)] Gellius *MAXIMUS* **was** also apparently an imperial claimant in Coele Syria following the elevation of **ELAGABALUS**. He was the son of a doctor – presumably of equestrian rank – L. Gellius Maximus, of a family long settled in Pisidian Antioch. He was legate of the IVth (Scythian) Legion, but his reign was fairly short and he was killed in 219. He does get a mention, as 'Gellius', under **DIADUMENIANUS** in the HA.[309] Nothing is known of the family.

⋆

Imperial Claimant under Alexander I

TAURINUS
231

TAURINUS, like *VERUS* is only a *cognomen* and he was called *tyrannus* (usurper or pretender) by Polemius Silvius but was apparently the unwilling choice of the soldiers according to Victor.[310] Presumably this happened in 231, when **ALEXANDER** was amassing forces for his campaign against Artaxerxes of Persia. A former suffect consul, he was probably acclaimed in Syria where he may have been governor, and on the collapse of his revolt subsequently drowned himself in the Euphrates. The name (garbled as Verconius Turinus by the HA) evokes that of the senator attested in 155, Statilius Cassius Taurinus[311], surely the brother of the Statilius Taurus who was attested a year later. He was a member of the Arval Brethren and a patrician by creation. He was very likely the son of another Statilius Taurus who was a senator of praetorian rank in 117. The T. Statilius Silianus who was also an Arval Brother (in the reign of **CARACALLA** or **ELAGABALUS**[312]) must have been a close relative too. Indeed, Sir Ronald Syme, writing of this whole group of imperial claimants says that they 'may have asserted an illustrious ascendance'.[313]

---

309. Dio, 79. 7, 1-2; HA *V. Diadumenian.* 9,1 cf. 8, 4-9; PIR² G130 cf. G123, G. 131

310. Polemius Silvius *Laterculus* II. 30-31; Aurelius Victor 24.

311. PIR² S523; FS 3128

312. ILS 5039; PIR² S848. The alternative is that he could belong to the (presumably unrelated) Statilii Maximi. A family of greater prominence in the Antonine era.

313. Syme (1971) 159, n. 6

Whether these 2nd/3rd century Statilii were descended from the Statilii Tauri of the early empire is difficult to be sure, although both were patricians, and both of Imperial creation. The likelihood is that they were in some way, although there are two or three generations completely missing between the reign of **CLAUDIUS** and the senator of 117. The youngest recorded member of the Julio-Claudian group, in some way descended from the ancient patrician families of Valerius Messalla and Cornelius Sisenna, was Sisenna Statilius Taurus, a youthful *salius Palatinus*, a patrician in AD38 and later an Augur.[314] The family are believed to stem from T. Statilius, an Epicurean senator proscribed in 43 whose son, T. Statilius Taurus, became one of **AUGUSTUS'S** early marshals, consul (ii) in 26BC.[315] His two grandsons, Titus and Sisenna, were consul in AD11 and 16, the latter being the father of the augur.[316] The last attested males amongst the descendants of Augustus' marshal were Taurus Statilius Corvinus, consul in AD45 and his cousin T. Statilius Taurus who held office the year before. Whilst the former probably had no male heir – his much-married sister the empress Statilia Messallina (see above **Table XI Brief Lives**) had at least two children who bore the name – there may have been descendants of the latter who have dropped from record.

An attempt at a reconstruction of the family from the senator of 117 will be found in the adjacent box, **Table XXXII(a)**

TABLE XXXIII: THE POSSIBLE CONNECTIONS OF TAURINUS

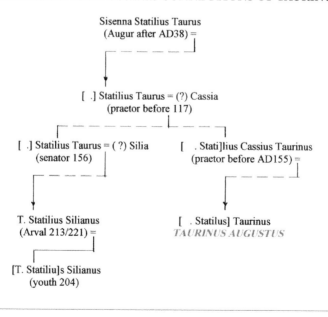

---

314. FS 3140 cf. PIR² S852

315. Wiseman (1971) No. 413

316. Early Tauri: PIR² S613, 851, cf. ILS 893, 7404 & FS 3141-2. The consul of AD11 was grandfather of the Empress Statilia Messallina.

Imperial claimant supposedly under Alexander I

[URANIUS
?231]

Uranius, of servile origin is said by Zosimus[317] and Georgius Syncellus[318] to have been an imperial claimant in Edessa also during the run-up to **ALEXANDER'S** Persian expedition, and thereby assumed to be the father of the later imperial claimant at the same city, *(URANIUS) ANTONINUS IV*, see below, **part V(a)**. This was once thought to be re-inforced by coin typology, but subsequent scholarship has demonstrated otherwise.[319] Thus, although *URANIUS* seems to have existed, he must be identified with his later namesake, in **part VI.**

∗

Imperial claimant under Alexander I

SELEUCUS
?231

SELEUCUS occurs only in two late sources[320]; he seems otherwise to be unknown. It is possible he could have been the general who led a rebellious legion from Egypt to join **ALEXANDER SEVERUS** in 232. If so, he would be of equestrian rank, Egypt being barred to senators. If not, then he may be identifiable with [C.(?)] Jul[ius] Ant[onius] Seleucus[321], under **ELAGABALUS** who was propraetorian legate in Lower Moesia and after that – promisingly for this identification – consular legate in Coele Syria at just this date. He is thus also possibly to be identified with the contemporary Antonius Seleucus v. c. *consularis noster.*[322]

His name suggests a descent from Seleucus IV Philopator, King of Syria 187-175BC via the Egyptian Royal house and either the children of Antonius and Cleopatra or the descendants of C. Julius Antiochus Epiphanes, last King of Commagene (AD38-72).

317. 1.12
318. p. 674
319. Fink (1939) 329; but for a doubt about this see Syme (1971) 159, cf.. Settipani (2000) 443
320. Polemius Silvius *Laterculus*, II. 30-31 & *Chronica Minora*, 520-523.
321. PIR² I154, where the identification with this imperial claimant is doubted; cf. Syme (1971) 159..
322. Gilliam, J. F., in *American Journal of Philology* LXXIX (1958) 231 f.

There were a number of mediatised royal houses in the second century senate, and such connections might indeed impel a man to aspire to the purple, following the successful example of such as **ELAGABALUS** and **ALEXANDER**, bearing in mind that the Royal House of Emesa was probably regarded as somewhat less illustrious than those of Syria and Commagene.

[.] **Jul[ius] Ant[onius] Seleucus** was suffect consul in the early 3rd century and was probably of the family of the Julii Maiores, descended in the female line from the daughter of **MARCUS ANTONIUS**. If this identification can be accepted, then the Commagenian connection would be through the female line.

The only other senatorial candidate might be M. Flavius Vitellius Seleucus, consul in 221; if he usurped, as a former ordinary consaul, it is unlikely that a writer like Herodian would have omitted to mention it.[323].

＊

---

323. Syme, *loc.cit*, n. 6.

The Imperial Succession
Maximinus I
Gordianus I
Gordianus II
Maximus II
Balbinus
Gordianus III

Imperial claimants
Magnus I
Quartinus
Sabinianus

MAXIMINUS I
(Known to history as Maximin Thrax)
21st March 235 – 24 June 238

Background

It is extraordinary that **MAXIMIN**, usually known additionally as 'Thrax' (The Thracian) was the first emperor to have risen to the purple from the ranks of the army and the first successfully to govern the empire without once visiting its capital. He was the second (following **MACRINUS**) to succeed as a non-senator. The HA claims that he was an exceedingly large man with an innate confidence in his own ability and a military talent that his superiors had recognised by promoting him swiftly being, at the time of his elevation, Prefect of the Recruits (*praefectus tironum*).[324] This, though, would suggest that he was less of a battle-hardened general as a military bureaucrat.

C. Julius Verus MAXIMINUS was born in 172 or 173[325], allegedly in a village near Oescus (near Pleven, Bulgaria), a part of the area of *Colonia Trebelliana* in Lower Moesia. He is alleged to have started life as a shepherd boy but because of his prodigious size and strength, recruited into the army under **SEPTIMIUS SEVERUS**. In fact he almost certainly enlisted in an entirely conventional manner when of age. By sheer ability, he rose to the rank of prefect and then later, legate of the *Legio* II Traiana, in Egypt, from whence senatorial officers were barred by an edict of Augustus. In Alexander's Eastern campaign he was prefect of Mesopotamia. He was prefect of Recruits in 235, which would seem like a demotion of sorts; perhaps it was, and rankled, which might explain his leadership of the revolt.

---

324. Haegemans (2010) 52-56.
325. PIR² I619; his age is given by Zonaras, XII, 16.

Reign

MAXIMINUS I was given an Imperial acclamation and hailed as Augustus 21st March 235, **ALEXANDER** being killed the next day.[326] His style as Augustus was: **Imperator Caesar C. Julius Verus Maximinus Pius Felix Invictus Augustus.**[327] This was confirmed by the senate 25 March 235, which body also recognised him as *Pontifex Maximus* and granted him the tribunician and proconsular power, renewable on 10th December, before which date he had received a second imperial acclamation.[328] In 236 he began the year as ordinary consul, assumed the surname **Germanicus Maximus** and associated his son as heir; thereafter he received two more Imperial acclamations. In 237 he was further styled **Dacicus Maximus** and **Sarmaticus Maximus** and was hailed as imperator for the fifth and sixth times, following these with an eighth acclamation in 238.[329] His wife, who almost certainly predeceased him, probably prior to his elevation to the purple, was **Caecilia Paulina**.[330] She always appears on coins with Divine honours, probably voted her by the senate at the Emperor's request.

The reign began with reluctant recognition by the senate, a body that he heartily seems to have despised, thus ending any pretence that the senate might have in determining policy or supporting the *princeps*. Nevertheless, he seems to have left in place the policies and personnel of his predecessor's régime, and mounted an immediate punitive expedition across the Rhine to deal with the Germanic tribes (specifically the Alemanni), which was successfully achieved, despite a pair of attempts to overthrow him, by imperial claimants *MAGNUS* and later *QUARTINUS* (see below), one involving a group of senators and their military contemporaries, the other by the destruction of his Rhine pontoon bridge, leaving him on the far side with little support, on the assumption that the Barbarians would do the rest before **MAXIMIN** could react effectively. Both failed dismally and in their wake (perhaps understandably) the cruelty of the new Emperor in dealing with these conspiracies became more marked. Furthermore, the Alemanni at this time constituted very little threat and there is the consequent suspicion that the new Emperor chose to attack them to earn easy honours to bolster his authority in Rome.

Nevertheless, having dealt with these Germans, the new Emperor then turned his attention to the Danube frontier, also apparently in turmoil, with Barbarians taking advantage of the troop reductions occasioned by **ALEXANDER'S** eastern campaign. Here he defeated the Dacians and Sarmatians 236-237, gaining more honours.

Both these campaigns were, however, costly and the exactions required by the Imperial fisc to cover the ever-increasing military expenditure were much resented in civilian circles, especially at Rome, where the aristocracy's attitude to him was one of socially grounded distaste combined with resentment at being not only fleeced but also comprehensively

---

326. See note above about the insecure nature of this date.
327. ILS 490
328. CIL. VI. 2001, 2009
329. ILS 488
330. ILS 492; PIR² C91 ; they married c. 213

by-passed. The fisc being unable to supply sufficient funds, the Emperor resorted first to extortion and confiscations, which only served to exacerbate tensions with the governing *élite*. His second resort was to antagonise the lower echelons of society by cutting back on several of the benefactions traditionally handed out to the Roman masses, like the *annona* (corn dole). He also further debased the coinage, which increased inflation.

His son, **Maximus**, serving as a military tribune in the army elsewhere, was summoned to the Emperor's side and given the name and title of Caesar probably in 236, thus designating him his heir. The HA also has the young Caesar betrothed to Julia Fadilla an alleged descendant of **ANTONINUS PIUS**.[331] If this unlikely match be accepted, it would show **MAXIMIN** repeating the strategy of both Julia Mamaea and Julia Soaemias in trying to ally a prince perceived to be well outside the loop of the mainstream governing class with a matron from the highest echelons of the senatorial aristocracy, preferably – as here – with previous Imperial connections.[332]

C. Julius Verus Maximus was born c. 214/215, serving as military tribune under his father in Egypt and was made heir with the style **C. Julius Verus Maximus Nobilissimus Caesar,** to which the senate (in all probability) added *Princeps Iuventutis*. He was hailed at least once as *imperator* and bore all the same victory epithets as his father: **Germanicus Maximus, Dacicus Maximus** and **Sarmaticus Maximus.** He was co-opted – presumably *in absentia* and in one case supernumerically - into two priestly colleges. Despite somewhat unreliable evidence he seems not to have become co-Augustus with his father.[333]

In the event, the exactions and confiscations pushed the *elite* too far, and one rather footling incident set off the rebellion (and rapid suppression) of the two **GORDIANI** and then the senate's nomination of the joint emperors **BALBINUS** and **MAXIMUS II,** resulting in the Emperor and his son hurrying towards Rome with an army, determined to extirpate these impertinent aristocrats. Both father and son had been declared public enemies (*hostes publici*) by the senate April 1st or 2nd 238, but were effectively sole rulers again from 12/13th April when the co-emperors **GORDIAN I & II** died, to 22nd April when the senate appointed **BALBINUS** and **MAXIMUS II. MAXIMIN** and Maximus Caesar were killed by their own troops on or about 24th June at the siege of Aquilaea, leaving no known issue.[334] It is this final debâcle that encourages one to wonder at the real quality of **MAXIMIN'S** abilities as a general, that he was so rapidly defeated by what was, in essence, a bunch of part-timers led by amateurs.

---

331. *V. Due Max.* 27, 6

332. She was actually a cousin three times removed from Pius (PIR² I668 & stemma p. 317) being great-great-grand-daughter of P. Julius Lupus (*ibid.*, I389) second husband of that Emperor's mother, Arria Fadilla. For the early generations of this family see **Table XX Brief Lives**. As the match is considered unlikely in the extreme, no table has been offered here.

333. PIR I620

334. Herodian 8, 5

Family

The Emperor **MAXIMIN** is thought actually to have been born and bred in a Thracian part of the province of (Lower) Moesia, attached to the latter by **DOMITIAN** in 86; contemporary references to him as a barbarian or 'semibarbarus' may reflect this, although it should be remembered that his father was said to be of Gothic descent. He was also said to have been a Roman citizen, although of lowly origins. In fact, Syme points out that most of this is fiction driven by a bad press. He considers him to have been a person of Roman descent – as the traditional form of his name might suggest - long settled in the Lower Moesian area.[335] He is really the precursor of the great run of Illyrian emperors that dominated the second half of the century and beyond, up to the death of **LICINIUS I.** The barbarian parents ascribed to him by the HA were furnished with the names of Micca and [H]abiba, the mother allegedly an Alan woman, and are considered to be entirely fictitious. No other relations are known in any source.

✶

Imperial claimant under Maximinus I

MAGNUS
Late March – early April 235

MAGNUS emerged as imperial claimant as the leader of an anti-**MAXIMIN** faction in the Rhine army, a section of which – perhaps appalled by the fate of the young **ALEXANDER** to whose family at least they were devoted – acclaimed him on hearing the news of the murder.[336] He was apparently a patrician ex-consul but one who must, in the event, have lacked conviction as a potential ruler, for he was refused recognition by the senate, although they may have been cowed by **MAXIMIN** or by the propect of the new emperor wreaking a dreadful revenge, as had **SEVERUS I.** They therefore officially deposed him - if we may trust the HA.[337] We might, however, doubt this, as they were quick enough to recognise the two **GORDIANI** later. His identity is, however, fairly clear, for a senator C. Petronius Magnus who appears on a list of patrons of the City of Canusium in 223 seems at a later date to have had his name erased, something only a *damnatio memoriae* could explain. He was praetor between 211 and 217, but the date of his suffect consulship is not clear. As an ex-consul in 235 it might have been held c. 218/223.[338]

Unfortunately, there were several families of senatorial Petronii at this – as most – dates, and no evidence has yet emerged to link *MAGNUS* with any of them.[339]

---

335. Syme (1971) 186
336. Herodian 7, 1. 4-8 ; PIR² M100
337. *V. Max.* 10. 1-6
338. ILS 6121, cf. PIR² P286
339. A descent from T. Pactumeius Magnus (suffect consul 183) seems possible, cf. PIR² P27, 28 & 29

Furthermore, the *cognomen* Magnus is fairly common too. There was another Magnus, a patrician suffect consul in the following generation who could have been a son, and of course, the family of **PETRONIUS MAXIMUS** and **OLYBRIUS** is riddled with people called Magnus, thought by some modern scholars to derive from a connection with **MAGNUS MAXIMUS** (see below, sections **V(d) and VII, Tables XLVII, LVIII(a) & LXIII Brief Lives**). This claimant is, however, the possible argument against a descent from **MAGNUS MAXIMUS**, albeit that so far, no genealogical connection between this Petronius Magnus and the first Petronii of the fourth century has yet emerged. In any case, *MAGNUS'S* attempt failed miserably and he was executed by **MAXIMINUS I**.

∗

Imperial claimant under Maximinus I

QUARTINUS
235/236

QUARTINUS, another ex-consul, attempted to seize power in 235 or 236, encouraged by a mutiny amongst the Osrhoenian auxiliaries, formerly fanatically dedicated to **ALEXANDER**.[340] The HA claims he was a former tribune of a Moorish auxiliary unit, cashiered by **MAXIMIN**.[341] His revolt was put down by one Macedo[342] but only after six months.[343] If his period in power were true, it might be legitimate to enquire why this man issued no coins in his own name; the two **GORDIANI** managed it in only a couple of weeks!

Herodian calls him Quartinus, the HA Titus, from which it is perhaps possible to identify him as **T. Fulvius Quartinus**. If so it is conceivable that he was a brother or half-brother of P. Fulvius Macrianus[344] the father of the later imperial claimants *MACRIANUS* and *QUIETUS*, see below, **part V(c)**. *QUARTINUS* is said by the HA[345] to have been married to a Calpurnia, descended from the illustrious Calpurnii Pisones of the Republic, last securely recorded a century before. Were this snippet corroborated elsewhere, it might fit neatly with the later (alleged) imperial claimant *PISO II*

---

340. There is confusion about the exact date, but it probably happened much later than *MAGNUS'S* rebellion and could have lasted up to six months.
341. *Tyr. Trig.* [*TT*] 32, 1-2
342. Herodian, VII, 1, 9-10 portrays him as a treacherous advisor. Perhaps a son of [?C.] Ofilius Valerius Macedo, suffect consul before 198 and in 204 a *XVvir sacri faciundis* [FS 2567, cf. ILS 5050A & 5934]
343. HA, *V. Due Max.* 11. 2-4; *TT.* 32, 6
344. PLRE I. Macrianus 2
345. *Tyr. Trig.* 32. 5

(see below, **part V**) but as it is possible he was fictitious too, the matter can safely be discounted. There is no hint of any issue.

*

GORDIANUS I
22nd March – c. 13th (22nd) April 238

GORDIANUS II
22nd March – c. 13th (22nd) April 238
(Known to history as GORDIAN I & II)

Background

The Gordians would be relegated to the status merely of imperial claimants were it not for the fact that they not only minted coins in both their names, but managed to obtain recognition from the senate, too, albeit in all likelihood (and unwittingly) posthumously. Their elevation to the purple was through an unlikely and rather minor set of circumstances. Because the financial exactions of **MAXIMIN THRAX** were allegedly so harsh, these fell on the simpler farming folk of the provinces, not just on the great senatorial landholdings. The officers responsible for extracting this tribute were the provincial procurators, and the officer *en post* in the province of Africa Proconsularis managed, by using force and even killing people and in defiance of the proconsul, to arouse the ire of the local propulation to the extent that the local élite, led by a local town councillor, one Mauricius[346] resolved to assassinate him. This was done at Thrysdus (El Djem, Tunisia) whilst the procurator was supervising the payment of the levies on olive oil, attended by the farmers, greater landowners and their tenants.

Having burnt their boats and virtually guaranteed bloody reprisals from the Emperor, these turbulent locals resolved to offer the purple to the elderly proconsul, **M. Antonius GORDIANUS**. He at first attempted to refuse but soon realised what a difficult situation they were all in; after all, **GORDIAN** as governor of the province, had either to have the procurator's murderers killed and order further reprisals, or go along with them and hope to fortune. Being – all authorities agree - 80 (or in his 80th year) he felt he had nothing to lose and accepted the acclamation.

As it happens, his son was with him serving as legionary legate. This situation is attested a fair number of times in the early empire, except usually the son was a junior senator. Here, however, presumably because the governor was unusually old, he had persuaded his son to do the honours, although he, too, was an ex-consul and certainly not ordinarily obliged to serve in a capacity usually reserved for ex-praetors.

---

346. But note, named only in the HA, *Tres Gord.* VII, 4

M. Antonius Gordianus Sempronianus Romanus[347] was born probably in Cappadocia in c 159, probably of a senatorial family and presumably served as quaestor c. 187 and *aedile* c. 189, establishing that he was not of a patrician family. Whilst serving in this office the HA tells us that he gave twelve gladiatorial shows, one for each month, a colossally expensive undertaking, reflecting on the enormous wealth of the family.[348] He was *praetor* presumably c. 191-192, but the upheavals following the death of **COMMODUS** may have delayed the advancement of his career, for although the HA claims he was consul with **CARACALLA**[349], it must have been after 216 when he was still an ex-*praetor*, serving as legate of Lower Britain [Britannia Inferior]; the province of Britain had then just been split into two to reduce the number of troops available to possible imperial claimants.[350] He thereafter must have been suffect consul – perhaps c. 222 in the wake of the elevation of **ALEXANDER** – becaming governor of Africa c. 237, which was the usual interval after the consulship for such a prestigious position.

His son **M. Antonius Gordianus Sempronianus Romanus,** later **GORDIAN II**[351], was born c. 192 and probably served as quaestor on the recommendation of **ELAGABALUS** c. 220/221 going on to serve as urban *praetor* on the recommendation of his successor, probably in 226 or 228[352]; he was suffect consul under **ALEXANDER**, probably in 229, after which he would have governed a province. He then offered to serve as his father's legate in Africa from 237 and both were acclaimed Emperor 22nd March 238.[353] It would seem that the philosopher Philostratus dedicated his *Lives of the Sophists* to an Antonius Gordianus, whom modern scholarship considers must be the son, not old Gordian, for he also claims him as a descendant of the famous eastern senator, Herodes Atticus (born c. 102) which would be barely possible for the father, bearing in mind that the sources mainly agree that he was around 80 in 238.

Reign

Hence, on his acclamation, **GORDIAN I** associated his son, elevated as **GORDIAN II** with him in his rule as co-Augustus, probably in the hope that should he die or need military action, he was there by his side to give aid.

Having accomplished all this, envoys were sent to the senate at Rome to announce their elevation, and the senate duly acknowledged them, declaring, with unusual boldness, **MAXIMIN** to be a public enemy, thereby setting in motion a civil war. The senate ordered coins to be struck in the names of the two Augusti, confirming that, either on acclamation or by decree of the senate, **GORDIAN I** had been awarded the additional *cognomen* of **Africanus.**

---

347. PIR² A833
348. V. *Tres. Gord.* 3. 5
349. *Ibid.,* 4. 2
350. Birley (1981) 181-186
351. PIR² A834
352. HA, *Tres. Gord.* XVIII. 4-5. There is nothing inherently unconvincing about this part of the HA's account.
353. The consulship is confirmed by a milestone at Caesaraea Maritima; only the HA attests him as consul before his elevation, which is an example of it containing nuggets of truth.

He seems to have adopted the style **Imperator Caesar M. Antonius Gordianus Sempronianus Romanus Africanus Augustus**.[354] It is not known exactly when his envoys reached Rome, but around April 1st or 2nd he had been granted, jointly with his son (see below), the tribunician and proconsular power, and been acknowledged as Pontifex Maximus. The two were also granted the title *Patres Patriae,* all of which was included on their coins. He took his own life 12/13th April on hearing of the defeat of his son, and they were both deified by the senate 22nd April 238, the date the news of his death reached Rome. The career of the son closely followed that of the father after their acclamation in Africa on 22nd March, although he was not regarded as *pontifex maximus*. His Imperial style was, therefore, **Imperator Caesar M. Antonius Gordianus Sempronianus Romanus Africanus Pius Felix Augustus**[355] and he was killed leading his forces against Capellianus, governor of Mauretania, 12/13 April 238, and was later also deified by the senate. He appears to have married but we do not know the name of his wife. The HA, never to be outdone by history, also claims that he had 22 concubines by whom he had at least 66 natural children, which sounds like wishful thinking on the part of the anonymous author![356] These even included the future emperor **CLAUDIUS II** according to the *Epitome*.[357] The HA at least allowed him one legitimate son, which, however, it fails to name, perhaps having run out of inspiration.[358] If a son indeed existed, he must have perished with his father and grandfather at the hands of Capellianus, or otherwise oner might suppose **GORDIAN III** would not have been chosen to succeed **BALBINUS** and **MAXIMUS II.**

Unfortunately, before the deputation to the senate could return to Africa, news came that, acting on the orders of **MAXIMINUS**, Capellianus, had defeated **GORDIANUS II**. Their joint rule had lasted an estimated 22 days. Capellianus crowned his victory with a particularly bloody mopping up operation in Carthage. Officially, however, the reign lasted until news of their defeat and death reached the senate in Rome on or before 22nd April.

Apart from their coming to power and their demise, nothing is known of their reign in between. How they planned to neutralise **MAXIMIN** is difficult to estimate, for the odds were heavily stacked against their success. Blocking the grain supply would have been their only ploy, as *MACER* found in 69. Perhaps the subsequent successful defence of Italy by their successors, **MAXIMUS** and **BALBINUS**, gives the clue. It could have been done, but the fact that they were still in Africa nearly a month after their acclamation suggests that neither was imbued with the sort of dash that got **SEVERUS** to Rome with such aplomb in 193; their inaction seems with hindsight, to smack of the proverbial rabbit caught in headlights – but then, one was by the standards of the time, exceedingly old and the other middle aged.

---

354. ILS 493
355. ILS 493
356. *Ibid.* 19. 3
357. *Epitome* 34, 2
358. HA *Tres Gordiani.* VI. 3

Family

As might be expected, the HA makes extravagant claims for the antecedents of the Gordians. **GORDIAN I** was descended on his father's side, it avers, from the Gracchi – the assassinated aristocratic peoples' tribunes for 133 and 122-121 BC, Ti. and C. Sempronius Gracchus – and from his mother's side of the family from **TRAIANUS** - who was childless. It goes on to assert that **GORDIAN'S** father, grandfather and great-grandfather all held the consulship, as had his wife's father and grandfather, not to mention two of her great-great grandfathers.[359] Of course, none of this is so very remarkable amongst the senatorial aristocracy of any era. The point is, how much of it can be accepted and if some are elsewhere attested, is it possible to identify the people concerned?

The pedigree here is partly based on Oliver, J. H., *The Ancestry of Gordian I*.[360] The first thing is to establish whether there is any likelihood of **GORDIAN I'S** father being called Maecius Marullus as the HA asserts. The *cognomen* Marullus is found primarily as borne by the Eggii, a family originating from Aeclanum (Mirabella Eclano) in Italy which entered the senate under **CLAUDIUS** if not before. Just how closely related L. Eggius Marullus, who served before 47 as the magistrate responsible for the oversight of the Tiber[361] was to C. Eggius Ambibulus, recorded as a senator the year following, is not entirely clear; they may have been brothers, perhaps cousins.

Sir Ronald Syme, in the process of emphatically placing the author of the HA in the last decade of the 4th century, rubbished his constant use of the name Maecius as being a satirical throwback from the pretentiously ancestored Maecii of that era as lauded by St. Jerome.[362] Yet we find the Eggii and Maecii intertwined in the name of <u>C. Eggius [L.] f. Cor. Ambibulus</u> Pomponius Longinus Cassianus L. Maecius Postumus, consul in 126.[363] In all probability, he was born a grandson of M. Pomponius M. f. Cor. Bassulus, an equestrian poet of the early empire, although whether the intermediate generation was marked by a senator who married a lady – as did **NERO'S** great marshal Corbulo (see **Table VII(a) Brief Lives**) – from the distinguished republican house of the Cassii Longini as the grandson's name seems to imply, we have no proof. L. Maecius Postumus, suffect consul in 98[364] was the husband of an Eggia Ambibula who went on to marry <u>P. Calvisius Ruso</u> Julius Frontinus, suffect consul c. 84[365] and a great-grandfather of **MARCUS AURELIUS** (see **table XIX(b) Brief Lives**). It may be that her grandfather, the senator of 48, had an unrecorded son called Lucius who adopted the consul of 126, who also perhaps made it into the patriciate on **TRAJAN'S** accession.

All this is to establish that a man called Maecius Marullus is not necessarily to be dismissed as fiction, despite Syme's assertion that the author of the HA 'was amusing himself with mild

359. *Tres Gord.* II. 2
360. *American Journal of Philology* 89 (1968) 345-347
361. ILS 5926
362. Syme (1968) 162-163
363. ILS 1054
364. ILS 5027
365. PIR² C350, corrected in Birley (1987) 245

parody of the pretensions advertised by the Roman aristocracy.' After all, he was making a point, using plenty of rhetoric and irony in his inimitable way. Since Syme first wrote, however, an inscription at Corinth emerged naming Maecius Marullus and his father, a Corinthian rhetor and sophist, Maecius Faustinus.[366] Faustinus, as a man living in the time of **ANTONINUS PIUS**, could easily have been enfranchised by the consul of 126, taking his name and bestowing that of a member of his family on his son. Furthermore, bearing in mind that one of the Gordian Emperors (probably the younger) was the dedicatee of Philostratus, a Syrian Sophist, having a Sophist rhetor as a (great) grandfather would rather strengthen the supposition that Marullus could indeed have been **GORDIAN I**'s father.

Furthermore, the HA asserts a descent from the Gracchi and, in **GORDIAN I** and **II**, we find the name Sempronianus. Syme pointed out that this 'might have suggested a fable of Gracchan descent'. But, as he says in his next sentence, the HA 'seems to know nothing the the Gordians use of this name.' Whilst theoretically possible, such a descent would appear to be a speculation too far.

Likewise, the name 'Romanus', if inherited, calls to mind either P. Plotius Romanus, an early Severan suffect consul whose grandfather was a leading citizen of Ostia[367] or, somewhat less likely, from the younger Pliny's equestrian *protégé*, C̲. Licinius Marinus V̲o̲c̲o̲n̲i̲u̲s̲ R̲o̲m̲a̲n̲u̲s̲ who came from Spain.[368] Less reliance can probably be placed on his alleged kinswoman Sempronia Romana except to demonstrate the possibility of these two names coming together in contexts other than amongst the ancestors of the Gordians.

The final problem is the 'M. Antonius' with which the **GORDIANS**' names begin. Oliver suggests another distinguished Corinthian, M. Antonius Achaicus[369] or a member of his family, might have adopted him if not already related by marriage. This is attractive, but the Roman world was, thanks **to Mark Antony's** decade of dominance of the east, not short of people whose names began with M. Antonius.

What therefore of the HA's claims that three generations of Gordian I's antecedents had held the consulship? His father seems indeed to have held a suffect consulship under **COMMODUS** but if Oliver's reconstruction of his ancestry is correct, then that is all.[370]

Turning the the Emperor's mother, allegedly Ulpia Gordiana, there are far fewer clues. A literal 'descent from Trajan' we know to be absurd, the assumption triggered by the use of the *nomen* Ulpius, which was, thanks to the enfranchising activities of the Emperor **TRAJAN** also common throughout the Roman world (see **Table XVIII**).

Finally there is the *cognomen*. It may have derived from a connection with Ti. Claudius Ti. f. Quir. Gordianus, consul designate in 188 when he was legate of Numidia. He came from Tyana in Cappadocia (Kemerhisar, Turkey), although he may have derived his *cognomen* ultimately from Gordium in the province of Asia (Yassihüyük, Turkey). His inscription in

---

366. Oliver (1968) 345-347; contemptuously dismissed as "co-incidence" by Syme (Syme (1971) 169)
367. ILS 6138
368. Syme (1958) I. 81; PIR² L210. He was from Hispania Tarraconensis.
369. In Kent, J. H., *Corinth* VIII (1966) iii, 264
370. *Epigraphica* 33 (1971) 82; AE (1971) 62

Numidia is erased, perhaps precisely because of a relationship with the future emperor who was, after all, deposed by a subsequent governor of the provice.[371] This would also lend credence to Philostratus's assertion that **GORDIAN I** was descended from the senatorial sophist Herodes Atticus, for he is generally believed to have been close kin to Claudius Gordianus.

Finally **GORDIAN II** is supplied with an Empress with a challenging name, too. According to the HA she was called **Fabia Orestilla**[372] - said by the same unreliable source to have been great-grand-daughter of **ANTONINUS PIUS** and daughter of the otherwise unknown Annius Severus, which name with its happy concatenation of Antonine and Severan elements instantly engenders suspicion.[373] To reconstruct a possible descent for Fabia Orestilla it would be necessary to discard Annius Severus as her father and replace him with an unrecorded Fabius (not impossible) and suppose that he was married to Herodes Atticus's daughter (who is thought to have had a son by an unknown husband). Fabia's *cognomen* might be explained by kinship to the suffect consul Claudius Orestes, a brother or half brother of Ti. Claudius Pompeianus, consul (ii) 173, the new man from Syrian Antioch who married Annia Aurelia Galeria, daughter of **MARCUS AURELIUS**, see **Table XXIII Brief Lives**.

That the family survived in some branch (setting aside HA's assertion of the prolixity of the issue of **GORDIANUS II**) might possibly be evidenced by the Carthaginian senator Gordianus who fled to Rome when the Vandals took Carthage in 439 but whose son Claudius later managed to reclaim the family's estate in Byzacena.[374]

The table below, therefore, is only a suggested attempt at a reconstruction of the Gordian dynasty.[375] Settipani suggests that the grandfather of **GORDIAN I** was a M. Antonius [   ], praetor designate in 135 married to a Sempronia Romana, attested daughter of T. Flavius Sempronius Aquila, an Equestrian bureaucrat from Galatia by a neice of Herodes Atticus. It is not that far removed from **Table XXXIV**, but without the adoption there suggested.[376]

---

371. PIR² C880

372. *Tres. Gord.* 2. 2

373. *ibid.* 6. 4; 17, 4

374. Suggested by Conant 145, cf. PLRE II Gordianus 1. His grandson was Fulgentius, Bishop of Ruspe.

375. Where (enfr.) refers to enfranchisement by grant of citizenship.

376. Settipani (2000) 136-137, cf.pedigree p. 141 on the Maecii.

TABLE XXXIV: THE GORDIANS

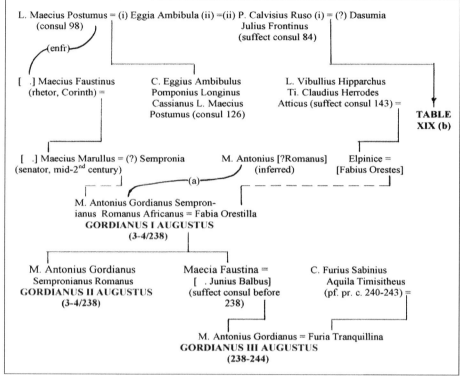

TABLE XXXIV: BRIEF LIVES

P. Calvisus Ruso Julius Frontinus

His marriage to Eggia is secure, that to Dasumia not directly attested. Yet by it he was ancestor of **MARCUS AURELIUS**. See **Table XIX(b) Brief Lives.**

C. Eggius [L.]f. Cor. Ambibulus Pomponius Longinus Cassianus L. Maecius Postumus

Born about 88, consul in 126, having been raised to patrician rank by **TRAJAN** in 98. It is thought he was a Maecius (son of the consul of 98) adopted by L. Eggius Ambibulus a son C. Eggius Ambibulus, a senator in the reign of **CLAUDIUS I** [ILS 1054]

C. Furius Sabinius Aquila Timisitheus

Highly competent praetorian prefect appointed by

GORDIANUS III in 240, but who died of natural causes on campaign in 243, a happenstance which probably sealed the young ruler's fate. His daughter married the emperor. See **Table XXX(b) Brief Lives.**

[C. Junius Balbus]

According to the HA an ex-consul who married the sister of **GORDIAN II**, but for whose existence no other attestation can be found. However, there was a C. Junius Balbus, sub-prefect of the vigils (assistant police chief) attested in 203. He could have had a senatorial son or nephew, so the name is at least credible [PIR[2] I733, 734]

Maecia Faustina

That **GORDIAN II** had a sister who was the mother of **GORDIAN III** there is no doubt. The problem is that we cannot bre sure if this was her name. She died with her son in 244.

[L.] Maecius Faustinus

A sophist rhetor at Corinth, early 2nd century. Possibly enfranchised by L. Maecius Postumus or a member of his family [Oliver (1968) *loc.cit.*]..

[L.] Maecius Marullus

Attested by an inscription at Corinth and, if the HA is right in supposing **GORDIAN I** to have been the son of a consul, a senator and suffect consul [cf. *ibid.* & Syme (1971) 4, 12, 169]

L. Maecius Postumus

Consul 98 and son of another L. Maecius Postumus; a good candidate to be the man who enfranchised Maecius of Coninth with Roman citizenship [FS 2324, 2325].

L. Vibullius Hipparchus Ti. Claudius <u>Herodes Atticus</u>

Athenian grandee and suffect consul in 143 [Pomeroy (2007) *passim.*]

*

MAXIMUS II
(Known to history as PUPIENUS MAXIMUS)
22nd April – 29th July 238

BALBINUS
22nd April – 29th July 238

Background

News of the demise of the two Gordians seems not to have reached Rome until 21st or 22nd April, **MAXIMIN THRAX a**gain being sole unchallenged ruler during that time, albeit outlawed by the senate. However, on 22nd April, the senate no doubt in apprehensive state, met to deal with the crisis, bearing in mind that the cruel emperor was likely to exact a terrible revenge on their number for their condemnation of himself and enthusiastic support for the Gordians. Indeed, as soon as news came that the Gordians had raised the standard of revolt, the senate appointed a panel of twenty ex-consuls (*vigintiviri*) to make arrangements for the eventuality of **MAXIMIN** invading Italy with a view to exacting a terrible revenge.

The senate deified the two late emperors, and nominated the two senior presiding consulars of the *vigintiviri* as joint emperors: **M. Clodius Pupienus Maximus** and **D. Caelius Balbinus Calvinus**, henceforth the emperors **MAXIMUS II** and **BALBINUS**. The first was a distinguished general, but of not particularly distinguished family, whilst the other was of illustrious family – or so we are told by HA.³⁷⁷ In fact, analysis of their

---

377. V. *Max. et Balb.* 2. 7, cf. PIR² C1179

families (see below) suggests that both were upper class patricians, the former a successful if rather strict general, the latter a notably able administrator. Being the senior members of the committee, they were, of course, getting on in years.

M. Clodius Pupienus Maximus was born c. 175 – Zonaras gives his age as 74 on accession, but the evidence seems not to bear this out. Herodian tells us **MAXIMUS** was of patrician rank, which would have given him an accelerated career; his son's career tells us that *he* certainly was patrician.[378] The HA claims **MAXIMUS** was "adopted as a son" by an unattested Pescennia Marcellina[379], which seems highly unlikely. He was, however, suffect consul in c. 215/217. He thereafter governed either Upper or Lower Germany, followed by Asia before becoming ordinary consul in 234, following this with the office of Prefect of the City (PUR), in which he was remembered, according to the HA, as being severe, if not harsh, but by Herodian as having exercised the office without bias.[380] The exact chronology of this post is not certain, but the way the urban populace reacted against him indicates that memories were still fresh and suggests that it was probably just after his second consulship rather than before it, which is more or less what one would expect.

D. Caelius Calvinus Balbinus[381] was born, probably at Rome, in between 165 and 170, although Zonaras[382] says 174, but this is generally accepted as being too late. He was suffect consul in 203, which would be about right for a man of distinguished family and – as alleged – a patrician. Thus he was a *Salius Palatinus* and would also have been quaestor c. 194/6, praetor c. 196/8. He served a second consulship – also suffect in this case – in 213. The HA tells us that he governed Asia, Africa, Bithynia, Galatia, Pontus, Thrace and 'The Gauls'.[383] Leaving aside Pontus – only created by **DIOCLETIAN** and thus exisiting when the HA was written, but not in **BALBINUS'S** time – this list is perfectly reasonable given the length of his service, although it seems in approximiately in reverse order of seniority, the most prestigious coming first. With **MAXIMUS** he co-adopted the young nephew of **GORDIANUS II** before the end of April.

Reign

MAXIMUS was nominated one of the *vigintiviri* by the senate late in March 238 and was appointed one of the two Augusti to replace the Gordians on 22nd April 238. Thereby he was invested with the proconsular and tribunician power, renewable on 10th December yearly. He had, with **BALBINUS**, jointly adopted as heir **GORDIANUS**, the nephew of **GORDIAN II** before the end of April. He was killed with **BALBINUS** in Rome 29th July

---

378. ILS 1185; PIR² C1179; XII, 17; Settipani rather daringly adduces his descent from the ancient republican patrician Claudii Pulchres: *op. cit.* 118-128 and pedigree p. 123

379. HA, *V. Max. et Balb.* 5. 7; cf., **Table XXVIII Brief Lives.**

380. Syme (1971) 171; Herodian 7, 10. 4, but who later agreed that he *had* been severe (*ibid.* 7, 10. 6). For the approximate year: Mennen (2011) 260.

381. FS1003; PIR² C126

382. *Op. cit.* xii, 17

383. V. *Max. et Balbin.* 7, 2

the same year. His imperial style was: **Imperator Caesar M. Clodius Pupienus Maximus Pius Felix Augustus.**[384]

After his acclamation, the career of **BALBINUS** exactly followed that of **MAXIMUS.** His Imperial style, however, was: **Imperator Caesar D. Caelius Calvinus Balbinus Pius Felix Augustus.** Both Emperors were also declared *Patres Senatus* – Fathers of the Senate and the office of pontifex maximus was given to each of them, an anomaly, but not without precedent.[385]

Unfortunately, neither the urban plebs nor the praetorians were too keen on being ruled by a pair of ageing patricians and consequently the former rioted and the latter failed to assist. In the end, it was made clear that the two new Augusti should share their rule with the nephew of **GORDIAN II**, who appeared to enjoy some popularity, was exceedingly rich – enabling the Emperors to pay a donative to calm febrile expectations – and who was thenceforth adopted jointly by them and nominated Caesar.

This done, action was essential, as **MAXIMIN** had already reached the borders of Italy. **MAXIMUS** therefore, gathered together a rather disparate body of troops, strengthened by the praetorian guard, and headed north, whilst two other *vigintiviri* managed to halt the irate Emperor outside the strategic city of Aquileia. This was an astute move, as **MAXIMIN** had to take it to be able to maintain his southward momentum. He offered an amnesty if it surrendered, but his reputation being as it was, the senatorial leaders within rejected it. A siege thus began, with the forces of **MAXIMUS** blockading the city and **MAXIMIN** investing it, but cut off from his supplies by the blockade.

After a desperate siege, the Italian elements within the army of **MAXIMIN** began to become unsettled at so long drawn out an affair against their follow countrymen and they began to conspire with elements of the Praetorian Guard to bring matters to a conclusion. The *Legio* II Parthica, mainly recruited from Campania, therefore took matters into their own hands and on 24th June killed the Emperor and his son, lifted the siege and took their heads to Ravenna where **MAXIMUS** had set up his HQ.

The ease with which the traditional ruling class, for decades increasingly out of the loop of supreme power, managed to bring about the fall of **MAXIMIN,** requires explanation. Traditional top-level patronage appears to have been important in spreading the revolt from Rome to the Provinces, and the Thracian's fall was hastened by the senate presciently siezing control of the Italian ports, constrainng his ability to re- supply and thereby blocking a significant channel of communication to the wider empire.[386]

MAXIMUS then disbanded his irregular forces, sent **MAXIMIN**'S legions back to their correct provinces and returned to Rome with a personal guard of Germans and the praetorian cohorts.

---

384. ILS 496; Syme (1971) 163-166, 173-178
385. PIR² 126, cf. Syme (1971) 163-166, 170-173.
386. Haegemans (2010) 34, 182-5, 191

The returning Augustus came back to an ovation (*ovatio*), which was only one stage down from a triumph – whilst his unfortunate colleague had been having trouble in Rome with discontent and unrest, exacerbated by a pair of senatorial delinquents, trying to be helpful, who put to death a group of praetorians without authority. Thus **BALBINUS** greeted his colleague with a diminished respect. The stage was thus set for them to fall out.

This they duly did, despite the increasingly insistent evidence of their coin issues that they were working in harmony. Nevertheless, discord was apparent and this, combined with **MAXIMUS'** unpopularity from his time as City Prefect, when he was known for his severity, the praetorian guard's dislike of emperors appointed by the senate but not approved by themselves and by **BALBINUS'** inaction over the senatorial murder of a number of guards during his colleague's absence, led to frustrations coming to boiling point. What clinched it was **MAXIMUS** proposing to deploy his personal German guards to protect the emperors from a praetorian-led mob, which had turned ugly at the conclusion of the Capitoline Games. **BALBINUS** rejected this proposal, assuming it was a ploy to get rid of him. Whilst they were arguing about this on 29th July 238, the praetorians entered the palace, dragged both of them out and killed them, proclaiming the youthful Caesar **GORDIANUS III** in their place.

Family: Maximus

MAXIMUS'S family presents us with a plethora of clues as to his origin, but few firm facts. The tale the HA peddles that he was the son of a blacksmith is pure fiction. The Pupieni appear to have come from Volterrae (Volterra). His wife's name is nowhere supplied by ancient sources, but from the first appearance amongst his children of certain names, we are on pretty firm ground in supposing her to be a Sextia and probably the daughter of T. Sextius Lateranus, consul in 197, himself the grandson of T. Sextius Africanus, consul in 112 and a member of an old senatorial family going back to one of Caesar's adherents, T. Sextius, who acquired his *cognomen* Africanus from a notable proconsulate of Africa 44-40 BC.[387] The fact that she was not named in any of the accounts of the events of 238 and that no coins were struck in her name strongly suggests that she was dead before her husband's elevation. Their daughter's name suggests that the Sextii had contracted a fairly recent marriage with the Cornelii Cethegi – a relatively obscure but ancient patrican family from the Republic still managing to survive in the later 2nd century.[388]

It is only possible to push back **MAXIMUS II's** male line one or possibly two generations but it is tempting to see a Statilia M[axim]a and her husband, a mid 2nd century senator whose *nomen* began [.] Pu[   ] as the emperor's grandparents, with the lady supplying him with his *cognomen* Maximus. There is also discoverable a freedman of a person called

---

387. Wiseman (1971) No. 102; *Classical Quarterly* (1964) 130-131; they were possibly a junior branch Republican family of consular rank, the Sextii Calvini: Syme (1987) 176.

388. They may have been a branch of the Cornelii Lentuli which revived the *cognomen* as they demonstrably had that of Scipio, both in the late 1st century BC. The name Cethegus survived into the 6th centiury amongst the Roman aristocracy.

L. Clodius Pup[ienus   ] whose status in unknown, date not closely assignable, but who could be the same man or a close relation.[389]

On the distaff side the name Clodius, originally the plebeian version of the patrician Claudius, looks as though it might have come in via the emperor's mother, whom we only know as Prima courtesy, however, of the HA and unconfirmed elsewhere. It is here suggested that she was called Clodia/Claudia Pulchra and have been a scion of this illustrious family for the survival of which in the early empire there is some support and would explain both the Clodius and Pulcher elements in the Emperor's name and in those of his probable issue and posterity. The appearance of the name Lateranus on both sides of Maximus's family might suggest that the Claudii/Clodii and Sextii may well have both descended from marriage with daughters of Q. Plautius Q.f. Lateranus, killed by Nero in 65 when consul designate without being allowed to embrace his children.[390]

The most interesting aspect is that not only did this emperor have issue, but that they and three generations afterwards bore elements of his name, which is rare. Even those rulers who did leave numerous descendants, like **MARCUS AURELIUS** or plenty of collaterals like the Julio-Claudians or the Severans, tended to see successors in the Imperial office a threat and slaughter them wholesale. Here, the succession of a minor, appointed before the praetorian guard managed to kill the joint emperors, seems to have obviated such a dire happenstance. By the time another soldier emperor had emerged in the person of **PHILIP I**, the grandchildren of so ephemeral a figure as **MAXIMUS** were probably thought to be entirely unthreatening to the new régime.

As is clear in the accompanying Brief Lives section, the use of the *signum* Gennadius by M. Ulpius Pupienus Silvanus seems to point to further continuity possibly even as late as the early 7th century.

---

389. Syme (1971) 174-175 quoting CIL.IX.5765 at Ricina
390. Syme *loc.cit.* Plautius Lateranus: Tac. *Ann.* XV 59

TABLE XXXV: THE FAMILY OF MAXIMUS II

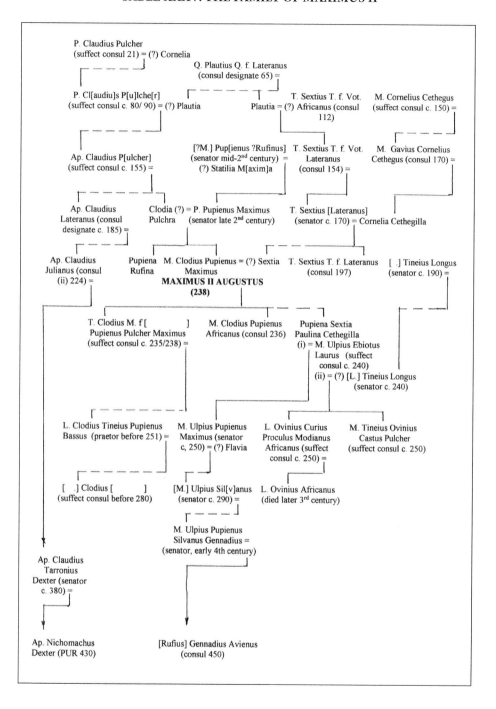

TABLE XXXV: BRIEF LIVES

Ap. Claudius Julianus
Suffect consul c. 200, consul again in 224 & PUR. He had a daughter Claudia Sabinilla, who claimed descend from Aeneas. His posterity survived into the fifth century [ILS 1184; PIR² C901].

Ap. Cl[audius] Lateranus
Noman possibly spelt *Clodius* if MAXIMUS' usage is anything to go by. When designated suffect consul had had served on a religious board, and had been propraetorian legate of *Legio* III Italica, raised 165 to serve in **MARCUS AURELIUS'** German campaign. His cognomen strongly suggests descent from Plautius Lateranus [ILS 3203] (qv).

Ap. Claudius P[ulcher]
Suffect consul in an unkown year mid-2nd century, is named on an inscription on which the upright of the first letter of his cognomen is visible: a 'P' for Pulcher seems plausible. [CIL XVI 131; PIR² C761]

P. Claudius Pulcher
Suffect consul in 21, grandson of P. Clodius, the troublesome peoples' triune of 58 killed in 52BC, so presumably no longer a patrician, as the tribune had himself adopted out of his own family to obtain plebeian status to run as tribune. His brother Appius was exiled in 2BC for adultery with Julia, daughter of **AUGUSTUS**. cf. also **Tables V & VIII** [FS2724; PIR² P 472]

P. Cl[audiu]s P[u]lche[r]
A suffect consul of the later Flavian period, on an inscription at Ostia; probably grandson of the foregoing [PIR² C986]

Ap. Claudius Tarronius Dexter
Certainly descended from Q. [T]arronius Q.f.

Fab. Dexter, a third century curule aedile designate, and himself a late 4th century senator [PLRE I Dexter 4, cf. PIR² T29]

Clodia Pulchra
All the evidence suggests a lady of this name as the Emperor's mother, although HA calls her Prima [HA *V. Max et Balb.* 5; Settipani 123, 392].

[.] Clodius [   ]
Suffect consul before 280; not enough left of the inscription for us to be sure he belongs to this family [PLRE I. p. 217., cf. PIR² C1153]

M. [Clodius] Pupienus Africanus
Consul 236 [ILS 466 ; Syme (1971) 174]

M. Clodius Pupienus Maximus
See above **MAXIMUS II AUGUSTUS**

T. Clodius M. f [   ] Pupienus Pulcher Maximus
Suffect consul c. 235/238, partron of Tibur (Tivoli), and a patrician. His son's inscription demonstrates (from her freedman's name) that he married a Tineia The missing name may be Lateranus[FS1253; ILS 1185; PIR² C1180. 1185]

L. Clodius Tineius Pupienus Bassus
Praetor before 251 [PIR² P1084]

M. Cornelius Cethegus
Suffect consul c. 150, he was proconsul of Asia twenty years later and a descendant of Ser. Cornelius Cethegus (consul 24) of an ancient branch of the great patrician house of the Cornelii going back to M. Cornelius M. f. Cethegus, pontifex maximus, who died in 211.

M. Gavius Cornelius Cethegus

Consul 170, died c. 180. It is by no means clear whether this man was the son of the preceding or merely adopted by him. If the latter, he was probably son of M. Gavius M. f. Pob. Squilla Gallicanus consul in 150 and great-grandson of C. Cornelius Gallicanus, suffect consul in 85 who is thought to have married the patrician heiress Cornelia Cethegilla Aemilia Plancina. The name and quite probably the bloodline survived into the 6th century, witness Fl. Rufius Nichomachus Cethegus (consul 504) and his probable descendant Cethegus, *patricius* and *vir gloriosus* at Rome in 598 [Brown (1984) 23.27.29. 222; Morris (1965) 88f; PLRE II. p.281; IIIA, p. 279].

Ap. Nichomachus Dexter

Widely considered a descendant of Ap. Claudius Tarronius Dexter, he was prefect of the City (PUR) in 430. [PLRE II Dexter 3]

L. Ovinius Africanus

His existence was recorded only in death, as a youth, mid to late 3rd century [PLRE I. Africanus 7].

L. Ovinius Curius Proculus Modianus Africanus

Sufferct consul c. 250. His wife's name is unknown but she was a sister of Claudiana Eusebia. Possibly the line continued: note the Africanus who held some kind of post in 326 and another, governor of Pannonia who was killed 385 [PIR[2] O123].

Q. Plautius Q. f. Lateranus

Son of Q. Plautius, suffect consul 36 but relegated from senate for being one of Empress Messallina's lovers in 48, but restored by Nero in 55. He was killed for involvement in Piso's plot. A kinsman of the Plautii Silvani (see **Table X** brief lives). He had children living in 65. [Tac. *Ann.* XI, 36; XIII, 11, XV, 49 & 59]

Pupiena Rufina

Recorded as a *clarissima femina* (*c.f.* = lady of senatorial rank) early/mid 3rd century, cf. [?Clod]ia Casta Si[Sabi]nilla, a girl in 204 [PIR[2] P804]

Pupien[i]a Sextia M. f. Paulina Cethegilla

Her name Paulina also suggests an Aemilian ancestry for her, presumably via her mother [PIR[2] P805]

[?M.] Pup[ienus ?Rufinus]

Senator mid-2[nd] century. Note also L. Clodius Pup[ienus] of Ricinsa, Picenum, living approximately 3[rd] century, for a possible relative [CIL IX. 5765].

P. Pupienus Maximus

Later 2nd century figure whose daughter was called Pupienia Rufina and who wife was, according to the HA, called Prima, see Clodia Pulchra above. The Emperor also had, according to the HA, four brothers and three other sisters, who failed to live to full maturity. [HA *V Max. et Balb.* V, 1; Syme (1971) 174 f., quoting CIL.VI. 25233]

[Rufius] Gennadius Avienus

Consul of 450, Avienus, who was said by Sidonius Apollinaris to be a descendant of the (Valerii Messallae) Corvini and of the late imperial Decii. It is likely that Avienus was an ancestor in some degree of another Gennadius, equally aristocratic, who was a successful general, *magister militum* of Africa and first *exarch* there 591-598. A Gennadius who was PUC in the early 7th century was probably his son. If all this can be accepted, it represents the continuing bloodline of **MAXIMUS II** enduring four and a half centuries, not to mention the bloodline of the Cornelii Cethegi from the early Republic [PLRE II. Avienus 4; III. Gennadius 1]..

Sextia

Probably to be identified with the Sextia Cethegilla who appears in three Roman inscriptions of the period.[CIL VI 11058, 11684 & 26529]

T. Sextius T. f. Vot. Lateranus (elder)

Consul 112, married Asinia, daughter of C. Asinius Pollio, a noble ex-praetor killed in the Year of the Four Emperors, and son of the multi-named Lateranus who was consul in 94, himself apparently adopted from a cousin's family by the T. Sextius Africanus who was made a patrician in 48 and suffect consul in 59, great- grandson of the Caesarian officer [FS3087 & p. 895; PIR² A1240, S659, 660, 668; Wiseman (1964) 130-131]

T. Sextius T. f. Vot. Lateranus (younger)

Consul 154, son of T. Sextius Africanus consul in 112 [FS 3088; PIR² 666].

T. Sextius Lateranus

Consul in 197 and a friend of **SEVERUS**, by whom, apparently he was enriched [Syme (971) 174]

Q. Tineus Clemens

Consul 196 and probably husband of an Ovinia. He was one of three consular brothers, all the third generation of their family, to hold that office. They originated from Roman stock settled in one of the eastern provinces, although ultimately Etruscan, probably specifically from Tibur (Tivoli) or Praeneste (Palestrina). The family were made patrician by **ANTONINUS PIUS** [PIR² T.223, cf. 227, 228-229, 231; Syme (1971) 165]

[L.] Tineius [Q.]f. Arn. Longus

Son of Tineius Longus, quaestor designate under **COMMODUS** and himself praetor under **SEVERUS,** which suggests that **MAXIMUS'S**

daughter may have been the eldest child and emphasises that the Emperor was getting on a bit by the time he assumed the purple. Pupiena may have been his second wife, however. The marriage is attested by the names of the sons, but Settipani suggests that a sister may have married T. Clodius Pulcher Maximus (qv) and thereby have become mother of the following. [PIR² T225; Settimpani (2000) 123]

M. Tineius Ovinus L. f. Arn. Castus Pulcher

Suffect consul c. 250 and a patrician by creation; his filiation supplies his father's *praenomen* [FS3262; ILS 1207; PIR² T226]

M. Ulpius Eubiotus Laurus

First (?) husband of Pupiena Sextia Paulina Cethegilla, a suffect consul in the second quarter of the 3rd century (c. 230) [Syme (1971) 174]

M. Ulpius Pupienus Maximus

A mid-3rd century senator, whose names make his descent from the Emperor clear. It might be reasonable to assume from the son's name, his wife, possibly Flavia, would have been a daughter of a putative Silvanus, conceivably suggesting descent from the other Plautii. [PIR² V564]

[M.] Ulpius Sil[v]anus

Governor of Lycia c. 290. It is possible that the Ulpius Silanus recorded by the HA under **AURELIAN** may be the same man. The Silvanus recorded in the *Passio St. Luciliani* as governor of Bithynia could conceivably be him, too, but the reliablility of much hagiography can often be on a par with the HA and this Silvanus is not elsewhere attested [HV *V. Aurel.* 19, 3; PLRE I. Silvanus 7].

M. Ulpius Pupienus Silvanus *signo* Gennadius

A senator and orator, fourth century (probably early), also patron of Surrentum (Sorrento). The

last element of the name is a *signum* (see intro-   names of several grandees [PLRE I. Silvanus 6; II.
duction) but is found later as an element in the   Avienus 4; III. Gennadius 1; Syme (1971) *loc.cit*].

*

Family: Balbinus

Our sources tell us very little about Balbinus, despite universal assertions that he was very
noble. The exception – inevitably – is the HA, which tells us that he claimed descent from
"Cornelius Balbus Theophanes", a reference to L. Cornelius Balbus, an *élève* of Caesar[391]. This
may merely be to explain the Emperor's additional *cognomen* – a diminutive of Balbus – or
it may, indeed, be the truth. Unfortunately the name in both forms is fairly common. The
father's antecedents may have included Q. Caelius Honoratus, suffect consul in 105, for a
man of this name was an exact contemporary of the future Emperor, and could have been
his brother or cousin. A rather less likely ancestor might have been L. Cael[ius Calv]inus,
suffect consul at an unknown 1st century date. If his name is not to be restored as L. Cael[ius
Ruf]inus (or even [Balb]inus), his mother or grandmother could just possibly have been
the last of the noble Republican Domitii Calvini.

Neverthless the resulting table is almost entirely speculative, therefore and should be
treated with some caution.

TABLE XXXVI: THE FAMILY OF BALBINUS

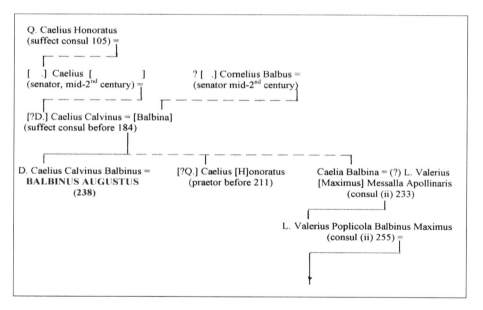

---

391. *V. Max et Balb.* VII. 3.

TABLE XXXVI: BRIEF LIVES

D. Caelius Calvinus Balbinus
See above **BALBINUS AUGUSTUS**

[D.] Caelius Calvinus
A suffect consul before 185, when he was Imperial legate of Cappadocia. As a *salius Palatinus* he was also a patrician. A descent from one of the ordinary consuls for 137, P. Coelius [sic] Balbinus Vibullius Pius has been canvassed by Settipani, but nor should the 1st century L. Cael[ius Calv]inus be entirely discounted [ILS 394; Settipani (2000) 224; Syme (1971) 172 n. 1]

Q. Caelius Honoratus
Suffect consul in 105.

[?Q.] Caelius [H]onoratus
A senator of praetorian rank recorded in 211.

[.] Cornelius Balbus
A senator who is probably an invention of the HA, as we find him writing to **MARCUS AURELIUS** praising the young **NIGER** in a piece of fictional correspondence. Perhaps he inspired the fiction that Balbus, his Spanish namesake, was an ancestor of **BALBINUS**. The names are common enough for the fiction to have masked a real senator of these names whose daughter *did* become the emperor's mother, of course. Such a marriage certainly might explain the HA's unlikely sounding story of a descent from L. Cornelius Balbus (suffect consul 40BC) [HA *V. Pesc.* 4, 1]

L. Valerius L. f. [Maximus] Messalla Apollinaris
Served a suffect consulship c. 214 and a second, ordinary consulship in 233. For his descent see below but he was also descended from two turbulent Neronian senators, P. Clodius Thrasea Paetus (suffect consul 56) and C. Helvidius Priscus (praetor 70).[PIR² V86]

L. Valerius L. f. Claud. Poplicola Balbinus Maximus
Consul for the second time in 255. His use of the name Balbinus may be a co-incidence and inherited from another family entirely, but the strong possibility remains that he may have been the emperor's nephew. This man, who was a patrician by creation and descended through a single female line from the ancient patrician house of Valerius Messalla, could trace his antecedents back to the regal period. The daughter of M. Valerius Messalla Messallinus (consul 3BC) married L. Vipstanus Gallus (praetor 17), of an emergent family, whose descendants increasingly assumed the full nomenclature of their grander relations. He had numerous descendants, who flourished into the 6th century, but the connection with **BALBINUS'S** family is not sufficiently attested to warrant setting them all out here [FS3424; ILS 1190-91; PIR² V121].

*

GORDIANUS III
(Known to history as GORDIAN III)
29th July 238 – 25th February 244

Background

As we have seen, after the proclamation of **BALBINUS** and **MAXIMUS II** the praetorian guard made much of the young nephew of **GORDIAN II** as they became increasingly restive. As a consequence, the two new emperors acquiesced in the situation and jointly adopted the youth as Caesar or heir apparent. The intention was no doubt to groom him to take over when the two old men should die. His style was probably (although no coin nor inscription has survived to prove it) **M. Antonius Gordianus Caesar**, although it is not known if the joint adopton of the lad led to any change in his nomenclature, as happened with previous imperial adoptions. If there was any change, it was no doubt rapidly dropped in the wake of the assassination of the two emperors on July 29th.

Reign

The reign of **GORDIAN III** is hampered by the lack of reliable sources, for Herodian's and Dio Cassius's accounts of the Empire had both ended at this point. Unlike **ELAGABALUS** and **ALEXANDER,** however, he was not, as far as is known, under the control of a manipulative mother; indeed, we hear virtually nothing of her.

The new emperor's style as officially adopted was **Imperator Caesar M. Antonius Gordianus Pius Felix Augustus** and he was unanimously acclaimed by the senate being given the tribunician and proconsular power and made Pontifex Maximus, probably on 29th or 30th July. These powers were renewable annually on 10th December as normal. He was also styled *invictus* and *pater patriae*.[392]

The reign was marked by a well-intentioned administration, seemingly carried out in partnership with the senate. **GORDIAN'S** good fortune, however, which is doubtless why the reign lasted as long as it did, lay in the fact that one of the praetorian prefects, C. Furius Sabinius Aquila Timisitheus - appointed in the aftermath of a crisis in Africa in 240 – effectively acted as **GORDIAN'S** regent and, by a happy chance, appears to have been a thoroughly decent man equipped with highly competent administrative and military skills. He was also, as speculated above - see **Table XXX (b)** - a probable nephew by marriage of **CARACALLA**. In due course, in 241 **GORDIANUS** married his daughter Sabinia Furia Tranquillina, who received the style of Augusta although there was no known issue, perhaps because of their youth or merely through the paucity of record.

Until 240, there was a period of consolidation, with a successful campaign fought in Lower Moesia, but in that year the crisis in Africa erupted. An imperial claimant, *SABINIANUS* (qv), proconsul of Africa, attempted – for whatever pressing reason is quite unclear – to

---

392. FS661; ILS 499-501; PIR[2] A835

repeat the action of **GORDIAN I** two years previously. It may be, as was suggested above (**Table XXII Brief Lives**) that this man claimed descent from **MARCUS AURELIUS,** which may have prompted him to act on his own account. This time, however, it was the governor of Mauretania, rather than Numidia, that suppressed the outbreak.

These events, however, might have been the spur behind a move, made the same year, by Shapur, crown prince of the newly re-instituted Sassanian Persian Empire. He seized the strategic border town of Hatra (al-Hadr, Iran). This was quickly followed by further aggressive moves on the part of the Persians, who no doubt perceived the empire as potentially without decisive authority at the highest echelons under a boy-emperor.

Timisitheus put in hand measures for a military expedition to the east in 241. As before, the reduction in manpower on the Danube and Rhine frontiers tended to have the knock-on effect of incursions in these sectors once the information reached the barbarians beyond. Thus, whilst gathering extra units from the Danube, Timisitheus conducted a pre-emptive campaign against the Goths. By 243, the expeditionary force was in Syria, which was cleared of Persian elements and not long afterwards, the Persians were decisively defeated in Mesopotamia at the battle of Rhesaina (Ras al-Ayn, Syria), the Romans recovering control as far as Nisibis and Carrhae, where Crassus had been defeated nearly 300 years previously, and which **MAXIMIN I** had granted away in his haste to return to Rome after assassinating **ALEXANDER.** Clearly thus far, the operation had been a success. That this was in large part thanks to Timisitheus is made clear by events that followed his death - probably from disease - later in that year.

The new Praetorian Prefect was a Roman citizen of Arab extraction, M. Julius Philippus. Almost all the (much later) Roman sources aver that, from this point, the Persian campaign was wound down and measures taken to undermine the Emperor by disaffecting the troops. Philippus, in the meantime, appears to have got himself appointed regent as well. An acute - and allegedly artificial - lack of supplies and some military reverses seem to have led to a mutiny at Circesium (Buseira, Syria) on the banks of the Euphrates, in which the soldiers were asked to choose between the 19-year old youth **GORDIAN** and the hoary commander, Philip, with the emperor having to plead for his life. The HA even claims that Philip was elevated to the purple as joint emperor with **GORDIAN** before the final *debacle.* The young emperor's only advisor, according to the same source, was the other Prefect, who the HA suspiciously names as Maecius Gordianus, otherwise quite unattested. Most likely it was C. Julius Priscus, the other prefect's brother, who also later made a stab at a claim to power as *PRISCUS* (qv). In the event, we are told that the soldiers chose **PHILIP** and **GORDIAN** was peremptorily put to the sword, his widow being suffered to survive, although we know nothing further of her.[393]

It might well be argued that much of this does not ring true. If Philip wanted the thone, one could imagine less complex ways of encompassing **GORDIAN'S** downfall. Furthermore, if the shortage of supplies was combined with 'military reverses', one cannot help feeling

---

393. HA. *Tres Gord.*, 30, 1-9.

that Philip was more likely to get the blame than **GORDIAN**. A Persian source, however, claims that Shapur had won a crushing victory as the culmination of a counter-attack NW of Ctesiphon (Al-Mada'in, Syria) early in the February and that **GORDIAN** had been killed in battle:

> When at first we [Shapur] had become established in the Empire, Gordian Caesar raised in all of the Roman Empire a force from the Goth and German realms and marched on Babylonia against the Empire of [Persia] and against us. On the border of Babylonia at Misikhe, a great frontal battle occurred. Gordian Caesar was killed and the Roman force was destroyed.

A bas relief rock carving depicting Shapur's triumph at Bishapur in the Shiraz region of Iran, long thought to depict the submission of **VALERIAN** makes a similar point showing **GORDIAN III** trampled beneath the hooves of Shapur's steed and **PHILIP** kneeling before the Great King offering tribute of 300,000 *denarii*. A fire altar dedicated to Ahura Mazda by one Abnun, dateable to this time also seems to celebrate the same Persian victory.

This indeed could be true, despite the tendency for such laudatory claims by Sharpur to include elements of exaggeration. In either case, there appears to be a propaganda war being waged. Perhaps, in truth, the campaign was indecisive for both sides. Now, it may be that **PHILIP** engineered the emperor's death in battle – that was to happen at least one more time in the coming years – or it may have been a genuine disaster caused by Philip's lesser military talents, but in either case the bizarre scene retailed by the HA fails to convince. Furthermore, if there had been a defeat, it was probably felt imperative that it should be airbrushed from the official accounts, so as not to undermine the new ruler's authority. Had **GORDIAN'S** arms met with unqualified success, it is hardly likely that either a mutiny would have occurred or that a triumphant Emperor would have been assassinated.

A death in battle or from disease would at least have explained the senate's ready acquiescence in **PHILIP'S** succession. Indeed, quite apart from his having been a possible battle casualty, a death from poison giving symptoms resembling those of a disease would surely have been a far more credible way of disposing of the young ruler than the farcical events described by the HA. Either way, **GORDIAN'S** reputation survived; **PHILIP** urged upon the senators the deification of his predecessor, to whom he had, apparently, erected a monument on the banks of the Euphrates. Nor is there any real hint in this reign that people looked upon **PHILIP,** unlike **MAXIMINUS**, as some sort of grim usurper. Most of the criticism was mainly directed against his origins on the south eastern fringes of the Empire.

No mention is made of any children of **GORDIAN III**, but Settipani certainly supposes that there might have been. The young emperor was sixteen when he married and nineteen when he died, so it is not biologically impossible. We have only the evidence of the unreliable HA to suggest that the Empress was present with the him when he died; it is far more likely that she remained in Rome and that if there was any issue, they would have been in her care. Settipani points to several people of high rank all called Gordianus: a senator living around 300 (337), St. Gregory the Great's father (died c. 570), great uncle (son of Pope (Caelius) Felix I, died young 485), and great-great uncle, a priest of a family church who died in 502 as being possible descendants. It is suggested that the name came through the blood line of the early 4th century *grande dame*, St. Paula.[394] This line could have descended just as well from **GORDIAN II** if the HA's account of his abundant issue is to be believed. But then, had they existed, surely one of them would have been dragged out of seclusion to succeed **MAXIMUS** and **BALBINUS**?

*

Imperial claimant under Gordian III

SABINIANUS
240

SABINIANUS was proconsul of Africa in 240, implying that he was a fairly senior senator and an ex-consul (he should have held office around 225/228), but only a suffect one, as his name does not identifiably appear on the surviving *fasti* – the official list of ordinary consuls, by which each year was named. There is very little authentic information about him, either, except that his imperial acclamation took place in 240 and that his rebellion had been suppressed at the hands of the loyal governor of Mauretania by the end of the same year.[395]

The reason that the troops to suppress Sabinianus had to be summoned from Mauretania was that the military situation was in some turmoil due to the aftermath of the Gordians' rebellion and its brutal suppression, and because the senate, on behalf of **GORDIANUS III,** cashiered the units that Capellianus had commanded in April 238.

Identifying this man is beset with fewer problems then usual. There are three possible candidates: an otherwise unrecorded Annius Sabinus and thus possible kin of **MARCUS AURELIUS'** collaterals and probably descended from the Flavian dynasty [see **part II(b) & Table XXII**], one of the Vettii Grati Sabiniani or the Asinii Rufini. Of these, whilst it might seem unlikely that the Annii would change their *cognomen* from Sabinus to Sabinianus, kinship to a past (and well regarded) emperor might seem a likely spur to taking a tilt at the purple. The Vettii Grati produced ordinary consuls either side of the fatal year 240 and it seems unlikely that they would have held any after that year had one of them attempted to seize the purple. C. Vettius Gratus Sabinianus was consul in 221; his son C. Vettius Gratus Atticus Sabinianus was consul in 242: unthinkable if his father had rebelled two years before, added to which, he himself was referred to as Vettius Atticus.[396]

---

394. PLRE II Gordianus 1 & 2; Settipani (2000) 139. Also the Pope's aunt, Gordiana, *ibid.*
395. HA. *Ibid..* 23, 4; PIR²S18
396. ILS 6110; his great-great grand-daughter married two emperors in succession: **MAGNENTIUS** and **VALENTINIAN I** (qv. *infra*).

This just leaves M. Asinius Sabinianus, who was suffect consul around 225 or a little later and was thus perfectly placed to serve as proconsul of Africa – if that is really the post held by the usurper in 240.[397] His family history is on record, going back to a friend of the historian Tacitus. He and one of the Annii must be equal contenders for the culprit. Lack of certainty, however, would seem to render any attempt to set out his connections a little premature. A final thought is that he could conceivably have been a kinsman of the man just made praetorian prefect, C. Furius Sabinius Aquila Timisitheus (see above). In which case, there may have been more to the business that meets the eye.

⋆

---

397. PIR² A1251 His full name isnow revealed as M. Triarius Rufinus Asinnius [sic] Sabinianus: *ibid.* Vol. VII p.4.

V
THE MILITARY ANARCHY 244-284

*

V(a)
THE SENATORIAL EMPERORS:
PHILIP I TO GALLIENUS

The Imperial Succession

Philippus I

Philippus II

Decius

Etruscus

Hostilianus

Gallus

Volusianus

Aemilianus I

Valerianus

Gallienus

Saloninus

Imperial claimants

Silbannacus

Sponsianus

Pacatianus

Iotapianus

[Marcus]

Priscus

Valens I

Antoninus IV

Ingenuus

Regalianus

Quietus

Macrianus

Valens II

Aemilianus II

Memor

[Antoninus]

If the year 238 had been hectic – like 193, another 'Year of the five Emperors' – the period following the assassination of **GORDIAN III** was worse, and things went downhill there-after too. Although the new emperor **PHILIP I** was an equestrian officer, the provinces were still largely governed by members of the senate who were at various stages in their careers. Therefore, it was from amongst them that imperial claimants were most likely to emerge. Thus the succession of emperors acknowledged by the senate was after **PHILIP I** almost exclusively of senatorial extraction, as were most of the extraordinary number who unsuccessfully or ephemerally grasped at power. It was only after **GALLIENUS** had barred senators from most imperial governorships that the balance changed abruptly.

The acceleration of regime change that occurred in the wake of **GORDIAN III's** assassination seems to have been triggered by the enigmatic events on the eastern frontier. As we have seen, the official version of **GORDIAN'S** campaign against the newly fledged Persian empire seems to have left something to be desired in its relationship to the actuality. At some stage after the death of Timisitheus, the Empire appears to have suffered a major military reverse in the Persian theatre and although the official story was of a successful campaign and a treaty, there can be little doubt that news soon spread along the military grapevine that there had been a shocking reverse. Its effect seems seriously to have diminished the prestige of the ruler, and encouraged a number of army commanders and others to feel that they could make a better fist of things. Therefore in the 24 years between the accession of **PHILIP I** and the assassination of **GALLIENUS**, there were no less than eleven acknowledged emperors (albeit that three were youthful heirs designate) and something like fifteen imperial claimants, although this number is less certain, as a number of these appear only in the HA and either probably did not exist or were not really imperial claimants at all. As in the previous section, bogus imperial claimants are listed for reference purposes (having been brought into existence by the HA, they do get mentioned occasionally in works of reference) but are here set within square brackets.

This accelerating instability encouraged those living beyond the frontiers of empire to try their luck within it, usually destructively, and that in turn encouraged impromptu acclamations. It also required ever-increasing sums of money to pay the armies and each imperial succession required a donative to whichever élite corps was supporting a claimant, usually the praetorians. The only way to square the circle in unsettled times was to debase the currency, a process begun by **CARACALLA**, so that by the time **PHILIP I** came to power, the new silver coinage introduced by **CARACALLA**, the *Antoninianus,* was almost entirely base metal merely washed over with silver, and usually referred to as billon. The *denarius*, also debased, had become almost worthless.

*

PHILIPPUS I
(Known to history as Philip the Arab)
25th Feb. 244 – 26th Aug. 249

PHILIPPUS II
May 247 – Sept. 249

Background

Whether **PHILIP THE ARAB** – so called from his origin – was guilty of treachery in having **GORDIAN III** deposed and killed, or whether the Persians were, for once, correct in claiming that the young emperor died in battle, he acceded with something of a cloud over him, exacerbated by the disadvantageous way the war against Sharpur was broken off.

This involved a payment of half a million *sestertii* – not that much, bearing in mind that the qualification for the senate was twice that – and an annual grant thereafter. But Philip could not afford to be dilatory in returning to Rome, as **NIGER** had been after 193: that way lay ruin – hence the treaty. It left the Romans with Lesser Armenia and Mesopotamia, so there was some advantage there to help save face. In addition, he appointed his brother-in-law Severianus as governor of ever-troublesome Upper and Lower Moesia and his brother Priscus he left behind in the east as governor of Mesopotamia, later appointing him Praetorian Prefect and 'ruler of the east', a most unusual title, but one that presaged the division of the Empire under the Tetrarchs half a century in the future.

M. Julius Philippus[398] was born in Trachonitis (Al-Lajat, Syria) c. 204, almost certainly the younger sibling. He was probably a senior army NCO, rising to deputy praetorian prefect under his brother from 242 or 243. He was promoted praetorian prefect by **GORDIAN III** late in 243, no doubt on the advice of Priscus, as Timisitheus' replacement. He was acclaimed emperor either as a result of plotting or possibly in the aftermath of a military setback, 25th February 244.

Reign

On arrival in Rome, **PHILIP** made his peace with the senate, obtained divine honours for his predecessor and gave him a lavish state funeral. He adopted the style **Imperator Caesar M. Julius Philippus Pius Felix Invictus Augustus.**[399] The senate confirmed him in office with the grant of the tribunician and proconsular powers (renewable, as usual, on 10th December each year[400]) and made him *Pontifex Maximus.*[401] Shortly thereafter, the senate further granted him the style **Persicus Maximus**. He was consul in 245, acclaimed

---

398. PIR² I461; see also Körner (2001) *passim*.
399. ILS 507; Körner (2001) 42-49.
400. Inscription quoted in JRS XCII (2007) 216.
401. ILS 506

Germanicus Maximus in 246 and **Carpicus Maximus** in 247, when he held a second consulship and soon afterwards raised his son to the rank of co-Augustus. He was married to a lady of senatorial rank, Marcia Otacilia Severa, created Augusta in 244.[402]

The son, **M. Julius Severus Philippus**[403] was born in 237 or 238, declared Caesar in spring 244 as **Nobilissimus Caesar M. Julius Severus Philippus** and styled *princeps iuventutis*.[404] In 247 he was made co-emperor and invested with the same powers as his father, including the chief pontificate as **Imperator Caesar M. Julius Severus Philippus Augustus**.[405] He was also consul with his father. His father held a third consulship in 248 with his son. At Rome itself the reign was marked by a number of impressive public works and lavish secular games to mark the thousandth anniversary of the founding of the City which fell in 248.

The Danube frontier seems to have been a continuing problem and in 245, the Emperor set out for Dacia, for his brother-in-law's efforts to stem the tide in the adjacent Moesias had proved ineffectual. He seems to have gained a complete victory over the Carpi in Dacia. The grant of the title by the senate in 247 of Germanicus Maximus alongside Carpicus Maximus suggests that he then went on to bloody the nose of the Quadi, a troublesome German tribe settled a little further north and west along the river.

Yet, even whilst the capital was indulging in an orgy of games, feasting and donatives in 248, it appeared that the Danube (and probably the Rhine) frontiers were still giving trouble. Three imperial claimants appeared in quick succession. Two, *SILBANNACUS* on the Rhine and *SPONSIANUS* on the Danube are only names, (although the former managed to issue some coins) but their actions should probably seen in the light of some desperate crisis on the frontiers rather than as a deliberate effort to remove **PHILIP.** Indeed, one may have been acclaimed to deal with the other, or as a result of having done so. *SPONSIANUS* certainly had this effect in Moesia, for another imperial claimant, *PACATIANUS* seems to have put himself forward in order to neutralise him. Underlying all this may have been resentment amongst the provincial governors and legates – all at this period mainly senators – over the appointment over their heads of **PHILIP'S** equestrian kinsman Severianus to both Moesias, perhaps exacerbated by incompetence on Severianus's part. This in its turn could well have persuaded *PACATIANUS* at least to have in his sights the removal of **PHILIP,** although his coin inscriptions suggest a (temporary) accommodation between them, unless such a development was wishful thinking on *PACATIANUS'S* part. However, he was assassinated by elements of his own forces before long.

It was a third century problem that a disaffected military unit might unexpectedly acclaim its general as emperor, leaving the unfortunate commander no choice but to pick up the ball and run with it; should a general demur, it would inevitably leave the soldiers open to an accusation of mutiny, the punishment for which was decimation. Thus a refusal

---

402. ILS 507
403. PIR² I462
404. ILS 512
405. ILS 511, 513

of imperial honours tended to guarantee a quick assassination, whilst acceptance was a gamble with the likelihood of a similarly fatal outcome – a classic Catch-22.

Any overbearing behaviour by Severianus gains credence when one turns to the activities of the Emperor's brother Priscus in the East. His incompetence and the perceived injustice of his exactions in the region caused an uprising under the locally credible imperial claimant *IOTAPIANUS* who not only claimed descent from Alexander the Great but kinship with **ALEXANDER SEVERUS**, too.

Faced with what had begun to look like military meltdown, **PHILIP** began to suffer what could have been nervous breakdown. Instead of the immediate military response one might have expected, he chose to go to the senate and offer to abdicate, a suggestion which was received in stony silence, one senator correctly suggesting that the usurpers would soon be killed by their own men, no doubt citing the recent examples of *SILBANNACUS* and *SPONSIANUS*. This, indeed, is precisely what happened, first to *PACATIANUS* then, probably the following year to *IOTAPIANUS* who, from his coin inscriptions, may have scored a victory - presumably fairly minor – over the Persians.

In the end he appointed a senator with Danubian connections, Decius, as supreme commander (*Dux*) of Moesia and Pannonia – effectively replacing Severianus, by this time presumably a dead duck – which put him in command a very powerful army.

In the event, Decius secured the Danube frontier once again by the end of 248 and it remained quiet until the Goths, Carpi *et al* perceived further unrest on the Roman side of the frontier and took their opportunities. The only trouble was that some unkown event caused Decius's army to proclaim him emperor in mid-June 249. **PHILIP,** however, rejected an offered arrangement through distrust of the claimant. Although weakened, we are told, by old age and some (unknown) infirmity, he gathered a considerable force – presumably from Gaul or Africa – and set out north to contest the claimant, by this time *en route* to Rome to consolidate his position.

If the ancient author called the Chronographer of 354 is to be believed in his estimate of the reign as lasting 5 years, 5 months and 29 days, **PHILIP** was killed in the subsequent battle near Verona around 26th August 249. The son, **PHILIPPUS II**, having reigned as sole emperor for some two weeks, was sought out and killed by a returning detachment of disgruntled praetorian guards at their camp in Rome early in September 249; the empress is thought by some sources to have survived.

The Christian writer Eusebius - repeated by St. Jerome in *Chronici Canones* - claims that **PHILIP** was the first Christian emperor. This is not accepted by modern scholars and, if one accepts the commonly believed account of his rise to the purple, he certainly failed to act like one. Nevertheless, we have the testimony of his contemporary, Bishop Dionysius of Alexandria, that he showed remarkable tolerance towards Christians, that the Empress intervened to save the life of St. Babylas, Bishop of Antioch.[406] Of course, if he *had* been a Christian, his position was by no means as secure as that of **CONSTANTINE I** in 313, and

---

406. Discussed in Körner (2001) 260-273.

he would surely have practised his beliefs discreetly. Yet no contemporary gossip picked it up and Eusebius was surely influenced by the contrast with his successor, **DECIUS,** who instituted a savage persecution. Yet it may be argued that this might have been done as retaliation against **PHILIP'S** perhaps perceived Christianity, or tolerance of it; the persecution was, in either case, probably incorporated an element of finding a scapegoat for the upheavals of the Empire, which were no doubt having an impact on all levels of society.

Family

Philip's family came from Trachonitis, on the southern edge of Syria, east of the Jordan. His native village, of which his family were chiefs, was later incorporated by the Emperor as a city called Philippopolis (today's Shabba). The fact that the family name was Julius indicates that they had received full citizenship before Caracalla's enfranchisement of the whole empire. As petty Arabian princes, their citizenship might indeed have gone back some considerable way further, possibly even to the earlier first century. We do not know the details of the Emperor's ancestry beyond his father however.

TABLE XXXVII: THE FAMILY OF PHILIP THE ARAB

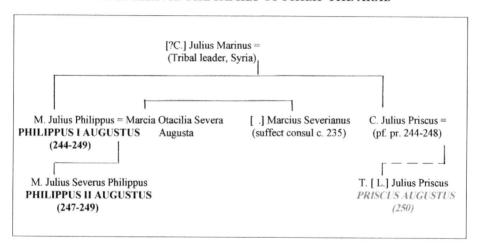

TABLE XXXVII: BRIEF LIVES

[?C.] Julius Marinus

Undoubtedly of equestrian status, he was a local tribal leader and probably died shortly before 244. He was deified not long after the reign began on the request of his son **PHILIP** and not only was the family's native city re-named Philippopolis, but a temple was erected there to Marinus [PIR² I 407; Körner (2001) 49-53]

M. Julius Philippus

PHILIPPUS I. AUGUSTUS see above.

C. Julius Priscus

The elder son, born before his imperial brother. This is because his appointment as praetorian prefect was probably on merit and came before that of **PHILIP**, which itself may well have been made as a result of canvassing. He was probably a senior army

NCO prior to appointment as praetorian prefect in 242/243, presumably with Timisitheus. He was styled a *vir eminentissimus* (*v. e.*) an equestrian rank at this period coming into common usage. With his senior colleague's death he was joined by his brother, **PHILIP**. In February 244 he was made governor (as *praefectus*) of Mesopotamia as well as retaining his praetorian prefecture. He was additionally made *rector Orientis* ('ruler of the East') before 248. What became of him in the rebellion of *IOTAPIANUS* is unclear. Even if he was able to survive, he was probably killed later on the orders of **DECIUS**. He married Tryphoniana and had at least one son, quite possibly the imperial claimant *PRISCUS* (qv) [PIR² I 488; Körner (2001) 54-59; Mennen (2011) 265]

T. Julius Priscus

Was an imperial claimant in Thrace as *PRISCUS*, killed 251, see below [PIR² I 489].

M. Julius Severus Philippus

See above **PHILIPPUS II. AUGUSTUS**.

Marcia Otacilia Severa

Said to have been daughter of Otacilius Sever[ian]us, governor of Moesia, but this may be a double for her putative brother, Severianus (qv). She may perhaps have been a descendant of M. Otacilius Catulus, suffect consul in 88. Her mother may well have been a Marcia, but Marcii are too numerous to enable us to be more positive as to her father-in-law's name. Bowersock thought her family perhaps Arabian, too. Attributions to him of a younger son Q. [Julius] Philippius Severus, a baby when his father fell, and a daughter Julia Server[ian]a seem not to be confirmed in the sources [Bowersock (1983) 123; Körner (2001)

[.] Marcius Severianus

The Empress's brother appears to have been the Marcius Severianus whom Philip appointed to govern the Moesias. He would have been suffect consul before that date [Körner (2001) 33, 63-64].

Imperial Claimant under Philip I

SPONSIANUS
c. ?February – c. 22ⁿᵈ April 248

SPONSIANUS would appear to have been an imperial claimant in Moesia (probably Upper Moesia), of which he may have been governor, or an equestrian military commander (*dux*), some time in the reign of the Emperor **PHILIP I**.[407] The events leading up to the acclamation of *PACATIANUS* (qv) would seem the most likely context. Nothing can be discovered about this claimant, nor can any clues be recovered from his name. There would appear to be no Sponsii amongst the Roman *elite* to explain it. He first came to notice with the discovery of an *aureus* in Transylvania in 1713 and, like all unique finds, it was long dismissed as a forgery, although it seems inherently unlikely a forger would choose a name so rare as *SPONSIANUS*. In recent years,

---

407. Körner (2001) 389-390

however, a very few *denarii* have also turned up, all with the same obverse and reverse, which suggests that this man did have an existence, still however, un-corroborated in any other context. The fact that he escaped the attentions of the author of the HA adds something to *SPONSIANUS'S* credibility.

His coins are unusual in that the imperial inscription occupies both faces of the flan, whilst the reverse bears no 'slogan', consisting only of two figures standing either side of an Ionic column supporting a statue with wheat ears (for plenty) issuant from either side of the base.

⋆

Imperial Claimant probably under Philip I

SILBANNACUS
?248

A man styling himself **Mar[(c)ius] Silbannacus** is known only from an exceedingly rare *Antoninianus* to have been an imperial claimant at about this period. Some reference books give his name as 'Marcus', but the abbreviation here is undoubtedly a *nomen*, not a *praenomen*, and Marcius or Marius are the only likely alternatives.[408] He may well have been an unrecorded governor of one of the Germanies (and therefore a senator) elevated by the troops on the Rhine frontier as a result of some forgotten crisis. Indeed, if his *nomen* really was Marcius, he might even have been a kinsman, perhaps another brother, of the Empress Severa (above). The year 248, immediately prior to the usurpations of *SPONSIANUS, PACATIANUS* and *IOTAPIANUS*, seems the most likely place for him, bearing in mind the style of the coin itself.

He adopted the imperial style **Imperator Mar[(c)ius] Silbannacus Augustus**.[409] The reverse depicts Victory, so he may have inflicted a surprise defeat on a German or Frankish invasion, prompting his men to acclaim him. A second issue features Mars *propugnator* and was also found in Gaul. Scholarly opinion is divided as to his exact *floruit*, under **DECIUS** being an alternative suggestion and preceding **POSTUMUS** is yet another theory. Harold Mattingly fairly convincingly dated it on style and quality to c. 248/250, however. The likelihood is that he was soon killed by his own troops. His name seems Celtic, so perhaps a man of Gaulish or even British extraction, and possibly not even senatorial. He had no known family or connections.

⋆

---

408. Körner (2001) 386-389
409. Coin, British Museum, believed to have been found in Lorraine acquired 1937. A subsequent example was found near Paris in 1996: Syvänne (2019) 41

Imperial claimant under Philip I

PACATIANUS
c. 22nd April – c. July 248

The rise of the imperial claimant **Ti. Claudius Marinus Pacatianus** on the Danube frontier, presumably again in (Upper?) Moesia, may be related to the swift rise and fall of *SPONSIANUS*, unless both were elevated at about the same time in adjoining provinces, in response to some crisis, perhaps a military setback. The removal of troops from the Danubian frontier in order to wage war against the Persians by Timisitheus seems to have come at a time when the barbarian peoples beyond were themselves coming under pressure from the east, and the resulting perceived weakness of the Empire's defences seems to have encouraged these tribes to test them. That they probably found them wanting might seem evident from the sequence of imperial claimants in the era and the subsequent defeat of the Emperor **DECIUS** in 251. That *PACATIANUS* was attempting to challenge **PHILIP I** as a primary aim would seem unlikely, especially in view of a coin type he issued bearing the legend *Victoria Augg.* ('the victory of the emperors'). The doubling of the last consonant of 'Augg.' indicates two emperors reigning together in at least supposed harmony. Either he anticipated coming to an arrangement with **PHILIP** or he actually did.[410] In which case, his uprising must have occurred prior to **PHILIP II** being made Augustus – or the news had yet to reach him. Probably he merely anticipated coming to an arrangement with **PHILIP**.

   Ti. Claudius Marinus Pacatianus[411] was son of [Ti.] Claudius Solemnis, suffect consul (presumably latish in life) c. 230. His mother may or may not have brought the name Pacat[ian]us into the family for, as we do not know the name of this man's grandfather, we cannot tell if he was Marinus, Pacatianus or something else entirely. *PACATIANUS* himself must have served as a suffect consul before c. 246/247, when he was presumably appointed governor of Lower or more probably Upper Moesia. Assuming his career was normal and that his family were not patrician, he would have been born c. 205, *quaestor* c. 233/234, *aedile* or peoples' tribune 235/236 and *praetor* c. 240 after which he would have served as commander of a legion or been governor of a lesser province. He was imperially acclaimed on or just after 22nd April 248 adopting the imperial style **Imperator Ti. Claudius Marinus Pacatianus Pius Felix Augustus**[412] and was killed in July or possibly August the same year. No wife is known, nor any issue, but one should note Claudius Julius Pacat[ia]nus[413] a senator who governed Campania at some unknown period in the later 4th or earlier 5th centuries as a possible descendant or kinsman.

---

410. The third alternative was that the mintmaster used an extant reverse die for **PHILIP I** & **PHILIP II**.
411. PIR² C390; Körner (2001) 282-288; Settipani (2000) 350 n. 2 & 351 fails to mention him.
412. Coin evidence. The 'Pius Felix' seems to have been added after an interval.
413. PLRE II. Pacatianus 2; ILS 6505. The names are by no means uncommon, however.

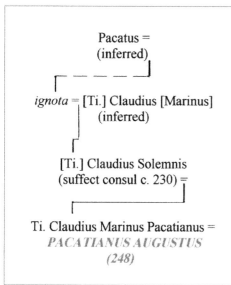

Pacatus =
(inferred)

ignota = [Ti.] Claudius [Marinus]
(inferred)

[Ti.] Claudius Solemnis
(suffect consul c. 230) =

Ti. Claudius Marinus Pacatianus =
PACATIANUS AUGUSTUS
(248)

His rebellion provided an opportunity for a renewed Gothic incursion which lasted nearly three years, causing the utmost chaos on the Danube and accounting for the lives of the Emperor **DECIUS** and his son, as well as that of the usurper *PRISCUS* (see below). All this may have been the reason that he was apparently killed by his own men in the late summer of 248. The senate, ignorant of his demise, later condemned him as a public enemy.

Left: **TABLE XXXVIII: THE FAMILY OF PACATIANUS**.

Imperial claimant under Philip I and Decius

IOTAPIANUS
c. June 248 – Sept. 249)

The name *IOTAPIANUS* clearly suggests that this ephemeral emperor rejoiced in a descent, like *AVIDIUS CASSIUS,* from the former Kings of Commagene [see **Table XXV Brief Lives**]. He also boasted a descent from Alexander, although whether Alexander of Macedon or **SEVERUS ALEXANDER** was intended has been the subject of debate; neither had he any (surviving) children, so descent from the family of one or the other rather than the individual was clearly intended; also, **ALEXANDER SEVERUS** was a contemporary.[414] He was an imperial claimant at Antioch whose position was brought about as a result of the rigorous exaction of increased taxation on the citizens of the east by Philip's elder brother, C. Julius Priscus, the *rector Orientis*. This is not necessarily something that would plunge the soldiers into ferment, but his measures may well have included trimming the soldiers' perks, reducing their opportunities for booty or merely a cut in pay. As we have seen when considering the life of **PHILIP I**, the east may also have still been feeling the effects of a serious military reverse in 244. It is presumed that *IOTAPIANUS* was the proconsul of Syria at the time of his elevation, and the fact that he seems to have maintained his position for over a year without coming to Rome to claim legitimacy and to try matters with **PHILIP** suggests that he was moderately successful, or merely that the developing crisis in the Balkans was taking the heat from him.

---

414. Aurelius Victor 29 ; Körner (2001) 277-282. Syme (1971) 202.

M. F[ulvius] R[usticus] Iotapianus must have been suffect consul c. 235/237 prior to being governor - as it would appear likely - of Syria and, as a probable patrician, he would perhaps have been born c. 202, become *quaestor* c. 228/230 and *praetor* 232/233. After imperial acclamation in around June 248, he took the style **Imperator Caesar M. F[ulvius] R[usticus] Iotapianus Augustus.** He appears to have achieved some kind of victory subsequent to his elevation, placing the appropriate slogan on his coins and an inscription at Palmyra probably reflects that. He was probably killed by his own troops late August or early September 249, and his head was subsequently brought before **DECIUS** in Rome later in September.[415] This suggests that *IOTAPIANUS'S* challenge was successfully crushed, perhaps by his own disaffected men, only a short time before, probably whilst **PHILIP** was trying to deal with **DECIUS.** We know nothing of a wife nor of any children, nor does the name recur.

Family

On his coins, *IOTAPIANUS* is called **M. F[   ] Ru[   ] Iotapianus**[416] which is usually expanded to read **M. Fulvius Rufus Iotapianus** although it might be argued that a somewhat better case might be made for his first *cognomen* to be expanded as **Rusticus,** the Fulvii Rustici being even then a prominent senatorial family of (created) patrician rank, whereas no other Fulvius Rufus is discoverable in the élite of this or any other period. If this is accepted, then one can point to Brixia in Italy as their ultimate place of origin.

The connection with Alexander the Great could well have been with Mithridates I. Callinicus, King of Commagene 96-70 BC [see **Table XXV Brief Lives**]. He married Laodice Thea Philadelpha, daughter of Antiochus VIII Gryphus, King of Syria 125-96 BC by Cleopatra Tryphaena, daughter of Ptolemaeus VII, King of Egypt 145-116 BC, grandson of Ptolemaeus V Epiphanes, fourth in descent from Ptolemaeus I, step-brother of **Alexander the Great.** Thus their posterity was descended from Alexander's step-brother, hence, in all probability, *IOTAPIANUS'S* claim.

Table XXXIX therefore, is merely an attempt at reconstructing *IOTAPIANUS'S* possible descent. In the **Brief Lives** section notes on the earlier generations, accessible elsewhere, have been omitted. Note that Settipani attaches Julia, presumed mother of the Imperial Claimant, to the dynasty of Priest-Kings of Emesa, and thereby claims *IOTAPIANUS* as second cousin of **ELAGABALUS.** This has its attractions, as the kinship might notionally have decided the claimant in his course of action.[417]

---

415. Aurelius Victor, *loc ,cit.*; PIR² I49
416. also on CIG 4483/IGR.III.1033, at Palmyra where his cognomen is expanded to 'Ru[ ]'
417. Settipani (2000) 447 & n. 6, 448 (table).

TABLE XXXIX: THE FAMILY OF IOTAPIANUS

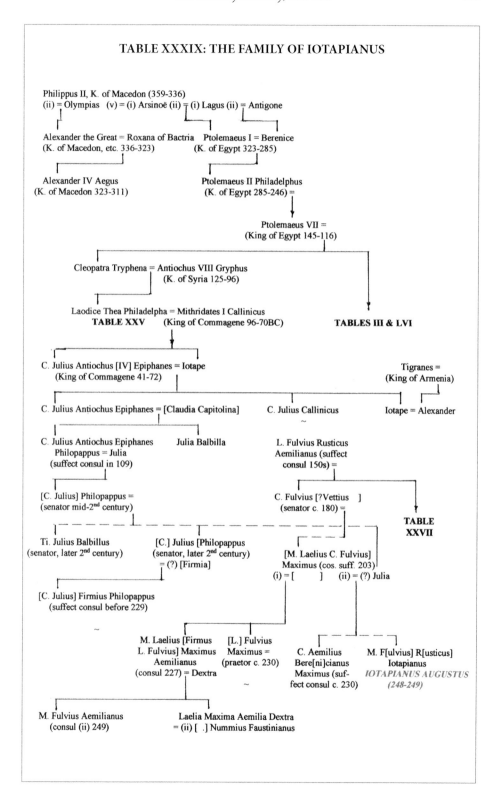

Philippus II, K. of Macedon (359-336)
(ii) = Olympias   (v) = (i) Arsinoë (ii) = (i) Lagus (ii) = Antigone

Alexander the Great = Roxana of Bactria   Ptolemaeus I = Berenice
(K. of Macedon, etc. 336-323)   (K. of Egypt 323-285)

Alexander IV Aegus   Ptolemaeus II Philadelphus
(K. of Macedon 323-311)   (K. of Egypt 285-246) =

Ptolemaeus VII =
(King of Egypt 145-116)

Cleopatra Tryphena = Antiochus VIII Gryphus
(K. of Syria 125-96)

Laodice Thea Philadelpha = Mithridates I Callinicus   **TABLES III & LVI**
TABLE XXV   (King of Commagene 96-70BC)

C. Julius Antiochus [IV] Epiphanes = Iotape   Tigranes =
(King of Commagene 41-72)   (King of Armenia)

C. Julius Antiochus Epiphanes = [Claudia Capitolina]   C. Julius Callinicus   Iotape = Alexander
~

C. Julius Antiochus Epiphanes   Julia Balbilla   L. Fulvius Rusticus
Philopappus = Julia   Aemilianus (suffect
(suffect consul in 109)   consul 150s) =

[C. Julius] Philopappus =   C. Fulvius [?Vettius]
(senator mid-2nd century)   (senator c. 180) =
    TABLE
    XXVII

Ti. Julius Balbillus   [C.] Julius [Philopappus   [M. Laelius C. Fulvius]
(senator, later 2nd century)   (senator, later 2nd century)   Maximus (cos. suff. 203)
    = (?) [Firmia]   (i) = [   ]   (ii) = (?) Julia

[C. Julius] Firmius Philopappus
(suffect consul before 229)
~

M. Laelius [Firmus   [L.] Fulvius
L. Fulvius] Maximus   Maximus =   C. Aemilius   M. F[ulvius] R[usticus]
Aemilianus   (praetor c. 230)   Bere[ni]cianus   Iotapianus
(consul 227) = Dextra   ~   Maximus (suf-   *IOTAPIANUS AUGUSTUS*
    fect consul c. 230)   *(248-249)*

M. Fulvius Aemilianus   Laelia Maxima Aemilia Dextra
(consul (ii) 249)   = (ii) [.] Nummius Faustinianus

TABLE XXXIX: BRIEF LIVES

C. Aemilius Bere[ni]cianus Maximus
Suffect consul c. 222/235 [CIL.XII.3163]

M. Fulvius M. f. Aemilianus
Suffect consul c. 238, consul (ii) 249; He was probably father of L [Fulvius] Aemilianus who was ordinary consul in 276 [PIR² F529; PLRE Aemilianus 2; Mennen (2011) 105].

[L. (?)] Fulvius C. f. Maximus
Praetor in the early-to-mid 3ʳᵈ century [ILS 1195]

M. F[ulvius] R[usticus] Iotapianus
See above *IOTAPIANUS AUGUSTUS*

C. Fulvius [?Vettius   ].
A later second century senator who may have married a Laelia, perhaps daughter of an obscure M. Laelius Firmus. He was brother or uncle of, or possibly identifiable with, C. Fulvius Rusticus Aemilianus, grandfather **of JULIANUS I** see **Table XXVII Brief Lives**. His father was L. Fulvius Rusticus Aemilianus a former suffect consul made a patrician by **MARCUS AURELIUS** by a second wife, Gavia Cornelia, descended from the Cornelius Scipio Orfitus family of the first century and claiming thereby an illustrious Republican ascendancy; the missing part of his name may therefore have been Scipio Orfitus. Another branch of the Fulvii Rustici were father and grandfather of the Empress Bruttia Crispina, see **TABLE V Brief Lives**. [PIR² F557].

Iotape
Probably [Julia] Iotape in full; she married in AD58 Alexander, King of Armenia, son of C. Julius Tigranes VI (58-68) and a descendant of Herod the Great, King of Judaea. Alexander's sister married the senator M. Plancius Varus.

Iotape had three children, C. Julius Agrippa, C. Julius Alexander Berenicianus and Julia Iotape. It has been suggested that *IOTAPIANUS* was descended from one of these sons, both of whom had distinguished senatorial careers [PIR² A500, I48, 130, 141].

Julia Balbilla
A poet and a friend of **HADRIAN** and his Empress [PIR² 650]

C. Julius Antiochus Epiphanes
Otherwise Antiochus IV, King of Commagene 41-72. He married his sister (as was the convention amongst Egyptian and Hellenistic ruling families) and was deposed for allegedly making overtures to Parthia in 72, retiring with his family to Rome [PIR² I149]

C. Julius C. f. Fab. Antiochus Epiphanes
Reconciled to **VESPASIAN** after fleeing to Parthia in 72 and enjoyed an honoured retirement in Rome. He married a daughter of Thrasyllus, a lady who is probably to be identified with Claudia Capitolina, a Roman matron of the period [PIR² C813, I150]

C. Julius C. f. Fab. Antiochus Epiphanes Philopappus
Archon at Athens 75/88, adlected into the senate by **TRAJAN,** later one of the Arval Brethren and made a patrician by 107; suffect consul in 109. He married Julia, a cousin of C. Julius Eurycles Herculanus, a scion of the former ruling dynasty of Sparta [PIR² I151, 302]

Ti. Julius Balbillus
Priest of the sun 199/201 and a senator. His name strongly suggests descent from **Ti.** Claudius

Thrasylli f. Quir. Balbillus a son of the astrologer Thrasyllus and of Aka, sister of Mithridates III King of Commagene (reigned 20-12BC), he was prefect of Egypt AD55-59. His sister married an *eques* called L. Ennius, and their daughter was the wife of **TIBERIUS'S** notorious praetorian prefect Macro (qv) [[ILS 1346, 4329 & 4331; FS 1241, 1170, 2001; PIR² C813]

[C. Julius] Callinicus
Younger son of Antiochus IV and retired to Rome following the mediatisation of Commagene, his *nomen* and *praenomen* are not in doubt but are not attested directly [PIR² 228]

[C. Julius] Firmius Philopappus
Suffect consul before 229.

[C. Julius] Philopappus
Senator mid-2nd century.

[C.] Julius [Philopappus]
Senator, later 2nd century. Apart from a daughter thought to have married [Fulivus] Maximus

(qv), it is thought that another may have married [Sex. Julius Maior] Antoninus Pythodorus a late 2nd century senator who was probably father of Julius Antonius Seleucus, possibly to be identified with the imperial claimant *SELEUCUS*, see below [PIR² vol. IV p. 232 & I154]

[M. Laelius] C. Fulvius C. f. Maximus
Patrician suffect consul of 203, descended from the Fulvii Rustici, originally from Mediolanum (Milan). He probably had two wives, of whom Julia would have been the second. He was later governor of Dalmatia, propraetorian legate of Lower Germany and Prefect of the City of Rome (PUR) but became a victim of **ELAGABALUS** in 222. [FS1769; PIR² F551; Morris (1965) 91-92]

M. Laelius [Firminus L. Fulvius] Maximus Aemilianus
Consul in 227, probably husband of a [Calpurnia] Dextra [FS1769]

[.] Nummius Faus[tin]ianus
Consul 262 [PLRE I. Faustinianus 1]

Alleged imperial claimant, possibly under Philip I

[MARCUS (I)]
?249

This emperor, mentioned by Zonaras as being acclaimed by the senate in the reign of *PHILIPPUS I* is spurious and a case of the author giving *PHILIPPUS'S praenomen* a life of its own.[418] A claimant called Severus Hostilianus is equally spurious.[419]

*

---

418. Zonaras XII, 18, cf. PIR² M271.
419. Körner (2001) 391-393.

DECIUS
26th Aug. 249 – 1st June 251

ETRUSCUS
May – 1st June 251

HOSTILIANUS
June – late November 251

Background

DECIUS was a senior senator of Pannonian origin, the second, after **MAXIMIN I,** of a long line of military men from what later became known as Illyricum (the region is so called on some of the Emperor's coinage, which makes much of his home area), although the only one of senatorial rank. He was also the first Emperor to have been killed in action fighting against an external enemy.

He was serving as Prefect of the City of Rome when **PHILIP I** selected him – because of his local origins – to go to the Danube frontier with oversight of the Moesias and Pannonia, to deal with *PACATIANUS* and the Gothic incursions which had taken place as a result of the usurpation, which he did with ruthless efficiency, although he had warned the Emperor before departing that his own elevation might result, which it duly did in June 249.

Once installed as an imperial claimant **DECIUS** is said to have written to **PHILIP** promising to return to Rome and resume his role as a private citizen. This story of the reluctantly acclaimed but high-minded usurper is not uncommon during the period, and little credence is to be attached to it, especially in that, as a senator, **DECIUS** probably looked down his nose at Philip, leaving aside any suspicions the senate might have held about his role in the deposition of **GORDIAN III.**

Reign

The new emperor was at first called **Q. Decius Valerinus,** subsequently, presumably by virtue of adoption by an otherwise unidentified C. Messius [   ] he became **C. Messius Q. Decius Valerianus.**[420] He was born c. 190 at Budalia (Martinci, Serbia) and was suffect consul in 232. He was subsequently appointed governor of Lower Moesia (c. 234), Lower Germany and Tarraconensis (Spain), the latter in 237/238. After this, he underwent his change of name before being appointed Prefect of the City by **PHILIP** in 247.[421] He was made Commander-in-Chief of the Danube frontier in summer 248 and was still theoretically *en post* when incontestably elevated to the purple as a result of the defeat of **PHILIP I** on 26th August 249. He reached Rome before the end of September and was recognised as Augustus by the senate. He was thereupon granted the tribunician and proconsular power,

---

420. FS 2440; ILS 490; PIR² D28 & JRS XCIII (2003) 233
421. Mennen (2011) 260, and marked 'uncertain', as only the HA attests his appointment.

renewable on 10th December yearly,[422] made Chief Priest and granted the extra name of **TRAIANUS**, the latter not necessarily at once, but certainly by 250, by his admiring former colleagues in the senate which gave him rather a lot to live up to.[423] His imperial style was therefore **Imperator Caesar C. Messius Q. Traianus Decius Pius Felix Augustus** to which **Invictus** was quickly added.[424] He was consul (ii) in 250 and (iii) in 251.[425] As recognition of his military efforts prior to his accession he was later granted the additional epithet **Dacicus Maximus.** He had married Herennia Cupressenia Etruscilla, and the senate made her Augusta on his accession. She was the daughter of Q. Herennius Etruscus, a Severan senator, perhaps by a daughter or grand-daughter of Cupressenius Gallus, suffect consul in 147. The name Perperna, one of those bestowed on the younger son, also suggests that the Empress was descended from M. Perperna, consul in 92 BC, although there is no certain senatorial trace of that old Etruscan family beyond the reign of Augustus.[426]

Nevertheless, much of the good work **DECIUS** had done on the Danube was put at risk by his having to fight it out with **PHILIP** outside Verona, so his accession was marred by further problems on the Danube, caused by the Gothic king Kniva leading a horde of followers into Roman territory and creating havoc, resulting in the desperate usurpation of *PRISCUS* at Philippopolis.

This was a blow to **DECIUS,** for he was busy numismatically trumpeting his Pannonian or – as he described it on his coins, Illyrian – origins, just as Kniva's people were reducing the area to chaos.[427]

He nevertheless, initiated a number of reforms, appealed extensively to imperial nostalgia, invoking the names of past deified emperors – perhaps impelled by the grant by his fellow senators of the additional name of **TRAJAN** – and tried to breathe new life into the pantheon of Roman gods, under threat from a number of monotheistic cults. To help achieve this, his *régime* required certificates of sacrifice from citizens to prove their pagan *bona fides*, which monotheists like the worshippers of the Sun or of Isis or Mithras were happy to go along with, but not the Christians, who largely refused. This inevitably led to a widespread persecution, in this case a pretty savage one, long remembered by the church after its emancipation in 313.

The Danubian crisis, despite being somewhat alleviated by a victory gained by **DECIUS'S** successor as C-in-C of both the Moesias, Trebonianus Gallus, kept rumbling on and the emperor decided to take an expeditionary force thence to deal with Kniva once and for all. He left a senior senator, P. Licinius Valerianus – later emperor **VALERIAN** – in Rome with special powers to hold the fort, made his sons Caesar, first Etruscus and slightly later Hostilianus, and took off for the Balkans with the former.

The elder son, **Q. Herennius Etruscus Messius Decius** was therefore traised to the rank

---

422. ILS 518
423. Syme (1971) 220
424. ILS 514, 515
425. AE (2003) 1415
426. ILS 521, 7043, cf. Syme (1971) 197.
427. Seaby (1971) IV p. 25 No. 43: the rev. legend reads Gen[ius] Illurici.

of Caesar and *princeps iuventutis* in May or June 250, **Nobilissimus Caesar** being added to the foregoing, and was consul with his father in 251.[428] He was born c. 233/234 and was unmarried. The younger son, **C. Valens Hostilianus Messius Q. Perperna** was born about 236/238. His names mark a break with convention, with the actual *nomen* coming after the *praenomen* and two *cognomina* and being succeeded by another *praenomen,* a pattern which became more common amongst the *élite* about a century later. He was appointed caesar at the same time as his brother as **C. Valens Hostilianus Messius Quintus Nobilissimus Caesar** also as *princeps iuventutis.*[429] Shortly before **DECIUS'S** final campaign, he appears to have been designated Augustus as **Imperator Caesar C. Valens Hostilianus Messius Quintus Augustus** and was recognised by the senate in July or August 251 as soon as news reached them of his father's and brother's death, when he was granted the tribunician and proconsular power, renewable in the usual way. It is less clear whether he was also made pontifex maximus.

The Balkan campaign had mixed fortunes, news of which seems to have prompted a rash of imperial claimants. The response in propaganda terms, and as a riposte to a military success against the German Carpi, was that **DECIUS** raised his son **ETRUSCUS** to the rank of co-emperor as **Imperator Caesar Q. Herennius Etruscus Messius Decius Augustus,** at which time he seems to have received the tribunician and proconsular power from the senate.[430] But in the end, the campaigning came unstuck; a trap laid by the Emperor with Gallus to crush Kniva as he returned to cross the Danube went completely awry and both father and son fell in battle at Abrittus (Razgrad, Bulgaria) in lesser Scythia on the far North Eastern edge of the Empire, not far inland from the Black Sea coast, between 27th May and 1st June 251. **ETRUSCUS** was in fact killed in action an hour or two before his father.[431]

Cynics claimed that **GALLUS** had betrayed them, but this seems unlikely, for the battle was going well until Kniva unexpectedly turned the tables. The senate, on receiving this news, deified both **DECIUS** and **ETRUSCUS**.

Gallus, whether he liked it or not, was immediately acclaimed emperor and, as with the deaths of **MARCUS AURELIUS, SEVERUS I, ALEXANDER** and **GORDIAN III,** a promising military situation was settled disadvantageously and in haste in order for him to hot-foot it back to Rome to legitimise his *régime.*

Technically, however, Decius younger son, **HOSTILIANUS** had succeeded, and on **GALLUS'** arrival he was duly confirmed as co-emperor and adopted by **GALLUS**, but had died, ostensibly of plague – not in itself particularly unlikely – by the end of November that year.

Family

Decius' family came from Lower Pannnonia, and he himself from Budalia near Sirmium (Sremska Mitrovica, Serbia). The fact that he was able to have a long and distinguished senatorial career

---

428. ILS 516
429. ILS 516, cf. coins.
430. *trib. pot., cos. des.,* ILS 519
431. JRS XCII (2007) & AE (2003) 1415.

suggests that the Decii were probably well to do and of Roman stock, settled in the province, although arguing from names, Syme preferred that he was of native stock, long holding the citizenship, and this part of the empire in which Syme had long taken a particular interest.[432] He was said to have been of 'consular descent', so the family may have reached high office after **MARCUS AURELIUS'S** Danubian wars. For his son to qualify for the senate, the father, whose name is unknown must have had a fairly spectacular equestrian career; Syme proposed Q. Decius Vindex, procurator of Dacia in the late 2nd century for his father.[433] Decius was thus probably born in Budalia simply because the family had travelled there to look after their estates.

The ancestry of the Empress is too obscure to be securely worked out, but somewhere along the line the *nomen* Hostilius, that of Perperna and the *cognomen* Etruscus came into her bloodline; the former is very scarce in the Imperial senate. Any attempt to suggest how she acquired these names is therefore doomed to failure for the lack of evidence.[434]

TABLE XL: THE FAMILY OF DECIUS

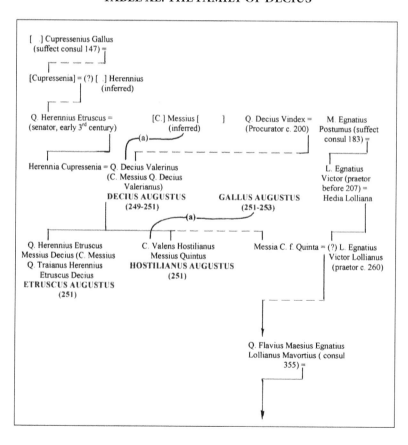

---

432. Syme (1971) 194-196

433. Syme, *loc.cit.* The consular descent may have been hyperbole, although the Empress could boast it.

434. The *Vita* of SS Calocerus & Parthenius calls her, erroneously, Tryphonia.

TABLE XL: BRIEF LIVES

[.] Cupressenius Gallus
Suffect consul 147.

Q. Decius Valerinus/C. Messius Q. Decius Valerianus
See above **DECIUS AUGUSTUS**

Q. Decius Vindex
Procurator of Dacia c. 200 [PIR² D29; Syme (1971) 194-196]

Q. Herennius Etruscus
Senator, early 3ʳᵈ century

Q. Herennius Etruscus Messius Decius (C. Messius Q. Traianus Herennius Etruscus Decius)
See above **ETRUSCUS AUGUSTUS**

[C.] Messius [   ]
It would appear that the Emperor's adoptive parent has eluded record completely. Perhaps a kinsman of L. Messius L.f. Rufus, a senator from Githigis in Africa who made it to the quaestorship and perhaps to a consulship if he can be indentified with L. Mes[sius   ] suffect in the 240s or a little before.

C. Valens Hostilianus Messius Quintus
See above **HOSTILIANUS AUGUSTUS**

Imperial Claimant under Decius

PRISCUS
c. November – December 250

T. Julius Priscus was governor (*agens vice praesidis,* usually abbreviated to *praeses,* a governor of equestrian rank) of Macedonia and Thrace, where **PHILIP I** had founded another city named after himself. There is a strong possibility that he was the cousin of **PHILIP II** (see above, **Table XXXVII Brief Lives**). During his governorship, to which he could have been appointed under his uncle's regime and, because of the chaotic situation at his fall, had not been removed, had to defend this Philippopolis from an attack by Goths under their king, Kniva, in winter 250/251, mainly as a result of **DECIUS** inflicting a not sufficiently decisive defeat upon them further north. Being in no way seriously impaired, Kniva had moved south to invest Philippopolis.[435] His position became critical and his troops mutinous. As a desperate last throw he declared himself Emperor around November 250, and used the authority he was thus perceived to have acquired to make terms with the Gothic king. Somehow, however, it all went completely wrong, and after a while the Goths sacked Philippopolis anyway, and *PRISCUS* was probably killed, although whether by his own men or the Goths is unknown. In July, he was posthumously declared a public enemy by the senate, ignorant of his death. His *praenomen* is wrongly given by Aurelius Victor as Lucius.

---

435. PIR² I489; Aurelius Victor, 29; Polemus Silvius, 39-40 who dates it all to 251; Zosimus 1, 23.1.

Were he really a nephew of **PHILIP I**, one might have thought one or more of the sources might have mentioned it, but the sources themselves are so scrappy and inadequate that this is not necessarily a bar. Indeed, kinship with the late Emperor might have encouraged him to adopt this rather unlikely and desperate solution to a long siege which did not seem to be going his way.

*

Imperial claimant under Decius

VALENS I
March-April 251

The imperial claimant *VALENS I* must have constituted a serious loss of face for the future emperor **VALERIAN** when the latter was left behind by **DECIUS** as home supremo, especially as he was a fellow senator and even possibly a kinsman. Worse, he was actually proclaimed at Rome with support of a faction of the senate, although we do not know what events brought this about; perhaps the contrast of the austerity of **DECIUS** after the munificence of **PHILIP I**. The date seems to have been late March 251.

[**Ti.**] **Julius Valens Licinianus** was a senator in 251 and because he does not seem to have been particularly well connected, we do not know much about his family. He must at least have been fairly senior, without doubt a former suffect consul, and he lasted days rather than weeks before being killed by the mob.[436]

The family of **Valens** may be known. Although the combination is not at all uncommon, the imperial claimant may be descended from the younger Pliny's equestrian friend Julius Valens.[437] If so, a couple of generations thereafter are missing before we reach the usurper's probable grandfather, [**Ti.**] **Julius Licinianus** a senator in 188/189.[438] He was father of **Ti. Julius Licinianus** senator in 223, when he was one of the patrons of Canusium.[439] He is thought to be the father of [**Ti.**] **Julius Valens Licinianus,** known as *VALENS I.* We know nothing of wife or children although two generatons down the line, **Julius Valens,** although of equestrian rank – he was a *vir perfectissimus* – was governor (*praeses*) of Nearer Spain under Diocletian and could have been a descendant for, at this period, anyone who wanted an official career needed

---

436. HA, *Tyr. Trig.* XX (where he was inserted out of sequence solely in order to pad out the number of usurpers in Gallienus's reign); Aur. Victor, 29, 3; *Epitome* 29,5; PIR² I610 cf. I380.
437. *Ep.* 5, 21, 2; PIR² I609.
438. PIR² I 379
439. ILS 6121; PIR² I 380.

to avoid the senate, members of which, since the time of **GALLIENUS,** had been to a large extent relegated to roles of minimal influence. Thus the connection is plausible, although the frequency of both names leaves a large element of doubt.

*

GALLUS
1ˢᵗ June 251 – August 253

VOLUSIANUS
November 251 – August 253

Background

C. Vibius Trebonianus GALLUS was born in Perusia (now Perugia, Italy) c. 206, becoming quaestor c. 235, probably *aedile* or peoples' tribune c. 237, praetor 240 and consul in 245. He had served as a legionary legate in Thrace 235/6. In 250 he was appointed governor of Upper Moesia. He was the senior commander in the combined force defeated at the Battle of Abrittus, on or around 1ˢᵗ June 251 and, having extricated his remaining forces from the chaos, regrouped and was acclaimed emperor by the relieved soldiers. Whether he encompassed the doom of his predecessors as was alleged in some sources, seems on the whole, doubtful.

Unfortunately, as with **PHILIPPUS I** and others, desperation to consolidate his position at Rome led to the conclusion of a hasty treaty, in this case on the Danube. Kniva was allowed to re-cross the frontier not only with his booty but with his Roman captives, many of them of high status, and an annual subsidy was to be paid. Probably **GALLUS** expected to be able to mount an expedition soon afterwards to rectify these matters but in the event it never materialised.

Reign

Acclaimed emperor on or about 1st June 251, **GALLUS** then returned to Rome and obtained recognition by the senate. He also adopted **HOSTILIANUS** and recognised him as co-Emperor (but without him being *pontifex maximus*), creating his own son **VOLUSIANUS** caesar and *princeps iuventutis*. He also persuaded the senate to deify his predecessors: in other words, he did everything by the book, including paying elaborate respect to the senate, somewhat side-lined since the death of **GORDIAN III**. On recognition he took the style **Imperator Caesar C. Vibius Trebonianus Gallus Pius Felix Augustus;** he added **Invictus** not long afterwards[440] being granted the tribunician and proconsular power, renewable 10ᵗʰ December yearly and the office of Pontifex Maximus. As with many of his

---

440. ILS 522; PIR² V403 & cf. AE (2006) 1249-50.

shorter-lived predecessors, we do not know how many imperial acclamations he received at his reign, although there was always one at the beginning. He was consul (ii) in 252. He had married Afinia M. f. Gemina Baebia[441] in all probability a descendant of L. Afinius Gallus, suffect consul in 62, also, like the Empress, a Perusian; her maternal grandmother was probably Baebia M. f. Nigrina.

Later, in November, his co-Augustus, **HOSTILIANUS** died of plague and **GALLUS** thereupon replaced him as Augustus with his son **VOLUSIANUS. C. Vibius C. f. Afinius Gallus Veldumnianus L. Volusianus** was at this stage probably an adult, and possibly already a senator. As emperor he was styled **Imperator Caesar C. Vibius Afinius Gallus Veldumnianus Volusianus Pius Felix Augustus** and was given the supreme pontificate jointly with his father and all the other usual powers.[442] He too held the consulship in 252 and again in 253. **GALLUS** also had a daughter, Vibia Galla.

The treaty with Kniva did not hold for long and the Danube frontier was soon again plunged into chaos. Worse, Sharpur I, King of Persia, emboldened by his apparent easy victory against **PHILIP I**, and seeing that Rome was in political turmoil, decided to try and destroy it, in the east if not further afield.

He was aided, as he no doubt calculated, by an outbreak of plague which began about this time and decimated civilian populations and the army alike. Thus, at a juncture of political weakness, the empire was suddenly made much more vulnerable by a drastic loss of man-power and consequent economic downturn. The result for central government, which seems to have largely continued to run the Empire perfectly well, despite the perturbations at the highest level, was a drastic drop in tax revenue, just when the army was continually having to be paid donatives and generally expanded to meet the external threats, themselves fuelled by the perceived internal chaos. It was, once again, the classic vicious circle.

Sharpur's campaign was successful; he had over-run the entire province of Syria by 253 and chaos in the east continued for a decade before being brought under control, just as the plague rampaged through the empire for even longer.

GALLUS comes over as a traditionalist in a context in which tradition had little chance of flourishing, but in his two years in power, he had little time to consolidate his *régime*. It may be too that, as a senior senator, his attempt to rule with the senate - many of the reverses of his fairly numerous coin issues bear the letters S C (*senatus consultum*) - was perhaps misplaced. At the beginning of 253 he also revived **DECIUS'S** persecution of the Christians, possibly as a means of diverting attention away from (or finding scapegoats for) the crises which beset his rule. Either way, the next effective imperial claimant, **AEMILIANUS** put paid to his well-intentioned efforts and his persecuion, catching the capital by surprise.

The usurper, governor of Lower Moesia, having successfully at last brought the Goths to heel, was acclaimed by his army and, as was *de rigueur*, immediately set out for Italy. **GALLUS** called on the former right hand man of **DECIUS**, P. Licinius Valerianus, now

---

441. ILS 527
442. ILS 522

governing Germany, to travel south and help him deal with **AEMILIANUS**, but he arrived too late to do anything for **GALLUS**. Heading a much inferior force, his soldiers killed **GALLUS** and his son at Interamna Nahars (Terni), just north of Rome early in August 253. Their men then went over to the challenger, mainly because, with the example of the demise of **PHILIP** at the hands of **DECIUS,** which had resulted in heavy loss of Roman lives inflicted by other Romans, no soldier wanted to kill comrades in arms. In the 4th century this situation altered. There were several engagements between rival claimants costing thousands of lives but, by that time, the make up of the armies was much more orientated towards barbarian recruits who had no such qualms - as long as they were paid. In the event, Valerianus still dealt with **AEMILIANUS**, but on this occasion to his own advantage and at a time of his own choosing.

Family

C. Vibius Trebonianus Gallus was, like most of his predecessors, a distinguished and aristocratic member of the senate. The family came from Perusia (Perugia), as did that of the Empress Baebiana, who was denied the title Augusta by the ever-correct Gallus because the mother of the co-Augustus **HOSTILIANUS** was still alive and bearing the title. Julius Caesar's lieutenant, C. Vibius Pansa (consul in 43 BC) and his father, also a senator, also came from Perusia, and Professor Wiseman adds that C. Vibius, a moneyer in c. 39BC, was also from there, and was probably related to Pansa.[443] His family and **GALLUS'S** were in the Tromentina voting tribe, as were the majority of the Vibii Vari, from which family, it is thought **GALLUS'S** was descended. A difficulty is raised in the person of a senator in the first decade or so of the 1st century AD, L. Vibius L. f. Rom. Varus Appianus, whose real father was either a patrician Claudius Pulcher (compare the *agnomen* of M. Valerius Messalla Barbatus Appianus, consul in 12, son of Ap. Claudius Pulcher consul in 38 BC and adopted by a Valerius, see **TABLE V Brief Lives**) or by an obscure Appius in the Romilia tribe.[444] If the Vibii deployed in the table (below) *were* descended from him, then they managed to revert to or remain in the Tromentina, Perusia's tribe, or the adoption was perhaps testamentary.[445] It is probably safer to regard L. Vibius Appianus as, say an uncle of the Claudian ex-praetor.

GALLUS retained close links with his home town although seems to have been descended from a stay-at-home cousin. Another probable ancestor is Ap. Annius Trebonius Gallus, consul in 108, son of Civil War general Ap. Annius Gallus (suffect consul and made a patrician 68) – another possible Claudian connection if the *praenomen* is anything to go by – who was related by marriage to the opulent Athenian senator, Herodes Atticus.[446] Settipani suggests that this family was descended from a clan of this name from Iguvium

443. Wiseman (1971) no. 490

444. IGR IV. 1353.

445. Taylor (1960) Romilia as an ancient voting district associated with the Vaticanus, 274; the Tromentina asssoiciated with Perusia, 165, 275; for testamentary adoptions, see Introduction.

446. Birley (1987) 113; PIR² A653, 692, 654

(Gubbio, Italy), and that the son of the consul of 108, Ap. Annius Gallus (suffect consul around 139) married a daughter of M. Atilius Metilius Bradua (also consul in 108) and that their daughter Appia Annia Galla married Herodes Atticus. He also adduces the Trebonian connection with a marriage between Gallus, the suffect consul of 67, and a daughter of P. Trebonius, who served similarly in 53.[447]

The table below suggests that the Trebonian connection was the Emperor's mother. To suppose that, because we are short of Trebonii between the suffect consul of 53 and the end of the second century, the alliance has to have been early is to ignore the sheer number of names permanently lost from the roll of senators in the intervening years, bearing in mind it was a body of six hundred. The survival, albeit without the benefit of recorded high office, of some Trebonii over that period is perfectly plausible.

But quite how **GALLUS** was descended from the Annii Galli remains impenetrable; possibly through the Vibii Vari. Whatever the connection was, evidence of it (except in the Emperor's name) is lost.

---

447. Settipani (2000) 472-473.

TABLE XLI: THE FAMILY OF GALLUS

TABLE XLI: BRIEF LIVES

Afinia M. f. Gemina Baebia

Daughter of an M. Afinius [   ] and in all probability a descendant of L. Afinius Gallus, suffect consul in 62, also, like the Empress, a Perusian; her maternal grandmother was probably Baebia M. f. Nigrina. [ILS 527]

T. Clodius Vibius Varus

Consul 160. He appears to have had one or more daughters.

C. Julius Lupus T. Vibius Varus Laevillus

He was propraetor of quaestorian rank in Asia

in 131/132 and probably married a daughter of his boss, the proconsul, C. Julius Alexander Berenicianus (suffect consul in 116) and grandson of Herod Agrippa, making him kin to **ELAGABALUS** and *IOTAPIANUS*, see **Tables XXXII & XXXIX**. A change of voting tribe in the grandson would suggest this man had a daughter who married a man with the *praenomen* Aulus and was perhaps otherwise called Pompilius Piso [PIR² I391].

P. Julius Lupus
See **Table XX Brief Lives**

A. Julius Pompilius A. f. Cor. Piso T. Vibius Varus Laevillus Berenicianus
Suffect consul in 180 [ILS 1111; PIR² I477]

[.] Junius Veldumnianus
Consul 272, probably to be identified with a Junius Veldumnianus who was PUR late in the 3rd century [PIR² I845; PLRE I. Veldumnianus 1, where his possible kinship to **GALLUS** is noted.]

C. Valens Hostilianus Messius Quintus
The younger son of the Emperor **DECIUS**, **HOSTILIANUS AUGUSTUS** on whom see **TABLE XL Brief Lives.**

C. Vibius L. f. [ ]
A Perusian and presumably but not certainly a senator. Name inferred from the filiation of his son. He married Proculeia, daughter of L. Proculeius A. f. [(?) Gallus] 'Titia gnatus' (i.e. his mother was a Titia) [ILS 6617]

C. Vibius C. f. Afinius Gallus Veldumnianus L. Volusianus
See above **VOLUSIANUS AUGUSTUS**

C. Vibius C. f. L. n. Tro. Gallus Proculeianus
Senator and patron of Perusia 205; possibly married a Trebonia. He may also have had a sister married to a Junius too. He pre-deceased his father [ILS6616].

C. Vibius Trebonianus Gallus
See above **GALLUS AUGUSTUS**

T. Vibius Varus,
In 47 an ex-praetor

[?T .] Vibius Varus
Suffect consul in 93. Possibly he or his son (qv) married to a Clodia, unless the appearance of this *nomen* in the nomenclature of his grandson reflected an origin with the Claudii Pulchres.

T. Vibius Varus
Suffect consul 134.

[L.] Vib[ius] Veld[umnianus] Perusian senator, mid 2nd century, "avus karissimae" ('beloved grandfather') of his grandson (qv), He could have been born a Veldumnius and adopted by an L. Vibius, who might indeed have been a brother of T. Vibius Varus suffect consul 134 (qv). It is also possible that he married a Salvia; certainly there was some link with the family of **JULIANUS I**, for note Vibia L. f. Salvia Vara, married to M. Nummius Umbrius Primus Senecio Albinus (consul 206) a sister of **DIDIUS JULIANUS,** see **Table XXVII Brief Lives** [ILS 6616].

*

AEMILIANUS I
(Known to history as AEMILIAN)
June – October 253

Background

A demand that the subsidies agreed by **GALLUS** to the Gothic leader Kniva be increased, led to an outbreak of fresh hostilities on the Danube frontier in early summer 253. **M. Aemilius AEMILIANUS** was the man on the spot, as governor of Lower Moesia and, with the promise of a hefty donative to his troops (probably to be paid out of the subsidy due to the Goths), quickly cleared the province of Gothic marauders before carrying the fight into Kniva's territory where he won a great victory.

This victory, coming on the tail of so many defeats, setbacks and partial successes, led to his being acclaimed emperor by his men. Unwisely leaving some Gothic elements still rampaging in Thrace, Aemilianus set out for Rome, **GALLUS** leading a force out from the capital to oppose the upstart. Instead, his troops murdered him and **VOLUSIANUS** before a trial of strength could be made.

   M. Aemilius Aemilianus was born at Girba on the island of Meninx off the north African coast either in 206 or 213.[448] His ancestors were Moorish, marking him out as the first Emperor of Moorish origin. It is also assumed that he was the first of his family in the senate, so his promotion would not have been as fast as that of a patrician or a member of an established family like **GALLUS**. Having been appointed governor of Moesia in 251, he must have previously held a suffect consulship, which is unlikely to have been prior to 240/241 (if he was born in 206) or 247/248 (if his date of birth was 213), the latter being on the whole more likely.

Reign

AEMILIAN was given the purple by his troops and received his first – and probably only – imperial acclamation from them possibly in June 253 (although the news took a month to reach Rome). He was nevertheless swiftly recognised by the senate late in July, after the fall of **GALLUS** and, from coin evidence, throughout the empire. He took the imperial style **Imperator Caesar M. Aemilius Aemilianus Pius Felix Invictus Augustus,** being made Chief Priest (*pontifex maximus*), granted the tribunician and proconsular powers, renewable on 10th December yearly and made Father of his Country (*pater patriae*). His wife, C[aia] Cornelia Supera, was recognised as Augusta, presumably on his accession. Her name would suggest that she was the daughter of a C. Cornelius Superus who is not otherwise known. There are no reports of any issue.

   Despite being condemned as a public enemy on acclamation in June, **AEMILIAN**, like **GALLUS,** was a senator and, once in power, attempted to rule as *primus inter pares* (first

---

448. ILS 528 ; PIR ² A330; *Epit.* 31, 1-3, cf. Zonaras, XII, 22

amongst equals) with them. Zonaras, however, calls him grovelling and ignoble, but as he was writing over a century later, such strictures have to be taken with some cynicism. Unfortunately, **VALERIAN,** who had been summoned to his aid in panic by **GALLUS,** carried on into Italy, despite receiving news of **AEMILIAN'S** success. **VALERIAN'S** army, specially strengthened to fight the Alemanni on the Upper Danube, seem to have acclaimed him emperor once their objective was clear to all. In October, as soon as they were in a position to confront the forces of **AEMILIAN,** the latter's officers killed him near Spoletum (Spoleto, Italy) in a carbon copy of the demise of **GALLUS** and **VOLUSIANUS** a few months before. At some stage in these proceedings, the HA alleges that another imperial claimant arose called Cyriades.[449] Almost certainly he is to be indentified with one Mereades who betrayed Antoich to the Persians and ended up being killed by them. No other source suggests that he assumed the purple.[450]

∗

VALERIANUS I
(Known to history as VALERIAN)
October 253 – June 260

Background

P. Licinius **VALERIANUS** *Colobius*[451] was born c. 195 and had held a suffect consulship. He may have married twice, since his presumed elder son bore none of the names associated with the family of the mother of **GALLIENUS**. If so, the marriage must have been c. 215 and very brief. The emperor's second wife, whom he married c. 217/218 was [Egnatia] Mariniana[452] daughter of Q. Egnatius Victor Marinianus, suffect consul before 230.[453] In 251 **VALERIAN** was appointed *censor* - the first non-Imperial holder of this important office for centuries – and was *princeps senatus* or 'father of the senate' which suggests that he was the most senior surviving ex-consul, which might in turn confirm that he served his consulship sometime around 230; the problem is that this information only appears in the HA, and is thus highly suspect. Probably he was merely an ex-consul serving in various capacities in the provinces, as one might expect. Thus in 251-252 he was governor of a Danubian province, since he was fighting Goths, and by 253 he was governing Rhaetia, unless he had been given an unspecified overall command by **GALLUS**. He was acclaimed by his troops in October 253 shortly before deposing **AEMILIAN,** and was recognised by the senate within days of the death of his predecessor, doubtless with the unspoken reservation that he was likely to last little longer and any of his three predecessors. The

---

449. HA Trig. Tyr. II. 1-4.
450. E.g., Ammianus Marcellinus *Roman History*, 23.5.3; John Malalas, *Chronographia*, 295-296
451. The *signum* Colobius is provided solely by *Epitome* 32, 1.
452. PIR² E39
453. PIR² E37

senate also pronounced a *damnatio memoriae* upon poor **AEMILIAN,** which might seem a little harsh for a man who had ruled respectfully of his fellow senators for only just over three months. In the event, any cynicism was mistaken about the likely length of the new Emperor's reign was soon dispelled, for **VALERIAN,** although a senator of aristocratic background, set about putting the empire back on its feet and, had it not been once again for the intervention of Shapur, King of Persia, might well have succeeded.

Reign

VALERIAN, described (by the HA) as careful, modest and serious, was recognised by the senate, granted proconsular and tribunician power, renewable yearly on 10th December, and was made pontifex maximus, taking the imperial style **Imperator Caesar P. Licinius Valerianus Augustus,** later expanded to **Pius Felix Invictus Augustus.** He also began to be styled 'Dominus', presaging his son's adoption of the style 'Dominus Noster'[454] which became the norm over ther succeeding years for emperors right up until the seventh century. He was consul (ii) in 254, also (iii) the following year and (iv) in 257. His wife Mariniana was made Augusta, but seems to have died shortly afterward, being deified by the senate.

    VALERIAN was probably the last emperor to have considered himself based in Rome; his son was hardly ever there through campaigning and, with successors who were not in origin senators, the ancient tie began to break down. Emperors henceforth tried to visit Rome, but hardly any were actually based there.

    Having settled matters there, however, the new ruler was obliged to tackle a full-blown crisis. The frontiers were in a shambles, for the Persians had captured Antioch and most of Syria, Armenia and Mesopotamia, and the Danube had seen two, possibly three armies removed and marched off to Rome and whilst most detachments no doubt were sent back, elements would have remained to bolster up each succeeding emperor: **DECIUS, GALLUS, AEMILIAN** and now **VALERIAN,** leaving the frontiers gravely at risk.

    The emperor immediately appointed his 35-year old son **GALLIENUS** – a competent general – as co-emperor and, in the face of mounting crises in both the northern frontiers and the east, the empire was informally divided between them in 256, **VALERIAN** at the same time appointing **GALLIENUS'** son Valerianus, junior, as Caesar, although when he died in 258, his younger brother **SALONINUS** was appointed in his place.

    GALLIENUS set out to restore the situation on the Danube and Rhine frontiers, which he did with some success, earning both emperors the additional style **Germanicus Maximus** in 257. **VALERIAN** himself went east to tackle the Goths who had become bold enough to begin raiding Asia (Minor) by sea and had even penetrated to the Crimea, disrupting Roman corn supplies in the process.

    Meanwhile, taking advantage of the chaos in the Empire, the Persians resumed their campaigning in the east. From the events, such as the capture and abandonment of Antioch, it is clear that Sharpur's main objectives were not to take the eastern portions of the Empire

---

454. PIR² L258

over, but to take advantage of the situation to take booty. Antioch had fallen in 256, but **VALERIAN** recaptured of the city in the following year. As we have seen, the reality of Sharpur's alleged puppet emperor, Cyriades (really a criminal chancer called Mareades) may safely be discounted an as example of the HA conjuring usurpers out of thin air to people his chapter called the *Thirty Tyrants*.[455] Thereafter, **VALERIAN** set about slowly clearing the entire area of Sharpur's forces and garrisons.

Even so, he had a hard time with the Persians, who were bolstered by success, lack of serious opposition and good morale. Whilst two civil wars were raging in the west, the Persians had made serious inroads into the east, especially Syria, with the result that *ANTONINUS IV* otherwise *URANIUS*, a successor of **ELAGABALUS** as priest-king of Emesa, had been constrained to offer himself as an imperial claimant with a mandate, at the very least, to keep Sharpur from sacking Emesa. On arrival, **VALERIAN'S** first move was to put down *ANTONINUS* who may have abdicated rather than been killed. Thereafter operations were hampered by poor morale, a devastated countryside and an increasingly virulent outbreak of plague. The emperor's capture, probably through betrayal rather than through a military failure, at Edessa in May/June 260, marks the low point in the entire history of the Empire prior to the collapse of the west in the fifth century.

VALERIAN was taken to Persia where various chronicles recount that he lived on in ignominy, being either used by Sharpur as a mounting stool or being covered with the skin of an ass. Later sources claim that he was flayed either alive or after his death and a straw stuffed mannequin fashioned from the result, thereafter on display for generations in one of the most important temples in the Persian capital. Professor Grant suggests that he may in fact have sought sanctuary with Sharpur after an army mutiny on acceptable terms, and that all the subsequent tales amounted to a smokescreen to disguise the actuality.[456]

*

GALLIENUS
29th August 253 – September 268

SALONINUS
c. July - November 260

Background
P. Licinius Egnatius Gallienus was born c. 218, was probably quaestor c. 246/7, *aedile* or peoples' tribune c. 248/9 and praetor c. 250/251. **GALLIENUS** was in Rome when his father replaced **AEMILIANUS,** and the senate created him Caesar about 26th August 253, adding **Nobilissimus Caesar** before his name. Within four days his father had raised him to the rank of co-augustus as **Imperator Caesar P. Licinius Egnatius Gallienus Pius Felix**

---

455. HA *Tyr. Trig.*. 2.
456. Grant (1985) 165

Augustus adding **Invictus** soon afterwards and preceding it with **Magnus** after 260.[457] He was also joint *pontifex maximus* with his father, receiving from the senate all the usual powers renewable on 10th December. He is one of the first emperors to be alternatively styled **Dominus Noster** before his *cognomen* in lieu of Imperator Caesar, a tradition continued for all his children. He was consul in 255, (ii) in 257, (iii) in 260, (iv) in 261, (v) in 263, (vi) in 265, (vii) in 266 and (viii) in 267. He was acclaimed *imperator* on accession and for the third time in 257, for the sixth time in 263 and no less than twelve times by 265. He added the *cognomen* **Germanicus** by 257[458], qualifying it with **Maximus** later and also adding **Dacicus Maximus** c. 264.[459] He married c. 243 Cornelia Salonina Chrysogone, from 253 styled Augusta[460], daughter of P. Cornelius Saecularis, consul (ii) in 260, whose wife was probably Saloni[n]a, daughter of the senator M. Salonius Longinus Marcellus.[461]

Sole reign

With his father's capture by or defection to Sharpur, a serious situation became desperate. In the west **GALLIENUS** had considerable success of the Rhine and against the Carpi in the areas on the northern and western edges of Dacia, but had to deal with an imperial claimant in the Balkans, *INGENUUS* who seems to have clung on to power there for well over two years. Worse, his attention to the Rhine frontier – or the subsequent drop in attention to it in favour of the middle Danube – caused a further imperial claimant to declare himself in Gaul, **POSTUMUS**, who, in the event, presided over a break-away Gallic empire which endured some 15 years.

In the post-**VALERIAN** east, a whole sequence of imperial claimants rose up, all attempting to step in and halt the slide, whilst at the same time exploiting at a Heaven-sent opportunity to grasp at supreme power: *MACRIANUS, QUIETUS, REGALIANUS* and *AEMILIANUS II* (qqv). Unfortunately in most cases, the military situation was too fragile for the claimant to attempt to patch up a treaty and head for Rome and recognition; in many cases the situation was certainly too fluid for donatives to be paid or booty to be taken, and claimants were cut down as quickly by their officers as they had been acclaimed in the first place. The only hope for such chancers was to try and carve out a polity and hope to come to terms or gain further advantage later.

As if that wasn't enough, whilst **GALLIENUS** was occupied in Dacia in 256-257, a confederation of Frankish tribes managed to breach the Rhine frontier in more than one place and embark on an unparalleled rampage through western Europe as far as the Straits of Gibraltar (and possibly Africa), looting and burning *en route*. This must have been the main spur to the acclamation of **POSTUMUS** not so long afterwards.

This catastrophe was not repeated until new years' eve, 406 when the same happened. The

---

457. ILS 536, 538.
458. ILS 541
459. ILS 552
460. PIR² C1499
461. CIL. IX. 2592

difference was that in 256 the empire had the resources and residual strength to recover. The Franks were eventually rounded up and persuaded to return back across the Rhine, but almost immediately that was done, and the Rhine defences re-strengthened, the Alemanni broke out of Raetia and invaded Italy itself. Fortunately, rapid reaction on **GALLIENUS'** part enabled him to win a crushing victory outside Mediolanum (Milan) and they were dispersed and re-settled.

Nevertheless, **GALLIENUS** also resorted to the dangerous stratagem of diplomacy, too, setting up a large group of Marcomannic tribes south of the Danube in Roman territory – the first such settlement known and a precedent for many such compromises in the fifth century. In the process, the HA peddles the unlikely tale that, as part of the treaty, he had felt constrained to marry the ruling prince's daughter as a sort of secondary wife, which, had it really happened, would have done nothing for his reputation at Rome, where he was already (apparently) viewed as a cruel and self-indulgent tyrant; the entire tale may therefore safely be ignored.[462] At the same juncture, as a measure of tactical consolidation, he also withdrew Roman control from the Agri Decumates, an important military zone lying between the Upper Danube and the Upper Rhine.

In reality, **GALLIENUS'** alleged faults were secondary, for 260 was the darkest single year in all Roman history prior to the fifth century. Yet his military and organising abilities and energy kept things on an even keel despite further barbarian incursions, those of the Persians and constant reports of imperial claimants. He was, we are told, extraordinarily unpopular with almost all levels of Roman society, yet by the time he eventually succumbed to the assassin's knife in 268 he had reigned fifteen years and turned the tide. He would appear, in retrospect, to have been the victim of much adverse criticism, probably because his re-organisation of the way the empire was administered, which reforms almost entirely sidelined the senate (as a source of tiresome imperial claimants) and hamstrung its members' traditional career path (*cursus honorum*).

Meanwhile, *INGENUUS* had been defeated by **GALLIENUS** in Pannonia in 258, and by the Emperor's equestrian 2i/c, Aureolus, at Mursa (on the River Drava, Croatia) in January 259, the fleeing imperial claimant being killed soon afterwards. Yet within a year, the Pannonian troops replaced him with *REGALIANUS*, governor of Upper Pannonia, but his grasp at power gave yet another tribe, the Roxolani of Sarmatia (the north western littoral of the Black Sea) the chance to over-run the province, **GALLIENUS** being busy in northern Italy throwing back the Alemanni at the time. Consequently, the soldiers, bottled up in Carnuntum (Bad-Deutsch Altenburg, Austria) by the Roxolani and other disaffected elements, eventually deposed and killed him. At this juncture, or a little before, the Emperor made his son **SALONINUS** Caesar. **P. Licinius Cornelius Saloninus Valerianus**[463] was born c. 245/6, created in 258/259 **nobilissimus Caesar**[464] and *princeps iuventutis* in place

---

462. HA V. Gall. 21.2; she was allegedly called Pip[ar]a.
463. PIR² L183
464. ILS 539, 558, 559

of his deceased elder brother. Although called Augustus on Alexandrian coins minted some time between 258 and 260, he only appears to have been formally declared emperor at Colonia Agrippina (Cologne) after the outbreak of the revolt of **POSTUMUS.**

All this Balkan activity meant that **GALLIENUS'S** C-in-C Rhine had to be 100% reliable and loyal, especially as the Caesar Saloninus had been installed at Colonia Agrippina (Cologne, Germany) as figurehead, under the keeping of one of the Praetorian Prefects, Silvanus. Unfortunately, in the fatal year of 260, Silvanus fell out with **POSTUMUS**, and the latter proclaimed himself emperor, following a crushing victory by the acting governor of Rhaetia over yet another bothersome tribe, the Semnones, which had placed much booty in his hands.[465] This provoked Silvanus into acclaiming **SALONINUS** as co-Augustus with his father. A confrontation began which resulted later that autumn in the death of **SALONINUS** and his mentor, and the triumph of **POSTUMUS.** It is doubtful if **SALONINUS'S** elevation ever received recognition by the senate in his lifetime, and thus he may not have received a vote of the usual powers and titles. He was certainly recognised, though and styled **Imperator [Caesar P. Licinius Cornelius] Salon[inus] Valerianus Augustus** but was killed late in the same year, when **POSTUMUS** took the city. He was unmarried, but subsequently recognised and granted divine honours by the senate.

At this stage too, **Q. Julius Gallienus**, believed to be the Emperor's youngest son, seems to have been briefly proclaimed Caesar, recorded on two types of very rare retrospective coins and struck to commemorate him with divine honours **Divo Caes[aris] Gallieno** and **Divo Caes[aris] Q. Gallieno.**[466] Although there is some doubt about the authenticity of at least one type, the person commemorated seems to have taken over from **SALONINUS** as **GALLIENUS'** heir and thus to have been nominated Caesar in around 260/261, just about the time that **POSTUMUS'S** *coup* was being played out. He might well have been extremely young and clearly died prematurely. Presumably his full style at death was **Nobilissimus Caesar Q. [Egnatius] Julius Gallienus**, although he may have had other names, omitted on coins.

GALLIENUS, despite an attempted invasion of Gaul, was unable in the end to offer effective remedial action (and was himself wounded in a seige) with the result that the western provinces of modern Germany, Belgium, Britain, France and Spain formed a breakaway political entity which was to endure for fifteen years for, once recovered from his wounds, **GALLIENUS** found he had other fish to fry.

Meanwhile, in the east, the provinces were collapsing before increased Persian raids, but Fulvius Macrianus, Valerian's right-hand man in the east, held the line at Samosata (Samsat, Turkey), having turned down the opportunity of rescuing the Emperor, which was probably a wise, if cautious, decision. **VALERIAN'S** other Praetorian prefect, Ballista, managed to inflict a signal defeat on the Persians at Corycus (Kizkalesi, Turkey) in Cilicia, following

---

465. The victor was M. Simplicinius Genialis, who may have made a brief bid for the purple after falling out with **POSTUMUS** and before being suppressed by **GALLIENUS**: Drinkwater (2007) 54-57.
466. RIC 2, RIC 1. It is quite unclear whence his *nomen* came from.

which Sharpur was forced to withdraw. Ballista clearly thought the situation needed an Augustus on the spot. Sensibly deciding that he was not the man for the job – contrary to the claim in the HA[467] - he persuaded Macrianus to accept the throne, but he in turn demurred on grounds of advancing years and lameness, suggesting his sons, *MACRIANUS* the younger and *QUIETUS*, both middle ranking officers, instead, and these imperial claimants seem to have acceded in September 260. The former, with his father, having set the East to rights, set out for the Balkans – presumably *en route* for Rome – but were defeated and killed there by the emperor's general Aureolus. In the chaos that followed the HA claims that there also arose two other alleged imperial claimants, Piso Frugi in Mursa (on the River Drava, Croatia), followed by his supposed nemesis, Valens[468], but both may safely be discounted as fictional. The Emperor's general Aureolus, was himself acclaimed (qv), although the circumstances may have required exceptional methods, for he was allegedly deposed, forgiven and re-instated by **GALLIENUS.**

Meanwhile, Odenathus, King of Palmyra, offered inducements by **GALLIENUS**, set to work to dispose of *QUIETUS,* whom he eventually bottled up in Emesa (Homs, Syria) where the citizens, fearing a devastating sack of the town, killed the young co-emperor. This left Odenathus free to deal with the Persians himself, which he did with some aplomb, although Egypt, part of *QUIETUS'S* domains, set up another imperial claimant to replace him in the shape of *AEMILIANUS II.* (An additional such claimant, Memor, although probably a real person, was never acclaimed Emperor as has been supposed). Meanwhile, in 264 **GALLIENUS** had celebrated a triumph in honour of Odenathus's success against the Persians.

By 267, Odenathus was complete master of the east, having additionally defeated the Persians at Ctesiphon itself the year before and in gratitude, **GALLIENUS** awarded him the title of *imperator* and 'Governor of the East', only for him to be cut down by an ambitious kinsman, *MAEONIUS*, who was swiftly despatched as a result. The story that he immediately declared himself an imperial claimant is confined to the HA and may also be ignored.[469] Odenathus' widow, **ZENOBIA** then declared herself her husband's successor in all his appointments and titles, something of which **GALLIENUS** did not approve but with which he was unable to deal. It has recently become apparent, too, that she later elevated her young son **VABALLATHUS** as Augustus between August 267 and August 268 simultaneously granting herself similar rank.[470]

This move came because in the winter of 268 a massive force of Goths invaded the Balkans, being joined by a large horde of Heruli, a Germanic tribe from north of the Black Sea. **GALLIENUS** rushed to meet them and defeated them at a significant battle at Naissus (Niš, Serbia) but not before they had sacked Athens.

---

467. *Tyr. Trig.* 18

468. *Ibid.,* 19-21, but note that a Piso did really exist then but was never an imperial claimant: PIR² P428, cf. C298; PLRE I Piso 1; Syme (1971) 270.

469. *Op cit.* 17.

470. Millar (1971) 16; that the process was more gradual than once thought, and patchier in its effects is attested by Mennen (2011) 240-246.

Taking advantage of this very serious diversion, the pardoned *AUREOLUS*, left in northern Italy to ensure that **POSTUMUS** was kept bottled up in Gaul, changed his allegiance at first to **POSTUMUS,** but in the end attempted to have himself acclaimed Emperor yet again, at Mediolanum (Milan). **GALLIENUS**, with all his characteristic energy, mopped up in Greece and the Balkans and returned to defeat *AUREOLUS* at the battle of Pontirolo (Italy), forcing his wayward general to fall back on Milan where the Emperor bottled him up. Then, just as he was about to administer the *coup de grace*, he was himself killed, after 28th August, probably very early September 268, by his own officers, a group of Danubian comrades-in-arms which he had actively promoted. They allegedly included the Praetorian Prefect Heraclianus, the generals Cecropius and Marcianus, along with the future emperors **AURELIANUS, PROBUS** and **CLAUDIUS II,** the latter, although not present, almost certainly up to his neck in it. The Emperor's brother Valerianus was also killed and the empress was despatched not long afterwards, as were any other close kin, the murder of whom was driven forward by the senate, vengeful after having been stripped of almost all its power and influence. The *coup*, which ushered in more than a century of non-senatorial soldier-emperors of a very different kidney, was nothing if not thorough. Furthermore, it marked an important watershed in the evolution of the monarchy. Nevertheless, **GALLIENUS** was reluctantly deified by the senate at the insistence of his successor.

In order to minimize disaffection in the east, **GALLIENUS** had lifted the persecution of Christians inaugurated by **DECIUS** and continued by **GALLUS** and his father. He re-organised the army to provide a central mobile corps to be based in Mediolanum so it could be deployed rapidly to potential trouble spots. This was mainly made up of armoured cavalry, and there was move towards cavalry elsewhere, lessons having been learnt from Sharpur's use of it, not to mention the Sarmatians. This unit was officered by professional soldiers of equestrian rank largely drawn from the Danubian provinces of proven ability; there was no longer any place for young tribunes of senatorial family.

In order to cut down on imperial claimants Gallienus removed senators' exclusive right to ranks like senior tribune (*tribunus laticlavius*) or legionary commander[471] and gradually increased the number of Imperial provinces governed by men of equestrian rank, who were styled *praesides* (singular *praes*), a process initiated by **SEVERUS**. He must have felt that men of lower rank would be less likely to grab at power like the average senior senator, keen to enhance the *dignitas* of his family. Furthermore, many senators had extensive *clientelae* (people obligated to them in various ways and dependants) not to mention estates scattered throughout the empire. Such support could be crucial in determining the likelihood of a successful bid for the purple. In this, **GALLIENUS** was to be proved wrong, of course. The lesson to be learned – as **MAXIMIN** or **PHILIP** could have told him – was that it was the army at a general's back that made an emperor, not his position in society.

With far fewer governorships and hardly any opportunities for military careers, the senate began to take up powerful civilian functions both in the administration and, eventually,

---

471. Webster (1969) 116-117

at court. It was to transform the *cursus honorum* and radically change the background of most emperors, at least until the 5ᵗʰ century.

Nevertheless, **GALLIENUS** had taken control of the empire at its lowest ebb, and this alleged enthusiast for poetry and philosophy managed, by energy, ability and single-mindedness, to set the state on the long haul back to health. One suspects that he is a much under-rated ruler, the usual negative attitude to him coloured by the hatred for him shown by classical chroniclers (mainly of senatorial rank), no doubt influenced by the rancour arising from his sidelining of the senate.

Family

The sources all seem to agree that the branch of the Licinii from which Valerian and his family stemmed was noble and Etruscan. Nevertheless, it is relatively difficult to pin his ancestors in the male line down. Even Valerianus's father's name is unknown. It is the family of Valerianus's wife, the Egnatii, who are provably distinguished. This particular inclination to favour kin when bestowing offices, especially the consulship, may provide a guide to the further reaches of **VALERIAN'S** family, however. **GALLIENUS'S** father-in-law enjoyed a second consulship in 260, and the fact that the otherwise obscure C. Salonius Lucullus held the ordinary consulship in 265 may well be explained if we postulate, as here, that he was the Empress Salonina's uncle. Again, P. Egnatius Marianus's name strongly suggests that he must be closely related to **GALLIENUS,** and that he was consul in 268 would appear to confirm it. HA gives **VALERIAN** an unattested 'noble kinsman' Valerius Flaccinus [*V. Prob.* 5.3].

Settipani has other ideas to offer. He supposes that Gallienus Concessus might be a grandson of M. Junius Maximus (a priest of the cult of Augustus in 180, and thus a patrician) and son of M. Junius Concessus Aemilianus by Licinia Galliena, a putative aunt of **VALERIANUS.** He also speculates that Concessus married a sister of the emperor **GALLUS** and that their sons might include Junius Gallienus recorded as a priest of the cult of the sun and Junius Veldumnianus, consul in 272.[472] He also suggests that Egnatius Victor was a son of the philosopher A. Egnatius Priscilianus.[473]

Yet the fact is that there are too few firmly attested relationships for us to be at all sure. The table given here attempts to set out the most convincing pattern of these.

Further reading:

Sylvänne, I., *The Reign of Emperor Gallienus: The Apogee of Roman Cavalry* (Barnsley 2019)

---

472. Settipani (2000) 355.
473. *Ibid.* 399-400.

TABLE XLII: THE FAMILY OF VALERIAN

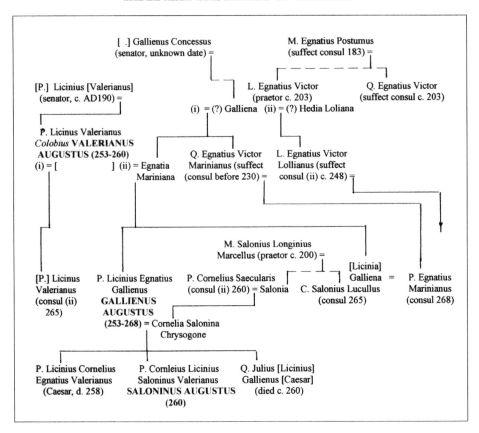

TABLE XLII: BRIEF LIVES

P. Cornelius Licinius Valerianus

Born c. 244, made *nobilissimus Caesar* 253/254 and *princeps iuventutis* but died unmarried in the earlier part of 258, being afterwards deified [ILS 538, 553; PIR² L184].

P. Cornelius Saecularis *Calliepius*,

Consul (ii) in 260, so perhaps suffect consul under **PHILIP I** [PIR² 1432; PLRE I Saecularis 1]

[P. Egnatius] Marinianus

He was probably [Egnatia] Mariniana's nephew and consul in 268. He was likely to have been **GALLIENUS'S** next heir at his death and could have been made Caesar, but no source mentions

it. Either way, the relationship was too close for comfort: he, too, seems to have been killed in the bloody aftermath of Gallienus's fall [PIR² E39; PLRE I. Marinianus 1]

M. Egnatius Postumus

Suffect consul 183, possibly a grandson of M. Egnatius Marcellinus, suffect consul in 116. The Egnatii Victores are not *certainly* his sons, however [PIR² E26; Settipani (2000) 399].

L. Egnatius Victor,

Senator in the late 2nd century, an ex-praetor, died in 218; the names of his sons suggest the names of his likely two wives. The dates of their careers suggest the order. The family were Italian, from Falerii (Civita Casstellana, Italy). There were two members of the family whose names occur on an inscription of this period or a little earlier as a series of initial letters: Q. E. G. Perpetuus and his son, Q. E. G. L. L. Tarronius Pisoninus. The E & G could be convincingly restored as Egnatius and Gallienus, a suggestion strengthened by restoring the son's Ls as Lucillus (or Lucilianus) and Lollianus. Bearing in mind the senatorial habit of polyonymy, these may be Victor Marianus or a brother, and a brother or cousin of the consul of 268. Even if the G should be restored by some name other than Gallienus, these men are still close kin to this Imperial house [FS1516; PIR² E35, P430, T30].

L. Egnatius Victor Lollianus

Suffect consul before c. 240 and again c. 248, and propraetorian legate of Pontus-Bithynia in 249 before becoming Prefect of the City (PUR) in 254. However, it has been suggested that the legate in Pontus (an ex-consul himself) must be a separate person, perhaps a son. He was almost certainly the ancestor of Q. Flavius Maesius Egnatius Lollianus Mavortius, consul in 355, ancestor of a considerable number of fifth and sixth century senators [PIR² E36 cf. *Roman Inscriptions 2006-2010* in JRS CII (2012) 216].

Q. Egnatius Victor

Suffect consul in 204. Possibly father and grandfather of the two enigmatic customers mentioned in the note about his brother Lucius, above, although if so, the Gallienus marriage must have occurred in the previous generation [PIR² E35].

Q. Egnatius [Victor] Marinianus

Suffect consul before 230 [PIR² E25 cf. 37]

Gallienus Concessus

The HA alleges that **GALLIENUS'S** grandfather

was called Gallienus, although it would seem more likely that, if this nugget bears any relation to the facts, it would have been the Emperor's great-grandfather who bore this name, as here. This man could have been the candidate as the Emperor's ancestor, if one accepts the dating given in PIR², but PLRE suggests that he belongs in the fourth or fifth century. Indeed, there are people called Gallienus around after the fall of the dynasty (as asserted by the HA), witness Junius Gallienus, a senator and priest of **AURELIAN'S** cult of the Sun a generation or so later. [HA *V. Gall.* 19, 3/8; PIR² G41, I75 ; PLRE I. Gallienus 2 ; PLRE II Concessus 1]

Q. Julius Gallienus

He is only recorded on two types of very rare coins, all retrospective and struck to commemorate him with divine honours. He might well have been extremely young and clearly died prematurely. There are no clues in his ancestry to explain the 'Q. Julius' element of his name; the combination was rare, although it might be reasonable to speculate that Licinius or Egnatius might have followed the *praenomen* in his full style, omitted on the coins.

[Licinia] Galliena

According to the HA the alleged assassin of an imperial claimant called Celsus. Her murderous exploit is a fantasy (as is Celsus, himself, the bearer of a name constantly in evidence in the HA). If she existed at all, there is some evidence to suggest that she may have been married to C. Salonius Lucullus, consul 265 [PIR² G266].

P. Licinius Cornelius Saloninus Valerianus

See above, **SALONINUS AUGUSTUS**

P. Licinius Egnatius Gallienus

See above **GALLIENUS AUGUSTUS**

P. Licinius Valerianus *Colobius*

See above **VALERIANUS AUGUSTUS**

[P. Licinius] Valerianus

Presumably born c. 216/217 and therefore suffect consul c. 252/253 before being (ordinary) consul (ii) for 265 He was killed probably at Rome (Eutropius says Milan) some time after his brother's murder, in September 268. We know of neither wife nor children. The Lucillus who was consul with Valerianus in 265 was also a kinsman of the Imperial family being a relative of Gallienus, the son of [Cn.] Egnatius Lucilianus, an ex-governor of Britain and possibly a brother of Egnatius Victor Marinianus. [PIR² E23, L257; PLRE I. Valerianus 14; Birley (1981) 197].

M. Salonius Longin[i]us Marcellus

Thought to have been father of Salonina, wife of Cornelius Saecularis. Nothing is known of his family, although a relationship to C. Salonius Matidius Patruinius, who married **TRAJAN'S** sister (see **Table XVIII Brief Lives**) is certainly conceivable [CIL. IX. 2592].

✶

Imperial claimant under Valerian

ANTONINUS IV
(Also known to history as URANIUS)
253-254

L. Jul[ius] Aur[elius] Sulp[icius] Ura[nius] Antoninus[474] appears to have seized power in Emesa in order to protect it from the depredations of the rampant Persian invaders, taking advantage of the chaos at the heart of the Empire and in the Balkans. That he was successful must stand to his credit both as a commander and as a ruler. However, he was by no means a tyro, as he was the priest king of the city state - the conical black stone brought to Rome by **ELAGABALUS** appears on one of his coins - and a successor of the psychotic Severan, clearly implying fairly close kinship. For the ruling family of Emesa and his possible place in it see **Table XXXII Brief Lives**. He also appears at an earlier juncture in Zosimus as an imperial claimant; it has subsequently emerged that this is a chronological misplacement of this man caused by numismatists' disagreements on dating the coin types.[475] If the later chronicler John Malalas is to be believed he is also to be identified with the Emesan High Priest of Aphrodite, Samsigeramus, certainly a name to be found amongst the members of the family of **ELAGABALUS**.

Some of his gold coins just give his name with *Conservator Aug.* or *Fecunditas Aug.* on the reverse, almost as if he was deliberately avoiding the actual imperial style.

---

474. PIR² I195; Syme (1971) 202.

475. Frank (1939) 329; Zosimus I. 12, 2 who wrongly claims he was of slave descent. Settipani asppears to accept that both were authentic claimants: *op. cit* 443-448, the one being father of the other.

Despite that, however, he wears a wreath but calls himself merely **L. Jul[ius] Aur[elius] Sulp[icius] Ura[nius] Antoninus** - no 'Imperator Caesar' nor 'Augustus', although he probably was so styled officially - claiming the tribunician power and the consulate ('Co[nsuli]s I'[476]), although these are unlikely to have been ratified by the senate in Rome. Some reverses also include the formula 'AUGG' confirming his imperial style and that he was either recognised briefly, probably by **VALERIAN**) or claimed that he had been.[477]

Accounts differ as to his fate. Those that suggest that he abdicated and was accorded an honourable retirement ring truest. For he saved the situation in Syria for long enough for **VALERIAN** to get there in force and begin to roll the Persians back. If that is the case, it is possible *ANTONINUS* was accorded some form of recognition by the senate which has - as has so much at this period - escaped record. Furthermore, he may well have been a senator and a former (suffect) consul.

Zosimus records an *ANTONINUS (V)*[478] as one of those who rebelled against **GALLIENUS** at the same time as *MEMOR* and *AUREOLUS* (qqv), probably to be identified as this man.

*

Imperial claimant under Valerian

INGENUUS
July 258 – January 259

Ingenuus[479] was an imperial claimant in Pannonia who was proclaimed at Sirmium (Sremska Mitrovica, Serbia) having rebelled in the summer of 258, thus before and not, as previously supposed, in the wake of the capture of **VALERIANUS**. There is, however, much debate about the chronology of events on the Danubian frontier at the beginning of the sole rule of **GALLIENUS**.[480] A senator of consular rank, he was the governor of Pannonia when proclaimed emperor by the legions of Moesia.

He was defeated by **GALLIENUS'S** general, Aureolus at Mursa (on the River Drava, Croatia) early in 259 and was probably killed by his own supporters in subsequent flight, although suicide cannot be ruled out. After an hiatus of some five months his rebellion was re-ignited by *REGALIANUS* (see below).

---

476. RIC 7
477. 'Saeculares Augg' RIC 7.
478. Zosimus I. 38, 1; PLRE I. Antoninus 1
479. PIR² I23; PLRE I. Ingenuus 1 which dates the rebellion to 260-261.
480. Barnes, T. D., in *Phoenix* 26 (1972) 160-161, supported by a consular date

He was perhaps son or grandson of the C. Julius Ingenuus, a senatorial youth who was recorded as military tribune of *Legio* III Italica which was stationed in Noricum in the later 2nd century.[481]

*

Imperial Claimant under Gallienus

REGALIANUS
August 260 – March 261

When Sir Ronald Syme reviewed the Emperors from the Danubian provinces – loosely Illyricum[482] – he seems to have overlooked *REGALIANUS*.[483] Almost our only information comes, inevitably, from the HA, which means that it is less than reliable, including Dacia being claimed as his place of origin.[484] With this latter fact, Sir Ronald elsewhere concurs, however.[485] We are also told he was commander – *dux* – in Illyricum but that he was acclaimed in Moesia. In fact, as his wife was a member of a grand senatorial family it seems far more likely that he was the senatorial governor of Moesia Inferior or Superior.

Reign
GALLIENUS, in the wake of *INGENUUS'S* rebellion, re-organised the Danubian defences but had to hurry back to Italy to deal with an influx of Alemanni, a Germanic people, leaving *REGALIANUS* there to complete his measures. This was just as well, for a tribe called the Roxolani, recently re-settled by **GALLIENUS** inside the Empire in this sector, rebelled and attacked the forces of *REGALIANUS*, who fell back on Carnuntum (Bad-Duetsch Altenburg, Austria). He only became an imperial claimant in around August 260 by the acclamation of his troops.

He held out for several months, managing to last long enough to issue coins, but his men, in desperation, killed him. Most (but not all) of his issues have, as part of their reverse legend, the formula 'AUGG.' suggesting that he was, at least temporarily, recognised by **GALLIENUS** after his father's demise.

REGALIANUS seems therefore unlikely to have been of Dacian stock, *pace* Sir Ronald, but would have been born c. 215, have entered the senate and eventually served as suffect consul at some date prior to 259 before being appointed governor of one of the Moesias. When acclaimed, he took the style **Imperator Caesar P. C[assius]**

---

481. PIR² I359
482. Syme RP III (1984) 892-898
483. PIR² C2. HA *Tyr. Trig.* 24 wrongly calls him Trebellianus.
484. *Tyr. Trig.* 10, 1-17.
485. Syme (1971) 211

Regalianus [(?)Pius Felix] Augustus. We might speculate as to whether he arrogated to himself the pontificate and the powers usually bestowed by the senate; in all probability he did, but the senate was never rash enough to recognise him. He was killed in the late winter or early spring of the year following.

Family

The HA claimed that *REGALIANUS* was kin to Decebalus, that King of Dacia who had been removed at great cost by **TRAJAN** 105-107, but this has to be discarded. On his coins he is merely 'P. C. Regalianus', where the C was long thought to strand for Cornelius, but a diploma of Severan date discovered relatively recently, introduces us to a hitherto unknown suffect consul, C. Cassius Regallianus, who may well have been this claimant's father. Hence the C in this case may reasonably be taken for Cassius. However, thanks to his desire to strike coins depicting his wife, Sulpicia Dryantilla (styled Augusta), a Lycian from a senatorial family, we can see that he was well connected.[486] The Empress was also a descendant of the sister of later 2nd century imperial claimant *AVIDIUS CASSIUS*, see **Table XXV Brief Lives**.

With this in mind, the table below, devoted to the family of the Empress, is derived with minor alterrations, from the *Prosopographia Imperii Romani,* as referenced in **Brief Lives**. Settipani suggests an alternative descent, inserting another generation between Sulpicius Pollio and Dryantilla, and making her grandmother Dryantilla a daughter of Ti. Claudius Agrippinus, the suffect consul of 151, and making Dryantius Antoninus his brother, but still married to Avidia Alexandria. He also assigns as mother to the suffect consul of 151 Julia Lysimache, a descendant of the tetrarch Trocondas III.[487]

---

486. DNP 1096.
487. Settipani (2000) 461-463,

TABLE XLIII: THE FAMILY OF DRYANTILLA

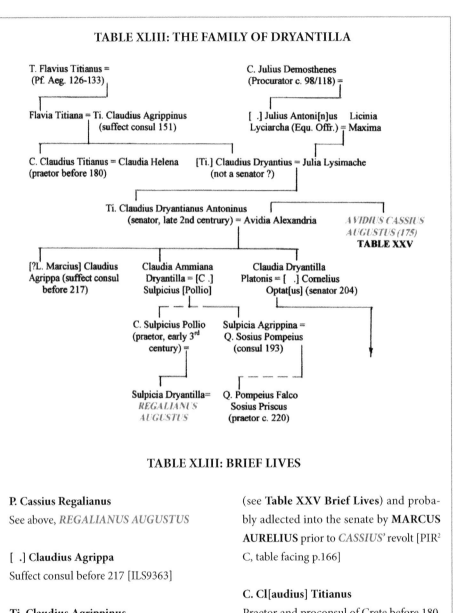

TABLE XLIII: BRIEF LIVES

P. Cassius Regalianus

See above, *REGALIANUS AUGUSTUS*

[.] Claudius Agrippa

Suffect consul before 217 [ILS9363]

Ti. Claudius Agrippinus

An arval brother and suffect consul 151
[FS1163].

[Ti.] Claudius Dryantius

Much of the family details given here are
from PIR [PIR² C858 & p. 166].

Ti. Claudius Dryantius Antoninus

Brother-in-law to *AVIDIUS CASSIUS*

(see **Table XXV Brief Lives**) and proba-
bly adlected into the senate by **MARCUS
AURELIUS** prior to *CASSIUS'* revolt [PIR²
C, table facing p.166]

C. Cl[audius] Titianus

Praetor and proconsul of Crete before 180.
He had a probable son, Ti. Claudius Titianus,
living 200 [FS1242]

[.] Cornelius Optat[us]

A senator in 204

T. Flavius Titianus

Prefect of Egypt, 126-133

[.] Julius Antoni[n]us

Equestrian officer, military tribune IVth Legion Scythica, mid 2nd century [PIR^2 I153].

Julia Lysimache

'Mater stirpis consularis' (Mother of a line of consuls) [PIR^2 I677].

C. Julius Demosthenes

A member of an opulent family from Lycia, he enjoyed a protracted career as an equestrian military officer, before being appointed procurator of Sicily by **TRAJAN** c. 103/114 [PIR^2 I288]

[L. Marcius?] Claudius Agrippa

Suffect consul before 217 Probably related to L. Marcius Celer M. Calpurnius Longus, a suffect consul of the mid-2nd century [ILS 9363 of 218].

Q. Pompeius Falco Sosius Priscus

Patrician and praetor c. 210/220 also a *salius*, possibly the same man or father of the Falco who was governor of Germania Superior 240 and thus at some stage a suffect consul. Barbieri considers this man to be the son of the related M. Roscius Lupus Murena, but this is now doubted. [ILS1106; FS2751; JRS CII (2012) quoting AE (230-05) 1866 ; PIR^2 P603]

Q. Sosius Pompeius Falco

Patrician by creation and son of the senator with the longest recorded Roman name (see **introduction**), and descended from a Flavian senator and, in the female line, from the Kings of Sparta. Consul 193, whose wife is attested as the great niece of the imperial claimant *AVIDIUS CASSIUS* see **Table XXV Brief Lives** [FS 2765; PIR^2 P655]

[C.] Sulpicius Pollio

As with his wife's family, he was from Lycia. Whilst he is affirmed as the husband of Dryantilla, it is not certain if he is to be identified with the suffect consul of late 2nd or early 3rd century date whose *nomen* only is recorded [FS 3194] .

C. Sulpicius Pollio

Praetor, early 3rd century; legionary legate and Arval brother in 218 [FS 3195 cf. 3194; ILS 5039; PIR^2 I017].

*

Imperial Claimants under Gallienus

MACRIANUS
c. 17th May 260 – April/May 261

QUIETUS
c. 17th May 260 – November 261

The man on the spot when **VALERIAN** made his undignified exit in spring 260 was [T.] Fulvius Macrianus, his equestrian *procurator arcae et praepositus annonae* - effectively his quartermaster general.[488] Indeed, he refused to mount a rescue of the unfortunate emperor because his military position was too weak; few sources present this as an act of self-promoting treachery, as anyone reading the history of the previous forty years might have supposed. Indeed, things were so chaotic that the elevation of a responsible general on the spot to the purple was inevitable, even if not desirable.

Macrianus was duly hailed as emperor at the urging of the barbarian praetorian prefect Ballista[489], but declined on the ground of age and infirmity – perhaps an unconvincing response, considering he had so recently been **VALERIANUS'** second in command in the campaign. Instead he proposed his two sons, present as legionary legates, **T. Fulvius Junius Macrianus** and **T. Fulvius Junius Quietus**[490] who had been appointed as military tribunes by **VALERIAN** according to the HA[491] but in fact were probably by then senators of praetorian rank. They were immediately recognised in the important provinces of Asia, Syria and Egypt, and with **GALLIENUS** under almost unsupportable pressure in the west, for a few months it rather looked as if the eastern part of the Empire was going to become a separate polity, rather presaging the formal division instigated under the Tetrarchs two generations later.

T. [or P.] Fulvius Junius *MACRIANUS* was an ex-praetor and legate serving under his father, who was robably acclaimed on 17th May 260. He was styled **Imperator Caesar Fulvius Macrianus Pius Felix Augustus**[492] but it is highly unlikely that he received any recognition from the senate. We can thus say that he assumed the powers and chief priesthood, although he and his brother could have set up some kind of conciliar body or quasi-senate at Antioch, appointing themselves consuls and no doubt allowing various opulent local magnates a share in the honours too, putting their skills to use in administering the vast swathe of territory they now controlled. According to papyri, they entered on to a second joint consulship on 17th May 261,

---

488. PIR² F549; PLRE I. Macrianus 2
489. An imperial claimant himself according to HA. *Tyr. Trig.* 18: a groundless supposition.
490. PIR² F546, 547; PLRE I. Macrianus 3, Quietus 2
491. *Op. cit., Tyr. Trig.* 12. 10
492. Coins

confirming that *MACRIANUS* was believed in Egypt at least then still to be living, although in fact he may have already met his fate; communications with the west were still poor at this time.[493]

Having stabilised the situation in Syria, it was then decided that the elder brother should go to Rome and establish his rule throughout the Empire, **GALLIENUS** being then (as far as they knew) struggling with the Alemanni on the Rhine and damaged goods in the light of the fate that had encompassed his father. *QUIETUS* was left with Ballista to hold the East.

MACRIANUS thus set out for the Balkans with his father as C-in-C, probably with the object of gathering extra support and reaching Rome to legitimise his position with the senate. They no doubt banked on using the corn imports from Alexandria, which they controlled, to add leverage to their ambitions. Unfortunately they arrived in Illyricum just as **GALLIENUS'S** general Domitianus was mopping up after helping Aureolus depose *REGALIANUS,* and were defeated by him in battle, both being killed in action some time after 17th May 261.

With his elder brother and father *en route* to Rome, **T. Fulvius Junius** *QUIETUS*[494] remained to consolidate the east, especially as Ballista had inflicted an unexpected defeat on Sharpur and driven him back across the Euphrates. As the younger brother he looks suitably youthful on his coins. He was probably also acclaimed 17th May 260 and styled **Imperator Caesar Fulvius Quietus Pius Felix Augustus**[495] with the other powers as for his brother, including an immediate 'ordinary' consulship. He was 'consul' (ii) from 17th May 261 but was killed at Emesa, probably in November that year. According to the HA he married and had issue, amongst whom was the mother of Cornelius Macer, a senator alleged to have been flourishing c. 300/315, but completely unattested elsewhere and therefore in all probability, entirely fictitious.[496]

Unfortunately, once his co-Augustus had been eliminated by **GALLIENUS** in 261, the Emperor managed to persuade the astonishingly loyal Prince of Palmyra, Odenathus, to field a force to overthrow *QUIETUS.* He thus appointed the Palmyrene supreme commander in the east and he was eventually able to surprise *QUIETUS* at Emesa and the young imperial claimant was killed by the citizens of the City who were not at all keen to endure the privations of a siege and the inevitable reprisals that the City's fall would have entailed.[497]

---

493. P. Oxy. 2710.

494. PIR² F547; PLRE, I. Quietus 1

495. Coins

496. *Op. cit.,* 14. 5 & 3, 5

497. The dates of these proceedings are to some extent confirmed by an Egyptian papyrus from Oxyrhincus, No. 2710, cf. Zonaras, 12. 24 & HA, *V. Gall.* III.4.

The family of Macrianus and Quietus

Stein adduces the descent of this family from an alliance in the mid second century between the Aurelii Galli and the Neratii Prisci, citing a number of pieces of circumstantial evidence.[498] If this could be better authenticated, it would give the two imperial claimants a connection with the fourth century consular Neratii and through them to the Empress Justina, second wife of **VALENTINIAN I** (see **Table LIV(b).**) Doubts obtrude, however, for the elder Macrianus was only an equestrian officer, albeit a very senior one, and thus is unlikely to have been able to boast a glittering array of consular ancestors, especially as there is nothing concrete to connect him with the man whom it is has been suggested might have been his father, L. Neratius L.[f. Gal.] Junius Mac[er], a senator and patron of Saepinum who married a Fulvia Prisca.[499] That his wife was probably of senatorial family and from the younger son's name, probably called Junia (and thus conceivably a daughter or sister of Junius Macer), is much more likely.[500]

*

Imperial claimant under Gallienus

AEMILIANUS II
November 261 – 31ˢᵗ March 262

With the death of *QUIETUS* in Emesa at the hands of Odenathus of Palmyra in November 261, Syria and Asia nominally were returned to the control of the Empire. However, in Egypt, L. Mussius Aemilianus Aegippus the Imperial prefect, who had thrown in his lot with the two claimants, must have realised that his only hope of escaping a terrible retribution for defecting from **GALLIENUS** to *MACRIANUS* and *QUIETUS* was to seize the purple himself, playing Egypt and its grain supplies as his trump card.[501]

L. Mussius Aemilianus who bore the *signum* **Aegippus** (probably from his office) was probably born c. 210/15 and rose rapidly through a distinguished equestrian career, ending up holding the second most important equestrian appointment after praetorian prefect, that of prefect of Egypt, in 258, appointed by **VALERIANUS**.[502] As such he bore the style of *vir perfectissimus* (vp) and was a zealous persecutor of Dionysius of Alexandria and the strong Christian community in Egypt generally whilst **VALERIANUS** was alive. He was still *en post* when *MACRIANUS* and *QUIETUS* were

---

498. PIR² IV (1966) p. 329
499. PIR² F565. HA tells us that the emperors' mother was a 'noblewoman' (13, 1
500. As proposed in two hypothetical variations by Settipani (2000) 327-328.
501. Aurelius Victor (32.4) is the only non-HA authority for his actually having assumed the purple.
502. HA *Tyr. Trig.* 22; PIR² M757; PLRE I. Aemilianus 6; his meteoric career: ILS1433.

proclaimed for he allowed their coins to be struck at Alexandria indicating his support for them. *AEMILIANUS II* was overthrown by his successor as prefect of Egypt, the *dux* (general) Aurelius Theodotus, probably at the end of March 262, certainly by the August. It seems strange that he issued no coins; after all **GORDIANUS I** was only emperor three weeks and still managed to issue some, albeit the senate authorised it, being on his side. Possibly *AEMILIANUS* was content to continue to issue those of *QUIETUS*, or contented himself with Alexandrine provincial issues. The alternative is that he never had himself acclaimed emperor at all, but merely held out against **GALLIENUS'S** forces out of necessity. He was killed on the orders of **GALLIENUS.** Nothing is known of his family, although they were probably of Italian stock.[503]

*

Imperial claimant under Gallienus

VALENS II
261-262

Proconsul of Achaia or Macedonia in 261, a praetorian governor called Valens appears to have raised the standard of revolt, possibly as a result of successfully defending Thessalonica from the marauding Goths, according himself the epithet **Valens Thessal[on]icus.** As he appears in the HA, one might be tempted to view him with some reserve were it not for the fact that he also appears in two other sources. HA says he was disposed of by Piso, probably in 262.[504] This Piso Frugi Thessalicus is said by HA to have been sent to put down the revolt by *MACRIANUS* and to have become an imperial claimant in *VALENS'S* place, and to have been a scion of the eminent republican family the Calpurnii Pisones and thus a kinsman of **PISO/GALBA II** (qv). Whilst this may be possible (there are no other Pisones known to have survived the 2nd century) he was probably only the governor of a neighbouring province who neutralised *VALENS'S* revolt, elevated to a claimant by the HA, keen to make up its total of 30.[505] HA also claims the senate voted Piso a statue for his pains, which is possible, but unlikely. The identity of *VALENS*, however, remains elusive, although HA claims him as a great nephew of *VALENS I.*

*

---

503. Syme (1971) 270 & n. 4

504. HA *Gall.* II.2 & *Tyr. Trig.* 19.1. *Epitome* 32.4 7 Amminanus Marcellinus 21,16.10; PLRE Valens 2

505. HA *Gall.* 2.2-4; *Tyr. Trig.* 19-21; on the relationship of Valens I & II, 20. 2. PLRE Piso 1

Imperial claimant under Gallienus

MEMOR
c. April 262?

Mentioned by Zosimus as an imperial claimant in Egypt at the same time as [*ANTONINUS (V)*] and *AUREOLUS*.[506] The most likely context for him is that he was a senior official of *AEMILIANUS II* and tried to continue his regime. If so, the attempt was nipped in the bud and Theodotus captured and killed him probably within weeks of *AEMILIANUS'* overthrow. He may never have actually become established as an imperial claimant before his demise. His career and family are totally obscure.

*

Imperial claimant under Gallienus

[ANTONINUS V]
262

Mentioned by Zosimus[507] as a usurper at the same time as *MEMOR* and *AUREOLUS* but probably he is a confusion with *(URANIUS) ANTONINUS IV* (see above). Otherwise location, career, family and fate are totally obscure.[508]

*

Imperial claimant under Gallienus

AUREOLUS
Autumn/winter 267 - August/September 268

M'. Acilius *AUREOLUS* was **GALLIENUS'S** right hand man, even from before his father's capture. Sir Ronald Syme, the supreme expert on the Danubian provinces considered that he may well also have come from Dacia Ripensis.[509] With **CLAUDIUS, AURELIAN** and **PROBUS** he seems to have been one of a group of brothers-in-arms,

---

506. Zosimus 1, 38; PLRE I. Memor 1
507. Zosimus, *loc.cit.*
508. PIR² A790; PLRE I. Antoninus 1. HA *Tyr. Trig.* 29 also inserts a fictitious claimant here, *CELSUS*.
509. PIR² A1672; Zonaras, 12, 24; Syme (1971) 211.

all Danubians of humble beginnings and all officers in the *elite* mobile cavalry corps created by **GALLIENUS** to act as the spearhead of a mobile, troubleshooting force based at Mediolanum (Milan), the perfect hub for reaching the likely hot-spots of the Rhine and Danubian frontiers. In 260, he defeated *INGENUUS* and the following year *MACRIANUS*.

In 262, whilst struggling to contain the chaos arising from the aftermath of the declarations it appears from some sources that he was himself acclaimed Emperor for a brief time in the Balkans in 262, but seems to have demised his honours to **GALLIENUS** and been forgiven. If this train of events is true, then it says much for his perceived loyalty to the Emperor and his effectiveness as a trouble-shooting general.

Nevertheless, sometime in spring 268 he decided to throw his lot in with the Gallic Emperor **POSTUMUS** only for this gesture to go un-acknowledged. However, having done so, he had compromised himself hopelessly with **GALLIENUS** and held out against him. He issued coins, not in his own name but in that of **POSTUMUS**.[510]

Eventually he was worsted by **GALLIENUS** at the Battle of Pontirolo, following which he fell back on Milan, at the siege of which City, **GALLIENUS** was finally assassinated by a group of officers. At a late stage, although according to two sources before the Emperor's murder, he finally declared himself Augustus.[511] Yet *pace* Zosimus and Aurelius Victor, it would make considerably more sense if his declaration had been as a result of this news. He might have still remained in hope of a reconciliation whilst his old comrade-in-arms lived. He was promptly declared a public enemy and soon afterwards submitted to **CLAUDIUS II,** only to be killed by the Emperor's men, possibly after a brief attempt to re-ignite his claim to the purple.

Said to have been of humble birth, his full name suggests that his father or an earlier ancestor was granted Roman citizenship by a member of the old republican noble family of the Acilii Glabriones or Avilae, members of which invariably used the archaic *praenomen* Manius (M'.) and which family continued in prominence throughout much of the Imperial period; one may well have been governing the relevant Balkan province before 217 (none are known but there are considerable gaps in the rolls of such office-holders), after which date everyone became Roman citizens. Nothing further is known of his family.

*

*

---

510. Drinkwater (1987) 145-147. Reverse legends, significantly, include slogans extolling the cavalry.
511. If we may accept the testimony of a single late *aureus*, recorded in 1718, since lost: *ibid.* 33, 146, n. 82.

V(b) & V(c)
BREAKAWAY POLITIES

The chaos that broke out once the news of the defeat and capture of **VALERIAN** had become public, not only led to a rash of imperial claimants but to a pair of what were effectively breakaway empires, run on typically Roman lines, but of which the rulers of both showed scant signs of risking everything by making a bid for supreme power in command of a (re-)united polity. The difference between them was that whilst the Gallic Empire, which flourished from 260 to 274, was never - despite attempts by a handful of later claimants, like *CARAUSIUS, MAGNENTIUS*, **MAGNUS MAXIMUS** and *CONSTANTINUS III* to revive the idea - to become an enduring entity in late Roman history. Yet that in the East showed a way forward that was taken up by the Tetrarchs and later by the sons of **THEODOSIUS I**.[512] The Imperial succession is, in these sections, treated as *sui generis* acknowledged, and the Emperors' named are listed in purple as recognised within their own polities, although none were recognised by the senate in Rome.

V(b)
THE FIRST GALLIC EMPIRE

The Imperial Succession
Postumus
Marius
Victorinus
Tetricus

Imperial Claimants
Laelianus
Faustinus

The North West provinces were never a viable political entity within the context of a Mediterranean empire, although the area made a perfectly good administrative unit - from the 4th century, the Praetorian Prefecture of Gaul – but even that ceased to be sustainable once the Rhine frontier had finally collapsed.[513]

The sources for the Gallic Empire are fragmentary and in some cases contradictory, but were drawn together convincingly by J. F. Drinkwater, whose chronology is followed below. It is thought that, like *MACRIANUS* and *QUIETUS,* the regime was underpinned by an expanded provincial council in lieu of a senate, members of which were given consulships as occasion and precedent demanded. The membership would have been of Gallic nobles,

---

512. Drinkwater (1987) 239ff.
513. *Ibid.*, 255.

municipal grandees and military men. At its height, under **POSTUMUS**, the Gallic empire encompassed the three Gallic provinces, the two Germanies, the two British provinces, Belgica and all the Spanish ones. After the first decade, most of Spain had been lost, as had Gaul south of the Alps and east of the Rhône. Yet the reason for the long endurance of this Empire was that none of its rulers were willing to chance their arm on making a bid to occupy Italy and take Rome.

Once this became obvious to **GALLIENUS**, he was able to let the Gallic Empire get on with securing the German frontier, confident that he would experience no stab in the back whilst active elsewhere; it suited his strategy in damping down the unrest the capture of his father had caused. Indeed, by 266/267, he could claim that there was 'everywhere peace' a fact he put on the reverse of one of his coin issues of the time. For this he certainly owed something to the Gallic Empire. Yet the sources are so unreliable and patchy that, for all we know, **GALLIENUS** and the Galllic rulers may indeed have reached an understanding, although if they did it did not extend to acknowledgement on their coin issues. An interesting point made by Drinkwater is that the Gallic mint was served by one or more of the finest die-sinkers in the long history of Roman coinage; the imperial portraiture is exceptional and culminates with a superb three-quarters head of **POSTUMUS** which is unparalleled outside the ancient east.[514]

*

POSTUMUS
July 260 – March 269

Background
POSTUMUS[515] was the governor of either upper or lower Germany – he is described using anachronistic terminology[516] – and was acclaimed emperor in May or very early August 260. Having **SALONINUS**, the son and titular representative of **GALLIENUS,** within his sphere of influence at Colonia Agrippina (Cologne) and with one of the praetorian prefects, Silvanus, acting as the young prince's minder, a major falling out was inevitable, and in the outcome, Silvanus and his charge died, and **POSTUMUS** was recognised by all the provinces of NW Europe.[517]

 M. Cassianius Latinius POSTUMUS may himself have been of Batavian or Gallic stock; his *nomen,* created from the adjectival form of Cassius, is certainly reminiscent of Gallic family names from this period. The 'Latinius' element might well have been senatorial Italian (the HA claims his father was also called Postumus[518]) and perhaps derived from his

---

514. Drinkwater (1987) 157-158; an example is in the British Museum.
515. PIR² C467; PLRE I. Postumus 2
516. *Dux* and *praeses* by the HA: *Tyr. Trig.* III. 9
517. Drinkwater (1987) 26-27.
518. HA *Tyr Trig.* 3-4; it makes Postumus a 'tribune' in 257.

mother. It may be, therefore, that he was at least a second generation senator and, if indeed Gallic, something of a rarity at this period. A Gallic ancestry might also help to explain his remarkable success. He served as suffect consul before 258, so had been perhaps born around 210 and would therefore have entered the senate in c. 232/4.

Reign

He became Emperor as **Imperator Caesar D[ominus] N[oster] M. Cassianius Latinius Postumus Pius Felix Augustus,**[519] had himself recognised as *Pontifex Maximus* and obtained a grant from his *consilium* of proconsular and tribunician powers, renewable, it would seem from coin evidence, on 10th December yearly, adhering to the tradition for this transaction. He appointed yearly consuls and himself held further consulships, in 261, 262, 266 or 267 and 269. He was thus able to govern his provinces in the traditional way through senatorial ex-magistrates although the exact detail is lost to us. By the beginning of 269 he had been consul five times, had held the *tribunicia potestatis* ten times and been granted the style of *Pater Patriae*.

It transpired that the new ruler was cannier than most imperial claimants, deciding to stay where he was and to consolidate those provinces that had adhered to his cause. **GALLIENUS** meanwhile, being beset by would-be successors elsewhere, decided for a time to let him be, possibly even recognising him, enabling him to retrench further. In 265, after **POSTUMUS** had managed to re-consolidate the Rhine frontier, **GALLIENUS** at last attempted to re-take his Gallic provinces, but after a good start, was wounded during a siege and withdrew, albeit in good order.

When *AUREOLUS* seized power in Milan, **POSTUMUS** refused to come to his aid, presumably because **GALLIENUS'S** general had led the campaign to unseat him in 265. This failure to grasp what must have appeared as a golden opportunity to seize the whole western empire might have represented a loss of prestige which perhaps led to his death early the following year at the hands of a group of his officers, following the suppression of the imperial claimant *LAELIANUS.* He was killed probably in March 269, ushering in a Gallic Year of the Four Emperors.

Family

Nothing is known of his wife and only the HA mentions any offspring, a son,[520] also Postumus, allegedly made Caesar and later Augustus. No other source has any of this and it may safely be ignored, although he may well have had a son, perhaps the senator Latinius Primosus recorded (along with Gordianus, a possible descendant of the ephemeral dynasty of that name) on an inscription from Rome of about 300.[521] It would appear that **VICTORINUS** was effectively the Emperor's intended successor, which would rather

---

519. Fulll names, ILS 560-562; CIL.II. 4943 etc.; on coins it is abbreviated to his *cognomen* only..
520. HA *Tyr. Trig.* 4.1. cf. PIR² C467;PLRE I. Postumus 1.
521. CIL VI. 37118.

suggest that there was neither son, son-in-law nor brother to hand who could have filled this role, although the remainder of his family could have been in Rome, cut of from his sphere of influence. A lack of coins bearing the image of an Augusta also suggests that he might have been a widower or bachelor by 260.

Imperial claimant under Postumus

LAELIANUS
January – March 269

At the beginning of 269, *LAELIANUS*, almost certainly **POSTUMUS'** governor of Upper Germany, rebelled and proclaimed himself emperor. The catalyst may have been the re-annexation to the Empire of **POSTUMUS'** Spanish provinces, assuming that this occurred so early in the year (or late in that preceding). The alternative cause might have been the refusal of **POSTUMUS** to go to the aid of *AUREOLUS* the previous autumn, an occasion he might have used to take over the entire west.

In any case, [C.] Ulpius Cornelius Laelianus,[522] without doubt a senator and a former suffect consul, either under **VALERIANUS** or as an appointee of **POSTUMUS.** He was styled after his acclamation **Imperator Caesar Laelianus Pius Felix Augustus** and was soon confronted by **POSTUMUS**, defeated in battle and besieged at his capital, Moguntiacum (Mainz). The city was eventually taken and *LAELIANUS* captured, although his subsequent fate is not recorded. He was probably killed along with **POSTUMUS,** if not executed beforehand. The length of his reign is not certain, but it was long enough to enable him to issue coins. **POSTUMUS** probably wanted to see the onset of spring before moving against him. We can say nothing of this man's family, unfortunately. The *cognomen* occurs in a branch of the senatorial Pontii in the 2nd century, but thereafter the name is not met with until this man. The HA, with its customary cavalier attitude to facts, calls him Lollianus and contributes not a single reliable fact about him.[523]

⁎

---

522. PLRE I. Laelianus 1; HA incorrectly calls him Lollianus (*Tr. Trig.* 5.)
523. *Tyr. Trig.* 5, 1-8.

MARIUS
March - June 269

Following the capture of Moguntiacum, **POSTUMUS** refused to allow his forces to sack the city, which caused sufficient resentment for an officer called **M. Aurelius MARIUS** to lead a revolt which ended in the murder of the emperor, the sack of the city and the elevation of the instigator, who then removed to Augusta Treverorum (Trier).

MARIUS'S name suggests descent from a family granted citizenship by **M. AURELIUS**, a member of his family, by **SEVERUS** after 195 or **CARACALLA** prior to 212. The HA claims that he was astoundingly low-born and a former blacksmith,[524] and the other related sources, Aurelius Victor and Eutropius, both label him as of common origin or a trades-man.[525] One suspects that, obscure though his family background may have been, he would have been chosen by the military for a good reason – probably because he was an officer and, as one source declares, *strenuus* – energetic. The same sources only credit him with a reign of between one and three days but, from the coins he issued and their quantity, he probably lasted three or four months before being killed by his troops and, after a two-day *interregnum,* replaced by **VICTORINUS.**[526]

He seems to have been acknowledged within the polity as emperor, and used the style **Imperator Caesar M. Aur[elius] Marius Pius Felix Augustus**.[527] He is known to have held the tribunician power (presumably by grant of the anti-senate established by **POSTUMUS**), but no coin records a consulship. Coin portraits show a man with close cropped hair and much in the mode of the Illyrian soldier emperors like **CLAUDIUS II** and his successors. Indeed, it is perfectly possible that he was from Illyricum. No concrete information has survived concerning his family.

*

VICTORINUS
June 269 – February/March 271

Background
VICTORINUS seems to have been the right hand man of **POSTUMUS** and may indeed have been his intended successor. He probably started out as the emperor's praetorian prefect, but can be assumed to have moved on by 267 in which year he served as (Gallic empire) ordinary consul with **POSTUMUS**.[528] The additional indication that he was

---

524. *Tyr. Trig.* 8. 1
525. Aur. Victor, 33, 9; Eutropius 9, 9. 2
526. Drinkwater (1987) 177-178
527. Coin evidence.
528. The year of the consulship could have been 266: Drinkwater (1987) 120

probably not praetorian prefect in the later part of the reign was that if he had been, he would probably have been on the spot during the unfortunate events at Moguntiacum. Had he been so, he would undoubtedly have either been killed or his accession would have followed seamlessly without the intervention of either the usurper or his ephemeral nemesis. As it was, he held back, kept his powder dry and, two days after the assassination of **MARIUS**, he was acclaimed emperor at Trier.

Reign

He styled himself officially **Imperator Caesar M. Piavonius Victorinus Pius Felix Augustus.** He served a second consulship in 270 and renewed his tribunician power twice after his accession.[529] Unfortunately, it was on **VICTORINUS'S** watch that **CLAUDIUS II** managed to re-assert control over most of Spain and some of Southern Gaul, causing the once great Gallic nation of the Aedui to go over to the new emperor at Rome. **VICTORINUS** determined to put an end to this piece of insubordination and resolved to bring the Aedui to heel, if only to prevent more Gaulish *civitates* (urban-centred tribal areas) from attempting to break away. This he achieved, although at the expense of a seven month siege of the cantonal capital, Augustodunum Aeduorum (Autun), which was subsequently sacked and its important inhabitants scattered into exile. The emperor returned in triumph to Colonia Claudia Ara Agrippinensium (Cologne).

Beyond that, **VICTORINUS'S** achievement was to consolidate what remained of the empire, and in this he was successful. The Rhine frontier remained quiet and in the end his undoing was excess. He was apparently something of a seducer of other officers' wives and in the spring of 271, went too far with the spouse of an official called Attitianus who encompassed his assassination.

At this stage, the late Emperor's mother (Victoria, or Vitruvia) took a hand. Whether Attitianus or anyone associated with him expected to be elevated to the purple we shall never know, for his mother acted with commendable speed and single-mindedness. She issued a generous donative to the army out of her own pocket, secured the deification of her son, resisted the temptation to emulate **ZENOBIA** and thus brought about the acclamation of the governor of Aquitania, **TETRICUS** who was almost certainly a close kinsman of his predecessor; it was the nearest the Gallic Empire was ever to get to a dynasty.[530]

Family

His origin probably lay amongst the higher echelons of the Gallic nobility, and his full name, **M. Piav[v]onius Victorinus** certainly suggests possible Celtic and certainly western provincial ancestry, especially the double 'v', rendered without fail on his coins, although

---

529. PLRE I Victorinus 12; the fictional child is *ibid.*, Victorinus 1a.
530. Aur. Victor 33.14 ; cf. HA *Tyr. Trig.*. VI. 3, VII. 1-2 He may have been a son-in-law or nephew although *Tetricus* 24.2 claims he was related to Victorinus's mother Victoria; possibly she had a sister who was **TETRICUS'** mother – but it is worth remembering that this *is* the HA..

not elsewhere, making his name well-nigh unique.[531] The HA's suggestion that he had a son, also Victorinus, whom he made Caesar, is generally thought to be spurious.[532]

*

TETRICUS
February/March 271 – March/April 274

Background

VICTORINUS' governor in Aquitania and probable close relative who, thanks to the decisiveness of Victoria, succeeded to the throne without any problem, was **C. Pius Esuvius TETRICUS**, a man said to have been of noble birth and senatorial status, prior to his service in the breakaway realm.[533] His name is, again, undoubtedly Gallic and derives from the Esuvii, a tribe mentioned by Caesar who inhabited much of what we know today as Normandy. The tribal name in turn from the deity Esus; **TETRICUS** may have been descended from a Prince of that people.

He was clearly a man whom the troops were prepared to accept, and indeed, coin evidence suggests that *en route* from his province to Trier, he seems to have inflicted a defeat on some German tribes, which had probably attempted an incursion in the wake of the death of **VICTORINUS.** The following year he had to deal with these tribes again before settling the Imperial capital at Trier rather than Cologne.

Reign

His Imperial style was **Imperator Caesar C. Pius Esuvius Tetricus Pius Felix Augustus**, and he is believed to have served his first (suffect) consulship in 272 (although it could have been somewhat earlier, as a private citizen), followed by an ordinary one in 273 and a third the year following. His *tribunicia postestas* was renewed four times before his fall.[534] In 273 his son, also called C. Pius Esuvius Tetricus, was nominated Caesar and thus heir designate as **C. Pius Esuvius Tetricus Nobilissimus Caesar** and made *princeps iuventutis*.[535] He shared the consulship with his father in 274. His elevation seems to have been preceded by some kind of crisis which was accompanied by a debasement of the coinage, previously running at a somewhat superior weight and fine-ness than that of the Empire at large. Young Tetricus was never accorded the rank of Augustus, so it is incorrect to refer to him as Tetricus II, as is often the case. The cause of this crisis is not really understood. Drinkwater suggests that by 273 the influence and financial support of Victoria had ended, quite possibly through her death, and that more coin was required to give the troops an increased donative.

---

531. Drinkwater (1987) 125-126.
532. *Tyr. Trig.* VII 1-2. He was put in to make up the number thirty in the title.
533. PIR² E99; PLRE I. Tetricus 1.
534. ILS 566
535. *Ibid.,* I. Tetricus 2; PIR² E100; ILS 567.

By the end of 273, the Emperor **AURELIAN** (see below) had restored order in the east and was in a position to bring the Gallic empire back into a re-united empire. Accordingly, as soon as winter had abated in 274, he advanced into Gaul. **TETRICUS** accordingly moved to meet his forces. Traditionally the battle at Châlons-sur-Marne was a pushover for **AURELIAN** but was followed by **TETRICUS** and his son being spared. The impression was that they had reached an accommodation with **AURELIAN** and had 'thrown the match' as it were, especially as their men were being suborned by their probable governor of Gallia Belgica, *FAUSTINUS*. This story is thought, however, to have been much influenced after the event by Aurelianic propaganda. In fact it seems that the battle of Châlons was hard fought, with heavy casualties and that although **TETRICUS** and his son *were* spared, they had previously been captured, humiliated and displayed in the emperor's triumph alongside the equally humiliated (but typically defiant) **ZENOBIA**.[536] Yet, after the triumph, both men were allowed to resume their places in the senate, the elder **TETRICUS** being soon afterwards being made *corrector* of Lucania - governor of a minor Italian sub-province - dying many years later.

*

Imperial claimant under Tetricus/Aurelianus

FAUSTINUS
274

It would appear that, after the Battle of Châlons-sur-Marne, a second revolt flared up, but that probably it was short lived and quickly crushed. This may have been the context in which the shadowy *FAUSTINUS* flourished. We know absolutely nothing about him; we can only guess that he was governor of Belgica, and the suggestion is Drinkwater's but resting on reasonably reliable reports of further Gallic unrest after **TETRICUS'S** deposition. Having tried to overthrow **TETRICUS** before his final battle, he may have escaped and attempted to keep the Gallic realm in being by declaring himself Emperor. The lack of coins would merely confirm the fact that his time in the sun was brief.[537]

Further reading:
Drinkwater, J. F., *The Gallic Empire; Separatism and Continuity in the North Western Provinces of the Roman Empire AD260–274* (Stuttgart 1987)

*

---

536. Drinkwater (1987) 42-43.
537. Drinkwater (1987) 43, 91, cf. Zonaras 12, 27.11.

VI (c)
THE PALMYRENE EMPIRE

The Imperial Succession
Zenobia
Vaballathus

Imperial claimants
[Maeonius]
Antiochus

Palmyra was a strategic lynch-pin of the Roman east, where the camel trains crossed and which acted as an inland port of exchange, the revenues from which endowed its rulers with great wealth.

The ruling dynasty of Palmyra, enfranchised by **SEVERUS I,** probably in the wake of the defeat of **NIGER**, assisted **GALLIENUS** in holding Syria and much of the east in the wake of the defeat and capture of the emperor's father in 260. Septimius Odaenathus was Prince of Palmyra 261-267, jointly Exarch of the East with his father Septimius Haeranes (died 267) from 251, appointed by **DECIUS**, having been adlected into the senate with the rank of ex-praetor. He was suffect consul *in absentia* between 252 and 257. He was twice victorious over the Persians, in 262 and 266, and also instrumental in eliminating the eastern *imperium* set up by *MACRIANUS* and *QUIETUS*, defeating the latter and stepping into his shoes with full imperial sanction of **GALLIENUS.** His second wife was Zenobia, by whom he had additional children, and who stepped into his shoes after he was assassinated at Emesa between August 267 and August 268.[538]

His coins show him attired like a Roman emperor, albeit laureate rather than with a radiate crown, and the obverse legends just show his name. The reverse of the best known type, however, bears the legend Pax Augustorum – the peace of the emperors, provoking the question why the plural *Augustorum*? The issue does not predate the capture of **VALERIANUS**, and thereafter there was no joint rule until much later. Was this the eastern dynast quietly asserting himself as co-Augustus with his ally, **GALLIENUS**?

---

538. PLRE I Odenathus 1; Zosimus 1, 39.2; Zonaras, 12, 27. HA. *Tyr. Trig.* 16 names a son by an earlier marriage as Herodes who, it claims declared himself emperor 266/267; nowhere else attested.

Possible Imperial claimant under Gallienus

[MAEONIUS]
267

The death of Odaenathus appears to have been encompassed by a jealous cousin,[539] named only in the HA as *MAEONIUS*. That work avers, perhaps predictably, that he promptly became an imperial claimant and had himself acclaimed emperor.[540] If so, his reign was short, for there were no coins. The likelihood is that the cousin, whether called *MAEONIUS* or otherwise, may well have murdered the dynast and his son, but is quite unlikely to have made a bid for the imperial purple; after all, his victim had been careful to avoid just that. On the whole this imperial claimant is best treated as a chimaera.

*

ZENOBIA
August 271-August 272

Background

ZENOBIA assumed power in the east on the death of her husband, rather as Victoria had done for **TETRICUS**, the difference being that whilst **TETRICUS** was an adult, her son **VABALLATHUS** was only a child of about 10 or 11. She therefore had to secure the succession and act as regent for the boy. Until 270 she made no claim to imperial power. either for herself or for her son, and in that she differed from previous would-be claimants in the east, like *ANTONINUS IV* and, like the Gallic emperors, she refrained from attempting to create an independent polity. Thus, matters proceeded smoothly and allowed first **GALLIENUS** and thereafter **CLAUDIUS II** to deal with problems elsewhere without having to worry about the east. But in 270 there was a change. For some reason, probably related to the security of her core dominions, **ZENOBIA** extended her control to encompass Arabia, southern Asia Minor and Egypt itself.

Reign

Early in 272 (or possibly any time after later summer 271[541]) she finally assumed the style of a Roman ruler, styling herself **Septimia Zenobia Aug[usta]** and simultaneously elevated her son **VABALLATHUS** to the purple as well. Despite this, in May 272 **AURELIAN** managed to recover Egypt, and a month earlier had prepared an expeditionary force to

---

539. Zonaras, 12, 24.
540. HA *V. Gall.* 13,1 & *V. Tyr. Trig.*15, 55-6 & 17, 1-3.
541. See the discussion of the matter in Southern (2008) 119-120.

re-take the rest of the east, starting at Byzantium (Istanbul), and going towards Palmyra via southern Asia Minor, where he paused briefly to invest Tyana (near Kemerhisar, Turkey); otherwise he met with little resistance until he reached Syria where he was obliged to join battle near Antioch at Immae, at Daphne and at Emesa (Homs, Syria). Zenobia was no pushover, although he spared most defeated cities and captured soldiery, thereby making it easier for backsliders to desert the Empress. Thus when the final confrontation took place at Palmyra itself, the emperor's clemency facilitated the capitulation of the city, once **ZENOBIA** had fled east and been captured, presumably with **VABALLATHUS.**

After her defeat, she was brought to Rome, paraded in **AURELIAN'S** triumph and then allowed to retire with honour, allegedly marrying again (to an un-named senator) and living to a considerable age.[542] The claim by Zosimus that she died *en route* from Palmyra to Rome may be discounted.[543] An alleged friend of **ZENOBIA,** a Seleucan merchant called Firmus is said to have seized Egypt in 272, after her fall, in an attempt to re-instate her *imperium*, but he was quickly defeated and killed by **AURELIANUS**. This story occurs only in the HA and should be discounted.[544]

*

VABALLATHUS
Late 271 or early 272 – 28th August 272

L. Julius Aurelius Septimius VABALLATHUS Athenodorus was the eldest son of **ZENOBIA,** ruling the east under her (for he was only 10 when he succeeded and 16 when he was deposed) as recognised official proxy for the Empire, at first as *Rex regorum corrector totis Orientis* (King of Kings and governor of all the East) and later as *consul imperator and dux Romanorum*.[545] After the death of **CLAUDIUS II** he seems to have largely gone independent, assuming the style *imperator*. When faced with the prospect of being neutralised by **AURELIAN,** however, under his mother's auspices he burnt his boats completely and by around February 272 had assumed the title of Augustus, becoming a fully-fledged imperial claimant, being styled **Imperator Caesar Vhabalathus Augustus** (*sic*), or (on a milestone) **Imp[erator] Caes[ar] L. Julius Aurelius Septimius Vaballathus Athenodorus,** a status briefly accepted by **AURELIAN** according to papyri found in Egypt. Less than a year later, however, he was captured and deposed when the Emperor took Palmyra, at the end of his fourth regnal year as *rex regorum* of Palmyra.[546] He is assumed to have survived in Rome with his mother and the rest of the family. He, or one of his brothers, may have married and had issue, for St. Jerome tells us that there

---

542. She was probably only in her early 30s when captured.
543. Zonaras, *loc. cit.*, supported by St., Jerome; Zosimus 1, 59.
544. PLRE I Firmus 1,cf. HA *Try. Trig.* 3, 1; *V. Aurel.* 32, 1-3 & *V. Probi* 24, 7 (born in Seleucia).
545. PLRE I. Athenodorus 2
546. Millar (1971) 16 & n. 164.

were descendants in Rome in his day in the early 5th century, and a little earlier Libanius wrote of a descendant in one of his letters.[547]

Family

ZENOBIA was apparently the daughter of a magnate called Septimius Antiochus, and claimed descent from the Kings of Syria, Marcus Antonius and Cleopatra VII of Egypt.[548] All this is, of course, perfectly feasible, including her descent from M. Antonius, whose daughter by Cleopatra married Juba king of Numidia and had issue, about whom we have very limited information and whose son Alexander became king of Armenia and married Iotape, daughter of the King of Media Atropene. This is similar to the ancestry claimed for him by her husband, Odaenathus II of Palmyra, although we can only be certain of his ancestry back to his grandfather, and probably his great-grandfather, Haeranes I, whom Settipani makes instead a putative great- uncle substituting the name of Nasor. However, he identifies this Haeranes as a man of this name of Dura Europos c. 160 whose ancestry he is able to project back a further three generations.[549] He also suggests that **ZENOBIA'S** father might well have been son of one [C. Julius] Malchus, great nephew of a Samsigeramus, connected to the Priest-Kings of Emesa and thus to **ELAGABALUS**.[550] From there, it is possible, as Dr. Settipani points out, that the Emesan princes were descendants of Antiochus IV, King of Commagene and thus notionally connected through him to C. Julius Ptolemaeus, King of Mauretania 23-40 and grandson of **M. Antonius** and Cleopatra on one side and of the North African Kings of the Massayles on the other.

With regard to Zenobia's descendants, Settipani identifies Herennianus and [He]rennia Clea[   ] as her children, but here they are regarded as the children of her second marriage to the unknown senator, clearly an Herennius.[551] He suggests that their daughter married a senator called Patavinus and was the parent of the recorded *grande dame* Lucia Septimia Patavinia Balbilla Tyria Nepotilla Odaenathiana.[552]

---

547. Thus supporting HA: *posterior etiam nunc Romae inter nobiles manent.* (27.2)
548. PLRE I. Zenobia 1. HA provides her with younger sons, Herennius and Timolaus, the former, inevitably, said to have been styled Augustus (15, *passim*).
549. Settipani (2000) 433-434.
550. *Ibid.* 436.
551. *Ibid.*, 443
552. CIL VIII 981

Imperial claimant under Aurelianus

ANTIOCHUS
February/March – April/May 273

Early in 273, whilst **AURELIAN** was dealing with an uprising amongst the Carpi in the Balkans, Marcellinus, his overlord in the East, appointed to damp things down after the collapse of the Palmyrene empire, was approached by a delegation of powerful Palmyrans led by one Apsaeus who urged him to assume the purple. Being no fool, he was non-commital and played for time, allowing him to send word of what was afoot to the Emperor. However, in the interval, being tired of waiting for his decision, Apsaeus and his *confrères* acclaimed one of their own, *ANTIOCHUS*, as emperor.[553] It is generally thought that this man was probably the father of **ZENOBIA**. In the event, the emperor managed to break off his campaign against the Carpi and return to Antioch rather more rapidly than the insurgents may have expected, and within a couple of months in all probability, Palmyra was re-taken and the uprising ended. No coins are known, which is ever a sign of a short-lived *régime*. Zosimus records that *ANTIOCHUS* was spared because the emperor 'considered him unimportant'.[554] Despite the HA recording that the City was razed, archaeology tells us that no such thing happened and that it continued to flourish at least until the reign of **IUSTINIANUS I.**

Further reading

Southern, P., *Empress Zenobia: Palmyra's Rebel Queen* (London 2008)

---

553. Southern (2008) 44, 152-153.
554. Zosimus 1, 61. 1.

TABLE XLIV: ZENOBIA AND HER FAMILY

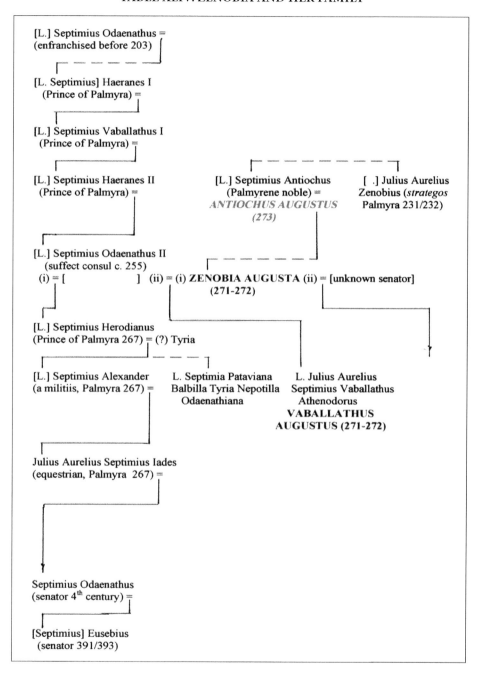

TABLE XLI: BRIEF LIVES

Julius Aurelius Septimius Iades
Called *Eques Romanus*, Palmyra, 267 but the chronology suggests that he must have been an infant then [PLRE I Iades 1]

L. Septimia Pataviana Balbilla Tyria Nepotilla Odaenathiana

On the inscription commemorating her, she is described as a *clarissima puella* – a girl of senatorial rank, suggesting that her father must have held senatorial rank, hence her suggested parentage as given here. The only real alternative is that she may belong a generation later. Her second *nomen* Tyria suggests her possible mother. The *cognomen* Balbilla raises the possibility of senatorial antecedents, perhaps from the brother of **HADRIANUS'S** poet friend Julia Balbilla, who was none other than C. Julius Antiochus Epiphanes Philopappus (suffect consul 109, see **Tables XXV & XXXIX Brief Lives**), descended from the Kings of Commagene. This might also explain the use of the name Antiochus in the family too. [ILS 1202, cf. FS2001,].

Septimia Zenobia

See above **ZENOBIA AUGUSTA**

[.] Julius Aurelius Zenobius *qui et* Zabdilas

Strategos (general) at Palmyra 231/245, latterly serving under Priscus, brother of **PHILIPPUS I.** He was also a senior local official at Palmyra. His father and grandfather, Zabdilas and Malchus, are not shown on the table. [PIR² I196]

[L.] Septimius Alexander

Served as an equestrian officer at Palmyra 267 [PLRE I. Alexander 19]

[L.] Septimius Antiochus

Palmyrene nobleman claiming descent from Cleopatra VII of Egypt and the Kings of Syria [Southern (2010) 5, 10].

[Septimius] Eusebius

Probably a senator in 391/393, when he was a recipient of a letter from the eminent Antiochene sophist Libanius and therein acknowledged as a son of an Odaenathus and a descendant of Odaenathus of Palmyra. A senator called Flavianus in the next generation claimed descent from King Samsigeramus of Emesa, according to the author Photius, so could possibly have been this man's son, in which case he had a grandson called Diogenes son of Eusebius, who married Cyrina and had children, including Theodora, a correspondee of Damasius around 500. [PLRE I. Eusebius 27; PLRE II Theodora 6; Settipoani (2000) 441]

[L.] Septimius Haeranes II

Prince & Exarch of Palmyra, died 267 [PIR² S329]

[L.] Septimius Herodianus

Prince of Palmyra from 267. His suggested wife Tyria would perhaps have been sister or daughter of Tyrius Septimius Azizus (a *v[ir] p[erfectissimus]* – an equestrian official – c 260/268) and possibly of Phoenician origin. He was killed with his father in unexplained circumstances in 267 [PLRE I. Azizus 1].

[L.] Septimius Odenathus

Enfranchised before 203 [PIR² S338]

[L.] Septimius Odaenathus II

Prince of Palmyra 261-267; adlected into the senate as an ex-praetor, c. 250/1; Exarch of Palmyra with father 251-267, suffect consul c. 252/257. Killed with his eldest son 267, possibly at Emesa [Southern (2010) 78-81]

Septimius Odaenathus

Probably a senator, 4th century, known only as the father of [Septimius] Eusebius (qv).

*

The Imperial Succession

Claudius II Gothicus

Quintillus

Aurelianus

Tactius

Florianus

Probus

Carus

Carinus

Numerianus

Imperial Claimants

Domitianus II

Bonosus

Proculus

Saturninus II

CLAUDIUS II
(Known to History as CLAUDIUS GOTHICUS)
September 268 – September 270

Background

M. Aurelius Valerius CLAUDIUS was born in Illyria 10th May, probably in 214 (he was 56 when he died), one of a group of cavalry generals under **GALLIENUS**, those especially promoted non-senatorial professional soldiers that he favoured in his far-reaching reforms of the military, which marked the beginning of a move away from an infantry-based army to a largely mounted mobile one, leaving the infantry increasingly to man the frontiers (*limes*). Syme said of them, 'brothers-in-arms, here, some perhaps from the same locality and related by ties of blood or marriage.'[555] The only certain thing we know about **CLAUDIUS'** career is that he was a tribune under **GALLIENUS** (probably of the *protectores,* the Emperor's personal bodyguard) serving at Ticinum (Pavia), although the HA adds that he was first appointed tribune under **DECIUS**, served in a legion (inevitably not one otherwise known to history) and under **VALERIAN** was appointed *dux* of the whole of Illyria. By and large

---

555. Syme (1971) 211. If only we knew the ties of blood and mariage in detail, it might throw more light on events between 268 and 284.

these details ring reasonably true, however.[556] Certainly the plot to assassinate the emperor may well have started out with a view to putting **CLAUDIUS** in his place. They chose the middle of the siege of Milan to strike because **GALLIENUS** was dealing with *AUREOLUS*, essentially a man of similar background to the group of assassins,one of their own.

Once acclaimed, he immediately put a stop to the senatorially inspired extirpation of the surviving family of **GALLIENUS** and insisted the senate should accord the late emperor divine honours, which they reluctantly did. Subsequently, **CLAUDIUS** refused to come to terms with *AUREOLUS* in Milan but he surrendered anyway, being later murdered by some soldiers because of his betrayal of **GALLIENUS,** whom they had admired.

Reign

The senate was quick to recognise the new emperor, and he took the style **Imperator Caesar M. Aurelius Claudius Augustus,** was granted the tribunician and proconsular powers (to be renewed on December 10th each year) and designated him ordinary consul for the beginning of the year following (269). The HA claims he had to deal with an imperial claimant called Ap. Claudius Censorinus, an aged senator, twice consul and terribly distinguished, acclaimed at Bononia and later killed by his own troops. There is no trace of his many magistracies on the record and his is dismissed by all commentators as fictional.[557]

Quite early in his reign **ZENOBIA** appears to have annexed Egypt and she had added Syria and southern Asia minor too by the time he died. This was mainly because the new emperor was obliged to turn his attention to events on the German frontier, where a victory early in 269 over a horde of Alamanni who had crossed **POSTUMUS'** realm and penetrated far into the empire accorded him an acclamation and the honorific **Germanicus**.[558] He also managed to detach Spain from the Gallic empire. A year later he was further acclaimed as **Gothicus** (which adhered to his name ever afterwards) after inflicting a crushing military defeat on a vast horde of Goths near Marcianopolis (Devnya, Bulgaria) on the lower Danube, completing a campaign started by **GALLIENUS** but against an enemy which had grown and become much more of a threat in the intervening period. He was almost immediately obliged to move to Sirmium (Sremska Mitrovika, Serbia) in preparation for a campaign against the Juthungi which tribe had made a threatening foray across the upper Danube, but died there of plague in September (some sources claim May) 270, although at least one account (inevitably) alleged murder. Eutropius said of him that he was a 'frugal and moderate man, a steadfast upholder of justice and well qualified to administer the state.'[559] His victory against the Goths earned him a golden shield and statue, and he was deified on his death by the senate on their own initiative.[560]

---

556. PLRE I. Claudius 11.
557. HA XXXIII, cf. Syme (1968) 157
558. ILS 570. He was acclaimed Parthicus, too :ILS 571
559. *Op. cit.,* 9, 11.
560. ILS 572.

The family of Claudius II.

Nothing is known about his family except that his brother (who briefly succeeded him) was **QUINTILLUS**. Nevertheless, the House of Constantine (qv) invariably claimed to descend from him, the first direct reference to which occurs in 310, forty years later, although an argument has been advanced for its appearance as early as 297.[561] Although both families appear to have come from Illyria, and some connection is of course possible, descent from Claudius, a mythical brother called Crispus or even a sister, is universally considered to have been adopted or exaggerated as a legitimating stratagem by **CONSTANTINE** or his father. The HA, however, supplies him with Illus, King of Troy and Dardanus as ancestors, not to mention other kinsmen: **CONSTANTIUS I CHLORUS** being the son of Eutropius, Dardanian husband of Claudia, daughter of Crispus, an alleged brother of **CLAUDIUS II**.[562] As **CONSTANTINE I** was probably born c. 250, this descent is impossibly long from a man (Crispus) who would have been born somewhere around 220. If the panegyricists of **CONSTANTINE** had thought about it, they could have declared that **CONSTANTIUS I**'s father had married the sister of **CLAUDIUS II**; that at least would have fitted the tight time-frame. Presumably there was enough genuine information then known to preclude deploying this hypothesis. It also alleges that **QUINTILLUS** had two sons (un-named) and a sister, Claudia Constantina but at least agrees that the emperor himself had no issue.

*

QUINTILLUS
September - October 270

Background

CLAUDIUS II's brother **M. Aurelius QUINTILLUS** was in command of troops in Italy at the time of the death of the former. It is possible that he was born in 229, for his age at death is recorded as 41 in one very late source.[563] Had **CLAUDIUS** been murdered, it is far more likely that a successor would have been proclaimed on the spot at Sirmium and indeed, some ancient sources aver that he had nominated **AURELIAN**.[564]

Reign

But, such was the euphoria created by **CLAUDIUS'** victories that **QUINTILLUS** was acclaimed by the army at Aquileia and received immediate recognition from the senate in the style of **Imperator Caesar M. Aurelius Claudius Quintillus Augustus**.[565] At first, eg.

---

561. See Drinkwater (1987) 79-80 & n. 171.

562. HA *V. Claud.* 11, 10, 13, 1-3, 9. Another sister, Constantia, allegedly married an 'Assyrian tribune'.

563. Banchich & Lane (2009) 122.

564. Zonaras 12, 26.

565. Zonaras claims he was elevated not by his soldiers but on the initiative of the senate, which seems less likely: *loc.cit.*

on the *aureus* issues, the name Claudius is absent, and it would seem that he was probably born plain M. Aurelius Quintillus, adding his brother's name after a fairly short interval to emphasise continuity. Eutropius remarked that his elevation was with the agreement of the soldiers and that he too was a man of 'singular moderation and grace', if anything even superior to his brother. Yet following his formal installation by the senate, he lasted only seventeen days, although another source claims 117) but in either case this was long enough to mint a number of coin issues, presumably to pay the soldiers a donative. It was not enough; it seems that it was **AURELIAN** instead who had the fate of the empire in his hands, and bowing to the inevitable, **QUINTILLUS** committed suicide, also at Aquilaea (which fact alone argues for the short account of the reign). HA claims he left two sons.[566]

AURELIANUS
(Known to history as AURELIAN)
September 270 – September/October 275

Background

It was widely reported that **AURELIAN** was the preferred and indeed nominated successor to **CLAUDIUS II,** but whose smooth accession to power was interrupted by the acclamation in Italy, with senatorial backing, of **QUINTILLUS**, although he subsequently measured his reign from the death of his old colleague-in-arms. **L. Domitius AURELIANUS** was apparently born in Moesia Superior[567] in humble circumstances on 9th September in or around 215. A full career is mapped out for him in HA, none of which can be taken at face value, especially the suffect consulship under **VALERIANUS** with as colleague the fictional Ulpius Crinitus 'of the house of **TRAJAN**' and by whom he had allegedly been adopted – quite an achievement for an equestian officer, however, high-flying.[568] Needless to say, whatever his career before 268, he appears to have been one of the *junta* of senior equestrian officers who encompassed the demise of **GALLIENUS** outside Mediolanum (Milan) that year. Yet even they are largely to be discounted for only the Praetorian Prefect Aurelius Heraclianus (who really did plan the assassination of **GALLIENUS**) can be attested with confidence.

Reign

Despite confusion amongst the sources, the death of **QUINTILLUS** and elevation and recognition of **AURELIAN** seems to have led to a rebellion in Rome. The spark appears to have been a decision by the new emperor to close the Rome mint prior to a re-organisation. The mint-master Felicissimus - an unfortunate name in the circumstances - seems to have led a riot which escalated into a fully-fledged revolt, the participants ending up fortifying

---

566. Eutropius, 9, 12 ; HA *V. Claud. loc.cit.*
567. Aurelius Victor, 35, 1. Eutropius says Dacia 'Ripensis', *op.cit.* 9, 13 but cf. Syme (1971) 210.
568. PLRE I Aurelianus 6; HA *V. Aur.* 10, 3, 14 & 38.4.

the Caelian Hill, before being dealt with savagely. The fact that numerous senators were caught up in all this suggests that possibly a pro-**QUINTILLUS** faction may have been involved and that the matter arose at the beginning of the reign. Nevertheless, the emperor's refusal to purge the senate for supporting **QUINTILLUS** and later merciful treatment of **TETRICUS** and **ZENOBIA** argues for an element of exaggeration in all this.[569]

He was finally recognised by the senate as **Imperator Caesar L. Domitius Aurelianus Pius Felix Augustus** to which his military prowess was sufficient for him to add also the title **Invictus**. He was confirmed as pontifex maximus and granted the tribunician power (renewable on 10th December following and on that date thereafter) and the proconsular *imperium*. He assumed the consulship for 271 with a descendant of **MARCUS AURELIUS,** Ti. Pomponius Bassus Faustinus (see **Table XXIV Brief Lives**) as a gesture of his intention to co-operate with the senate. He was consul again in 272 and 273. Having damped down the aftermath of the mint workers' rebellion, the emperor appointed a new mintmaster, C. Valerius Sabinus, and proceded to improve the weight and fine-ness of silver coinage, which had fallen from slightly debased silver, to billon and finally almost to base metal with only a 2% silver wash over each flan. This was boosted to 5% and the gold *aureus* was increased in weight to fifty per pound. The quality of the dies was also improved. He also initiated the building of a new defensive wall around Rome which now bears his name. He was also an adherent of the worship of the sun god Sol Invictus which seems to have been dominant in his native Danubian homeland. The idea seems to have been to unite the other cults within the monotheistic umbrella of Sol. The fact that the old Republican dynasty of the Aurelii had some role in providing priests for a similar cult at Rome may have influenced him in deciding to do so.[570]

AURELIAN had no time to stand still, however. He was immediately forced to deal with another incursion of the Juthungi, intercepting them on their way back from looting in Italy. Not that his attentions were on this occasion sufficient, for he was forced to intercept a second invasion of Italy, suffering an initial defeat in the process, but ultimately annihilating them. In between, he was obliged to deal with an irruption of Vandals in Pannonia. Thereafter, instead of fire-fighting, he was able to go on the offensive, re-organising the Danubian frontier, before dealing with the Palmyrene Empire and thereafter the Gallic one. On the Danube, he withdrew from the greater part of Dacia, re-creating the reduced province as Dacia Ripensis (Dacia Bankside) on the south of the river and incorporating parts on Moesia and Thrace. To keep the East quiet, papyri seem to indicate that by late 271 he had recognised **VABALLATHUS** of Palmyra as joint emperor, but this arrangement appears to have been overtaken by events by the end of August 272.

After successfully dealing with **ZENOBIA** he had to return to the Danube to destroy the Carpi, another barbarian people, but even before this was complete, he had also to deal with the brief resurrection of the Palmyrene polity under *ANTIOCHUS.* The Gallic

---

569. Eutropius 9, 14, 1.
570. White (2005) 132.

campaign, perhaps significantly, also flared up again, possibly under *FAUSTINUS* as well as *DOMITIANUS II*. By this stage **AURELIANUS** had been heaped with celebratory *agnomina*: **Arabicus, Carpicus, Parthicus, Palmyricus, Gothicus, Dacicus** (all followed by **Maximus**), the last being bestowed after his seventh renewal of his tribunician power, probably early in 275.[571] His coins acknowledged him as *Restitutor Orbis*, 'the restorer of the world', amongst other laudatory epithets, most of which in truth were probably deserved, despite one of two new imperial claimants popping up.

After this the emperor went to Germany and then on towards the East to deal with the Persians, who were showing signs of restiveness after the defeat of Palmyra, which had long acted as a useful deterrent in the area. Unfortunately at Coenofrurium near Perinthus (Marmara Ereğlisi, European Turkey) in Thrace in late September or early October 275 he was murdered by a faction of the praetorian guard at the instigation of his private secretary Eros, probably, like the demise of **VICTORINUS**, as the result of a private quarrel, rather than a planned change of *régime*. This is emphasised by the fact that there was no obvious successor waiting in the wings, and that a brief hiatus followed before the next emperor was identified and acclaimed. Once the succession had been resolved, **AURELIANUS** was promptly deified by the senate, although one inscription suggests that he was briefly subject of a *damnatio memoriae*, perhaps as a consequence of the brutal suppression of Felicissimus' revolt.[572]

Family

The Emperor's *nomen* suggests that his family had held the citizenship since before Caracalla's enfranchisement, but beyond that little can be said. His wife, known from coins and an inscription, was Ulpia Severina (who nomen probably gave the author of the HA the idea to conjure up Ulpius Crinitus again), styled Augusta during her husband's reign, during which she must have died, for she was acknowledged as *diva* after it.[573] However, he apparently had a sister who married and had a son, whom **AURELIAN** had killed for some unknown reason. The HA also includes this information, adding that the unfortunate young man also had a sister (who suffered a similar fate) and that there was another sister who left descendants, one of whom was Aurelianus, governor of Cilicia c. 300, but for whom there is no corroborative evidence.[574]

*

---

571. ILS 575, 576, 577, 579, 581, 582
572. ILS 585.
573. PLRE I Severina 2; ILS 587
574. PLRE I Aurelianus 1; HA *V. Aur.* 42.1, cf. Eutropius ix.4.

Imperial claimant under Aurelian

DOMITIANUS II
February – March 271

Although the transition of power from **CLAUDIUS II** to **AURELIAN** had all the appearance of having been smooth and trouble free, there were others trying to establish themselves in opposition. *DOMITIANUS II* was acclaimed, possibly in Gaul.[575] Conceivably his bid for the purple really belongs to the story of the Gallic Empire (qv above). Little is known of it beyond a brief report by Zosimus (not naming the claimant[576]), and a coin, not universally accepted as authentic, bearing the legend **Imp[erator] C[aesar] Domitianus P[ius] F[elix] Aug[ustus]**. Subsequent to its discovery, a second one turned up in Oxfordshire dateable to 271, rather validating the authenticity of its predecessor.[577] Nothing else is known of this man, bar the spurious claim in the HA that he was descended from **DOMITIANUS I**.[578]

*

Imperial claimant under Aurelian

SEPTIMIUS
271

Imperial claimant in Dalmatia early in the reign of **AURELIAN.** He was killed by his own men not long after his elevation.[579] There are no other clues as to his identity and no known coins.

*

---

575. The design of the coin and the quality of the imperial portrait suggest this strongly.
576. *Op.cit.* I. 49, 2, cf. HA *V. Gall.* 2, 6 & 13, 2; *TT.* 12,14 & 13,3.
577. *Daily Telegraph* 25/2/2004.
578. PIR ²D114; PLRE I Domitianus 1; HA *Tyr. Trig.* 12, 14..
579. Aurelius Victor 35, 3, Zosimus 1, 49. 2; PLRE I. Septimius 1.

Imperial claimant under Aurelian

URBANUS
c 271

URBANUS was an Imperial claimant in the reign of **AURELIAN**. Neither the time nor the location of his elevation has survived, nor have any coins (if any were minted) survived, and nothing is known of the man. He was quickly suppressed.[580]

＊

TACITUS
November/December 275 – June/July 276

Background

Most of the ancient sources claim that there was a substantial interregnum between the assassination of **AURELIAN** and the elevation of his successor. If so, the name of any *interrex* is unknown; if one was appointed by the senate he would have been the first since Ser. Sulpicius Rufus in 52BC. The period covered would have been October/November to December 275.[581] Furthermore, the next Emperor, **TACITUS,** is painted as an elderly senatorial nobleman, boasting his family connections with Cornelius Tacitus, the early second century historian. Syme managed to cut through all this, making the point that there was not likely to have been an interval of more than a week or so after the assassination.

Yet instead of an elderly nobleman elected by the senate, the new Emperor was almost certainly another Danubian general, but in this case one who had ended his career with suffcient renown to have been adlected into the senate, probably with the rank of ex-consul, and indeed, he appears on the *fasti* as ordinary consul for 273. The received story we have is of the old boy receiving the news that he had been named as emperor at his residence in Campania and entering Rome in civilian garb to be invested with the purple by the senate.[582] Syme was prepared to accept that he was by this stage in his career a senator, and may very well have been residing in Campania.

Reign

Once installed, he assumed the style **Imperator Caesar M. Claudius Tacitus Pius Felix Augustus,** was acknowledged as pontifex maximus, granted the tribunician power and

---

580. Zosimus 1, 49.2; PLRE I. Urbanus 1.
581. Aur. Victor 35, 9-12; coins; HA *V. Tac.* 1.1
582. Syme (1971) 237 f., cf. Zonaras 12, 28, Aurelius Victor 36, 1.

proconsular *imperium*.[583] He was also made consul designate for 276, appointed one M. Annius Florianus as his praetorian prefect, and punished **AURELIAN'S** assassins. He is also reported to have restored the senators' *cursus honorum* – their career path in the governing hierarchy, curtailed under **GALLIENUS**.[584]

He also seems to have remained in Rome until the new year, when he went out to the Balkans to join the army assembled by his predecessor in order to complete his mission to the east. He advanced into Asia Minor and encountered a strong force of Goths (actually Heruli) which he successfully defeated an achievement which promptly earned him the epithet **Gothicus Maximus**.[585] He continued to Tyana (Kemerhisar, Turkey) in Cappadocia where he died in July 276, either from disease, but perhaps more likely through assassination. On his coins he was accorded the title *Restitutor Rei Publicae* (restorer of the Republic), yet strangely, he was neither deified nor condemned by the senate on his death.

Family

There is little certain information about this emperor's family, although the HA claims him for Interamna Nahars (Terni, Italy) and with estates in Africa.[586] He was certainly no senatorial noble of distinguished lineage, nor any descendant of the historian Tacitus, as the HA would have us believe. One supposed reason for his assassination (if assassination there was) was that a relative called Maximinus had been appointed governor of Syria and whose remorseless exactions there had created widespread discontent.[587] Furthermore, he is said to have left behind sons (who would have been of senatorial rank) and that his successor, **FLORIANUS** was said to have been his uterine half brother.[588]

*

FLORIANUS
June/July – August/September 276

Background

FLORIANUS is, in reality, unlikely to have been the half-brother of **TACITUS**. His appointment as praetorian prefect to the emperor seems, on the other hand, entirely convincing. Thus, with the assassination of the old emperor at Tyana, whether he was complicit or not, as praetorian prefect, **FLORIANUS** was in the perfect position to be acclaimed as his successor.

---

583. ILS 590; PIR² C1036/PLRE I. Tacitus 3
584. Aur. Victor 37, 6.
585. ILS 591 (Cos. II, *trib. pot.* II).
586. HA *V.Taciti* 10, 3, 5 & 15, 1.
587. Zonaras 12, 28; Maximinus: PLRE I. Maximinus 1; killed before the emperor in June 276.
588. HA *V. Taciti* 6,8, 14, 3 ('many children') & 16, 4.

Reign

The emperor's brief reign was to take place entirely on campaign in the east as far as we can tell. Eutropius says of him that he reigned 80 days and 'did nothing worth remembering.' He was, however, quickly recognised by the senate in Rome and was styled **Imperator Caesar M. Annius Florianus Pius Felix Invictus Augustus** and recognised as pontifex maximus.[589] He was also no doubt granted the tribunician power and proconsular *imperium* renewable in the usual way.

Having succeeded and been acknowledged by the senate, still the ultimate validating authority, Florianus moved against the Heruli once more with the intention of finally driving them beyond the boundaries (*limes*) of the empire and ensuring that they caused no further trouble. This was going well when news reached the emperor that the commander of the forces in the East, M. Aurelius Probus, the successor in that post of **TACITUS'S** relative, Maximinus, had himself been acclaimed emperor by his men following a successful campaign against some turbulent allies of Persia and probably also as a result of the disaffection caused by Maximinus. He was quickly acknowledged throughout the eastern provinces, including Egypt.

Consequently, **FLORIANUS** was forced to place a subordinate in command of a holding operation against the Heruli and march to Syria with the bulk of his forces with the intention of snuffing the rebellion out. Probus, who commanded a much smaller force, cleverly declined to be brought to battle and by raids and skirmishing managed to demoralise the Emperor's army, which tactic was subsequently led to a revolt which led to **FLORIANUS** being killed by his own men at Tarsus in Cilicia (Turkey) after an 88-day reign, probably to avoid a bloody conflict. He was the third emperor to die within a space of 12 months, and this hiatus undid much of the good work done by **AURELIAN** in re-unifying the Empire. We know nothing of his family; the HA inevitably, claims he had many children.[590]

*

PROBUS
July/August 276 – September 282

Background

PROBUS, like **AURELIAN** managed to stop the rot, once he had secured his position, but managed to earn undying adulation from senatorial historians as something of a paragon, a man of virtue, gracious nature and fairness. The reasons for this are complex and not wholly agreed, although it is clear that he was regarded as just as fine a commander as **AURELIAN** but that the latter was the more abrasive character and was also noted for his

---

589. Eutrop. 9, 16; ILS 592; pontifical style and trib. pot. I: ILS 593. PIR² A649/PLRE I. Florianus 6.
590. HA V. *Taciti* 16.3-4.

short fuse.[591] That the two Augusti had once been comrades in arms seems highly likely and both may have been part of the group of Illyrian officers that encompasssed the demise of **GALLIENUS** only eight years before. **PROBUS** was acclaimed in Syria, probably as soon as news of the death of **TACITUS** and the elevation of **FLORIANUS** had reached him. Certainly, his early weeks seem to have overlapped most of the latter's reign. Unfortunately for so important a figure, most of what we know of **PROBUS** derives from the HA, which creates great difficulties in view of the complete inaccuracy (and in some cases utter fiction) with which the histories of some of his predecessors are endowed.

M. Aurelius **PROBUS** was born at Sirmium (Sremska Mitrovika, Serbia) on 19th August 232, according to a number of sources, including the HA.[592] He may have borne the *signum* Equitius, for this name appears as his *nomen* in Aurelius Victor and on one issue of coins, causing slight confusion, most easily thus explained.[593] His pre-imperial career, however, is only given in the HA, where it claims, perfectly plausibly, that he served as a tribune under **VALERIAN** on the Danubian frontier and also under **GALLIENUS**, miraculously managing to preserve both life and career through the various imperial claimants and barbarian incursions of those years. Later he is said to have served in Egypt under **AURELIAN** before being appointed to succeed Maximinus as *dux* or governor in the east.[594]

Reign

Despite their recognition of **FLORIANUS,** the senators were quick to recognise his successor, too; papyri confirm his recognised elevation as pre-dating 29th August 276. Once the news of **FLORIANUS'S** demise had reached them, therefore, he was recognised as pontifex maximus and granted the tribunician power (to be renewed annually, perhaps now earlier than in December) and proconsular imperium; he also assumed a suffect consulship. He was ordinary consul in 278, 279, 281 and 282. His regnal style was **Imperator Caesar M. Aurelius Probus Pius Felix Invictus Augustus.**[595] He was also officially recognised as *Pater Patriae*. The following year, following his finally settling the problem of the marauding Heruli which had put paid to the careers of his two predecessors, he was granted the *agnomen* **Gothicus**.[596] Two years later he was able to add **Maximus** and amplify his style to **Germanicus Maximus**, earned following two years hard pounding in clearing various Germanic peoples from Gaul and the Rhenish provinces, where they had taken advantage of the chaos of 276 by breaking through and causing unparalleled and widespread destruction, for which service his reputation in Gaul during the century following remained remarkably high out of gratitude.

---

591. Eutropius 9, 17.
592. PLRE I Probus 3.
593. Op. cit. 36,2; the coins were minted at Ticinum.
594. HA *v. Probi* 3,5; 4,2; 5,1, 6-7 & 9,5.
595. ILS596.
596. ILS594

He is said by HA to have continued **TACITUS'** reform of the senatorial *cursus*. He also re-consolidated the Rhône frontier. Then, in 279 he campaigned on the lower Danube, inflicting a defeat upon the Getae before moving on to Asia minor where a considerable and destructive band of outlaws (*bagaudae*) under an Isaurian called Lydius was causing similar destruction to that suffered by the citizens of Gallic provinces. Lydius was killed after a fairly lengthy seige of his fortified hideout before **PROBUS** was obliged to deal with further Persian incursions into Syria that the troubles with the outlaws had precipitated. This latter campaign we know only implicitly because in 279 he assumed the additional style of **Persicus Maximus.** After that, he was obliged to move swiftly on to Egypt to deal with a similar outbreak caussed by Nubian people called the Blemmyes, following which he had the marshes bordering the Nile in places to be reclaimed (a similar project had been initiated by him on the lower Danube, too) and he ordered numerous new bridges to be built and began restoring temples there too.[597]

He then returned to Rome, and might have considered the firefighting part of his reign finished, leaving him scope to get on with economic and infrastructure consolidation for, unlike **AURELIANUS,** he realised that ending the continuing military crises required more than a round of police actions and counter-attacks. He had already in Gaul begun the task of rebuilding and is credited with widespread initiation of viticulture there as well as in the provinces of the lower Danube, to help rebuild the economy of these areas. Unfortunately, it was probably at this stage, in 280 he was obliged to deal with a pair of imperial claimants, *BONOSUS* and *PROCULUS* at Colonia Agrippina (Cologne) in Germany, generating sufficient momentum as to threaten a new Gallic Empire. In the chaos engendered by their suppression, another claimant popped up too, which also had to be dealt with, but which did not require the Emperor's personal presence in its suppression.

Even as all this was happening in the North West, Syria was once again was the hub of a new revolt by its supreme commander, a Moor called *SATURNINUS* who became an imperial claimant. Fortunately, this man was murdered by his own officers after a few months, which enabled **PROBUS** to return to Rome once more in 281 and celebrate an impressive triumph over the Germans, whom he had also had to deal with once again, in the wake of the revolt at Cologne. In 282 (when he was consul for the 5th time and held the tribunician power for the 7th) he again set out for the east, to repair any damage caused by the revolt of *SATURNINUS,* and also with the intention of dealing a hammer-blow to the turbulent Persians. He sent one of his praetorian prefects to the upper Danube to ensure order there. However, early in September, this man, **CARUS**, was acclaimed by his troops, and **PROBUS** was obliged to turn back to deal with this. Unfortunately, years of draining marshes and undertaking public works under strict military discipline, thus depriving them of the opportunity for plunder, had left the army (or at least the praetorian guard) disenchanted and his advance party threw their lot in with **CARUS** and, when news of

---

597. We rely on the (probably fictitious) epitaph from his alleged tomb near Sirmium retailed by the HA (*V. Probi* 21) for most of this information, although much of it is, again plausible and some is borne out by archaeology.

this reached the main army, it encouraged the men to turn on their emperor, especially
as he had paused at his birthplace (Sirmium) to get the troops to repair a reservoir and
ditches damaged by winter rains. Whilst it may have been a mere mutiny rather than a
revolt linked to **CARUS'S** acclamation, the result was the same: the soldiers chased him
to a signal tower not far from the city and slaughtered him there. The date of this is very
uncertain; all we can say is that he died between 28th August and 31st December 282, thanks
to Alexandrian coins issued for his 8th year. If the story of his burial in a large tumulus
nearby can be accepted, it is likely that he was held in somewhat higher esteem by his
fellow provincials than his men, and that they decided to commemorate him in this way.
He was subsequently deified by the senate.[598]

Family

Aurelius Victor names the father of **PROBUS** as Dalmatius but the HA credits him with
kinship with **CLAUDIUS II** and posterity, who settled at Verona and 'were desitned to
become leaders of the senate.'[599] A convincing case has been made for at least the existence of a daughter by Mommaerts and Kelley who strongly suspect that the widespread
aristocratic use of the name Probus amongst a tightly-knit group of families in the fourth
and fifth century west (especially Gaul) and in the seventh in Constantinople, was due
to this daughter having made a glittering marriage to the future consul of 314, Petronius
Annianus.[600] If this postulation is accepted, then this bloodline unites a whole group of more
or less short lived emerors and indeed might explain why they aspired to the purple at all.
Table XLV, based on this postulation, therefore sets out the bare bones of this remarkable
nexus. The details of the families of these rulers will, of course be set out in the approriate
place in the sections below. The fourth century and earlier lives are appended here.

It is important to point out, however, that this postulation has not gone unchallenged,
especially concerning the Anician family, although that is an aspect which does not strongly
effect the reconstruction itself.[601] Note, though, a variety of sources, from the HA and (much)
later, endow the emperor with other, unattested kin: Maximus for a father, a son, Domitius
(mentioned in late saints' lives), a brother, Domitius (in HA), another, Calocerus, Bishop
of Byzantium [*sic*], two distaff nephews, [H]adrianus and Demetrius (military martyrs
according to Nicephorus) and a half sister, Claudia. None can be otherwise authenticated,
however and have been omitted from **Table XLV**.[602]

*

---

598. CIL I² 255
599. HA *V. Probi* 24, 1-3: Maximus for a father and a son, Domitius (mentioned in late Saints' lives) a brother,
     Domitius, two un-named distaff nephews (Nicephorus i. 773) and a half sister, Claudia.
600. Mommaerts & Kelley (1992) 111-121.
601. Eg. Cameron, A., *Anician Myths* in JRS CII (2012) 133-171.
602. Nicephorus *Historia Ecclesiastica* i. 773; *Acta Sanctorum*; HA, *loc.cit.*

TABLE XLV: THE POSTERITY OF PROBUS

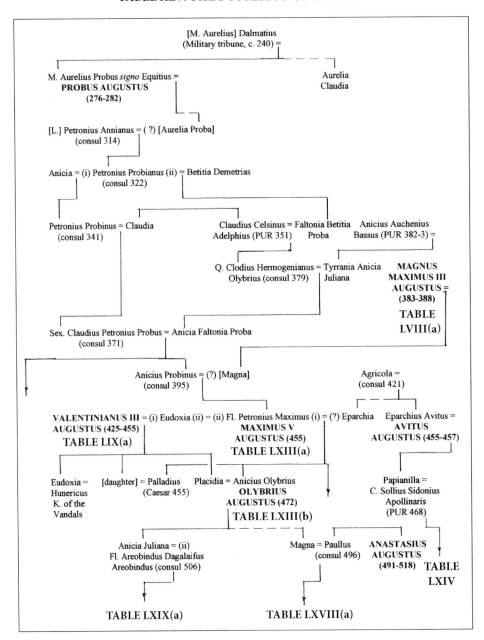

TABLE XLV: BRIEF LIVES

Anicius Auchenius Bassus

We are told his father and grandfather were both consuls, and it is probable that his father was Amnius M.' Caesonius Nicomachus Anicius Paulinus, consul in 334 and his grandfather Amnius Anicius Julianus, consul in 322. The family – clearly Anicii in the male line – were descended from Q. Anicius Q. f. Faustus, suffect consul in 198. Either he or one of his immediate descendants had been raised to patrician rank. Bassus, a Christian, was praetor, then proconsul of Campania and Prefect of the City of Rome (PUR) 382-383. He was father of several children. [PIR² A595; PLRE I. Bassus 11, Julianus 23, Paulinus 14]

Anicius Probinus

He became consul at a very young age, in 395, the office having become by this time largely ceremonial and hideously expensive to hold. He then went on to be proconsul of Africa which, with Asia, had been left to be governed by senior senators after most of the remainder had been reserved for equestrians in the reforms of **GALLIENUS.** He was also a poet. Settipani suggests that he must have married the daughter of **MAGNUS MAXIMUS,** cutting out Mommaerts & Kelley's introduction of the Ennodii shown here. [PLRE I Probinus 1; Settipani (2000) 382-383].

Aurelia Claudia

Known only from the HA, which fails to accord her a husband, but claims that she gave her brother a decent burial. She may not have existed at all [HA *V. Probi* 3, 4].

[M. Aurelius] Dalmatius

Originally a soldier, but promoted to tribune. He married a lady of higher rank than himself. He seems to have retired to Egypt. He is named by Aurelius Victor, but the remaining information is from the HA and thus suspect. He would have been born c. 200 and would have owed his promotion to **SEVERUS ALEXANDER.** The name makes one wonder if **PROBUS** had more than one marriageable daughter (or aunt), bearing in mind that **CONSTANTIUS I** had a younger son bearing the name, who in turn bestowed it on his son [PLRE I. Dalmatius 1, cf. 6/7].

M. Aurelius Probus [?*signo* Equitius]

See above **PROBUS AUGUSTUS**

Betitia Demetrias

Parents not securely identified, perhaps grand-daughter of C. Betitius Pius Maximilianus, a junior senator in the mid 3rd century and a descendant of C. Neratius Proculus Betitius Pius Maximilianus, a senator who was one of the patrons of Canusium (Canosa di Puglia) in 223 and of a family from Aeclanum (Quintodecimo, Mirabella Eclano) [PLRE I. Demetrias]

Claudius Celsinus *signo* Adelphius

His wife, a Christian, was a poetess; he himself was *corrector* of an Italian province c. 330, *consularis* (governor) of Numidia, served as proconsul (again, where is unknown) and became PUR in 351 [PLRE I. Celsinus 6/7]

Sex. Claudius Petronius Probus

Probably the most illustrious and competent senatorial aristocrats of the fourth century, his glittering career is more reminiscent of one of the famous consular magnates of the early empire, even though the titles of the most senior posts held had changed out of all recognition. He was born c. 330; was quaestor, then urban praetor, suffect consul before 358 when he was proconsul of Africa, going on to become praetorian prefect (governor of a group of provinces) four times, in Illyricum, Gaul, then of Illyricum, Italy and Africa combined, a post to which he was re-appointed following a seven year gap. He was ordinary consul in 371, although the *fasti* do not accord him an indication that he had been consul before, but the status of suffect consuls had become devalued sufficiently for this to have become the norm. He fled to Thessalonica when **MAGNUS MAXIMUS** invaded Italy in 388 and died shortly afterwards [PLRE I. Probus 5; Matthews (1967) 487-488].

Q. Clodius Hermogenianus Olybrius

Son of Clodius Celsinus Adelphius, he was a Christian, *consularis* of Campania in the 350s, proconsul of Africa 361, PUR 369-370, Praetorian Prefect of Illyricum 378 and consul in 379. He died between 384 and 395. It is not clear if Olybrius was part of his full name or a *signum*; in either case, it continued down through the family into the 6th century [PLRE I Claudius 7 & Olybrius 3].

Eparchia

The marriage is speculative, and the name an assumption; she may, as Settipani suggests, have ben called Palladia, a name which crops up amongst the couples' descendants, cf. **Table LXIII(a)** [Mommaerts & Kelley, *loc.cit.*; Settipani (2000) 383].

[L.] Petronius Annianus

He was consul in 314 and praetorian prefect of Africa 315-317. It is likely that this great late Roman dynasty came originally from Ausculum (Ascoli Piceno). Their descent can be reliably derived from L. Petronius L. f. Fab. Annianus, an equestrian officer adlected into the senate with the rank of ex-praetor some time before 244, thus possibly under **GORDIAN III** and probably this man's grandfather or great-grandfather. Settipani however, speculates that his father might have been instead L. Publilius Petronius Volusianus, a suffect consul from the late 3rd century and a daughter of **DIOCLETIAN'S** patron Annius Annullinus. [PLRE I Annianus 2; Settipani (2000) 376-377]

Petronius Probianus

Proconsul of Africa 315-316, thus probably suffect consul some time before, and possibly praetorian prefect of an unknown group of provinces before holding a (?) second consulship in 322, following this with the Prefecture of the City of Rome (PUR) 329-331 [PLRE I. Probianus 3]

Petronius Probinus

His career prior to his consulship in 341 is not known, but he served as PUR 345-346 [PLRE I Probinus 2]

*

BONOSUS
280

PROCULUS
280

At some stage in the reign of **PROBUS**, two frontier commanders in Germany had themselves proclaimed emperor, most probably in spring 280. *BONOSUS* was commander of the army on the Rhine and the acclamation took place at Colonia Agrippina (Cologne). Quite how *PROCULUS* fitted in is obscure. They may have commanded the armies in the two Germanies and thought to make their bid jointly. To confuse matters, Aurelius Victor omits *PROCULUS* entirely, although he is mentioned by Eutropius.[603] Most of our information, unfortunately, comes from the HA and is not to be relied upon. Included is the fact that *BONOSUS* was a career soldier, said to have been of British descent, son of a schoolmaster or similar, who had married a Goth and settled in Spain. *PROCULUS* came from Albingaunum (Albenga, Liguria) and was of noble family, although later on he is said to have had Frankish blood.[604] It may indeed be that they were one and the same. He (or they) was or were quickly supressed and killed by **PROBUS**, so probably their reign lasted a month or six weeks or so; there was apparently no time for any coins to be minted, for instance.

Predictably, the HA provides both these imperial claimants with families. *BONOSUS* was said to have also married a Goth (perhaps a relative!) called Hunila and had two sons, both spared by **PROBUS**.[605] *PROCULUS* was married to Vituriga (alias Samso) and they were parents of Herennianus, related to one Maecianus and the family continued at Albingaunum.[606] All plausible enough, but lacking any corroboration whatsoever.

*

---

603. *Op. cit.* 9, 17
604. PLRE I Proculus 1
605. PLRE I Bonosus 1 & Hunila based on HA *V. Firmi* 15,2, 3 & 7..
606. PLRE I Herennianus 2 & Vituriga; HA *loc.cit.* 12, 3, 4, 7 & 13, 5.

Imperial Claimant under Probus

SATURNINUS II

c. December 280 – c. March 281

SATURNINUS was allegedly an old comrade in arms of **AURELIAN**, whom that emperor appointed either to govern Syria or to be C-in-C forces on the eastern frontier (*dux limitis orientis*). He became an imperial claimant by military acclamation in the east, and was acknowledged throughout the region, minting coins at Alexandria. He seems to have been killed at Apamaea (Qalaat al-Madiq, Syria) in Syria by his own officers before **PROBUS** could divert from other problems and deal with him. Zonaras would have him an African (whether his term 'Moor' is accurate is anybody's guess).[607] His coins tell us that his *nomen* was Julius, which leads PLRE I to suspect that he may be identifiable with **C. Julius Sallustius Saturninus Fortunatianus**.[608] This man is kown from an inscription in Africa (confirming Zonaras) and was propraetorian legate (and thus a senator) in Numidia under **GALLIENUS**, commanding that emperor's *Legio III Augusta*. He was probably one of the last such office holders before this and other military posts were closed to senators. Not only had he thus served but he had also been suffect consul, c. 260. His inscription, also tells us that, after his stint in Numidia, he had been *comes* (military courtier) of an emperor who is not named, but could be any from **GALLIENUS** to – as HA suggests – **AURELIAN**. The HA contains much about this man, mainly patently fictitious, although part of it relates to his not being permitted to enter Egypt which, as the man whom we suspect of being this imperial claimant was a senator, would probably reflect the truth, rather than his having been of modest background and trained as a rhetorician as the HA claims.[609] His imperial style was **Imp[erator] C[aesar] Jul[ius] Saturninus Aug[ustus]**, as on his coins.

For once the HA fails to endow him with any family but, if he can be identified with Fortunatianus, then we are able to say something about his background. He was probably a grandson or great-grandson of Sallustius Saturninus, who served as a procurator under **SEPTIMIUS SEVERUS**, possibly via a female line. Alternatively he might have descended from T. Julius T. f. Fab. Saturninus, another procurator, who served in Germany under **MARCUS AURELIUS** and whose probable brother, C. Julius Saturninus, was suffect consul at about the same period.[610] He was certainly married to Vergilia Florentina. It is suspected that C. Julius Fortunatianus, an *egregius*

---

607. PLRE I Saturn inus 12; Zonaras 12, 29.
608. *Op. cit.*, Fortunatianus 6 cf. PIR² I540/546
609. HA *V. Firmi et al*, 7, 3 & 9, 2-4. NB The Saturninus of HA *Tyr. Trig.* 23 is entirely fictional.
610. PIR² I 319, 548, 547

vir (equestrian) may have been his son and we know that this Fortunatianus also had a son called C. Mevius Silius Crescens Fortunatianus who was a *clarissimus puer* (boy of senatorial rank). It may be that *SATURNINUS* had doffed his senatorial status (or done so on behalf of his son) in order to continue a military career, and that the grandson reverted to senatorial status, perhaps because his mother (presumably a Mevia or a Silia) was of that standing.

*

CARUS
September 282 – May 283

CARINUS
282 – July/August 285

NUMERIANUS
May 283 – November 284

Background

Once **PROBUS** had been killed, **CARUS** was unchallenged, and thus must have enjoyed fairly wide support in the army. **M. Aurelius [Numerius] CARUS** had been born in Narbo (Narbonne) in Gaul c. 225, so was not of the charmed circle of Danubian or Illyrian officers who had dominated the purple since the fall of **GALLIENUS,** although like them, he was a non-senatorial career officer, but one who had also had a civil career, albeit only according to the HA.[611]

Reign

He was soon in Rome where he obtained from a compliant senate the tribunician and proconsular powers, renewable annually, was confirmed as pontifex maximus and held a suffect consulship, followed by an ordinary one with his elder son **CARINUS** at the beginning of 283. Both sons were initially styled Caesar (*nobilissimus Caesar*: 'most noble Caesar')[612], and the elder had become co-Augustus, probably by the beginning of 283. **CARUS'S** style was **Imperator Caesar M. Aurelius Carus Invictus Pius Felix Augustus.**[613] **CARINUS'S** was similar: **M. Aurelius Carinus Pius Felix Augustus.**[614] At some stage in his short reign he decided to style himself *Deo et Dominus* (God and Lord), as on an issue

---

611. PLRE I. Carus/PIR² A1473; HA *V. Cari* 5,2 (a senator) cf. 5.3 (praetorian prefect).
612. ILS601; PLRE I Carinus & Numerianus; PIR² A1473 & 1564.
613. ILS598
614. ILS607

of *aurei*, the first time this style had ever been applied to an emperor. It was not to be the last; up to that time, one had to at least have been dead prior to deification.

Once the campaigning season had started, **CARINUS** was left in charge of the western part of the Empire, whilst **CARUS** and **Numerianus,** the younger son, departed for the east to mount a punitive expedition to Persia. As the frontier had been quiet during *l'affaire SATURNINUS*, this was probably mounted more for prestige than anything else. Unfortunately, with the invasion force well inside the Persian Empire after a successful invasion and the capture of the capital, Ctesiphon, **CARUS** died, allegedly from a lightning strike near Ctesiphon. Others thought that he was murdered either by his son or the praetorian prefect, L. Flavius Aper (Numerianus's father-in-law[615]). As the invasion was on a roll, as it were, this would seem like an inopportune moment to eliminate a rival for power, and the sheer unlikeliness of death by lightning might suggest that this is what indeed happened. A third possibility is that his death was encompassed by some kind of Persian fifth columnist, although this seems as unlikely as the lightning strike. Either way, the result was that **NUMERIANUS** was now declared co-Augustus with his brother. His father was deified by the senate and granted the posthumous suffixes **Persicus Maximus** and **Germanicus Maximus**.[616]

Imperator Caesar M. Aurelius Numerius Numerianus Pius Felix Invictus Augustus (born c. 253) was able to mop up and arrange treaties after his accession, the Persian campaign having essentially been successfully completed prior to his father's death. He then withdrew the army to Syria, where the Emperor had to nurse his eye, which had developed a serious infection after sustaining what was probably a minor wound in the fighting in Mesopotamia en route to Persia. After a while, as the army moved slowly back to Rome, **NUMERIANUS** was obliged to travel in a closed litter, and by the time they had reached Sirmium (Sremska Mitrovika, Serbia), he had obviously died, for in the heat a distinctive stench was emerging from the litter. Either he had been carried off by his infection or had been opportunistically murdered by his scheming father-in-law, Aper, who was certainly widely suspected of murdering the young man. Whatever the truth, a kangaroo court of senior officers put him on trial but he hardly had time to be heard before, on 20th November, the troops acclaimed one Diocles, then commander of the household mounted guard (*protectores domestici*) as emperor. He moved swiftly to have Aper disposed of. A dispassionate eye might indeed discern the hand of Diocles, who now became an imperial claimant as **DIOCLETIANUS**, in the entire sequence of events, with Aper – who after all was a member of the imperial family – framed and conveniently disposed of.

Meanwhile, the elder brother, **CARINUS** was still firmly in control in the West, where he had gained a considerable victory of the Germans, and in consequence he added **Germanicus Maximus** to his imperial style. He also defeated the Quadi on the Danube frontier, leading him to return to Rome in 284 to celebrate a triumph. He then seems to

---

615. PLRE I. Aper 2/3. If these men are one and the same, Aper had previously been governor (*praeses*) of Pannonia Inferior. He was probably also an Illyrian. HA says he was murdered.
616. ILS596, 609; he had had his tribunician power renewed for the first time prior to his demise.

have proceeded to Britain, although there seems to be little independent record of why exactly he felt obliged to do so. As a result he also added the style **Britannicus Maximus**.[617]

At this stage he had to deal with an imperial claimant, *JULIANUS II* in Illyricum (and, it would seem, another, *JULIANUS III,* in northern Italy, see below) which he dealt with early in 285, leaving him clear to face the advancing **DIOCLETIAN** at the head of what was essentially a victorious but smaller army. In July they met in battle on the river Margus (Great Morava, Serbia), during which **CARINUS** seems to have been victorious, but at the crucial moment of victory he was struck down by a group of officers fearful of what the future might hold with him triumphant, for the emperor was a notorious seducer and was reported by Eutropius to have put to death many innocent men through false accusations.[618] It may be his staff saw the makings of another **COMMODUS** in him. In either case, his army went over to the defeated **DIOCLETIAN** without demur and, although no one knew it at the time, a whole new era was about to dawn and the chaos of the previous five decades was shortly to end. All three of Rome's shortest-lived dynasty suffered a *damnatio memoriae* and had their inscriptions erased.

Family

We do not know what **CARUS'S** father was called but he is assumed to have been a Gaul, and the occurrence of the *nomen* Numerius in the younger son's nomenclature has suggested to some that the Emperor's original *nomen* was Numerius and that he assumed M. Aurelius as an imperial style on acclamation, just as most emperors from the fourth century tended to adopt Flavius. He also had a daughter, Paulina, who may have been twice married. **CARINUS'** Empress was called Magnia Urbica, and she appears to have died with her husband.[619] Either he, his brother (who married the daughter of L. Flavius Aper), or their attested sister Paulina had a son, known only from coins as *Divus Nigrinianus nepos Cari* (the deified Nigrinianus grandson of Carus). The lack of imperial titulature for him has led to the suggestion that he was a young son of **CARINUS** who survived into **DIOCLETIANUS'S** reign and was deified on his death as a gesture of conciliation towards the supporters of the short-lived dynasty.[620]

A possible relation or descendant was Numeri[an]us, perhaps significantly governor of Gallia Narbonensis in 358/359.[621] Later hagiography has also connected SS. Cantius, Cantianus and Cantianilla (martyred near Aquileia c. 304/306) with the family of **CARUS**. They were certainly siblings and their martyrdom was recorded by St. Maximus and preserved in a sermon of St. Ambrose less than a century later. What is less likely is that they were members of the Anician family (on which see below) and what is even more spurious is the claim that they were orphaned nephews of **CARINUS**.

---

617. ILS608. This could have been as a result of one of *CARAUSIUS'S* early successes

618. *Op. cit.,* 9, 19.

619. PLRE I Paulina 1/2; Urbica 1. HA claims he had 9 wives! [*V. Cari* 16, 7]

620. PLRE I. Paulina 1 & Nigrinianus 1; also mentioned on an inscription CIL VI. 31380.

621. PLRE I Numerius 1. His name is given as Numerius by Ammianus but by John of Antioch.

Whilst we know that **CARINUS** was obliged to deal with an imperial claimant called *JULIANUS* there are discrepancies concerning the place at which the imperial claimant was killed and in his nomenclature. Thus it seems sensible to fall in with the suggestion of PLRE I that there were *two* imperial claimants of this name who appeared in the wake of the deaths of **CARUS** and **NUMERIANUS**, and thus rivals of **CARINUS** and **DIOCLETIANUS.**[622]

TABLE XLVI: THE FAMILY OF CARUS

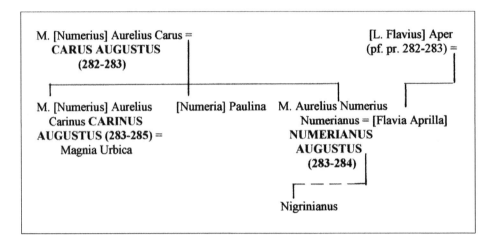

JULIANUS II
May/June 283 – September 285

We are faced with two contemporary imperial claimants of the same name, and to allocate them numbers in the grand sequence, it is necessary to separate them. It seems most likely that the first imperial claimant is that mentioned by Zosimus as having seized power in Pannonia on the death of **CARUS** in May or June 283.[623] He was probably praetorian prefect up to that point on a special command on the Danube.

His full name was **M. Aur[elius]** *JULIANUS* according to the coins he had minted at Siscia (Sisak, Croatia) and he was probably another of this cadre of Illyrian officers who seem to have had a monopoly on the purple (and attempts at the purple). He styled himself **Imperator Caesar M. Aurelius Julianus Pius Felix Augustus** and the reverse of his coins *Pannoniae Aug[ustus]* (Emperor of the Pannonian [provinces]) seems to suggest that he viewed himself as ruler of a Pannonian Empire along the lines of **POSTUMUS'S** in Gaul and **ZENOBIA'S** in the East. He seems to have survived

---

622. PLRE I Julianus 24 & 38.
623. Aurelius Victor, 39, 10 cf. PLRE 1 Julianus 38.

unmolested until **CARINUS** set off to deal with **DIOCLETIANUS** in spring 285, when he was subsequently hunted down, defeated and presumably killed in Illyricum. We have no knowledge of any family.

*

Imperial claimant under Carinus

JULIANUS III
c. July – September 284

Zosimus mentions this man first, as having seized power in Italy, although analysis would suggest that he post-dated *JULIANUS II* by up to a year.[624] **Sabinus** *JULIANUS* was *corrector* (junior provincial governor) in northern Italy, and was aclaimed by the troops in there, presumably in summer 284, on receiving the news of the death of **NUMERIANUS**. He was subsequently and probably very rapidly defeated by **CARINUS** at Verona (probably on his way back to Rome to celebrate his triumph), without, it would appear, having had time to mint any coins. Nothing further is known about him.

*

---

624. Zosimus 1, 73.1 cf. PLRE 1 Julianus 24.

THE TETRARCHY,
THE HOUSES OF CONSTANTINE & VALENTINIAN

*

VI(a)
THE TETRARCHY

The Tetrarchs
Diocletianus
Maximianus I
Galerius Maximianus II
Constantius I
Maxentius
Severus II
Maximinus II Daia
Licinius
Valens III
Martinianus

Imperial Claimants
Amandus
Carausius I
Allectus
Domtianus III
Achilleus
Alexander II

DIOCLETIANUS
(Known to history as DIOCLETIAN)
20th November 284 – 1st May 305

Background

In November 284, the imperial cavalry commander Diocles had gone from being a senior officer to imperial claimant. It was to take him a further twelve months to secure recognition as emperor, and no one sitting in the senate at Rome or in the officers' messes of the wider Empire can have expected him to last any longer than **AURELIANUS** or **PROBUS** at best. Yet he became the first man to don the purple since **ANTONINUS PIUS** to manage two whole decades. He was also the man who transformed many aspects of the way the empire functioned, attempted to stabilise the economy and transformed the supreme office from a notional *primus inter pares* to in institution that ruled through naked unambiguous power. He was also notable for having abdicated and died in his bed.

Born probably in 236 or 237 (on 22nd December) in Illyria, probably at a village in Dalmatia later re-named Diocleia in his honour, it is unclear what his full name actually was prior to his accession. Various accounts of his origin exist: that he was said to have been of obscure birth; that he was the son of a *scriba* (clerk) and that he was the freedman of a senator called Anullinus. In fact all these *could* be true. For example, one might reasonably reconstruct his original name from his later name which was C. Aurelius Valerius Diocletianus. If one assumes that 'Aurelius' was assumed, as with **CARUS,** as a formal imperial style (going back to **SEPTIMIUS SEVERUS'S** desire to associate his family with **MARCUS AURELIUS**), then one is left with C. Valerius Diocles as likely. If one could identify a senator called C. Valerius Anullinus living in the mid-3rd century, then one might be on fairly firm ground. **DIOCLETIAN'S** father, if slave, could easily have been a *scriba* in a noble household and then given his freedom, at which point he would probably have assumed his former master's *praenomen* and *nomen*. And his own given name as *cognomen*. PLRE suggests, however, that Anullinus might well have been the father of C. Annius Anullinus, consul in 295.[625] Yet there were also Cornelii Anullini recorded not so long before and M. Valerius M..f. Anulla is on record in the earlier 2nd century. Thus a senator called C Valerius Anullinus cannot be ruled out bearing in mind the diminishing number of senators' names known to us as the 3rd century progressed. Indeed, it may even be that C. Annius Anullinus was polyonymous and included Valerius amongst his no doubt resplendent array of names.

Whatever his precise origin however, Diocles served as a soldier from before 270, rising in rank through service under **AURELIAN** and **PROBUS**, possibly including an important command in Moesia. He is also thought to have served as suffect consul or have been granted consular rank in 283 by **CARUS** when he was also probably made commander of the *protectores*. He was thus the first acknowledged emperor to come to the purple when of senatorial rank since possibly **TACITUS,** certainly since **GALLIENUS**. He was quite probably also the first freedman.

Reign

Following his elevation to Augustus (albeit at first only as an unacknowledged imperial claimant) he seems to have very sensibly sat tight and waited for **CARINUS** to come to him, just as *JULIANUS II* was doing in Pannonia. Neither seems to have been tempted to take the other out, to use today's *argot*. Yet ten months after his acclamation, he unexpectedly became the beneficiary of the assassination of **CARINUS**, thus snatching victory from the jaws of defeat. He was sensible enough to seek reconciliation with those who backed his dead rival (hence the deification of **CARUS'S** probable grandson) although he did not stop the senate from pronouncing the *damnatio memoriae* upon all three of his predecessors.

---

625. PLRE 1 Anullinus 1& 3.

DIOCLETIAN hardly ever set foot in Rome, although the senate was quick to recognise him, grant him the tribunician and proconsular power, acknowledging him as *pater patriae* and making him pontifex maximus.[626] He repaid them by continuing the trend of his predecessors and excluding them completely from the administration of the Empire.[627] His formal style was **Imperator Caesar C. Aurelius Valerius Diocletianus Pius Felix Invictus Augustus.**[628] He was consul (ii) in 285 in the place of the deceased **CARUS**, and ordinary consul in 287, holding seven further such consulships in 290, 293, 296, 399, 303, 304 and 308. His wife was called Prisca and they had a daughter, Valeria.[629] After only a few months in power, during which he made a successful punitive expedition against the German tribes on the Rhine frontier (earning himself the additional style of Germanicus Maximus), he nominated an old comrade-in-arms, **MAXIMIAN**, as co-ruler with the usual style of Caesar, although he himself remained the senior of the two and his colleague always dutifully deferred to him. This clearly worked well, and on 1st April 286 his new colleague was raised to the rank of Augustus. He adopted the *signum* Jovius, bestowing that of Herculius on his colleague.

*

MAXIMIANUS I
(Known to history as MAXIMIAN)
1st April 286 – 1st May 305,
May – November 308 & 310

Background

As with his older comrade, we do not know what the rest of the new emperor's names were before he assumed the imperial style of **Aurelius Valerius Maximianus Nobilissimus Caesar** on his appointment as **DIOCLETIAN'S** junior colleague.[630] He clearly adopted two names exactly as borne by his colleague (probably acknowledging a notional, if not formal, adoption of the one by the other) and they also co-ordinated their birthdays, presumably the younger man's being brought into line with **DIOCLETIAN'S**. As Augustus, his style was modified to **Imperator Caesar M. Aurelius Valerius Maximianus Pius Felix Invictus Augustus**, and he was acknowledged as *pater patriae*.[631] The office of pontifex maximus was again divided, being also bestowed upon him, and he was granted the tribunician and proconsular powers enjoyed by his senior colleague, renewable yearly, as had been the custom since 27BC.

---

626. His only certain visit was in late autumn 303
627. Arnheim (1972) *passim*.
628. ILS616.
629. PLRE I Prisca 1; a suspect source names her as Eleutheria; conceivably she could have borne this name too.
630. *Ibid.*
631. PLRE I Maximianus 8

MAXIMIAN was born near Sirmium (Sremska Mitrovica, Serbia) probably c. 243/245, marking him out as yet another Illyrian. Syme suggests that he may have been a relative of the emperor **TACITUS**.[632] He appears to have served with **DIOCLETIAN** under **AURELIAN** and **PROBUS,** although it is not clear what position he held prior to his elevation. Conceivably he had been appointed praetorian prefect by **DIOCLETIAN** after his successful *coup* against Aper on the death of **NUMERIANUS**. Both emperors retreated from the monotheistic worship of Sol (the Sun God) much favoured by most of their Illyrian predecessors, and revived the ancient religion of the empire. To re-inforce this they allowed themselves divine *signa*: **DIOCLETIAN** adding to his name **Jovius** and his colleague, **Herculius,** which also neatly underscored their relationship to each other.

Joint reign

The two Augusti went on to campaign remorselessly, with **DIOCLETIAN** active in the east and **MAXIMIAN** in the west, both emperors accumulating imperial salutations and triumphal *agnomina* in some profusion. Each one earned, eg **Sarmaticus Maximus,** was borne by both although only one of them would have actually earned it. **DIOCLETIAN** spent 286-290 campaigning on the Danube frontier and then on the Persian one. **MAXIMIAN** meanwhile had internal problems to unravel as well, for a serious outbreak of brigandage manifested itself in Gaul, led by a vagabond called *AMANDUS* who had the temerity to declare himself emperor before he could be suppressed. However, at virtually the same time, another claimant appeared, this time in Britain. This was *CARAUSIUS*, who had been given an extraordinary naval command with a brief to clear the Channel and North Sea of pirates, presumably Germanic, for Britain and the channel coasts had been suffering from frequent and damaging raids. This he seems to have done with much aplomb, but in 286 he succumbed to the temptation to become an imperial claimant and, like **POSTUMUS**, decided to stay in Britain, although his sway eventually included large parts of the northern Gallic coast for a while, including the naval base at Boulogne. **MAXIMIAN**, being busy following the problems posed by suppressing *AMANDUS*, and fighting on the Rhine frontier, was obliged to leave him be until things quietened down. For his part, *CARAUSIUS* sensibly did not risk an invasion beyond the parts of Gaul he controlled in the hope of establishing his *imperium* more widely. **MAXIMIAN** was consul in 287, 288, 290, 293, 297, 299, 303, 304, and 307.

It became clear to the two Augusti that although the original notion was for **MAXIMIAN** to succeed **DIOCLETIAN**, they were both getting on, and they therefore decided to appoint a subordinate each, to act as deputies (Caesars), each one to be allocated a sphere of influence, thus creating a formal four-way rule, or tetrarchy. In due course the Augusti would be succeeded by their Caesars in a smooth change-over, a scheme which showed more faith in human nature than perhaps it warranted. The arrangement was also cemented by a series of marriages. Thus **MAXIMIAN** in the west appointed his praetorian prefect **CONSTANTIUS** as Caesar, and **DIOCLETIAN** appointed **GALERIUS**. The latter married

---

632. Syme (1971) 247.

the former's daughter Valeria (thenceforth Galeria Valeria), whilst Constantius divorced his wife in order to marry **MAXIMIAN'S** step-daughter. **MAXIMIAN'S** son **MAXENTIUS** also married the daughter of **GALERIUS** (see **Table XLVII**, below).

Thereafter, imperial control began to be asserted in earnest, despite a tribal rising in Africa and the continuing problem posed in the NW by *CARAUSIUS* and his successor *ALLECTUS* who was eventually dealt with very effectively by Constantius, the western Caesar who recaptured the Gallic possessions of the breakaway empire in 293 and in 297 invaded Britain and eliminated *ALLECTUS*. In 296, the new Persian ruler, Narses seized Roman Armenia, and invaded Syria. The Caesar Galerius, sent to sort matters out, was heavily defeated and was publicly reprimanded by **DIOCLETIAN** for risking battle with an inferior force. The setback caused consternation in Egypt, always vulnerable to Persian attack since the days of Darius, and L. Domitius *DOMITIANUS* was acclaimed emperor there in the general panic. He was killed (in circumstances of which we know nothing) in December 297, his place being taken by a successor, Aurelius *ACHILLEUS*. He was dealt with by **DIOCLETIAN** personally in spring 298. Meanwhile, Galerius redeemed himself by winning a stunning victory over the Persians in Armenia, resulting in a favourable peace with held for four decades. Nevertheless, constant campaigning was necessary to ensure peace along the frontiers.

Imperial claimant under Maximianus

AMANDUS
286

The *bagaudae* or brigands seem to have been a phenomenon of provincial life whenever government was in dispute or weakened in some way. Consequently, in the period of transition from **CARUS** to **DIOCLETIAN** and with *JULIANUS III* active in northern Italy, an outbreak took place in Gaul led by a man called Amandus and supported by one Aelianus. So entrenched had they become by 286 that *AMANDUS* began styling himself Augustus and issuing coins, albeit with rather blundered legends: *Imp. C[aesar] C. Amandus P[ius] F[elix] Aug[ustus]* and *Imp. S. Amandus P[ius] F[elix] Aug[ustus]* from which we might reasonably conclude that his full name was something like C. S[   ] Amandus.[633] He was, however, quickly suppressed by **MAXIMIAN**, but in later hagiographies was alleged to have been a Christian.[634]

*

DIOCLETIAN now turned his attention to the re-organisation of the Empire itself. The size of the provinces was reduced (once again on the notion that governors having

---

633. PLRE Aelianus 1 & Amandus 1. Some older sources credit him with the *nomen* Silvius, for which no proof.
634. Abbot Babolenus in Duchesne, *Rerum Franciarum* i., 662.

too much power provided them with the wherewithal to become imperial claimants) and they were grouped in twelve dioceses, each under the control of a civilian governor called a *vicarius*. One result was that Italy, previously long free of taxes, lost its tax-free status (except for the immediate environs of Rome itself); another was to re-inforce the impotence of the senate, which was left with only two of the provinces assigned to it by **AUGUSTUS** and they were much reduced in size. The armed forces were taken out of the hands of the provincial governors and diocesan *vicarii* completely and was henceforth to be controlled independently. The army was also divided between the border garrisons (*limitanei*) and the more mobile reserve field army which had a near preponderance of cavalry and could be sent on demand to tackle problems that needed more than just the border units. These were the *comitatenses*, notionally part of the Emperor's personal bodyguard (although they were in fact much more numerous than that), and the *palatine*, elite infantry. The old legions by this time had been reduced in size, had their equipment thinned out and were mainly allocated to border units, or *limitanei*. Personnel were increasingly drawn from the wilder provinces and from barbarian tribes, due to the exemptions allowed to mainstream citizens.

Furthermore, price-fixing was introduced in an attempt to stabilise the currency, the coinage was reformed and jobs were made practically hereditary as were town councillorships. The revised coinage included an *aureus* struck at the standard of 60 to the pound, a new silver coin of drastically improved silver content known as the *argenteus*, and a new large bronze coin, the *aurelianus* valued at 10 *denarii*. A price edict was issued in 301, which attempted to establish the legal maximum prices that could be charged for goods and services. This was an exercise in futility as maximum prices proved impossible to enforce. Worse, the Edict was reckoned in terms of *denarii*, although no such coin had been struck for over 50 years.

All this achieved some stability, but price fixing is invariably deleterious in the longer term and fixing people in places and professions prevents the free movement of personnel to wherever they might be needed, which was one of the problems that lay behind the difficulty of army recruitment. Added to which, Christianity, then rapidly gaining ground in the east and to a lesser extent in the west, was leading to people opting out of mainstream life completely, mainly by taking the tonsure or holy orders and refusing military service. This eventually led to a decree of 298 requiring all in imperial service to publicly sacrifice to the gods on pain of dismissal. Then in 304 a further edict or rescript required everyone, Christians included, to offer sacrifice on pain of death, which triggered the last great persecution of the Christians, although it was enforced a lot more harshly in the east than in the west. The Caesar Galerius has subsequently received most of the blame for this, but one can hardly absolve **DIOCLETIAN** himself. On the whole, however, the Tetrarchy worked remarkably well – until **DIOCLETIAN** decided, in 305, to abdicate, and persuaded the ever-loyal **MAXIMIAN** to follow suit. Thereafter, things began to unravel, rather messily, although the concept of Tetrarchy tottered until after 337.

Having retired to his enormous palace at Split, in Dalmatia, close to his birthplace, the emperor re-entered public life briefly only once, to attend a conference of the tetrarchs at Carnuntum (Bad Deutsch-Altenburg, Lower Austria) in November 308, the year in which he held his final consulship. The tetrarchic system was showing signs of falling apart, mainly thanks to the acclamation of **CONSTANTINE I** at York in 306, and the taste for power exhibited by **MAXIMIAN**, who attempted to resume the purple to counterbalance this threat, in support of his son **MAXENTIUS** who had also seized power in the west. **DIOCLETIANUS** was asked to re-assume the purple, but he refused point blank. He returned to his palace and died there 3ʳᵈ December 311.

⋆

Imperial Claimants under Maximianus

CARAUSIUS I
October/November 285-293

Background

CARAUSIUS was born in the low countries, of a people called the Menapii, and became an experienced mariner. He also proved himself a capable soldier, too, serving under **MAXIMIAN** against *AMANDUS* and his *bagaudae*. At some stage, he had received a commission to equip a fleet and suppress the German pirates which were affecting the Channel and North Sea. There is some suggestion that this may have been a commission of **CARINUS'S**, but if not, it would have been under **MAXIMIAN**. His exact position cannot be determined, despite plentiful contemporary references to him; he may have been prefect of the *Classis Britannica* (British Fleet) and then have had a wider brief as *dux*.[635] It was certainly under him as *dux* that his admiral, operating out of Boulogne, cleared the seas of pirates, and recovered much booty, but instead of returning the stolen property either to those from whom it had been taken or to the Imperial fisc, he kept most of it himself, lavishly rewarding his sailors. Having been tipped off about his impending arrest on **MAXIMIAN'S** orders for this piece of *lesé majesté* he thereupon technically became a pirate himself,[636] being acclaimed emperor in 285 and seizing northern Gaul and the whole of Britain.[637] It may even be that this *coup* was the spur that led **DIOCLETIAN** to promote **MAXIMIAN** from Caesar to Augustus in April 286, in which case *CARAUSIUS'S* acclamation may have taken place in autumn 285. The new imperial claimant's name is not wholly clear, as it is given (in its fullest form) as **M. Aurelius Ma[ ] Carausius**, where the Ma[ ] element may or may not be expanded to the Gallic name Mausaeus, although Maius, Magius or Marius are all possible.[638] The name Carausius itself seems to be of Celtic origin, and in him it makes its first appearance on the pages of history- but not the last.

635. Birley (1981) 311-312.

636. He was referred to as *archipirata* in a hostile panegyric.

637. PLRE I Carausius

638. *Roman Inscriptions of Britain* (RIB) 2291.

Reign

The claimant's style appears to have been **Imperator Caesar M. Aurelius Ma[   ] Carausius Pius Felix Invictus Augustus**, and he probably assumed the M. Aurelius element on his acclamation, as **CARUS** also probably did (cf. above). Whether he assumed the title of pontifex maximus is not clear, but he did award himself two consulships during his seven years in power.[639] He also attempted to gain acceptance as co-ruler with **MAXIMIAN** and **DIOCLETIAN**, possibly before the former mounted an attempt to dislodge him which failed, possibly due to the weather in the channel (his excuse), but more likely because *CARAUSIUS* had defeated him in northern Gaul. Whether his overtures were accepted (presumably to buy time in which to regroup and mount another campaign) we do not know, for the sources are universally hostile after the event, but the British claimant did produce a famous issue of coins bearing the profiles of himself, **MAXIMIAN** and **DIOCLETIAN** with a legend CARAUSIUS ET FRATRES SUI (Carausius and his brothers).

In any case, it would appear that during his reign Britain was quiet, and local memories of him must have been most favourable for one finds British aristocrats bearing his name in the 5th and 6th centuries, most notably on an inscription from remote Penmachno, in North Wales: *Carausius hic iacit in hoc congeries lapidum* (Here lies Carausius in this heap of stones).[640] The spectacular sequence of stone built and many-towered shore forts, stretching from Bitterne (Hants.) to Brancaster (Norfolk) as well as along the Gallic coast, may well be a part-legacy of Carausius' reign, although whether built as part of the campaign against the German pirates or as a security measure after the Britannic Empire had come into existence is not wholly, clear. Some were already in existence, dating possibly to the time of **AURELIAN** or even **CARUS'** enigmatic British venture, but the remainder form a coherent strategic pattern and the balance of evidence is in favour of many of them to have been built at this period.[641]

CARAUSIUS' loss of the continental port of Boulogne and its extensive hinterland to the Caesar Constantius c. 292/293 may however have been the trigger for the seizure of power by *ALLECTUS* which resulted in *CARAUSIUS'S* murder in the latter year. Then again, the panegyricists would have us believe that the ambitious subordinate believed he would be recognised in some way by Constantius and the senior Augusti if he rid the island of the tyrant. Perhaps he believed he would be made Caesar. In the event, of course, he was deluding himself. Nothing is known of this imperial claimant's family nor of any wife or children – unless of course the survival of his excessively rare name implies progeny.

*

---

639. Coin evidence.
640. Thomas (1994) 205, where he suggests this man was a priest and the date c. 500.
641. Casey (1994) 115-126.

ALLECTUS
293 - 296

The assassination of *CARAUSIUS* may well have been the result of the loss of that ruler's continental possessions. Nevertheless, *ALLECTUS*, his nemesis, still controlled two or more provinces, for it is not known when Britain was further subdivided from the two provinces into which it was divided in c. 213 into the four recorded in c. 313. This could have happened under **POSTUMUS**, or as part of **DIOCLETIAN'S** re-organisation, although that probably had not occurred until after 296. We do not know this imperial claimant's other names, for no inaugural minting of coins has turned up, which as tradition tended to demand, usually incorporated the ruler's full imperial style.[642] We do know he was *CARAUSIUS'* chief ally and either his *rationalis summa rei* (chief financial officer) or more plausibly his praetorian prefect. The two of them had attempted to reform their currency to match that being undertaken in the wider Empire. That he survived for as long as three years is down to the fact that **CONSTANTIUS** and the other Tetrarchs had to be sure that the Germanic tribes to the east of the Rhine would not rise to support him or take advantage of an attempt to end the secession by invading Gaul. Furthermore, there having been an unsuccessful attempt to dislodge *CARAUSIUS* earlier in c. 289, no chances could be taken, and a sufficiently powerful force had to be readied. The fact that *ALLECTUS* had to be dislodged at all, suggests that there was little local opposition to his *coup*.

ALLECTUS styled himself simply **Imperator Caesar Allectus Pius Felix Augustu**s; he held a consulship in 294 and, despite the loss of Bononia (Boulogne) by his predecessor, seems to have still had control of large parts of Gaul. He seems also to have continued work on the Saxon Shore forts begun by his predecessor, and he began the construction of an imperial palace beside the Thames in the SW angle of the City of Londinium.[643] When the invasion did come, the Caesar **CONSTANTIUS** sent two fleets, led by his praetorian prefect, Julius Asclepiodotus.[644] *ALLECTUS* seems to have been wrong-footed by being under the impression that only one fleet had arrived (having evaded his own experienced fleet in a channel fog near Insula Vectis (Isle of Wight) and hurried to meet the invaders. Another fleet seems to have outflanked him and he was killed in battle, in spite of support by Frankish mercenaries, who took the most casualties.

*

---

642. PLRE I Allectus
643. Casey (1994) 127, 134.
644. PLRE I Asclepiodotus 3. He was consul in 292.

DOMITIANUS III
August 296 – 2nd December 297

This imperial claimant, **L. Domitius** *DOMITIANUS*, appears as passing from his year one to his second year in August 297, so must be presumed to have seized power in Egypt when **GALERIUS** was experiencing his little difficulty with the Persians. He was probably prefect of Egypt at the time, although we have no record of him in this office, but the sources for the period are scrappy in any case. He may have died in early December 297, when his ally *ACHILLEUS* seems to have taken over, by which time he was under siege at Alexandria by **DIOCLETIAN**. The sources do not mention that he was killed by his own men, as most usually happened in such circumstances, so he may have died of natural causes or in battle.[645] We know nothing of his origin or family.

*

ACHILLEUS
2nd December 297 – July 298

[M.] **Aurelius** *ACHILLEUS* was a *vir perfectissimus* and the *corrector* (equestrian governor) of an Egyptian province (probably Aegyptus) in September 297. He is named as the imperial claimant instead of *DOMITIANUS III* in several sources, but was probably his successor after 2nd December 297. As the siege of Alexandria lasted for eight months[646] his reign must have ended, no doubt bloodily, in June or July 298, depending on exactly when it began.[647] No coins survive from his time (if any were minted) but his imperial style was no doubt **Imperator Caesar Aurelius Achilleus Pius Felix Augustus.**

*

EUGENIUS I
303

The commander of a unit of 500 infantrymen engaged upon harbour work at Seleucia, *EUGENIUS* was proclaimed emperor by his men. He subsequently advanced on the provincial capital, Antioch, but was defeated and presumably killed in battle, or dispatched immediately thereafter. The year is thought to have been 303.[648] He issued no coins and nothing is known either of his origins or his family.

---

645. PLRE I Domitianus 6.
646. Eg.: Eutropius 9, 22—23 & Orosius VII, 25.4.8.
647. PLRE I Achilleus 1.
648. PLRE I Eugenius 1.

TABLE XLVII: THE IMPERIAL SUCCESSION 284-383

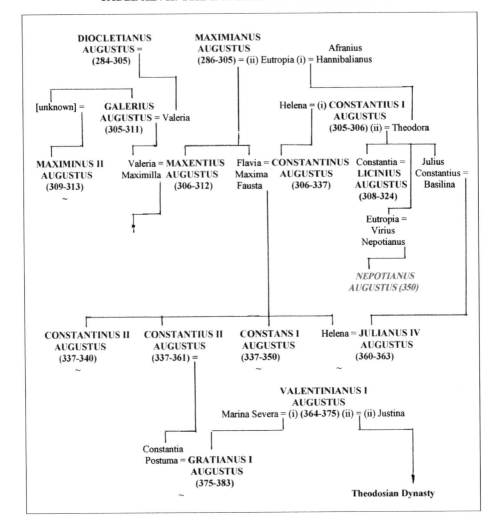

Note that in the table above, only the connections between the various rulers are shown. Their fully detailed families will be found in the tables that follow.

The continuation of the Tetrarchy

The consequences of the retirement of the two Augusti in 305 were entirely foreseeable. The two men appointed to rule in their place, **GALERIUS** and **CONSTANTIUS I** were chosen for their loyalty and competence. In turn, the retiring emperors, rather than the newly elevated ones, chose as the two Caesars, not their protéges' sons (who were not only fully adult and, as it turned out, competent) but two other old comrades-in-arms **SEVERUS** and **MAXIMIN** and again, alliances were cemented by marriage. Thus the sons of **MAXIMIAN** and **CONSTANTIUS**, **MAXENTIUS** and **CONSTANTINE**, were passed over in favour of two cronies of **GALERIUS** and **DIOCLETIAN** but, thanks to the tortuous series of dynastic marriages, they were nevertheless bound tightly into the nexus of the tetrarchic imperial family. It was inevitable that at some time or another one or both of the two who had been passed over would make a bid for power.[649]

The first to break ranks was **CONSTANTINE.** He had served under **DIOCLETIAN** as a senior tribune, and then as a senior commander against the Sarmatians under **GALERIUS.** When the new Caesars were announced, he obtained permission to travel west to serve under his father. In letting him go, **GALERIUS** was committing a grave error. The two then went to Britain to campaign against the Picts. After obtaining a considerable victory, **CONSTANTIUS,** unwittingly imitating **SEPTIMIUS SEVERUS,** died of disease at York. At this point **SEVERUS** should have become unchallenged emperor in the west, but the troops at York acclaimed **CONSTANTINE** instead. This was not in the plan. As a fire-fighting measure, **GALERIUS** appointed **CONSTANTINE** Caesar to **SEVERUS.** Later in the same year, **GALERIUS,** short of revenue, was rash enough to remove the privileged tax-free status of Rome, causing an outcry, exploited by **MAXENTIUS** the son of **MAXIMIAN** to seize power himself, effectively threatening the position of **SEVERUS.** He then appointed his supposedly retired father as his colleague. They then recognised **CONSTANTINE** as Augustus, but had too few troops at their disposal to achieve very much against **SEVERUS,** who in due course was ordered by **GALERIUS** to crush the uprising. He advanced on Rome, where his troops unexpectedly deserted to the revered **MAXIMIANUS** (doubtless aided by the promise of a donative – retired emperors were hardly likely to be hard up) and **SEVERUS** was captured, forced to abdicate and later killed. To cement all this, Fausta, sister of **MAXENTIUS** was duly obliged to marry **CONSTANTINE.**

GALERIUS was hardly likely to take all this lying down, but an attempt to wrest power in the west away from **MAXENTIUS** failed almost as dismally as that of **SEVERUS.** Yet in spring 308, **MAXIMIAN** decided to stop playing second fiddle to his son and had himself acclaimed senior western Augustus, but this ploy failed and he was forced to flee to his son-in-law, **CONSTANTINE.** He then prevailed upon **GALERIUS** to fetch **DIOCLETIAN** out of retirement in an attempt to resolve the issue. The result was more of an arrangement on paper: **GALERIUS** remained Augustus in the East and appointed another old crony, **LICINIUS** to replace **SEVERUS** in the west with **CONSTANTINE** as his Caesar and **MAXIMIN DAIA** as eastern Caesar. This left **MAXENTIUS** still in control of Italy and Africa as unofficial Augustus and **CONSTANTINE,** whilst officially Caesar, had already been acclaimed as Augustus two years before. Needless to say, this left uncertainty into which an imperial claimant called *ALEXANDER* arose in Africa to challenge **MAXENTIUS** and it took nearly two years to dislodge him. Yet even as *ALEXANDER* was being dislodged, **MAXIMIAN** seized his chance whilst **CONSTANTINE** was conducting a spring campaign against the Franks, and escaped from house arrest with him, to go south to Arelate (Arles) where for the third time he was proclaimed Augustus. On hearing that his son-in-law was coming after him, however, he

---

649. The entire idea of the Tetrarchy being a formal quasi-constitutional arrangement has been challenged by Lead-better (2009).

moved south to Massilia (Marseilles), where the citizens had no intention of being involved in a siege and turned the old boy over to **CONSTANTINE.** It was given out not long afterwards that he had committed suicide by hanging in late 309 or early 310. **MAXENTIUS,** in a gesture of filial piety, had him deified by the senate. One result was that **MAXIMIN DAIA** was raised to the rank of Augustus and when a year later **GALERIUS** died, he split the rule of the east with **LICINIUS,** who was palmed off with the Balkan and Danubian provinces. A year later again and **CONSTANTINE** had eliminated **MAXENTIUS,** followed by **LICINIUS,** who defeated **MAXIMIN** the same year, leaving, just two Augusti. There things were left until 324.

*

MAXIMIANUS II
(Known to history as GALERIUS)
1st April 305 – 30th April 311

Reign

GALERIUS was apparently called C. Galerius Maximinus *signo* Armentarius before being called upon by **DIOCLETIAN** and **MAXIMIAN** to assume the role of Caesar. Thereupon he assumed the former's *nomen* and the latter's *cognomen* to become **Nobilissimus et Fortissimus Caesar C. Galerius Valerius MAXIMIANUS** the latter name being the one he always seems to have borne officially, even though he was universally known as **GALERIUS,** both by contemporaries and all later chroniclers. He was born c. 254 at Romulianum near Serdica in Dacia (the name was that of his mother, bestowed upon the region (*pagus*) by him when emperor in her honour;[650] it is now Gamzigrad, Serbia) and was originally a herdsman; although his mother's name (Romula) is known, that of his father is lost to us. He too served in the army under **AURELIAN** and **PROBUS.** On being made Caesar he was obliged to divorce his first (anonymous) wife, by whom he had had a daughter, Valeria Maximilla, and marry **DIOCLETIAN'S** daughter Valeria. As Augustus, he was endowed with the tribunician and proconsular powers and the duplicated office of pontifex maximus. His style then became **Imperator Caesar Galerius Aurelius Valerius Maximianus Pius Felix Invictus Augustus.**[651] He also adopted his sister's son, his caesar, **MAXIMINUS II DAIA.** He bore the triumphal epithets of **Germanicus Maximus II, Sarmaticus, Persicus, Britannicus, Carpicus, Armeniacus, Medicus and Adiabenicus,** each with **Maximus** added, and had been the holder of eight consulships, in 294, 297, 300, 302, 305, 306, 308 and 311.[652] He died of what appears to have been a particularly revolting affliction at Nicomedia (Izmit, Turkey) 30th April 311. His reign was most notable to Christian writers for the vigour with which he persecuted Christians, although he is said to have repented on his death bed.

---

650. PLRE I Maximianus 9; FS1804; Syme (1971) 212, 226. Title as Caesar: ILS 630, 633, 635.
651. ILS653.
652. ILS642.

TABLE XLVIII: DIOCLETIANUS & MAXIMIANUS

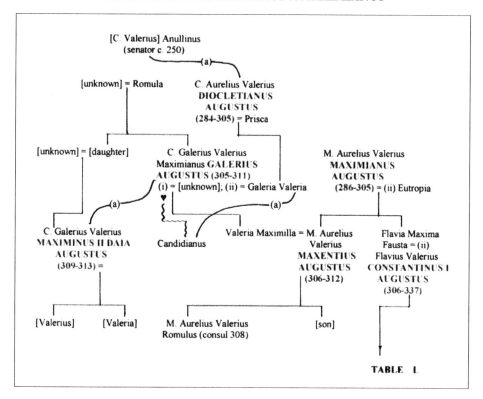

CONSTANTIUS I CHLORUS
1st April 305 – 25th July 306

Background

Flavius Valerius CONSTANTIUS was born in Illyria on 31st March in an unknown year, probably c. 250. The supposed descent from Eutropius and a sister of **CLAUDIUS II** may be discounted, early though it appears; there is no hint as to the names of his parents, although the recurrence of Julius amongst his descendants may suggest a likely name for one of them. Neither do his origins have to be that humble, for after military service as a member of the *protectores* and then as a senior tribune, he was made *praeses* (governor) of Dalmatia possibly by **AURELIANUS** where an inscription supplies his original full name as above.[653] He served as a *dux* (general) under **PROBUS** if we may trust the HA.[654] He married Flavia Julia Helena, a Bithynian, and mother of his son **CONSTANTINE I**, but was forced to divorce her in order to marry **MAXIMIAN'S** daughter Flavia Maximiana Theodora (by whom he had six further children) when he was made Caesar in March 293.

---

653. PLRE I Constantius 12
654. *V. Probi* 22, 3. Plausible, but unproven.

Thereafter he called himself **C. Flavius Valerius Constantius Nobilissimus Caesar** *signo* **Herculius** and had responsibility for NW Europe, being endowed with the tribunician and proconsular power.[655]

Reign

His first task as Caesar was to eliminate *CARAUSIUS* and *ALLECTUS*, which he succeeded in doing in 296, having also won two victories over the German tribes on the east bank of the Rhine, mainly the Alemanni, recruiting one of their princes, Crocus, and his men into his auxiliaries or *protectores*. **CONSTANTIUS** was called *chlorus* (pallid) only from the sixth century, but he won a favourable reputation amongst Christian writers of the 4th century through his attempts to ameliorate the consequences of the anti-Christian edicts of his colleague **GALERIUS**. He was named western Augustus in succession to **MAXIMIAN** in April 305. He was thereafter styled **Imperator Caesar C. Flavius Valerius Constantius Augustus**, becoming pontifex maximus, later adding the *agnomina* **Germanicus Maxdimus II, Sarmaticus Maximus II, Persicus Maximus II, Britannicus, Carpicus, Armeniacus, Medicus**, and **Adiabenicus,** each qualified by **Maximus**. The following year he campaigned particularly successfully against the Picts in Britain with his son **CONSTANTINE** as a senior commander. Having come back to Eboracum (York) after the conclusion of the Pictish campaign, he became ill and died there 25th July 306 only in his second year of extraordinary powers. He was six times consul in 294, 296, 300, 302, 305 and 306. After his death he was deified by the senate.[656]

An interesting coda relates to his death. He was allegedly buried in Wales and, after his defeat of Llewellyn ap Gruffydd in 1282, King Edward I had the Emperor's monument drawn to his attention and the following year the remains of **CONSTANTIUS** were taken to Segontium (Caernarfon) and there re-buried in the church. The author of the 9th century *Historia Brittonum* indeed mentions the burial (but calling the person commemorated **CONSTANTINE (II)** the son of **CONSTANTINE I**, presumably in error, despite mentioning the name as being so inscribed).[657] How much credence we may give to either the *Historia Brittonum* account or the identification of the re-burial in 1283 is impossible to say. There may have been a late Roman funerary monument somewhere in Wales to a Constanti[n]us who was perhaps merely *assumed* to be either **CHLORUS** or **CONSTANTINE II** but was in reality some forgotten officer, administrator or post-Roman warlord of that name. After all, **if CONSTANTIUS I** had died in York, he would hardly need to be buried 150 miles away in Wales.

---

655. ILS 648/649; ILS 637 gives his *praenomen* (erroneously) as Marcus.
656. ILS652.
657. Knight (2014) 170; Morgan Evans (2014) 174 quoting *Historia Brittonum* 25.

TABLE XLIX: THE SIBLINGS OF CONSTANTINE

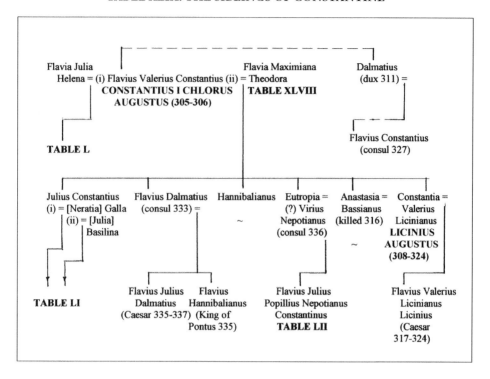

TABLES XLVIII & XLIX: BRIEF LIVES

Anastasia

Baths at Constantinople were named after her [PLRE I. Anastasia 1]

C. Aurelius Valerius Diocletianus

See above, **DIOCLETIANUS AUGUSTUS**

M. Aurelius Valerius Maxentius

See below **MAXENTIUS AUGUSTUS**

M. Aurelius Valerius Maximianus

See above **MAXIMIANUS I AUGUSTUS**

[M. Aurelius] Valerius Romulus

Still a boy in the years immediately prior to his father's elevation, he was consul 308 & 309, but this was not recognised as such outside the west; he is thought to have died in 309, and was deified by the senate. There is uncertainty about his nomenclature, only a single coin giving 'M. Aurelius' but which calls him *nobilissimus Caesar* although he was never made Caesar by his father as far as is known, being referred to merely as *nobilissimus vir* (most noble man) [PLRE I Romulus 6].

Basilina

She was of noble birth, and still young when she died not long after the birth of the future emperor, her second son and third child. Unlike her husband, she appears to have been an Arian Christian [PLRE I Basilina]

Bassianus

Nominated Caesar in the west by **CONSTANTINE** in 316, but rejected by **LICINIUS**. Incited to revolt by his brother Senecio (see **Table LII Brief Lives**) and in the aftermath, killed [PLRE I Bassianus 1]

Candidianus

Illegitimate son, born c. 296. Adopted by his stepmother Galeria Valeria Augusta and betrothed to the young daughter of **MAXIMIN II.** Executed on the orders of **LICINIUS** in 313 [PLRE I Candidianus]

Constantia

An Arian Christian, she married **LICINIUS** at Milan in 313. The younger Licinius may have been adopted by her. [PLRE I Constantia 1]

Dalmatius

A very senior commander serving as *comes* or *dux* in Illyricum in 311 and although serving under **LICINIUS,** possibly a brother or other close relative of **CONSTANTIUS I.** [PLRE I Dalmatius 2]

Eutropia

A Syrian, she was living in 325 [PLRE I Eutropia 1]

Flavia Julia Helena

St. Helena was born c. 250 at Drepanum (later renamed Helenopolis, now Hersek, Turkey) in Bithynia where she came from a family of lowly station and was probably originally merely the mistress of **CONSTANTIUS I,** who was obliged to divorce her when he became Caesar in 293. She was retrospectively created Augusta in 324 or 325. In 326, having attempted to encompass the death of Fausta in revenge for the death of the Caesar Crispus, she was converted to Christianity and thereupon went to the Holy Land where she discovered the Holy Sepulchre, over which she erected a magnificent church, and the True Cross (which on the other hand is not mentioned by her contemporary Eusebius, but is alluded to by St.

Ambrose, a figure who wrote two generations later on). She built other churches and the province of Helenopontus (formerly Pontus, a former kingdom in Anatolia) was named after her. She died c. 330. The Church later recognised her as a saint.

Flavia Maximiana Theodora

She was the probable daughter of Afranius Hannibalianus (**Table L Brief Lives**) and thus of senatorial rank. She probably assumed the first two of her names on her marriage in 293 [PLRE Theodora 1].

Fl[avia] Maxima Fausta

Born in Rome c. 288/90, in 307 she married **CONSTANTINE I**. Later she told her husband about **MAXIMIAN'S** conspiracy against him. She hosted the Synod of Rome, 313 at her palace on the Lateran. She was made Augusta after her marriage. Some sources suggest that Minervina and not Fausta was the mother of **CONSTANTINE II**. She was blamed for the death of Crispus Caesar and was subsequently put to death [PLRE I Fausta]

Flavius Constantius

He was praetorian prefect of **CONSTANTINE I** in the east 324-326, from 326-327 in Italy under Constantius Caesar and was consul in 327. He is assumed to be a close kinsman of the emperor from his name and his consulship; his place on the pedigree above is to some extent speculative [PLRE I Constantius 5].

Flavius Dalmatius

Consul and censor in 333, following which he served as a senior commander on the Eastern frontier 334-335 [PLRE I Dalmatius 6]

Flavius Hannibalianus

Educated with his brother Dalmatius at Toulouse under Exsuperius. He was later made *nobilissimus* by **CONSTANTINE I** and in 335 King of Kings of the People of Pontus, but was killed at Constantinople in the wake of the emperor's death in 337 [PLRE I Hannibalianus 2].

Flavius Julius Dalmatius
Made Caesar 18th September 335 but in 337 he was killed at Constantinople on 3rd September in the aftermath of the death of **CONSTANTINE I**; he was an issuer of coins [ILS 720; PLRE I Dalmatius 7].

Flavius Julius Popillius Nepotianus
See below *NEPOTIANUS AUGUSTUS*

Flavius Valerius Constantinus
See below, **CONSTANTINUS I AUGUSTUS**

Flavius Valerius Constantius
See above **CONSTANTIUS I AUGUSTUS,**

Flavius Valerius Licinianus Licinius
Born July or August 315, made Caesar 1st March 317 hence his appearance in some books as Licinius II, but deposed and spared in 324 when his father, defeated, retired to Thessalonica. Nevertheless, **CONSTANTINE I** had him executed in 326 anyway [PLRE I Licinius 4].

Galeria Valeria
If she bore the name Galeria prior to her marriage to **GALERIUS** in 293, she was probably a fairly close relation of his, perhaps through her mother. Made Augusta in 305, she fled to **MAXIMIN II DAIA**, but in refusing to marry him, lost her property and was exiled. In 313 **LICINIUS** intended to kill her, but she fled again and hid, but in January 315 was caught and executed. She was a Christian, childless, but the adoptive mother of Candidianus [PLRE I Valeria].

C. Galerius Valerius Maximianus
See below **GALERIUS AUGUSTUS**

C. Galerius Valerius Maximinus Daia
See below, **MAXIMINUS II AUGUSTUS**

Galla
She was half-sister of Vulcacius Rufus (consul 347), sister of Neratius Cerealis (consul 358) and was married by 325. Her elder son (whose name is not known for certain) was killed at Constantinople in 337 in the wake of the death of **CONSTANTINE I** [PLRE I Galla 1].

Hannibalianus
He probably died relatively young as he appears to have received no honours and his name is not amongst those killed at Constantinople in 337, so he had probably died by then [PLRE I Hannibalianus 1].

Julius Constantius
He was a Christian who left property to the church at Ephesus. He married Galla before 325 when Gallus Caesar was born. Consul 335 and one of the first of the new patricians, he also was killed in 337. [PLRE I Constantius 7]

Minervina
Concubine of **CONSTANTINE I** who later married him c. 290 and was mother of Crispus Caesar (and possibly of **CONSTANTINE II**. It is not known whether she died before 307 or was divorced then [PLRE I Minervina]

Valerius Licinianus Licinius
See above, **LICINIUS AUGUSTUS**

Virius Nepotianus
He is assumed to have been the son of the consul for 301 of the same name; he himself was consul

in 336. Probably he was dead by the time his presumed son was acclaimed in Rome in 350. The family go back for certain to the later 2nd century, Q. Virius Font[eius] Nepotianus being most likely his direct forebear. The contemporary Virii Lupi were probably related and had an equally long history. The family originally appears to have originated in Florence. [PLRE I Nepotianus 7, cf. 5 & 6]

*

MAXENTIUS
28th October 306 – 28th October 312

Background

Born c. 287, before his elevation, he was **M. Valerius MAXENTIUS,** *vir clarissimus*[658] (although *puer clarissimus* would have been more to the point), his father's status giving him senatorial rank and indeed, he lived at Rome, had a house on the Via Labicana and was only 19 when proclaimed emperor. In 305 he married Valeria Maximilla the daughter of **GALERIUS**, who bore him two sons, one called Romulus and the other whose name we do not know.[659]

Reign

On acceding to the purple, his style changed to **Imperator Caesar C. (but sometimes M[arcus]) Aurelius Valerius Maxentius Pius Felix Invictus Augustus**, and was granted the proconsular *imperium* and tribunician power as well as being declared pontifex maximus, making a total of four holding this office at this juncture, rather making a mockery of the state's chief priesthood.[660] In view of the youth of **MAXENTIUS,** it would seem that, however disappointed he may have been about being passed over as one of the new Caesars in 305, only a man of the stature and maturity of his father could have masterminded his acclamation in the autumn following the elevation of **CONSTANTINE**, who had been in the same situation, but who was a decade or more older. His first move was to be acclaimed as *imperator caesar* – the usual prefix for emperors since **AUGUSTUS** – but it was only when **GALERIUS** refused to recognise him that he added the epithet *augustus,* in April 307.

He saw off an attempt **by SEVERUS II** to eliminate him and controlled Italy, Sicily, Corsica, Sardinia, Africa Proconsularis and those African provinces to the west of it, although he did have to contend with the imperial claimant *ALEXANDER II* there. Soon, to boost his authority, his father came out of retirement and brokered an alliance with **CONSTANTINE**. Then, after his son's final elevation to the rank of Augustus, he attempted to replace him completely, but was thwarted and fled to the court of his new ally, committing

---

658. CIL XIV 2825
659. ILS667
660. ILS670

suicide in 310 after a failed attempt to re-enter the fray in late 309. Once **GALERIUS** and **SEVERUS** had died, the way was open for **CONSTANTINE** to move against **MAXENTIUS**, who on being heavily defeated at the Battle of the Milvian Bridge outside Rome, was drowned in the rout. It was the sixth anniversary of his coming to power; he was still only 25. He was consul in 308, 309, 310 and 312. His younger son is thought to have either survived or died with him; Romulus, probably his designated heir, seems to have died before him, probably of natural causes.

Imperial claimant under Maxentius

ALEXANDER II
308 – summer 310

Alexander was a Phrygian equestrian officer (he was styled *vir perfectissimus*) of fairly advanced years who was appointed *vicarius* of the diocese of Africa at some stage prior to 308, in all probability from 303. His tenure probably lasted until 308 because, in that year **MAXENTIUS,** doubting the loyalty of the army in the province, demanded that he send his son to Rome as a hostage. Alexander thereupon refused and was instead acclaimed emperor by his troops. His imperial style was **Imperator Caesar L. Domitius Alexander Pius Felix Augustus.** One of his coin issues described him on the reverse as *SPQR Optimo Principi*, a remarkably old fashioned conceit; surely he could not have viewed himself as a new **AUGUSTUS**? An inscription from before his elevation gives his name as Val[erius] Alexander.[661] It is suggested that he changed his name on becoming an imperial claimant; alternatively he may have had other names, as was still then fashionable even for non-senators. Either way he may have dropped the 'Valerius' element in order to distance himself from the Tetrarchs almost all of whom bore this name. Thanks to the turmoil elsewhere, it seems that he was not dislodged until **MAXENTIUS** was able to send a force to Africa under the elderly ex-governor of the senatorial province of Africa Proconsularis C. Ceionius Rufius Volusianus (consul (ii) in 314), made praetorian prefect for the purpose, supported by the equestrian commander Zenas, who defeated and killed him, presumably along with his unfortunate son, whose name has not survived.[662] Volusianus' appointment demonstrates that **MAXENTIUS** at least was not prepared to stick to **GALLIENUS'S** ordinance excluding senators from senior military and other positions, a relaxation continued by **CONSTANTINE I.**

*

---

661. PLRE I Alexander 17, 20. The claimant, also *vicarius* of Africa could conceivably have been a separate person.
662. PLRE I Volusianus 4, who was back in Rome by October 310 & Zenas 1.

SEVERUS II
August 306 – March/April 307

Sir Ronald Syme characterised **SEVERUS II** as a 'low-born drinking companion of **GALERIUS**'[663]; that he probably lacked charisma is underscored by the rapid desertion of his troops when he tried to dislodge **MAXENTIUS** in spring 307. He is the only Tetrarch who was not related (as far as we know) to any of the others. He was born in Illyricum (where else?) probably around 260 and rose rapidly in the army, being a senior commander before he was chosen as Caesar by **GALERIUS,** taking office on 1st March 305.[664] His promotion to Augustus as a response to the acclamation in Britain of **CONSTANTINE** probably occurred in August 306. His full original name is not known, but as Emperor he was styled **Imperator Flavius Valerius Severus Pius Felix Augustus.**[665] He was granted the tribunician and proconsular powers as Caesar, and was consul in 307. He does not appear to have been pontifex maximus. We do not know the name of his wife, because she had died or been divorced prior to his accession, but they did have a son, [Flavius Valerius] Severianus, who survived him.[666] He later attached himself to **MAXIMIN DAIA** but was executed by **LICINIUS** after **MAXIMIN'S** fall. **SEVERUS** himself was taken prisoner by **MAXENTIUS** in spring 307 and was killed or forced to commit suicide at Rome, 16th September that year.

*

MAXIMINUS II DAIA
(Known to history as Maximin Daia)
1st May 310 – July/August 313

Described as a semi-barbarian of low birth, and originally called Daia, **MAXIMINUS II** was born 20th November 270 and seems originally to have been an infantryman, then a member of the *protectores* and later a tribune, prior to his coming to wider notice. He was appointed Caesar by his maternal uncle **GALERIUS** and in the process adopted the names **Galerius Valerius Maximinus Nobilissimus Caesar,** or **C. Valerius Galerius Maximinus** *signo* **Iovius.** He was also made *princeps iuventutis.* He was raised to the rank of augustus in the wake of the elevation of **LICINIUS**, again at the behest of **GALERIUS.** He was given the proconsular and tribunician power, made pontifex maximus and was consul in 307, 311 and 313.[667] He was given responsibility for the east, and as augustus kept it, with **LICINIUS** squeezed between him and **CONSTANTINE I** and **MAXENTIUS.** He also continued the persecution of the Christians initiated by **GALERIUS**, although with

---

663. Syme (1971) 212
664. ILS646
665. PLRE I Severus 30
666. PLRE I Severianus 1.
667. This last consulship appears to have been suffect.

reduced intensity. However, once the former had eliminated the latter, **LICINIUS** was emboldened to do likewise with **MAXIMIN,** defeating and killing him (and, presumably his children) in summer 313.[668]

He was married with a son born in 305 and a daughter born the previous year. As his wife was never recognised as Augusta (which is presumably why her name is lost to us) she may have died relatively young, perhaps in childbirth.

*

LICINIUS
11th November 308 – 324

Background

LICINIUS was from Dacia Ripensis and of peasant stock. He was born c. 265 and made his career in the army, serving with **GALERIUS**, with whom he had shared a tent on campaign and to whom in the long run he owed his position as Augustus. He had fought against the Persians in 296-297 as **GALERIUS'S** second in command. He was sent as a legate or envoy to **MAXENTIUS** at Rome in the wake of the demise of **SEVERUS,** but was never called upon to be a Caesar in the tetrarchic system, being hurriedly appointed emperor in the wake of the crisis conference at Carnuntum in 308.

Reign

His original name is lost to us – it might have been Licinius Licinianus, or similar, but with his elevation to the rank of augustus, he assumed the name and style **Imperator Caesar C. Valerius Licinianus Licinius Pius Felix Invictus Augustus**. He was therefore granted the tribunician and proconsular power, made pontifex maximus and was consul in 309, 312, 313, 315, 318 and 321 (in the east only).[669] He was also later styled **Sarmaticus Maximius** and **Germanicus Maximus**.[670] At first given sovereignty over the Balkan provinces only, in 313 he took inspiration from **CONSTANTINE'S** elimination of **MAXENTIUS** and moved against **MAXIMIN II** in the east, quickly overcoming him and executing him (and his children). From 313 for eleven years he and **CONSTANTINE** divided the empire east-west between them, and he had of course, married his colleague's sister in 313, by whom he had a son, Val[erius] Licinianus Licinius, born in summer 315 and often called **Licinius II**, although he was never augustus. The younger Licinius was consul at the tender age of four in 319 and again in 321 (latterly in the east only) and who was on 1ˢᵗ March 317 was declared Caesar along with **CONSTANTINE'S** sons Crispus and Constantinus (later **CONSTANTINE II**).[671]

---

668. PLRE I Maximinus 12
669. PLRE I Licinius 3
670. ILS678, 679.
671. ILS680, 712.

The era of co-operation between the two emperors was never particularly friendly or open, and in 315, **CONSTANTINE** provoked a breach by proposing his nephew Bassianus as Caesar in the west. **LICINIUS** refused, fearing that such a move might shut out his own son, with the result that poor Bassianus (see **Table XLIX Brief Lives**) was killed on the pretext of trying to forment revolt out of wounded *amour propre* in not becoming Caesar, and in 316 **CONSTANTINE** invaded the Balkans hoping to dispense with his colleague altogether. He carried all before him at the first encounter, leading **LICINIUS** to set up his commander **VALENS** as co-augustus in opposition to **CONSTANTINE**. A second battle, at Hadrianople (Edirne, European Turkey), in the wake of this was indecisive, and the two had to come to terms at Serdica (Sofia, Bulgaria) on 1st March 317 when the three under age Caesars were appointed and poor **VALENS**, who had served his purpose, was killed out of hand. One result was that **LICINIUS** became less inimical to the Christians. Yet he was still a pagan himself and a close friend of pagan philosophers and others within his sphere of influence, whilst his imperial colleague was actively promoting Christianity. Rightly suspicious of **CONSTANTINE'S** motives, he feared that Christians were acting as a fifth column inside the eastern polity and from c. 320, started purging them from his bureaucracy and army. He also suspected the bishops of disloyalty and began executing them. This led to another open breach with **CONSTANTINE**, who this time met his opponent at the second battle of Hadrianople, 3rd July 324, defeating him soundly.

LICINIUS fled to Asia, and appointed the commander of his guard, **MARTINIANUS** his co-emperor. **CONSTANTINE** came after him again, crossing the Bosphorus and inflicting a second defeat on him at Chrysopolis (Üsküdar, Turkey) 18th September 324. Within a week, **LICINIUS** and **MARTINIANUS** surrendered at discretion to **CONSTANTINE** at Nicomedia (Ismit, Turkey). He was spared, sent into exile at Thessalonica but killed anyway by the ever fickle **CONSTANTINE,** being hung in spring the following year. Later that year a similar fate befell **MARTINIANUS**. Young Licinius was also spared, but in typical Constantinian fashion was executed anyway in 326. An illegitimate son of **LICINIUS**, later legitimated, was also spared, but in 336 was reduced to servile status and sent to work in the women's quarters of an opulent residence at Carthage.[672]

*

---

672. PLRE Licinius 4. It was probably the safest place for the son of a fallen Augustus, with an eventual prospect of manumission.

VALENS III
c. 10th October 316 – 8th January 317

MARTINIANUS
July – September 324

This man, whose original name may well have been [**M.**] **Aurelius Valens**, was a senior army officer serving **LICINIUS** as *dux limitis* (border commander) in Dacia. He was appointed co-ruler with **LICINIUS** a few days after the battle of Cibalae on 8th October 316, taking the style **Imperator Caesar M. Aurelius Valerius Valens Pius Felix Augustus**. It was to him that fell the task of re-grouping **LICINIUS'S** army, to act as a decoy for his colleague to mount a second attack and whose generalship probably led to the welcome stalemate between the two antagonists. His reward, however, once the ensuing peace agreement had been made, was to be disposed of – permanently.[673] Whether this took place before the end of the year when the hostilities actually ceased, or on 1st March 317 when the treaty was actually signed, is not entirely clear. In either case, he lived long enough to issue coins. Nothing is known of any family.

Although neither **VALENS III** nor **MARTINIANUS** received recognition from the senate or in the west at all, least of all from **CONSTANTINE,** they do not really count as imperial claimants, having been raised up and dispensed with (albeit in a cavalier fashion) by a legitimate ruler in the person of **LICINIUS.** Before his elevation **MARTINIANUS** bore the entirely new office of chief minister, (*magister officiorum*) which was to became commonplace in the following years. His imperial style was **Imperator Caesar Martius Martinianus Pius Felix Augustus** although one issue of *follis* places an 'S' between C[aesar] and his name, thought by some to suggest 'Sextus'; it is more likely to have been a blundered die. He was appointed under virtually identical circumstances to **VALENS II**, following the defeat of **LICINIUS** at the second battle of Hadrianopolis 3rd July 324, and surrendered to **CONSTANTINE** after his defeat at Chrysopolis on 18th September.[674] He was exiled and later killed. Nothing is known of any family.

*

---

673. PLRE I Valens 13.
674. PLRE I Martinianus 2.

Constantinian dynasty
Constantinus I
Constantinus II
Constans I
Constantius II
Nepotianus
Julianus IV
Jovianus

Imperial Claimants
Magnentius
Decentius
Carausius II
Genseris
Vetranio
Silvanus

CONSTANTINUS I
(Known to history as Constantine the Great)
25th July 306 – 22nd May 337

Background

CONSTANTINE was born at Naissus (Niš, Serbia) 27th February 272, only three years after **CLAUDIUS II** had defeated the Goths there - which may explain his later desire to be acknowledged as one of that ruler's kinsmen - and followed his father into the army. As a keen young cavalry commander he served under **DIOCLETIAN** as a senior tribune in Asia and Palestine, later acting as a commander under **GALERIUS** against the Sarmatians.[675] In this early part of his career he probably married Minervina (by whom he had Crispus). After his elevation and later recognition by **GALERIUS**, he was obliged to divorce her and marry, in March 307, Fausta, by whom he had the future Emperors **CONSTANS I** and **CONSTANTIUS II**; his son **CONSTANTINE II** was born in the same year as **CONSTANTIUS**, so was probably illegitimate and the result of a liaison with a concubine. For the remainder of his family see **Table L.**

In the wake of the defection and disposal of the errant ex-tetrarch **MAXIMIANUS,** he decided to publicise his supposed descent from the family of **CLAUDIUS II,** which

---

675. PLRE I Constantinus 4.

later ages tended to treat as fact.[676] It may well be asked why he chose **CLAUDIUS** and not **AURELIANUS** or **PROBUS** from whom to forge a descent; the answer (apart from, perhaps, his birth in the city where the Goths received their come-uppance) may be that the two families did have some kind of connection and that **CONSTANTINE** merely chose to magnify and embroider it to bolster his own prestige at the expense of **MAXENTIUS,** against whom it was now imperative that he move. His embracing of Christianity as a result of a vision on the eve of the Battle of the Milvian Bridge was just another astute move, but one that might not be so ground-breaking as might at first sight be thought, for the name his younger half-sister, Anastasia (born between 293 and 306) has peculiarly Christian overtones. The thought occurs that she might have been a sibling of the full blood and that Helena's family may have had some Christian connections, if not the future discoverer of the True Cross herself. Either way, the Emperor's *in hoc signo vincit* moment was astutely timed and was followed through in the policy of the remainder of his reign from the Edict of Milan in 313 to his death-bed baptism.

Prior to his elevation he was **C. Flavius Valerius Constantinus**, although his *praenomen* changed, to both Marcus and Lucius.[677] After elevation (as augustus) he was recognised by the Tetrarchs as caesar as **Fl. Valerius Constantinus Nobilissimus Caesar**, but a year later this was modified on recognition as Augustus to **Imperator Caesar Divi Constantii f[ilius] Flavius Valerius Constantinus Pius Felix Invictus Augustus,** to which were added *pater patriae* and pontifex maximus, with the senate granting the usual annually renewable tribunician and proconsular powers. In 312 he added the *agnomen* Maximus and in 324 Victor in lieu of Invictus.[678]

Reign

On his recognition as Augustus he was saluted as **Germanicus Maximus**, this title being re-conferred thrice more in 308, 314 and 328, along with **Sarmaticus Maximus** (323 and 334) **Gothicus Maximus** (328, 332) and finally **Dacicus Maximus** in 336, these reflecting the incessant need to pacify the more volatile border regions of the empire. He was also made consul on recognition in 307, holding the consulship again in 312, 313, 315, 319, 320, 326 and 329 – eight times in all.

The first act following the ousting of **MAXENTIUS** was to agree the Edict of Milan with a reluctant **LICINIUS** in February 313, ending the persecution of Christians and putting the empire under the protection of God. He thereafter patronised churches and expended much time and effort attempting to bring unity to the fissiparous church through councils, inducements and diplomacy.

---

676. The HA gives **CLAUDIUS II** a sister Constantia & a third brother, Crispus whose daughter Claudia marries the Dardanian Eutropius, parents of **CONSTANTIUS I**: *V. Claud.* 13, 9; Eutropius and Zonaras make Claudia, the daughter of **CLAUDIUS II**: Eutropius 9, 22; Zonaras 12, 26f.
677. CL.VIII. 1781 (Marcus); *ibid.* 9042, 10064 (Caius) and ILS 690 (Lucius).
678. ILS699, 702.

With the defeat of **LICINIUS** and **MARTINIANUS,** the now sole emperor decided to establish a new imperial capital at Byzantium on the Bosphorus, in a sense the virtual pivot between Europe on one hand and Asia and Africa on the other. This would be called Constantinopolis (Constantinople, since 1923 Istanbul) and would be the seat of power, armed with a second senate and hence mirroring this and other institutions in the old capital. This made strategic sense, and also set the scene for the division of the Empire, later to become permanent. The new city was inaugurated with great ceremony in May 330.

CONSTANTINE completed the military and administrative reforms begun by **GALLIENUS** and refined by **DIOCLETIAN**, separating the military and civilian spheres completely. The title of praetorian prefect was henceforth applied to a civilian supremo with oversight of a group of Dioceses. Likewise the army, already divided between border troops (including the remnants of the old Imperial legions) and a mobile centrally based trouble-shooting force (along with the emperor's personal troops, replacing the praetorian guard, now finally abolished), were placed respectively under a Master of the Soldiers (infantry: *magister militum*) and a Master of Cavalry (*magister equitum*) both answering to the emperor and under whom came the *duces* (commanders). Nevertheless, he completely reversed the policy of **DIOCLETIAN** of excluding senators from office, re-opening to them administrative careers and employing them in the highest offices, also up-grading equestrian governor's rank (*praeses*) to consular status, to entice the senatorial aristocracy back into the mainstream administration of the Empire, a policy which his successors continued, although its effects were less apparent at first in the East.[679]

Meanwhile, the reach of hereditary trades was extended, even to the army, which was an unfortunate policy albeit designed to make up for the shortage of manpower caused by the wars of the later 3rd century and major outbreaks of plague. On the other hand a successful re-organisation of the currency was promulgated. The *aureus* was replaced by the *solidus* (although this may have happened as early as 301[680]). In 309 this was standardised at 72 *denarii* to the (Roman) pound, a rate which continued unchanged throughout the empire until the eleventh century. Nevertheless, the *denarius* had long ceased to exist as a coin and was reduced to a unit of account, with 4 and 25 being the value of the two base metal denominations, the latter being the *nummus* which was fixed as the maximum daily wage of a labourer in 301. The silver coin, briefly the *aurelianus,* was re-graded as the *argenteus* fixed at the same weight in silver as a first century *denarius* but actually worth 100 of them.

He also erected a barrage of ritual around his person, giving the emperor near sacred status and surrounding himself with a hierarchy of courtiers. Henceforth, suppliants were to prostrate themselves before his person (*proskynesis*), viewing himself as God's vice-ger-ent on earth. The evolution of this (which may have begun to some extent as early as the reign of **SEPTIMIUS SEVERUS**) was in part to raise the status of the monarch from the first among equals (*primus inter pares*) of **AUGUSTUS** to a remote and awesome figure

679. Arnheim (1972) *passim.*
680. Hartley *et al* (2006) 57.

making revolt or assassination all the more difficult and heinous. Hence his coin image moved from a 3rd century-style radiate crown, or laureate head, to the use of a diadem, occasionally a plain looking band around the head, but more often decorated with a double row of pearls and sometimes with plaques.

Despite this, he continued to encourage his subjects to come to him with petitions and appeals. **CONSTANTINE** was generous, but hot-tempered, which occasionally led to rash decisions, and he was especially impatient with the theological disputes amongst his Christian subjects, but he was also a reformer who laid the foundations (building upon those of **DIOCLETIAN**) that enabled the empire to renew and survive a further 1,100 years in the east and 150 years in the west, a considerable achievement when viewed in the context of the near melt-down of the third quarter of the previous century.

The Roman Empire never solved the problem of succession adequately. It began with the dynasty of Caesar and Augustus, and veered thereafter between the dynastic and military dictatorship, although even then, sons were usually designated as successors, even if few managed to succeed their fathers. **DIOCLETIAN**, like **AUGUSTUS**, left only a daughter and had to cobble together a dynasty on that basis, but ended appointing successors, allegedly on merit, to the exclusion of the nexus of alliances he had brought into being. In the end the hereditary principle asserted itself.

The Senate and the Patricians

The old definition of a patrician (*patricius*) as a member of a family descended from one of the original members of the Regal senate and entitled to certain privileges, or as a member of a family subsequently raised to that status by one of the dynasts or emperors, ceased to apply from the reign of **CONSTANTINE**, although its social cachet and importance must have been in steep decline from the later third century with the ending of the senate's leading role in running the Empire. Constantine opened up all official posts to senators' sons (which led to the virtual disappearance of the equestrian order), graded the enlarged senate into ranks, in ascending order *vir clarissimus* (as all senators from the 2nd century), *vir spectabilis* and *vir illustris* or *inlustris*. The very highest rank to which a person outside the Imperial family could aspire was the new rank of patrician, held only for life. One of the first **CONSTANTINE** ever created was his unfortunate cousin Julius Constantius, killed in 337 (see above **Table XLIX Brief Lives**).

Family

CONSTANTINE'S family were fairly young, and until his elimination in 326 as the result of what appears to have been a plot on the part of the Empress Fausta (mother of two of his half brothers), his eldest son Crispus was the obvious heir.[681] He is known to have had at least one child, although no names have survived and their fate is unknown. If they did survive early childhood the likelihood is that they would have been killed.at about the

---

681. PLRE I Crispus 4; he was consul in 318, 321 and 324.

same time as their father. Several half-siblings and nephews of the Emperor (see **Tables XLVIII & XLIX**) were appointed Caesars in a pallid reflection of the tetrarchic system: Bassianus (316, killed 316), Flavius Hannibalianus (*rex regorum*, 335, killed 337), Flavius Julius Dalmatius (335, killed 337), Flavius Claudius Constantinus (317, succeeded 337), Flavius Julius Contstantius (324, succeeded 337), and Fl. Julius Constans (333, succeeded 337). This was a clear recipe for the trouble that loomed as he breathed his last at his palace at Ankyrona (near Izmit, Turkey) 22nd May 337. After he was dead, he was deified by the senate, although it might seem anomalous that a man who died a Christian should be drafted into a pagan pantheon. A coin type was even issued with the late emperor's veiled head as a god and on the obverse and the deceased ruler galloping Heavenward in a quadriga and the hand of God emerging to gather him up. Talk about hedging one's bets.

On the emperor's death, there was an interregnum of almost four months, during which the Caesars Hannibalianus and Dalmatius, realising that they were being sidelined by the Emperor's surviving sons, were involved in a mutiny at Constantinople along with Julius Constantius, another cousin, ex-consul and patrician (but not actually a Caesar), but this was nipped in the bud by the late Emperor's last right hand man, the Praetorian Prefect Ablabius.[682] Julius Constantius, Hannabalianus and Dalmatius were all put to death along with other members of the family on 3rd September. Consequently **CONSTANTIUS II, CONSTANS I** and **CONSTANTINUS II** were jointly declared co-emperors on 9th September (see **Table L and Brief Lives**). The dynasty had just 23 years to run.

---

682. PLRE I. Ablabius 4. He was an upwardly mobile Cretan, who rose to the senate and a consulship in 331; daughter became Queen of Armenia and his grand-daughter was a sister-in-law of **THEODOSIUS I** (qv)

TABLE L: THE POSTERITY OF CONSTANTINE

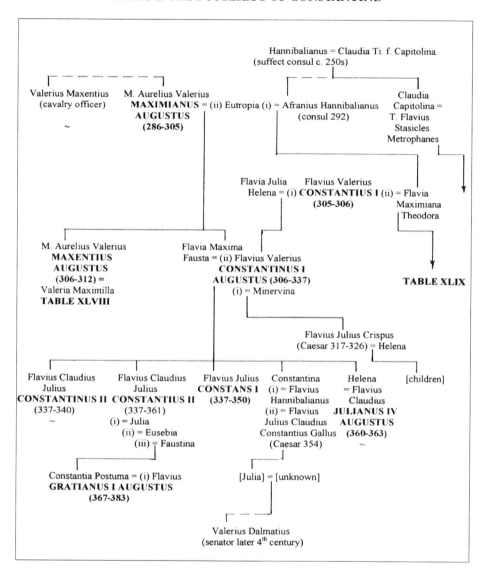

TABLE LI: JULIAN THE APOSTATE

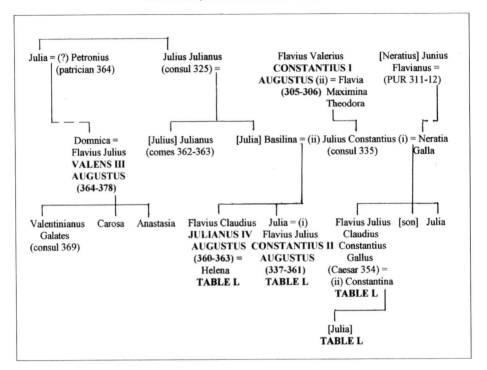

TABLES L & LI: BRIEF LIVES

Afranius Hannibalianus

Possibly from Asia, born c. 250 and probably the son or grandson of the suffect consul in the mid 3rd century (cf. below) He had served as an officer under **PROBUS** and in 286 was named Praetorian Prefect with Asclepiodotus, who later re-took Britain from *CARAUSIUS* in 296. It is assumed that he and Asclepiodotus were both adlected into the senate with the rank of praetor; they were made consuls for 292, and Hannibalianus was Prefect of the City (PUR) 297-298 and first husband of the Empress Eutropia. He may have had issue by another marriage, too. As their daughter (who was probably called Afrania originally before assuming a Tetrarchic name on her marriage) married in 293, she must have been born c. 275, leaving Hannibalianus plenty of opportunity to re-marry. The continuity of the *nomen*

might suggest that *SYAGRIUS* (see **Table LXVI**) could have been a descendant [ILS 8929; PLRE Hannibalianus 3, cf Settipani (2000) 379-380]

Claudia Ti. f. Capitolina

There is some uncertainty about the relationships of this family of Claudii. Capitolina's father was probably Ti. Claudius Marathonius (suffect consul in the earlier 3rd century), her mother a grand-daughter of [?Ti].Claudius Capitolinus, a praetor in the late 2nd century and himself probably son of Claudius Bassus Capitolinus, suffect consul in the third quarter of the 2nd century. Another Claudius Capitolinus, possibly a senator, from Philadelphia, Arabia in the late 1st or 2nd century, could have been a close relation. Capitolinus, consul in 274 might well have been this woman's brother [ILS 9258; PLRE I. Capitolinus 1].

Flavius Hannibalianus

See above **Table XLIX Brief Lives**

Flavius Julius Claudius Constantius Gallus

He was born in Etruria, 326; his life was spared by Ablabius in September 337 because he was very ill and not expected to survive. He was proclaimed Caesar 15th March 351, when he changed his name to Flavius Claudius Constantius, although he was always referred to as Gallus. He was subsequently degraded from his rank and executed in 354 aged 28. There is no direct evidence for wife and children, but a daughter is suggested above, and a second daughter, Anastasia (claimed as a forebear of the Emperor **ANASTASIUS I**) is sometimes alleged, see **Table LXVIII(a)** [ILS 737; PLRE I Constantius 4].

Flavius Julius Crispus

He is also referred to as Fl. Claudius Crispus and Fl. Valerius Crispus. He was born c. 305, educated in Gaul under Lactantius (a venerable rhetor, scholar and author) and married Helena in 322, by whom he had at least one child. Made Caesar at Serdica (Sofia, Bulgaria) 1st March 317 with his brother **CONSTANTINE (II)** and was consul in 318, 321 and 324. He was killed on his father's orders, probably at the instigation of his stepmother in February 326 [PLRE I Crispus 4].

T. Flavius Stasicles Metrophanes

PIR places this man, who came from Tralles (Aydin, Turkey), and his wife, a little earlier than suggested here, but as one son was called Capitolinus, the above arrangement would appear not unreasonable. Another son was T. Flavius Clitosthenes (suffect consul in the later 3rd century) and P. Aelius Sempronius Metrophanes (late 3rd century senator) was probably a grandson on the distaff side. Ther family descended from T. Flavius Clitosthenes Claudianus, a notable of Thera in the early 2nd century, whom Settipani suggests may have been descended from one Kleitosthenes who married Asclepias, daughter of Dorotheus, late in the first century BC [Settipani (2000) 380].

Hannibalianus

Also from Asia, as was his probable [grand]son; he was suffect consul in the 250s. His daughter is attested and from whom his wife's name is adduced. Settipani suggests that he may have been descended from P. Afranius Flavianus, suffect consul c. 110, an Ephesian [PIR² H14; Settipani (2000) 331-332].

Julia (daughter of Julius Constantius)

Settipani suggests she was married to [Vettius] Justus, governor of Picenum 352/361

Julius Consatantius

See above, **Table XLIX Brief Lives.**

Julius Julianus

He was originally of equestrian standing and had served as Prefect of Egypt by 314 and a praetorian prefect the year following, with the senator Petronius Annianus (see **Table XLV Brief Lives**). He was Praetorian prefect again under **LICINIUS** until 324, but was so much admired for his administrative competence that **CONSTANTINE** spared him and made him consul in 325 [PLRE I Julianus 35]

[Julius] Julianus

A Christian born c. 320, governor of Phrygia before 362, *Comes* of **JULIANUS IV** in the east 362-363 where he emulated his master and apostasised, dying in office shortly afterwards. His wife was also Christian [PLRE I Julianus 12]

[Neratius] Junius Flavianus

Prefect of the City 311-312 [PLRE I Flavianus 10, cf. Settipani (2000) 330]

Petronius

An army officer serving in an élite regiment in the east before 364, when he was made a patrician in order to lead a campaign against Persia. He was so cruel and avaricious, however, that he drove a number of senior people to support an imperial claimant, *PROCOPIUS* in 365 [PLRE I Petronius 3]

Valentinianus Galates

Born 18th January 366, probably in Galatia, and made consul aged three in 369. He died of natural causes in c. 370 [PLRE I Galates]

Valerius Dalmatius

A Pannonian who was governor of Lugdunensis Tertia (Gaul) and who may well have gone on to be praetorian Prefect, although the remainder of his career is not known to us. His name strongly suggests descent from the House of Constantine [PLRE I Dalmatius 8]

Valerius Maxentius

Served as a cavalry commander very late in the 3rd century; his name strongly suggests a link with the family of **MAXIMIANUS.**

⋆

CONSTANTINUS II
(Known to history as Constantine II)
9th September 337 – March 340

Background

Flavius Claudius CONSTANTINUS was born at Arelate (Arles, France) in February 317, probably to a concubine of **CONSTANTINE,** as his next brother **CONSTANTIUS II** was born six months later to the Empress. The use of the name Claudius in this generation of the family is an expression of the claim made on behalf of **CONSTANTINE** that he was descended from (or from the family of) the emperor **CLAUDIUS II.**

Reign

After the three brothers were proclaimed co-emperors on 9th September 337 (after some months of rule in the name of their father carried on by loyal ministers like Ablabius) **CONSTANTINE II** was allocated the revived Gallic Empire insofar as he given rule over Britain, Gaul and Spain. His brother **CONSTANS I** had the remainder of Europe and Africa as his area of competence, whilst **CONSTANTIUS II** ruled the East, although the eldest brother was notionally senior augustus with theoretical overlordship of the entire empire. From being declared Caesar at less than a month old in March 317 as **Flavius Claudius Constantinus Nobilissimus Caesar,** he took the style as Emperor of **Dominus Noster Flavius Claudius Constantinus Pius Felix Augustus,** and all three brothers were granted tribunician and proconsular power by the senates of Rome and Constantinople. He rapidly added **Alamanicus** to his style after pacifying the tribes on the Rhine frontier.[683]

---

683. ILS724

His first consulship was in 320, and he held the office again in 321, 324, 324, 329 and 339. He married before 335, but we know neither the name of his empress (who may therefore have died or been divorced before his accession) nor of any children.

It would seem that he was unable to exercise his authority over parts of the Empire beyond those in his immediate control and in order to assert himself over (or rid himself of) his brother **CONSTANS**, he invaded Italy in spring 340, but was killed in an ambush near Aquileia.

*

CONSTANS I
9th September 337 – 18th January 350

Background
Having fought off his elder brother's attempt at controlling his part of the empire, **CONSTANS** was able to enlarge his own with the addition of his sibling's remarkably short-lived Gallic empire. The empire was now once again, as from 313 to 324, divided between east and west. **Flavius Julius CONSTANS** was born to the Empress Fausta in 320, was educated at Constantinople and taught Latin by Arborius, the uncle of the eminent Gallic author and statesman, Ausonius. He was proclaimed Caesar on Christmas day 333 at Constantinople as **Flavius Julius Constans Nobilissimus Caesar**.[684]

Reign
On elevation to the purple with responsibility for southern Europe and Africa he was styled **Dominus Noster Flavius Julius Constans Pius Felix Augustus.** Like his brothers he received the usual powers which were probably not customarily renewed annually by this time. He took the additional style of **Sarmaticus** following a successful military campaign on the Danube in 338.[685] He was consul in 339 and 346. Having taken control of the whole of the west at the tender age of 20, he ruled without major upset, although was increasingly criticised for his immorality. He also suffered from arthritis despite having an overwhelming penchant for the chase. Playing on these supposed grievances, and whilst the eastern emperor's attention was diverted by a hard campaign against the Persians, in mid-January 350 **CONSTANS** was murdered in the palace as a result of a conspiracy organised by his army commander *MAGNENTIUS*, who promptly declared himself Augustus in his place. He had neither wife, nor children.

*

---

684. PLRE I Constans 3, where the possibility is expressed that his date of birth was actually 323, making him just 14 (rather than 17) when he acceded to power.
685. ILS724; campaign, Zonaras 13, 5. 28.

MAGNENTIUS
18th January 350 – 10th August 353

Background

Fl[avius] **Magnus** *MAGNENTIUS* was a professional soldier who rose high in imperial service. The sources are united in calling him a barbarian (and attributing to him in consequence, numerous negative attributes) but differ in whether he was the son of a German or a Briton. The latter might seem the more likely, however, and this tradition asserts that he was born at Ambianum (Amiens, Gaul) and that his mother was Frankish – hence perhaps the accusation that he was German. He was probably born in 303. His earliest soldiering was done as a member of an infantry regiment (probably one of the old legions) on the North West borders, but under **CONSTANTINE I** he advanced rapidly becoming a *protector* (officer in the Imperial guard). At the time of his becoming an imperial claimant he was *comes rei militaris* that is, imperial military advisor/commander with the *Ioviani* and *Herculani* (field army regiments constituted under the first Tetrarchs) under his command in Italy.[686]

Reign

On being proclaimed, he styled himself **Dominus Noster Magnus Magnentius Imperator Augustus Pius Felix**, although this changed twice, to the much more traditional **Imperator Caesar Magnus Magnentius Augustus** and then the more pretentious **Dominus Noster Magnentius Invicto Principi Victor et Triumfatus** [*sic*] **Semper Augustus**.[687] Whether he managed to obtain recognition by the senate at Rome is doubtful, or **CONSTANTIUS II** would surely have wreaked a terrible revenge upon its members, whereas it is claimed that this is precisely what *MAGNENTIUS* did after the failure of **NEPOTIANUS'** revolt. *MAGNENTIUS* at first hoped that he would obtain recognition from **CONSTANTIUS II** in the east, especially as the latter was hard pressed, and hence his adoption of the additional name of Flavius. In this he failed. Furthermore, he had a reputation for brutality, and his usurpation caused consternation in Rome, where the nephew of **CONSTANTINE I** declared himself an Imperial claimant that summer, but in the event lasted barely a month before one of *MAGNENTIUS'S* marshals suppressed him. He then appointed **Magnus** *DECENTIUS*, apparently his younger brother, Caesar, to hold the west whilst he moved against **CONSTANTIUS II**.[688] He served as consul in 351 (recognised only in the west) and again in 353, which was only recognised in the Gallic Empire area. In September 351

---

686. PLRE I Magnentius
687. ILS 743, 744 & 742.
688. PLRE I Decentius 3.

he fought an excessively bloody battle at Mursa (on the River Drava, Croatia) on the Danube, which was a Pyrrhic victory for the Eastern emperor, for the imperial claimant, although defeated, remained in the field with some of his forces intact. He retreated to Gaul and once again recreated a Gallic Empire, dormant since 340, and managed to hang onto it until the opening of the campaigning season of 353, when **CONSTANTIUS II** came after him again, defeating him near Lugdunum (Lyons). He committed suicide 10th August 353 to avoid being handed over to **CONSTANTIUS**. He left a widow, a young lady of impressive senatorial ancestry called Justina, who soon afterwards married the future emperor **VALENTINIAN I** (see **Table LIV** and **Brief Lives**).

*

DECENTIUS
?May - 18th August 353

Background

DECENTIUS was probably made Caesar in the wake of the revolt of *NEPOTIANUS*. His appointment was in order for *MAGNENTIUS* to have a reliable commander in his rear whilst he attempted to resist **CONSTANTIUS.** He was styled **Dominus Noster Flavius Decentius Nobilissimus Caesar**, the name Flavius again suggesting that his appointment preceded the refusal of **CONSTANTIUS** to countenance such impertinence.[689] He was consul (recognised only in the area of the former Gallic empire) with his brother in 353. He suffered a reverse against the Franks in his brother's absence and found Trier, to which he had fallen back, closed to him thanks to a *dux,* Poemenius changing his allegiance (and thought by some, on numismatic evidence to have become an imperial claimant, although this is highly unlikely).[690]

Reign

It is probable that, with the Eastern emperor advancing toward Gaul in spring 353, *DECENTIUS* was appointed co-ruler with his brother; had he declared himself augustus only after *MAGNENTIUS'S* death, it is unlikely we would have the one inscription styling him **Dominus Noster Magnus Decentius Caesar Pius Felix Semper Augustus** - the Flavius seems to have been dropped once recognition had eluded the two western rulers.[691] After the death of *MAGNENTIUS*, he escaped with some other units, no doubt aiming, as successor, to rescue the situation but soon realised his cause was hopeless and also took his own life near Agedin[c]um (Sens) eight days later.

*

---

689. ILS746
690. Ammianus 15, 6; Kent (1959) 105-108
691. ILS747

NEPOTIANUS
3rd – 30th June 350

Background

At Rome the assassination of **CONSTANS** and the acclamation of *MAGNENTIUS* went down very badly, and what appears to have been a clique of senatorial grandees thought that, with a grandson of **CONSTANTIUS I** amongst their number, there might be a chance of dislodging the usurper, or at least keeping him pinned down until **CONSTANTIUS II** could intervene. Their candidate was Flavius Julius Popillius *NEPOTIANUS* Constantinus, whose father Virius Nepotianus, consul in 336, had married **CONSTANTIUS'S** daughter Eutropia. He probably survived the counter-coup killings at Constantinople 3rd September 337 either because he was in Rome or due to his extreme youth, for he was probably born c. 328/333.

Reign

The self-appointed avenger of the House of Constantine entered Rome (having probably been acclaimed at his suburban villa) at the head of an armed force composed mainly of gladiators, and was recognised by the senate on 3rd June 350, thus legitimizing his rule. He cannot, despite his brief tenure of the purple, be regarded as an imperial claimant, having been recognized by the senate and having tried to stand up to a murderous usurper. The senate, to which he belonged by birth, the first such emperor since **GALLIENUS** almost a century before, no doubt accorded him the annually renewable proconsular and tribunician power. There appear to be no lapidary inscriptions to him surviving, but coin evidence provides him with two main imperial styles: **Fl[avius] Pop[illius] Nepotianus Augustus** and **Fl[aviu]s Nep[otianus] Constantinus Augustus**[692]; one shows him, most unusually for the time, bare headed, the other laureate. These suggest that he assumed the *agnomen* Constantinus subsequent to his elevation in order to bolster his claim to legitimacy. The lack of a depiction of a diadem or radiate crown along with the use of a contemporary prefix, like *dominus noster,* might also suggest that his senatorial sponsors saw themselves as asserting a long-departed influence and reverting to more traditional style of the principate. He also issued coins in the name of **CONSTANTIUS II** and in one account made his son **Popilius Nepotianus Nigrinianus** caesar. After attempting to resist, the Prefect of the City, Fabius Titianus, a supporter of *MAGNENTIUS*, fled, leaving the new ruler to establish his position. But *MAGNENTIUS* quickly dealt with the situation by sending a force to Rome under the command of his *magister officiorum*, Marcellinus. In the ensuing rather one-sided encounter on 30th June, the hapless augustus was killed, his head put on a lance and paraded around the city *pour encourager les autres*, no doubt. His mother, Eutropia, possibly a prime mover in the matter, was also killed the day afterwards, along with his son and other members of the Constantinian family in the capital along with a large number of other people involved, most of them senators.

---

692. PLRE I Nepotianus 5

Family

Current research supposes that the senator Q. Virius Egnatius Sulpicius Priscus, married a Fonteia, probably of the family of D. Fonteius Frontinianus L. Stertinius Rufinus, suffect consul in 162 or 163, and that their son, Q. Virius Font[eius] Nepotianus was **NEPOTIANUS'** immediate ancestor.

TABLE LII: THE CONNECTIONS OF NEPOTIANUS

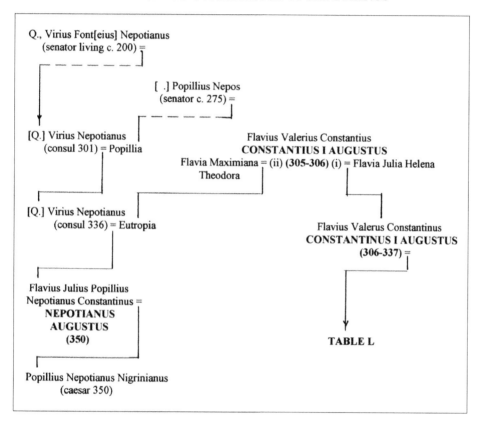

TABLE LII: BRIEF LIVES

Flavius Julius Poillius Nepotianus Constantinus
See above, **NEPOTIANUS AUGUSTUS**

Flavius Valerius Constantinus Augustus
See above, **CONSTANTINUS I AUGUSTUS**

Flavius Valerius Constantius Augustus
See above, **CONSTANTIUS I AUGUSTUS**

[.] Popillius Nepos
Senator living c. 275. We cannot be absolutely sure of this man's *floruit*; he could have been a contemporary of Nepotianus, in which case the latter's wife may have been his sister.

Q. Virius Font[eius] Nepotianus
Senator living in the reign of **SEPTIMIUS SEVERUS**. His ancestry goes back to N. Italian

Q. Virius Larcius Sulpicius [Priscus], praetor 180, probably brother of governor of Britain L. Virius Lupus (in 197). The former was father of Q. Virius Egnatius Sulpicius Priscus. The origins of the Sulpicii Prisci are unclear [PIR² F582]

[Q.] Virius Nepotianus
 Consul 301; thought to have been a direct descendant of Q. Virius Fonteius Nepotianus [PLRE I Nepotianus 6]

[Q.] Virius Nepotianus
Quite why the Imperial family singled this otherwise obscure senator out to marry a princess of their house is not known, although his appointment to a consulship in 336 was undoubtedly a consequence of the alliance. Presumably spared through being safely in Rome when so many members of the Imperial family were slaughtered on the death of **CONSTANTINE I** [PLRE I Nepotianus 7]

*

CONSTANTIUS II
9ᵗʰ September 337 – 3ʳᵈ November 361

Background
Flavius Julius CONSTANTIUS was born 7ᵗʰ August 317 in Illyricum, son of **CONSTANTINE I** and the Empress Fausta, proclaimed Caesar 8ᵗʰ November 324 and held the first of his consulships two years later aged nine. **CONSTANTIUS** was thrice married. In 335 he wed a daughter (whose name is not known) of Julius Constantius (see **Table XLIX Brief Lives**). She either died or was divorced by 353 when he married Eusebia. She was the daughter of Flavius Eusebius, consul in 347 and her two brothers, Flavius Eusebius junior and Flavius Hypatius, undoubtedly benefitted from her new station being also made consul together in 359 and appointed Patricians.[693] An Arian Christian, she died c. 360 and in the year of his death the Emperor married Faustina, by whom he had his only surviving child, the posthumously born Constantia.[694]

Reign
CONSTANTIUS II was elevated to the rank of Augustus on 9ᵗʰ September 337, when his style was **Imperator Caesar Flavius Julius Constantius Pius Felix Augustus.**[695] He also styled himself similarly but inserted **Divi Const[antini] f. Val[erius] Maximian[us] n[epos] Divi Claud[ii] pron[epos]** also adding **Sarmaticus** and **Persicus.**[696] He held the consulship in 326 aged nine, and thereafter in 335, 342, 346, 352, 353, 354, 356, 357 and 360. Once his sole reign had begun in 354 he assumed the venerable title of *pontifex maximus.*[697] The

---

693. PLRE I Eusebia; Eusebius 39 & 40; Hypatius 4. The family were from Thessalonica.
694. PLRE I Faustina & Constantia 2.
695. ILS732; PLRE I Constsantius 8.
696. ILS725.
697. FS1694.

first part of his reign was spent fighting the Persians on the eastern frontier, not always successfully. A century or so before, some of his military predicaments would have led to an immediate rash of imperial claimants, but it is to his credit and to the respect generated for the dynasty that this hardly happened. The one major exception was the acclamation of *VETRANIO* the *magister peditum* of **CONSTANS** in Illyricum in 350. This was dealt with, following the death of **CONSTANS,** by **CONSTANTIUS II**, and ended, most unusually, with the imperial claimant's abdication and pardon; no blood was shed, unlike the battle of Mursa a year later, the casualties of which were so severe as to leave the Roman army fatally weakened and henceforth increasingly dependent on barbarian mercenary units.

The overthrow of his brother **CONSTANS** was such as to incline **CONSTANTIUS** to appoint a new colleague and in 351 he made his cousin and brother-in-law **Flavius Claudius Constantius Gallus** Caesar, when he was known as **Flavius Claudius Constantius Nobilissimus Caesar** (see **Tables L & LI Brief Lives**). He was consul in three consecutive years, 352-354. This arrangement was sealed with Gallus's marriage to the emperor's sister Constantia but, thanks to his 'cruelty and violent disposition' he proved a broken reed and was degraded from office in 354, being subsequently executed.[698]

Having had to dispense with the dubious assistance of Gallus, it became clear to **CONSTANTIUS** that he still needed a co-emperor and, on 6th November 355, he appointed Gallus's pagan younger half-brother **Flavius Claudius JULIANUS** as Caesar (qv below).[699] This was probably in immediate response to the appearance of another imperial claimant, *SILVANUS* at Cologne (Colonia Agrippina) in Lower Germany on the Rhine frontier, earlier in 355. Both he and the shadowy imperial Claimant *CARAUSIUS II* in Britain were probably elevated by their troops in response to the destruction of *MAGNENTIUS* and *DECENTIUS* in 353 and **CONSTANTIUS'S** subsequent return to the east. **JULIANUS** was, in consequence, sent to the Rhine to sort matters out, which he did with considerable success, becoming popular as a result with both the army and the local élite. Needless to say, this led to **CONSTANTIUS** feeling threatened. His reply was to attempt to curb **JULIANUS'S** power which had the predictable result of him being acclaimed Augustus by his forces in 360. On his way to deal with his presumptuous kinsman, however, the emperor died on 3rd November 361, apparently of disease, leaving **JULIANUS** sole emperor.

---

698. Aurelius Victor 42, 9.
699. PLRE I Julianus 29

Imperial clamant under Constantius II

VETRANIO
1st March - ?November 350

VETRANIO was of peasant birth from Lower Moesia and apparently illiterate, despite having risen to high command as *magister peditum* in Illyria and had been *en post* for a considerable time; he was elderly when he was acclaimed at the very end of February 350, by the army at Sirmium (Sremska Mitrovica, Serbia). This was as a result of the news reaching them that **CONSTANS** had been deposed and killed by *MAGNENTIUS*. His imperial style (from coins) was **D[ominus] N[oster] Vetranio P[ius] F[elix] Aug[ustus]**, although on a single issue he is styled **nobilissimus Caesar** only, suggesting an attempt to style himself as the official caesar of **CONSTANTIUS II**. Subsequently, he negotiated unsuccessfully with *MAGNENTIUS* for recognition but, when the army of **CONSTANTIUS II** was near Serdica (Sofia), the latter appealed, as a son of **CONSTANTINE,** to the imperial claimant's army. *VETRANIO* thereupon cast off his diadem and opened negotiation to end the stand-off. This resulted in his being allowed to abdicate and retire honourably, the emperor realising that the old commander's acclamation had helped his own cause in tying up *MAGNENTIUS* whilst he disengaged himself from the east and moved to the Balkans. This probably occurred late in the year, perhaps November. After his abdication he retired to Prusa (Bursa, modern Turkey) and died in 357. Nothing is known of his full name or his family.

*

Imperial claimants under Constantius II

CARAUSIUS II
c. 354/358

CARAUSIUS II was only known from a single coin found at Richborough of a familiar *fel[ix] temp[orum] reparatio* ('return of happy times') type that could only date from the mid-350s, but the authenticity of which was long doubted.[700] The recent discovery of about twenty other examples, some from primary deposits, and all from Britain, suggests that this man and his possible successor have to be added to the list of imperial claimants. The likelihood is that he was acclaimed in Britain or Northern Gaul in the wake of the elimination of *DECENTIUS* and if so, probably before the incident of *SILVANUS* (qv). The coins read **Domino [Nostro] Carausio C[a]es[ar]** a unique way

---

700. *Numismatic Chronicle*, 3rd ser. vol. VII (1887) 191 and cf. H.V. Sutherland, *'Carausius II', 'Censeris', and the Barbarous* Fel. Temp. Reparatio *Overstrikes, ibid.* 4th ser. Vol. IV/V (1945).

of styling an imperial claimant, or even a recognised emperor for that matter. The lack of the epithet Augustus in inexplicable, although the use of Caesar suggests that he was appointed by an augustus as *DECENTIUS* had been by *MAGNENTIUS.* Could he have been made Caesar by the latter in his brief period ruling Gaul alone, or was he a true stand-alone imperial claimant? The name might suggest either a descendant, perhaps a grandson, of *CARAUSIUS I,* or a man wishing to identify himself with his namesake, itself suggesting that this was a very British imperial claimant who wished to go it alone, as had been the case in 286.

However, the reverse inscription would seem to run counter to this. It presents a familiar bronze type of **CONSTANTIUS II** coin with the Emperor holding a phoenix and *labarum* standard on the prow of a vessel, the rudder of which is held by Victory. The inscription, uniquely, reads: **domin/conta /no** suggesting a blundered attempt at **Domin[o Nostro] Con[s]tan[ti]o** which contrary to any successionist ideas, might betoken a claimant rebelling against other usurpers and proclaiming his support for **CONSTANTIUS II.** Several further coins again have the legend altered. He has been furnished with a wife, Oriuna and daughter Flavia, but these are very much in the HA mould and should be discarded; the claimant himself is still clouded with doubt.

GENCERIS
c. 358

GENCERIS is known from being named on a single variant of the coins noted above and is assumed to represent the name of a successor of *CARAUSIUS II,* assuming that either man actually existed. Neither are named in any other context, most notably in Ammianus Marcellinus. Their absence from his pages is the most telling argument (if by no means conclusive) against them. The most recent overview of the subject is by Casey who does not quite commit himself.[701]

*

---

701. Casey (1994) 165-167.

Imperial claimant under Constantius II

SILVANUS
11th August – 8th September 355

Following the suppression of *MAGNENTIUS*, **CONSTANTIUS II** returned east, leaving trusted lieutenants in charge of the more sensitive frontier areas. On the Rhine he left his *Magister Peditum* (Infantry general) *SILVANUS* who had earned his promotion through his desertion of *MAGNENTIUS* to the cause of the House of Constantine. Following an intrigue in his HQ at Milan, however, he was forced to assume the purple at Colonia Agrippina (Cologne) in August 355. Whether he obtained recognition from the senate at Rome (within his sphere of command) is not known but it seems unlikely, or reprisals against its members would have been recorded once order had been restored, and memories of the events of 350 were doubtless still raw there. As emperor, his style was **Dominus Noster Imperator Cl[a]udius Silvanus Augustus**.[702] The *nomen* Claudius may have been added on accession as a sop to the House of Constantine.

The imperial claimant was a Christian, the son of Bonitus, a Frank, the commander of the *Legio* VII Claudia in Moesia Prima under **CONSTANTINUS I,** who later promoted him to a senior post, probably a *dux*.[703] He was a senior tribune commanding an élite regiment when he defected to **CONSTANTIUS** in 351 prior to the Battle of Mursa. The following year he was made *magister peditum* in Gaul and later (it would appear from a decree addressed to him) was promoted to *magister militum*, a relatively new post combining the offices of *magister peditum* with that of *magister equitum*. He had responsibility for the West. Whilst the Emperor was staying at his base, Milan, *SILVANUS* was at Cologne dealing with the German frontier. His acclamation was provoked by a coterie of corrupt courtiers altering despatches and fermenting doubt in the Emperor's mind about his loyalty. The end of the revolt came about after 28 days through an emissary from the Emperor, Ursicinus, betraying the claimant's trust during negotiations, having him dragged from a church service and hacked to pieces. 'Such was the end,' wrote Ammianus Marcellinus, 'Of a commander of no small merit, who was driven by fear of the slanders in which a hostile clique had ensnared him in his absence, to adopt extreme measures in self-defence.'[704] His wife and young son were however saved, although we do not know their names, suggesting that the Emperor may have soon afterwards realised that the matter had been unjustly provoked by his own officials.[705]

---

702. ILS748, cf. ILS 1460 where he is merely Silvanus Augustus.
703. PLRE I Bonitus 1, cf. 2.
704. *Op. cit.,* 15.5.29
705. The 'young son' perhaps Silvanus, a *dux* and local governor in Africa in 393: PLRE I Silvanus 5.

The whole episode has been doubted by one recent commentator, on the grounds that *SILVANUS* issued no coins, but as the gates of the city containing the nearest mint, Trier, were closed against him, this would seem no bar to the authenticity of the matter. Furthermore he is named as Augustus in two inscriptions and alluded to in a third.[706]

*

JULIANUS IV
(Known to history as Julian the Apostate)
February 360 – 26th June 363

Background

By being sent by **CONSTANTIUS II** to Gaul, **JULIAN** was being dealt a very poor hand by his cousin. Much of the western currency had been demonetised by a decree, partly to remove memories of *MAGNENTIUS* and *DECENTIUS*, but also to prevent **JULIANUS** from getting enough cash together to make a donative to the troops on the German frontier with a view to making a claim on the purple. There had also been the usurpations of *CARAUSIUS II* (if we can accept the reality of it) and *SILVANUS*, which had left the troops demoralised (exacerbated by the lack of cash to pay them) and the border Germanic tribes eager to make mischief. **JULIAN** was a far superior general than his cousin (who had been slogging away at the Persians with very mixed success on and off since his accession) and soon reduced the Rhine and related borders to order, gaining much popularity in the process, which only went to increase **CONSTANTIUS'** distrust. As a result **JULIAN'S** remit and powers were reduced, with the result that early in 360 he was acclaimed emperor by his troops at Lutetia Parisiorum (Paris).

Flavius Claudius JULIAN has been born in May or June 332 to Julius Constantius and (Julia) Basilina, a noblewoman of unknown family, and an Arian (later orthodox) Christian who died not long after his birth. Her father is thought to have been Julius Julianus, consul in 325, who may well have been the uncle of **VALENS'** wife (see **Table LI**). He escaped being culled in the *putsch* of 3rd September 337 by his tender age. He had a lengthy education in rhetoric and philosophy which convinced him that he was a traditional pagan. He also wrote extensively. He was made caesar 6th November 355 and shortly afterwards was married to Helena, one of **CONSTANTIUS'S** sisters. His style thereafter became **Julianus Nobilissimus Caesar** and as such he was consul in 356, 357 and 360.

Reign

CONSTANTIUS II seems at first to have been prepared to recognise his junior colleague's acclamation but, after a considerable delay, he changed his mind and started out to supress him, very conveniently dying early on in the process at Mopsucrenae in Cilicia (Turkey)

---

706. CIL.X. 6946. On him see PLRE I Silvanus 2, also Aur. Victor 42, 16, Zonaras 13, 9 & Eutropius 10, 13.,

on the 3rd November of the year following. This had the advantage of leaving **JULIAN** as sole emperor and of preventing a great deal of bloodshed. The new sole emperor was styled **Dominus Noster Flavius Claudius Julianus Pius Felix Augustus.**[707] By 361 he had been hailed as *imperator* seven times. He re-instated the old Roman Pantheon, giving it the place it had enjoyed until 313 as the official state religion and deprived Christianity of its special status, taking the on the role and title of pontifex maximus. This earned him the epithet 'The Apostate' from Christian chroniclers. He was granted the tribunician and proconsular power by the senate, given the style *pater patriae* and, like all his predecessors prior to **CONSTANTINE** was adlected into all the priestly colleges not to mention being acknowledged as pontifex maximus.[708] He served a fourth consulship in 363. He also reformed the civil service and administration generally, saving money and enabling him selectively to reduce taxes. For his family connections, see **Table LI** and **Brief Lives**, above.

In March 363, he led a concentrated and well organised expedition to the east to force a final showdown with the Persians, bearing in mind that for twenty five years his predecessor had not really prevailed against them decisively. The Persians were accordingly defeated before Ctesiphon, their winter capital. The main Roman force then moved northwards to join up with reinforcements with the intention of making a final offensive and bring the matter to a conclusion, but became seriously bogged down by the terrain and adverse climate. Furthermore, whilst en route, the emperor was wounded, apparently in a skirmish. **JULIAN'S** wound became infected and he died, probably from septicaemia on 26th June. There were no children, nor surviving close kin, and the House of Constantine, except for the two year old daughter of **CONSTANTIUS II**, was at an end after 57 years. Nevertheless, a new dynasty was about to emerge, to re-inforce its claim through that very link.

∗

IOVIANUS
(Known to history as Jovian)
27th June 363 – 16th February 364

Background

The shock of the Emperor's death, deep in enemy territory, must have heartened the Persians and struck apprehension into the Roman staff officers. The next day, the aged Saturninius Secundus *signo* Salutius, praetorian prefect of the East, was offered but declined the purple, and the army instead chose **JOVIAN.** Nevertheless his election caused consider-able surprise, Ammianus Marcellinus suggesting that he was wrongly identified with the homonymous head of the Civil Service (*primicerius notariorum*), whose name also had been canvassed (and who was executed after his namesake's elevation for suspicious behaviour).

---

707. ILS753; PLRE I Julianus 29.
708. FS1676

JOVIAN was then *Primicerius Domesticorum* (commander of the household troops) having been promoted to that position by **JULIAN** prior to the campaign from a less senior position in the *domestici*.[709]

JOVIAN was born in 331 at Singidunum (Belgrade, Serbia) so maintaining the tradition of Balkan emperors. His father was Varronianus, who was a tribune of the *Joviani*, one of the new military units founded by **MAXIMIAN**, and after which the boy was named. The father had risen to become a distinguished *comes* of **CONSTANTIUS II** and it is said that it was thanks to his father's reputation that **JOVIAN** was singled out to replace **JULIAN**. Varronianus himself died in late summer 363 (see **Brief Lives**, below).[710]

Reign

The new Augustus took the style of **Dominus Noster Flavius Jovianus Victori ac Triumfatori Semper Augustus**.[711] He received recognition of the senate and therefore may safely be assumed to have been granted the tribunician and proconsular powers and despite being a Christian, he also became *pontifex maximus,* but reversed most but not all of **JULIAN'S** pro-pagan enactments. He began to introduce penalties against paganism, too, whilst maintaining a theoretical freedom of conscience.[712] He was ordinary consul with his young son, Flavius Varronianus for 364, and the latter was given the style *nobilissimus*, but not accorded the rank of caesar, probably out of regard for his tender years.

JOVIAN chose to make a disadvantageous peace with the Persians rather than risk continuing the campaign, which made him very unpopular, although he was only making the best of a tight corner into which **JULIAN'S** unexpected demise had landed them. That having been achieved, the army withdrew very slowly to Antioch before proceeding towards Constantinople. It was on this journey, that the Emperor died of carbon monoxide poisoning as a result of a brazier having been put into his tent for warmth and accidentally not being removed; surprisingly, none of the sources suggest that this was an assassination. The date was 16th February 364. His widow, who was probably called Charito, went into retirement with her two sons, and she and one son appear to have been still alive in 380.

---

709. PLRE I Jovianus 3.
710. PLRE I Varronianus 1
711. ILS757: 'Ever victorius and triumphant'.
712. FS p. 689.

TABLE LIII: THE FAMILY OF IOVIANUS

TABLE LIII: BRIEF LIVES

Candidus

Arian bishop in Lydia and a recorded relation of **IOVIANUS** [PLRE I Candidus 1]

Flavius Iovianus

See above **IOVIANUS AUGUSTUS**

Flavius [?Lucillianus]

The Emperor's younger son. It is not clear whether it was he or his brother who was recorded as living 'in fear of his and his mother's life' in 380.

Flavius Varronianus

Elder son of **IOVIANUS** with whom he was consul in 364, although very young. It is not clear whether it was he or his brother who was recorded as living 'in fear of his and his mother's life' in 380, although another source claims **VALENTINIANUS** had his eyes put out to be on the safe side. [PLRE I Varronianus 2]

Ianuarius

Like Candidus, an *adfinis* (close relation) of **IOVIANUS,** from his career, possibly a first cousin rather than an uncle. He was probably made *magister militum* (or *comes rei militaris*) in Illyricum by the emperor, and was proposed as a replacement for him in 364, as was his successor *en post*, Flavius Equitius [PLRE I Ianuarius 5].

Lucillianus

Made *comes rei militaris* (Imperial advisor on military matters) in the east under **CONSTANTIUS II** in 350 to keep the Persian campaign going whilst the emperor went to deal with *MAGNENTIUS*, defending Nisibis (Nusaybin, Turkey) against Persian counter-attacks. Gallus made him *comes domesticorum* (chief guard commander) in 354 and he was later sent on an embassy to Persia 358-59. **CONSTANTIUS II** appointed him *magister militum* in Illyria in 360, where he was captured by **JULIAN**, after which he retired to Sirmium (Sremska Mitrovika, Serbia) before being appointed *magister equitum et peditum* (effectively his old position) by **JOVIAN** to take command in the west, but was killed in 364 at Rheims (Durocortorum) in a mutiny. He was probably from Pannonia, like his son-in-law [PLRE I Lucilianus 3]

Varronianus

A native of Singidunum in Pannonia (Belgrade, Serbia), he was tribune of a unit originally raised by **MAXIMIAN**, but was appointed by **CONSTANTIUS II** as *comes domesticorum* in which post he was very highly regarded. He died shortly after his son's elevation to the purple [PLRE I Varronianus 1]

Further reading:

Alföldi, A., *The Conversion of Constantine and Pagan Rome* Trans. Mattingly, H. (Oxford 1948).

Hartley, E., Hawkes, J., Henig, M. & Mee, F., *Constantine the Great, York's Roman Emperor*, York Museum Exhibition Catalogue, (York, 2006).

Murdoch, A., The Last Pagan: *Julian the Apostate and the Death of the Ancient World* (Stroud 2003)

Pohlsander, H. A., *The Emperor Constantine* (London 1996).

*

THE HOUSE OF VALENTINIAN &
THEODOSIUS THE GREAT

The Imperial Succession
Valentinianus I
Valens IV
Gratianus I
Valentinianus II
Magnus Maximus III
Victor
Theodosius I

Imperial Claimants
Valentinus
Firmus
Procopius
Marcellus I
Eugenius II

VALENTINIANUS I
(Known to history as Valentinian I)
26th February 364 – 17th November 375

Background

There was a ten day interregnum after the unexpected death of **JOVIAN** – after all, had he been done away with, a conspirator would have been proclaimed immediately. The generals and courtiers met to decide on a successor. Their choice, after much deliberation, fell on a former *comes* of **JULIAN** whom the emperor had later banished, but who had been recalled by **JOVIAN** and appointed a senior commander in Galatia. Having been summoned to the conclave and having accepted, **VALENTINIAN** took a month before astounding the army high command by selecting his portly, sluggish and illiterate younger brother **VALENS** as his co-ruler.

The new emperors were the sons of Gratianus, a giant of a man of humble origin from Cibilae in Pannonia (Vincovci, Croatia), who had risen through the ranks to become a senior commander (*comes rei militaris*) in Britain under **CONSTANS. VALENTINIAN** himself was born in 321 and seems to have served with his father before being appointed to a tribunate in Gaul in 357, after which **CONSTANTIUS II** promoted him and posted him to Mesopotamia c. 360 before **JULIAN** made him a *comes* although, after his recall, he reverted to the rank of tribune. He was married to Marina Severa at the time of his elevation and father of a son. After he had become emperor he re-married Justina, the widow of the imperial claimant *MAGNENTIUS*, by whom he had another son and three daughters (see below **Table LIV** and **Brief Lives**).

Reign

The new emperor took the style **Imperator Caesar Dominus Noster Flavius Valentinianus Pius Felix Maximus Victor ac Triumfatori Semper Augustus** and this was acknowledged by the senates at Rome and Constantinople, which granted both emperors tribunician and proconsular powers.[713] Although an orthodox Christian, he also took the office of pontifex maximus. He held a modest four consulships, in 365, 368, 370 and 373, all jointly with his brother. A few months after his accession, the two brothers split the empire between them along the same lines as had **VALERIAN** in 253, **DIOCLETIAN** in 286, and **CONSTANTIUS II** in 340, **VALENTINIAN** taking the West and his uncouth brother the East.

He spent almost all of the reign campaigning and, in having to pay for the increased military requirements, began squeezing the civilian population remorselessly, also launching a series of treason trials against the plutocratic but largely impotent western senators – the old aristocracy – not because (as he alleged) that they were using pagan magic and soothsayers to hatch plots against him, but because he needed to sequestrate their estates in order to raise cash to pay the army. This showed the way that the imperial administration had begun the move to rehabilitate the senatorial class under the House of Constantine but then, after 363, all this went into reverse as a military clique took over and governed much more pragmatically and to some extent reactively. Where a smattering of members of recently ennobled families could have expected high bureaucratic and military appointments before, now most such positions went to Pannonians/Illyrians, rather as they had in the post-**GALLIENUS** period.

Consequently, **VALENTINIAN** fought a whole series of campaigns on the Rhine, mainly with considerable success, securing the frontier for a generation, making treaties, launching punitive expeditions, strengthening forts, garrisons and cities. During this period he was also forced to deal with a serious crisis in Britain caused by barbarians running amok in 367 and then by an imperial clamant, *VALENTINUS*, all sorted out by his able *comes*, Theodosius, who later went on to solve a series of revolts in North Africa too, provoked by flagrant corruption in the administration and which culminated in the acclamation of yet another imperial claimant, *FIRMUS*. These events, though, led the Emperor to add to his formal style **Germanicus, Alemannicus, Francicus** and **Gothicus** all suffixed by **Maximus.** The latter is a reminder that, having settled the Rhine, **VALENTINIAN** then turned his attention to the Danube, where he was obliged to fight more campaigns than he needed to because of his lack of diplomatic skills and quick temper. Indeed, a manifestation of the latter before a stubborn delegation of Sarmatians caused a stroke which

---

713. ILS760, 771.

killed him on 17[714] November 375.[714] His eight-year-old son by his first wife, **GRATIAN,** had been proclaimed co-ruler with him on 24th August 367 and at 16, succeeded him as sole (Western) emperor.

VALENS IV
28th March 364 – 9th August 378

Background

Whilst his brother hardly sent Roman biographers into ecstasies over his character, abilities and habits, **Flavius VALENS** was universally regarded as the inferior man, in looks, capability, deportment and disposition. He was born the younger son of Gratianus c. 328 and enjoyed a fairly torpid military career before, in the early 360s, he was appointed a middle ranking officer in the Imperial guard (*protector domesticus*). On his acclamation, **VALENTINIAN** made him *tribunus stabuli,* a military court appointment with oversight of the procurement of mounts and draught horses for the army everywhere. He was plucked from these none-too-heavy responsibilities on 28th March 364 by his brother and made co-ruler, later with responsibility for the eastern half of the Empire. On his accession he was already married to Domnica, and by her he became father to Valentinianus Galates, Carosa and Anastasia.

Reign

VALENS seems to have been recognised, along with his brother, in all the usual powers of the emperor and also seems to have been acknowledged as pontifex maximus.[715] His style was **Imperator Caesar Dominus Noster Flavius Valens Semper Augustus** although he later added **Victoria ac Triumfator** like his brother, placed before 'Semper'.[716] He also held six consulships, in 365, 368, 370 and 373 (all jointly with his brother) and in 376 and 378 as well. He was, however, unswervingly loyal to his brother, which contributed much to internal stability. The beginning of his reign was, however, marred by the emergence of *PROCOPIUS,* an Imperial claimant with tries of kinship to the House of Constantine, at his capital, Constantinople, which he had just left to deal with a breakdown in **JOVIAN'S** peace treaty with the Persians. This diverted the Emperor until the following spring, but as a consequence of their support of *PROCOPIUS,* there was now a problem of an influx of Goths, which took until 369 to sort out, resulting in a treaty following a ruinous defeat of the barbarians.

Thereafter **VALENS** was able to re-apply himself to the problems of the east, which had been exacerbated by Shapur II, the Persian King, taking advantage of the problems

---

714. PLRE I Valentinianus 7
715. FS1715; PLRE I Valens 8.
716. ILS760

caused by *PROCOPIUS* to seize control over Armenia, then under the rule of a Roman client king, Arsaces III, formerly married to Olympias, daughter of **CONSTANTINE'S** Praetorian Prefect, Ablabius. This made him a first cousin by marriage of the future emperor **THEODOSIUS I** and a kinsman of the imperial claimant *FIRMUS,* demonstrating the empire-wide reach of the new aristocracy created by the reforms of **CONSTANTINE.** The only other potential claimant with whom **VALENS** had to deal was a senior civil servant called Theodorus who had the misfortune to be told by an oracle that he would succeed **VALENS,** which led to the young man's execution for treason. He never had any pretensions to become an imperial claimant however.[717]

Although Shapur was roundly defeated, the problem of Armenia continued to simmer in the background, keeping the Emperor in the area, whilst he sent a *comes*, Lupicinus, to deal with problems amongst the Goths on the Danube, seriously exacerbated by the westward surge of the Huns from the Steppes, which spooked the former into seeking to re-locate across the river. Aided by the *dux* of Moesia, Maximus (probably to be identified with the future emperor **MAGNUS MAXIMUS**), the transfer was so appallingly mishandled that the Goths rebelled and **VALENS** was obliged to rush back to the Balkans to deal with it. His brother had also just died, but the latter's successor, the pious and rather unwarlike **GRATIAN,** scored a substantial victory on the Rhine, and diverted some troops to aid his uncle. Unfortunately, before they could link up, **VALENS**, very poorly advised, got himself into a position where conflict was inevitable and, in the ensuing (second) Battle of Hadrianople (Edirne, European Turkey), the under-strength Roman force was completely annihilated by a hugely superior horde of Goths. The Emperor himself was killed. The date was 9th August 378 and the defeat was regarded as the most catastrophic Roman defeat since Cannae in 216BC. Furthermore, it utterly emasculated the Roman army in the eastern part of the Empire.

---

717. PLRE I Theodorus 13. This incident took place in 371/372.

TABLE LIV(a): THE HOUSE OF VALENTINIAN

TABLE LXII

TABLE LIV(a): BRIEF LIVES

Anicius Olybrius

See below **OLYBRIUS AUGUSTUS**

Constans

He was C-in-C Thrace 412 and still in office when made consul (for the East) in 414 with the future **CONSTANTIUS III**; their names and the

fact that they served their consulships together strongly suggest kinship

Flavius Aëtius

See below **Table LIX(a) Brief Lives**.

Flavius Bassus [*signo*] Herculanus

He was chosen for husband of the fiercely ambitious Princess Justa because of his good character and rewarded with a consulship for 452 [PLRE II Herculanus 2]

Flavius Constantius

See below, **CONSTANTIUS III AUGUSTUS**

Flavius Gratianus

See below, **GRATIANUS I AUGUSTUS**

Flavius Julius Connstantius

See above **CONSTANTIUS II AUGUSTUS**

Flavius Magnus Magnentius

See above *MAGNENTIUS AUGUSTUS*

Flavius Placidius Valentinianus

See below **VALENTINIANUS III AUGUSTUS**

Flavius Theodosius

See below, **THEODOSIUS I AUGUSTUS**

Flavius Valens

See below, **VALENS III AUGUSTUS**

Flavius Valentinianus

See above **VALENTINIANUS I AUGUSTUS**

Flavius Valentinianus

See below **VALENTINIANUS II AUGUSTUS**

[Flavius] Valentinianus Galates

Child consul in 369, died 370, see above **TABLE LI Brief Lives.**

Gaudentius

Born 440, of senatorial rank in 454 when to be betrothed to the emperor's daughter. Carried off to Carthage by King Gaiseric in 455 and not heard of after c. 460 [PLRE II Gaudentius 7]

Grata

Unmarried in 375; still living in 392 [PLRE I Grata]

Gratianus

Born in Cibalae, Pannonia (Vincovci, Croatia) probably c 295, he became a professional soldier, rising to become an imperial *comes rei militaris* and commander of a force which saw combat in Africa and then in Britain in the 340s. He was retired to his native city when he entertained *MAGNENTIUS* there in 351. He died between 364 and 367 and a statue was erected in his honour at Constantinople [PLRE I Gratianus 1; Birley (1981) 331-332]

Hunericus

Son and heir of Gaisericus, Vandal King in Africa, whom he succeeded in 477 and died 484. He had no surviving male issue by his first wife, a daughter of King Theodoricus of Italy, but by Eudocia whom he married in 442 had two sons, cf. Hildericus, **TABLE LIX(a).** Succeeded by his nephew Gunthamundus [PLRE I Hunericus; Conant (2012) 23].

Justa

Unmarried in 375 and probably still living in 392 [PLRE I Justa 1]

Justina

Suggested by Settipani as daughter of [Vettius] Justus and, possibly Julia, daughter of Julius Constantius, consul 335, see **Table L** [Settipani (2000) 330].

Magnus Decentius

See above, *DECENTIUS AUGUSTUS*

Palladius

Appointed Caesar by **PETRONIUS MAXIMUS** and probably killed with him later that year [PLRE II Palladius 10]

Petronius

An infantry commander prior to 364, and then promoted and made a patrician. He was sent to the east by **VALENS** in 364, but was much hated for his cruelty and greed, thus partly contributing to the support for *PROCOPIUS*. Not heard of after 365 [PLRE I Petronius 3]

Petronius Maximus

See below, **TABLES XLV & LXII MAXIMUS V AUGUSTUS**

Theodosius

Born in 414, died an infant in 415 and buried in a silver coffin near Barcino (Barcelona) [PLRE II Theodosius 5]

*

TABLE LIV(b): THE EMPRESS JUSTINA

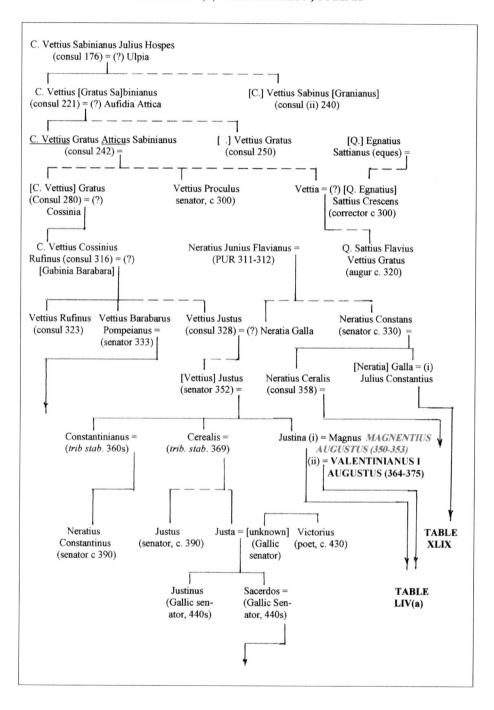

TABLE LIV(b): BRIEF LIVES

Cerealis

He seems to have succeeded his brother Constantinianus in the important court appointment of *triunus stabuli* in 369 and as such played an important part in the acclamation of **VALENTINIAN II** in 375 [PLRE I Ceralis 1].

Constantinianus

He succeeded his brother-in-law, **VALENS** in the position of *tribunus stabuli* in 364 and served until killed in Gaul in 369 [PLRE I Constantinianus 1].

[Q.] Egnatius Sattianus

An equestrian from Beneventum.

[Q. Egnatius] Sattius Crescens

A senator and *curator rei publicae* (public guardian, appointed on an occasional basis to sort out the finances and governance or any city of province) of Lucania and Bruttium, SE Italy c 290/300 [PLRE I Crescens 4].

Flavius Magnus Magnentius

See above *MAGNENTIUS AUGUSTUS*

Flavius Valentinianus

See above **VALENTINIANUS AUGUSTUS**

Justa

An attested but anonymous daughter, assumed to have married an unknown husband, but whose father in law was called Nicetus. Her husband was Victorius' brother and she was the mother of two sons, the name of one of whom suggests her relationship to Cerealis. A shift of such families towards Gaul (in this case marriage to a senator with estates in Gaul – Aquitania) was partly due to the diminishing importance of Rome and partly because the Imperial capital had long since

moved north to Mediolanum (Milan) and then to Ravenna (qv)

Justinus

Gallic senator, 440s and heir with his brother of their uncle Victorius [PLRE II Justinus 2]

Justus

Senator, c. 390, of noble birth and a pagan who was *vicarius* of the Diocese of Africa [PLRE I Justus2]

[Neratia] Galla

See above, **Table XLIX.**

Neratius Cerealis

Born about 295, he rose to be prefect of the corn supply in 328. He escaped the rule of *MAGNENTIUS* by being with the emperor in the Balkans, but was made Prefect of the City as soon as the claimant had been dislodged, in 352; he was consul in 358. He was father of the senator Neratius Scopius and was half brother of Vulcacius Rufinus, consul in 347. He was still alive c. 380 [PLRE I Cerealis 2].

Neratius Constans

The name of this senator of c. 330 is not securely known, although that he was a Neratius is not in doubt.

Neratius Constantinus

Senator c 390 he was patron of Saepinum (Altilla) in Italy, from whence the Neratii originally came [PLRE I Constantinus 10].

[Neratius] Junius Flavianus

The family descended out of Saepinum, the first known from there being an equestrian of late republican date called C. Neratius Sex. f. and the first known senator being T. Neratius Pansa, from the reign of **CLAUDIUS I,** from whom this man is thought to have been descended, although there are two gaps in the family tree which cannot be filled on present knowledge. The family were created patricians in 74. He was Prefect of the City from 311 to 312 [PLRE I Flavianus 10]

Sacerdos

Gallic senator, 440s, living with his brother (and co-heir of their uncle Victorius) on their estates in Aquitania [PLRE II Sacerdos]

Q. Sattius Flavius Vettius Gratus

He was not only an Augur (a very prestigious religious position for a senator) but *corrector* (junior governor) of Lucania and Bruttium in SE Italy. c. 320 [FS2982; PLRE I Gratus 3]

C. Vettius Cossinius Rufinus

Known as a member of a patrician family (of the traditional, albeit created, variety) through having been a *salius Palatinus*. He had a full career, probably amongst the first senators able to resume anything such since the reforms of **CONSTANTINE**, culminating in the Prefecture of the City in 315 followed the consulship in 316. He was patron of Atina, in Italy, from whence the family may have originally come [PLRE I Rufinus 15].

[.] Vettius Gratus

Consul 250 [PIR¹ V328]

[C. Vettius] Gratus

Ordinary consul 280 and probably married to a daughter of Cossinius Rufinus [PLRE I Gratus 1]

C. Vettius C. f. Volt. Gratus Atticus Sabinianus

Raised to the patriciate by **ALEXANDER SEVERUS**, before 225, and consul 242. From the nomenclature of his posterity, he either married a Naevia or a daughter of C. Asinius Lepidus Praetextatus, whose connections would seem to have reached back into the republican patriciate [ILS 6110; PIR¹ V322/329]

C. Vettius C. f. C. n. Volt. [Gratus Sa]binianus

Consul 221. His son's name probably derived from a marriage with a daughter of the senator Aufidius Atticus. Settipani suggests an intervening generation, via C. Vettius Gratus Sabinianus, quaestor in c. 194. He also suggests that this man's son, C. Vettius Gratus Atticus Sabinianus, a boy in 194, would be the brother of the consul of 221, whereas here it is accepted that they are one and the same [cf. FS3474; PIR¹ V331; SEttipani (2000) 333 n.1]

Vettius Justus

Consul 328. It is here proposed that he married a Neratia Galla, which would explain the fondness for Gallus/Galla amongst the long posterity of **VALENTINIAN I** [PLRE I Justus 4]

[Vettius] Justus

Senator and *consularis* (governor) from 352 of the Italian province of Picenum following *MAGNENTIUS'S* defeat and until 361 when he was executed by **CONSTANTIUS II** for letting on about a dream in which his daughter gave birth to the imperial purple. As it happens, she certainly *did* give birth to an emperor, so the story was probably made up in the aftermath! Settipani sets out a complex descent for these Vettii from the late first to the early sixth century. [PLRE I Justus 1; Settipani (2000) 335].

Vettius Proculus

Senator, c 300, who was given charge of the Empire's roads in Italy (*curator viarum*) [PLRE I Proculus 13]

Vettius Rufinus

Consul 323 [PLRE I Rufinus 24]

C. Vettius C. f. Volt. **Sabinianus** Julius Hospes

Suffect consul in 176 and a *Sodalis Titii*. It seems likely that he was born an equestrian Julius Hospes and adopted by a descendant of C. Vettius Sabinus Granianus, who had served as quaestor of Achaea in the reign of **TRAJAN**. If so, he was almost certainly a descendant of T. Vettius P. f. Serg. Sabinus, praetor in 59BC, whose father Publius was probably the *triumvir monetalis* who issued coins c. 97BC. The change of voting tribe from Sergia to Voltinia suggests that the adoption was a formal one, and not testamentary [Pflaum (1962) 115-116; Wiseman (1971) No. 482].

[C.] Vettius Sabinus [Granianus]

Served as suffect consul probably under **SEVERUS ALEXANDER,** Prefect of the City in the tumultuous year 238 and consul (ii) in 240. Described (but in HA) as 'from the Ulpian family' implying kinship to **TRAJAN** which on the face of it, seems unlikely and is not borne out by the names used by the family [PIR¹ V333].

Victorius

Gallic poet, c. 430 and uncle of Sacerdos and Justinus (qqv) and, by clear implication, brother of the unknown husband of Ceralis's daughter [PLRE II Victorius 3]

*

Imperial claimant under Valentinian I

VALENTINUS
368

Nothing is known of this man's background except that he was a Pannonian; the likelihood is that he was a senior officer of some sort, promoted by **JOVIAN** or one of his successors. The great late fourth century consul and letter-writer, Q. Aurelius Symmachus had a nephew and an uncle called Valentinus, but neither fit the description of this claimant, although a connection cannot be ruled out entirely, Pannoniasn origin or not.[718] He committed some serious offence and, instead of being executed, his brother-in-law Maximinus, then praetorian prefect, persuaded the Emperor to exile him to Britain where, with other exiles, he planned a rebellion. Quite how closely this was linked to the 367 barbarian rampage already alluded to is not known, but there certainly seems to have been a link. Maybe *VALENTINUS* was hoping to stir unrest and then triumphantly put it down seeking to benefit from the chaos or its aftermath. The rebels obtained the support of elements of the army in Britain, but it is not made clear if he was actually styled Augustus or not. It would seem very unlikely that any rising would have worked if he hadn't, and the whole affair was subsequently hushed up, so the information may have been lost as a result. There are no coins, however, so his time in the sun must have been short - probably under a month. After a relatively short period, he was captured with the other ringleaders by the comes Theodosius, and handed over to the C-in-C for the Diocese, the *dux Britanniarum* Dulcitius, for execution.[719] There is some suggestion that **MAGNUS MAXIMUS** served under Theodosius or Dulcitius in putting down this outbreak.[720]

TABLE LV : THE CONNECTIONS OF VALENTINUS

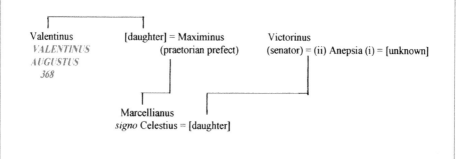

---

718. Cf. Settipani (2000) 412.
719. PLRE I Valentinus 5, cf. Zosimus iv. 12. 2.
720. Birley (1981) 337-338, 349.

TABLE LV: BRIEF LIVES

Anepsia

A Roman lady of senatorial rank, she agreed to her daughter's marriage in 370. She also sheltered Avienus (probably a relation of the famous contemporary man of letters, Q. Aurelius Symmachus) who was accused of adultery, an accusation she herself faced shortly afterwards, and was executed for it. Probably this was all part of **VALENTINIAN'S** drive to enrich the state at senatorial expense [PLRE I Anepsia].

Marcellianus *signo* Celestius

A man of senatorial rank and a military commander in the Balkans with the rank of *dux* c. 373. He was remembered for having invited the King of the Quadi to a banquet as an opportunity to murder him [PLRE I Marcellianus 2].

Maximinus

Born at Sopianae in Pannonia (Pécs, Hungary), he started out as a lawyer before governing two junior provinces, Corsica and Sardinia, which qualified him to enter the senate. He then governed Tuscia (Tuscany, Italy) before becoming prefect of the corn supply and in 370 *vicarius* of Rome (governor of the provincial area) and then praetorian prefect of the Gallic provinces for five years. He was subsequently executed by **GRATIAN** for unknown reasons, although he is said to have become brutal and arrogant in later life [PLRE I Maximinus 7]

Valentinus

See above, *VALENTINUS AUGUSTUS*

Victorinus

Apparently a senator who used his rank (of which we know nothing beyond his actual status) to get a number of senators, put on trial at the behest of **VALENTINIAN,** acquitted. He was a close friend of Maximinus [PLRE I Victorinus 5].

*

Imperial claimant under Valentinian I

FIRMUS
c. 372-375

The son and heir of Nubel, King of the Moorish people in Mauretania, *FIRMUS* was a thoroughly Romanised member of a large and influential local tribe. He fell out with the *comes* of Africa, Romanus, who was corrupt and consequently went to considerable lengths to deny *FIRMUS* a hearing at Court. In the end, the Moor's restraint collapsed and, with the backing of several allied peoples and two important military units, declared himself emperor late in 372 or early 373, being acknowledged in the surrounding provinces, too.[721]

---

721. PLRE I Firmus 3

He retained control well into 375, when the *comes* Theodosius, fresh from sorting out problems of a similar nature in Britain, arrived at the head of re-inforcements, refused to treat with him and after a series of sanguinary encounters, defeated him, following which *FIRMUS* committed suicide. He seems to have issued no coins, probably because his area of influence did not include a city with a mint. His family claimed descent from C. Julius Juba (or a sibling) son of C. Julius Ptolemaeus, King of Numidia 23-39 the son of C. Julius Juba II, King of Numidia and Mauretania 25BC-23 and his first wife, Cleopatra, daughter of Cleopatra VII of Egypt and **M. Antony**. Juba II himself was a descendant of the famous Numidian King Massinissa, d. 146BC.

TABLE LVI: THE FAMILY OF FIRMUS

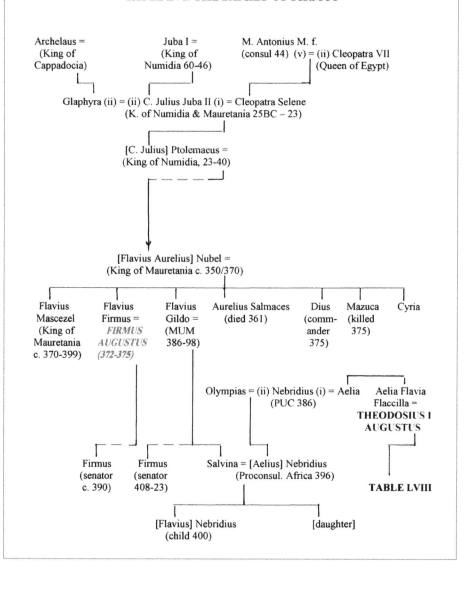

TABLE LVI: BRIEF LIVES

[Aelius] Nebridius

Proconsul. Africa 396 and presumably the son of his father's first marriage [PLRE I Nebridius 3]

M. Antonius M. f.

See above **TABLE I Brief Lives**

Archelaus Philopatus Ktistes

Archelaus surnamed Philopatus Ktistes was King of Cappadocia, a descendant of Mithridates VI King of Pontus, and was installed in 36BC by **M. Antonius** but deserted him at Actium and kept his throne. He died in 17 [PIR² G176].

Aurelius Salmaces

Born in 306, originally his name was rendered as Sammac; he owned a fortified *latifundus* (country house estate) called Petra, 'built in the manner of a city' in the family kingdom and used it as a base to assert his loyalty to Rome. He died in 361 at Altava (Lamoricière, Algeria) in Africa Caesariensis.

Cleopatra VII

Queen of Egypt, see **Table III Brief Lives**

Cyria

Supported her brother's revolt with her own money [PLRE I Cyria].

Dius

Commanded part of *FIRMUS'S* forces in the final encounter with Theodosius, 375 [PLRE I Dius].

Firmus

Senator c. 390 & thought to be the man so named on an amphitheatre seat at Carthage [PLRE I Firmus 3].

Firmus

Senator serving as a legate to the proconsul of Africa, Enno[d]ius, c. 408-423 [PLRE II Firmus 1]

[Flavius Aurelius] Nubel

Sub-king (*regulus*) of Mauretania c. 350/370, born in the land of the Jubuleni (hence perhaps his genealogical claims), and a Christian. The Flavius Nuvel (*sic*) who was a retired cavalry officer at this approximate period is considered to have been a separate person by PLRE and thus may have been a close relation, but Conant considers them to be one and the same, in which case Nubel/Nuvel was an *ex praepositus*, and son of Saturninus, *vir perfectissimus* and himself son of Florus [Conant (2012) 294-295; PLRE I Nubel, Saturninus 6].

Flavius Firmus

See above *FIRMUS AUGUSTUS*

Flavius Gildo

He fought for Theodosius against his siblings in the campaign to end the régime of *FIRMUS*, 373-375. His commander's son **THEODOSIUS I** appointed him a *comes* and later *magister utriusque militium* (supreme commander) in Africa in 386. In 397 he switched his allegiance to the Emperor of the East, **ARCADIUS** and cut off the corn supply to Rome, leading to his being declared a public enemy by the senate but was defeated by a force under his brother Mascezel, whose children he had had killed in the collapse of *FIRMUS'S* revolt [PLRE I Gildo]

Flavius Mascezel

King of Mauretania c. 370-399; appointed *dux* to crush his brother Gildo 397 [PLRE I Mascezel].

Juba I

Installed by **Pompey** as King of Numidia 60-46 but deposed by **Caesar**. He claimed descent from King Massinissa (d. 148).

C. Julius Juba II

He was also nephew of King Iempsal, grandson of King Gauda, himself grandson of Massinissa. As a child paraded in the triumph of Julius Caesar, and later brought up in his household and then that of **Octavianus** who, as **AUGUSTUS** installed him as King of Numidia & Mauretania in 25BC. He married Cleopatra Selene c. 23BC and had Ptolemaeus (qv) and a daughter who was probably called Drusilla. On Cleopatra's death he married Glaphyra who divorced him in 7BC to marry Archelaus, ethnarch in Judaea and the brother of her first husband, Alexander. He died in 23 [PIR² C1148, I65]

C. Julius Ptolemaeus

At first joint ruler with his father, he was King of Numidia 23-39, he was assassinated at the behest of **CALIGULA** at Rome in 40 [Barrett (1989) 116-118].

Mazuca

Fought alongside *FIRMUS*, but was mortally wounded and captured by Theodosius [PLRE I Mazuca]

Nebridius

His first wife, Settipani suggests could have been, with her sister the empress Flaccilla, a sister of Fl. Afranius Syagrius, consul in 382 (see **Table LXVI** below). Nebridius was prefect of the City (of Constantinople) 386 in which year he married Olympias, but died not long afterwards. [PLRE I Nebridius 2; Settipani 418]

Olympias

Daughter of Seleucus, a former *comes* and grand-daughter of Ablabius, who executed most of **CONSTANTIUS II's** cousins at Constantinople 3rd September 337. She is remembered as a friend of St. John Chrysostom [PLRE I Olympias 2]

Salvina

Held hostage by **THEODOSIUS I** in an attempt to keep her father in line and in the process was mar-ried to Nebridius, by whom she had a son and a daughter. She was widowed in 400 but still living in 404 [PLRE I Salvina]

Flavius Theodosius

See below**, THEODOSIUS I AUGUSTUS**

*

PROCOPIUS
28ᵗʰ September 365 – 27ᵗʰ May 366
MARCELLUS I
27ᵗʰ May – early June 366

The Emperor **JULIAN** is said to have acknowledged this imperial claimant as a kinsman and at some stage to have promised *PROCOPIUS* the succession, should he die without issue. Both matters are retailed by Ammianus Marcellinus, so there would seem no reason to doubt them, although the mechanics of this kinship are not exactly known; probably it was through through his mother.[722] He was born in Cilicia around 326 of noble family and brought up at Corycus (Kız Kalesi, Turkey). His wife was Artemisia, by whom he had a family, from whom descended the future Emperor **ANTHEMIUS**, although she was reduced to poverty in the wake of the usurpation of her husband. In 358, **CONSTANTIUS II** had appointed him *tribunus et notarius* (senior civil servant) and sent him on an embassy with **JOVIAN'S** father-in-law Lucillianus to Persia. Subsequently, he seems to have reached a high position in the service and **JULIAN,** presumably out of familial solidarity, made him *comes* and appointed him to command a military unit on the eastern frontier.

After the accession of **JOVIAN**, he voluntarily relinquished his claim on the succession and was given the task of organizing the funeral of his predecessor at Tarsus, after which he retired with his family to his estates. Unfortunately, **VALENTINIAN** and **VALENS** considered him a threat, so he fled to the Chersonese (Crimea). Eventually, he seems to have decided that as he was a marked man in any case, he might as well make a bid to fulfill **JULIAN'S** promise to him after all, and returned to Constantinople. Here, with the support some of the senate and two resting military units, he was proclaimed **Dominus Noster Procopius Pius Felix Augustus** on 28ᵗʰ September. The population supported him because he promised to relive the crushing taxation the new emperors had imposed to pay for the military campaigns of **JULIAN** and **JOVIAN** and his kinship with **the House of CONSTANTINE** was no doubt also a powerful spur for many. He was also backed by 3,000 Goths who were bound by treaty to the heirs of **CONSTANTINE**. Troops assembled by a worried **VALENS** in Asia also went over to him and the Eastern emperor seriously considered abdication. Although his resolve was stiffened by his *magister equitum* Lupicinus (the same who later bungled the transfer of the Goths across the Danube), *PROCOPIUS* made all the running militarily, until the non-arrival of Egyptian corn supplies that he had promised (without necessarily being able to deliver), which caused his support to slip, coupled with the necessary re-imposition of heavy taxation. **VALENS** also got the upper hand in a propaganda war, and by the spring managed to win two victories over his opponent, the second

---

722. PLRE I Procopius 4 quoting Amm. Marc. 23, 3.2 etc. (and repeated by other writers)

being achieved in the teeth of defeat through serious defections. The imperial claimant was captured and executed on 27TH May 366.

MARCELLUS, a cousin, whom *PROCOPIUS* had appointed protector, on hearing that the claimant was dead, had himself proclaimed in lieu. He was soon caught by the Emperor's forces and also killed, probably early in June. We do not know the details of the relationship between the two, however, and *MARCELLUS* had no time, it would seem, to issue any coins.[723]

*

TABLE LVII: PROCOPIUS & ANTHEMIUS

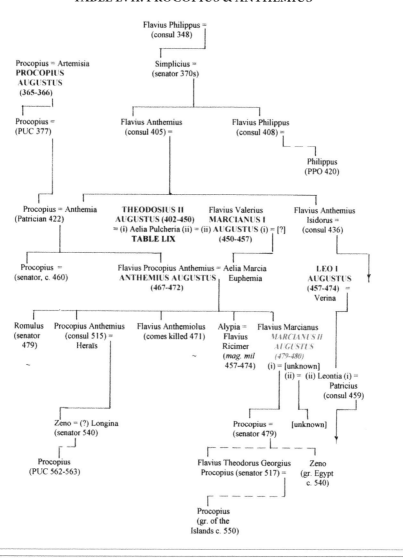

---

723. PLRE I Marcellus 5

Aelia Marcia Euphemia

Only daughter, married c. 453, styled Augusta 467-472 [PLRE II Euphemia 6].

Flavius Anthemiolus

Probably the eldest son, although if his mother was Euphemia, he would have been still just in his teens when sent to Gaul in command (as *dux* and *comes*) of an army to meet Euric, the Visigothic King at Arelate (Arles), in which action he was killed, August 471[PLRE II Anthemiolus].

Flavius Anthemius

Finance minister to **ARCADIUS** 400, *magister officiorum* (head of administration) in 404 and made praetorian prefect of the East 405-414, Eastern consul 405 and a Patrician by 406 [PLRE II Anthemius I].

Flavius Anthemius Isidorus

He was proconsul of Asia 405/410, prefect of the city (of Constantinople) 410, praetorian prefect of Illyricum 424, Eastern consul in 436 and father of Flavius Anthemius Isidorus Theophilus, himself governor of Arcadia in 434. The consul was dead c. 446/447 [PLRE II Isidorus 9; Theophilus 6]

Flavius Philippus

Mocked as the son of a sausage maker from Egypt, Philippus learnt shorthand and became a junior bureaucrat, rising to be praetorian prefect of the East in c. 344-351 and consul in 348. He was sent on an embassy to *MAGNENTIUS*, but ended up under house arrest with him, where he died in 351 [PLRE I Philippus 7].

Flavius Philippus

A magistrate before 388, he was prefect of the City of Rome c. 391, and western consul 408 [PLRE I Philippus 8 & *ibid*. II Philippus 9].

Flavius Procopius Anthemius

See below ANTHEMIUS AUGUSTUS

Flavius Ricimer

His father was a prince of the Suebi, his mother a member of the Visigothic Royal House, her father being the Visiogthic King Vallia and his uncle was Gundobadus, King of the Burgundians. He had served as an officer under Aëtius with the future emperor **MAJORIAN** before becoming a military *comes* in 456 being shortly afterwards appointed Western *magister militum* by **AVITUS** in 456, but was appointed in addition a *comes* and patrician by the Eastern Emperor during the interregnum following the fall of **AVITUS** in 459. Thereafter he became the sole effective power in the West once **MAJORIAN** had failed to defeat the Barbarians, deposing him as well as all his successors until his own death in 472. He was also consul in the West for 459 [PLRE II Philippus 7, Ricimer].

Flavius Theodorus Georgius Procopius

Governor of Lower Palestine (Palaestina Secunda) with the rank of *consularis* and a senator in 517/518. His parentage is not certain, but his name certainly suggests descent from this family [PLRE I Procopius 9].

Flavius Theodosius

See below, **THEODOSIUS II AUGUSTUS**

Flavius Valerius
MARCIANUS I AUGUSTUS

Leo
See below **LEO I AUGUSTUS**

Leontia

Younger sister of Ariadne. wife of the Emperor **ZENO**. Imprisoned with her husband on the failure of his revolt 480. All their children were daughters, but their names are not known. Her first marriage, to the caesar Patricius was annulled when her husband was overthrown in 471 [PLRE II Leontia 1].

Flavius Marcianus
See below *MARCIANUS II AUGUSTUS*

Julius Patricius
Son of Flavius Ardaburius Aspar, the powerful *magister utriusque militum* (MUM) in the East in the 430s, and eastern consul 459. In 470-471 **LEO I** made him caesar to keep his father loyal, hence his marriage to the Emperor's daughter . He was deposed when Aspar was murdered in 471, when he may have been killed too, although the best source claims he was spared [PLRE II Patricius 15].

Philippus
Praetorian Prefect in Illyricum 420-421; he is just a name, so although it is likely he may have been a son of the consul of 408, it is far from proven [PLRE II Philippus 2]

Procopius
See above, *PROCOPIUS AUGUSTUS*

Procopius
Possibly the Eastern senator who was a relative of **VALENS**. He was prefect of the City of Constantinople in 377 [PLRE I Procopius 5 cf. 7, 8 & 9]

Procopius
Known to be a descendant (presumably grandson) of the Imperial claimant, and thus probably the son of the foregoing. His wife is attested in a poem of Sidonius Apollinaris, and he was made either *dux* or military *comes* in the East, fighting the Persians, from whom he rescued the army. He was subsequently made a patrician and master of the soldiers in the east, continuing until 424 [PLRE II Procopius 2].

Procopius
Senator, c. 460 [PLRE II Procopius 4].

Procopius
A senator 479, it is not known if he was with his father in 484, after his third deposition and flight to the Isaurian fortress of Papirius (near Isnebol, Turkey). If he was, he was probably killed when it was captured in 488, but he could have remained in Constantinople or even have been sent with his father to Rome from Papirius. Nor is it known if he was married and had issue, but he was certainly old enough and it is here suggested that he did [PLRE II Procopius 5].

Procopius
Governor of the (Aegean) Islands c. 550 [JRS CII (2012)]

Procopius
Prefect of the City of Constantinople 562-563 when he interrogated suspects involved in an attempt to assassinate **JUSTINIAN I** [PLRE III Procopius 3]

Procopius Anthemius Ant[hemii] f.
In 479/80 took part in the revolt of his brother, the imperial claimant *MARCIANUS II,* but escaped to the Goths in the West and later to Rome, then in the hands of the barbarian King Odoacer . He returned to Constantinople under **ANASTASIUS I** and was made a patrician, later being appointed Eastern consul in 515 [PLRE II Anthemius 5/9].

Romulus

Took part in the proclamation of *MARCIANUS II* as a senator in 479-480, subsequently escaping to Rome [PLRE II Romulus 3]

Simplicius

A senator in 358 when he was exiled from court for consulting an oracle concerning the chances of becoming emperor. Restored in 364 as a person of great influence [PLRE I Simplicius 4]

Verina

Aelia Verina (the *nomen* may have been assumed after she became empress) was sister of *BASILISCUS* and had also a sister who was married to a man called Zuzus, later a rebel.

She married **LEO I** before he assumed the purple. She was styled Augusta and died during a siege of Papirius c. 484. [PLRE II Verina]

Zeno

A senator, he was betrothed to Longina, sister of the Emperor **ZENO**, but it is not clear if they got married or not in the end. **JUSTINIAN I** made him *praefectus augustalis* (governor of part of Egypt) but he was dead by 548 [PLRE II Zeno 3]

Zeno

Made Governor of. Egypt c. 540 but was defrauded at his death of his estates by **JUSTINIAN I** [PLRE III Zeno 1]

*

GRATIANUS I
(Known to history as Gratian)
24th August 367 – 25th August 383

Background

GRATIAN, who was named after his grandfather (see **Table LIV(a)** above), was born on 18th April 359 when his father was serving at Sirmium (Sremska Mitrovica, Serbia), He was made consul aged 6 in 366 with the style *nobilissimus puer* (most noble boy) and proclaimed co-emperor with his father 24th August the year following, as a result of **VALENTINIAN** falling seriously ill whilst campaigning against the Alemanni on the Rhine frontier. This caused a certain amount of apprehension amongst the general staff but, on recovering, the Emperor disingenuously informed them that his son's ability to rule would flow from his nobility of character and sense of justice and that in any case, he would grow into the role of commander. It spoke volumes when, on the next campaign, **GRATIAN** was left behind with his tutor, the cultivated Gallic senator, D. Magnus Ausonius, whom his former charge later made consul in 379.[724]

Reign

Yet he was not, as it turned out, an obviously martial youth, more one with a tendency to piety. The Empire's two senates confirmed his elevation and he took the style **Dominus Noster**

724. PLE I Gratianus 2

Flavius Gratianus Felix Semper Augustus and he was presumably endowed with tribunician and proconsular powers, although whether the senate had much say in this by this date is debatable.[725] He was also made pontifex maximus (much more likely to have been conferred or at least acknowledged by the senate, still at this date predominantly pagan), but he renounced the title later in his reign, in 382.[726] The new Emperor was consul for a second time in 371, and thereafter in 374, 377 and 380. In 374, at fifteen, he married Constantia, last surviving member of the previous dynasty, thus very emphatically securing the place of his own family. The union produced a son (whose name we do not know) but he died before his mother, who died early in 383 and **GRATIAN** re-married Laeta, but there were no further issue. When his uncle was killed by the Goths, he and his half-brother **VALENTINIAN II** continued to divide the Empire between them, **GRATIANUS** taking the west, which was a better situation than in 375, when **VALENTINIAN II** was first elevated by **VALENS** without consulting **GRATIAN**. Indeed, the events of 378 ulitmately eventuated in the young emperor at least taking the field, and he won a considerable victory (much aided by his *magister militum*, the Frankish-born Merobaudes) over the most southerly tribe of Germans at Argentaria (Colmar, Alsace). It perhaps earned him the additional style of **Germanicus Maximus**, although it is not recorded, and these usages were beginning to fall into desuetude.[727]

Yet the crisis in the east following Hadrianople was too serious for **GRATIAN'S** slender military skills, so he took the prudent step of appointing the son of one of his father's leading commanders, Theodosius, the man who had sorted out Britain and then *FIRMUS,* but who had fallen foul of a palace intrigue resulting in the Empress Justina having him killed in 377. His son, also Theodosius, had served very successfully as *dux* in Moesia, but had retired to the family estates in Spain after his father's demise, but was at this juncture recalled and made co-Augustus (East).

Later **GRATIAN** moved his court from Augusta Treverorum (Trier) to Mediolanum (Milan) and visited Rome regularly, which was not as welcome as it sounds, for the young man managed to combine a love of the arena and his blond barbarian personal bodyguards with a renewed persecution of paganism, which resulted in the alienation of the resurgent senatorial aristocracy. Furthermore, his increasing reliance on barbarian officers and advisors combined with his naturally un-martial nature also alienated the army in the North West, especially after his departure to Milan, and the outbreak of a fresh problem on the Rhine in 383 coincided with the appearance of an imperial claimant, **MAGNUS MAXIMUS**. Faced with the choice, important elements of his army defected to the newcomer, forcing **GRATIAN** to flee east, but he was overtaken by the *magister militum* of **MAXIMUS** who killed him 25th August 383 at Lugdunum (Lyons).

*

---

725. ILS 778

726. FS1685. He was probably the last emperor to bear it, cf. FS pp. 61-65.

727. But were revived under **JUSTINIAN**.

VALENTINIANUS II
(Known to history as VALENTINIAN II)
22nd November 375 – 15th May 392

The younger son of **VALENTINIAN I** was born 2nd July 371 at Trier and was named after his father. He was proclaimed Augustus on 22nd November 375, five days after his father's death.[728] For most of his life he was under the influence of the dowager Empress Justina, various ministers and, after 379, his older and much more experienced co-ruler **THEODOSIUS I.** Furthermore, during his reign, the Eastern part of the empire began to gain predominance over the west. **VALENTINIAN II** was recognised as emperor by the court, the army and, no doubt, by the senates. He adopted the style of **Imperator Caesar Dominus Noster [Flavius] Valentinanus Pius Felix Semper Augustus.**[729] He was made consul in 376 and again in 378, 387 and 390. On the death of **VALENS** (when he was still only eight) he succeeded as sole Augustus in the east, his rule being exercised by a close-knit group of courtiers who had either avoided or survived the Battle of Hadrianople. Yet the entire east was in turmoil: there were Goths rampaging through Thrace and the Balkans, and only a modest force had been sent by **GRATIAN'S** advisors to help - prudently, as it turned out, from the point of view of the security of the west. This led to the senior emperor (still himself only nineteen) appointing **THEODOSIUS I** as his half-brother's co-ruler at the beginning of 379.

From then on, the older man was to make all the running; **VALENTINIAN** was increasingly to become a cipher, representing the continuity of the regime and Imperial family, although the senior man soon married his colleague's sister Galla. A complicating factor was that the emperor was an Arian Christian, taking his lead from his mother, earning him the enmity of the charismatic St. Ambrosius, Bishop of Milan, whose implacable opposition finally prevailed.

Once **MAGNUS MAXIMUS** had become established in the West - essentially reviving the Gallic Empire of 120 years before – his faith became a stick to beat him with both by **THEODOSIUS** and **MAXIMUS,** bitter rivals though they were but united in their detestation of the youthful ruler's lack of orthodoxy. It was only when Justina died, c. 387/388, that **THEODOSIUS** was able to persuade him to return to orthodoxy. By this time, military affairs, and effectively much of the running of the Empire, lay in the hands of a triumvirate of very able and highly motivated Frankish generals, led by Arbogastes, fiercely loyal to **THEODOSIUS,** but openly contemptuous of the young emperor. Consequently, when **VALENTINIAN** attempted to assert himself and exercise his *imperium*, he was suddenly found dead in his apartments on 15th May 392. Officially it was suicide, but nobody was fooled. **THEODOSIUS** was now sole emperor. Effectively, he had engineered a gradual, well orchestrated and successful rolling *coup*.

*

728. PLRE I Valentinianus 8
729. ILS781 & coins. Flavius was not consistently used.

MAXIMUS III
(Known to history as Magnus Maximus)
June 383 – 28th July 388

VICTOR
384 – c. 1st August 388

Background

MAGNUS MAXIMUS is frequently labelled an imperial claimant, but in a largely unchallenged and universally acknowledged reign of over five years, his legitimacy was as strong as most other rulers of the era. He started out as an imperial claimant though, and from Britain, too, as had **CONSTANTINE the Great**, whom he regarded as having set a wholly valid precedent.

His date of birth is not known, but having a young family, it may reasonably by assumed that he must have been born, in Hispania Gallaeca (Galicia, Spain), around 340. His recorded kinship with **THEODOSIUS**, although not specified, was probably reasonably close, as he served under that emperor's father in Britain in 367-369, when it has been suggested that he was the officer who suppressed the imperial claimant *VALENTINUS*, although this remains unproven.[730] They served together again in the war against the imperial claimant *FIRMUS* in Africa a few years later, co-operating with the claimant's loyal brother, Gildo (see **Table LVI Brief Lives**). He was also probably the Maximus who assisted the incompetent Lupicinus in trying to re-settle the Goths on the SW side of the Danube in the run-up to the Battle of Hadrianople. Later, in c. 380, **GRATIAN** made him *comes rei militaris* in Britain (C-in-C armed forces), the island by then divided into four, perhaps even five provinces.[731] His title is thought to have been, on slightly later evidence, *dux Britanniarum* (C-in-C the British provinces). He appears to have inflicted a heavy defeat on the Picts and the Scots in northern Britain. Quite what impelled him to become an imperial claimant, traditionally whilst at Segontium (Caernarfon, Gwynedd), is not known, but it was probably a combination of the general dissatisfaction, especially amongst the military, with **GRATIAN'S** rule, not to mention his coterie of barbarian officers, and the announcement by **THEODOSIUS** that his eldest son, **ARCADIUS** would be his co-ruler, something it was widely suspected **MAXIMUS** had expected to be, on the grounds of ties of kinship and shared service. Either way, the event took place in autum 382 or, as previously believed, in spring (probably June) 383, following an incursion across the Rhine of Alemanni under Fraomar, conceivably engineered by **MAXIMUS'S** Gothic lieutenant, Andragathius to provide an excuse for the planned *coup*. Birley indeed suggests that he had crossed to Gaul before being acclaimed.[732]

---

730. Birley (1981) 349.

731. Early Welsh legend tells us that he was in Britain for seven years prior to his usurpation, making his appointment c. 377, immediately after the Danubian affair, unless the legend combined his three years from 367 with his four years from c. 380. By no means to be relied upon, but an interestingly precise detail [*The Mabinogion: The Dream of Macsen Wletic*].

732. Birley (1981) 351; the revised (earlier) date: Cameron (1968) 97.

Reign

Having staked his claim, **MAXIMUS** crossed to the continent to confront the forces of **GRATIANUS**. Sulpicius Severus, quoting St. Martin of Tours, who knew **MAXIMUS**, tells us that the Emperor took the acclamation of the soldiers – which apparently came as a surprise – as a reign of necessity, imposed upon him by the will of God. He appears also to have undergone baptism prior to his elevation, telling Pope Siricius that he had gone directly from the font to the throne. The assertion that he wholly or partially denuded the Island of troops is unlikely to be strictly true, although he would have crossed with sufficient forces to confront the Emperor, and these troops would have been mobile units (*comitatenses*), not the former legions, now constituting the *limitanei* guarding the northern border and elsewhere.[733] Furthermore, as a competent commander he would surely have sent such vexillations back once he had taken over command of **GRATIAN'S** forces. This he managed without serious bloodshed by the defection to his cause of the Emperor's Moorish cavalry, probably a pay-off from the years in Africa supporting Gildo. **GRATIAN** himself, his army fatally weakened, bowed to the inevitable and fled, but was caught and killed by Andragathius on 25th August.[734]

The newcomer styled himself **Imperator Caesar Dominus Noster Magnus Maximus Pius Felix Augustus**. At this point, **MAXIMUS** settled his court at Augusta Treverorum (Trier) and sent an embassy to **THEODOSIUS** who, although apparently discomforted by the murder of his western colleague, was busy with Persian perturbations on his eastern frontier, and was obliged eventually (in 386) to accept his old comrade-in-arms's *de facto* position. For his part **MAXIMUS,** in a deal brokered by St. Ambrose, senatorial former provincial governor and strong-minded Bishop of Milan, agreed to respect the realm of **VALENTINIAN II** in Italy and the Balkans. Circumstantial evidence suggests that, although he did not control Italy, he obtained some degree of recognition from the senate, by which, in later decades, his memory appears to have been held in some respect. In the light of these two factors, it would seem quite anomalous to regard **MAXIMUS** as a usurper; the imperial claimant had arrived, established himself in a manner very similar to that of **POSTUMUS** over a century before and ruled what in effect was a revived Gallic Empire, unchallenged for five years and recognised (however grudgingly) by the Eastern Emperor. Despite the accord which secured him recognition, both sides took precautions against a push south by **MAXIMUS**: **VALENTINIANUS'S** *magister militum* Bauto fortified the Alpine passes against a surprise attack, whilst **MAXIMUS** for his part set out his stall by naming his young son **Flavius VICTOR** as co-augustus, probably in 384.[735] The two adopted the style **Dominus Noster**

---

733. The evidence rests on the later *Notitia Dignitatum* which places an infantry unit with links to North Wales (the [*pedites*] *Seguntienses*) stationed in Illyricum. But the transfer of such units (in both directions) was entirely normal in the 3rd and 4th centuries.

734. PLRE I Andragathius 3

735. He is called Magnius Victor Maximus [*sic*] on some coins, and the name Flavius was probably assumed on his elevation to Augustus The mainly hostile contemporary sources call him a child, but his coin portraits show a youth in his early teens [PLRE I Victor 14].

Magnus Maximus et Flavius Victor Invictis et Perpetuis Augusti.[736] The elder man seems also to have adopted the *agnomen* **Britannicus Maximus** too.[737] No doubt they accepted the tribunician and proconsular powers, probably from the western senate, but possibly from a provincial council-cum-senate, but the position of pontifex maximus was not conferred, for **MAXIMUS** was a zealous Christian and indeed, acted very aggressively to the southern Gallic Priscillianist sect, being the first Christian Emperor to condemn a Christian (Priscillianus himself) for heresy. Thereafter the office of pontifex maximus remained unfilled until its apparent abolition in the first decade of the fifth century, the title being later assumed by the popes. He was recognised consul (in the west only) in 384 and again in 388.

The rule of **MAXIMUS** is nowadays accepted to have been very successful. The Alemanni were put in their place and his good relations with several barbarian leaders ensured peace, during which the economy prospered, and he also remitted taxation to some extent and built up good relationships with the senatorial nobility within his *imperium*. He also streamlined the provincial administration, subdividing one the provinces of Lugdunum. He may even have been responsible for the creation of the fifth British Province; if so, it must have acquired its name Valentia (from the former western emperor) after his downfall. Ancient authors were critical, but by no means uniformly so, Orosius and Sulpicius Severus giving us a much more favourable picture of him.[738]

The end of his reign was caused (not unsurprisingly) by ambition, spurred by religious orthodoxy. In 387 he invaded Italy, the *causus belli* being the eradication of Arianism in the Empire, in the persons of **VALENTINIAN II** and his mother. He took Milan, forcing Justina and her son to Aquileia from whence they fled to **THEODOSIUS** in the East. **MAXIMUS** was now in control of all **VALENTIANUS'S** part of the empire except much of Illyricum. He had his position confirmed by the senate at Rome which he visited in person, extended his reforming government to his new dioceses, although his HQ remained at Milan. For his part, **THEODOSIUS** resolved not to drive him back into the Gallic Empire area, but to crush him completely, so took his time making preparations. It was not until June 388 that he made his move into the Balkans, countered by his adversary. The outcome was that the Western ruler was worsted in two out of three battles, and was captured at Aquileia.

The defeated emperor had some reasonable hope of having his life spared by **THEODOSIUS,** who enjoyed a reputation for clemency and, when confronted by the eastern emperor, emphasised the point that he had sought and obtained his acquiescence in his position and had only moved into Italy in the interests of orthodoxy and the good of the empire. Whatever **THEODOSIUS** had decided to do, however, was forestalled by his officers who, taking no chances, took **MAXIMUS** and executed him shortly afterwards. Meanwhile, **VICTOR** had managed to escape capture, but only for a few days, when he too, despite his tender years, was taken and summarily dispatched.

---

736. ILS788; PRE I Maximus 39.
737. Birley *loc.cit.*
738. Quoted in Haarer (2014) 167.

Family

The family of **MAGNUS MAXIMUS** came from Gallaecia (Galicia) in Spain, and was closely related to that of **THEODOSIUS,** although how is not known.[739] He had an uncle (whose name is not known) so his father was unlikely to have been Count Theodosius's younger brother or else the sources would have mentioned it. Yet it was a close enough relationship for **MAXIMUS** to presume upon it and for him to have risen through the army with the future emperor under the elder Theodosius's command. Probably they were first cousins, perhaps once removed and on the distaff, as the names borne by **MAXIMUS'S** family are not found amongst **THEODOSIUS'S.** His mother was pensioned by **THEODOSIUS** after his fall, which strongly suggested that she was the familial link.[740] A possible reconstruction is shown in **Table LVIII(a).**

We also hear little of an empress, which we would have expected to have done had he had a wife living, yet Sulpicius Severus, without naming her, describes her as a pious woman who waited silently upon St. Martin whilst her husband entertained him to supper. This could refer to the lady later identified as Helena and, whatever her name, the date could be much earlier than the encounter when **MAXIMUS** was emperor, for St. Martin became Bishop of Tours in 371 and had served as a junior officer in the army in Gaul under **JULIAN.**[741] The absence of her name on coins or in inscriptions surely suggest she had died prior to his acclamation, leaving the young **VICTOR,** who was more likely in his early teens than an infant, according to his coin portraits. **MAXIMUS** also had a mother living (not named, nor, it would seem, made Augusta, as was fairly normal) and daughters. Not only are they mentioned by St. Ambrose (but again, unfortunately not by name) as being entrusted to a relation of **THEODOSIUS** after the death of **MAXIMUS,** but one was apparently cured by St. Illidius (3rd) Bishop of Augusto Nemetum (Clermont) before 385.[742] Indeed, the suggestion that one daughter made a glittering senatorial marriage, perhaps to Anicius Probinus (rather than Ennodius, *pace* Mommaerts and Kelley), is to some extent confirmed by a remark of the Byzantine historian Procopius, who claimed that Petronius Maximus (**MAXIMUS V,** see below and **Table XLV** above) was a descendant of **MAGNUS MAXIMUS.**[743]

However, the mention of a wife and daughter bring us to one of the most problematic aspects of the Emperor's family, which takes on a whole new dimension in Welsh legend. The entire complex skein of ancient genealogies is customarily either written off as too unreliable and written down too late to be of the slightest value, or is merely ignored; certainly their reliability has to be held in great doubt, although recent philological work has revealed

---

739. He was previously long accredited with the middle name Clemens, but this has now been established as a misreading of one of the ancient sources: Birley (1981) 348.
740. Birley (1981) 352, quoting St. Ambrose, *Epistulae* 40.32.
741. PLRE I Martinus 3
742. Quoted in Morris (1972) 419.n 2.
743. Proc, *HB* 1, 4.16. **Table XLV**, based on Drinkwater & Elton (1992) clearly has too many generations between Magnus **MAXIMUS III** and Petronius **MAXIMUS V,** who was born c. 390. The former's daughter must have been born c. 368 and cannot have married before 385 or 386, which would make her the mother, not the grandmother of **PETRONIUS MAXIMUS,** cf. **Table LVIII(a)** below.

archaic elements with the presumption that they embody much earlier written material. Yet it would seem entirely wrong to take the latter course, so **Table LVIII(b)** in **Appendix I** gives the Emperor's legendary family (which has numerous variations) according to Welsh legend and the inscription of the pillar of Eliseg at Valle Crucis, Powis, attempting to retain the more credible and earlier recorded elements, as largely accepted by J. H. Ward (and rejected by Anthony Birley).[744] It therefore merits its place if only for the sake of completeness, with conflicting elements reconciled. Some of the Welsh material is eminently reasonable, could we but confirm it from other sources, the impression being given almost of a closely related coterie of what appear to be serving senior Roman staff officers, just like the kin of **VALENTINIAN I** and **VALENS** (above, **Table LIV(a)**) but other elements appear as clearly fantastic.[745]

The most important element is, however, **MAXIMUS'S** wife, who is named as a British woman (or a Roman woman living in Britain) called Helena, which commentators dismiss as merely a double for St. Helena, the mother of **CONSTANTINE I**. Yet, if we remember that the Emperor spent a couple of years in Britain in 367-369, when he was probably in his late 20s, and thus at a most suitable age to be wed, his marriage to a British resident is not so unlikely as it might seem and, of course, the name of the Augusta Helena was by then sufficiently revered as to have inspired the nomenclature of numerous female infants.

*

TABLE LVIII(a): THE FAMLY OF MAGNUS MAXIMUS

---

744. Ward (1972) 277-289, cf. Birley (1981) 352 n. 35.

745. Matthews (1975) 175 & n. 3, where these connections are given little credence, albeit with a caveat.

TABLE LVIII(a): BRIEF LIVES

Anicius Probinus

Consul 395; see above **TABLE XLV Brief Lives**. There is not room between the probable birth of **MAGNUS MAXIMUS** c. 345 and that of **PETRONIUS MAXIMUS** c. 396 for more than one generation, so the suggestion of an intervening one wherein Enno[d]ius (proconsul of Africa 395) married **MAGNUS MAXIMUS'S** daughter cannot be possible.

Antonius Maximinus

Governor of a new province in Spain, probably created bv **MAXIMUS** (and partly named after him). His inscription is in Gallaecia, suggesting that was where he came from and, combined with his name strongly suggests that he was a close kinsman of the Emperor [*Panegyrici Latini*., 12, 24, 1; PLRE I Maximinus 9].

[Flavius Anicius] Petronius Maximus

See below **MAXIMUS V AUGUSTUS**

Flavius Eucherius

 Presumably of Spanish origin, he was *comes sacrarum largitionum* (treasury secretary) in the west under **GRATIAN** 377-379 and was appointed consul 381 by his nephew shortly after the latter's elevation to the purple. He appears to have retired to the east, where he was recorded in 395 [PLRE I Eucherius 2].

Flavius Theodosius

Celebrated Spanish born *comes* 368-369 and *magister militum* in the west 369-375, who was executed on false grounds at Carthage in 375 [PLRE I Theodosius 3].

Flavius Theodosius

See below **THEODOSIUS AUGUSTUS**

Flavius Theodosius

See below **THEODOSIUS AUGUSTUS**

Magnus Flavius Victor

See above **VICTOR AUGUSTUS**

Magnus Maximus

See above **MAXIMUS III AUGUSTUS**

Marcellinus

When **MAXIMUS** was acclaimed Emperor, he was living within the area governed by **VALENTINIAN II** but was allowed to travel to his brother. He was appointed a *comes* and dined with St. Ambrose in 386 before commanding part of the army in the final confrontation with **THEODOSIUS,** in 388, after which he was either killed in action or subsequently liquidated [PLRE I Marcellinus 12].

Thermantia

Nothing is known of **THEODOSIUS'S** mother except that she died c. 389/391 [PLRE I Thermantia 1]

Unknown

A powerful *comes* of his nephew 383-388 [PLRE I Anonymus 36]

Victor

Comes of **MAXIMUS** 386-388, he met St. Ambrose at Mogontiacum (Mainz) in 386 and went to Milan later to broker peace. Probably **MAXIMUS'S** son was named after him [Sulpicus Severus, *Vita Martini* 20, 4; PLRE I Victor 6]

THEODOSIUS I
19th January 379 – 17th January 395

Background

THEODOSIUS was, as far as we know, the first emperor of Spanish origin since the accession of **HADRIANUS** two hundred and two years previously, and was the son of **VALENTINIAN I's** cavalry commander who had been executed through the unfortunate machinations of others, following his successful overthrow of *FIRMUS* in 375. His son by Thermantia was born around 346 at Cauca (Coca) in Gallaecia, one of the Spanish provinces, and followed his father into the army. His career seems to have been highly successful, although no doubt aided by the success of his father. He was appointed *dux* in Moesia Prima in 373/374 but retired in 375 after his father's death to his family's Spanish estates, which suggests that the family were aristocratic, if only in local terms. There he married his fellow Spaniard Aelia Flaccilla around 376, and had two sons. He was summoned back by **GRATIAN** in 378 to be *magister militum* in Illyria, in the aftermath of the defeat at Hadrianople and acquitted himself with considerable success, leading the Emperor to raise him to be his co-Augustus with responsibility for the east on 19th January the year following.[746] Bearing in mind his kinship with **MAGNUS MAXIMUS** and the subsequent rivalry between them, it may be that **GRATIAN** had one or other of them in mind and that **MAXIMUS,** being a little older, felt aggrieved at being passed over.

Reign

THEODOSIUS took the style **Dominus Noster Flavius Theodosius Pius Felix Augustus**[747], and was endowed with the tribunician and proconsular powers, probably automatic by this stage, for a formal vote in the two senates may have become superfluous and served a consulship in 380 followed by two further terms in 388 and 393. On accession, the empress assumed the additional name of Flavia and was styled Augusta, the first Empress to enjoy this rank since St. Helena. She died in 386 at Constantinople. The emperor thereupon married Galla, the youngest of the three sisters of his western colleague, **VALENTINIAN II,** thus legitimising the rule of his family and securing a series of familial connections going back to **DIOCLETIANUS** (see **Table XLVII** above). There were two sons, Gratianus and Iohannes (who died as infants) and a daughter, Galla Placia.

Like his probable cousin, the new Emperor was a redoubtable defender of Christianity, but his later soubriquet of 'The Great' was earned on the battlefield. After a four year campaign, he roundly defeated the Goths in the Balkans, finalising affairs by a treaty reached in 382. This seemed like the end of the problems posed by these particular Goths (the Visigoths) but in fact, by settling them within the empire - the Hunnic pressure to their eastern flank had not abated since the decade before - under the authority of their

---

746. PLRE I Theodosius 4
747. ILS783

own king, a risky precedent had been set. Furthermore, should **THEODOSIUS** wish to draw upon their military services, it would be as allied, not as integrated units of the army, as before, another complicating factor. It may well be that the measure was conceived as a temporary one, which the emperor planned to resolve in the medium term, but in the event, this never happened. He also managed to secure a long lasting peace on the eastern frontier with the Persians. This freed him to deal with his western colleague.

His strategic military intentions were diverted by his efforts from 387 to crush **MAGNUS MAXIMUS,** which he achieved at Aquileia the following summer. Furthermore, as **VALENTINIAN II** was something of a cypher when it came to effective rule, affairs in the west remained in the hands of senior officers of Barbarian origin. One reason for their being favoured was that they were felt unlikely to declare themselves imperial claimants, being barbarian, but in this **THEODOSIUS** overlooked the role of the catspaw claimant put up by an ambitious general. As we have seen, this barbarian command monopoly was challenged by the western emperor in 392 and as a result **VALENTINIAN** was killed, leaving **THEODOSIUS** as sole emperor.

In 390 **THEODOSIUS** took a terrible revenge on the citizens of Thessalonica for causing a spot of bother: murdering the Goth Bothericus, his army commander in the area. This resulted in his immediate excommunication by the Bishop of Milan, St. Ambrose, whose authority within the church at the time was unchallengeable exceeding, by force of character and consistency, even that of Pope Siricius. The emperor was forced into the humiliating position of having to do penance for his crime, which he seems to have done without repercussions for the redoubtable prelate. During this period the emperor stayed for nearly two years in the west and was received in Rome for an extended visit with great enthusiasm. Nevertheless, this great bastion of paganism was disappointed in 392 when the Emperor issued an edict banning pagan practices throughout the empire. Interestingly, though, he preserved the magnificent temples for other purposes or as works of art: the first known example of a conservation-minded ruler. Unfortunately, his Christian successors failed to emulate his example during the following century.

Meanwhile, having disposed of **VALENTINIAN II**, the general Arbogastes needed to keep hold on supreme power, especially as **THEODOSIUS** was unlikely to acquiesce in his bringing about the ruin of his brother-in-law. The western strong man was both a pagan and a barbarian, so he needed an emperor. He chose *EUGENIUS*, and for two years **THEODOSIUS** essentially ignored events in the west whilst building up strength for yet another round of civil conflict. He also nominated his younger son, the 8 year old **HONORIUS** as co-emperor with his elder brother to secure the succession. Eventually his forces met Arbogastes' army on the river Frigidus, not so far from Aquileia, where he had defeated **MAXIMUS** twelve years before, and trounced him in a two day battle which once again tore the manpower heart out of the Roman Army so high were the casualties on both sides.

The emperor pardoned most of the associates of the imperial claimant, although Arbogastes was killed on 7th September. He thereafter made dispositions, whereby in the event of his death, the empire would be divided by his sons. Probably this was a similar arrangement as that made by **VALENTINIAN I,** and by no means intended to be permanent. In the event, the younger son, **HONORIUS**, was summoned to Milan at the beginning of 395 with the intention of being formally invested as co-emperor with his elder brother and father. In the event, **THEODOSIUS** took ill and died unexpectedly soon after his arrival. The division of the empire was about to become permanent. Only **JUSTINIAN** was to rule more than just the east again.

For the *family of* **THEODOSIUS I** *see* **Tables LXIX(a) & LIX(b).**

Further reading:

Sivan, H., *Ausonius of Bordeaux: Genesis of a Gallic Aristocracy* (London 1993)
Williams, S. & Friell, G., *Theodosius, The Empire at Bay* (London 1994).

Imperial claimant under Theodosius I

EUGENIUS II
22nd August 392 – 6th September 394

Background

Arbogastes realized, once he had encompassed the end of **VALENTINIAN II** in May 392, that he could never rule on his own account, and the hostile reaction to events in the west at Constantinople made him realize that he needed an imperial claimant to legitimize his rule. In August he selected a man of senatorial rank, the *magister scrinii* (head of the civil service) *EUGENIUS* to assume the role. His place of origin is unknown, but he had originally been a teacher of rhetoric, but had risen high enough to become a *vir clarissimus* by 385 under **MAGNUS MAXIMUS** and reached his final bureaucratic post in 390.[748]

Reign

On elevation, the imperial claimant styled himself **Dominus Noster Flavius Eugenius Pius Felix Augustus**.[749] He received the tribunician and proconsular power, probably from the senate itself, and served an immediate suffect consulship, recognized in the west but not in the east. Apart from being middle aged, nothing is known about him, except that he had a wife (presumably never recognized as Augusta) and children, who were spared after the Battle of the Frigidus, mainly through the intercession of St. Ambrose. *EUGENIUS* adopted a policy of toleration towards paganism and as the creature of an Arian, a blind eye was turned there, too. The temples were all re-opened and he became popular with the majority of the senatorial aristocracy who were still pagan, all of which hardened **THEODOSIUS** against the old cults, which asserted themselves with a vengeance after he had regained control of the west. After the battle of the Frigidus, the imperial claimant, captured, was summarily executed at the feet of the Emperor. Arbogastes escaped but was hunted down and killed the next day.

---

748. PLE I Eugenius 6
749. ILS7

The Imperial Succession
Honorius
Constantinus III
Constans II
Constantius III
Johannes I
Valentinianus III
Maximus V

Imperial Claimants
Marcus II
Gratianus II
Maximus IV
Iovinus
Sebastianus
Attalus
Heraclianus

HONORIUS
10th January 393 – 25th August 423

Background

The new western emperor was born on 9th September 384, and was thus but a boy when he acceded to the imperial purple as the colleague of his father and elder brother. Indeed, the chief problem for the Theodosian dynasty is that, apart from its founder, each representative came to power as a child and, had any of them even had the potential to rule effectively as **THEODOSIUS** had done, they never had the chance, day-to-day government being in the hands of senior, mainly barbarian, generals interfered with by determined female relations. Neither were in the business of taking the risk of allowing these young emperors to assert themselves or even acquire the necessary skills. In being nominated as co-emperors as children, **HONORIUS** and his brother **ARCADIUS** in the east were following a trend started by **VALENTINIAN I** in nominating his sons as children, and the trend accelerated throughout the fifth century. Increasingly, the emperor's role started to become ceremonial, like oriental emperors of more recent times, whilst powerful court factions strove to control and execute policy. In the end, it opened the way for powerful generals to dominate the government and nominate children of the dynasty and later, harmless bureaucrats (when there was no dynasty).[750] It fatally weakened the west, although imperial power recovered in the east after two successive child emperors. As it turned out, in the case of **HONORIUS,** it is doubtful whether, with all the advice and training in the world, he would have emerged as an effective ruler in his own right.

Prior to his elevation **HONORIUS** was styled **nobilissimus puer** and in 386, aged 13 months served as consul before being proclaimed Augustus on 10th January 393.[751]

Reign

Flavius HONORIUS was styled in a somewhat *retardataire* style as **Imp[erator] Caes[ar] D[ominus] N[oster] Honorius Perp[etuus] Aug[ustus]**, although in some cases his *nomen* was also inserted.[752] He served further consulships in 394, 396, 398, 402, 404, 407, 409, 412, 415, 417, 418 and 422. In 395, he married the elder daughter of Flavius Stilicho, the Vandal-born commander who had succeeded Arbogastes in the West. She died in c 407/8 and he then married her sister Thermantia in 408, but she divorced him after his acquiescence in the murder of her father, without whose outstanding skills as a military commander (he was *magister militum* in the west for a considerable thirteen and a half years, from 394 to 407) the west might have succumbed permanently to the waves of barbarians who began to surge across the western provinces following his downfall. Both marriages were childless, which was to produce further problems for the future.

In fact, the first six years of the reign were peaceful, thanks to the effective settlements made by the two emperors' father and his reputation, which to some extent lived on after him. However, in 401, the Goths who had been settled south of the Danube in Thrace after 378, acquired a new, young and ambitious king in Alaric, and began to move westwards, raiding northern Italy in that year, but were successfully repulsed by Stilicho. Nevertheless, the court moved from vulnerable Milan to impregnable Ravenna on the Adriatic, but still in northern Italy, and remained there for much of the rest of its existence. In 405, the Goths tried once more but Stilicho again drove them out. Yet the respite was brief, for on new year's eve 406, the Rhine froze over and the Alemanni, Vandals, Alans, Sueves and Burgundians, pressed in the east by advancing Huns, crossed in force and began to ravage Gaul, before entering Spain in 409. This time their aim was not plunder but settlement.

The commanders on the spot were overwhelmed (their names have not come down to us), and local concern led to the acclamation of **CONSTANTINE III** (later grudgingly recognised as co-ruler), his predecessors and successors, leading to yet another revival of a polity greatly resembling the whilom Gallic Empire, this time as a matter of survival. Stilicho was tied up with the breakdown of a treaty he had made earlier with Alaric, and the Goths again had to be ejected from Italy, but this time it was not so straightforward, and any military reserves were still thin on the ground, due to the appalling losses at the Battles of Hadrianople and the

---

750. McEvoy (2013) 326-329
751. The date is given as 23rd January in some sources, cf. PLRE I Honorius 3.
752. ILS793-795.

Frigidus. As a consequence, understrength efforts to regain control of Gaul and the North West were ineffective. Meanwhile, Stilicho was keen to re-unite the empire after the death of **ARCADIUS** in 408, planning on a regency for the latter emperor's infant son. Unfortunately a group of **HONORIUS'S** advisers suggested he was more interested on placing his own son Eucherius (eminently qualified as a great-grandson of the *comes* Theodosius) on the throne instead, and he was arrested and executed by an officer called Heraclianus 23rd August 408.

All the while, Alaric, keen to be granted a semi-autonomous polity within the empire in return for honours, security and military aid, was pressing the senate (which he revered as having some kind of primacy which it had in practice long lost) and the Imperial government for a settlement, investing Rome threateningly, but not proceeding any further. But negotiations broke down and in the end he opted for setting up his own regime centered on Rome. Alaric managed to carry the senate and most of the people with him, outraged as they were at the lack of support they had received from **HONORIUS'S** government, by now vainly engaged in trying to contain **CONSTANTINE III** and the barbarians he seemed not to be able to repel. Therefore, Alaric elevated the Prefect of the City, Priscus *ATTALUS*, to the purple. He thereupon made Alaric his *magister militum* and together they marched on Ravenna to depose **HONORIUS**. The latter however was saved by an unexpectedly rapid response to an appeal for military re-inforcements from the government of the infant **THEODOSIUS II** in the East, resulting in the prompt arrival of six legions at Ravenna. A stalemate followed, and in 409, the *comes* in Africa (murderer of Stilicho and future imprerial claimant) *HERACLIANUS*, cut off the grain supply to Rome in a gesture of loyalty to **HONORIUS**. Alaric, furious, insisted on sending a detachment of his troops to Carthage to teach him a lesson, but *ATTALUS*, honourably but unwisely, refused to sanction a barbarian invasion of Africa, resulting in his immediate deposition and, from 24th to 26th August 410, the sack of the city, an act that in truth had a much more profound effect on people's morale than practical problems for the Empire.

The sack lasted three days and was pretty restrained, especially by ancient standards. Once finished, Alaric took Galla Placidia, the half-sister of **HONORIUS**, hostage and retreated south, intending to cross to Sicily from whence he proposed to invade Africa and teach *HERACLIANUS* a lesson. In the event, this never happened, for a storm prevented him from reaching Sicily and he then took fever *en route* and died in September at Consentius (Cosenza) in modern Calabria.[753]

If anyone thought that **HONORIUS** would lose control of the west completely, the death of Alaric would prove them wrong. At the right moment a new *magister militum*, Constantius, was appointed and within a year had disposed of **CONSTANTINE III**, although the Gallic secession had another two years to run before it was finally put to rest, after six very turbulent years. Unfortunately 413 also saw the loyal *HERACLIANUS*[754] declare himself an imperial claimant and he sailed for Italy intent on overthrowing **HONORIUS** himself. This time the venture failed through lack of resolve, and thereafter an uneasy peace was preserved,

---

753. PLRE II Alaricus 1
754. Heraclianus II was a seventh century member of the Heraclid dynasty, and beyond the scope of this work.

aided by a treaty formally settling Alaric's Visigoths under imperial suzerainty in Spain, thus bringing Gaul to some kind of stability. Alaric's half-brother succeeded him, falling in love and marrying their long term hostage, the princess Galla Placidia, but died (along with their infant son) not long afterwards. His successor, Walia, returned Galla to her family, and in due course the *magister militum* Constantius (also a long term admirer of the princess) also married her. At her insistence he was briefly made co-emperor as **CONSTANTIUS III** (a move rejected by the court in Constantinople) but after his death his widow, whose beauty and allure must have been considerable, discovered that the Emperor her brother had also fallen for her and was becoming a nuisance, so she moved to the East. Not long afterwards **HONORIUS** fell ill and died on 26th August 423, leaving a power vacuum. This was promptly filled by a man who, like *EUGENIUS,* was the head of the civil service, **IOHANNES**. Although recognised by the senate, the east did not and he lasted only some eighteen months before an army from Constantinople arrived, deposed him and installed as emperor the young son of **CONSTANTIUS III** and Galla Placidia, Valentinian.

TABLE LIX(a): THE FAMILY OF THEODOSIUS I (WEST)

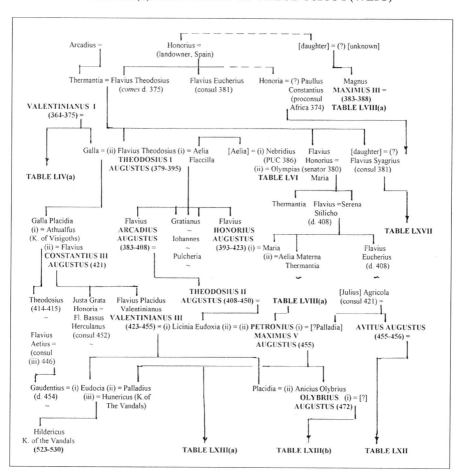

TABLE LIX(a): BRIEF LIVES

Aelia Flaccilla

Of Spanish origin, she adopted the Flavia element of her name on being made Augusta in 379 and was mother of a daughter and four sons, of whom two died young. Famous for her charitable works and her piety. She died 386, when a statue was erected to her in the senate. Settipani suggests that she and her sister may have been siblings of Fl. Afranius Syagrius, consul 382 (see **Table LXVI** below) [PLRE I Flaccilla; Settipani (2000) 418].

Aelia Materna Thermantia

When she was in her teens she was made *nobilissimus puella*, and she married **HONORIUS** after the death of her elder sister in 408. After the fall of Stilicho, she was sent back to her mother in Rome, where she died in July 415. She may have remarried and had issue [PLRE II Thermantia].

Anicius Olybrius

See below **OLYBRIUS AUGUSTUS**

Athaulfus

He was a Gothic nobleman, married to the sister of Alaricus, King of the Visigoths, whose puppet emperor, the imperial claimant *ATTALUS,* made him cavalry commander in 409. He was elected King of the Visigoths on the death of Alaricus later in 410. Sometime prior to 414, his wife died (or was otherwise disposed of) and he married Galla Placidia (qv), but died in September 415 [PLRE II Athaulfus]

Avitus

See below **Table LXIV AVITUS AUGUSTUS.**

Eudocia

Elder daughter; her betrothal to Hunericus was probably in 442 or 443, but the marriage did not happen until after she had married Palladius Caesar in spring 455 and he had died a month or so later. In the meantime she had married Gaudentius, the son of the *magister militum* Aëtius (qqv) who must have died in the wake of his father's murder. She died in Jerusalem in 471/2 [PLRE II Eudocia1].

Flavius Aëtius

The last great general and mainstay of the western empire in the reign of **VALENTINIAN III**. He was born c. 390 at Durostorum, Lower Moesia (Silistra, Bulgaria), thus firmly in the later Roman tradition of generals of Danubian origin. His father was Gaudentius of a noble local family and his mother an upper-crust Italian lady. His father, a cavalry general in Gaul, had been killed in a mutiny, probably whilst trying to re-impose the control of **HONORIUS.** As a young officer, Aëtius was held hostage by both the Visigoths and the Huns, giving him an excellent insight into their ways. He was instrumental in clearing up after the death of **JOANNES I** (under whom he had originally served) and was appointed *comes* and *magister militum* in Gaul 425, gaining a wider remit in 429, serving until 454, and being created patrician in 435. He married the Visigothic princess Pelagia formerly the wife of the *comes* Bonifatius and still alive in 451. His greatest achievement was the breaking of the power of the Huns in 451, and containing the expansion of the Visigoths in Gaul. He was consul three times, in 432, 437 and 446 (all in the west) and two future emperors served under him, **AVITUS** and **MAIORIANUS**. His relationship with **VALENTINIAN III** soured in summer 454, possibly due to plotting by **PETRONIUS MAXIMUS,** and he was killed by the Emperor's own hand September 21/22 that year [PLRE II Aëtius 7]

Flavius Arcadius

See below **ARCADIUS AUGUSTUS**

Flavius Bassus Herculanus

Nothing is known of his antecedents, but he was regarded as a 'safe pair of hands' as a husband for the Emperor **VALENTINIAN III's** sister, who had ambitions to be empress. They married in 449 or 450. He was appointed consul (west) in 452, but nothing more is known of him. If there had been any children who lived to maturity, we should have heard of them, but note the 6th century consul Arcadius Placidus Magnus Felix (see below **Table LXIII(a) Brief Lives**), whose names evoke the sort of alliance between the house of **PETRONIUS MAXIMUS** and that of **THEODOSIUS** that this marriage might have produced [PLRE II Herculanus 2].

Flavius Constantius

See below **CONSTANTIUS III AUGUSTUS**

Flavius Eucherius

At the time of the elevation of **THEODOSIUS I** to the purple he was *comes sacrarum largitionum* (imperial finance minister) having been appointed by 377 and served until 379. He was made consul in 381 and was living in the East in 395 [PLRE I Eucherius 2].

Flavius Eucherius

The only son of the general, he was born at Rome c. 387. In 396 he was given the rank of *tribunus et notarius* (a senior civil service rank). It was hoped that he would marry Galla Placidia and become emperor, but his father fell in 408. He escaped to Rome but was killed there [PLRE II Eucherius I]

Flavius Honorius

Elder brother of the emperor **THEODOSIUS I**, he was dead before his brother's elevation. He held senatorial rank [PLE I Honorius 2].

Flavius Honorius

See below **HONORIUS AUGUSTUS**

Flavius Pacidus Valentinianus

See below **VALENTINIAN III AUGUSTUS**

Flavius Probus

An extremely learned man of distinguished family, whose name clearly indicates descent from the family of **PETRONIUS MAXIMUS,** cf. **TABLE LVIII(a).** He was a *vir inlustris* by 512 and was Western consul in 513 [PLRE II Probus 9]

Flavius Stilicho

The first great general of the Theodosian dynasty. His father was a cavalry officer under **VALENS** of Vandal descent. He was a military tribune c. 383, after which his rise was fast, culminating in his appointment as *magister militum* (possibly in Thrace) in 392, being promoted to the same office throughout the west and made a *comes* in 394 which offices he held until his death. He was *vir inlustris* from the same year and was western consul in 400 and 405. He dealt with great success with the sudden upsurge in barbarian migrations and their consequent incursions into the empire, although by 406-407 was becoming stretched due to his intention to re-unite the empire for **HONORIUS** which meant that he was relatively powerless to deal with the Gallic secessions. This led to his fall and murder in front of the emperor by *HERACLIANUS* in 408. If it is true that he wanted his son Eucherius to become emperor, it is strange that his career was never developed, despite his sister being empress. He was a Christian, noted for his efficiency and honesty [PLRE I Stilicho].

Flavius Syagrius

It is difficult to distinguish the elements of this man's career from those of his near namesake (and probable kinsman), Flavius Afranius Syagrius, consul the year after him. Both were probably of Gallic extraction and the sons of senators, and presumably cousins. He was the sole survivor of a military expedition across the Rhine in 369, but was *magister officiorum* a decade later and praetorian prefect of Italy 380-382, during which time he held his consulship. He seems to have died in office c. 382. He was ancestor of *AEGIDIUS* and *SYAGRIUS* the two rulers of northern Gaul 461-486, see **Table LXVI** [PLRE I Syagrius 3].

Flavius Theodosius

Much of his career is set out above. He was a Spanish officer, who fought with **MAGNUS MAXIMUS** in Britain and was made *comes rei militaris* (West) 368-369 and then promoted to *magister militum* (commander-in-chief) in which he was highly successful and in which he remained until executed at Carthage on a trumped up charge in 375.He was bapitsed a Christian late in life [PLRE I Theodosius 3].

Flavius Theodosius

See above **THEODOSIUS I AUGUSTUS**

Flavius Theodosius

See below **Table LIX(b) THEODOSIUS II AUGUSTUS**

Galla Placidia

Born in 388, she also bore, at some time after her birth, the *nomen* Aelia before Galla, probably in honour of her father's first wife. She was living in Rome when taken hostage by Alaricus in 410 and married his brother-in-law in 414, by whom she had a son who died as a baby. She managed to get repatriated in 416 and married **CONSTANTIUS III** on 1st January 417, having by him two children. She also had a niece called Singledia, presumably the daughter of one of Athaulfus's siblings. In 421 she was granted the style of Augusta, but she went with her family to Constantinople in 422, returning as regent for her son in 425; she died 27th November 450. She built two churches and owned a palace at Constantinople [PLRE II Placidia 4].

Gaudentius

Only son of Aëtius (qv) born at Rome c. 440. He was carried off to Africa by Gaisericus, King of the Vandal kingdom there and is not heard of again [PLRE II Gaudentius 7].

Gratianus, Iohannes & Pulcheria

All three died in childhood [PLRE I Pulcheria].

Hildericus

King of the Vandals 523-530. He was born c. 456, succeeded Thrasamund in May 523, and immediately ceased the persecution of Catholic Christians acknowledging the suzerainty of the empire by minting coins bearing the image of **JUSTIN I.** He was heavily defeated by a Moorish army was consequently deposed in May 530 and imprisoned by Gelimer, who had him murdered in September 533, shortly before the *comes* Belisarius destroyed his kingdom. He left children (and therefore descendants of **THEODOSIUS I**) living at Constantinople in Procopius's time. He also had an anonymous brother, whose left sons Hoamer (blinded 530, killed 533) and Euageës (killed Sept. 533 having had a daughter Damira, who died an infant) [PLRE II Euagees, Hildericus, Hoamer; Conant (2012) 34].

Hunericus

Eldest son of the Vandal King Gaisericus see above **TABLE LIV(a) Brief Lives**

[Julius] Agricola

A gallic nobleman of senatorial family, possibly based in Narbo (Narbonne); there is slight doubt about his first name, which was particularly popular amongst the Gallic élite. He may have been the son (or a descendant) of Philagrius (see **Table LXIV** below). He was praetorian prefect in the west before 418 (in Gaul specifically in the latter year) and consul (West) 421 [PLRE II Agricola 1].

Justa Grata Honoria

Born the eldest child of **CONSTANTIUS III** and Galla Placidia, late 417 or 418, she was accorded the title Augsuta, probably from 425. She was fiercely ambitious, faced disgrace in 449 for having an affair with her estates' factor (being possibly pregnant by him), hence her betrothal to a senator, Herculanus. She thereupon secretly sent word to Attila the Hun, asking him to come and avenge her. She narrowly escaped execution, but was hastily married to Herculanus c. 450. Attila regarded her as betrothed to him and invaded, triggering a chain of momentous subsequent events [PLRE II Honoria].

Licinia Eudoxia

Born 422, she married **VALENTINAN III** (to whom she had been betrothed since 424) on 29th October, 437 and was made Augusta in 439. She re-married (against her wishes) in spring 455 to **PETRONIUS MAXIMUS** but, after his death in May, was carried off to Africa by Gaiseric (whom she may have actually invited to come to Rome after her second marriage) only returning to Constantinople in 462. She died there c. 493 [PLRE II Eudoxia 2].

Magnus Maximus

Note that the relationship to **THEODOSIUS I** shown here is a less satisfying alternative to that given above in **Table LVIII(a)**.

Nebridius

See above **TABLE LVI Brief Lives**

Palladius

Created **nobilissimus caesar** in spring 455 by his father and presumably killed in the chaos assiociated with the sack of Rome by Gaiseric at the end of May that year [PLRE II Palladius 10].

Paullus Constantius

A distinguished senator and husband of an Honoria, believed to have been the aunt of **THEODOSIUS I.** He was proconsul of Africa in 374, dying in office 6th July 375. His wife appears to have predeceased him and both were buried at Salona (near Solin, Croatia) where they no doubt had an estate. They left two children, both senators, Paulinus [?Vetran]io and Antonius Paulus, both of whom served as their father's legates in Africa [PLRE I Constantius 11, Paulus 8 & Paulinus ...io].

Petronius Maximus

See below **MAXIMUS V AUGUSTUS**

Placidia

The Emperor's younger daughter, she probably married in 454 or more likely after her father-in-law's accession in 455. She and her mother were carried off to Cathage by Gaisericus in 455 but sent on to Constantinople later, where she was recorded as living in 478 [PLRE II Placidia 1].

*

A SECOND GALLIC EMPIRE

The freezing of the Rhine on the last day of 406 was an opportunity for those Germanic tribes settled on the east side of the river to grab the opportunity to cross *en masse* into the Diocese of Gaul. Whether this was an opportunity for which they had planned, or whether it was sheer opportunism, or whether indeed the leaders of the various people consciously colluded is not really known. The effectiveness of it would seem, with hindsight, to betoken some kind of co-ordination in the event of the river freezing, in itself a phenomenon to which both sides were no doubt used. Nevertheless, it seems to have caught the military commanders at Cologne and Trier completely unawares and before long the Franks, Burgundians, Sueves, Alans and Vandals had broken out of the frontier zone and were busy rampaging across the Gallic Provinces, causing chaos.

Furthermore, the aim of these peoples was, like Alaric's, to settle within the empire, for they were being impelled by the Huns crowding from the East, which meant that the numbers involved were huge, even if the fighting strength of each 'nation' was only a proportion of the whole. The situation closely resembled the incursion of 256, and the reach of the incursion - right down to the Gates of Hercules - was similar. In 256, **GALLIENUS** had been able to deal with it to some extent, but in the medium term the turmoil, insecurity and discontent it bred had the same result. In 259 **POSTUMUS** was acclaimed and the first Gallic Empire was born, lasting some 14 years. What was different in 407 was that the central government of **HONORIUS** - in reality, Stilicho – had its hands full elsewhere, and was not in a position to intervene. The reaction, therefore, was similar but events moved faster.

Essentially an imperial claimant arose in Britain rather than on the continent, who crossed the Channel with the laudable intention of rectifying the situation. For roughly six years, Gaul was governed under a series of imperial claimants who desperately tried to stem the barbarian tide whilst at the same time coping with rivals and with those barbarians who clearly would never return. There was a general lack of co-ordinated action, resulting in disagreements and fissiparous tendencies in the body politic. Whilst it could be argued that both *CARAUSIUS I* and **MAGNUS MAXIMUS** founded Gallic empires too, in reality the former's never included the whole of Gaul, despite the wide dissemination of his coinage, let alone Spain and the Rhineland, whilst **MAGNUS MAXIMUS'S** *imperium* was not one content to remain lodged within the NW provinces. In 407, the impression given is that these fire-fighting imperial claimants were content by and large to remain within the NW provinces where indeed they had their hands full.

The fact that these imperial claimants at first arose in Britain was simply that, with barbarians overwhelming the border provinces of the two Germanies and Belgica, there was every chance that Britain would be cut off. Furthermore, potential claimants commanding on the Rhine may have been discredited by the incursion, or killed attempting to halt it. It is a measure of the assimilation of Britain within the empire that the prospect of independence was the last thing anyone appears to have desired.

*

MARCUS II[755]
?Autumn 406 - January 407

The reduction of troops on the Rhine frontier and a demand from Stilicho to the authorities in Britain to contribute detachments to re-inforce his efforts against the Eastern imperial government seem to have led to the acclamation of one *MARCUS.* Birley has said that it was 'reasonable to suppose' that he was one of the three senior Roman commanders in Britain: the *Comes Britanniarum* (Count of the Britains), the *Comes Litoris Saxonici* (Count of the Saxon Shore) or the *Dux Britanniarum* (C-in-C Britain) and points out that Sheppard Frere considered that he was in fact holder of the first of these positions.[756] One ancient source says of the third of this sequence of three imperial claimants, that

> 'They appear to have chosen Constantine thinking that, as he had this name,
> he would firmly master the imperial power, since it was for a reason such
> as this that they appear to have chosen the others for usurpation as well.'[757]

This would suggest that this particular *comes* (if *comes* he was) reminded them of **MARCUS AURELIUS**, then still well remembered as a doughty defeater of barbarian attacks.

His acclamation is thought, on critical evaluation of the somewhat challenging evidence, to have occurred in 406 not 407, possibly in the autumn, when unrest on the frontier first became apparent in military circles in the Western Empire. He did not last very long, 'because he did not agree with the soldiers' character', and was presumably assassinated. The chronology of the sequence of British acclamations suggests that he must have been disposed of by some time in January 407.[758] Nothing whatever is known about this man's origin or family. By this date the name was most likely a *cognomen* rather than a *praenomen*, as was more usual in this period.[759] If any coins were minted, they failed to survive.

*

---

755. He is here accorded a number only to distinguish him from the questionable *MARCUS (I),* allegedly an imperial claimant under **PHILIPPUS I** (qv)
756. Birley (1981) 342 & n. 2; cf. PLRE II Marcus 2.
757. *Op. cit.* 343, quoting Sozomen.
758. *Ibid.*, 344, & n. 15.
759. Cf. PLRE I Marcus 2, 3,& 4. A 'citizen of the Island of Britain' according to Orosius *Adv. Pagan.* vii. 40, 4.

GRATIANUS II
c. January – April 407

The loss of *MARCUS* must have thrown up a difficulty, if he really had been *Comes Britanniarum*. No doubt he appointed one of the officers on the strength in the British provinces as his replacement. Yet with his death or deposition, we are told the clique of officers who brought about his demise allowed his successor to be chosen from amongst the civilian leaders of British provincial society. Perhaps Sozomen was right, and the name was everything; after all, for all his faults, had not **GRATIAN (I)** defeated and virtually annihilated a mass of German tribesmen who had crossed the Rhine in 378?

Thus the new imperial claimant, raised to the purple in the weeks or days following the reception of the news of the barbarian invasion of Gaul, was called *GRATIAN*, and was a *municeps* – probably a leader of one of Britain's *civitates* (tribal capitals)[760], from which we might reasonably suppose that he was of Roman-British stock. As we have absolutely no other information, it may be that, as with other instances of 'regime change' - *CARAUSIUS* springs to mind – he may have been appointed to a senior post by *MARCUS,* as a *comes*, perhaps a fiscal officer, like *comes sacrarum largitionum* from which dizzy eminence he was encouraged, like *ALLECTUS* to replace his benefactor.

All we know beyond that, is that he was in power for about four months before being deposed by the army. What could have been going on during that time? Again, no coins were minted, although whilst no bullion was able to reach Britain, apparently cut off from the Continent, base metal coins could have been issued. One might wonder why not. As *GRATIANUS* was no soldier, presumably this was the reason no effort was made to cross the Channel and try to restore order. Zosimus claims that the British establishment were at first primarily concerned that the barbarians would turn upon them. Perhaps the new claimant launched a diplomatic offensive to try to find out from Ravenna what was going to be done to protect the island. It may be that, with no progress being made, the army got restive and disposed of *GRATIANUS,* nominating a candidate of their own instead. That man was **CONSTANTINE III.** The date was probably some time in April 407.

*

---

760. PLRE II Gratianus 3.

CONSTANTINUS III
(Known to history as Constantine III)
c. April 407 – August 411

CONSTANS II
c. February 410 – March 411

Background

The new British imperial claimant **Claudius CONSTANTINUS** must have been born not later than 360, in view of the fact that he had a mature elder son and a grown up, if still youthful, younger one. He may, therefore have cut his teeth serving under **MAGNUS MAXIMUS** in Britain and in Gaul, perhaps afterwards serving in a variety of theatres in the wider Empire. The magic of the name, as we have seen, may indeed have impelled **CONSTANTINE** into the purple yet, in view of the lack of magic attached to his two predecessors, it might seem more plausible to suppose that he had probably engineered a coup against *GRATIANUS* as a result of the lack of action in a developing crisis. He is said, however, to have been *infima militia* (of the meanest soldiers) which does not seem at all likely. His entire career suggests that he was probably an experienced officer, which would strengthen the case for his having engineered his own acclamation as imperial claimant. He may have begun his career as a squaddy but, by the time of his elevation he was probably fairly senior in the island from well before the crisis in some significant military capacity, and perhaps promoted to *comes Britanniarum* by *MARCUS* as his replacement.

Reign

Either way, he seems not to have left Britain for the continent immediately, remaining in the island and making dispositions to secure the place once he had removed the field army to the continent. Although the sources imply that he completely denuded the Diocese of troops, it seems likely (supported by archaeology) that, as with **MAGNUS MAXIMUS**, he left at least the frontier forces *in situ* - thus Hadrian's Wall and the Saxon Shore forts probably remained manned, if, in the latter context, on a reduced basis using locally recruited militias.[761] He probably crossed to the continent in early summer of 407. His dispositions included the appointment of joint *magistri militum*: one of his subordinate commanders, Justinianus, and a Frankish officer, Nebiogastes, sending them across the channel in advance to take command of what remained of the Gallic army.[762] In the event, they had to deal not only with the barbarians roaming around northern and western Gaul, but attempts by **HONORIUS** to neutralise this imperial claimant on his northern

---

761. Collinson & Breeze (2014) 61-72
762. PLRE I Justinianus 1, PLRE II Justinianus 1 & Nebiogastes.

flank. Had the government in Ravenna recognised **CONSTANTINE** more immediately, more might have been achieved. Instead, within a few months, **HONORIUS'S** general Sarus had defeated and killed Justinianus and later killed Nebiogastes after tricking him into a parley, instead of allowing them to sort out the barbarians.[763]

The new emperor's full style was **D[ominus] N[oster] Flavius Claudius Constantinus P[ius] F[elix] Aug[ustus]** but we are even less well informed about the underpinning of his regime than we were about **POSTUMUS** a century and a half before: did he call a council or senate of Gallic grandees? Did he nominate consuls and so forth? The course of events probably suggest that some kind of assembly of the great and good was constituted, but no consuls have ever been identified except for **CONSTANTINE** himself. In 409, the 3rd consulship of Eastern emperor **THEODOSIUS II** was not recognised, and the imperial claimant himself held his first *in lieu*. Towards the end of 407, Justinianus was replaced by another Frank, Edobichus and Nebiogastes by a Briton, Gerontius, both much more competent and probably fellow officers of **CONSTANTINE**.[764] They soon forced Sarus to lift the siege of Valentia (Valence) which city he had invested after disposing of Nebiogastes, as drove him back into Italy.

Most accounts of what transpired thereafter give a highly confused picture, and as such probably represented the situation on the ground fairly accurately. The Barbarian hordes seem to have ravaged westwards rather than southwards, leaving **CONSTANTINE** to move south to secure those parts of Gaul untouched by the chaos, finally fixing his capital at Arelate (Arles). That he lasted as long as he did suggests that he did a fairly competent job in the circumstances. He was only really challenged when the going became very rough. He must have also undertaken some stabilisation of the Rhine frontier, which although more notional than actual after 407, still seems to have been manned to some extent.

Having secured Gaul as well as he could, in 408 **CONSTANTINE** elevated his elder son, **Constans** to the rank of **nobilissimus caesar**, having caused him to leave the monastic life which he had embraced at some earlier stage. He then sent him, with Gerontius as his *comes*, into Spain to settle matters there in 408. He swiftly put down all resistance and then garrisoned the Pyrenean passes to prevent the barbarian tribes, by this time in western Gaul, from entering Spain. Constans then returned to Gaul. This period of stability, combined with a period of extreme weakness and peril on the part of the official western government in Ravenna, led to **HONORIUS** grudgingly recognising **CONSTANTINE** as co-emperor by sending him an imperial robe and agreeing to serve with him as joint consul for 409. Yet it was in that year, probably in the summer, that things began to unravel. Constans returned to Spain with another *magister militum*, Justus - conceivably a son of the unfortunate Justinianus[765] - to relieve Gerontius. Unfortunately, the entire thing somehow went seriously wrong;

---

763. Drinkwater (1998) 284 ff.
764. PLRE II Edobichus & Gerontius 5
765. The concordance in their nomenclature, as with *CONSTANTINUS* and *CONSTANS*, is highly suggestive.

Gerontius took offence and, having won the support of his troops, began plotting against **CONSTANTINE** by colluding with the barbarians whom the latter had finally managed to settle in Gaul. The outcome was that he enrolled a large number of them into his forces in Spain, which was the thin end of the wedge, and from that year, the Pyrenean border became exceedingly porous.

This was read at Arelate as an act of rebellion, whereupon, Gerontius, an 'experienced soldier and stern disciplinarian' raised his *domesticus* (second in comand) *MAXIMUS* to the purple in Spain in 409. Yet for the time being, **CONSTANTINE** and *MAXIMUS* successfully ruled Gaul and Spain in an uneasy peace, although it would appear that in 410, the *régime* of the Gallic emperor suffered a set-back. In that year control of Britain slipped out of *CONSTANTINE'S* grasp. From the very confusing accounts, it would appear that the administration he had left behind there, presumably a *vicarius* (diocesan governor), provincial governors and the three senior military command-ers[766], appears to have been ousted by an anti-Constantinian *putsch* (presumably led by another imperial claimant whose name has not been preserved[767]), and the new administration then appears to have written to **HONORIUS** pledging their loyalty to him and asking for help in defending their shores and borders. The response was the famous rescript of 410 (fixing the chronology), bidding the cities of the diocese to look to their own defence for the time being. That 'time being' turned out to be a trifle open-ended and direct control appears never to have been more than tenuously resumed over the British provinces.

Late in 409 or early 410, one of **HONORIUS'S** disloyal commanders, Allobichus - another Frank – encouraged the Gallic rulers to join him in overthrowing **HONORIUS**, and in spring 410 **CONSTANTINE** made the same mistake as **MAGNUS MAXIMUS** and crossed into Italy, leaving Constans behind to look after affairs in Gaul. It was presumably at this stage too that Constans was elevated to the rank of co-Augustus with his father bearing the style of **D[ominus] N[oster] Constans P[ius] F[elix] Augustus**; his younger brother **Julianus**, who was probably only in his early 20s, was made **nobilissimus Caesar**. From coins, it would appear that both he and his father still considered themselves recognised co-rulers of the West with **HONORIUS**.

Meanwhile, in Italy, the claimant beat a hasty retreat after the plot against **HONORIUS** was uncovered and the disloyal Frank executed. However, the temporary absence of **CONSTANTINE** in Italy had encouraged Gerontius and *MAXIMUS* to attempt to take control of Gaul from him. At the beginning of 411 they crossed the Pyrenees and attacked besieged Vienna (Vienne), on the fall of which **CONSTANS** was killed. These upheavals in Gaul provided the government in Ravenna with an opportunity to pull

---

766. The two *comites: Britanniarum* and *Litoris Saxonici,* and the *dux Britanniarum.*

767. Those commentators who have risked speculating on British events from this point would suggest the person who has come down to us as Vortigern (see **Table LVIII(b)** in **Appendix 1**) was the claimant, but it need not be so. Events may have been a lot more complex at this stage

things round, and Allobichus's much more competent successor as *magister militum,* Constantius, was sent to attack **CONSTANTINE'S** capital, Arles. As he approached, the city was already invested by *MAXIMUS,* who, on realising this, raised the siege and retreated back to Spain. With things going wrong, **CONSTANTINE'S** praetorian prefect, Decimius Rusticus connived with a Gallic notable called *JOVINUS,* posted on the Rhine frontier to keep order there, to have the latter declared emperor in **CONSTANTINE'S** place.[768] Meanwhile, the latter's last hope was the arrival of re-inforcements from the Rhine under the ever loyal Edobichus, but Constantius, realising this, made a lightning march up the Rhône valley and confronted the Frank, whose forces handed him over and deserted to *JOVINUS.*

Realising that the game was up, the Gallic ruler took holy orders and then negotiated a surrender with Constantius, including a safe conduct for himself and his younger son, Julianus. On nearing Ravenna, however, the party were intercepted, and the pair were executed on the spot.[769] Despite having received a bad press as being the catalyst for the abandonment by the Empire of the Diocese of Britain, Prosper of Aquitaine could write of this that **CONSTANTINE** had defended the frontiers of Gaul better than eny emperor since **MAGNUS MAXIMUS,** Zosimus adding that until this crisis, the Rhine frontier had been neglected since the time **of JULIAN**.[770]

Family

CONSTANTINE may have been a Briton, but we certainly cannot be sure, although his name suggested, to those who were familiar with the early Welsh pedigrees, that he belonged to the post-Roman ruling dynasty of Dumnonia (modern Devon and Cornwall). Indeed, from that perspective, with the name Geraint (Gerontius) alternating with Custennin (Constantinus) in the king-lists, it could be argued (or not certainly denied) that the *magister militum* Gerontius could possibly have been a fairly close relation of **CONSTANTINE** himself. There had been, indeed, plenty of precedent. All we can tell for certain is that the claimant had no living wife (or he would without doubt named her Augusta and issued coins bearing her image), two certain sons of whom, **CONSTANS II** was married for, after the defeat of rebel forces in Spain in 408, he left his wife and household in Caesaraugusta (Zaragosa) whilst he returned to Arelate; their fate in unrecorded. As with **MAGNUS MAXIMUS,** early Welsh genealogical works and legends provide the Emperor with further family. See **Table LX** below.

*

768. PLRE II Rusticus 9. He was a friend of Sidonius Apollinaris's family, and quite probably a close relative of the poet and politician Decimius Magnus Ausonius (consul in 379): Sivan (1993) 60 f..

769. PLRE II Constantinus 21; Constans 1 & Julianus 7.

770. Prosper, year 412, Zosimus 6, 3, both quoted in Knight (2014) 167.

MAXIMUS IV
c. June 409 – Sept. 411 & c. July 419 – February 421

Background

Having decided to make a break with **CONSTANTINE III,** his former *magister militum* Gerontius for some reason decided not to have himself acclaimed, possibly because his reputation for severe discipline meant that the move would not be wholly popular with his troops. He therefore chose his *domesticus* and dependent, *MAXIMUS* as emperor at Tarraco (Tarragoña), probably in early summer 409. His style was (from a modest coinage of silver *siliquae* minted at Barcino (Barcelona) c. 410): **D[ominus] N[oster] Maximus P[ius] F[elix] Aug[ustus].**

Gerontius's first task, originally under **CONSTANS II** as Caesar, had been to overcome a pro-**HONORIUS** uprising amongst the local élite in the Gallaecian region, led by a group of the emperor's relations, Theodosiolus, Didymus, Lagodius and Verianus. They were quickly put down, the first two being captured and the latter, who escaped, going to Constantinople. Once **CONSTANS** had returned to Gaul for the second time, with *MAXIMUS* installed, Gerontius felt able to pursue a more aggressive policy. He settled the barbarians that were already in Spain, and greatly enlarged his forces with them before going to war against **CONSTANTINE.**

Reign

It would appear, from all the evidence, that the new imperial claimant was mainly a figurehead with Gerontius, a first class commander, making all the running: arranging treaties with the Vandals in Spain, conspiring to de-throne **CONSTANTINE III,** besieging Vienna and killing **CONSTANS II.** Had he been the prime mover in these, he would without doubt have been killed when the army mutinied. As it was, when the retreat from Arelate led to the army turning on their British general, Gerontius killed his wife Nunechia and then killed himself. *MAXIMUS* seems to have survived, in some sources as Emperor, until some time in 412, before going to ground. He is said to have lived quietly on an estate in Spain (presumably Gallaecia) amongst the very Vandals whom the local grandees had accused Gerontius of introducing into their diocese.

In July 419, however, we find another *MAXIMUS* appearing in Spain as an imperial claimant. It is not absolutely certain that this is the same man as *MAXIMUS IV* but the circumstantial evidence strongly supports it.[771] This time, he was empurpled by the ruler of the Vandals, Gundericus, whose people had been forcibly moved after a spat with the Sueves, both peoples having been settled by Gerontius in Gallaecia. Gundericus's people were moved to Baetica, another Spanish province, and the Gothic auxiliaries who had policed the move withdrew west of the Pyrenees. Thus in about July 419, *MAXIMUS* was trotted out and restored whilst the nominal *vicarius* of the entire diocese was expelled.

---

771. PLRE II Maximus 4 & Maximus 7.

The *comes Hispaniarum* Asterius, fresh from sorting out the Sueves, seems to have been able to deal with the claimant before the appearance the Western government's *magister militum per Gallias* (C-in-C Gaul) Castinus, sent to straighten things out. Asterius took the ever useful Gothic auxiliaries with him and fought a series of running battles, in which *MAXIMUS* was captured, probably in February 421. His nemesis was made a patrician as a reward.[772] Castinus then took over. Initially successful, by refusing to compromise he later suffered a crushing defeat, which sealed the future of Roman Spain for ever and allowed the Vandals to settle where they had triumphed (hence modern Andalsusia).[773]

MAXIMUS was, however, sent back to Italy where he was slaughtered in the arena as part of the Emperor's thirtieth anniversary games, 10th January 423.

Family

MAXIMUS is described as a 'dependent' of Gerontius (meaning close relative), and is often thought of as his son, which may well have been so. The only reason to doubt it is that if Gerontius was held responsible by the Roman population of Spain for allowing the barbarian in, then why would they have let his son live? The answer may lie in the gratitude of the Vandals, amongst whom he seems to have lived for the eight years between his reigns and who elevated him to the purple a second time when showing defiance to a Roman administration which they felt had not dealt fairly with them. Added to this, there is the suggestion, albeit embedded in the much later and largely untrustworthy Welsh genealogies, that Gerontius and **CONSTANTINE III** were also close kin.

The two names crop up amongst the Cornovii, which people had their capital at Viroconium (Wroxeter, Salop.) but a significant group of whom John Morris considered were transferred to the far South West of Britain to expel an incursion of Irish as part of the upheavals and make-do-and-mend settlement in Britain of the years 407/410. Hence, therefore, the subdivision of Dumnonia (the emergent polity covering the whole of the British South West) called Cornovia (later mutating through several stages into modern Cornwall) and its double, Cornouaille, across the channel in Brittany.[774] This is re-inforced by the fact that, in Susan Pearce's words, 'All the traditions of the royal line of Dumnonia relate to early ancestors firmly rooted in Wales', citing Eudaf Hen (Roman equivalent, approximately Octavius Priscus), Cynan (Conan/Caninus), Helen (alleged wife of **MAGNUS MAXIMUS**) and [G]adeon being associated, like **MAGNUS MAXIMUS** himself, with *Aber Seiont* (Caernarvon) and even citing Geoffrey of Monmouth's description of Eudaf as 'Duke of the Gewissei', suggesting Eastern mid-Wales, thus the heartland of Powys.[775]

---

772. Kulikowski (2000) 123 ff.
773. Livermore (1971) 85
774. Morris (1973) 69.
775. Pearce (1978) 143 cf. Dark (2000) 148 & Russell (2017) 238-239.

Sozomen, in his description of the deaths of Gerontius and Nunechia, also tells us of their close aide, Alanus who died with them.[776] The passage rather reads as though he might be another close relation, perhaps her brother. If so this is an example of yet another name found in the later Breton/Cornish annals, alongside those of Geraint and Custennin.

It is therefore entirely possible, though entirely unproven, that these three imperial claimants were close kin and that from them, somehow, the shadowy early medieval kings of Dumnonia and even parts of Brittany descended. The traditional Welsh genealogies would have them descend from Eudaf Hen via his son Caninus [Conan/Cynan Meriadoc], who was, in their eyes, a brother-in-law of **MAGNUS MAXIMUS**.[777] It may also be that they had started out as a group of locally recruited senior officers serving in Britain in 406/407. **Table LX** is an attempt to suggest how these important characters could have been linked, but note that it is largely speculative.

*

TABLE LX: CONSTANTINE III & GERONTIUS

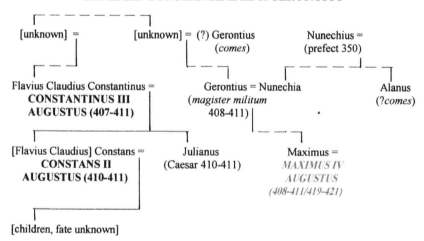

TABLE LX: BRIEF LIVES

Alanus

Friend and companion of Gerontius, possibly a *comes* of *MAXIMUS,* therefore. Tellingly. he was prepared to die together with Gerontius and Nunechia [Sozomen IX.13]

Flavius Claudius Constantinus

See above *CONSTANTINUS III AUGUSTUS*

[Flavius Claudius] Constans

See above *CONSTANS II AUGUSTUS*

Gerontius *comes*

A *comes* of *MAGNENTIUS,* possibly *comes rei militaris,* exiled to Arelate 353/353 [PLRE I Gerontius 1]

---

776. Sozomen IX. 13 (not in PLRE II)

777. See Appendix I Table LVIII(b). The Welsh sources are Jesus MS 20, 10-11 & *Bonedd y Saint* 26.

Gerontius

A native of Britain, a probable former comrade-in-arms and *comes* of **CONSTANTINE III** but nominated *magister militum* in Gaul appointed to succeed Justinianus in summer 407. On his subsequent career, see above. It is quite possible he was a son of the elder Gerontius (who may have been a Briton, was not necessarily so) and would have been born about the time Gerontius was exiled to Arelate. Probably he was somewhat older than **CONSTANTINE**, which may be why he eschewed the purple in favour of his probable son, *MAXIMUS* [PLRE II Gerontius 5]

Julianus

Younger son, made *nobilissimus* in 408, and *nobilissimus caesar* in 410, killed with his father 411. Their heads were displayed at Carthage, perhaps to keep *HERACLIANUS* in line [PLRE II Julianus 7]

Maximus

See above *MAXIMUS IV AUGUSTUS*

Nunechia

A Christian killed by Gerontius at her own request, with Alanus, to prevent herself falling into the hands of the soldiers [PLRE II Nunechia]

Nunechius

Praetorian prefect in Gaul of *MAGNENTIUS* and a senator. He led a delegation to **CONSTANTIUS II** to negotiate a settlement between the two emperors, but was detained by the latter. His subsequent fate is unknown He would almost certainly have served in tandem with the elder Gerontius and both were quite possibly former comrades-in-arms of *MAGNENTIUS'S*. [PLRE I Nunechius].

*

JOVINUS
July 411 – c. later March 413

SEBASTIANUS
(Known to history as Sebastian)
c. October 412 – c. mid-March 413

Background

In Gaul, with **CONSTANTINE III** in trouble, there was disaffection amongst the troops on the Rhine, this time comprising levies of Burgundians, Alans, Alamans and Franks which had been re-organised by him after the crisis of 407. Probably they had not been paid, itself no doubt a symptom of the upheavals being experienced throughout the north western provinces. Nevertheless, to remedy the situation, Guntiarius, the Burgundian chief, and Goar, his Alan opposite number, raised a Gallic noble senator, *JOVINUS* to the purple at Mundiacum (Muntzen, near Tongres) in Germania Secunda. He was probably **CONSTANTINE'S** *comes rei militaris* or governor there. One of his other supporters was Athualfus, leader of the Visigoths, still resentful about his people's treatment in

Italy by the government of **HONORIUS**. The Gallic nobility also supported him (he being of their number) and Decimius Rusticus, who had deserted **CONSTANTINE III** now joined him. Indeed Rusticus may even have been a kinsman, which might explain his willingness to change horses in the middle of such a choppy stream.

Reign

The new imperial claimant styled himself **D[ominus] N[oster] Iovinus P[ius] F[elix] Aug[ustus]** although as with **CONSTANTINE, CONSTANS** and *MAXIMUS*, we know of no certain governmental structures in place in the continuing break-away empire that might have validated styles or awarded consulships and suchlike, but there almost certainly was such a body, composed of the senatorial nobility and the military *élite* based in Gaul (and Spain to 410).

After the demise of his rival at Arles, *JOVINUS* appears to have taken a grip on the situation, but his chief problem was with the contending barbarian chieftans upon whose co-operation he depended to keep his *régime* stable in Gaul. This was fine up to a point, but Athaulfus, who had with him the Princess Galla Placidia, the daughter of **THEODOSIUS I**, began to make demands over and above the others (his imperial hostage being freely used as a bargaining chip), especially as he managed to dispose of **HONORIUS'S** former general, Sarus, who had defected to *JOVINUS*, but whom Athaulfus destroyed, with his men, in revenge for past encounters. Promoting Athaulfus as his right hand man would have undoubtedly had put the noses of Goar and Guntiarius out of joint, so instead, he made his brother *SEBASTIAN* his co-ruler in 412, to demonstrate to the Goth that he already had a deputy and successor.

SEBASTIAN'S style was, as was now the norm, **D[ominus] N[oster] Sebastianus P[ius] F[elix] Aug[ustus]**. As a consequence, early in 413, a very miffed Athaulfus secretly sent to **HONORIUS** and offered him the heads of both imperial claimants in return for a treaty with his people, which offer, needless to say, was readily accepted. Athualfus was as good as his word, returning to Gaul, killing *SEBASTIAN* and capturing his brother, sending him to Narbo, where Claudius Postumus Dardanus, **HONORIUS'S** praetorian prefect (nominally of all Gaul), who had been discreetly supporting Athaulfus after his defection back to **HONORIUS**, had him executed, duly despatching their heads on to Ravenna. Both were subsequently sent to Carthage to join those of **CONSTANTINUS III, CONSTANS II** and that of the recently executed *HERACLIANUS*.[778]

Aftermath

These executions marked the end of the short-lived second Gallic empire after some seven years. Henceforth **HONORIUS** was once again able to reign over an undivided west, even if his control over Britain, portions of Gaul and large parts of Spain was rather more titular than effective.

---

778. PLRE II Jovinus 2 & Sebastianus 2.

Family

The two imperial claimants were brothers, but nothing is known of their careers prior to their elevation, although, as suggested above, *JOVINUS* was probably an appointment of **CONSTANTINE III's** on the Rhine frontier. They had a third brother, Sallustius, who was also executed in 413. There is a suggestion that they were descended (presumably grandchildren) of the consul of 367, Flavius Iovinus, who had been appointed *magister equitum* by **JULIAN** in 361, served as troubleshooter in Britain in his consulship year and who appears to have been a Gaul of distinguished family.[779] Consentius, a rhetor at Narbo in the 440s, had indeed married a lady (whose name is lost to us) who was a descendant of the consul of 367. It is here suggested that she was the daughter of *JOVINUS* or one of his siblings. It is therefore possible tentatively to suggest a possible family for the two imperial claimants, below **Table LXI**

*

TABLE LXI: JOVINUS & SEBASTIAN

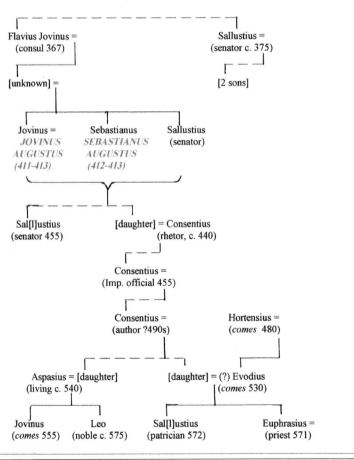

---

779. Birley (1981) 373-374. He retired to Rheims and founded a church there.

TABLE LXI: BRIEF LIVES

Aspasius

A Gallo-Roman nobleman, attested as father of Leo and Jovinus by Venantius Fortunatus. The name of his elder son suggests descent from Fl Jovinus via the Consentii [PLRE III Aspasius]

Consentius

A poet, a man of senatorial rank and a native of Narbo (Narbonne) whose wife was a descendant, Sidonius Apollinaris tells us, of the consul of 367, Fl. Jovinus [PLRE II Consentius 1]

Consentius

Son of the foregoing and addressee of a poem from Sidonius, an old friend. The failure of Sidonius to mantion the imperial claimant may well have been his closeness in time to that event which it may have been tactful to omit from his effulgences. He became *tribunus et notarius* (junior under-secretary) under **VALENTINIAN III** who sent him on embassies to the court of Constantinople. He retired, but was recalled by **AVITUS** as *cura palatii* (major domo). He again had retired to his estates by 466 and was still living in the 470s [PLRE II Consentius 2]

Consentius

A man of senatorial rank (*vir clarissimus*), a fifth century Gallic author and probably related to the two preceding [PLRE II Consentius 3]

Euphrasius

A priest at Clermont (also spelt Eufrasius), who hoped to be appointed bishop there in 571 but was unsuccessful. He was related to a Frank called Beregisil, possibly his brother-in-law. His family was local and of senatorial descent [PLRE III Eufrasius]

Evodius

A priest at Clermont of noble family who failed to become bishop of Gabalitana (Javols), but was later made *comes* of Clermont in succession to his father [PLRE III Evodius]

Flavius Jovinus

Served as *magister equitum* of **JULIAN** 360, serving under his successors until made consul in 369. He suppressed the mutiny which killed Lucillianus, **JOVIAN'S** father-in-law in 364, and led a successful campaign against the Alemanni in 366, which earned him his consulship, during which he served in Britain. He built a church at Rheims [PLRE I Jovinus 6].

Hortensius

A man of senatorial rank appointed *comes* of the Auvergne based at Nemetum, later Civitas Avernum (Clermont) following a sack of the area by Frankish King Theodoricus. He probably married a daughter of Magnus Felix, grandson of **PETRONIUS MAXIMUS** [PLRE II Hortensius 2 & **Table LIX(a)** above]

Jovinus

See above *JOVINUS AUGUSTUS*

Jovinus

A comes of the Frankish king, he was appointed a patrician by the King Sigibert 573/574 and made governor of Provence. He was still alive and clashing with the Frankish authorities in 581 [PLRE III Iovinus 1].

Leo

A Gallo-Roman of senatorial descent, but nothing is known of his life [PLRE III Leo 10].

Sallustius

A man of senatorial rank who served as prefect of the City of Rome 387. He was in correspondence with Q. Aurelius Symmachus from which we learn that he had two sons, the younger of whom married in 398. There is no certainty that he was related to Fl. Jovinus, however [PLRE I Sallustius 4]

Sallustius

A Gaul; and a man of senatorial rank, he was executed along with his siblings in 413 [PLRE II Sallustius 2]

Sal[l]ustius

A senator of high rank (a *vir inlustris*) living at Narbo in 455 where he was a generous benefactor to both church and state [PLRE II Sallustius 6].

Sallustius

Of a senatorial family from the Auvergne he was appointed *comes* of Civitas Avernum (Clermont) by the Frankish grandee Chramn in 555 and was probably still in office five years later. Later a patrician [PLRE III Sallustius].

Sebastianus

See above *SEBASTIANUS AUGUSTUS*

*

The collapse of the Second Gallic Empire is generally thought to mark the end of direct imperial involvement with Britain. No official troops meant that no money was coming into the province, although modern thinking believes that the money economy survived with the coin in circulation in 407 for at least a generation.[780] Ken Dark has argued convincingly that a typical late antique society survived in most of Britain throught the fifth century and in the north, west and south west for at least another century beyond that.[781] Yet high-spending officials were withdrawn, being replaced only by locally based ones. Other commentators have, however, claimed that a much more sudden economic collapse occurred.[782] Nevertheless, there can be little doubt that those living in the province still thought of themselves as part of the empire, even though direct involvement with the structure of government had been largely lost. Our (admittedly inadequate) sources tell us that, whatever form of government remained, felt sufficiently involved with the empire as to expect imperial assistance long after the withdrawal of the provincial army in c. 406/411.[783]

The references in the sources to the province succumbing to the rule of 'tyrants' suggests that whoever took over after the fall of **CONSTANTINE III** – usually named as Vortigern, with even more shadowy characters bobbing up in his wake – might be so termed and who may reasonably be classified as 'tyranni' and thus recognised imperial claimants. The British ruler Vortigern, we are told in a late source, *tenuit*

780. Dark (2000) 144; cf. the wear on much of the later Roman coinage excavated in Britain, eg. those from the age of **VALENTINIAN I** recovered from Derventio in the 1960s & 1970s & curated by the author at Derby.
781. Dark (2000) *passim*.
782. Halsall (2013) 96f.
783. Barnwell (1992) 68-69 quoting Gildas, *De Excidio* 15-20.

imperium in Britannia (held imperial power in Britain) in 425.[784] How they actually styled themselves and indeed saw themselves is open to question, and outside of legend, none made a bid for power beyond Britain, unlike **CONSTANTINE.** Hence, it seems safer here to overlook their claims.

⋆

Imperial Claimants under Honorius

ATTALUS
November 409 – May/June 410 & 414 – June 415

Background

Priscus *ATTALUS* was a senior and very distinguished pagan senator whose family came originally from Greece. He was born c. 360/365, and late in the reign of **THEODOSIUS I** he had served as a provincial governor, for he held the rank of *vir spectabilis* on receipt of his first surviving letter from Symmachus in 394. Four years later he was one of a deputation from the senate to **HONORIUS**, and fulfilled the same role again in 409 after the first siege of Rome by Alaric, the Gothic king. As a result, he was appointed *comes sacrarum largitionum* (chief finance minister) for the western Empire, but about six months later was further appointed prefect of the City of Rome. It was whilst he was in this office that the second siege of Rome began and he was singled out by Alaric to be his puppet emperor late in the year, probably in November.

ATTALUS was extremely wealthy and had estates in Greece as well as a villa at Tibur (Tivoli) and a town house on the Mons Caelius at Rome.[785] There is no mention of a wife, so she probably had died or divorced prior to her husband's accession.

Reigns

As emperor, the new imperial claimant was first of all baptised a Christian, although by an Arian Gothic bishop, for most of the migrating tribes which came into the Empire at this period, if they were Christian at all, were of the heretical Arian persuasion. *ATTALUS* assumed the rather obsolete senatorial style **Imp[erator] Priscus Attalus P[ius] F[elix] Aug[ustus]** on his coins. One might have assumed that he would have become consul on the next available opportunity, but the western consul in 410 was Tertullus, who was probably a son or brother. This was recognised neither by Ravenna nor Constantinople, although no alternative western consul seems to have been appointed, except in the polity of **CONSTANTINE III.** *ATTALUS* was

---

784. According to the much later *Historia Brittonum* 66: Morris (1980) 80.
785. PLRE II Attalus 2

acclaimed by the senate (at the command of Alaricus), to which he delivered a long and elaborate discourse, and may even have been formally accorded the tribunician and proconsular powers at the same time. Whether this recognition made him an acknowledged emperor is a matter of debate, but as the long-serving legitimate western emperor failed to acknowledge his status, he remains here an imperial claimant only, senatorial support (possibly under duress) notwithstanding.

One issue of his coins bears the reverse legend *Invicta Roma Aeterna* (Eternal unconquered Rome) which seems gloriously ironic when one bears in mind that some time after the issue was made, Alaric sacked the City, even though he pulled his punches (the more lurid accounts of the incident are all by later Christian writers with an axe to grind). *ATTALUS* made some appointments, notably Alaric, who became *magister militum*, a position for which he had asked **HONORIUS**, but which had been denied, precipitating the sack, during which the princess Galla Placidia was taken hostage. *ATTALUS* then sent Alaric to take control of northern Italy and to invest Ravenna, which, coming at a critical period in the affairs of **HONORIUS** forced a recognition of *ATTALUS* as co-Augustus.[786]

Meanwhile the latter set in train measures to secure Africa. In this latter task, the Gothic king believed his emperor was dragging his feet. As a result, his disaffection drove him to re-open negotiations with **HONORIUS** with the result that in summer 410 the claimant was deposed, although (unusually) no harm came to him. However, what with becoming an Arian and having presided over the sack of Rome as Alaric's creature (he wrote panegyrics for him), he could hardly return home, so remained with the Visigoths, even after their king had died and been succeeded by his brother-in-law Athaulfus.

After having supported *JOVINUS* and *SEBASTIANUS* and then betrayed them, Athaulfus remained in Gaul campaigning for **HONORIUS** against the Vandals, but in summer 414 after a squabble with the court at Ravenna over his unauthorised marriage to Galla Placidia, he once again elevated *ATTALUS* to the purple, on this occasion without the prospect of recognition as co-ruler. However, when the Goths retreated into Spain in 415, they abandoned poor *ATTALUS* (but not Galla Placidia), leaving him to fall into the hands of the imperial government. He was deposed, mutilated (thumb and forefinger of his right hand only – he was let off rather lightly) and led in a rather empty triumph celebrated by **HONORIUS** in June 416 (probably on the first anniversary of *ATTALUS'S* second deposition) before being exiled to the Lipari Islands, after which no more is heard of him.[787]

*

---

786. He retains his status as an imperial claimant not because his recognition was fleeting but because his second reign was completely un-recognised.
787. This was the last recorded triumph ever held in the western empire.

TABLE LXII: THE FAMILY OF ATTALUS

[Insteius] Tertullus =
(PUR 359-361)

P. Ampelius = (?) [Insteia]
(PUR 371-372)

Priscus Attalus =
ATTALUS
AUGUSTUS
(409-410/414-415)

Ampelius =
(senator 390-394)

Ampelius =
(senator c. 409/415)

Tertullus
(Consul 410)

[daughter]

6th century Ampelii

TABLE LXII: BRIEF LIVES

Ampelius

A senator, known to Symmachus and mentioned by him in a letter, c. 390-394 [PLRE I Ampelius 1].

Ampelius

Son of *ATTALUS*, although not known to have been named as his father's heir or made Caesar. He was a senator and was kept in the Visigothic entourage c. 409/415. It is possible he left a family, however, as there was a number of Ampelii flourishing in Rome under King Theodericus in the early 6th century: one was prefect of the corn supply at Rome 523/526, later a *vir illustris*; another was also of the same rank and living in the first half of the 6th century, whilst a third was a *vir magnificus* and a judge in Apulia under **JUSTINIAN** in 559, as well as a Tertullus who was a patrician c. 522 (he also had a son, Placidus). It is impossible to establish any connection and there seem to be no likely kin in between this man and these later homonyms. Nevertheless, they certainly suggests a possible connection [PLRE II Ampelius 1, cf. 4, 5, Placidus 3 & Tertullus 2, also *ibid*. III Ampelius 1, 2].

P. Ampelius

Originally a pagan native of Antioch but of a senatorial family. It is most unusual for a senator to bear a *praenomen* and *nomen* alone, and although this is how he must have been known to his friends (e.g. Symmachus) it would seem likely that he had a *cognomen* too; the western senatorial families were sticklers for traditional orthography much of the time, although they played games with the elements of them. Ampelius served as a provincial governor c. 355, possibly of Cappadocia, then of Achaia in 359/360, after which he was at court in Constantinople from 360 before serving as proconsul of Africa 364 and prefect of the City of Rome 371-372, in which office he was popular, despite imposing strict regulations on bars and restaurants. His son – presumably the future imperial claimant – is attested as having been born prior to 366 [PLRE I Ampelius 3]

[Insteius] Tertullus

Thought to have been grandson of Attius Insteius Tertullus, prefect of the City if Rome 307-308, and son of [Insteius] Tertullus proconsul of Africa in 326, he was Prefect of the City of Rome 359-361. The suggestion in the reconstruction of the family of *ATTALUS* is that the *cognomen* Tertullus came into the claimant's family through a marriage with this man's family. The Insteii can be traced with reasonable confidence back to L. Insteius [L. f. Hor.] Tertullus (master of a priestly college 214), conceivably a grandson of M. Insteius Bithynicus, suffect consul in 162 [PIR[2] I30, 38; PLRE I Tertullus 2 cf. Tertullus 1, 5 & 6].

Priscus Attalus

See above *ATTALUS AUGUSTUS*

Tertullus

A popular senator, he was appointed consul (West) at Rome by Attalus for 410 and is said to have expressed ambitions to assume the purple himself but was later executed, probably in the wake of *ATTALUS'S* deposition. All this, and the fact that he was a pagan, strongly suggests that, if he was not a son of the imperial claimant, he may have been a brother. Furthermore his *cognomen* suggests descent from the Insteii Tertulli. [PLRE II Tertullus 1]

*

Imperial claimant under Honorius

HERACLIANUS
c. November 412 - 7th March 413

Appointed *comes* of Africa in 408 by a grateful **HONORIUS** mainly, it would seem, as a reward for killing Stilicho with his own hands at Ravenna on August 22nd that year, his behaviour towards Rome (which relied on the export of corn from his diocese) left much to be desired. Nevertheless, he remained loyal to **HONORIUS** throughout the period of *ATTALUS'* rule and even sent him financial assistance. *ATTALUS* sent a replacement for him to Carthage called Constans, whom *HERACLIANUS* killed, leading to the delay in taking the diocese over that contributed to the deposition of *ATTALUS*. *HERACLIANUS* was rewarded with the consulship (west) for 413, but hardly had he been designated than he declared himself an imperial claimant, and stopped all exports of food to Italy.

We do not know how he styled himself, as there are no inscriptions and he seems not to have issued any coins. He did collect a large fleet and sailed to Italy to depose

HONORIUS, but on landing he was defeated, and as a result he abandoned his fleet and army, and retired to Carthage in a single vessel, where he was murdered on 7th March 413. His consulship was annulled, his supporters persecuted and his property (which was not enormous) seized.[788]

The only facts we have about his family is that he had a daughter who married Sabinus, his second-in-command and who ended up in exile.

*

CONSTANTIUS III
8th February – 2nd September 421

Background

Flavius CONSTANTIUS was yet another Danubian general, albeit of Roman descent, having been born at Naissus in Dacia Ripensis (Niš, Serbia) c. 366, becoming a junior officer under **THEODOSIUS I**, and distinguished himself in numerous campaigns. He appears at court in 409, where he had one of Stilicho's assassins killed. By 411 he was a *comes* and *magister militum* throughout the western empire, a post he held until 421. He was also made *vir illustris* and held the consulship (West) in 414. The following year he was made a patrician (if indeed not so promoted earlier).

He was an implacable foe of the Visigoths, especially Athaulfus, of whom he was jealous for having married Galla Placidia, whom he coveted, and this coloured his military policy. He attacked the Visigoths in Gaul, driving them from Narbo (Narbonne) and forcing them across the Pyrenees (obliging them again to abandon *MAXIMUS IV*). When Athaulfus died, his successor, Walia, made a treaty with him and repatriated Galla, whom he wed (largely against her will, one suspects) on 1st January 417, at which juncture he entered into his second consulship. She was made Augusta and they had two children, Pulcheria and the future emperor **VALENTINIAN III**. At her insistence he was elevated to be co-emperor with **HONORIUS.** He then negotiated the settlement of the Visigoths in Aquitania (418). He was consul a third time in 420, being then described as **Flavius Constantius vir clarissimus et vir inlustris patricio et tertio consulis**.[789]

Reign

On his elevation to the purple he took the style **Dominus Noster Invictus Princeps Constantius [Augustus]** on accession.[790] The convention when a new emperor was acclaimed was that his statues were sent to the senate and court of the other half of the

---

788. PLRE II Hercalianus 3.
789. ILS801.
790. ILS809; PLRE II Constantius 17

empire for formal recognition. The unilateral elevation of **CONSTANTIUS** and the influence over the young emperor of his sister Pulcheria ensured that these were rejected in Constantinople, a slight which humiliated the new augustus. He therefore made preparations to impose himself in the east by force, thereby re-uniting the Empire, but died of pleurisy on 2nd September. He was known for his incorruptibility and stern demeanour, although it appears he also enjoyed social occasions and found life at court after his accession stifling and confining. Yet for a decade or more he had dominated political and military life, seen off four imperial claimants and stabilised the rule of **HONORIUS**, in short a man of considerable distinction.

Family
See above **TABLE LIX(a)**; nothing is known of his ancestry except that it was Roman and Danubian.

*

IOHANNES I
(Known to History as John [I][791])
20th November 423 – March 425

Background
When **HONORIUS** died unexpectedly of dropsy on 15h August 423 there was a power vacuum in the west which was technically a reversion to a re-united empire, under the eastern emperor, **THEODOSIUS II**. Indeed it was at his court that the nearest heir in blood to the Western empire was closeted with his mother: **CONSTANTIUS III**'s son **Valentinian**, **HONORIUS**'s nephew. Bearing in mind the fragile stability achieved by **CONSTANTIUS** in the West, his successor as *magister militum*, Castinus clearly recognised the urgent need for a western emperor. Being a capable and ambitious man he probably reckoned that a competent civilian of not too eminent a background might be ideal, leaving him to exercise power behind the throne, as with *EUGENIUS* almost three decades before. With hindsight it might be that he would have been better advised to choose a man within the wide family circle of the Theodosian dynasty, for on that basis, recognition of what he had done would be more likely to have been forthcoming from the court in Constantinople. As it is, he chose a senior civil servant on unimpeachable integrity called **JOHN**.

At the time of his elevation, which occurred after an interregnum, (or united rule) of three months, **JOHN** was *primicerius notariorum* (chief of the civil service).[792] Nor was he the last senior bureaucrat to be raised to the purple by an ambitious commander-in-chief.

---

791. Most late Roman/Byzantine historians omit this John (and Constantine III) from the East Roman numbering sequence eg. John I = John Tzimiskes (969-976) and Constantine III = son of Heraclius I (2-5/641)

792. PLRE II Ioannes 6

We know nothing of his family or background, either; he is not even credited with a wife and it may be that the lack of family ties commended him to Castinus – no relations to over-promote nor children expecting honours and position or likely to make future claims on the purple. Two late sources claim he was of barbarian stock, either Vandal or Goth, but this may well be the working out of prejudice against a man who, in the East at least, was regarded as a usurper.

Reign

The new Western ruler was acclaimed at Rome (rather than Ravenna) on 20th November 423, the occasion being driven by Castinus, although discreetly enough to escape being blamed directly for it in the ancient sources. The fact that he was promoted and made consul (West, not recognised in the East) for 424 seem to speak for themselves, however. He was styled in the usual way as **Dominus Noster Iohannes Pius Felix Augustus**.[793] As he was in Rome, it seems likely that he was swiftly recognised by the senate and, if still applicable, granted the annually renewable tribunician and proconsular powers. He was designated for a further consulship (West) for 425, but when he assumed the *fasces* he was not, rather predictably, recognised by the Eastern court. He then moved the court back to Ravenna and awaited the outcome of a delegation to **THEODOSIUS II** requesting recognition. This was not forthcoming, and was accompanied by the raising of the infant prince **Placidus Valentinianus** as caesar. Although he was not recognised in the East, he was unchallenged in the west, and it seems reasonable not to label him an imperial claimant as such. He was regarded as having been chosen in the traditional way to succeed a deceased emperor. The lack of recognition though could only mean one thing, that an expedition would soon be on its way from Constantinople to topple him. The signs were, too that each half of the empire was beginning to go its own way.

Little is recorded of his 18 month reign, except that Castinus had previously fallen out with his colleague Bonifatius, who retired in a huff to Africa, but was appointed *comes* by the Empress Placidia, to whom he remained loyal. An expedition to dislodge him seems to have been unsuccessful but not a disaster, as Castinus survived it, reputation intact. The emperor showed tolerance to all Christian sects - Arians and Donatist included - which needless to say alienated the Catholic hierarchy in Rome. In Gaul, he appears to have caused offence by subjecting priests to the jurisdiction of secular courts.[794] One favour he did bestow upon the empire was the appointment of a young officer called Aëtius as *cura palatii* (guard commander); it was an inspired choice.

Indeed, in character, Procopius the 6th century historian, records that he was both gentle, sagacious and thoroughly capable of valorous deeds[795] This, however, did not avert the

---

793. Coins, where his name is invariably spelt with the 'h'.

794. John Matthews, *Western Aristocracies and Imperial Court AD 364 - 425* (Oxford: Clarendon Press, 1990), pp. 379f

795. Procopius, *De Bellorum* III.3.6. Translated by H.B. Dewing, *Procopius* (Cambridge: Loeb Classical Library, 1979), vol. 2 p. 25

inevitable. An army from the east invaded, invested Ravenna, which appears to have been betrayed from within, and which fell in March 425. Meanwhile, Aëtius had been sent north to hire 60,000 Hun mercenaries, but they arrived back in Italy days after the fall of Ravenna. He engaged with the eastern forces, but a truce was arrived at, under the terms of which the Huns were paid off, and Aëtius took command of Gaul as *comes* and *magister militum*.

Poor **JOHN**, however, was captured and, after being taken to Aquileia, where Galla Placidia and her children were awaiting the outcome, was ritually humiliated before being executed, probably in April. The empire then became re-united yet again under **THEODOSIUS II**, whilst preparations were made for the installation off a new regime.

*

VALENTINIANUS III
(Known to history as Valentinian III)
23rd October 425 – 16th March 455

Background
Placidus **VALENTINIANUS** was born 2nd July 419 and was recognised by **HONORIUS** as his heir in 421/422, when he was accorded the style of **nobilissimus**, although this was not at first recognised by the Eastern court. However, he was shortly afterwards taken to Constantinople by his mother, the dowager empress Galla Placidia in 422. After **JOHN** had become emperor, he was at last recognised as the potential western emperor by being accorded the title **nobilissimus caesar** at Thessalonica *en route* to back Italy on 23rd October 424. After the fall of Ravenna and the death of **JOHN**, he remained in a kind of constitutional limbo until proclaimed emperor in the autumn of 425.

Reign
By the autumn of 425 matters were ready for the virtual re-constitution of the western empire. As Ravenna had been sacked in retribution for the events of the reign of **JOHN**, it had been rendered uninhabitable, and the Imperial capital moved back to Rome, for the first time since the 3rd century, whilst Ravenna was put to rights. Eventually, on October 23rd 425 the six year old **VALENTINIAN** was acclaimed Emperor. Yet he never really came into his own either, being intellectually weak, martially and maritally inadequate as well as personally indecisive. He took the style **Dominus Noster Placidus Valentinianus Invictissimus Pius Felix Augustus**[796] and his mother, made Augusta for the second time (**HONORIUS** is believed to have stripped her of the style in 422/423), acted as regent for him until around 438/440. He served as consul, first in 425 as a belated ordinary consul (**JOHN'S** tenure not having been recognised) then in 426, 430 and after that at five yearly

---

796. ILS 804, 806, 816. PLRE II Valentinianus 4.

intervals: 435, 440, 445, 450 and 455. His thirty year reign marked the final descent of the west into a pale shadow of its former self. The enmity between the army commanders Aëtius and Bonifatius led to endless intrigue, with the latter coming perilously close to being an Imperial claimant whilst serving as C-in-C Africa. Bonifatius also re-inforced his sparse forces with an army of Vandals to defend Africa, which ultimately had the result that in 439, the barbarians over-ran all of the northern African provinces up to and including Africa Proconsularis, in the process establishing an autonomous kingdom, which lasted until it was reclaimed in 530.[797] One result was that Rome's grain supply had either to be bought at a premium from the Vandal kingdom or from other imperially controlled outlets, adding to the problems the West was already experiencing.

Meanwhile, Gaul was still seething with barbarian groups and was thoroughly unsettled, and Aëtius had his work cut out for over a decade trying to reconcile the expectations of mercenary groups like the Burgundians, whilst trying to confine the Visigoths to Spain and keep the remaining parts of Gaul free from vicarious raids, sieges and other upheavals. On the whole, he did tolerably well, but never quite managed to subdue and settle the entire diocese. Even the British called upon him in the later 440s to come to their aid against the Saxons, but he was too tied up with events between the Rhine and the Pyrenees to be able to help, although the appeal rather underscored the belief that whatever administration then existed in Britain, its leaders still considered themselves part of the empire.

VALENTINIAN'S greatest test was the invasion of the Huns, provoked by the appalling behaviour of the Emperor's sister, Justa Grata Honoria, whose dealings with Attila, the Hunnic chieftain, caused him to mount an invasion of Italy in order to claim her as his bride. The Huns had been a serious threat to the stability of the East up until then, but their departure westwards allowed the East some respite. At first, diplomatic means were tried, including the grant to Attila of the honorary rank of *magister militum.* Nothing worked, however, and the threat grew. Eventually, Aëtius managed to cobble together a large force of disparate barbarians (mainly Visigoths) along with regular troops, and defeated Attila decisively at the Battle of the Catalaunian Plains (by Les Maures, a ridge west of Montgueux) in Gaul in 451. Nevertheless, the Hun tried again in 452, taking Aquileia and Mediolanum (Milan) before agreeing to withdraw after the personal intervention of Pope Leo. Fortunately for practically everyone, he died of a stroke the following year and his empire rapidly began to crumble.

VALENTINIAN had been betrothed as a child whilst still living in Constantinople, to the daughter of **THEODOSIUS II,** Licinia Eudoxia, and eventually married her there on 29th October 437, when she was aged fifteen. They had two daughters, Eudocia and Placidia.[798] She was proclaimed Augusta at Ravenna (by this time rebuilt and fit for the court to return) in 439.

---

797. PLRE II Bonifatius 3. He divorced his first wife, Pelagia (allegedly a barbarian), by whom he had a daughter, who promptly married Aëtius, giving him a son Gaudentius, and probably also a daughter.
798. PLRE II Eudoxia 2, Valentinianus 4.

The distinguished and resplendently noble senator **Petronius MAXIMUS** plotted the downfall of Aëtius, whose power he coveted, especially as, in early 454, the *magister militum* had agreed with the Emperor to a marriage between their children, which would have virtually guaranteed Aëtius the succession. As a result of a plot of fiendish complexity, the great general was killed in the palace by the emperor's own hand 21st or 22nd September 454. The crowning irony was that, in demanding appointment to Aëtius's vacant posts himself, **MAXIMUS** was refused. The Emperor's own assassination on 16th March, in the Campus Martius at Rome the year following, by a pair of barbarian officers, could therefore be seen as well nigh inevitable.

Family
See above **Table LIX(a)**

*

MAXIMUS V
(Known to History as Petronius Maximus)
17th March – 31st May 455

Background
PETRONIUS MAXIMUS was the first member an old senatorial family to accede to the purple other than as an imperial claimant since the elevation, 202 years before, of **VALERIAN** and **GALLIENUS** in 253; although no ancient source tells us precisely who his parents were. However, modern scholarship has pieced together a pedigree which is taken as accepted, even without attestation.[799] Names, a great deal of circumstantial and indirect evidence make this descent virtually certain, his kin and much of his posterity established to the satisfaction of most scholars. Some of the uncertainty may have been because he was in his own time so well known that further explanation was considered un-necessary and secondly, because his reign ended in such devastating failure, much that would interest us was merely omitted. For his ancestry, see **Tables XLV & LVIII(a)**.

His father is believed to have been Anicius Probinus (consul in 395) and he may have been descended from the emperors **PROBUS** (possibly) and **MAGNUS MAXIMUS** (more certain, being recorded by Procopius). He was born c. 396 and was praetor in 411, when he was about 15, the magistracy having become very notional by this stage and merely a platform for ther recipient's family to give lavish games. At 18 he was appointed *tribunus et notarius* (a prestigious civil service sinecure) followed by the responsible post of *comes sacrarum largitionum* (keeper of the privy purse) c. 416-419 and the prefecture of the city

---

799. Mommaerts & Kelley (1992) 111-121; Settipani proposes a slightly different but perhaps less convincing solution.

420-421 (one was normally *en poste* for eighteen months). He served in this role for a second time later, probably in the 430s, when he undertook repairs to the basilica of St. Peter. In the early 430s he served as praetorian prefect (of which part of the west is not clear) and held his first consulship in 433 with the eastern emperor **THEODOSIUS II** as colleague. Then from 439 to 441 he was again praetorian prefect, this time of Italy. In 443 he held a second consulship (west) during which and for the two years following, he undertook the construction of a new forum at Rome on the *Mons Caelius*. By 445 he had been created a patrician. His career, for a senator especially, was exceedingly distinguished, but it seems to have given him imperial ambitions and having, it was said, encompassed the fall of Aëtius, his only rival, he was thereafter in a position to dictate the succession to the childless **VALENTINIAN**.

The story from the fall of Aëtius to the death of **MAXIMUS** has all the elements of tragic grand opera. Following the death of the general at the hands of the Emperor himself, **MAXIMUS** lobbied hard to be appointed *magister militum* in his place (a first for a senatorial aristocrat) along with a third consulship, but the emperor refused and appointed Majorian (subsequently emperor). According to John of Antioch, **MAXIMUS** then used the rape of his wife (whom he names as Lucina, but not elsewhere attested[800]) by the Emperor as a motive for the his assassination, the deed being accomplished very publicly by the two officers, thought to be in his pay, in the *Campus Martius* on 16th March 455. It was to prove one ambition too far.[801]

Reign

Following the murder of **VALENTINIAN III**, **MAXIMUS** moved to make a donative to the army and neutralise the ambitions of **MAJORIAN,** being acclaimed the following day. He immediately set about consolidating his dynastic position by marrying the Empress Eudoxia (apparently against her will) and marrying his son Palladius to the late emperor's daughter, widowed by the fall of her father-in-law Aëtius, which appears to have brought his son Gaudentius to ruin, too. It seems likely that his younger son and the future emperor **OLYBRIUS** (the relationship is nowhere attested but is generally accepted) had by this time already married the younger princess, Placidia.[802]

MAXIMUS took the style **Dominus Noster Petronius Maximus Pius Felix Augustus** and as a leading member of the senate, would undoubtedly have had himself voted the usual powers and probably was declared consul designate for the year following, although this is not directly attested. His eldest son, Palladius, was made **nobilissimus Caesar** at approximately the same time. Although he was unable to obtain recognition from the eastern court, he was acknowledged in the west, and despite his method of coming to power can hardly be called an imperial claimant.

---

800. She must have died or been divorced by the time of Maximus's accession, however and is more likely to have been called Palladia and to have been a sister of **AVITUS** (qv), thus explaining the appearance of Palladius as the name of one of his sons.

801. PLRE II Maximus 22.

802. The chronicler Hydatius only says Palladius was married to a daughter of **VALENTINIANUS III;** Conant *inter alia* favours Eudocia (*op. c.it.* (2012) 27).

He appointed his probable ex-brother-in-law, the Gallic senator Eparchius Avitus (the future emperor **AVITUS**) as *magister militum* and despatched him to Gaul to conclude a treaty with the Visigoths and to bring a detachment of them to strengthen the armed forces at the new emperor's disposal. To this end, the Emperor seems to have minted an unusual amount of gold coin both at Rome and Ravenna, undoubtedly to pay the Gothic auxiliaries and the donative to the troops already on hand. There are no known base metal or silver coins from this reign, however.

Unfortunately, his reluctant empress, in emulation of her sister-in-law's appeal to Attila, apparently called upon the Vandal King Gaiseric to come to her aid. In the event, he was only too pleased to do so, and arrived in Italy before **AVITUS** had returned with the Visigothic reinforcements. **MAXIMUS** had insufficient troops at his immediate disposal to defend the City and decreed its evacuation. The prospect of being present in a major sack by the feared barbarians turned the population against him, and he was killed in a tumult either on 22nd or the 31st May, being apparently torn limb from limb and his remains hurled into the Tiber. It is assumed that Palladius died with him.[803] Gaiseric entered the City two days later and looted it, although a full sack was avoided thanks to the intercession, yet again, of Pope Leo and, no doubt, of the princess he had come to rescue.

Family

MAXIMUS himself had no doubt as to the antiquity and nobility of his lineage.[804] There seems little reason to doubt Mommaets and Kelley's suggestion that the emperor was a son of Anicius Probinus, consul in 395 by, presumably the daughter of **MAGNUS MAXIMUS** (or his grand-daughter as they propose, and is shown on **Table XLV**). His paternal grandparents were the grandee Sex. Claudius Petronius Probus, who held most of the great offices of state prior to his consulship in 371 and his wife Anicia Faltonia Proba, daughter of Q. Clodius [*sic*] Hermogenianus Olybrius, consul in 379 and the heiress of Anicius Auchenius Bassus, of a family going back to a first consul under **SEVERUS I** and very possibly to a family pre-eminent at Praeneste during the republic, from which another branch had produced a consul, L. Anicius Gallus, who held office in 160BC. Olybrius was also the nephew of the wife of Petronius Probinus, consul in 341 and father of Sex. Petronius Probus.

Bearing in mind the consistency of nomenclature within the known kin of Petronius Maximus, the often dismissed assertion by the 6th century Eastern historian Procopius (followed by several other authors of the time) that he was a descendant of **MAGNUS MAXIMUS** cannot be dismissed as fable. Furthermore the suggestion by Mommaerts and Kelley that he was also descended from **PROBUS**, is equally plausible, given the good press that emperor received from the late fourth century historians and the frequency of the names Magnus, Maximus and Probus amongst his kin, posterity and those thought to be closely related, see **Tables XLV & LVIII(a)**.[805]

---

803. PLRE II Palladius 10.

804. ILS 809

805. *Op.cit.* 111-120, cf. HA *V. Probi* 24, 3, viewed cynically by Syme (1968) 11.

Another factor is the assignment of **OLYBRIUS** as a son of **MAXIMUS**, following Mommaerts & Kelley. In this Settipani differs in seeing him as a son of Anicius Probus, praetor 424 and grandson of Anicius Hermogenianus Olybrius, consul 395, himself one of the sons of Sex. Claudius Petronius Probus, which seems, like Mommaerts & Kelley's descent of **PETRONIUS MAXIMUS** from **MAGNUS MAXIMUS** to be packing in as generation too many.[806] In following the latter (with small variations) the following table would seem to make a more convincing case.

*

TABLE LXIII(a): PETRONIUS MAXIMUS

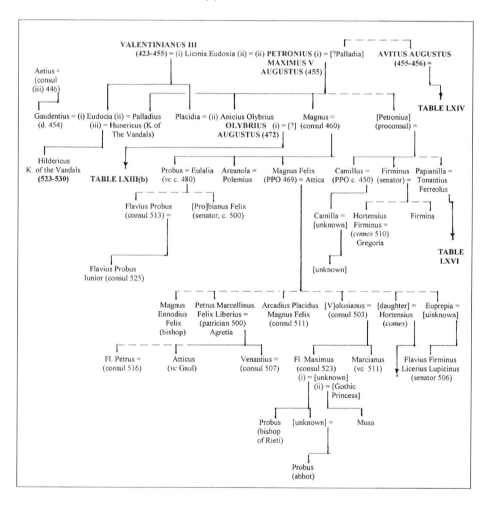

---

806. Discussed at length in Settipani (2000) 381-382 n. 16.

TABLE LXIII(a): BRIEF LIVES

Araneola

She married Polemius in the 460s [PLRE II Araneola]

Attica

Daughter of Placidus, the governor of a minor, probably Italian, province, since he is called a [*correc*]*tor*. The name suggests that he may have belonged to the grand senatorial family of the Rufii.[Mathisen (2003) 61]

Atticus

Recorded as a Gallo-Roman noble of senatorial descent, whose epitaph was composed by the poet Venantius Fortunatus [PLRE III Aticus]

Camilla

A widow with a young son, she was in financial difficulties in 512 when Ennodius, her relation, obtained help for her [PLRE II Camilla].

Camillus

Known to have been a nephew of Magnus (qv) and a son of [Petronius], he was a native of Arelate (Arles), a *vir inlustris* and a former praetorian prefect (probably of Gaul) when attending a dinner given by **MAIORIANUS** with Sidonius in 461 [PLRE II Camillus]

Eudocia

See above **TABLE LIX(a) Brief Lives**

Euprepia

Lived at Arelate (Arles) c. 475/508; the name of her husband is unknown (he was son of Firminus), but their only child was Flavius Licerius Firminus Lupicinus, educated by her brother Ennodius at Pavia and at Milan [PLRE II Euprepia; for the revised relationships see

Mommaerts & Kelley (1992) 112 f.].

Firmina

A woman of very high rank and relation of St. Ennodius, who had helped restore church property after the conquest of Italy by Theodericus in 490 [PLRE II Firmina]

Firminus

A *vir inlustris* living at Arles in the 460s and a friend of Sidonius Apollinaris[PLRE II Firminus 4]

Flavius Aetius

See above **TABLE LIX(a) Brief Lives**

Flavius Firminus Licerius Lupicinus

A senator with literary leanings b. c. 485/490, and still in education in 504. Although his father's name is not known, his paternal grandfather was a senator called Licerius, a name suggested by PLRE as closely cognate with that of **GLYCERIUS** (see below) and thus conceivably related [PLRE II Licerius, Lupicinus 3]

Flavius Maximus

According to Cassiodorus and Procopius, he was a member of the Anician family and a descendant of our **MAXIMUS**. He married twice, the second time to an Ostrogothic princess (the name of neither wife is known) in 535 the year he was western consul (without an eastern colleague). He was made a patrician in 523 with the qualification *vir illustris*, and the Ostrogothic King Theodahad appointed him *primicerius domesticus* (major domo) also in 535. He was the last man to hold games in the arena at Rome. He was killed in Campania by the Goths in 552 shortly after Narses had recovered Rome from them on behalf of **JUSTINIAN**, by which time he had been accorded the style *vir magnificus* by the Emperor. His children were: Probus (later Bishop of Rieti) and an unknown son, who had a son, Probus (an abbott at Rome c. 600) by his first wife, and a daughrer, Musa, by his second. They received part of his inheritance in 554 [Moorhead (1992) 163; PLRE II Maximus 20].

Flavius Petrus

He was of distinguished family who held minor office under King Theodericus, but was made *vir inlustris* in 510/511 allowing him to be enrolled into the senate (actual membership of which was restricted by then to men of the very highest rank). He was western consul (without an eastern colleague) in 516. His name and career strongly suggest that he may have been a son of Petrus Liberius (qv) [PLRE II Petrus 28]

Flavius Probus

An extremely learned man of distinguished family, whose name clearly indicates descent from the family of **PETRONIUS MAXIMUS** [cf. **TABLE LVIII(a)**]. He was a *vir inlustris* by 512 and was western consul in 513 [PLRE II Probus 9]

Flavius Probus Junior

All that is known of this man is that he was consul (west) in 525. The use of 'junior' strongly suggests that he was the son of the preceding, coming to the consulship at a very young age on the back of his father's eminence [PLRE II Probus 10]

Gaudentius

See above **TABLE LIX(a) Brief Lives**

Hildericus

See above **TABLE LIX(a) Brief Lives**

Hortensius

See above **TABLE LXI Brief Lives**

Hortensius Firminus

Comes civitatis of Clermont 510; his wife may have been a relation of St. Gregory of Tours.

Hunericus

See above **TABLES LIX(a) & LIV(a) Brief Lives**

Licinia Eudoxia

See above **TABLE LIX(a) Brief Lives**

M. Maecilius Flavius Eparchius Avitus

See above **Table LXII AVITUS AUGUSTUS.**

Magnus

His name reflects his supposed descent from **MAGNUS MAXIMUS III**; his mother Palladia was the daughter of Agricola (consul 421) and sister of **AVITUS**. He was *magister officiorum* (head of the bureaucracy) in Spain in the earlier 450s, praetorian prefect of Gaul in 458 and consul in 460. Sidonius Apollinaris considered him a good egg [PLRE II Magnus 2]

Magnus Ennodius Felix

A prolific letter writer, poet and biographer, St. Ennodius (his name is sometime rendered Magnus Felix Ennodius) was born c. 473 some commentators considering his father being Firminus, but this is doubted by Mommaerts & Kelley on a sound surmise. Indeed, in his correspondence he names numerous relatives but rarely tells us exactly how they were related to him. By 503 he was ordained deacon and by 513 was Bishop of Ticinum. He died in 521 [PLRE II Ennodius 2]

Magnus Felix

Received letters from **AVITUS'S** kinsman Sidonius Apollinaris and **MAGNUS MAXIMUS'S** alleged descendant Faustus, Bishop of Riez. He was praetorian prefect of Gaul by 469 the year he was made a patrician. He was still alive in 485 [PLRE II Felix21].

Marcianus

A senator at Rome to whom King Theodericus enabled the restoration of part of his and his siblings' inheritance in 511 [PLRE II Marcianus 14].

Palladius

See above **TABLE LIX(a) Brief Lives**

[Petronius]

A senator and a proconsul, probably of Africa c. 430s, referred to by Sidonius Apollinaris, but never named. Father of Camillus, a praetorian prefect before 457 and later a *vir inlustris*, known from his attendance at a banquet held by the emperor **MAJORIANUS** in 461 It is likely (altrhough unprovable) that he married a sister of St. Perpetuus (Bishop of Tours) and had other sons : Firminus , a senator at Arelate (Arles), possibly also Leontius and Ruricius (Bishop of Limoges, married to Hiberia daughter of Ommatius and father of two sons) as well as a daughter, Papianilla, the wife of Tonantius Ferreolus (praetorian prefect of Gaul 451-453) and thus a putative ancestor of Charlemagne. Certainly his posterity can be traced through several generations into the 6th century [PLRE II Ferreolus, Firminus 3, Leontius 15, Papianilla 1, Ruricius & Anon. 42]

Petrus Marcellus Felix Liberius

A senator of distinguished family, an 'honest and forthright man', he was born in the early 460s and died aged 89 but was still living in 554. Settipani is vague about his ancestry except to suggest that his maternal grandfather was the western consul for 463, Caecina Decius Basilius. Here Mommaerts & Kelley is followed. He married Agretia and was appointed praetorian prefect of Italy by King Theodericus 493 serving until 500, during which time he settled the King's Gothic followers on land sequestrated from Roman estate owners with notable tact. He was then made a patrician, was praetorian prefect of Gaul 510-534. He served **JUSTINIANUS I** in a number of delicate diplomatic missions and was twice named C-in-C of an army to be sent to Italy in 549 before being sent to drive the Goths from Sicily. In 552 he was appointed commander of an army sent to re-take Spain and by the time of his death had received the style of *vir gloriosissimus* from the emperor [PLRE II Liberius 3; Settipani 197]

Placidia

See above **TABLE LIX(a) Brief Lives**

Polemius

Of noble Gallic stock and grandson of Nymphidius. He was said by Sidonius Apollinaris to have been a descendant of the author Tacitus and the poet Ausonius, both distinguished senators of Gallic origin. The assertion, although perfectly possible, is not supported by any corroborative evidence. He served as praetorian prefect of Gaul 471-472 [Mommaerts & Kelley (1992) 115; PLRE II Nymphidius 1, Polemius 2].

[Pro]bianus Felix

His name is only known from a seat in the Flavian amphitheatre, and probably a *vir illustris* and his paternity is only suggested on account of his names. He will have been living c. 500 [PLRE II Felix 22]

Probus

A senator who had been a fellow student with Sidonius Apollinaris, whose cousin he married before 469. His wife Eulalia (remarkable for the severity of her character) was probably the daughter of a senator called Simplicius. Probus probably lived near Narbo [PLRE II Probus 4, Simplicius 8]

Probus Maximi f.

A friend of St. Gregory the Great and Bishop of Reate (Rieti), died c. 571, later canonised.

Probus

See **Table LXIII(b) Brief Lives**

Tonantius Ferreolus

See **Table LXVI Brief Lives**

Venantius

A *vir illustris*, he was given a senior titular court dignity and made consul in (west) in 507 mainly on the merits of his father. He held his consulship with the Emperor **ANASTASIUS**. A patrician called Venantius, living in 587./588 who married an Italica (a late 4th century Anician name) may have been this man's grandson, in which case his children were Antonia and Barbara, living in Sicily 601. Settipani suggests that Heliodorus, a Sicilian notable living in 681/85, and son of another Barbara, a lady of patrician rank, was probably a descendant. [PLRE II. Venantius 2; III. Antonina 3, Barbara, Venantius 2; Brown (1984) 253 Barbara 1 & 262; Settipani (2000) 197]

[V]olusianus

A *vir clarissimus* at the start of his career (c. 480) but consul (west) in 503 and made patrician and *vir magnificus* by 510 and died at easter 511 [PLRE II Volusianus 5]

*

VII(b)
THE LAST WESTERN EMPERORS

The Imperial Succession
Avitus
Maiorianus
Severus III
Anthemius
Olybrius
Glycerius
Julius Nepos
Romulus

Imperial Claimants
Marcellus II
Marcellinus II
Romanus I
Masties

Third Gallic Empire
Aegidius
Syagrius

The last generation of the empire in the west marked the rapid slide of imperial power from the hands of the emperor into the those of barbarian *generalissimos* allied to the gradual erosion of imperial control over the provinces outside Italy and Illyricum. In 455, only Mauretania (nominally), Hispania Tarraconensis, the Balkan provinces (some rather nominally), most of central and southern Gaul, Sicily, Sardinia and Corsica remained under direct control. Meanwhile, the Vandals ruled Africa Proconsularis and, although they issued coinage bearing the head of Honorius, they did not even make a pretence of being under Roman suzerainty, unlike the Sueves in Spain, the Visigoths in Aquitania and the Burgunduans in SE Gaul. Armorica appears to have joined Britain in throwing off its allegiance (or being effectively abandoned), the two Germanies were under the control of the Franks. Furthermore, the situation was still fluid, with peoples continuing to be on the move, leaving the imperial government having to juggle diplomacy (mainly from a position of weakness) and military might. On the whole, neither really succeeded, and the foundations were gradually laid for the successor kingdoms, which were to emerge in western Europe over the following couple of centuries.

AVITUS
9ᵗʰ July 455 – 17ᵗʰ October 456

Background

The rather gentlemanly (but thorough) looting of Rome by Gaiseric lasted two weeks following the death of **MAXIMUS**, and the West was left with a power vacuum. Notionally, however, the empire was united under the eastern Emperor, **MARCIAN**. Nevertheless, there needed to be authority in Italy to direct the clearing up and re-establish authority, before other barbarian peoples could take advantage of the crisis. One might have expected the senate to elevate an emperor, but they seem not to have done so or, more likely, none of their number was prepared to take the risk after that what had happened to **MAXIMUS**. Indeed, many of the senators had probably fled Rome with **MAXIMUS**, some of the most senior and eligible to Constantinople and probably had not had a chance to return. In other words there was probably not even a quorum.

The only person in a position to do anything was **MAXIMUS'S** *magister militum* **AVITUS**, who was still at the Gothic court at Tolosa (Toulouse) negotiating with King Theoderic II for a force of men wherewith he could relieve Rome. In fact, **AVITUS'S** relationship with the Gothic royal house went back a long way, and it was the King who urged his to assume the purple. **AVITUS'S** son-in-law, the senator and author Sidonius Apollinaris, reported that the King said to **AVITUS** that

> 'We do not force this [honour] upon you but we say to you that we are a friend of Rome; with you as emperor, I am her soldier.'

Theodericus wanted Roman support for a planned attempt to dislodge the Sueves from Spain; beyond that, their interest more or less converged.

[**M. Maecilius**[807]] **Eparchius AVITUS** himself was a member of a very eminent and noble senatorial family with roots in Gaul. They owned an estate called Avitacum near Augustonemetum (Clermont-Ferrand) and, by its alliances both before and after his time, this family managed to act as a genealogical bridge between the Gallic and Roman nobility. He was almost certainly an exact contemporary of his kinsman **PETRONIUS MAXIMUS**, studied law as a youth and, aged about 20, was sent as an envoy to **CONSTANTIUS III**, then in Gaul, to seek tax relief for his home region, at that time being harried by various semi-barbarian bands of freebooters, which was granted. Not long afterwards he visited his kinsman Theodorus (possibly an elder brother) who was a hostage with the Visigoths and swiftly became a favourite of King Theodoric I. In 430-431 he served as an officer under Aëtius against the Juthungi and was appointed to a much more senior command in 436 for that general's campaign against the Burgundians. Although we do not know what post he held, it qualified him as a *vir inlustris* and in 437 he was appointed *magister militum* in Gaul, defeating a force of marauding Huns near Clermont and lifting Theoderic's siege

---

807. The *praenomen* and *nomen* are given in earlier sources but are now rejected as unsubstantiated.

of Narbo (Narbonne), which he may have achieved more by diplomacy than by force of arms, given his long-standing friendship with the king. In 439 he was appointed to the less warlike post of praetorian prefect of Gaul, after which he retired to his estates c. 440, although in 451 he was recalled by his old commander to engineer an alliance between the Romans and the Visigoths to oppose the Huns, which he successfully achieved.

He was finally brought out of retirement by **MAXIMU**S to become *magister militum* again in order to raise a substantial force of Visigoths to relive Rome, then under threat from Gaiseric. It was from this position that he accepted the advice of his old fiend's son, Theodoric II to assume the purple.

Reign

The new emperor of the west was acclaimed by the Visigoths at Tolosa (Toulouse) and a few days later was officially proclaimed by the Gallic leaders in assembly (shades of **POSTUMUS** *et al.*) at Arelate (Arles) 9th July 455, six weeks after the death of his predecessor. He then spent some time gathering a viable army together (with the help of the Visigoths) and set out for Noricum,[808] just freed from Attila and the Huns, chaotic and over-run with other disorganised barbarians, which he recovered and settled before proceeding to Italy, entering Rome 21st September to a mixed reception.

Nevertheless the senate accepted him as one of their own and no doubt went through the motions of granting him the usual powers. He took the style **Dominus Noster Avitus Perpetuus Felix Augustus.** Unfortunately he failed to obtain recognition from the Eastern court, so his serving as Western consul in 456 was not recognised at Constantinople, and two eastern consuls served as well.[809]

He appointed Flavius Ricimer,[810] a Suevic prince with family connections to both the Burgundian and the Visigothic royal houses, as well as a recently retired Roman commander called Majorian as *comites*, the former as field army commander and the latter as commander of the Imperial Guard. The two had both served with **AVITUS** under Aëtius and were used to working together, although Sidonius rightly described Ricimer as 'a most ferocious' barbarian. By appointing him to a position of power, the new emperor was letting a cuckoo into the nest.

Ricimer's trouble was that he was fiercely ambitious and that he was a Sueve, and thanks to **AVITUS,** the Visigoths had been given *carte blanche* to enter Spain and clear them out of the diocese, which they had proceeded to accomplish very thoroughly, pushing the Suevic principality back toward the NW of the peninsular, a train of events which could hardly have endeared the emperor to him.

Once installed, **AVITUS** needed to get the Vandals out of his hair, for they were still blockading Italy, hence his appointment of two experienced men to command the armed

808. Sidonius claims it was to Pannonia.
809. PLRE II Avitus 5
810. PLRE II Ricimer 2

forces. He therefore issued an ultimatum to Gaisericus, but the onset of winter prevented any retaliation, and by the following spring, Ricimer managed to defeat him at sea and then cleared Sicily of Vandals, receiving the appointment as *magister militum* in recognition of his success. The lifting of the Vandal blockade was one thing, but it coincided with a severe famine in Italy, which the emperor and his civil service were hard put to alleviate. The senate, too, had lost faith in him, for all his appointments were of Gallic friends, relations and supporters, denying the Italian senators the career opportunities they expected for themselves and their families, especially as, with so many provinces over-run by barbarians, the number of provincial governorships had contracted alarmingly. Furthermore, the large barbarian element of the army which the emperor had brought with him was using up scarce resources when grain and other supplies were in short supply.

Ricimer and Majorian therefore raised the standard of rebellion, and **AVITUS'** new *magister peditum* (infantry commander), a Visigoth called Remistus, was assassinated. Unlike the rebellions of the previous two centuries, however, there was no imperial claimant, suggesting that nominal rule from the east was a possible option giving more freedom to whichever non-imperial strongman was in the driving seat in Italy. **AVITUS,** however, moved north with what troops he could muster and faced his two disaffected generals before Placentia, where he was roundly defeated, taken prisoner and deposed on 17th October 456. He was subsequently obliged to accept the bishopric of Placentia (Piacenza), and died, apparently of natural causes, in Gaul the following year.

Family

We are rich in information about the imperial family of **AVITUS**, simply because his son-in-law Sidonius Apollinaris wrote about his friends and relations in rich profusion, even though he omits occasionally to tell us people's names or specify the degree of kinship they bore to him or to each other. Nevertheless, he is a lot more informative on this latter topic than St. Ennodius, upon whom we are forced to rely for some of the kin of **MAXIMUS**, his predecessor.

AVITUS was said to be a descendant of Cn. Julius Agricola, famous as the conqueror of Scotland in the 80s, about whose illustrious career his son-in-law Cornelius Tacitus wrote; they too were Gauls. This is of course possible, but the nuts and bolts of the descent is never vouchsafed to us, nor is there anything like enough evidence for us to speculate on any such connection. The use of by the family of the name Agricola may have prompted them to claim the link, or may have reflected a genuine belief within the family. We only know of his grandfather, Philagrius (also claimed as an ancestor by other Gallic noble families), but the probable occurrence of the name Hesychius amongst his offspring might lead us to speculate that a daughter or sister of the Flavius Hesychius who was *comes* and *prefectus annonae* (commissioner of the corn supply) under **JULIAN** (the Apostate, under whom Philagrius also served) may have married the Gallic patrician and thus have been the grandmother of **AVITUS**.[811] Furthermore, the name Maecilius (if we can accept it as authentic) might suggest

---

811. PLRE I Hesychius 5

a descent in some manner from M[a]ecilius Hilarianus who was consul in 332 and a possible descendant of Maecilius Fuscus, who governed Britain under **GORDIAN III**.[812] More relatives are known of the Emperor than can be shown on the table below, simply because their relationships to him are much less certain even than those that are shown as speculative.

Furthermore, there were almost certainly descendants living in the seventh and early eighth centuries too, like Avitus, Bishop of Clermont, who died c. 690. He and his brother St. Bonitus (an ex-prefect of Provence and his successor as bishop) were sons of Theodatus and a Syagria, almost certainly a member of the family of the imperial claimant *SYAGRIUS* (see **Table LXVI,** below).

TABLE LXIV: THE FAMILY OF AVITUS

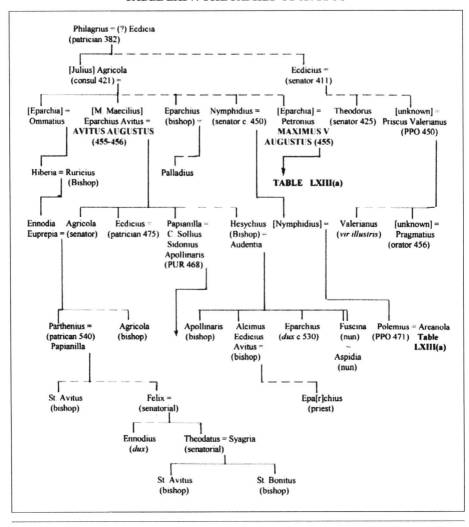

---

812. PLRE I Hilarianus 5; Birley (1981) 197, suggesting an Italian or African origin. Note also Pliny the Younger's Gallic friend of praetorian rank, Maecilius Nepos, another Gaul: Plin. *ep.*. ii.,3, etc.

TABLE LXIV: BRIEF LIVES

Agricola

Vir clarissimus of Clermont, c. 475, later a priest. He married Ennodia Euprepia a daughter of Ruricius, also a *vir clarissimus*, related to the Anicii and Bishop of Limoges c. 485-507 Ruricius's mother was a member of the Pontii Leontii of Burdigalia (Bordeaux) and his grandfather was probably Flavius Constantius Felix, consul in 428 [PLRE II Agricola, 2 Ruricius]

Agricola

A *vir clarissimus*, born 497, later Bishop of Cabyllona (Châlon-sur-Sôane) c. 537-580 and of a senatorial family [PLRE III Agricola 1].

Alcimus Ecdicius Avitus

Related to Sidonius Apollinaris, thus probably as here, a brother-in-law, born at Vienna (Vienne) c. 460, where he succeeded his father as Bishop c. 494, dying in 518. He was the godson of Claudius Mamertus, (St. Claudius) who baptised him [PLRE II Avitus 4]

Apollinaris

Related also to Parthenius (qv) and Ferreolus (see below **TABLE LXVI Brief Lives**). He was made Bishop of Valentia (Vence) c. 500, serving until after 517 [PLRE II Apollinaris 5]

Areanola
See **Table LXIII(a)**

Aspidia

A nun from the age of 12 and a recipient of her brother Avitus's letters [Schanze & Wood (2007) 5].

Audentia

Sidonius Apollinaris tells us that she and Papianilla were *consobrini*, taken to mean sisters by Mommaerts and Kelley but here interpreted as sisters-in-law [Sidonius Apollinaris, *Letters*. 3, 7; PLRE II Audentia 1; Mommaerts & Kelley (1992) 111]

Avitus
See above, **AVITUS AUGUSTUS**

Avitus (I)

Born 511, he was a friend of Gregory of Tours. He was the 18th bishop of Clermont, France, and he ordained Gregory as a deacon. He held the see 572-594 and is recognised as a saint.

Avtius (II)

Bishop of Clermont, dying in 689; he is also recognised as a saint. [Wood (1994) 81-82].

Bonitus

Bonitus, described as *ex senatu Romanii* (of Roman senatorial stock), had a distinguished civil career before being plucked from the governorship of the Auvergne to succeed his brother as Bishop in 689. He resigned a decade later after expressing doubts about the legitimacy of his elevation, died in a monastery in 706 and was canonised [Wood (1994) 82-84, 243]

Ecdicius

Estate owning grandee in the Arelate area, who received the fugitive Edobichus, the general of *CONSTANTINUS III*, and made away with him in 411 [PLRE II Ecdicius 1]

Ecdicius

Attached to the Imperial court under **ANTHEMIUS**, but returned to Clermont, where he defended it against a superior force of Visigoths, and later fed 4,000 people from the produce of his own estates during a famine in Burgundian territory. **JULIUS NEPOS** made him patrician and probably *magister militum* attached to the court in 474. He failed on this occasion to prevail against the Visigoths, and was replaced in 475 by Orestes (see **TABLE LXV(b) Brief Lives**). He was a friend and frequent guest of Sidonius [PLRE II Ecdicius 3]

Ennodius

He was *comes* of Poitiers under King Childebert II in 577 and in 585 was appointed *dux* by the same king, but dismissed in 587. He was acting as prosecutor at a trial in Metz three years later. There is no certain proof of his kinship to the two bishops [PLRE III Ennodius 2]

[Eparchia]

All we know is that Ommatius married a sister of the Emperor; her name can only be speculated about [Mommaerts & Kelley (1992) 111]

[Eparchia]

The arguments for her marriage to **MAXIMUS** are strong; if so, she committed suicide in 454 or 455; if on the latter date, probably as a consequence of her rejection in favour of the Empress Licinia Eudoxia [Mommaerts & Kelley (1992) 118, 119].

Eparchius

Bishop of Clermont before 470; brother of an Avitus (here suggested to be the emperor) and possibly father of a Palladius, which name would seem to re-inforce his kinship to **AVITUS** [Mommaerts & Kelley (1992) 111]

Eparchius

Born c. 504 and made *dux* in the Périgord region c 530, but later took the tonsure and was also ordained priest settling at Iculisma (Angoulême), dying c. 581 and later being canonised [*Greg. HF* VI.8]

Epa[r]chius

Described as *ex genere senatoriis* (of senatorial descent), he was a priest at Ricomagensium (Riom) in the Auvergne but had sobriety problems [PLRE III Epa[r]chius]

Felix

Apparently a citizen of Massilia (Marseilles) and *senatorius filiis* (son of a senator) and a friend of the poet Venantius Fortunatus. He may be identifiable with a Felix there who had a son, Marcellus, later (581) Bishop of Ucetia (Uzès) [PLRE III Felix 3 Marcelllus 6].

Fuscina

She was unmarried, having entered a convent at the age of eight, although was the recipient of letters from her brother Avitus [PLRE II Fuscina].

Hesychius

A man of 'senatorial status', who enjoyed an administrative career in the Empire before becoming Bishop of Vienna (Vienne) after 475, and who had died by 494. The names of his children strongly suggest that he must have been a son of the emperor **AVITUS** or less probably a nephew. [PLRE II Hesychius 11; Shanzer & Wood (2002) 439]

Hiberia

Joined her husband in entering upon a very devout way of life, and ferrred to by called 'Sarah' by at least one friend. Mommaerts & Kelley challenge the assertion that she did not have daughters, even if only wo sons are named [Mathisen (1999) 22-23]

[Julius] Agricola

His *nomen* is not entirely certain, but certainly likely. He was of a distinbguished Gallic family from the region around Narbo (Narbonne), and we first encounter him as praetorian prefect in the west, an appointment that he received prior to 418, in which year he served a second appointment as praetorian prefect this time in Gaul. He held the consulship in the west in 421 [PLRE II Agricola 1]

[M. Maecilius] Eparchius Avitus

See above **AVITUS AUGUSTUS**

Nymphidius (I)

Gallic nobleman and senator living c. 450, and grandfather of Polemius (qv) [PLRE II Nymphidius 1]

[Nymphidius (II)]

We only know that Polemius (qv) was the grandson of Nymphidius (qv), but we lack the name of the intervening generation, assuming the descent is indeed male line. Possibly another Nymphidius, eg. the man of his name who was a former official of Massilia (Marseilles) who died in 489 [PLRE II Nymphidius 2]

Ommatius

Descended from a Gallic family of Patrician rank (that is, a forebear must have been accorded he late imperial rank) and notable only because Sidonius Apollinaris invited him to a birthday party [PLRE II Ommatius 1]

Parthenius

A grandson of bishop Ruricius (qv), he was born c. 485, married by 507 and was recorded as having been a relation of Bishop Apollinaris of Vence (qv). When still young he conducted a successful embassy to the Ostrogothic King Theodoricus at Ravenna and this led him to a number of official appointments culminating in his being made patrician and *vir illustrissimus* (most illustrious man) by 542 or somewhat earlier. He discovered his wife

was being unfaithful with a man called Ausanius and had them both put to death. The Frankish King Theodebertus made him *magister officiorum* in Gaul, but he made himself deeply unpopular by imposing swingeing taxes and after the King's death in 548, he was put to death by an angry mob [PLRE II Parthenius 3; Mathisen (1999) 29].

Petronius Maximus

See above **MAXIMUS AUGUSTUS** & **Tables LXIII(a) & (b)**.

Philagrius

He may have been of Gallic origin, and first comes to notice as a *notarius* (civil servant) in that region c. 360. **JULIAN (IV)** sent him on a delicate mission to kidnap the German prince Vadomarius, after which he was in the Emperor's retinue in the Persian campaign. **THEODOSIUS I** then appointed him *Comes Orientis* (Eastern army commander) in 382 and he was made a patrician some time after that, retiring to an estate in Gaul where he had a fine library [PLRE Philagrius 2, 4].

Polemius

See above, **TABLE LXIII(a) Brief Lives**.

Pragmatius

Noble, wealthy and handsome, he was celebrated for his skill as an advocate in the courts. When his father-in-law was praetorian prefect, he joined his council or advisers becaming a *vir illustris*. He was, in his turn, praetorian prefect before 456 [PLRE II Pragmaius]

Priscus Valerianus

An ancestor had already held patrician rank, whereby his family was held by Sidonius to be of patrician status, which attests to the fact that, after the total eclipse of the old style patrician status in the time of **CONSTANTINUS I** a new patriciate was emerging, carrying almost as much prestige but no mechanisms guaranteeing accelerated promotion. His family are otherwise largely unknown (even his patrician ancestor being a matter for speculation) apart from Bishop Eucherius of Lyons, another senatorial grandee with a wife and four children. Sidonius also tells us he was related to **AVITUS**, but whether this was after his daughter's marriage or previously is not clear; the possibility exists that he too was a descendant of Philagrius. He was appointed praetorian prefect for Gaul probably under **VALENTINIAN III** [PLRE II Valerianus 8]

Ruricius

A man of senatorial rank and born c. 440, he was married before he end of 469. He had an estate at Gurdo (Gourdon, near Cahors), but in c. 477 after having at least two children (two sons are mentioned) he and his wife sought a religious life and by 485 he had been appointed Bishiop of Augustoritum (Limoges). He was a prolific letter writer, a friend of Sidonius Apollinaris and he died c. 507 [PLRE II Ruricius; Mathisen (1999) *passim*.]

C. **Sollius Modestus Sidonius Apollinaris**

Like **AVITUS**, but unlike most of his contemporaries, he appears to have borne a typical early imperial senatorial name but, as we only have single names for most of the remainder of his family, it is difficult to know whether they regarded themselves as Sollii, Sidonii or something else. He stands out in late antiquity as an exceptional author, poet, and prolific writer of letters, without whose surviving effulgences we would know considerably less about the late Western Empire. He was born c. 430, and although the name of his father (who had been

praetorian prefect of Gaul 448/449) is lost to us, his grandfather Apollinaris had held the same position under **CONSTANTINE III** 408/409. In 456 he composed and delivered a panegyric on his father-in-law **AVITUS**. Out of loyalty he opposed **MAJORIAN**, but was later reconciled to him, composing a panegyric on him too and being appointed by him *tribunus et notarius*, later becoming the emperor's friend and a *comes*. In 468 he was appointed Prefect of the City of Rome by **ANTHEMIUS** and became a patrician then or some time before. He was elected Bishop of Clermont in 469 and died in the early 480s [PLRE II Apollinaris 6]

Syagria

Apart from her marriage, nothing more is known about her. A possible descent for her is set out in **Table LXVI** [*Greg. HF* IV.46].

Theodatus

Noted, with his wife, in the Life of St. Bonitus [*Vita*, I, 1-2; *Greg HF* IV. 46]

Theodorus

His relationship to **AVITUS** is not wholly clear, but it seems likely that he was a cousin rather than a brother. He was of senatorial family therefore and around 425 was sent as a hostage to the Visigothic King Theoderic I where he was later visited by the future emperor [PLRE II Theodorus 12].

Valerianus

All that is known about this man is that he was a *vir illustris* and received a letter from Alcimus Ecdicius Avitus, Bishop of Vienna (Vienne) to whom he was almost certainly related. He was still alive in the 490s [PLRE II Valerianus 4]

*

MARCELLUS II
457

Simultaneous with the deposition of **AVITUS**, or so it would appear, we have a laconic reference in a letter of Sidonius Apollinaris (one of **AVITUS'S** numerous Gallic appointments) to a 'Marcellan conspiracy' (he actually wrote '*...de cupessendo diademate coniuration Marcellana*'[813] which seems a clear suggestion that some other Gallic notable called Marcellus was put up as an imperial claimant, probably *in lieu* of **AVITUS**. Yet no coins were issued, and nothing else is known, so it must be assumed that the bid ended very rapidly in failure. The identity of Marcellus (the best MS does not, it is now agreed, read Marcellinus, which would have implied that the *magister militum* of Dalmatia was somehow involved, which seems on the face of it highly unlikely) is quite unclear.[814] There were a number of Gallic aristocrats around at this period of that name, and only the Marcellus who was praetorian Prefect of Gaul c. 441-443 stands out as a possible candidate, yet we have no evidence that he was still living fifteen years later. The entire episode is a mystery.

*

MAIORIANUS
(Known to history as Majorian)
1st April 457 - 2nd August 461

Following the deposition of **AVITUS** on 17th October 456, the empire was technically once more united under the eastern emperor **MARCIAN.** Majorian and Ricimer were thereafter effectively **MARCIANUS'S** viceroys in the west, but crucially, Ricimer was the senior partner as *magister militum*, whereas his colleague was merely *comes domesticorum* – commander of an imperial guard without an emperor to protect. Nevertheless it would appear that they were content to exercise full powers under the eastern court for the duration of that autumn and winter. However, in February, Ricimer laid down office and accepted the title of patrician from **MARCIAN** and Majorian succeeded him as *magister militum*. It may be, however, that being subordinate to Constantinople cramped their style and restricted what they felt they needed to do to protect the west and, if possible, restore it. Therefore, on 1st April, Majorian assumed the purple at Columellae, near Ravenna, although for some reason he was not formally acclaimed in Ravenna itself until 28th December, and in

---

813. Sidonius Apollinaris, ep. I , 11 6
814. MacGeorge (2002) 64-65.

between used his military rank, probably because he was reluctant to assume the supreme office without the agreement of Constantinople. It is possible that the formal installation followed recognition.

The new Emperor, **Flavius Julius Valerius MAIORIANUS**, was of Roman stock, was relatively young (born c. 415), and had enjoyed a career in the army under Aëtius, seeing action against the Visigoths and the Franks in the 440s, but by the time of his old commander's murder he had retired to the country, probably in Gaul; Sidonius claimed that the jealousy of Aëtius's wife had brought about his retirement. He was made *comes domesticorum* by **VALENTINIAN III** after the murder, and was considered a possible successor when the Emperor was killed. Instead, **MAXIMUS** confirmed him in his post, as did **AVITUS**. On 28th February he succeeded Ricimer as *magister militum*.[815] Shortly afterwards, he won a victory over a substantial incursion into Italy of Alamanni from Rhaetia.

Reign

MAJORIAN adopted the style **Dominus Noster Julius Maiorianus Perpetuus Augusutus**[816], and was acknowledged by the senate and no doubt granted by them those powers that were traditional and which he would have exercised with or without their sanction, although he was theoretically one of their number. He was acknowledged by the eastern court sometime between April and December 457, most probably the latter. He was western ordinary consul for 458. His elevation led to considerable discontent in Gaul, where the deposition of their man **AVITUS** caused much resentment. According to Sidonius, this led one *MARCELLUS* to make a bid for the purple (qv. above) details of which are entirely lacking in the sources.[817] However, no more is heard of this and it is to be presumed that it fizzled out without serious repercussions. Certainly, **MAJORIAN** was obliged to assert himself in southern Gaul before being able to find acceptance.

It is often said that Ricimer ruled the west through a series of 'puppet emperors', but the reality was somewhat more complex. For a start, **MAJORIAN** was no puppet. He was a military man of proven success, a member of an established senatorial family, and virtually the equal of his friend and brother in arms Ricimer. The difference was that Ricimer had the ultimate hold over the largely barbarian-recruited army through his own family connections, and when the chips were down, it was likely that Ricimer's will would prevail. Yet **MAJORIAN** was faced with a declining population throughout the west, and the crushing burden of taxation to support the army was leading, amongst other things, to younger sons being forced into the church to save the expense of raising them, further restricting the number of people who could marry and raise children. He passed a number of laws to deal with this, remitted taxation and issued a decree against the dismantling of historic buildings in Rome on the pretext that the stone was required for 'public works'. This must

---

815. PLRE II Maiorianus.
816. ILS810
817. Sidonius Apollinaris, *Letters* I. 11, 6.

be the first piece of official conservation legislation ever passed in Western Europe, and was highly enlightened if, in all probability, largely ignored.[818]

The most pressing military problem was still the Vandal occupation of Africa and the economic problems it posed to Italy. The Emperor recruited the *comes* of Illyricum, Marcellinus (in reality a semi-independent dynast, for the Emperor's hold on the province was shaky to say the least), to clear Sicily of Vandals, which was successfully accomplished. **MAJORIAN** meanwhile entered Spain and reclaimed much of the peninsula, before preparing an expeditionary force to invade Africa via Mauretania from Carthago Nova (Cartagena). This was done with the full co-operation of the somewhat chastened Visigoths, and demonstrated that although the Western Empire no longer enjoyed direct control over all its provinces, it was successfully operating a form of federal empire or temporary commonwealth of associated and theoretically subject polities, of which Visigothic Spain had been one. The Vandal ruler Gaiseric, however, managed to neutralise this effort by destroying part of the fleet before it could set sail and by laying waste much of Mauretania so that it would not be able to sustain an invading army. In the event, this bought the Vandal kingdom a breathing space of some 70 years before the eastern emperor was successfully able to dislodge the Vandals after nearly a century in possession.

Nevertheless, the Emperor turned his attention to Gaul. Although there was still chaos and areas where the Empire's writ was tenuous, yet Cologne had been finally lost only in 457, during the interregnum, and **MAJORIAN** clearly expected to be able to restore matters even at this late stage; indeed, Hugh Elton has set out to show how that aim was not necessarily the Chimaera that one might have been led to suppose.[819]

Indeed, **MAJORIAN** had all the natural ability and qualities the Imperial office required at this time and could have pulled things back, at least in Gaul, but the fly in the ointment was his patrician, Ricimer. It seems to have occurred to the patrician that his imperial colleague was too independent-minded and competent for the barbarian to be able to pursue his own agenda, which centred on aggrandising himself and if possible loosening the hold the Visigoths had on his own people, the Sueves in Spain. With the excuse of the failure of the Vandal expedition as his cue, Ricimer intercepted and deposed the Emperor on 2nd August 461 and five days later had his former friend and comrade-in-arms put to death.

Family

Little is known about the family of **MAIORIANUS**, except that Sidonius Apollinaris tells us that his maternal grandfather, also Maiorianus, was *magister utriusque militum* in Illyricum under **THEODOSIUS I**, meeting with considerable success against the various swarming

---

818. In times of crisis, the practice was to demolish all or part of a building to remove the bronze cramps which anchored the ashlar blocks together to melt down. If there were marble veneers, these could be removed (and ground up to make lime) and the bronze fixings re-cycled. The last recorded instance was that by the Eastern Emperor **CONSTANS III** in the 660s which led to the collapse of many buildings: Llewellyn (1993) 157-8.

819. Elton (1992) 167-178.

and mingling tribal upheavals of the Danubian littoral.[820] It may be that he was recruited from **THEODOSIUS'S** Spanish friends or family circle like **MAGNUS MAXIMUS**, but he could also have been himself Illyrian, so long a breeding ground of Roman military leaders. Nor do his two other names (bearing in mind that the *praenomen* Flavius was by this date more of an honorific than a real name) give us any real clue, both being remarkably common even at this period. We hear nothing of a wife, nor of any children. Indeed, he may have been unmarried, as at one stage he was canvassed as a husband for Placidia, the elder daughter of **VALENTINIAN III**, a possible reason for his 'retirement' prior to the murder of Aëtius.

✻

SEVERUS III
(Known to history as Libius Severus)
September 461 – 14th November 465

Background

The demise of **MAJORIAN** once again left the empire technically united under the emperor **LEO I** and with Ricimer firmly in charge in the west. Yet the latter seems to have realised that he could not govern effectively without either official recognition from the East or an emperor through whom he could exercise power. Furthermore, the death of **MAJORIAN** had as bad an effect on Gaul as the deposition of **AVITUS** five years earlier. The *comes* and *magister militum* in Gaul, a native grandee with impeccable senatorial roots, *AEGIDIUS*, refused to recognise Ricimer's next nominee, **SEVERUS III**, and all but southern Gaul was thenceforth lost to what was, in effect, a third Gallic Empire and one, more to the point, that was to outlast the main western imperial polity by six or ten years. Whilst there is debate as to whether *AEGIDIUS* was a full-blooded imperial claimant or not, the fact was that he and his son controlled central and northern Gaul, latterly from Noviodunum (Soissons), for the next 25 years and the terminology used by contemporary commentators does not preclude their having been viewed as of imperial standing. Indeed, Ricimer may have hesitated as to whom to put forward for the purple, for *AEGIDIUS'S* claim was impeccable, but was probably rejected for the same reason as **MAJORIAN** had met his fate – he was just too competent; another possibility was that the man we now strongly suspect to have been a younger son of **PETRONIUS MAXIMUS,** Olybrius, had married the younger daughter of **VALENTINIAN III**. As her elder sister had been abducted from Rome by Gaisericus, who had married her, the Vandal King was now a member of the former dynasty and brother-in-law of Olybrius, this would also have guaranteed the acquiescence of the Eastern court. But in the end, Ricimer went for a cypher.

Libius Severus, possibly nicknamed *Serpentius*, was a senator and his family came from

---

the Lucanian region of Italy, but we have no information as to any career he may have enjoyed prior to his elevation.[821]

Reign

Flavius Libius Severianus SEVERUS was proclaimed on November 19th, although his actual elevation in the west might well have followed after only about a month from the deposition of **MAJORIAN,** for it may be that the pattern followed with the elevation of the latter prevailed here, too: the new emperor may have been acclaimed in September and an embassy sent to Constantinople to seek confirmation from **LEO**. When this was not forthcoming, he was probably given an official elevation and installation, with the usual endorsement by the senate, as recorded on 19th November. His style was **Dominus Noster [Imperator] Libius Severus Perpetuus Augustus.**[822] The new Emperor served as consul in 462 with **LEO I,** although as far as the latter was concerned there was no Western consul.

The acclamation of **SEVERUS** rekindled the ire of Gaisericus, who wished to have his brother-in-law **OLYBRIUS** as emperor of the West, so he renewed his harassment of the Italian mainland. Countering this was becoming increasingly difficult, especially as, with the loss of most of Gaul, a vast amount of potential tax revenue was not available to the Court. This must partly at least explain the lack of activity recorded for this reign, combined with the loss of control over most of Gaul, Africa, Spain and the North and North West. Only Dalmatia, part of Illyria plus Italy and Sicily, Sardinia, Corsica and southern Gaul remained under direct control.

SEVERUS himself died at Rome, after a life of religious rectitude, on 14th November 465, allegedly from drinking from a poisoned chalice at the instigation of Ricimer, but more probably, as Sidonius tells us, from natural causes. Murdering him, in the absence of the slightest motive, would not, for the patrician, have been in the least profitable.

Family

Nothing is known of the Emperor's family; there is mention neither of wife nor children, nor antecedents. His *nomen* Libius is a late imperial mutation from the more resonant name of Livius, last met with in an imperial context in **GALBA,** and precious few Livii are recorded in the senate after that period.

*

---

821. PLRE II Severus 18
822. ILS 811 & coins.

AEGIDIUS
November 461 – October/November 465

AEGIDIUS was a Gallo-Roman aristocrat who adapted to the new opportunities available to senators of distinguished family by the breakdown of the west by choosing a military career. He was probably born during the upheavals of the period of the rule of **CONSTANTINE III** and must have decided on a career of arms. He is known to have served with Aëtius, along with **MAJORIAN** and **AVITUS.** He became *magister utiusque militum* and *comes* in Gaul, appointed by **AVITUS** in 456. The position was something of a poisoned chalice but, despite losing control of Colonia Agrippina (Cologne) in 457 and subsequently Augusta Treverorum (Trier), both to the Franks, he managed to save Arelate (Arles) from the Visigoths. When **SEVERUS III** was proclaimed, he refused to recognise him, and then threatened to invade Italy, only being prevented by an outbreak of conflict on the part of the Visigoths, which he subsequently put down with aplomb. He was apparently distinguished both by his prowess and conduct.[823]

He now ruled what appears to have been a third breakaway Gallic empire, not dissimilar to that controlled by **CONSTANTINE III** only a lot smaller. He faced down the attempt by his replacement (appointed by **SEVERUS**) Agrippinus to take over and continued to exercise his *imperium*, winning a major encounter with the Visigoths at Aurelianum (Orléans) in 463. At this juncture he could have conquered the Visigothic kingdom, or he could have returned Gaul to Imperial control but, tellingly, he did not; he was content, like **POSTUMUS** and **CONSTANTINE III** (at first), to hang on to what he had got. Later though, he opened talks with the Vandals with a view to forging an alliance against the Visigoths.

He made his capital at Noviodunum (Soissons) and allied himself with the Franks, newly settled in the area. The Franks for their part acknowledged him as their over-lord, referring to him as *rex* – King.[824] Professor Fanning, however, has shown that the terminology employed (chiefly by Gregory of Tours[825]) is misleading, writing:

> 'It would be extremely rash to suggest that Aegidius and Syagrius were in fact Roman Emperors, but it is clear that Gregory of Tours and the *Liber Historiae Francorum* were using language that meant just that.'[826]

Regrettably, no inscriptions survive and neither man minted coins in his own name, yet it would be logical not to treat this brief Gallic dynasty as anything but serious imperial

---

823. See also MacGeorge (2002) 82-110.
824. Barnwell (1992) 70
825. Greg. *HF* 2, 27.
826. Fanning (1992) 296-297.

claimants.[827] Nevertheless, we know nothing of his style of address, nor whether, like **POSTUMUS** he had an assembly and nominated consuls; desperate times may have precluded such embellishments to the *régime*. Fanning's point about style and title however, might be seized on as valid for other extra-imperial but non-barbarian commanders of the period like the British warlord and correspondent of Sidonius, Riothamus in Gaul, as well as such shadowy characters as Vortigern and Ambrosius Aurelianus in Britain, all styled by later writers as *reges* (Kings), and as frequently as *tyranni*.[828]

AEGIDIUS was noted for his courage, good character and faith, but died in autumn 465, although accounts vary as to how this came about, one version favouring poison, another death in an ambush, but Gregory of Tours suggesting that he fell victim to an outbreak of plague.[829]

On the death of *AEGIDIUS*, his son *SYAGRIUS* stepped seamlessly into his shoes.

⋆

SYAGRIUS
October/November 465 – 486

Background & reign

The death of his father saw the son, *SYAGRIUS* succeed to his power, but how he styled himself is lost to us, but as Professor Fanning has pointed out, it would have been anything but *rex* (king). It may well be that the father made him a *comes* and *magister militum* under him, although a later source refers to him as patrician. He was born about 430 and therefore succeeded to power aged roughly 35. He may have had the *comes* Paulus as his *magister militum*, for we find this man successfully leading Roman troops, along with Franks under King Childericus I, against the Visigoths and then in 469 defeating Odovacer (later to overthrow **ROMULUS** in Italy) and taking Juliomagus (Angers), where he was killed in action.[830]

SYAGRIUS'S imperium, originally covering most of central and northern Gaul, was reduced by numerous conflicts to an east - west area stretching from the Atlantic coast, with the Loire as its southern border and probably excluding the Brittany to the Meuse/Scheldt Channel littoral. Nevertherless with Arbogastes in Trier as *comes* as late as 477, it may be that he had managed to re-establish control in the east too, no doubt with Frankish support.[831] Later, the western portion of his polity was lost and

---

827. MacGeorge (2002) 143. He and his son issued coins in the names of the western emperors.
828. Jordanes calls Riothamus *rex: Getica*, xlv. 237-238.
829. PLRE II Aegidius; Gregory of Tours, *Historia Francorum* II.18.
830. PLRE II Paulus 20; he is a prime candidate to have been made a consul of this breakaway polity.
831. PLRE II Arbogastes,; he was son of Arigius and a descendant of the Arbogastes who served **THEODOSIUS I** as *magister militum.* His appointment could have been a Frankish one, but if so, he was an odd choice, with friends like Sidonius Apollinaris: MacGeorge (2012) 75.

the Seine became the western edge of his empire – mainly the old province of Belgica Secunda[832] with parts of Gallia Lugdunensis and Germania. In 476, after the deposition of **ROMULUS** by Odovacer, the latter and *SYAGRIUS* sent embassies to Constantinople seeking recognition, which underlines the point that the Gallic ruler considered himself an imperial claimant. In the event, eastern emperor **ZENO** recognised Odovacer as Patrician on petition of the senate, but rejected the claims of the Gaul.

His alliance with the Franks fell apart after 481 under the rise of the young, energetic and charismatic new King, Chlodovechus (Clovis/Louis I) who was bent on expansion and continuing co-operation with *SYAGRIUS* had no part in this. Thus in 486, the two sides met in battle near Soissons, the Roman ruler came off worst, and was forced to seek refuge at Tolosa (Toulouse) with Alaric II of the Visigoths. This move led to an ultimatum from Clovis to Alaricus, who had no stomach to take on the Franks (when he did, in 507, he was killed and Visigothic rule in Gaul was effectively ended) and responded favourably to a demand to hand *SYAGRIUS* over. He was put under house arrest but was clandestinely executed in 487.

As it happens, the rule of *SYAGRIUS* managed to outlast the final Emperor of the west by six (or in some estimations ten) years. Clovis was recognised by the eastern emperor as patrician and honorary consul, maintaining the fiction that the west was still united as a sort of federation under the rule of Constantinople.

Family

The family may have been senatorial before the time of the two 4th century consuls called Syagrius, at least in the distaff line. Alternatively, they may have been amongst the eminent Gauls who entered public life in the wake of Ausonius, the tutor of **GRATIAN**.[833] The name Afranius, though, might imply a possible blood link with Afranius Hannibalianus the first husband of the Empress Eutropia (see above **Table XLVII Brief Lives**).[834] The name may have come into the family via one or other of the two consuls' mothers as suggested below. The name Syagrius, moreover would appear to have been a late Roman mutation of the early empire Suagrius, encouraging the suggestion that both Syagrii could have had Suagr[i]us, prefect of the City of Rome in 275 as a forebear.[835] There must too have been at least one missing generation between the consul Syagrius and *AEGIDIUS*. This gap could conceivably be filled from a rather later Frankish poetical genealogy quoted by MacGeorge:

> 'Primus rex Romanorum Allanius dictus est / Allanius genuit Pabolum / Pabolus Egetium / Egetius genuit Egegium / Egegius genuit Siagrium per quem Romani regnum perditerunt.'[836]

---

832. Some commentators consider his empire rather smaller at its end, eg. James (1988) 67-71.

833. Sivan (1993), 115, 133-134.

834. Settipani proposes a descent from Hannibalianus, consul in 292, an ex-praetorian prefect: op.cit. 279-380.

835. Ibid. 380, although this seems like a long shot, as PLRE I gives his name as Suagrus, seemingly a *cognomen*.

836. MacGeorge (2002) 80. It ends, 'by whom the Roman kingdom was lost.'

We have already met an 'Al[l]an[ius]' amongst the possible kin of Gerontius and for 'Pabolus' we should of course read Paulus. 'Egegius' is clearly *AEGIDIUS* but, if one reads 'Egetius' as Aëtius, then we are moving inexorably into the realms of fantasy, bearing in mind that Aëtius is not known to have had more than one son, Gaudentius, see **Table LXIII(a) Brief Lives**. Furthermore, had *AEGIDIUS* been a son of Aëtius, it is exceedingly unlikely that no writer of the time would have mentioned it. Yet the etymology of 'Egetius' seems exceedingly close to 'Aegidius', in which case it is possible that the poem celebrates the fact that *AEGIDIUS* bore the same name as his father who was the son of a Paulus, of whom there are a number of possible candidates towards the end of the fourth century. If we could accept this, then 'Allanius' would have to have been a brother of one or other of the consular Syagriuses to enable the chronology to fit. On the whole it is better to proceed on the basis that the poem is just too untrustworthy to be relied upon.

Through the wife of Tonantius Ferreolus (praetorian Prefect of Gaul in 451), *AEGIDIUS* and *SYAGRIUS* were connected with the families of **AVITUS** and probably **PETRONIUS MAXIMUS**. Furthermore, there was a considerable number of late antique Gallic persons of senatorial rank (a distinction clung to long after the demise of the senate itself in the early years of the 7th century) who are known to have descended from the Syagrii, although the exact relationships between them is unclear, with the result that **Table LXVI** contains a preponderance of speculation over attested links, and has to be treated with caution, although these insecure relationships are based on the work of others and upon circumstantial evidence.

It is interesting to note too that Tonantius Ferreolus was claimed as an ancestor by Charlemagne. This is normally treated with enormous scepticism by most scholars but, just as the claim (put forward by the 6th century historian Procopius) that **PETRONIUS MAXIMUS** was descended from **MAGNUS MAXIMUS** is accepted as highly probable by Mommaerts and Kelley amongst others, the claim of Charlemagne might in its turn be just as plausible if not more so. After all, if Charlemagne had wished to confect a false pedigree (like that of **CONSTANTIUS I** from **CLAUDIUS II**) he would surely have derived a line of descent from a named emperor or a person whose name carried some resonance in his own time, rather than one of several only fairly memorable upper crust Gallic praetorian prefects.

For the record, Charlemagne's supposed line is traced from an otherwise unknown daughter of Tonantius Ferreolus, Lucilia (Ferreolus is only recorded as having had sons) and a Frankish husband, Vaubertus. Their son (common to other suggestions) Ansbertus[837] is said to have married Blithilde, a daughter of the Frankish King Chlothar I (died 561), and of their five claimed offspring, St. Arnulf of Metz, a former Mayor of the Palace in the Frankish Kingdom of Austrasia and later Bishop there, became

---

837. Or grandson, Arnoald, son of Ansbertus

the father-in-law of St. Begga who married his son Ansegis, Charlemagne being the great-grandson of their son Pepin II.[838]

King Chlothar's daughter is not attested, and as he had six known 'wives' and only one named daughter, one or more certainly *could* have existed and in those days be reasonably well remembered.[839] Begga was daughter of Pepin I, otherwise Pepin of Landen. It is the forebears of St. Arnulf that are commonly called into question, whereas Begga's mother Itta (Iduberga) was certainly recorded and is acknowledged as being of a Gallo-Roman senatorial family, although we do not know which one. Another proposed line of descent has been proposed by Settipani from Ansbertus and Blitilde, through their son Arnoald, Bishop of Metz (died 640), his son being Arnulf of Metz, father of Angisel who married St. Begga.[840] He also proposes that their grandson, Charles Martel married Rotrude, for whom he adduces a descent from Syagrius, a son of Tonantius Ferreolus. The matter is unlikely ever to achieve a satisfactory resolution, yet is not on the whole all that unlikely.

---

838. Descent : Proc. *BV* I. 4,16 ; Mommaerts & Kelley (1992) 118; Constantine & Claudius see above; Arnulfus: PLRE III Arnulfus, Ansegis; Wood (1994) 261.

839. A claim to descend from the previous dynasty was probably a much more important ingredient of the genealogy than one from a GalloRoman, although it carried no real legitimacy under Salic law..

840. Settipani (2014) 20-23; modifications have followed from Kirk *et al.* Kelley (1947) rejected the descent of Arnulf from Aronald, but Settipani (1989) felt able to accept it.

TABLE LXVI: AEGIDIUS & SYAGRIUS

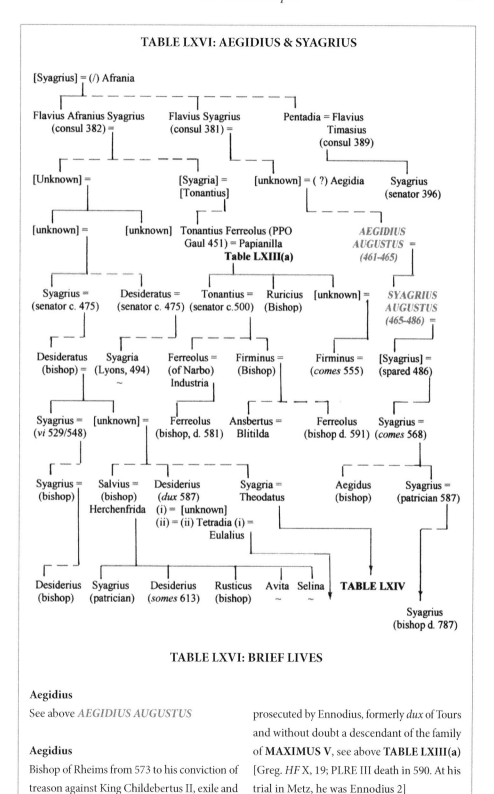

TABLE LXVI: BRIEF LIVES

Aegidius

See above *AEGIDIUS AUGUSTUS*

Aegidius

Bishop of Rheims from 573 to his conviction of treason against King Childebertus II, exile and prosecuted by Ennodius, formerly *dux* of Tours and without doubt a descendant of the family of **MAXIMUS V**, see above **TABLE LXIII(a)** [Greg. *HF* X, 19; PLRE III death in 590. At his trial in Metz, he was Ennodius 2]

Desideratus

A friend and probable relation of Sidonius, living mid to later 5th century [PLRE II Desideratus]

Desideratus

Bishop of Verodunum (Verdun) 529-554, later canonised. He or his anonymous wife may have had a connection with the Desiderius [*sic*] who was a *vicarius* under **MAGNUS MAXIMUS**, and which may explain the occurrence of the name amongst his posterity [Greg. *HF* III.34; PLRE I Desiderius 2]

Desiderius

He served as a *dux* under King Chilpericus from c. 574 changing sides at least twice subsequently and each time obtaining a pardon. He appears to have been a talented but fierce and ruthless commander. He was latterly based at Albigensium (Albi) but was killed in action fighting the Visigoths at Carsaco (Carcassonne) in 587. His second wife was maternally descended from the ancient senatorial nobility and was formerly married to the Gallo-Roman noble Eulalius of Clermont by whom she had two sons. She engrossed all of Eulalius's property when she left him and was condemned for it after Desiderius' death, and their children (whose names are lost) were declared illegitimate [PLRE III Desiderius 2, Tetradia; *ibid.* II Eulalius 2].

Desiderius

A member of a Gallo-Roman noble family, although his exact parentage is uncertain. He was Bishop of Vienna (Vienne) 596-607, suffered exile 603-605 and death as a result of falling out with the Visigothic Queen Brunichildis, wife of Frankish King Sigibertus I [PLRE III Desiderius 4]

Desiderius

He was a *comes* of King Chlotharius II, also *comes civitatis* (city governor) of Massilia (Marseilles), later head of his civil treasury, and also succeededhis brother Syagrius as governor of Provence 629/630. He then followed his murdered other brother Rusticus as Bishop of Cadurcorum (Cahors), dying in office in 650 [PLRE III Desiderius 5]

Ferreolus

A man of senatorial rank at Narbo (Narbonne) c. 525/550. Said to have married Industria of Narbo. They also had a son, Ansbertus (whose name suggests a Frankish marriage, perhaps Ferreolus's mother) who, by his wife Blitilda, may have been father of Ferreolus died 581, (qv), but as it is not entirely certain whether he was son of grandson of his namesake [Settipani (1990) 20].

Ferreolus

Born at Narbo (Narbonne) and later elected to succeed his uncle Firminus (qv) as 5th Bishop of Ucetia (Uzès) to his death in 581. He admitted Jews to the City and invited them to dinner, but was forced to back track on such enlightened moves by the king, Childebertus I. He was later canonised [Greg. HF VI, 7; Wood (1994) 25].

Ferreolus

By 579 he was elected 5th Bishop of Lemovices (Limoges) and died in 591. He restored the church of St. Martin at Brive after it had been wrecked in a conflict. He, too, was later canonised [Greg. *HF* V, 28 & VII, 10]

Firminus

Born at Narbonne 516 and elected 4th Bishop of Ucetia (Uzès) in 538 in succession to his uncle Ruricius (qv). He died in 553 and was succeeded by his nephew St. Ferreolus (qv). He was later recognised locally as a saint with particular resonance in times of plague.

Firminus

Although a grandson of Tonantius Ferreolus (qv) his father's name is unknown. He married the daughter of a former *comes,* Britianus and his wife Caesaria. He was appointed *comes* of the Auvergne c. 555 but deposed by the renegade Frankish Prince Chramnus only to be restored to office in 560 by Sigibertus I. He fought several campaigns for the King, only losing one battle, and re-taking Arelate (Arles). In 571-572 he was sent as an envoy to **JUSTIN II** to settle a peace treaty. He failed to prevent the suicide of his brother-in-law the *comes* Palladius in 573 [PLRE III Firminus 1]

Flavius Afranius Syagrius

He was almost certainly of Gallic stock and a senator, perhaps rising to prominence under the influence of the Gallic poet-statesman Ausonius and became proconsul of Africa c. 379-381, in which year he served as *comes sacrae largitionum* (finance minister) as well as prefect of the City, going on to be consul in the following year and praetorian prefect of Italy. He was said by Sidonius Apollinaris to have held three prefectures, so probably held his third after 382, probably under **MAGNUS MAXIMUS**. He was a friend of Auso-nius and was buried in Lugdunum (Lyons) [PLRE I Syagrius 2]

Flavius Syagrius

He is first discovered serving as a *notarius* (senior clerk) in Gaul, but was cashiered by **VALENTINIAN I** for being the only survivor of a disastrous expedition across the Rhine. He was restored to favour under **GRATIAN I** (doubtless, like his kinsman, through the influence of Ausonius or one of his circle) becoming *magister officiorum* in 379 and praetorian prefect of Italy the following year. He was also consul in 381, but seems to have died in office in 382 [PLRE I Syagrius 3]

Flavius Timasius

He served as an officer under **VALENS**, but was appointed *comes* and *magister equitum* (cavalry commander) by **THEODOSIUS I** in 386, adding command of the infantry as well in 388, remaining in office until 395. As such he commanded part of the army against both **MAGNUS MAXIMUS** and *EUGENIUS I,* serving with Stilicho in the latter case. He was also consul in 389. He was brought low by a legal case at Constantinople in 396 which resulted in his exile to Siwa Oasis in Libya, from which he attempted to escape, but seems to have perished in the desert, for he, nor his son Syagrius (qv) who set out to rescue him, was ever seen again. In view of his son's name, his widow Pentadia may well have been sister of one or other of the consuls of 381/2 [PRE I Timasius].

Papianilla

Clearly related to the Papianilla who married Sidonius Apoollinaris, probably an aunt; her sister is thought to have married **AVITUS** which effectively united the Aviti, the Syagrii, the Sidonii and the Petronii; their descendants were to dominate Gaul over the following two centuries as commanders, administrators and bishops [PLRE II Papianilla 1].

Ruricius

Elected 3rd Bishop of Ucetia (Uzès) in 533, but died after only five years to be succeeded by his nephew Firminus (qv).

Rusticus

Bishop of Cadurcorum (Cahors) from 623 until he was murdered in 630, to be succeeded by his brother the *comes* Desiderius [PLRE III Rusticus 6]

Salvius

A noble Gallo-Roman who died c. 618 [PLRE III Salvius]

Syagria

A rich noble Gallo Roman lady of Lugdunum (Lyons) who in 494 contributed a considerable sum to ransom captive Italians held by the Burgundians. She also founded churches and monasteries, which largess rather suggests that she was childless. As she was of Lyons, it is possible that her father was Syagrius, the 'Solon of the Burgundians' (qv). She may be the same as a Syagria who, by her husband Latinus had a son, Gundobadus, whose name perhaps commemorated descent from the Burgundian king and *magister militum*. [PLRE II Syagria]

Syagrius

Son of Timasius and a senator, who is said to have escaped arrest in 396 when his father was tried and perished in attempting to rescue him from Siwa. Nothing was heard of either man again [PLRE I Syagrius 1].

Syagrius

A friend of Sidonius and known to have been a great grandson of Fl. Afranius Syagrius (consul 382), he lived on an estate called Taionnacus (Teonnac) in Aeduan territory and was criticised by Sidonius for eschewing the public life that his illustrious ancestry imposed upon him. But he seems to have rectified this later, learning German with amazing rapidity and acting extensively as a judge and arbitrator in

Burgundian territory, becoming, as Sidonius put it, the 'Solon of the Burgundians' [PLRE II Syagrius 3].

Syagrius
See above *SYAGRIUS AUGUSTUS*

[Syagrius]

Son of the imperial claimant, who was legend says, spared by Clovis in 486.

Syagrius

His relationship to his father is attested by Gregory of Tours who adds that he murdered the man who had brought about his father's death. He was a *vir illustris* in Gaul and a signatory to the proceedings of the Council of Arausio (Orange) in 529 and was still alive in 548, by which time he had become Bishop of Gratianopolis (Grenoble) [Greg. *HF* III. 34; PLRE III Syagrius 1]

Syagrius

Comes civitatis of Pictavis (Poitiers) but killed in action there in 568.

Syagrius

Metropolitan and bishop of Autun 560-600, he was host to St. Gregory *en route* to England to begin his mission there. He baptised Chlotharius II and in his time the see was given precedence over all others in Gaul bar Lugdunum (Lyons). He was later canonised.

Syagrius 587

A Gallo Roman noble and *comes* in the Burgundian Kingdom under Guntram in 587, who in that year sent him as envoy to **MAURICIUS** at Constantinople, who made him a patrician and titular governor of Provence, with the intention of bringing it back within the Empire's direct control; this appears to have failed. Despite the assassination of *SYAGRIUS*, the family evidently prospered under Frankish rule. A descendant, Syagria, made a large donation of land to the monks of Novalesa Abbey in 739. 'The last known member of the Syagrii was an abbot of Nantua who was mentioned in 757.'[841] [PLRE III Syagrius 2].

Syagrius 787

Founder of the Abbey of St. Pons, Cimiez, in Provence, Bishop of Nicaea (Nice) 777 to his death in 787 and supposedly a kinsman of Charlemagne, although precise the relationship, assuming it existed, is lost (it was probably through a marriage). He was later canonised.

Syagrius

He came from Albi and served at the court of Chlotharius II, who made him *comes civitatis* of Civitas Albigensium (Albi) and he later became patrician and governor of Provence, dying *en post* 629/630 [PLRE III Syagrius 3].

Theodatus

A *vir clarissimus* in 599.

Tonantius

Inherited his father's estate at Prusianum and lived there with his brothers. [PLRE II Tonantius]

Tonantius Ferreolus

His antecedents are uncertain but recorded as 'very noble' and descended from patricians, according to several references in the correspondence of his kinsman and close friend Sidonius, where the latter probably means Constantinian patricians rather than the old, hereditary, ones. There were two early saints called Ferreolus (the only precursors for the name) one martyred (with his brother Ferrutio) at Vesontio (Besançon) in 212 and another two generations later, an army officer, martyred at Vienna (Vienne). Conceivably they were members of the family. He was Praetorian Prefect of Gaul in 451-453 and owned an esatate called Pusianum, near Nemausus (Nîmes) and another near Segodunum (Rodez). He fought against Attila in 451 and raised the siege of Arlate (Arles) in 453 by use of diplomacy. He was warmly remembered as praetorian prefect for reducing taxation. In 469 he was in Rome. He had several sons [PLRE II Ferreolus & cf. **TABLE LXIII(a)**]

ANTHEMIUS
12th April 467 – 11th July 472

Background

The death of **SEVERUS III** left yet another vacancy in the Western Empire, although hardly a power vacuum, as Ricimer still tightly grasped the reigns. Again the Empire was technically united, under the Eastern emperor **LEO I**, with the barbarian patrician in the West behaving as emperor in all but name, yet even at this pass nobody could imagine the West without an emperor.

---

841. Musset (1965) 127

The problem with the succession was that Gaiseric was still pressing the case for his brother-in-law **OLYBRIUS**, and denying him was inevitably going to lead to further aggression on the part of the Vandal ruler, especially on the coasts and hence supply lines of Italy. In the end, the choice was left to **LEO**, who in spring 467 finally decided to send the patrician **ANTHEMIUS**, a descendant of the imperial claimant under **VALENS, PROCOPIUS** (see above **Table LVII**).

The new Western emperor was the son of the *magister militum* Procopius and was married to Aelia Marcia Euphemia, the daughter and heiress of the late eastern emperor, **MARCIAN**. Probably Leo was keen enough to send **ANTHEMIUS**, effectively neutralising an able grandee with an excellent claim to **LEO's** throne. Although an Eastern senator of high rank, he had made his career in the army, and by 453 his father-in-law had appointed him *comes rei militaris*, and he served on the Danubian frontier. He did a sound job restoring the defences there and on his return in 454 he was promoted to *magister utriusque militiae* (commander-in-chief), which he held until his appointment as western emperor and patrician. He was Eastern consul in 455 sharing with the Western emperor **VALENTINIAN III**. It would have been expected that the husband of the emperor's only daughter would had succeeded seamlessly to the purple on the death of **MARCIAN**, but in fact it was said that his reluctance at the time and the opposition of his rival and fellow *magister utriusque militum* Flavius Ardaburius Aspar, led to the elevation of **LEO I**, as a compromise, and under whom **ANTHEMIUS** continued to serve, distinguishing himself against the Ostrogoths and the Huns.[842]

Reign

He arrived in Italy with an army, conveyed in a fleet, and was formally proclaimed on 12th April. The only thing against him was that the Empire had been divided for almost a century and people saw him as a foreigner, calling him *Graeculus* (Greekling). Once arrived in Rome, however, he was invested with the insignia of office, granted the usual powers by the senate and took the style of **Dominus Noster Procopius Anthemius Pius Felix Perpetuus Augustus**.[843] His wife, who seems to have died shortly after he came to power, was made Augusta.[844] He served a second consulship in 468, followed by his son Marcianus the following year with the future Eastern emperor **ZENO**.[845]

The first development was that Ricimer married the emperor's daughter Alypia, presumably to cement their working relationship. The intention of the entire set up from the point of view of **LEO** was that with an experienced general as emperor, allied to a ferocious and capable barbarian C-in-C, the war could be taken to the Vandals in Africa so that the running sore of Gaiseric and his raids could be ended. In fact, **ANTHEMIUS** had to fight on two fronts, for his direct hold on Gaul was by this time confined to the Rhône valley and the Auvergne, and

---

842. PLRE II Anthemius 3
843. ILS 812, 815 and coin issues, only one of which, uniquely, gives his name as Procop[ius] Anthemius.
844. Coin evidence only.
845. The son Marcianus received a second consulship from his father in 472 this time as eastern nominee.

the Visigothic king was now the able and determinedly anti-Roman Euricus. He reckoned that with the constant changes of emperor, the West would be a pushover, and he was not far off the mark. Twice **ANTHEMIUS** campaigned against him, and twice gained little or nothing, and in the process his son Anthemiolus was killed in action. Furthermore, the attempt to re-conquer Africa was also a complete failure and inevitably Emperor and patrician fell out, attempts at reconciliation with the Vandal kingdom being on the whole fruitless. The last of these attempts was negotiated by the distinguished senator, exiled to Constantinople, **OLYBRIUS** (almost certainly the younger son of **PETRONIUS MAXIMUS**), brother-in-law of the Vandal ruler. This too, broke down, resulting in Ricimer proclaiming the mediator emperor, in opposition to his own father-in-law, in April 472. Thereupon he laid siege to Rome for five months, finally entering the City on July 11th, at which point **ANTHEMIUS** was killed, according to John of Antioch, in cold blood by Ricimer's nephew, Gundobad, King of the Burgundians. Despite the catastrophic end to his reign, however, it would be unfair to describe **ANTHEMIUS** as Ricimer's puppet. The emperor was a distinguished and competent commander, raised by **LEO,** not by the western patrician, and by no means beholden to him. His problem was that neither he nor Ricimer, experienced soldiers, had any longer the resources (despite the Emperor's eastern detachments) to overcome either Euric or Gaiseric and their inevitable failure was only ever going to end in tears.

Family
See above, **Table LVII**

Imperial claimant under Anthemius

ROMANUS I
470

ROMANUS was *magister officiorum* in the West and had, by 470, been made patrician, probably by **ANTHEMIUS**. However, later that year Cassiodorus reports that he was somehow involved in a conspiracy against the emperor, possibly engineered by his friend Ricimer, which resulted in his being proclaimed emperor himself. However the matter was swiftly put down and the hapless pretender arrested and put to death. We know nothing of his earlier life nor of his family background. Needless to say, there were no coins issued in his name so we can only guess at the style he employed as Augustus.[846] As a result, Ricimer rose in revolt, but after some threatening manoeuvrings, a reconciliation was effected which lasted until 472.

*

---

846. PLRE II Romanus 4. His bid for power was also reported by John of Antioch and the much later Lombard historian Paul the Deacon.

OLYBRIUS
11ᵗʰ July – 2ⁿᵈ November 472

Background

Anicius OLYBRIUS was recognised as a leading member of the senate even before he was forced to leave Rome on the fall of his father in 455. He was in all probability a descendant of three other emperors, too; his family could hardly have been grander or better qualified, by the standards of the time, to become emperor. Yet that, and his kinship to the troublesome Gaiseric were his qualifications. Unlike his predecessor, he was not an experienced soldier nor even, like his father, a distinguished administrator. But he was married to the younger daughter of **VALENTINIAN III**, Placidia, making him, as we have seen, brother-in-law to the Vandal king of Africa, who had ceaselessly promoted his cause as western emperor from the time of the fall of **MAJORIAN** in 461, setting the rest of his family free at that time.

OLYBRIUS was made a patrician and eastern consul in 464 - there was no western consul that year, merely two eastern ones, but the fact that **OLYBRIUS** was really a western senator probably justified it. **LEO I** commissioned him to go to Rome to make peace between Ricimer and **ANTHEMIUS** and having done that he was supposed to go on to Carthage to sign an accord with Gaiseric too. Instead, he got caught up in the events of Italy, finding himself entering Rome as Emperor on 11ᵗʰ July 472. He was almost certainly designated as western consul for 473 (with **LEO** as eastern colleague), but having died before the beginning of that year, the western consulship remained vacant.

Reign

It is not known what sort of reception the new Emperor received from his fellow senators, but no doubt it was favourable, as he was one of their own, and they installed him and accorded him the powers required. He took the style **Dominus Noster Anicius Olybrius Pius Felix Augustus.**[847] He had established himself when first elevated by minting coins at Mediolanum (Milan), but what precisely he did during the long siege of Rome is not known, but it is likely that he was present during at least part of it. Once installed, his only recorded act was to confer the title of patrician upon young Gundobad, the son of Ricimer's sister. As his Burgundians at this time formed the backbone of the army, it guaranteed the soldiers' loyalty. Thus, when the Emperor died from natural causes at the beginning of November, it was Gundobadus who held all the cards.

Family

The Emperor's antecedents are dealt with in **Tables XLV** and **LXIII(a)** and his posterity mainly in the East is included in **Table LXIII(b)**, descending to people alive at the time of the death of the Emperor **MAURICIUS**, the last strictly Roman emperor dealt with in this

---

847. Coin evidence.

work. If one can accept the conjectural sections, there is a near 400 year descent from the earlier 3rd century (M. Aurelius Dalmatius) to c. 602, almost four centuries. From Anicia, first wife of Petronius Probinus consul in 322, it is possible to trace a descent from the probably senatorial father of Q. Anicius Q. f. Faustus, a suffect consul in 198 who was given patrician status by **SEPTIMIUS SEVERUS**.[848] In his turn, his forebear may have been Q. Anicius Faustus, a *duumvir* (town councillor) at Uzappa (Ab'd el-Melek), in Africa living early in the second century.[849] The family were settlers there and the name (and probably bloodline) went back to Praeneste, in Italy. Q. Anicius Praenestinus was the first recorded senator of the *gens*, had served as curule aedile in 304BC and was probably of a different branch of the family which were senatorial until at least the end of the Republic.[850] But Olybrius's ancestry does not stop there, for the consul of 198 married [Sergia] Paulla, daughter of L. Sergius Paullus, consul (ii) in 168, probably great grandson of L. Sergius Paullus, suffect consul under **CLAUDIUS I** before 46.[851] Beyond that, however, we cannot go.

The imperial links were maintained by **OLYBRIUS'S** posterity, too. His daughter married the brother of the Emperor **ANASTASIUS**, whose great grand-daughter married the brother of **JUSTIN II**. Another marriage brought a link to the notorious Theodora, empress of **JUSTINIAN**. Another distinction for this extraordinary family is that they also produced a pope, in the person of Vigilius (pope 537-555), younger son of the praetorian prefect Ioannes who married a daughter of another Olybrius, himself a praetorian prefect in 503.[852] It is possible that the male line was eventually snuffed out in the slaughter of the aristocracy, especially those with connections to the previous dynasty, initiated under **PHOCAS** from 602.

---

848. PIR² A595
849. ILS1263
850. Plin. *NH* xxxiii, 17. The African settlers (and those at Pisidian Antioch) were unlikely to have been direct descendants of this man.
851. ILS5926. They were also raised to patrician status by c. 150: Syme, RP III 1325.
852. The pope was thus a great-grandson of the Emperor **OLYBRIUS**.

TABLE LXIII(b): THE POSTERITY OF OLYBRIUS

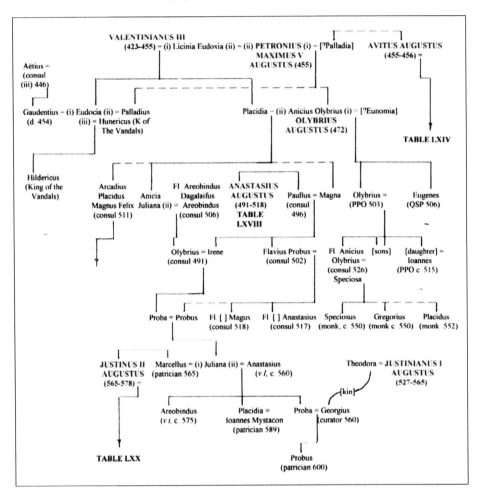

TABLE LXIII(b): BRIEF LIVES

Anastasius

See below **ANASTASIUS I AUGUSTUS**

Anicia Juliana

Born at Constantinople c. 462, she refused an offer of marriage from Theodericus, King of the Ostrogoths in Italy and married c. 479 being created a patrician in her own right as a member of an Imperial family, thus styled *patricia*. Significantly, she appears in the frontispiece of the Vienna Dioscurides (a herbal of c. 512) as an

empress. She built many churches and undertook numerous good works and died c. 527/528 when her household eunuchs became monks [PLRE II Juliana 3; Kiilerich (2015) 99-107]

Anicius Olybrius

See above, **OLYBRIUS AUGUSTUS**

Arcadius Placidus Magnus Felix

His name was recorded in full on the back of a seat in the Flavian Amphitheatre from the early 6th century, and was re-discovered in the 1990s. His names clearly suggest his antecedents: Arcadius Placidus from the House of **THEODOSIUS** and Magnus Felix from that of **PETRONIUS MAXIMUS.** King Theodericus promoted him to office carrying the style of *vir illustris* before 511, in which year, recorded as Flavius Felix, he was made consul (West). Bearing in mind the weight of imperial and senatorial nomenclature he carried, the consular senator Petronius might have been a son; he was the father of another illustrious man bearing a Theodosian name: Pope Honorius (625-640). Exactly how Felix's descent may have come about is impossible to discern precisely. What is suggested here is accepted as the most likely. [Mathisen (2003) *passim*; PLRE II Felix 20].

Areobindus

Vir illustris c. 575/600 [PLRE III Areobindus 5]

Eugen[et]es

An orator, *vir illustris* and literary man, the precise form of his name is not clear. He practised in the courts and was appointed *quaestor palatii* (QSP=palace treasurer) by King Theoderic 506, becoming *magister officiorum* in the west the following year [PLRE III Eugenes]

Flavius Aëtius

See above **Table LIX(a) Brief Lives**

Flavius Anastasius Paulus Probus Sabinianus Pompeius Anastasius

His names indicate his close kinship with Emperor **ANASTASIUS**. He was eastern consul in 517 and his diptych survives [PLRE II. Anastasius 17/Anonymous 4]

Flavius Anastasius Paulus Probus Probus Pompeius Anastasius

See **Table LXVIII(a) Brief Lives**

Flavius Anicius Olybrius

He was sole consul in 526, being recognised in both halves of the empire (albeit that the West was no longer under the direct control of the East, King Theodoricus acted like a viceroy, appointing senators to high imperial offices. His paternity is not certain. [PLRE II Olybrius 7]

Flavius Anicius Petronius Olybrius

His nomenclature is by no means certain, although his parentage is. He was born c. 480, served an entirely nominal (Eastern) consulship in 491 aged about ten. He seems to have been exiled after the *Nika* riot but was recalled and restored to his estates in 533, by which time he was already a patrician [PLRE II Olybrius 3]

Flavius Areobindus Dagalaifus Areobindus

Although of Gothic descent, the family had been senatorial since the time of his great great grandfather, Dagalaifus, consul in 366. This man's grandson and great grandson were both consuls, and his mother Godisithea, daughter of another Barbarian-descended grandee Ardaburius (consul 447). His consular diptych (as eastern consul in 506) survives, and he was previously married, his first wife's name being lost, although he had two sons by her. He also served as magister *militum per Orientem* (C-in-C East) 503-505 when he fought with mixed success against the Persians and Armenians. When in retirement, a mob, dissatisfied with **ANASTASIUS** marched on his town house in 512 shouting 'Areobindus for emperor!' but although they found Juliana at home, Areobindus had wisely gone into hiding, thus avoiding the dubious distinction of becoming an imperial claimant. He probably died not long afterwards. [PLRE I Dagalaifus; *ibid.*, II Areobindus 1, 2, Dagalaifus 2].

Flavius Placidus Valentinianus

See above, **VALENTINIAN III AUGUSTUS**

Flavius Probus

He was eastern consul for 502 at a young age, but went on to become *magister militum* in 526 by which time he appears to have been made patrician. Like Areobindus in 512, when the *nika* riot broke out in 532, he made himself scarce (not wishing to be a third ephemeral emperor in the family), fearing that the mob would want to elevate him to the purple. Not finding him at home, the mob instead burnt his house down. He was exiled after order was restored, but pardoned in 533. He was still living in 542, and was an adherent of the monophysite heresy [PLRE II Probus 8]

Flavius Anastasius Paulus Probus Moschianus Probus Magnus

Sole consul in 518, commemorated by a surviving ivory diptych which shows us that he was normally called Flavius Magnus [PLRE II Magnus 3]

Flavius Moschianus

His place on the pedigree above is not wholly certain; he may have been the brother of Secundinus (consul 511), as suggested in PLRE II Stemma 9. He was possibly *magister militum* in Illyricum in 482, and certainly consul in 512 [PLRE II Moschianus 1, 2]

Gaudentius

See above **Table LIX(a) Brief Lives**

Georgius

He is known to have been related to the Empress Theodora, but exactly how is not clear. He was *curator divinae domus Marinae* from 560 to 562 [PLRE III Georgius 7, Proba 2]

Gregorius

Noble and well educated, he gave everything away and entered the monastery then recently founded by St. Benedict near Terracina [PLRE III Gregorius 1]

Hildericus

See above, **Table LIX(a) Brief Lives**

Hunericus

See above, **Table LIX(a) Brief Lives**

Ioannes

Son of one of Ennodius's numerous acquaintances, he was still a student as the 6th century opened, but was a *vir spectabilis* (the lowest senatorial rank). He was governor of Campania in 507/511, later *comes sacrae largitionum* (keeper of the privy purse) to King Theodericus, and praetorian prefect of Italy, during which time he repaired the senate house and actively protected the poor from exploitation. He had died by 527. He had two sons Reparatus and Vigilius, of whom the elder served as prefect of the City (of Rome) c. 527 going on to be appointed by **JUSTINIANUS I** praetorian prefect of Italy in 538, in which office he was captured by the Goths the following year and summarily put to death. The younger son was ordained deacon by 531 and became papal representative at Constantinople due to his exalted familial connections, but returned and was elected pope in 537, dying in 555, yet another astonishing distinction for the Anician family [PLRE II Ioannes 67, Reparatus 1 & Vigilius 4; Brown (1984) 32; Kelly (1986) 60-61].

Ioannnes *qui et* **Mystacon**

He was from Thrace and his nickname referred to his moustache. He first comes to notice as *magister militum* (C-in-C) in Armenia, 579-582, then again on the eastern frontier, but achieving little against the Persians, he was transferred to Thrace in 587 and then to Armenia, again with the title patrician (589/590-591) [PLRE III.Ioannes 101].

Juliana

Went into exile with her father in 532 and a monophysite; was again exiled by her brother-in-law to a monastery , but was ultimately pardoned. Settipani suggests a separate Juliana married Marcellus, and makes her a possible daughter of Flavius Magnus, consul in 518 and suggersts that she was the mother by him of Helena, a woman of consular rank living in the 7th century [PLRE III Helena 2, Juliana 1; Settipani (2000) 423]

Justinus
See below **JUSTIN II AGUSTUS**

Magna
Her paternity is nowhere attested, but the frequency with which the names Magnus/a, Probus/a and Placidus/ia occur amongst her descendants makes this attribution virtually certain [PLRE II Magna].

Marcellus
Patrician 565, see below **Table LXX Brief Lives**

Olybrius
Yet another well-connected acquaintance of St. Ennodius and himself something of a poet. He was a leading member of the senate and died in office whilst serving as praetorian prefect of Italy under King Theodericus [PLRE II Olybrius 5]

Palladius
See above, **Tables LIX(a) & LXIII(a) Brief Lives.**

Paullus
He was Eastern consul without a Western colleague in 496 [PLRE II Paulus 26]

Petronius Maximus
See above **PETRONIUS MAXIMUS AUGUSTUS**

Placidia
See above **Table LIX(a) Brief Lives**

Proba
Known to have had sisters [PLRE III Proba 1]

Probus
He and his wife are both thought to have been relatives of **ANASTASIUS**; he is possibly the son of Probus, consul in 502 [PLRE II Probus 8; III Probus 1]

Probus
He is supposed to have founded the church of St. John the Baptist at Constantinople where he built 'splendid palaces'; a patrician c. 600 [PLRE III Probus 4.]

Speciosus
A 'famous' monk in Italy and a *vir clarissimus*. His name suggests he might have been a close relative of the patrician Speciosus, thrice Prefect of the City (of Rome) and Western consul in 496, whom Moorhead identifies as a member of the family of **OLYBRIUS** and who coujld possibly have been one of his un-named uncles of or perhaps a brother-in-law of Olybrius the Praetorian Prefect of 503 (qv). PLRE II connects him with the *clarissima femina* Speciosa, herself certainly as *adfinis* (relation) of the same Olybrius, this Speciosus' grandfather (cf. above) [PLRE II. Speciosa, Speciosus 1; III, Speciosus 2].

Theodora
See below **Table LXIX(b)**

⋆

GLYCERIUS
3rd March 473 – 19th June 474

Background

The death of **OLYBRIUS** left the inevitable power vacuum in the west, now in chaos, and notionally the empire was once again united under the Emperor **LEO I,** whose effective viceroy was the Burgundian chancer, Gundobad. He took his time deciding on his next move, before finally elevating his *comes domesticorum* (commander of the guard) to the purple at the beginning of March the following year.

From subsequent events it seems likely that, **GLYCERIUS** had probably been appointed to his position by **OLYBRIUS** sometime in the middle of 472; the appointment conferred the status of *vir illustris*. We have little information as to his origin, bar the inference from subsequent events that his mother lived at Ticinum (Pavia), suggesting that may have been his home town as well. The presumption is that he was a senator (albeit probably of recent creation), rather than a military man risen to the top through martial competence. With the Western empire in meltdown, the senate had, especially since the death of **VALENTINIAN III,** become the only recruiting ground for competent administrators, governors and even generals, a strange reversion to its pre-fourth century role. After the West had finally collapsed, senators still formed the backbone of the bureaucracy and administration of the successive régimes of Kings Odovacer and Theoderic, just as their coevals in Gaul (largely separated by the collapse from much actual participation in the senate in Rome) formed the underpinning of the Frankish, Burgundian and Visigothic kingdoms' administration for the folowing two centuries.

Reign

The new appointment – a puppet emperor this time if ever there was one – was proclaimed at Ravenna but may not have been recognised by the senate at Rome, for although his coins were minted at Ravenna and Mediolanum (Milan), none were minted at Rome. In other words, it is possible that he was not even acknowledged throughout Italy He was formally styled **Dominus Noster Glycerius Augustus Felix Perpetuus Augustus**[853] and it seems likely that he was Western consul for 474, although it does not show up on the *fasti*, probably because the Eastern emperor refused to acknowledge his elevation.[854]

Six months after his elevation, **LEO I** died, leaving as his successor his young grandson, **LEO II** and with the latter's father **ZENO** as co-emperor, leaving the unacknowledged **GLYCERIUS** as senior Augustus in the whole empire. His chief achievement was that, faced in early 474 with an invasion of Ostrogoths under king Videmer II, he managed through diplomacy to divert them from a planned descent on Italy and to go to Gaul instead. This had the effect of their

853. Coin evidence.
854. PLRE II Glycerius

uniting with the Visigoths, but at the cost of further losses of territory directly controlled by the Empire in southern Gaul. The very ineffectiveness of the emperor led to much unrest in Italy, including a riot at Ticinum in which a mob threatened to burn down the house of the Emperor's mother. Imperial reprisals were only diverted by the entreaties of the local bishop.

At this juncture, Gundobad's father died, and he returned to Gaul to reclaim his patrimony as co-ruler of the Burgundian people, leaving the Emperor without any real support. Simultaneously the Eastern Court sent, rather as they had **ANTHEMIUS** in 467 and **OLYBRIUS** in 472, another general to reclaim the west. This was the patrician and *magister militum* **JULIUS NEPOS**, who landed with an army at Portus, near Ostia at the Tiber's mouth, in June 474. **GLYCERIUS** appears to have travelled from Ravenna to Rome and offered to abdicate in order to re-unite the Empire, an offer which was accepted. He was, like **AVITUS**, offered and accepted the see of Salona, in Dalmatia (Solin, Croatia), which he still held six years later. Apart from the fact that his mother was living when he was elevated to the purple, we know nothing for certain of his family. Barnish, however, has suggested that he might have been connected with Licerius [= Glycerius], a contemporary, whose son seems to have married the sister of Ennodius and whose grandson was Fl. Firminus Licerius Lupicinus.[855]

∗

JULIUS NEPOS
(December 473/19th June 474 – 9th May 480

Background

The Eastern general sent by **ZENO** was probably of Western senatorial family, for his father had been a senior commander of **MAJORIAN** in Gaul in 458/459 who was praised by Sidonius. His uncle, Marcellinus, had been *magister militum*, whose command was extended by **MAJORIAN, LEO I** and **ANTHEMIUS** at various times, but which was primarily based in Dalmatia, where he may have had estates. **NEPOS** appears to have inherited the authority of Marcellinus in Dalmatia and may have been appointed or merely recognised as *magister militum* (West) by **ANTHEMIUS** when his uncle was killed in 468; he was certainly holding such an appointment (from the eastern emperor) when he descended on Italy in 474. He was also then patrician. He was nominated as new Western Emperor during the last illness of **LEO I,** probably in December 473; his commission was to take Italy and depose **GLYCERIUS,** which, after a delay until the start of the next campaigning season, he duly did.

Reign

Having received the submission of **GLYCERIUS, NEPOS** was actually proclaimed emperor on 19th (some sources say 24th) June 474. He was accepted and installed by the senate and was perhaps even granted the usual tribunician and proconsular powers, for the senate was

---

855. PLRE II Licerius & Lupicinus 3 ; Barnish (1988) 155 & n. 214.

a notable repository of arcane traditions and such a confirmation would have endowed its members with a taste for the authority that august body once enjoyed and to some extent had regained. He adopted the rather *recherché* style **Dominus Noster Julius Nepos Pater Patriae Augustus**.[856] He may also have served a (Western) consulship in 475, but his name does not appear on the *fasti*, and it may be that, as with **GLYCERIUS**, such a move was not sanctioned by the Eastern court, although why that might have been, seeing that he was their man, is difficult to say. Perhaps actually taking the Western throne may not have been in the eastern emperor's game-plan, although he certainly seems to have been recognised at some stage.

His main preoccupation was to try and prevent the Visigoths under their new, anti-Roman and anti-Catholic king, Euric, taking over the Auvergne, still part of the Empire. One of the sons of the Emperor **AVITUS**, Ecdicius[857], a stalwart loyalist, was made patrician and *magister militum* and in 474 managed, against fearsome odds, to relieve Arelate (Arles), but was less successful the following year, not helped by the fact that although **NEPOS** had some Eastern army units to support him, there were no significant military resources available to assist him. Nevertheless, Ecdicius was relieved of his responsibilities, and was replaced by Orestes. This man was yet another hardened soldier of Danubian stock, who had also once served as the secretary of Attila the Hun.

Having been appointed patrician and *magister militum* in the place of Ecdicius, Orestes acted unpredictably. Instead of marching to the relief of Arelate (which duly fell to the Visigoths), to neutralise the threat from Euric (which he thus failed to do), he turned his forces instead against **NEPOS** at Ravenna and laid siege to the city. **NEPOS** realised that he was the victim of a *coup* and on August 28th 475 wisely took ship with his entourage to Dalmatia, where he was well-known and appreciated, with the intention of regrouping there prior to making an attempt to return to Italy to eject Orestes, who had proclaimed his young son **ROMULUS** emperor in the place of **NEPOS**.

This he signally failed to achieve, unless the Eastern court withdrew the support he would have required. Thus for the following five years he ruled Dalmatia and those parts of neighbouring provinces where the writ of the western empire still ran – southern Pannonia south of the Sava, Histria and parts of Noricum – and, after the fall of **ROMULUS** tried once again to obtain the assistance of **ZENO,** the Eastern emperor, to regain his position. This too failed to get off the ground, probably because **ZENO** was happier to accept a united Empire than have a western colleague who could only function with the allocation of scarce military resources. Thus **NEPOS**, who had not abdicated, remained a nominal, semi-acknowledged western emperor with only limited effective reach. Nevertheless, his mini-empire in the Balkans acted as a useful buffer state to help shield the eastern empire from problems from that quarter, whilst they dealt with the perturbations caused by the Ostrogoths in northern Pannonia and Dacia Ripensis. In 477, under his nominal rule, *MASTIES* was imperial claimant in Numidia, but was suppressed by the Vandal kingdom after a few months.

---

856. ILS814; coins: D[ominus] Noster] Jul[ius] Nepos P[ius] F[elix] Aug[ustus].
857. Table LXIV Brief Lives

This relatively stable state of affairs, however, all came to an end on 9th May 480, when **NEPOS** was unexpectedly assassinated at his palace at Salona (Solin) by two *comites* called Viator and *OVIDA*, allegedly put up to it by the exiled and resentful **GLYCERIUS**, still serving as the local bishop. *OVIDA* then continued the *imperium* of **NEPOS** (whether as emperor or merely as a sort of warlord is unclear) but he succumbed to an attack by Odoacer at the end of 482, being put to death on 27th November (or 9th December).[858]

NEPOS' (or *OVIDA'S*) death left only *SYAGRIUS* as holding any imperial power in the Western Empire, the remains of which had fallen into the hands of the Hunnic adventurer Odovacer in 476.[859] A decade later, Clovis the Frank finished the job. Thenceforth, it existed only as a constitutional construct, with barbarian successor kings acting as nominal appointees of the Eastern Emperor. It was going to take three generations before the *reconquista* could begin, although it has been convincingly argued by Arnold that the deposition of Odovaccer by Theoderic in 493 was effectively a restoration the Empire in the west which lasted until the coming of the forces of **JUSTINIAN**.

Family

A temporal gulf separates **NEPOS** from the Julii Nepotes, who were senators in the mid to late second century, and any such connection seems inherently unlikely; nor is it certain that Julius was a *nomen* in the traditional sense. However, as he was apparently the heir to his uncle Marcellinus, who was an important power broker (if not warlord) in Dalmatia, it may well be that his own family were also from Salona or nearby. Indeed it may be that *OVIDA* was some kind of relation, perhaps of **NEPOS'S** mother. The name is Germanic. We also know that his wife (of whom we hear nothing during his reign, implying she may have died before he took power) except that she was related, very probably a niece, of the Empress Verina, the wife of **LEO I** and sister of the rather dim but persistent imperial claimant *BASILISCUS*.

TABLE LXV(a): THE FAMILY OF NEPOS

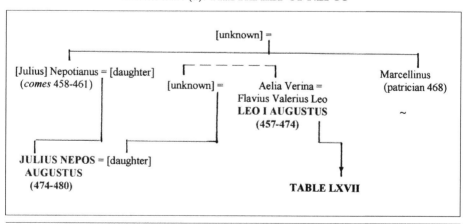

858. PLRE II Viator 1.
859. PLRE II Odovacer.

TABLE LXV(a): BRIEF LIVES

Aelia Verina

See below **Table LXVII Brief Lives.**

Flavius Valerius Leo

See below **LEO I AUGUSTUS**

Julius Nepos

See above **JULIUS NEPOS AUGUSTUS**

[Julius] Nepotianus

Probably from Dalmatia, he was appointed *comes* and *magister utriusque militiae* (adviser and C-in-C) under **MAJORIAN** in 459. He was active in Gaul and met with the approval of Sidonius Apollinaris. He was joint commander of a largely Visigothic army which defeated the Sueves in Spain the following year. He was succeeded by a Gallic noble, Arborius (conceivably a member of the family of the 4th century consul Ausonius) in 461 and appears to have died in 465 [PLRE II Nepotianus 2]

Marcellinus

He was a pagan of noble birth and well educated; he first comes to notice as *comes rei militaris* (senior army commander) in Dalmatia. He was a friend of Aëtius and had probably served under him, but he rebelled against **VALENTINIAN III** when his friend was killed, setting himself up as an independent commander in Dalmatia. He seems to not to have been the man canvassed as imperial claimant in Gaul on the death of **AVITUS** (see *MARCELLUS II* above). It would appear however, that there is less evidence (than for example with *AEGIDIUS*) that he was an imperial claimant. He merely seems to have ignored orders from Rome or Ravenna and bided his time, possibly with support from the Eastern Court. He accepted the authority of **MAJORIAN** in 457 and **ANTHEMIUS** in 468, underlining his support of the policies of the East towards the West. In 461 he was appointed *magister militum* and recognised as such by **LEO I**; he drove the Vandals out of Sicily in 465 and in 467 accompanied **ANTHEMIUS** to Rome, being made patrician on arrival. In 468 he cleared Sardinia of Vandals but was assassinated in Sicily in August 468 [PLRE II Marcellinus 6; MacGeorge (2002) 64-65]

Imperial claimants under Julius Nepos

MASTIES
c. 477 – 516

After it became clear that there were to be no further western emperors, the *dux* (leader) of the Romans and Moors in Numidia proclaimed himself emperor, and according to his monumental inscription datable to 516, he maintained himself as *imperator annis XL* (emperor 40 years) and had been *dux* for 67 years! He came from Arris (Arris Batne, Algeria) and must thus have been born c. 425, being appointed *dux* not before 449 (when Numidia was still under the sway of the western empire) which was probably an acknowledgement by the governor of his position as ruler of the Moors, probably on the death of his predecessor. His self-proclaimed elevation to the purple, after the example of *AEGIDIUS*, may have been made in conjunction with a revolt against the Vandals which began in the Aurès mountains in 477, resulting in his controlling an independent political entity. As a native ruler, he may well have been related to *FIRMUS* and his family (see above, **Table LVI**). Nothing further is known of this man nor of his family, except that the Vandals, who wasted the province in 468, seem to have left him to his own devices, and that he died in 516.[860]

*

OVIDA
9th May 480 - December 482

With Viator, *OVIDA* was a Germanic, possibly Gothic *comes* of **NEPOS** (of whom conceivably a relative) who, for some unknown reason decided, with his colleague, to do away with his master and personally took over in his stead, lasting until overthrown by Odovacer, probably in revenge for his assassinastion of his kinsman **NEPOS**, in December 482.[861] Whether he styled himself Augustus and was thus an imperial claimant, or merely gave himself some honorific like *magister militum* is not clear. On precedent and circumstantial evidence the former would seem the more convincing. No coins are known, however, although this is not wholly surprising.

*

ROMULUS AUGUSTUS
31st October 475 – 4th September 476

Background
NEPOS was driven out of Ravenna on 28th August 475, but the new Patrician Orestes did not do anything about replacing him for two months, during which time, as on several previous such occasions, the empire was united, at least notionally. As a native-born Roman rather than a barbarian, it is strange that Orestes did not himself don the purple, but it may be that he appreciated how devalued the currency of the western throne had become. It may be, too, that he was hoping for recognition of his position from **ZENO** in the east, but if so, it was not forthcoming. That being so, he may have decided to elevate his young son (thought to have been about 14) to the Imperial dignity.

Reign
It is not clear if the senate was involved at any stage, but probably it acknowledged the new Emperor and perhaps voted him the empty powers tradition dictated. His style was **Dominus**

---

860. PLRE II Masties; Conant (2012) 278, 280, 287, 293.
861. PLRE II Ovida

Noster Romulus Augustus Pius Felix Augustus which amply demonstrated the extraordinary decision taken to bestow the additional *cognomen* Augustus upon him, and not just append it as a title as had been the case ever since the death of **NERO**. Probably it was felt to be symbolic, attached as it was to the lad's given name and no one could have foreseen that he was going to be the last western Emperor. Indeed Orestes' actions would have been taken with confidence; after all, he had diverted from attacking Euric in order to depose **NEPOS**, so he probably thought that, with luck, he might be able to start a dynasty. Needless to say, colloquial usage soon reduced the Emperor's new name to Augustulus ('Little Augustus') which, bearing in mind his youth, was thought most apposite. **ROMULUS** was probably nominated as consul for 476 by the senate in Rome, but this would have been rejected by the eastern court, which only acknowledged its own, the Empress Verina's brother *BASILISCUS*, but in fact, the latter's consulship was annulled when he attempted a *coup*, and another of Verina's relations, Armatus, served the year out and there is no mention in the *fasti* of **ROMULUS**.

Orestes managed to negotiate a reasonably favourable peace accord with Gaiseric, which allowed Italy to recover economically, with grain shipments restored at last, although the price to be paid was much higher than when the province of Africa had been under direct imperial control. The one concession seems to have been that the Vandals were to continue to hold their enclave of Lilybaeum on the far western tip of Sicily, which was merely a recognition of a *de facto* state of affairs in any case. This treaty, however, encouraged the barbarian levies serving in Italy as Orestes army - mainly Heruli, Scirians and Torcilingi - to make demands for land in Italy on which to settle. Orestes then miscalculated, thinking that this was a negotiating ploy, especially as he was most disinclined to concede anything like as much as this in the heartland of the western empire. The troops' leader was the Hun soldier of fortune Odovacer. He was married to a niece of the Empress Verina and therefore closely related to **NEPOS**. His motive for what happened next might even have been notionally on behalf of **NEPOS,** although there is not enough evidence to be sure. He had served under Ricimer against **ANTHEMIUS** however, and had subsequently been made an officer of the *domestici* (the Imperial Guard), before serving in an unknown but very senior capacity under Orestes. He told his men that if they made him their King, he would guarantee their land allocation, and on 23rd August 476, they duly acclaimed him King, although of quite what is unclear, although he was effectively King of Italy.

Having become king, he led his army to face Orestes at Ticinum (Pavia), drove him out, sacked the city but cornered and captured him at Placentia (Piacenza) on 28th August, Orestes being put to death summarily. The Hun leader finally took Ravenna and captured the Imperial court on September 4th, Orestes' brother and deputy, Paulus, being killed. He spared young **ROMULUS**, however, on account of his youth, granted him a pension and packed him off to live in Campania in the villa built by L. Licinius Lucullus in the 60s BC.[862] He and his mother were recorded as still alive and enjoying the pension (renewed by King Theoderic) in 511, aged about 51.

---

862. PLRE II Romulus 4; Paulus 23. We do not know what rank or position was enjoyed by Paulus, probably *comes*.

With (as it turned out) the last western emperor gone - saving the legitimate ruler, **NEPOS** largely impotent and holed up in Dalmatia - that part of the empire was henceforth governed by barbarian kings, mostly seeing themselves as heirs of the previous Roman governors of the relevant provinces and technically viceroys of the emperor in Constantinople. Indeed, until not that long beforehand, Visigothic Gaul seems to have remained part of the Roman Diocese of Septem Provinciae (Provence) and it is even thought that Constantinople sent representatives to the Gallic Council.

Furthermore in the (slightly) changed circumstances, local aristocrats had offered their services with some alacrity to their new barbarian overlords in order to fill various posts (previously in the gift of the local praetorian prefect) on their behalf so that their career opportunities might not be curtailed through the senate in Rome henceforth lying in a different polity. In Italy, too, matters continued much as before and did so until the cataclysms resulting from the *reconquista* of the eastern emperor **JUSTINIAN** in the mid-6th century (on whom and whose family and connections, see below).

Family

The family was, it seems, from a remark in a letter of St. Ennodius, descended from the Valerii Messalae, whom he calls the Corvini, a *cognomen* favoured by this ancient patrician family in the republic and early empire.[863] The only obvious concatenation of a Valerius of this family and a Romulus is via a presumed union between a sister of Flavius Pisidius Romulus (PUR 406) and the senator Valerius Hermonius Maximus, whose father Valerius Poplicola, praetor in 375, may be considered a clear descendant of the old patrician Valerii, or at least a *soi disant* one.[864] Fl. Pisidius Romulus was probably the grandson of Fl. Romulus, consul 343, but there seems to be no clear evidence to connect him with the *comes* Romulus of 440.[865] The emperor's paternal grandfather, though, as a native of Pannonia, was unlikely to have been of senatorial lineage, but the Romulus name may have come down in this way to his maternal grandmother.

Interestingly, Settipani makes a convincing case, based on the *cognomen* of the western consul for 530, Orestes, for his being a grandson of the boy emperor.[866] Bearing in mind that the ex-emperor could have married at 25, say in 485, a daughter could have been of marriageable age by 505, allowing a recorded marriage with Avienus in 512. The son, serving a consulship at 18, would have occasioned little surprise in this era: it had become the norm, the office having become entirely honorific. The matter is safest allowed to rest there, although **Table LXV(b)** includes Settipani's suggestion that (with two postulations) the short-lived but aristocratic Pope Severinus could well have been a descendant.[867] The

---

863. Barnish (1988) 127, quoting Ennodius, *Ep.* I 9.4.

864. PLRE I Maximus 37, Poplicola 1, 2, cf. II. 1 & Romulus 5.

865. PLRE I Romulus 1, 2. The name of the uncle of the consul of 530, Flavius Ennodius Messala would seem to bear Ennodius out.

866. Settipani (2000) 164 & n 1.

867. Settipani (2000) 196-197.

name Avienus implies a descent from the illustrious orator Q. Aurelius Symmachus, consul in 391, whose family favoured the name. The occurrence of Probus in the nomenclature of the consul of 530 clearly suggests a descent from Sex. Claudius Petronius Probus, and thus from **MAGNUS MAXIMUS** and very possibly **PROBUS** cf also **Table XLV**.

TABLE LXV(b): THE FAMILY OF ROMULUS AUGUSTUS

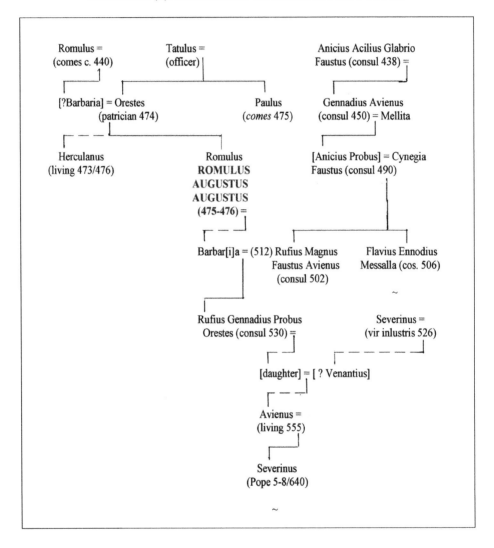

TABLE LXV(b): BRIEF LIVES

Anicius Acilius Glabrio Faustus

Presumed to have been a descendant of the consul for 191BC, M.' Acilius Glabrio and son of Anicia Proba, aunt of **PETRONIUS MAXIMUS,** see above Tables LIX(a) & LXIII(a). He was consul in 438 and several times PUR [PLRE I Proba 1 & II Faustus 8]

Avienus

All that we know of this man is that he was Roman and of noble family, living c. 555/580 [PLRE III Avienus]

Gennadius Avienus

Said by St. Ennodius to have been descended from the 'Corvini', consul in 450 and alive in 468. He married Mellita and also had a daughter Stephania [PLRE II. Avienus 4; Stephania]

[Anicius Probus] Faustus

Consul in 490, Praetorian Prefect of Italy 512; married to Cynegia, about whose family little is known. [PLRE II Faustus 9; Cynegia 1]

Flavius Ennodius Messalla

Close kin to [St.] Magnus Felix Ennodius, whose name also suggests a descent from **MAGNUS MAXIMUS** in the same way that this man's brother's does and his own commemorates his descent from the Valerii Messallae. Western consul in 506 [PLRE II Messalla 2]

Herculanus

This supposed son of Orestes appears in a late chronicle in a confused account of happenings in 473 which are so obviously inaccurate that most commentators reject the reality of this man altogether. If he did exist, he was perhaps an older brother of the emperor, which might pre-suppose his death prior to 475 [PLRE Herculanus 1].

Orestes

Served as secretary to Attila 449-452, possibly in the wake of having been given as hostage to him at some stage and because he was clearly well educated. He was twice sent to Constantinople on embassies by the Hunnic king. He must have subsequently found a position at the eastern court, before being sent, probably as a *comes*, to Italy with the forces accompanying **NEPOS,** who subsequently in 475 made him patrician and *magister militum,* which position he held subsequent to his son's succession as emperor. He was killed by Odovacer 28th August 476 [PLRE II. Orestes 2].

Paulus

In Ravenna in 476 whilst Orestes was away negotiating with the Vandals and later with his own troops, probably as a *comes* and in charge of his nephew. He was killed by Odovacer on 4th September 476 [PLRE II Paulus 23]

Romulus

He was an elderly *comes* in 449 when he was sent on an embassy to parley with Attila by Aëtius. [PLRE II Romulus 2].

Romulus

See above **ROMULUS AUGUSTUS**

Rufius Gennadius Probus Orestes

Western consul in 530, made a patrician by **JUSTINIAN** by 546 and exiled to Sicily the following year. His splendid ivory consular diptych is in the V & A [PLRE III Orestes]

Rufius Magnus Faustus Avienus

Western consul in 502, suggesting he was the elder son, and later Praetorian prefect of Italy

527-528, dead by 545. His marriage to Barbara [sic] in 512 is attested [PLRE Avienus 2]

Severinus

A *vir inlustris* in 526/534, he was probably the son of another Severinus, consul in 482 and grandson of Severinus, consul in 461 [PLRE II, Severinus 3 & 5; III Severinus 1]

Severinus

Born c. 580, elected pope in May 640, but carried off on 2nd August that year. He was almost certainly kin to his predecxcessor, Honorius I, whose father was an ex-consul called Petronius, suggesting descent from Sex. Claudius Petronius Probus, **MAGNUS MAXIMUS** etc.[PLRE III Severinus 2]

Tatulus

He was a native of Pannonia and lived near the River Sava. It seems that he had served in the army, and from the status of his son, he was probably a middle-ranking officer [PLRE III Tatulus]

Further reading:

MacGeorge, P., *Late Roman Warlords* (Oxford 2002)

Murdoch, A., *The Last Roman, Romulus Augustulus and the Decline of the West* (Stroud, 2006)

*

VIII(a)
THE HOUSE OF THEODOSIUS

The imperial succession
Arcadius
Theodosius II
Marcianus I

Whilst the Western half of the Empire had begun to creak at the seams almost from the day of **THEODOSIUS'S** death in 395, the east, after a slightly bumpy start, withstood the pressures of barbarian migration, the declining revenues, secessionist problems and over-mighty barbarian generalissimos and indeed became stronger over a similar period. The reasons for this are exceedingly complex and much disputed in some respects, too, but for the two centuries under review it was not only able to consolidate, but attempt a re-conquest of the Western Empire, over which the Eastern Emperors still had a notional sway. Africa was successfully regained, as was Italy, but the fierceness of the Gothic kings' resistance was unexpected and resulted in a phyrric victory, the Empire regaining a province and former capital, utterly wrecked by incessant conflict and open to further incursions from the North. Southern Spain was also wrested from the Visigoths, but was eventually - beyond the period under scrutiny here - allowed to slip once again from imperial control. Yet in the event, the east was to survive for a thousand and fifty eight years after the final division of the united polity.[868]

*

ARCADIUS
9th January 383 – 1st May 408

Reign
Raised to the rank of co-emperor with his father **THEODOSIUS I** aged just six, **Flavius ARCADIUS** succeeded to the eastern empire, according to the division devised by his father, on the latter's death on 17th January 395, when aged about 18. In the meantime, he had been educated by the elderly philosopher and senator Themistius and a monk called Arsenius.[869]

The new emperor was short and swarthy, indolent and of no great intellect, which left a more than usually extensive power vacuum. Just as Stilicho had stepped into the breach in the West, so in the east, **ARCADIUS** found a support in the dubious abilities of Flavius

---

868. 1,066 years if one counts until the demise of the successor mini-Empire of Trebizond which fell in 1461.
869. PLRE I Arcadius 5

Rufinus. He was a Gaul who had been his father's *magister officiorum* (chief minister), and who had been made praetorian prefect of the entire Eastern Empire by **THEODOSIUS I** in 392, the year he had also held the consulship. Although accused of corruption and indeed treason at intervals throughout his tenure, his administration was generally sound. His ambition expressed itself in that he was plotting a betrothal of his daughter to the Emperor. However, this was thwarted by his enemy, the elderly eunuch Eutropius, who was *praepositus sacri cubicula* (chief chamberlain of the household).

When Alaricus took advantage of the death of **THEODOSIUS** to ravage Greece, Macedonia and Thrace, Rufinus went without a bodyguard to try and bargain with the Gothic ruler, but became alarmed when a western army under Stilicho (who was speciously claiming to have been left as guardian of both young emperors) appeared, to aid him in repelling the Visigoths. Whilst away from the capital, Eutropius found a good looking young woman of part barbarian extraction and married her to **ARCADIUS** 27ᵗʰ April 395. This was Aelia Eudoxia, daughter of Bauto, a retired Frankish general who had held the consulship with **ARCADIUS** in 385. This put Rufinus's nose seriously out of joint, and precipitated his fall for, in withdrawing from Thrace, Stilicho had persuaded Rufinus's general Gaïnas (another barbarian) to lead the army of the East back to Constantinople and then kill Rufinus, which he duly did on 27ᵗʰ November, and in the Emperor's presence: hardly an auspicious start to the reign.

ARCADIUS took the imperial style **Imperator Caesar Dominus Noster Flavius Arcadius Perpetuus Augustus.**[870] Whether the Eastern senate granted proconsular *imperium* and tribinician power is not at all clear, but he was fully acknowleged. He had held his first consulship in 385, almost two years after having been made co-emperor, and then he served again in 392, 394, 396, and 402. The Eastern government, however, was carried on by a triumvirate of Gaïnas, the Empress and Eutropius, an alliance stabilised by mutual loathing. Matters came to a climax during a rebellion by Gothic settlers in Phrygia (Asia minor) which Gaïnas used to bring about the fall of the all-powerful eunuch (with the Empress's connivance) in 399. The following year, though, he over-reached himself in trying to grasp supreme power and rule through a weak emperor (anticipating Ricimer) and, in staging a *coup,* failed to anticipate the mood of the Constantinopolitan populace, who were fed up with barbarian soldiers all over the place, and was heavily rebuffed. Escaping to the North, he fell in with the Huns, who despatched him and, as a gesture of goodwill, sent his head to the emperor.

The fall of Gaïnas resulted in the Emperor granting the beautiful Eudoxia the style of Augusta (400), but she was never popular, and was not trusted by the church in sentiments expressed by the forthright St. John Chrysostom, who called her a Jezebel, and a loose woman, who was bringing the Imperial house into disrepute. However, she died on 6ᵗʰ October 404 in childbirth. The religious friction stirred up by Chrysostom was made worse by the hostility and indifference of **ARCADIUS,** who became particularly unhelpful when the Pope and his brother sent a delegation from Rome to mediate. They were treated badly and sent back. It was this that persuaded the ever ambitious Stilicho to declare war on the East in 406, only to

---

870. ILS797 : *imp.caes.*, 793, 794 : *perp aug.* & 795: Flavius Arcadius.

have his invasion thwarted by lack of resources, the irruption of barbarian tribes across the Rhine on new year's eve that year, and the appearance of the three British imperial claimants. In its turn, this was just as well, for **ARCADIUS** died unexpectedly on 1st May 408.

TABLE LIX(b): THE FAMILY OF THEODOSIUS I (EAST)

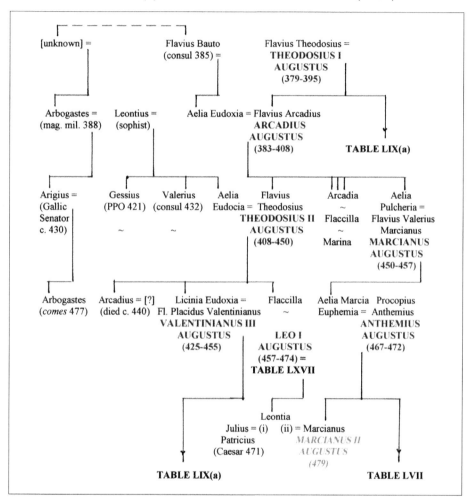

TABLE LIX(b): BRIEF LIVES

Aelia Eudocia

See below, *sub* THEODOSIUS II AUGUSTUS

Aelia Eudoxia

She was well educated in the capital and married 27th April 395, being made Augusta 9th January 400 and died 6th October 404; see also above [PLRE II Eudoxia 1].

Aelia Marcia Euphemia

Sole child of **MARCIAN** by his first marriage, she married **ANTHEMIUS** in around 453 and became Augusta on his accession in 467 when she appears on coins so styled. She is not heard of subsequent to his assassination and may have died entirely naturally between c. 469 and 471 [PLRE II Euphemia 6].

Aelia Pulcheria

Born 19th January 399, Pulcheria played a leading role in the education and guidance of her brother the Emperor from a young age (around 15) and remained a strong power behind the throne. She was styled *nobilissima puella* by 414, the year she was created Augusta on 4th July. She and her sisters took vows of celibacy, although she arranged for ther succession of **MARCIAN** in 450 and went through a form of marriage with him in order to secure the succession. The sources suggest that this did not compromise her virginity! She died in July 453. [PLRE II Pulcheria]

Arbogastes

A Frank and a keen pagan, he rose through the military to become in 380 *comes rei militaris* (chief military advisor) to **GRATIAN I** and fought under Bauto and the future emperor **THEODOSIUS I** against the Visigoths. He later, before 388, took over as *magister militum* (C-in-C) from Bauto, to whom he was almost certainly related, possibly a nephew. He led the campaign against **MAGNUS MAXIMUS** and captured the Emperor in 388. He brought about the death of **VALENTINIAN II** and encouraged the pagan imperial claimant *EUGENIUS*, who kept him *en post*. He was defeated by **THEODOSIUS I** and committed suicide. He took an active part in senatorial politics at Rome and elsewhere, involving the distinguished senator Virius Nichomachus Flavianus in his bid to stage a revival of paganism [PLRE I Arbogastes].

Arbogastes

A Gallic noble of senatorial rank and a friend of Sidonius Apollinaris, who praised his literary skill. He was then serving in Trier as *comes Trevirorum*, appointed by the Frankish King Childericus I [PLRE II Arbogastes].

Arcadia, Flaccilla and Marina

All three were persuaded by the Augusta Pulcheria (qv) to dedicate their lives to God (no doubt to giver herself a clear run) in pursuit of which they remained celibate. Flaccilla was born 17th June 397 and died before 408. Arcadia died in 444, and Marina, born 10th February 403, died on 3rd August 449, having built a palace in Constantinople [PLRE II Arcadia 1, Flaccilla 1 & Marina 1].

Arcadius

Recorded as living in 439 and died before his father. It is possible, from circumstantial evidence, that he may have married or been officially betrothed, but to whom is not clear [PLRE II Arcadius 1].

Arigius

A Gallo-Roman noble who was father of the younger Arbogastes (qv) but it is not entirely clear whether the elder Arbogastes was his father or father-in-law [PLRE II Arigius 1].

Flaccilla

Died whilst still in her childhood in 431 [PLRE II Flaccilla 2].

Flavius Arcadius

See above **ARCADIUS AUGUSTUS**

Flavius Bauto

A Fankish soldier of fortune with stern military qualities and a contempt for personal wealth, whom **GRATIAN I** made *magister militum* (C-in-C) some time prior to 380 and who fought under **THEODOSIUS I** against the Goths. **MAGNUS MAXIMUS** accused him of inciting various barbarian groups to attack him c. 384. One source claims that Arbogastes was a son of Bauto, but this is thought not to have been so, although that they were fairly closely related seems highly likely, as here. He was consul in 385 with **ARCADIUS** but had died before 388, by which time Arbogastes had succeeded him as western *magister militum*. [PLRE I Bauto].

Flavius Placidus Valentinianus

See previous section **VALENTINIANUS III AUGUSTUS**

Flavius Theodosius

See above **THEODOSIUS I AUGUSTUS**

Flavius Theodosius

See below **THEODOSIUS II AUGUSTUS**

Flavius Valerius Marcianus

See below **MARCIANUS I AUGUSTUS**

Gessius

Having your sister become empress could be useful. Eudocia worked hard to get her two brothers good jobs. Gessius was made Praetorian Prefect of Illyricum between 421 and 443, after which year his sister moved away from the Court to Jerusalem and her influence waned [PLRE II Gessius 2].

Julius Patricius

Despite his name, Patricius was an Alan by descent, having been the son of Flavius Ardaburius Aspar and brother of Ardaburius the younger and Herminericus. He was eastern consul in 459 with Ricimer and in 470 was made **nobilissimus caesar,** effectively heir to the throne, by **LEO I,** as an inducement to retain his father's loyalty. To seal the arrangement he married Leontia, the Emperor's daughter. When his father was murdered, he was deposed and had his marriage annulled, but was allowed to return to a private station, although other sources alleged that he was killed with his father and eldest brother [PLRE II Patricius 15].

Leo

See below **LEO I AUGUSTUS**

Leontia

She was born after her father assumed the purple, c. 458 and married Julius Patricius in 470 as a twelve year old which, when dynastic politics were involved was nothing unusual. After this was annulled in 471 and before 479, she married *MARCIANUS II*. She supported her husband's imperial claim, becoming titular Empress therefore, and shared his imprisonment in Isauria after the failure of the bid in 480. They had three daughters (see **Table LXVII Brief Lives**) [PLRE II Leontia 1]

Leontius

A Sophist philosopher at Athens of high reputation; his pupils included his daughter, the future Empress Eudocia, but had died before she had married **THEODOSIUS II** [PLRE II Leontius 6].

Licinia Eudoxia

Born in 422 she married 29th October 437 and was made Augusta eighteen months later at Ravenna She favoured **MAIORIANUS** to succeed her husband but was forced to marry **MAXIMUS V** instead, in spring 455. She was abducted by Gaisericus and lived at Carthage until released c. 462. She died between 462 and 493 [PLRE II Eudoxia 2].

Marcianus

See below *MARCIANUS II AUGUSTUS*

Procopius Anthemius

See previous section, **ANTHEMIUS AUGUSTUS** and **Table LVII.**

Valerius

He, like his brother, benefitted from his sister's time as Empress. He was appointed *comes res privatae* (personal secretary to the Emperor) in 425, held the consulship in 432 (with Aëtius) and *magister officiorum* (first minister) in 435. He was still living twenty years later [PLRE II Valerius 6].

THEODOSIUS II
10th January 402 – 28th July 450

Background

The son and heir of **ARCADIUS** was born 10th April 401 and was hurriedly raised to the rank of Augustus by proclamation 10th January following, whilst still a baby. Shortly afterwards the Eastern empire came under the control of the Anthemius, grandfather of the emperor **ANTHEMIUS** and a grandson of the praetorian prefect of **CONSTANTIUS II,** Philippus in his turn the son, it was said, of an Egyptian sausage maker. He was *comes sacrarum largitionum* (keeper of the privy purse) in the East from c. 400, was advanced to *magister officiorum* (chief minister) in 404 and praetorian prefect (East) a year later. In 406 he was also made patrician. He was virtual ruler of the Eastern Empire and was noted for his readiness to listen to advice and for his prudent administration. He rebuilt the walls of Constantinople 404-413, hence their name, the Theodosian Walls. He held the consulship in 405 with Stilicho, with whom he had worked when young, in a gesture of solidarity with the Western adminstration. In short, there was no better person to oversee the transition when **ARCADIUS** died in 408.[871]

Reign

Flavius **THEODOSIUS** was proclaimed at the age of just seven and took the style **Dominus Noster Flavius Theodosius Invictissimus Augustus**.[872] He held the consulship in 403 and thereafter no less than 17 more times in his reign.[873] Anthemius was displaced after about fourteen years in control, probably at the conniving of the Emperor's imperious sister Pulcheria. She wielded sole effective power thereafter until her death in 453.

On turning twenty, the Emperor married the daughter of an eminent (but recently deceased) Athenian pagan Sophist intellectual called Leontius. Her original name was Athenaïs, but she adopted Eudocia instead after adult baptism, her father having been a pagan. Beautiful, eloquent and an accomplished poet, she had caught the eye of the Emperor's sister Pulcheria whilst staying at Constantinople in pursuit of a legal case relating to her father's estate. As a result, they married on 7th June 421, when she assumed the honorific *nomen* Aelia. On 2nd January 423 she was proclaimed Augusta. Subsequently she appears to have clashed with her sister-in-law Aelia Pulcheria. At the same time, she was also obliged to cope with her kinswoman Galla Placidia and her children, self-exiled from the attentions of **HONORIUS**.

Although Placidia returned to the West after the defeat of **JOHN**, in the long run, Pulcheria triumphed, using her court eunuchs to undermine the empress, especially after the latter returned from a thanksgiving trip to Jerusalem (undertaken following the

---

871. PLRE II Anthemius 2.
872. ILS 804. 806 (the latter as consul xv (435); *invictissimus* = most unconquered.)
873. In 407, 409, 411, 412, 415, 416, 418, 420, 422, 425, 426, 430, 433, 435, 438, 439 & 444.

marriage of Licinia Eudoxia to **VALENTINIAN III**) with large amounts of Christian relics, having founded two churches and brought the relics of the protomartyr St. Stephen back to Constantinople. Her resentful sister-in-law smeared her with false charges of adultery and she eventually retired back to Jerusalem in 443 and died there 20th October 460.[874]

The Emperor, meanwhile, took no active role in the state, although unlike his father, who had been thoroughly indolent and unlovable, **THEODOSIUS** was bookish, a talented illuminator of manuscripts, mildly religious, a keen huntsman and personally charming. In anyone other than an emperor, this would no doubt have marked him out as an outstanding character, but in his position it constituted perceived weakness when strength was required. He did take an interest in what was going on, though but was generally content to let his sister and her picked men run the Empire.

Yet the eastern Empire managed to escape the baleful calamities which encompassed the west. Furthermore, a treaty was arrived at with the Sassanian court in Persia which was intended to guarantee peace for a century and actually succeeded in producing something resembling quietude for the remainder of the reign and beyond. On the other hand, the Balkans were constantly in turmoil, with various barbarian tribes making incursions or causing trouble. Yet **THEODOSIUS'** generals were able to exploit their energies in using the most effective of groupings to hold in check the increasingly troublesome Isaurian tribesmen, who had long been within the Empire but were uncivilised and turbulent.

The reign was also notable for the re-codification of the law. This had not been done since the time of the Tetrarchy and in the meantime much law had become redundant and more had been formulated through precedent via the court or Imperial rescripts (mandatory advisory notes to administrators in the emperor's name). In 429 a commission was set up to regularise the law for both parts of the Empire. A draft was produced in 435, refined and then published as the Theodosian Code in 438, being promulgated simultaneously by the senates of Rome and Constantinople on 15th February. It remained current in the West for over a century (although in the Visigothic areas of Gaul and Spain, a revised version of 507 was promulgated) and in the east until a much more root-and-branch revision was undertaken in the reign of **JUSTINIAN I**.

The last decade of **THEODOSIUS'S** long reign was clouded with renewed problems on the Danube frontier. The Huns had for some years been paid a modest tribute by the Empire to keep them quiet, but after Attila took over rule with his brother in 437, attacks and raiding began along the frontier, which by 441 demanded corrective action. In 447 the brother died, leaving Attila to his own devices, and he immediately demanded the tribute be doubled. The the Emperor understandably demurred, with the result that the Huns unleashed a veritable *blitzkrieg* across the Danube and down through the Balkans to the very walls of Constantinople, by-passing the capital and into Asia Minor, causing immense damage. Having created a desert, lack of forage soon led the Huns to drift back to their homelands on what we know as the Hungarian plain for, although exceedingly fierce and uncivilised, the supply side of fighting was not something of which they had the least

---

874. PLRE II Eudocia 2.

concept. Subsequent negotiation saw Attila's demands rocket to unheard of heights. Yet Imperial intelligence was such that the Huns' intention to trash the west became known, and the Imperial negotiators banked on Attila's reluctance to again raid south and east, when he was poised to wreak his mischief on the west. Furthermore, there had been such destruction that there would have been little in it for the Huns had they tried a repeat performance. Thus in 450, they moved West, and the Eastern Empire breathed a sigh of relief. And, thanks to Aëtius, they were never to trouble the Empire seriously again.

And it was in the middle of the negotiations with Attila, that the Emperor, out hunting, met with a fall, and was killed.

Family
See **TABLE LIX(b)** above.

*

MARCIANUS I
(Known to history as MARCIAN)
25ᵗʰ August 450 – 27ᵗʰ January 457

Background
As soon as news broke of **THEODOSIUS'S** death, there was an hiatus. Conventional wisdom would expect power to pass to the husband of the emperor's heiress, **VALENTINIAN III.** This would have re-united the empire, which was not thought desirable by Pulcheria, nor did she have any sort of high opinion of her Western kinsman. She herself was, in fact, the heiress on the spot, but the Empire was not yet ready for an empress in her own right; that had to await the accession of **IRENE** three hundred and fifty years later. Again, as when **ARCADIUS** had died, the east was in capable hands, for the Augusta's chief support was Flavius Ardaburius Aspar (consul 434, see **TABLE LIX(b) Brief Lives**, above). In fact, the late emperor had allegedly named (or been made to name) **MARCIANUS** as his preferred successor when on his death bed, but being named was not enough. Pulcheria agreed with the choice, took the initiative and early in August married him, although the arrangement included the preservation of the 51-year old Augusta's chastity.

Flavius Valerius Marcianus was born the son of a military man from Illyria - still clearly a breeding ground for military emperors – in 392.[875] He followed his father into the army, enrolling at Philippopolis and was commanding a unit of his own as a tribune by the time he went on campaign against Persia, some time before 420. On his return he was transferred to the *domestici* (Imperial guards) under the command of Aspar and his father Ardaburius, serving 15 years, including the fruitless campaign against Gaiseric 431-434, when he was captured by the Vandals and met the king. Thereafter he entered the (Eastern) senate. He

---

875. He may have been Thracian rather than Illyrian; there is also uncertainty about his *nomen* Valerius: PLRE II Marcianus 8].

was essentially a 58-year old *ex-tribunus* (retired colonel) when raised to the purple, and had already been married (his wife had presumably died) with a daughter living but no son.

Reign.

MARCIAN I was crowned by the Patriarch of Constantinople, with his new wife seated in full splendour beside him: the first religious coronation of a Roman Emperor; previously the ceremony had been carried out in front of the assembled Court in the palace or with decreasing frequency, in the senate at Rome. The new Emperor took the style of **Dominus Noster Flavius Marcianus Pius Felix Augustus** and held his first and only consulship in 451.[876]

His reign is notable because several problems were resolved, first amongst them being the refusal to pay tribute to the Huns and their subsequent removal to the West. The Emperor is often accused of isolationism, of abandoning the West to its fate, but recent opinion has revised this position and it is thought that he gave quite a bit of covert assistance to the campaign by Aëtius against Attila who, indeed, was considering taking the Eastern Empire on again when he died in 453. By this time the Emperor had forged alliances with the Ostrogoths, whom he settled as federates south of the Danube to act as a buffer should the Hunnic leader resume hostilities. He also took measures to re-populate and rebuild the cities destroyed by the destructive Hun rampage of 447. Indeed, he left the east in good political and financial health. This was helped by the cessation of the Hun tribute, enabling the emperor to cut the property tax (which endeared the senate towards him) confine the holding of the ruinously expensive praetorship to the sons of *illustres* only (who could afford the required lavish games), ended the sale of government posts and remitted all old (mainly tax) debts, which aided a wider constituency. Assets also piled up through the notable lack of military expenditure on campaigns; the decision to stay out of the chaos following the assassination of **VALENTINIANUS III** was a canny one. Essentially the emperor was lucky as well as wise.

Discord in the church was making itself felt at the start of the reign, which was settled by **MARCIAN** calling the Council of Chalcedon in 451, which established orthodoxy of doctrine, making a modest compromise concerning the nature of Christ to keep the majority of Monophysite Christians within the church. In the short term there was unrest at the result, mainly because the Emperor was so uncompromisingly Christian, but under his successor, these died down, although Monophysitism managed to survive and make its influence felt for at least another century and a half.

The Emperor made no provision for a successor, however, and died on 27th January 457, leaving the Empire theoretically united under **AVITUS**, although his daughter and sole heiress had just married the future Western ruler **ANTHEMIUS** who might have been considered as a likely contender for power.

Family
See above **TABLE LIX(b).**

---

876. ILS824

The imperial succession
Leo I
Leo II
Zeno
Anastasius I

Imperial claimants
Basiliscus
Marcus III
Marcianus II
Leontius
Petrus

LEO I
7th February 457 – 18th January 474

Background

The obvious successor to **MARCIANUS** was his son-in-law, the future western emperor **ANTHEMIUS**, who had been appointed *magister utriusque militae* (C-in-C) by his father-in-law when he became emperor. Possibly his succession would have cramped Aspar's style, but the future emperor did retain his appointment under the next *régime*, which suggests that the two generals got along well enough. Perhaps **ANTHEMIUS** was sensible enough to turn the idea of succeeding down. In fact, the *magister militum* Aspar acted quickly. As a man of Alan (German) descent, there was no possibility of his own accession to the purple being acceptable, so he was obliged to act in the manner of Ricimer, and rule through a nominee. Yet he chose not a malleable child but another seasoned soldier, **LEO I,** who was proclaimed emperor eleven days after **MARCIAN'S** death.

The new Emperor was born in 400/401 in Thrace, of Dacian descent. Essentially, therefore, he was another Danubian general in the mould of the successors of **CLAUDIUS II.** Like his predecessor, **LEO** seems to have been an ex-tribune and at the time of his elevation was in command of a unit of auxiliary levies at Selymbria (Silivri, Turkey, a suburb of Constantinople) and also a *comes*. He was by then married and had a daughter. Another followed in 457 and a short-lived son six years later.

Reign

Also like his predecessor, **LEO** was installed and crowned in the Cathedral by the Patriarch of Constantinople, whose position had been formalised and enhanced at the Council of

Chalcedon. The new Emperor took the style **Dominus Noster Leo Pius Felix Perpetuus Augustus.**[877] He held his first consulship in 458 with **MAJORIAN** as colleague, demonstrating his desire to make a rapprochement with the west and at the same time acknowledging the legitimacy of his western colleague. He subsequently held the consulship again in 462 (with **SEVERUS III**), 466, 471 and 473, on the latter occasion alone. Although he had been raised up by Aspar, the new Emperor forbore to become his creature, and sought to diminish the Germanic influence at court and in the army, on the whole with some success. That this did not result in all-out conflict reflects on the realism of the patrician and the tact of the Emperor. He instead recruited Thracians to the Imperial Guard, henceforth called the *excubitores* (sentinels) replacing the largely ceremonial *scholae*, and he recruited Isaurians - a rough, half-savage people, who occupied the mountainous interior of southern Asia Minor - to replace the Germans in the élite units of the field army. One senior commander of these levies in particular, Tarasicodissa, was made *comes domesticorum* (guard commander), marrying the Emperor's daughter Ariadne in 467 at which time he was appointed *magister militum* in Thrace.

In 468, **LEO I** set out to make a new attempt to extirpate the Vandal kingdom of Gaiseric, He installed the trusted and competent **ANTHEMIUS** as Western Emperor and recruited Marcellinus, the uncle of **JULIUS NEPOS** to assist. He then had a mental blip (or was browbeaten by the empress) and entrusted the entire enterprise, mounted on a massive scale, to his brother-in-law *BASILISCUS*, the heterodox sibling of Verina, who had made common cause against the Emperor's reforms with Aspar. Apart from such obvious *lèse majesté*, *BASILISCUS* was a Roman of impeccable pedigree but eminently unsuited to command, being slow-witted and indolent; he also had eyes on the purple. Needless to say, the entire African episode was a disaster, resulting in obloquy for *BASILISCUS* and bad odium for Aspar, who was accused of soft pedalling the expedition to preserve his fellow Arian, the Vandal King. Yet within two years, the Emperor's other daughter had been allowed to marry Aspar's younger son Julius Patricius, who was soon afterwards declared **nobilissimus caesar** (effectively heir presumptive) and *BASILISCUS'S* life had been spared by the entreaties of his sister. Yet within months, in 471, Aspar's elder son Ardaburius was caught red-handed conspiring to suborn the Isaurians, and he and his father were summarily killed; Patricius was stripped of his rank of Caesar but (unusually) survived. This was followed by a final purge of Germanic elements at court and in the army.

In autumn 473, the Emperor, now about 75, was failing, and he nominated the Empress's kinsman **JULIUS NEPOS** to the throne of the West (which the latter delayed taking up until the following spring) but inexplicably passed over his closest confidant and son-in-law, the patrician and *magister militum* Tarasicodissa (now calling himself the more Greek Zenon, or **ZENO**) and named the Isaurian's son Leo, aged seven, his heir. He died, on 18th January 474.

---

877. ILS810 & coins.

TABLE LXVII(a): THE FAMILY OF LEO I & ZENO

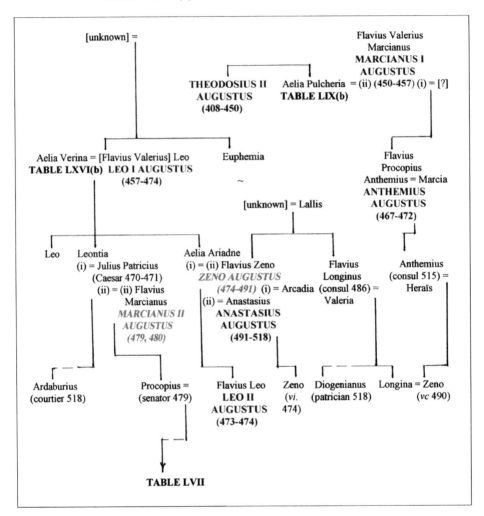

TABLE LXVII(a): BRIEF LIVES

Aelia Pulcheria

See above **TABLE LIX(b)**

Aelia Verina

She was of conventional Roman background and married Leo before 457. At some stage, probably from **LEO**'s coronation, she was created Augusta. She died in the seige of Papyrius in 484 [PLRE II Verina]

Anastasius

See below **ANASTASIUS AUGUSTUS**

Anthemius

See above **TABLE LVII Procopius Anthemius**

Arcadia

Probably first wife of **ZENO** and not, as stated in the one ancient source that mentions her, his second, in view of the fact that Ariadne outlived him [Arcadia 2].

Ardaburius

Eldest son of Flavius Ardaburius Aspar (*magister militum* 431-471 and consul 434) and grandson of Flavius Ardaburius (*magister militum* 424-425 and consul in 427), of Alan descent and an Arian. He was probably born c. 420, was praetor in 434 and eastern consul in 447. He was appointed *comes rei militaris* in 450 by **MARCIAN I** and *magister militum per Orientem* (C-in-C on the Eastern frontier) in 453, serving until 466. He had been appointed patrician before his appointment. He was killed with his father in 471 [PLRE II Ardaburius 1, 3 & Aspar].

Diogenianus

Recorded as a relative of Empress Ariadne, and thus probably a son of Longinus. He was *comes* in 492, commanding the guard in the war against the Isaurians, but was subsequently exiled for unknown reasons. He was recalled by **JUSTIN I** made patrician and *magister militum per Orientem* (C-in-C of the Eastern frontier) in 518 [PLRE II Diogenianus 4].

Euphemia

Unmarried and lived in Constantinople, where she had a statue of her brother erected by her house [PLRE II Euphemia 3].

Flavius Leo

See below **LEO II AUGUSTUS**

Flavius Longinus

He was appointed *magister militum* in 485 on his return from captivity after a rebellion, and campagned against the Tzani (otherwise the Macrones, a warlike tribe in Colchis, on the east side of the Black Sea). A leading senator, he was also one of the last non-emperors ever to have held two ordinary consulships, in 486 and 490. Only the name of his mother, Lallis is known, but by his wife Valeria he had a daughter Longina. He

had hoped to succeed his brother as emperor, but was by-passed, possible due to personality flaws, recounted in two ancient sources, and was exiled by **ANASTASIUS** to Egypt. One source claims he was sent to the Thebaïd in 491, where he starved to death in 499, another claims he was sent to Alexandria, ordained into the church in 492 and also died in 499. He may also be the familial link with Artemidorus, a noble easterner who decided to settle in Rome under Theodericus and rose to be Prefect of the City in 509. Cassiodorus implies that he was a relation of **ZENO** and so might be a son of this man or perhaps a son or close kinsman of Anthemius (qv) the consul of 515 (which would better fulfill Cassiodorus' use of the term 'noble') [Moorehead (1992) 154; PLRE II Artemidorus 3, Longinus 6].

Flavius Valerius Leo

See above **LEO I AUGUSTUS**

Flavius Marcianus

See below *MARCIANUS II AUGUSTUS*

Flavius Procopius Anthemius

See above, **ANTHEMIUS AUGUSTUS**

Flavius Valerius Marcianus

See above, **MARCIANUS I AUGUSTUS**

Flavius Zeno

See below **ZENO AUGUSTUS**

Julius Patricius

See above **TABLE LIX(b)**

[Leo]

The Emperor had a son in 462, although it is not certain what the child was called. He died in 463 aged five months [PLRE II *sub* LEO 6].

Leontia

See above **TABLE LIX(b)**

[Aelia] Marcia [Euphemia]

She married **ANTHEMIUS** in 453 and was styled Augusta from 467, but may have died before her husband's fall, for she is not referred to again in the sources [PLRE II Euphemia 6]

Procopius

Little known about this man except that a person called Theosebius went about the East claiming to be Procopius; one might wonder why [PLRE II Procopius 5]

Zeno

Son of the emperor's first wife, but although touted as a successor to his father, he was totally unsuitable, being vicious, licentious and immoral. He died fairly young before 474, probably from excess. He may also have had two sisters, Hilaria and Theopiste [PLRE II Zeno 4]. Crawford (2019) 29-39]

Zeno

We know he was betrothed to Longina, but it is not confirmed that they married, although the possiblity is strong. He inherited vast wealth from his family and **JUSTINIAN** appointed him, sometime beewteen 527 and 548, *prefectus augustalis* – governor of Egypt, which by this time had become a separate diocese. He is believed to have died in office [PLRE II Zeno 3].

⁎

LEO II
December 473 – 17ᵗʰ November 474

LEO II was born in 467 and was proclaimed **nobilissimus caesar** in October 473, being raised to co-emperor by his grandfather two months later, by-passing **ZENO**, his father. He became sole ordinary consul for 474 on 1ˢᵗ January. On the death of the senior Augustus **LEO I** on 18ᵗʰ January, he became sole emperor. He took the style **Dominus Noster Flavius Leo [Junior] P[ius] F[elix] Aug[ustus]**.

On 9ᵗʰ February 474, prompted by his mother, he helped to crown his father co-emperor. Coins were struck with the legend **D N Leo et Zeno PP Aug**., but with the bust of **ZENO** on the obverse, although some issues were struck with Leo alone. He was still only 7 when he fell ill and died in the November of that year, possibly on 17th.[878]

⁎

---

878. Coins; PLRE II Leo 7.

ZENO
9th February 474 – 9th April 491

Background

The new emperor was an Isaurian, one of a people long within the Empire and since 212 Roman citizens, dwelling in the mountainous interior of southern Asia Minor and noted for their savagery and turbulence. They had first been subdued by Sulla's ally, P. Servilius Vatia Isauricus (consul 79BC) in 76-75, being acclaimed *imperator,* accorded the honorary *agnomen* Isauricus and celebrating a triumph for his pains in 74. Originally called **Aricmesius Tarasicodissa**, he was born in 425 at an unlocated place called Rhusumblada, but we only know the name of his mother, Lallis. Neither is his early career at all clear, but it was probably military, and in 466 he was sent to Constantinople on a delicate diplomatic errand, and remained in the capital, having been rewarded with a senior commission in the guards as *comes domesticorum.* He changed his name to **ZENO** because it would aid his careeer and because a patrican called Zeno was also an Isaurian and was greatly respected.

Inevitably, after his appointment, a number of Isaurians were attracted to Constnatinople, and formed the core of the re-establishment of the armed forces initiated by **LEO I.** His wife had presumably died by this time and he married the Emperor's daughter Ariadne in 467. He was shortly afterwards apointed *magister militum* for Thrace and held a consulship the following year (469), before the end of which he was moved to command the whole army of the Eastern Empire. He may have been behind the murder of Aspar in 471, although if so, he saved the life of his future grandson-in-law, the patrician's youngest son Herminericus. He was made patrician and then in 473 appointed commander-in-chief at court. On the death of **LEO** his 6-year-old son proclaimed him emperor on 9th February 474, probably with the connivance of his mother.

Reign

The new emperor adopted the style of **Dominus Noster Flavius Zeno Perpetuus Augustus**, and he held a second consulship in 475, adding a single further one in 479. In 475 he encouraged the eminent senator Severus to negotiate a highly advantageous peace treaty with the Vandals almost concurrent with that negotiated by Orestes from the western court. Elevated to the rank of patrican to lend *gravitas* to his mission, he secured the return of large numbers of Roman captives and arranged freedom of worship for orthodox Christians in Arian Carthage.

The first crisis arose through the Empress Verina having taken a lover, Patricius (not Aspar's son but a senator who had been *magister officiorum* under **LEO I**), whom she intended to marry and raise to the purple once she had got rid of her son-in-law. As the Isaurians had turned out to have been less then a blessing in the capital - reverting to type on frequernt occasions – their unpopularity had rubbed off on the Emperor. The dowager Empress therefore colluded with her brother *BASILISCUS* to depose him, which she did by persuading him to escape to Isauria with his family by a crude stratagem on 9th January 476. However, *BASILISCUS*, aided by **ZENO'S** friend, the *magister officiorum* and patrician Illus, seized control of the situation, and made himself emperor whilst having the sense to have Verina's admirer Patricius liquidated. However, due to the sheer incompetence and lack of authority of the imperial claimant, most of his supporters gradually switched their allegiance back to **ZENO,** who was restored in August 477.

ZENO pardoned his mother-in-law (unwisely) and eventually banished her to Isauria. A period of calm and reconstruction followed, during which the Emperor declined to assist **NEPOS** in regaining possession of Italy (and the rather sleight-of-hand recognition of Odovacer as patrician). Then in 479, another imperial claimant in the shape of **ANTHEMIUS'S** son *MARCIANUS II* seized power and **ZENO** was only saved by a last minute intervention, again by the patrician Illus, who drove the claimant and two of his brothers out of the City, and although they renewed their bid in Asia Minor, they were ultimately unsuccessful. At this stage, **NEPOS** was assassinated and **ZENO** became ruler of a united Empire, albeit that he had little direct control over the west. Yet his ability to impose his authority was still being constantly challenged, not only by his distantly exiled mother-in-law but by his own wife, who was behind an attmept to kill Illus in 482 mainly, it would seem, out of familial piety. Illus suspected the Emperor was also behind the plot and fled east, only to join forces with the man sent to dispose of him, the patrician *LEONTIUS*, the latter, ironically, ending up as imperial claimant at Antioch before being driven out by an expeditionary force of Goths led by Ioannes and Theoderic the latter the future King of Italy. Despite this, they managed to hole up in Isauria, which became thenceforth for a while a breakaway mini-empire for four years before being crushed in 488, the dowager empress inlcuded in the general slaughter.

According to the historian of the Goths, Jordanes, when the ruler of Italy, Odovacer, was threatened by the advance of the Ostrogoths under Theoderic in 487, **ZENO** wrote commending the newcomer to the (Western) senate and Roman people.[879] The idea, it would seem, was that Theodericus, as *magister militum*, should rule Italy in place of **ZENO** until such time as the Emperor could arrive and re-establish full imperial authority in the West. In the event, **ZENO** died fefore the operation was complete and in the pause before his successor's authority was properly established, Theoderic had dug in. Nevertheless at the time it was understood that there was one Empire, of which Theoderic's kingdom was just one part.[880]

A final running sore which affected the reign was the Monophysite heresy and the Emperor's inconclusive attempts to find a compromise which would avoid the fragmentation of Christendom. He died with the matter unresolved after a period of waning faculties, on 9th April 491, leaving the sucession to be decided by his widow.

---

879. Moorhead (1992) 249.
880. Barnwell (1992) 137.

Family

By about 460 the future emperor was married to his first wife, Arcadia (died by 466) and was father of his son, another Zeno. He also had an illegitimate son (whose name is not known) who married and had a daughter (equally anonymous) who, some time after 474 (chronology would suggest c. 477/478 at the earliest), married Herminericus, who was the youngest son of Aspar and a very youthful consul in 465. They lived in exile in Isauria until they returned to Constantinople from 491. **ZENO** himself remarried Ariadne, the daughter of **LEO I** in 467.

⁎

Imperial claimants under Zeno

BASILISCUS
9ᵗʰ January 476 – August 477

MARCUS III
c. October 476 – August 477

Background

Despite his disastrous performance in Africa trying to dislodge Gaiseric, *BASILISCUS* had not lost his lust for supreme power, his slow-witted and trusting nature notwithstanding. With the help of his sister, the dowager emperess, he was able to enter Constantinople unopposed on 9ᵗʰ January 476, proclaiming his son *MARCUS* as **nobilissimus caesar.** He was recognised universally including by the senate, of which he was *princeps*, or *caput* as the position was by then called.

The new imperial claimant, **Flavius** *BASILISCUS,* had a military career at first, being appointed *magister militum* in Thrace 464-468 during which time he held the consulship in 465 *in absentia* with Aspar's youngest son Herminericus. He was also made patrician at about this time, and commanded the anti-Vandal expedition of 468-469. He was pardoned in 471 when he aided the Emperor asgainst Aspar. Nothing is known of his wife Zenonis, and although they seem to have had other children, only *MARCUS* is named.[881]

Reign

BASILISCUS, having obtained the recognition of the eastern senate, ought thus perhaps not to be classified as an imperial claimant at all, although truth be told, his elevation by *coup* and downfall bear all the marks of one. That his predecessor was able to return to power marks him out, despite this, merely as a claimant.

---

881. PLRE II Basiliscus 2

He was styled **D[ominus] N[oster] Basiliscus P[ater] P[atriae] Aug[ustus]**[882] and his wife Zenonis was made Augusta. He also held a second consulship in 476. His first act after having Patricius killed, which lost him Verina's support, was to raise taxes which also lost him the support of the population at large. His reaction was to elevate his son *MARCUS* as co-emperor, but his flaunting of his Monophysite religious sympathies thereafter began to exacerbate an already tense situation. As part of his attempt to make his particular brand of Christian heresy the new orthodoxy, he re-instated Timotheus, the former Bishop of Alexandria, ousted for non-conformity in 460, and attempted, on his advice, to reverse the decisions of the Council of Chalcedon and abolish the Patriarchate of Constantinople. At this juncture a large area of the capital was razed by a serious fire. By this, time Illus was conspiring with the dowager Empress to bring **ZENO** back, a happenstance *BASILISCUS* countered by making his unmartial and ne'er-do-well nephew Armatus consul, patrician and *magister militum* with a commission to nip the planned restoration in the bud and on the promise of promotion and the rank of **nobilissimus caesar** for his son **Basiliscus Leo**. In August 477, **ZENO** returned to Constantinople in triumph, and *BASILISCUS* with *MARCUS* and their families being exiled to Limnae in Cappadocia (Gaziri, Turkey) where they were confined in a dried up reservoir and allowed to starve to death.[883] The Caesar Basiliscus Leo was deposed in 478 and ordained, ending up as Bishop of Cyzicus.[884]

Family

All we know about the family of Verina and *BASILISCUS* is that they were of distinguished Roman stock. There are other gaps in our knowledge, too. We know Armatus was the Empress's nephew, but not the names of his parents, so we do not know if his father was a brother or sister of Verina. It is also known that **JULIUS NEPOS** was related by marriage to the Empress and it is here suggested that he may have been married to a sister of Armatus. There is also some reasonably persuasive circumstantial evidence that Odovacer himself may have had a connection, and it is also here suggested that his father, who spent some time in Constantinople at the crucial period, may also have married a sister of the future empress, although one (not wholly reliable) source claims his mother as a Scirian. If so, she may have had a sister married to a brother of Verina or other close connection. This might also explain the role of Odovacer's brother Onoulfus, a protégé of Armatus whom he murdered in 477 on the orders of **ZENO**.

---

882. Coin evidence.
883. PLRE II Marcus 4
884. PLRE II Basiliscus 1

TABLE LXVII(b): THE CONNECTIONS OF THE EMPRESS VERINA

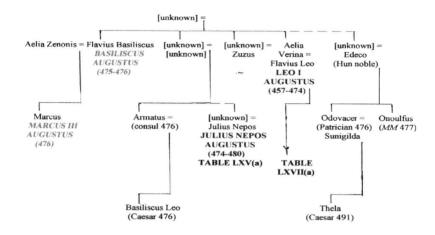

TABLE LXVII(b): BRIEF LIVES

Aelia Verina

Married **LEO I** before he became emperor in 457 and made Augusta in that year. Her subsequent machinations are recounted above. She died during the seige of the fortress in Isauria where she and *LEONTIUS* were holed up in 488 [PLRE II Verina].

Aelia Zenonis

She was proclaimned Augusta on her husband's assumption of supreme power, and she died with him in Cappadocia [PLRE II Zenonis].

Armatus

He owed his career to his family connections rather than any real competence. He was *magister militum* in Thrace 469-474, and a prime mover in the elevation of *BASILISCUS* to the purple, possibly because he was the lover of the Empress Zenonis. The Imperial claimant confirmed him in office at court. He was consul in 476 with *BASILISCUS* as colleague. He was confirmed as *magistrer militum* at court for life and his son proclaimed **nobilissimus caesar** in

return for backing **ZENO**. He was also created patrician, but the Emperor had him murdered – a popular move apparently – soon afterwards [PLRE II Armatus].

Basiliscus *qui et* Leo

Made **nobilissimus caesar** by **ZENO** in return for the betrayal of his father, and assumed the additional name of Leo as a result. He was deposed after the death of Armatus and was made to take ordination, eventually rising to become Bishop of Cyzicus. See also above [PLRE II Basiliscus 1].

Edeco

He was a Hun and a noble of the sub-tribe of the Sciri and married to a lady of that race too, but only on the say-so of a chronicler who wrongly branded him a Thuringian, so his wife could even have been Roman. He fought under Attila, making a considerable reputation for himself as a commander. He was sent to Constantinople early in 449, staying until high summer. After Attila died he and his son Onoulfus led their sub-tribe against the Ostrogoths and were twice soundly defeated, after which he appears to have returned to Constantinople. The career of his son strongly suggest that he was related by marriage with Verina's family [PLRE II Edeco].

Flavius Basiliscus

See above *BASILISCUS AUGUSTUS*

Julius Nepos

See above **JULIUS NEPOS AUGUSTUS**

Marcus

See above, *MARCUS III AUGUSTUS*

Odovacer

He was born c. 433 and married c. 455. He seems to have remained in Gaul after the death of Attila and around 463 he was in Gaul at the head of a band of Saxons who captured Juliomagus Andecavorum (Angers) and held it for some time until the Frankish King Childericus I took it from them and they were subsequently defeated by a Roman force. He then joined the Roman army and was in Noricum in 469-470, where he met St. Severinus He subsequently served in Italy under Ricimer, becoming an officer in the Imperial bodyguard. He turned on Orestes in 476 when refused land for his men to settle and ended up being proclaimed their King 23rd August (see above *sub* **ROMULUS AUGUSTUS**). He accepted the title of patrician from **ZENO** 476 or 477 but ruled Italy as *rex* (king) until his death in 493, although from 490, following two defeats by the Ostrogothic leader Theodericus, he was beseiged in Ravenna. In 493 he agreed with Theodericus to a joint rule, but was killed shortly aferwards on trumped up charges by the latter [PLRE II Odovacer].

Onoulfus

Brother of Odovacer, he may have had a marriage connection with the house of the Empress Verina. He came to Constantinople after being defeated, with his father, by the Ostrogoths, c. 466, and was quickly and otherwise inexplicably taken up by Armatus, who had him appointed *comes* and then *magister militum,* serving in Illyricum. He murdered his patron at the instigation of the Emperor in 477. Some time after 480 he went to Italy to serve under his brother but was killed following Odovacer's death at the hands of the forces of the Ostrogothic king Theodericus in 493 [PLRE II Onoulfus].

Sunigilda

She may have been a Goth and probably married Odovacer c. 455 and was mother of his son. After his death, Theodericus, who succeeded him as King of Italy, imprisoned her and starved her to death [PLRE II Sunigilda].

Thela

Thela (or Ocla) was the only known offspring of Odovacer and was made **nobilissimus caesar** c. 490 when beseiged with his father in Ravenna. It is possible that the latter was tempted to become an imperial claimant, perhaps in the hope of attracting support from Constantinople. Thela was given as a hostage to Theodericus in 493, was exiled to Gaul after the murder of his father, but he was killed after returning to Italy some time later [PLRE II Thela].

Zuzus

Apart from the fact that he was one of the leaders of *BASILISCUS'S* rebellion agianst **ZENO,** little is known about him [PLRE II Zuzus].

*

MARCIANUS II
(Known to history as Marcian II)
December 479; c. March – May 480 & c. April – June 484

Background

Flavius *MARCIANUS* was one of the sons of the Western Emperor **ANTHEMIUS,** by the daughter of **MARCIAN I,** after whom he was named. Born c. 444, he was consul with **ZENO** (before he became emperor) in 469 and for a second time, nominated by his father as Emperor, in 472 but, confusingly, as Eastern consul. The year before, **LEO I** had made him *magister militum* at court and patrician on his marriage to his daughter Leontia, then about 14. He survived his father's destruction by remaining at Constantinople, where he supported the revolt of *BAILISCUS* but turned against him later.[885]

Reign 1

MARCIAN II was the only imperial claimant to have had three reigns, albeit all fairly short. Late in 479 he himself raised the standard of revolt against **ZENO,** exploiting a wave of unpopularity against him in the capital, fuelled by resentment of **ZENO'S** treatment of Verina and in any case, he argued, he himself was not only the son of an Emperor, but was married to a woman who was *porphyrogenita* – born in the purple – unlike the Empress Ariadne, who was born *before* her father **LEO'S** accession. These were not exactly copper-bottomed reasons for seizing power by any estimation. Nevertheless, probably in December 479, he gathered a motley force of barbarian and Roman troops, supported by three senior commanders and by his brothers, the patrician Procopius Anthemius and Romulus. The Emperor's guard was under the command of the patrician Illus, who was defeated and retired across the Bosphorus. The operation was thus a complete success as far as it had gone, but at the crucial moment, hesitation and poor management caused his support to slip away and after a few days he was captured by Illus and was sent to Caesarea in Cappadocia where he was ordained as a priest. It is just possible that he had been designated as eastern consul for 480, and had the distinction reversed by **ZENO,** for there was no eastern consul for that year.[886] Of his brothers, Romulus escaped to Rome, where no more is heard of him, but Procopius Anthemius escaped to Thrace where he was sheltered by the Gothic *magister militum* Theoderic Strabo, nephew of the wife of Aspar, after which he joined his brother in Rome. After the accession of **ANASTASIUS** he returned to Constantinople and held the eastern consulship in 515; his son also had a distinguished career, but neither was ill-advised enough to revive the family's imperial aspirations.

---

885. PLRE II Marcianus17

886. Nor for that following, although Trocundus was rewarded for his efforts with the eastern consulship for 482.

Reign 2

After a few months, *MARCIAN* managed to escape from Caesarea, and he then gathered together another mixed force, this time of farmers, peasants, retired veterans and chancers. Declaring himself once again emperor, he entered Galatia and laid seige to Ancyra but, after some time, the defending forces, under the Isaurian Illus's brother, Flavius Appalius Illus Trocundes, managed to drive him off and after a few weeks cornered him and accepted his surrender. **ZENO**, perhaps worried that a harsh punishment might lead to more unrest, exiled him and his wife to his native Isauria, where he was imprisoned in a fortress called Papirius.

Reign 3

The patrician and *magister utriusque militum* Illus was virtually in full control of **ZENO'S** government from 479, and his popularity alarmed his fellow Isaurian, the emperor. Furthermore the latter had fallen out with the Empress Ariadne over the treatment of the dowager Empress Verina. In 483 therefore, Illus was dismissed and his property confiscated, and early in the year following he rebelled. His first move was to consolidate his position in Isauria, proclaim *MARCIAN* emperor yet again and make overtures to Odovacer, the Persians and the Armenians for help. Alarmed, **ZENO** despatched the *magister militum* in Thrace Leontius (another Isaurian) with an army to put the rebellion down, but on reaching Illus, was pursuaded to join him in opposing the Emperor.

At this juncture, *MARCIAN* was for a third (and final) time deposed in favour of *LEONTIUS* (qv), and with *LEONTIUS*, Illus, his wife (the ex-empress Leontia), ended up under protracted seige at Papirius in Isauria, from whence he was instead despatched to Italy with an embassy to accelerate any help Odovacer might feel inclined to provide. After that, we hear no more of him. Possibly he settled in Italy (where he may well have had property) and resumed the life of a senator at Rome under the settled regime of the Hun monarch. The fate of his wife is likewise unknown; if she went with him to Italy she will no doubnt have survived with him, but if she remained at Papirius, she was presumably killed along with the other members of *LEONTIUS'S* court in 488 when the fortress fell.

At no time did *MARCIAN II* ever issue any coinage, and as a result we are ignorant of the manner in which he was styled, although **Dominus Noster Flavius Marcianus Pius Felix Augustus** seems most likely.

Family

The imperial claimant was probably twice married and had a son, Procopius, by his first union and daughters with Leontia. See above **Table LVII** & **Brief Lives.**

*

LEONTIUS I
19th July 484 – September 488

Background

Leontius was another Isaurian military man, relatively young and well educated, who was described as handsome, although pock-marked, long haired, with a straight nose, good eyes and polite manners. In 484 or somewhat earlier he was appointed *magister militum* in Thrace. He was also a patrician and an honorary consul, which latter was an honorific which had largely superseded the holding of suffect consulships in the east from the time of **LEO I,** the first recorded dating from 475.[887]

Soon afterwards, he appears to have been commissioned to move east to supress the revolt of Illus, **ZENO'S** old friend, who had turned against him and who was at the time *magister militum* in the East. Illus had just elevated *MARCIAN II* to the purple (for the third time) and had the support of the duplicitous old empress dowager Verina. Once ensconced in the vicinty of Illus's forces, a parley was held, and the upshot was that *MARCIAN II* was deposed in favour of *LEONTIUS I.*

Reign

The old Empress crowned *LEONTIUS* at Tarsus on 19th July 484, after which they moved to Antioch, occupying the city from 27th July to 8th August, when new coins were issued. His imperial style was **Dominus Noster Leontius Perpetuus Augustus.**[888] Illus and the new imperial claimant were subsequently worsted in a battle with the forces of Iohannes (John the Scythian), sent to suppress them by **ZENO,** just outside Antioch and, as a result of which they withdrew to a near-impregnable fortress in the Isaurian uplands called Papirius. There they were subsequently beseiged for four years by the Imperial force.

At some stage during the seige, the ex-Emperor *MARCIAN II* was able to leave in order to travel to Italy in the hope of obtaining help from Odovacer. This seems to have failed, after which we hear no more of him. After an act of betrayal ended the seige, the imperial claimant, Illus, and the dowager Empress (and possibly the family of *MARCIAN*) were all captured and executed, *LEONTIUS'* head being sent to Constantinople for public display.[889]

Family

No known family.

---

887. PLRE II, 1246. Crawford (2019) 2091.

888. Coin evidence. Only three *solidi* from his issue are known; they are greatly outnumbered by fakes.

889. PLRE II Leontius 17, cf. Kadellis (2015) 62-63.

ANASTASIUS I
11ᵗʰ April 491 – 9ᵗʰ July 518

Background

The death of **ZENO** left a power vacuum, as so often happened in the fifth century, for the old Emperor was childless, having lost both of his known sons, **LEO II** and Zeno, long before his own demise. This left the Empress Ariadne holding the ring, surrounded by men with good claims to rule, either from close kinship with previous ruling families, ancient nobility or military merit. In the former categories could be numbered Procopius Anthemius, Flavius Longinus and Flavius Probus amongst others. Perhaps wisely, she ignored them all and chose one of the three senior officials of the court's corps of ushers, the *silentiarii*, called **ANASTASIUS,** a man not of the highest rank being a mere *vir spectabilis* and then aged 61. Nor was he even a member of the senate, for by this date in the east, *spectabiles* were not necessarily eligible. As he was getting on in years, he was probably thought of as a stop-gap candidate too.

    ANASTASIUS came from Dyrrhachium (Durazzo, Albania), having been born in 430 and was of a rather heterodox family, his uncle being an Arian, his mother a Manichaean and he himself a Monophysite. His father's name is not known, but Alan Cameron has plausibly suggested it was Pompeius, especially in view of its recurrence amongst his descendants.[890] It is likely that the family were in some way influenced by the sojourn of the Goths in the area (who were Arians) although most of his nephews and nieces were Chalcedonians, unlike Probus (consul 502) and the younger Caesaria. As for Manichaeanism - a dualistic belief in which the world is considered inherently evil and that access to special knowledge (*gnosis*) is required to access spiritual good - the Emperor's mother may have come from the east, where these beliefs had originated and at one time had seemed likely to challenge Christianity as the displacer of paganism in the Empire. The result was that the new emperor was not an orthodox, or Chalcedonian Christian, but a Monophysite, a heresy much favoured in the regions of the Empire nearest to Persia. He was keenly interested in religion, too and at one point had been suggested as Bishop of Antioch. He had also fallen foul of the Patriarch of Constantinople by offering classes in his beliefs.

    He managed to join the Imperial court as one of the *silentiarii*, who were only some thirty in number and were the officials who enabled the court to function smoothly. He presumably had a family member or patron who enabled him to make this career move, for the corps carried great prestige and by 491 he was one of the three *decuriones* or officers in overall charge. He was nicknamed Dicorus, because the pupils of his eyes were of different colours (blue and black in his case).

Reign

ANASTASIUS was chosen by the dowager empress and proclaimed in the senate on 11ᵗʰ April, two days after the death – unlamented – of **ZENO.** He took the style **Dominus**

---

890. Cameron (1978) 259-260

Noster Flavius Anastasius Pater Patriae Augustus and he held his first consulship in 492, following with two further consulships in 497 and 507. On 20th May his rule was further secured by his marriage to the Empress Ariadne, being crowned by the patriarch after having been obliged to sign a declaration that he would reign as an Orthodox Christian.[891]

His first act thereafter was to neutralise opposition. The only serious threat to his rule was the late Emperor's brother Longinus who, despite being described as 'stupid, arrogant and licentious', occupied high esteem amongst his fellow senators and had the support of his namesake, the Isaurian *magister officiorum*, also Longinus (of Cardala). He was promptly exiled, but in their reports of what happened next, contemporary accounts diverge. That he was merely exiled to southern Egypt and there starved to death seems inherently unlikely on its own. Another account, though, merely labels him as an Isaurian rebel whom the Emperor captured, which implies that a reference to Longinus of Cardala was really intended. As his chief cheerleader, the latter indeed immediately rebelled but as he was nowhere said to have proclaimed himself an imperial claimant, one is inclined to favour the account of Zonaras which states that it was **ZENO'S** brother who proclaimed himself emperor, but who was captured at the Battle of Cotyaeum in Phrygia and then exiled to Alexandria, ordained and died in 499. There is, however, no real evidence that he did actually declare himself Emperor.[892] The Isaurian revolt continued without him, however, and was not completely extinguished until 498.

Having successfully moved the tiresome Ostrogoths on to Italy in 490, their place was taken by the Bulgars (often referred to as Huns in contemporary chronicles) who raided across the Danube from about three years later. The potential and actual destruction they caused led to the Emperor ordering the construction of a defensive work to protect the capital from the Propontis to the Black Sea (called the Long Walls), and the strengthening of the existing Danube forts. Furthermore, the Persians, under a new King, Cavades I (488-531) finally broke the long peace between the two empires and this led to a war from 502 to 506, from which the Romans emerged generally with the advantage, leading to a new treaty between the two. In the west, Theoderic was recognised as king of Italy at the third attempt in 497, though **ANASTASIUS** subsequently fell out with him in 505-510 over which of them controlled Pannonia. It was at this period (c. 507/511) that the Ostrogoth had himself described on an inscription at Tarracina uniquely as *semper Augustus*. Whether this qualified him as an imperial claimant is doubted by most commentators. More likely it was a piqued reaction to the emperor's favouring of Clovis, King of the Franks (whom he appointed consul in 508), after his defeat of the Visigoths at this time.[893]

Macedonius, Patriarch of Constantinople, was in 511 replaced by a Monophysite on the Emperor's orders, which provoked riots in Constantinople and the revolt of the *magister militum* in Thrace, Vitalianus, who used his army in an attempt to force Chalcedonian orthodoxy on the emperor. Negotiations, also involving the Pope, eventually collapsed and

---

891. PLRE II Anastasius 4
892. *Op.cit.* 14, 3.20
893. Heather (1989) 108f.; Moorhead (1992) 186, quoting CIL X 6850-6852; Barnwell (1992) 95. For a persuasive case that Theodericus should be seen as imperial, see Arnold (2018) *passim*.

Vitalianus was defeated in Thrace in 515, in the wake of which he went on the run (he was to recur again during the next reign). An attempt to replace the Patriarch of Jerusalem with a Monophysite in 516 also provoked riots but again the Emperor backed down.

Although **ANASTASIUS** was well known to be careful with his money, on accession he nevertheless remitted two burdensome and unpopular taxes, applied stringency to the Imperial finances and improved efficiency in tax collection, with long term beneficial effects, although specific acts of parsimony occasionally led him into difficulties. In 494 he also reformed the coinage, including an increase of the availability of bronze, previously in short supply. By the time of his death in 518 the treasury had a surplus of 320,000 lbs. of gold.

Family

According to the panegyrics composed by the poets Christodorus and Priscianus, the family were alleged to descend from **Pompey** (on whose family see **Table I**) which would make him kin to **MARCUS AURELIUS**, but this was mere flattery, probably arising from the use of the name Pompeius by the family, and is one of the pieces of circumstantial evidence that Alan Cameron deployed in suggesting that this was probably the Emperor's father's name.[894] Other sources suggest that his mother was called (Anastasia) Constantina, but this name fails to recur in the family and is less plausible. A final assertion is that the Emperor's mother's family descended from Constantius Gallus (see **Table LI Brief Lives**) via a daughter called Anastasia; this, too is complete fiction.

ANASTASIUS had no children by the Empress Ariadne (who was past child bearing age when they married), but an illegitimate son (whose name is not recorded) who lived to maturity only to be killed in a theatre riot in 501.[895] Nevertheless, his family by 518 was not short of suitable heirs. As the Emperor's nephew Pompeius was married to an Anastasia, it may be that this is how the names came to be connected with the Emperor's parents. If **ANASTASIUS** had enjoyed so resplendent an ancestry, it is highly unlikely that he would have been born to a non-senatorial family. Furthermore, if a family like that had survived the passage of centuries and the occasional proscription of imperial rivals, it would surely have remained near the centre of power.

Nevertheless, the family of **ANASTASIUS** gained a place at the heart of the administration and managed to maintain it well beyond the Emperor's demise in 518, as set out in the two sections of **Table LXVIII** below. More significant, however, is the marriage between Magna and the Emperor's brother Paullus. Although her parentage is nowhere directly attested, the strong likelihood that she was a daughter of the Emperor **OLYBRIUS** seems inescapable (see **Table LXIII(b) Brief Lives**). Not only is her own name one that is firmly embedded in the Petronian/Anician dynasty, already postulated as being descended from the Emperors **PETRONIUS MAXIMUS, MAGNUS MAXIMUS** and **PROBUS**, but the frequent recurrence of the names Magna/Magnus, Proba/Probus and the Placidia/Placidus

---

894. Cameron (1978) 259-260.
895. *Ibid.*, 271 n. 31.

amongst her descendants seem highly significant.[896] With Placidia as her probable mother, too, a potent Theodosian descent is also intermixed amongst her posterity.

TABLE LXVIII(a): THE FAMILY OF ANASTASIUS I

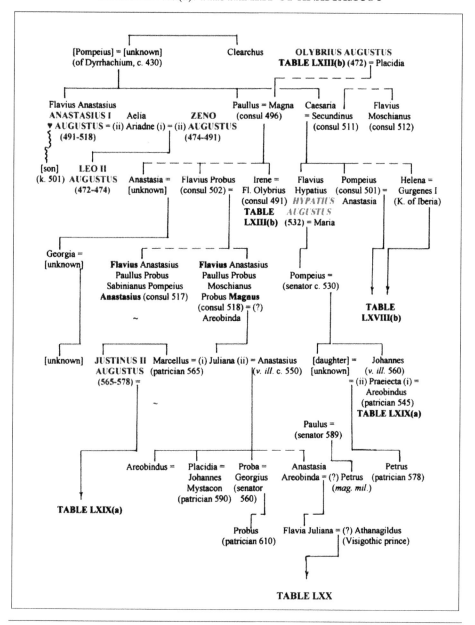

---

896. A small caveat has to be expressed with respect to Flavius Magnus and Flavius Anastasius. One bore the name Magnus and the other, *inter alia*, Sabinianus, and the possibility of a blood connection with the *magister militum* in Illyricum in 479/481, Sabinianus Magnus [PLRE II Sabinianus 4, 5] cannot entirely be discounted. However, the family is still persuasively replete with Probuses and Placidias to make the point..

TABLE LXVIII(b): THE FAMILY OF ANASTASIUS 2

TABLES LXVIII(a) & (b): BRIEF LIVES

Aelia Ariadne

See above, *sub* **ZENO AUGUSTUS**

Anastasia

Described as a *consularis femina*, meaning that her husband, whose name is not known to us,

was or had been consul, which restricts him to a fairly narrow field of candidates. She is thought to have been a monophysite [PLRE II Anastasia 2]

Anastasia

A *patricia* in rank, and mother of more than

one child; the probable names of two daughters have been identified, along with the anonymous existence of a third. She was a close friend of Anicia Juliana, the daughter of **OLYBRIUS AUGUSTUS** (see **TABLE LXIII(b) Brief Lives**) and was devoted to orthodox religion and good works. She founded a monastery on the Mount of Olives at Jerusalem, to which she retired and where she died [PLRE II Anastasia 3].

Anastasia

Admired by the Emperor **JUSTINIANUS**, a feeling not shared by the empress, in itself enough to drive her into exile at Alexandria where she too founded a monastery, from which she fled into the desert and lived as an anchorite when she heard of the death of Theodora in 548. Died unmarried 576 [PLRE II Anastasia 4].

Anastasia Areobinda

Said by one recent commentator to have been the wife of Petrus (qv), brother of the Emperor **MAURICIUS.**

Anastasius

Senator 548. He was betrothed to Belisarius's daughter in 543 and they married five years later but there is no mention of any issue. If there was, they would probably have fallen foul of the emperor and, as the source is Procopius, we can be fairly sure that he would have told us [PLRE III Anastasius 8].

Anastasius

Nothing is known of him except for his name. Nevertheless, his pivotal position in more than one imperial family would have ensured that he was at least a *vir illustris* and quite probably a patrician. Settipani suggests that he might have been the son of Fl. Anastasius (qv). [PLRE III Anastasius 9; Settipani (2000) 425]

Antonina

Reputedly the daughter of a charioteer and an actress at Constantinople, she was born c. 484 and had been around a bit before she married Belisarius, having had a number of natural offspring, too, e.g. Photius (honorary consul in 541), a daughter who married Ildiger (a general in the 540s) and another child whose own daughter was courted by a *magister militum* in the 550s. She was a *patricia*, the catspaw of the Empress Theodora, and an immoral meddler, yet on several occasions aided Belisarius on his campaigns. She broke up her daughter's marriage in 549 and died a widow after 565 [PLRE III Antonina 1].

Areobindus

He was the son of Dagalaifus and grandson of Areobindus, consul in 506 and thus was another descendant of **OLYBRUIS AUGUSTUS** (see **TABLE LXIII(b) Brief Lives**). He was a senator and patrician, and was made *magister militum* in Africa 545 where his inxperience led to his betrayal and death [PLRE III Areobindus 2].

Athanasius

Raised a Monophysite, he became a monk and in 566 narrowly missed being made Bishop of Alexandria. He thereafter became more heretical still, using his immense wealth to woo supporters [PLRE III Athanasius 5].

Caesaria

Probably born in the mid-5th century. Cameron gives her a daughter, also Caesaria, who died in 556, being then married with a family. Her husband may well have been Petrus, an honorary consul and patrician who went to Persia to negotiate the end of hostilities in 576 and who is known to have been somehow related to **ANASTASIUS**. Certainly the younger Caesaria was also somehow related to the emperor, but as she came from Samosata (Samsat, Turkey, now beneath the waters of the Atatürk dam), she probably was not a daughter of Caesaria senior [PLRE II Caesaria 1, 3; III. Petrus 6, 17; Cameron (1978) 273, 275].

Clearchus

All that is known about the Emperor's uncle is that he was an Arian, possibly through a Gothic marriage somewhere in the family [PLRE II Clearchus 4].

Demetrius

An honorary consul and a keen builder of churches. Professor Prince Kyril Toumanov considered that the consulship was bestowed in an effort to secure his loyalty on the death of his brother, King Stephanus, who had been in a state of near permanent revolt against the Empire [PLRE III Demetrius 9].

Flavia Juliana

Supposedly the daughter of Peter, brother of the Emperor **MAURICIUS** and wife of the exiled Visigothic prince, Athanagildus, on both of whom see below, **Table LXX Brief Lives.**

Flavius Anastasius

See above **ANASTASIUS I AUGUSTUS**

Flavius Anastasius Paullus Probus Moschianus Probus Magnus

Magnus was sent into exile with his family at some unknown stage, but was sufficiently rehabilitated by 518 to have served as consul (without a Western colleague) in that year. His relationship to Anastasius (qv below) is not attested but considered exceedingly likely on grounds of nomenclature and the fact that they served successive consulships. He is perhaps to be identified with the Probus who married Proba, the great-grand-daughter of **OLYBRIUS**, see **Table LXIII(b)** [PLRE II Magnus 5].

Flavius Anastasius Paullus Probus Sabinianus Pompeius Anastasius

Anastasius was a *vir illustris*, commander of the mounted Imperial guard and eastern consul.in 517. His and his brother's full names are only known because their ivory consular diptychs have survived, upon which they are inscribed. From this it may reasonably concluded that many of these later Roman princes and other aristocrats must all have had plentiful names, most since entirely lost to us. Cameron considers him the son of Sabinianus, consul in 505 (himself son of Sabinianus Magnus, *magister militum* in Illyricum 479-481) which is an alternative way of explaining the name Magnus recurring in the family. The present table is based on the alternative view of PLRE II/III. Settipani considers him to have been the father of Anastasius second husband of Juliana (qqv) [PLRE II Anastasius 17, Sabinianus 4 & 5, cf. Cameron (1978) 261; Settipani (2000) 425].

Flavius Belisarius

See box below *sub* **JUSTINIANUS I AUGUSTUS**

Flavius Hypatius

See below *HYPATIUS AUGUSTUS*

Flavius Moschianus

He was a senior commander in Illyricum in 482 either as *comes rei militaris* or *magister militum*, but the remainder of his career, apart from the ordinary consulship in 512 (probably bestowed at the end of his career through his kinship with the Emperor), is quite unknown to us. The relationship to Secundinus is nowhere actually attested, but PLRE II considers his consulship the year following that of Secundinus as being highly suggestive of their having been siblings. Cameron considers them unrelated, treating the *magister militum* as the father of the consul. [PLRE II Moschianus 1, 2; Cameron (1978) 261].

Flavius Olybrius

See above **TABLE LXIII(b) Brief Lives.**

Flavius Probus

Not only a nephew of the Emperor, he was also of the highest nobility through his mother, if the persuasive proposition that Magna was a daughter of **OLYBRIUS** is correct. He was probably born c. 470 and first comes to notice holding the consulship in 502 as a colleague of the western consul Rufius Magnus Faustus Avienus, who from his name was probably also a distant cousin. In 526 he was a patrician and probably *magister militum*, leading an embassy to the Huns to persuade them to defend Gurgenes I of Iberia. Two years later he was acquitted of slandering **JUSTINIAN I,** but he consequently went into hiding when the *Nika* riot started, in case the mob decided to declare him Emperor. This is approximately what happened, but the multitude, finding him not at home, merely burnt his house down. Nevertheless, he was still exiled, but pardoned in the following year; he was still active in 542. He was of Monophysite persuasion in religion, but is credited with the foundation of the church of St. John the Baptist at Constantinople and as the builder of splendid palaces [PLRE II Probus 8 cf. PLRE III Probus 4].

Georgia

Although this great heiress married, we know nothing of her husband, except that he was a patrician as she herself was styled *patricia* in consequence. Settipani identifies her father as Pompeius, consul 501, however. She had an equally anonymous daughter [PLRE II Georgia; Settipani (2000) 419].

Georgius

A man of senatorial rank who in 560-562 was probably *curator domus Marinae* (controller of one of the imperial properties, which carried the rank of *vir illustris*) and said to have been a kinsman of the Empress Theodora, which was not necessarily something to shout about socially. His tenure of office seems to have ended with an accusation of slandering the emperor [PLRE III Georgius 7].

Gurgenes I

This Bagratid Prince, ruler of Iberia (otherwise Kartl'i, or western Georgia) c. 526 was a Christian, the Iberians having been converted well before the Edict of Milan, who rebelled against the suzerainty of Persia when the king tried to impose the Persian cult of Ahura Mazda and its mortuary practices upon his people. He was defeated and fled, eventually arriving in Constantinople. He made a second marriage there (he was accompanied in exile by a son, Peranius) to a princess called Helena, referred to as 'the emperor's daughter', probably meaning an otherwise unrecorded niece of **ANASTASIUS**. If so, this would provide him with an impressive Roman ancestry, see **Appendix III**. Prince Toumanov identifies him with King Vakhtang I Gorgasil (d. 523) on the basis that the conventional chronology is slightly too late. Thus Armenian tradition has Gorgasil as a separate person from Gurgenes, who marries a daughter of the Emperor **LEO I** [Braund (1994) 282-285, 287 n .75; PLRE II Gurgenes].

Gurgenes II

Son of Leo and usually identified with King Guaram I of Iberia. Earlier he was Prince of Klarjet'i (Eastern Georgia) but in the uprising of the Armenians against Persia he too was forced to go into exile in Constantinople. When the Iberians revolted from Persia in 588 he was restored as their ruler by **MAURICIUS** with the roman rank of *curopalates* (originally the person in charge of the Imperial palace, but from the time of **JUSTINIAN I** an honorific title ranking only just below Caesar). He died at about the same time as the Emperor **MAURICIUS** was killed [PLRE III Guaram I].

Helena

Second wife of Gurgenes, otherwise Vakhtang I Gorgasil, King of Iberia and mother of Leo and Mithridates (qqv). She is referred to as 'the emperor's daughter' by which it seems clear that she was almost certainly a niece of **ANASTASIUS I.** The question arises as to exactly whose daughter she was. The probability (as shown in **Tables LXVIII (a) & (b)**) is that she was the sister of Pompeius and *HYPATIUS.* As such she would also have been a grand-daughter of the Emperor **OLYBRIUS,** which might make the import of 'the emperor's daughter' yet more convincing. Her descendant, Georgius, King of Georgia (acceded 1014), was thus a probable descendant of some of the great patrician republican houses; a possible reconstruction of this putative descent will be found in **Appendix III** [PLRE III Leo 9, Mihrdat; Toumanoff (1963) 368-9]

Irene

She was an *inlustris femina*; her relationships are attested by Nicephorus, *Breviarium* [PLRE II Irene].

Johannes

He married Praeiecta in 546/548 but had died by 566 or 567. No high offices are known but as the husband of the emperor's niece, he was clearly of senatorial rank, and therefore at least a *vir illustris.* Settipani suggests that it was Praeiecta who was daughter of Pompeius and John the husband. [PLRE III Ioannes 63; Settipani (2000) 419].

Johannes

His relationships are given in John of Ephesus's *Ecclesiastical History*. He was also a relation of Petrus (qv) with whom he was sent to Persia in 576, by which time he had been made a patrician

and honorary consul. He was also a Monophysite [PLRE III Ioannes 90].

Johannes *qui et* Mystacon

A Thracian, his nickname Mystacon derived for his prominent moustache, He was appointed *magister militum* in Armenia from 579 to 583 and in Thrace in 587, before returning to Armenia in the same capacity from 589/590 until some point after 591, by which time he had been made a patrician. He was instrumental in the restoration of the Persian King Chosroes II [PLRE III Ioannes 101].

Juliana

She was obliged to go into exile with her father Magnus (qv); she also endured persecution as a Monophysite and was exiled a second time c. 572 by **JUSTIN II.** She ranked as a *patricia* [PLRE III Juliana 1].

Justinianus I

See below **JUSTINIANUS I AUGUSTUS**

Justinus II

See below **JUSTINUS II AUGUSTUS**

Leo

Son of Gurgenes I of Iberia by Helena; nothing is known of his career except that he was father of Gurgenes II [PLRE III Leo 9]

Leo

See above **LEO II AUGUSTUS**

Magna

As Paullus was the only recorded brother of **ANASTASIUS I,** it is presumed that this lady, attested as married to a brother of the emperor, was his wife; nothing obtrudes to suggest otherwise. Her name makes the likelihood of her having been a daughter of **OLYBRIUS** inescapable, especially as her son and both grandsons were called Probus (and one called Magnus too). She is thus a pivotal link in the descent of a number of late Roman luminaries, not only having a number of distinguished (and otherwise) imperial forebears, but also, through the Anicii, a resplendent republican and patrician ancestry, on which see **Appendix III** [PLRE II Magna].

Marcellus

He was apparently still a young man when he married Juliana (he would have been born c. 513/515) and was thus still relatively young when appointed *magister militum* in 544 and sent to the East. He next appears in the same capacity in Thrace in 562 to defend Constantinople from a large force of Bulgars who were ravaging the province. In 565 he was made patrician on his brother's accession, but he seems to have died by 582 or else he would surely have been a candidate for the purple on his brother's demise [PLRE III Marcellus 5].

Mithridates

Nothing known of his career and he is known only because he was named as the uncle of Gurgenes II. Apart from Peranius, he had two other half-brothers, one anonymous and another called Dach'i [PLE III Mihrdat].

Paullus

Alluded to but not actually named as the husband of Magna (qv). He was consul in 496. Priscian (*Panegyric on the Emperor Anastasius*) mentions his offspring [PLRE II Paulus 27].

Paullus

Recorded as a senator in 589, he may well have been the un-named husband of the daughter of Pompeius, son of *HYPATIUS* especially as both seem to have had a son calleċ Petrus. In which case he was also the father of the emperor **MAURICIUS** (qv) [PLRE III Paullus 23]

Petrus

Honorary consul before 576, when he was part of a diplomatic mission (with Johannes) to Persia. He was a *vir gloriosissimus*, as senators were by this date styled and also, it would appear, a patrician. He was a Monophysite, a fact that led to a gap in his career between 571 and c. 575 when **JUSTIN II** launched a persecution. He may well be identifiable with Petrus, *magister militum* and the Petrus married to Anastasia Areobinda and brother of the emperor **MAURICIUS** cf., Paulus, above. [PLRE III Petrus 17 = Petrus 29 = 55].

Placidia

Her name, being eminently Theodosian (and at this period otherwise unique), does much to confirm her descent from the Emperor **OLYBRIUS** and Placidia, the daughter of **VALENTINIAN III** (see **Table LXIII(b))** via Magna (qv) [PLRE III Placidia].

Pompeius

Eastern consul in 501 with the Western patrician Flavius Avienus Junior, he suffered the indignity of having his house torched during the religious riots in 512. He was *magister militum* in Thrace around 517 where he suffered a defeat by a barbarian army. Despite this, he was a patrician with the rank of *vir magnificus* in 519 and he was *magister militum* again in 528, commanding reinforcements on the Eastern frontier in support of his brother. He was involved in the *Nika* riot in 532 and executed with his brother *HYPATIUS,* his corpse being thrown into the sea and his property confiscated, although it was later restored, much depleted, to his family [PLRE III Pompeius 2].

Pompeius

A man of senatorial rank living c. 530 [PLRE III Pompeius 1].

Proba

Her relationships are set out in Nicephorus' *Breviarium*, but of her life nothing has come down to us [PLRE III Proba 2].

Probus

On 5th October 610, Probus, a patrician, along with the palace *curator*, Photius, entered the Imperial Palace and seized the Emperor **PHOCAS** and delivered him to **HERACLIUS I**, who had him summarily executed. He is probably to be identified with the Probus whose seal, with a cruciform monogram, has survived. If this man can be accepted as a son of Proba and Georgius, then the blood line of the Petronii survived the depredations meted out to the high aristocracy by **PHOCAS** [PLRE III Probus 7, cf. 6].

Secundinus

We know nothing of his origins, but in 492 he was appointed Prefect of the City (of Constantinople) no doubt as a result of his brother-in-law's accession to the purple, which appointment suggests that he was a man of senatorial rank in the first place. By 503 he had been made a patrician and was consul in 511 with Western colleague Flavius Felix (Arcadius Placidus Magnus Felix, see above **Table LXIII(b).**). Three years later he was involved in negotiations to get his son back from the clutches of the turbulent Vitalianus [PLRE II Secundinus 2].

Stephanus I

Son of Gurgenes II (Guaram I), he rebelled in 607 or 608 against Roman overlordship of Iberia, to the throne of which he had succeeded in 602, and ruled independently until 626, when Persia re-asserted itself, to which he submitted, keeping his throne. In 627 he was killed defending Tiflis (Tblisi) against a successful attempt by **HERACLIUS I** to restore Roman suzerainty [PLRE III Stephanus 55].

Theodora

See below *sub* **JUSTINIANUS I AUGUSTUS**

Zeno

See above **ZENO AUGUSTUS**

Imperial claimants under Anastasius I

BURDUNELUS
496-497

The *Consularia Caesaraugusta* for the year 496 carries an account of the attempt to claim the western purple by one *BURDUNELUS* – the name means little mule, and is thus probably not the claimant's actual name – who 'became a tyrant' in Spain, then mainly under Visigothic control. The location of the outbreak has been suggested as Caesaraugusta (Zaragoza). He clearly had some support, but by the following year he lost this (how, we are not told) and elements of his former entourage eventually turned him in to the Visigothic authorities in Tolosa (Toulouse). Bizarrely here he was burned to death – perhaps more accurately roasted – in a bronze bull.[897]

*

---

897. PLRE II Burdunelus, cf. Thompson (1982) 177.

PETRUS
506

A curt entry in the same western chronicle informs us that one *PETRUS*, undeterred by the gruesome fate of *BURDUNELUS*, attempted to hold Dertosa (Tortosa) in Spain against the Goths and had been killed by them. As probably with the previous claimant in the area, his name suggests a member of the local Roman élite, and again, the description of him as *tyrannus* is the normal term for a usurper, i. e. an imperial claimant. Whether he set himself up as a potential western emperor or merely as a local one with the hope of resisting Gothic expansion and consolidation is not known.[898]

*

---

898. PLRE II Petrus 25 cf. Barnwell (1992) 69. *Tyrannus* is the normal Latin shorthand in the later empire to describe imperial claimants, cf. Vortigern (above) and the African claimants (below).

The imperial succession
Iustinus I
Iustinianus I
Iustinus II
Tiberius II
Mauricius
Theodosius III

Imperial claimants
Hypatius
Stotzas I
Stotzas II
Guntharis

IUSTINUS I
(Known to history as Justin I)
10th July 518 – 1st August 527

Background

The new emperor was proclaimed within 24 hours of the death of **ANASTASIUS,** and then only because of a slightly bizarre set of circumstances. The old emperor had no idea whom to appoint as his heir, despite the existence of a number of entirely suitable candidates, including three nephews who, according to the *Anonymous Valesianus*, managed to eliminate themselves in various ways. Thus the same source claims he next resolved to nominate as his successor the first person to enter his chamber the following morning. Against all the odds, this happened to be the *comes excubitorum* **Justinus.** Under the reformed arrangements, he held the position of commander of the crack troops which comprised the Imperial Guard, as the *scholae,* who previously had that position, were by this date, entirely ceremonial.

The Emperor died shortly after this modest stratagem had been played out, on 9th July. His chamberlain Amantius (a eunuch) put the *comes* Theocritus forward, but **Justinus** outmanoeuvred him and managed to stage-manage his own acclamation the following morning, with the result that Theocritus tried to stage a counter-coup, but this was nipped in the bud and the principals summarily executed.

The new emperor was an unlikely candidate by late imperial standards, although had he been acclaimed in the third century, he would have been considered par for the course. Like his predecessor, he was getting on in years, being was about 67 and entirely illiterate, having been born into Thracian peasant stock at Bederiana, near Naissus (Niš, Serbia) in the province of Dardania, part of the Diocese of Dacia Mediterranea. He and two companions are said by Procopius to have travelled to Constantinople to enlist in the army. He must have been endowed with considerable ability for, having been enrolled in the palace guard, he was soon commissioned and by the mid-490s had been made *comes rei militaris,* fighting as 2i/c to a succession of commanders in the Isaurian War, then in the Persian war of 503-504 and finally at the siege of Antioch in 504/505.

In 515 he was made Imperial Guard Commander, as which he transferred his military skills to naval warfare, helping to defeat Vitalinus at sea, routing part of his fleet. His appointment carried senatorial rank, which represented an impressive rise for a man who was obliged to use a stencil to sign his name. Nevertheless, the hyper-critical Procopius labelled him a donkey.[899]

Reign

The new Emperor acted swiftly to eliminate Theocritus. His other potential rivals were the late emperor's three nephews, of whom Probus and Pompeius seemed to have no imperial ambitions but the third, *HYPATIUS*, without doubt did harbour such ambitions, but was safely out of harm's way on the eastern frontier as *magister militum*. **JUSTIN** moved quickly to make a donative to the troops of five *solidi* per man, paid for out of **ANASTASIUS'S** replete treasury.[900]

He was proclaimed in the style of **Dominus Noster Justinus Pater Patriae Augustus** by the senate and his wife, Lupicina (by whom he had no surviving children) was given the additional name Euphemia and made Augusta.[901] He held the consulship for 519 with the Goth Eutharicus Cilliga as western colleague, a man whom he made his 'son at arms', suggesting that he acquiesced in his father-in-law, Theodericus's, designation of him as successor designate as ruler of the West. He held a second and final consulship in 524.[902]

The new emperor moved swiftly to effect an ecclesiastical settlement, and before the end of his first month, Chalcedonian Orthodoxy was restored and the Monophysite faction sidelined. The was an essential move to free **JUSTIN** for a trial of strength with the disaffected but equally orthodox former *magister militum* Vitalianus, who was still causing trouble in the Balkans, the more so because he considered he had a claim upon the purple too. **JUSTIN** made his peace with him, confirmed him in office, made him patrician and designated him as consul for 520. He was then put to work to settle outstanding difficulties with the church in the West which he managed to achieve successfully, albeit at the price of the *amour propre* of the Eastern faction, but one the emperor thought worth paying to achieve unity. Nevertheless, Vitalianus was always seen as a threat and was eventually murdered in the palace in July 520 along with two members of his staff, probably in the initiative of the Emperor's nephew the future Emperor **JUSTINIAN I**, who had been the *eminence*

---

899. PLRE II Justinus 4.
900. Generally, these donatives were made on accession and when a consulship was held by the Emperor to make a five or ten year anniversary, a tradition that was dropped by **JUSTIN I:** Burgess (2011) XIV *passim*.
901. PLRE II Euphemia 5
902. Moorhead (1992) 201; Fl. Rufius Opilio, an aristocrat, was his western colleague.

grise behind the ecclesiastical accords. The ambitious nephew acted very competently as **JUSTIN'S** secretary of state, whilst at the same time ensuring his own place in the succession.

As the reign went on, **JUSTINIAN'S** influence was seen to be increasingly pre-eminent hence, no doubt, Procopius's donkey jibe. After 520 and the elimination of Vitalianus, the emperor's nephew was virtually sole ruler of the empire, being made *magister militum* and patrician. He was later styled *nobilissimus* (most noble), a title normally coupled with that of *caesar* but here used separately for the first time to indicate someone on the brink of succession, or at least fitted for it, as the term *capax imperii* had been five centuries before. Probably after the empress's death, which seems to have occurred early in 527, **JUSTINIAN** was at last made co-emperor and formally adopted as **JUSTIN'S** son (the first imperial incidence of this formal procedure since the third century), thus avoiding a succession crisis when the old Emperor finally expired aged 77 on 1st August.

Family

Whilst the Emperor's family background was obscure and lowly, the Empress's was equally so. Of barbarian stock, sold into slavery and put into concubinage, she was later freed and subsequently married **JUSTIN**. Yet she was very moral and upright if a trifle unrefined, and she had no interest in affairs of state. She did, however, see Theodora, the future wife of **JUSTINIAN**, for what she was, and refused to approve their marriage. Needless to say, she was dead by April 527, when the future emperor was finally able to marry her. If the emperor and empress had any children, they had died prior to **JUSTIN** becoming emperor. Yet like **ANASTASIUS**, the imperial family was quite extensive thanks to the Emperor's two siblings marrying and having children. Unfortunately, we do not have the names or either, but **JUSTINIAN** was the son of his daughter and there were three sons born to the other sibling, whose gender is not known, but who was probably male. **JUSTINIAN'S** sister's children however, triply married into the family of **ANASTASIUS** and **OLYBRIUS** thus anchoring the new Imperial house to several earlier ones, and thereby strengthening its perceived right to rule. As a consequence, the number of imperial claimants significantly reduces compared with the situation in the previous era.

⋆

IUSTINIANUS I
(Known to history as Justinian I)
1st April 527 – 14th November 565

Background

JUSTINIAN reigned for a little over 38 years which, although falling short of the total of the reign of **THEODOSIUS II** by ten years, exceeded the length of the reigns of all his other predecessors bar **AUGUSTUS** himself (41); only **HONORIUS** (30) and **CONSTANTINE I** (31) came close. He is important because he again reformed and codified Roman law and for his attempt, only partially successful, to re-integrate the lost western provinces into the Empire.

JUSTINIAN was the son of his predecessor's sister, whose name is lost to us. She married a man called Sabbatius, about whom nothing whatsoever is known.[903] As he was born in 483, before his brother-in-law had achieved any more than modest eminence, Sabbatius was probably of middling rank, although unlikely to have been in such a lowly station in life as that in which **JUSTIN** had been born. He was probably dead well before his son became part of the Imperial family, otherwise we would have heard more of him, ties of blood in high office carrying the weight they did. Furthermore, the future emperor was born at a fortress called Bederiana (now Bader) hard by Tauresium (Gradiste, Macedonia), suggesting his father may have been an army officer but not necessarily a native of the area (i.e. a Thracian). **JUSTINIAN'S** full name, Fl. Petrus Sabbatius Justinianus, appears traditional (albeit that the *praenomen* is Christian and the Flavius probably an imperial honorific) but may well have been amplified after the family's rise to eminence.

At the time of his uncle's elevation to the purple, **JUSTINIAN** was serving in the ceremonial *scholae*, having become one of their officers. Indeed, when **ANASTASIUS** died, one of those proposed for the purple was the elderly and distinguished general Flavius Patricius (consul 500), but he was unacceptable to **JUSTIN'S** men, the *excubitores*, from whom the old boy had to be rescued by the quick thinking of **JUSTINIAN,** who was himself promptly put forward over his uncle, an honour from which he was quick to distance himself.

He was almost immediately thereafter made a *comes* and, following the murder of Vitalianus which he appears to have masterminded, he became *magister militum* (effectively chief of the general staff) as well. This elevated him to the senate and the rank of *vir illustris*; he also held the consulship in 521 and the celebrations and games accompanying this were held with conspicuous generosity, which did his popularity no harm at all. He was also made patrician at about this period and this raised him in rank to the relatively new style of *vir magnificus*. He was made **nobilissimus** and, after the death of the empress, he married and was made co-Augustus with his uncle, who died exactly four months later.[904]

His new bride, unlike the Empress Euphemia, was to loom large in the affairs of state, thanks to the account of her by Procopius who knew her. Born c. 495, she was originally from Cyprus, and became an exotic dancer with a reputation for her erotic performances and louche lifestyle. In this she followed in the steps of her anonymous mother, who had married Acacius, keeper of the animals for the Green circus faction. She had two sisters and at least two children, a daughter and a son, Johannes. She had gone to Libya c. 518 as the mistress of the governor, Hecebolus, but they fell out and she returned home via Alexandria, paying her way as an *orizontale*. On her arrival she had, however following a stopover in Alexandria, got religion and Monophysitism at that. She met **JUSTINIAN** and became his mistress. He got his uncle to elevate her to the rank of *patricia*, and he married her once the empress had died and **JUSTIN** had had time to amend the long-established law against senators marrying actresses. They were certainly married by the time **JUSTINIAN** had become co-emperor in April 527.

---

903. PLRE II Sabbatius
904. PLRE II Iustinianus 7

Thereafter she took an active role in government, attending the Imperial Council (*consistorium*), advising the emperor and exercising the power of make or break, life and death over his associates. She comes over as essentially insecure, her control freakery deriving therefrom with all the capriciousness and mental *chiaroscuro* that comes with it. Indeed, if the hostile account of Procopius is to be believed, she was everything her husband was not. He was hard working, generally affable and fiscally careful, whilst she was extravagant, slothful, haughty and capricious.

Reign

JUSTINIANUS I was acclaimed by the senate and court as sole emperor on 1st August 527. His style was **Dominus Noster Iustinianus Pater Patriae Augustus,** later adding in 539 **Alanicus** and **Vandalicus** having re-conquered Africa and **Alamannicus, Gepidus** and **Langobardicus** as the reign progressed.[905] He served a second consulship in 528 and two more in 533 and 534 before the institution was essentially abolished after the (western) consulship of Fl. Anicius Faustus Albinus Basilius Junior in 541.[906] Thereafter all consulships were honorary, except for newly acceded emperors who usually held an inaugural consulship. Years were counted not by consuls' names but the number of years after Basilius, thus *post consule Basili* I, II etc., until **JUSTINIAN'S** death.

Most commentators see four events (called pillars by Scott) marking out the reign: the codification of Roman law, the building of Hagia Sophia cathedral in Constantinople, the closing of Plato's Academy in Athens, and the re-conquest of the West. The chronicler John Malalas mentions all four, the latter briefly, but this aspect has been magnified by Procopius's account which focuses on the *reconquista*.

The first major achievement of the reign was the thorough revision of the legal code, much more far reaching than that published under **THEODOSIUS II.** It was carried out with remarkable celerity in 528-529 by a committee chaired by the corrupt, flawed but efficient and remarkably able jurist Tribonianus, who was *quaestor sacri palatii* (lord chancellor or chief legal officer) 529-532 & 535-542, producing the *Digest* and the *Institutes*.[907] Despite Tribonianus's alleged paganism, the Emperor ensured that nothing in the finished work would be incompatible with Christian teaching.

There was also a thorough reform of the tax system, coupled with a centralisation of bureaucracy, done to improve revenue and to increase efficiency. This was masterminded by another major figure, but also perceived to be corrupt, John the Cappadocian.[908] As will emerge, there was to be much for the treasury to fund. There was also a crack-down on paganism (leading to the closure of the Athens academy) and other heresies (but not Monophysitism, *pace* the Empress) which was pursued with too much rigour, resulting in a

905. Barnwell (1992) 95
906. The previous year (540) had been the last with two consuls, west and east.
907. PLRE III Tribonianus 1
908. PLRE III Ioannes 11

major revolt in northern Palestine by the Samaritans, the suppression of which devastated much of the province. After five years of rule, there was much discontent, especially in the capital, exacerbated by laws limiting the privileges of the circus factions, which struck at the heart of the celebrity culture that the ever-popular circus inspired.

The third pillar arose as a consequence of another event consequent on the tax reforms (and other irritants). These accumulated grievances that burst forth one day at the Hippodrome in Constantinople on 13ᵗʰ January 532, where a demonstration caused an over-reaction on the part of the authorities which in turn spiralled out of control, with a vast mob chanting *nika! nika!* (victory, victory!). This gave the name to the event (thus euphemistically called the *Nika* Riot) which rapidly broadened out into eight days of extreme disorder, during which much of the city was destroyed by rampaging and resentful mobs (largely comprising peasant and city dwellers, alike dispossessed by the harshness of the new imperial tax regime) mainly by fire, and during which the nephew of **ANASTASIUS I,** *HYPATIUS,* was raised to the purple, largely against his will. The uprising (for such it had become) was only ended because the Empress persuaded her husband not to flee as he was minded to do, and because two generals, Belisarius and Mundus, who were fortuitously passing through the city *en route* to new postings, took charge of the counter *putsch.* In this they were aided by the grand chamberlain, the Armenian eunuch Narses, who took the initiative in bottling a vast concourse of rioters in the hippodrome which had become a sort of headquarters of the rioters, allowing the two generals systematically to butcher the lot – allegedly between 20,000 and 50,000 people. Needless to say this was salutary and the riot swiftly collapsed. Later *HYPATIUS* and his brother Pompeius were arraigned before **JUSTINIAN** who was inclined to forgive them (they had been implicated largely against their will after all). Theodora however, demurred and, typically, demanded their execution, which followed in short order, their corpses being thrown into the Golden Horn.

In rebuilding the shattered city, the Emperor spared no expense, and the major public buildings, churches and infrastructure were renewed on a more impressive scale, notably the spectacular and revolutionary cathedral of St. Sophia (Hagia Sophia), designed (probably in advance of the riot) by Anthemius of Tralles and Isidorus of Miletus and still a major building of international importance to this day, preserved by its conversion into a mosque in 1453 and secularisation as a museum by Mustafa Kemal Pasha in the 1920s.

In mentioning Belisarius, it is worth noting that the early military business of the reign had been a campaign against Persia, led by him in his first command (replacing the absent imperial candidate of 528, Probus, a prince of the house of **ANASTASIUS**), although he obtained mixed results and was soon replaced. It was on returning from his second command that he came to be in Constantinople during the *Nika* riot, a happenstance that did no harm to his prospects, for the Emperor chose him to lead a new expedition to Africa to attempt to dislodge the Vandal kingdom. This was the first step in the fourth pillar, the *reconquista*. If successful, this venture was to be the first in a series of planned campaigns envisaged by **JUSTINIAN** to recover the Western Empire. Yet Belisarius was to turn out to be the greatest commander of his age or indeed of any other age of the Empire.

Belisarius

Flavius Belisarius was the ultimate hero: handsome, affable and generous. He came from a family from Germana (Saparevska, Bulgaria) in the Balkans and was born around 500, although we do not know the names of his parents. He married Theodora's friend Antonina c. 521 and their only child was Johannina (qv), although they had stepchildren (cf. Antonina, **Table LXVIII(a)** and **Brief Lives** above). In 533 he also adopted a Thracian member of his household (possibly a relative) as his son. This was Theodosius, who became Antonina's lover and died in 543. Belisarius was, even in his own time, celebrated as a great general. The result of this was that **JUSTINIAN** (egged on by the empress) was constantly suspicious that he might prove to be a threat and be at the centre of a conspiracy or even himself become an imperial claimant.

He first comes to notice as an officer in the imperial guard (*protectores*) in the early 520s, becoming *dux* (senior commander) in Mespotamia in 527 and being promoted to *magister militum* in the east in 529 which appointment ended following a non-strategic defeat by the Persians in 531. As a commander, despite this, his judgement was exceptionally sound; he proved to be shrewd and at his best in difficult situations, added to which he was also exceptionally brave. He was a fine tactician and able to make best use of inadequate resources, a useful talent in the age of **JUSTINIAN**.

His reward for services during the *Nika* riot was re-appointment as *magister militum* in the East, which appointment he held until 542. As such, he led the successful expedition to re-conquer the province of Africa from the Vandals, which triumphed through a combination of excellent leadership and a policy of conciliation towards the inhabitants. He returned to celebrate a triumph, the first non-imperial one since the reign of Augustus. He was made consul in 535, patrician and styled *vir excellentissimus*. As consul, he was despatched to the west again to re-conquer Italy, and began by taking Sicily (putting down a revolt in Africa the while) and entering Rome on 9th December 536, after which he had to endure a siege until March 538. Ravenna fell in 540, after which he was recalled to Constantinople.

The following year he led a campaign against Persia, but was disgraced and dismissed on the orders of the Empress. He was rehabilitated as *comes sacri stabuli* (effectively Imperial Master of Horse) in 544, being sent back to Italy as C-in-C, but with far fewer troops. He was made honorary *magister militum* but was effectively retired until, in 559, he was sent out to put down a revolt in Thrace by a group of disaffected Huns but with a very small and inadequate force. He managed this with complete success, again retiring thereafter, although he spent the first half of 563 under house arrest under suspicion of conspiracy. He was exonerated in the July and died in March 565. The legend that he was disgraced and blinded, leading to him becoming a beggar at the gates of the city may be safely discounted.[909]

---

909. PLRE III Belisarius I

The Italian campaign was only launched after the death of King Theoderic in Italy who, it has to be remembered, was theoretically ruling a part of the Empire as the Emperor's appointee. He had been a made patrician and was a former *magister militum* who had finally received imperial recognition in 493. His death in 526 and that of his dissolute grandson Athalaric eight years later, plunged the benevolent Ostrogothic regime into doubt from the point of view of its continued loyalty to Constantinople. This was the opportunity which the Emperor commissioned Belisarius to take. Much of Belisarius's good work there was undone in the 540s by imperial incompetence and the accession of a capable Gothic King, Totila.

Belisarius's second campaign from 544 to 549 was less successful due to lack of resources, and he was recalled after the death of Theodora, then his chief supporter. The situation was restored by the elderly eunuch Narses with John, the nephew of the former rival of **JUSTIN I**, Vitalianus, who fought a series of effective campaigns from 552 to 556, albeit with a much larger army. The result was the restoration of Italy, a small part of Gaul (essentially the *côte d'azure*) and much of southern Spain, but at the cost of the dereliction of most of Italy, both countryside and cities, the weakening of its defences and the deleterious effect of a reformation of its governance by a pragmatic sanction which established a viceroy (later called an Exarch, qv. *sub* **JUSTIN II**) at Ravenna. This last left the western senate at Rome completely by-passed in such a way that within three generations it had virtually ceased to exist and the ancient Italian senatorial aristocracy dispersed or impoverished (except for those families which had wisely migrated to the East).

The continuous conflict in Italy, perturbations in reclaimed Africa and constant warfare on the eastern borders with Persia were a severe drain upon the fisc, exacerbated by an apocalyptic plague in the 540s (originating in NE Africa) which killed millions (including the empress) and seriously depleted the reserves of manpower upon which the empire could draw. That so much was achieved was, in the circumstances, little short of miraculous. **JUSTINIAN** associated his nephew **JUSTIN** with his rule from c. 562, entrusting him with several delicate tasks and clearly marking him out as his successor. The old Emperor died aged around 83 on 14th November 565 and was duly succeeded by **JUSTIN II**.

TABLE LXIX(a): JUSTIN & JUSTINIAN

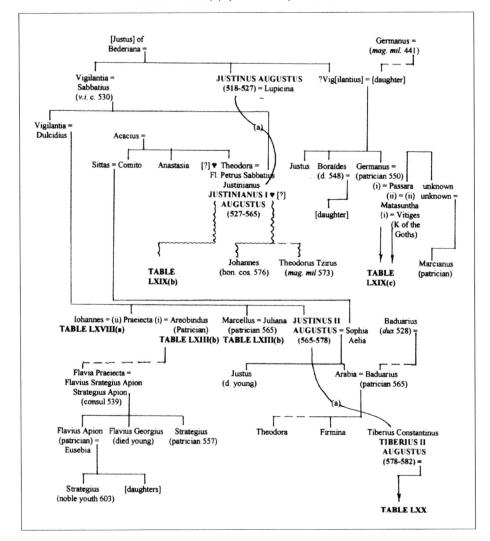

TABLE LXIX(a): BRIEF LIVES

Acacius

See below **Table LXIX(b)**

Anastasia

See below **Table LXIX(b)**

Arabia

Apart from her marriage and children, nothing is known of her life [PLRE III Arabia].

Areobindus

See above **Table LXIII(b)**

Baduarius

He was *dux* in Scythia with the rank of *magister militum* in 528 when he fought against marauding bands of Huns and Bulgars at various places around the Black Sea littoral. Nothing is known of his family, but the rarity of his name might plausibly suggest that he was either father or grandfather of the younger Baduarius [PLRE III Baduarius 1]

Baduarius

Quite possibly a son (as suggested above) or grandson of the preceding, he was *cura palatii* (imperial palace commander, a post that later became much grander and entirely honorific), appointed by **JUSTIN II** on his accession, as his successor in the post. As the emperor's son-in-law he was also made a patrician in the same year and *magister militum* the year following, in order to lead an army recruited from the Gepidae (a Balkan people) against the Lombards. He commanded an army against them again after they had migrated to Italy, largely through the consequences of his earlier foray in the northern Balkans. This time he suffered a defeat in which he was killed or captured and then killed [PLRE III Baduarius 2]

Boraïdes

Although we are told about his family connections, we learn neither the name of his wife nor his daughter, whom he cut out of his will, and who **JUSTINIAN** thereafter championed to the irritation of his brother Germanus, who was the chief beneficiary; it may be that the daughter became a Monophysite and that her father held fiercely orthodox views. After the *Nika* riot in 532 he, with his brother Justus, seized *HYPATIUS* and dragged him before the emperor. He died in 548 [PLRE III Boraïdes]

Comito

She was seven years old when Acacius died and was put on the stage by her anonymous mother as soon as possible thereafter. She married Sittas in 528, so probably born c. 512/514 [PLRE III Comito].

Dulcidius

His name is sometimes (wrongly) given as Dulcissimus. He was dead before his son acceded to the throne [PLRE III Dulcidius].

Eusebia

She was recipient of letters from Pope Gregorius (St. Gregory the Great) and was probably daughter of Rusticiana, a patrician lady at Constantinople who is thought to have been the grand-daughter of the philosopher and statesman Anicius Severinus Manlius Boëthius (consul 510) and his wife, also called Rusticiana, a descendant of Q. Aurelius Symmachus (consul 395) [PLRE II Boethius 5, Rusticiana 1; PLRE III. Eusebia 2, Rusticiana 2; Cameron (1978) 269]

Firmina

Only known from a late 6th century inscription [PLRE III Firmina].

Flavia Praeiecta

Her descent from the other Praeiecta is nowhere confirmed, but she was married to a great noble of Egyptian descent (where she owned an estate) and was styled *hypatissa* (= *consularis*) as befitted the wife of an ordinary consul – and one of the very last. She was also a *patricia*. The name Georgius amongst her sons might suggest that the Georgia (daughter of Anastasia) married to an unidentified husband might have actually been the wife of Pompeius the son of *HYPATIUS*, see above **Table LXVIII(a)** Praeiecta's probable father was also a descendant of *HYPATIUS* [PLRE III Praeiecta 2].

Flavius Apion

He was known to Pope Gregory the Great (thanks to his wife Eusebia, qv). He was made honorary consul (ordinary ones having been allowed to lapse by **JUSTINIAN I** after 541) and in 609 a patrician, probably on the strength of his illustrious family and connections to the ruling house, another reason to support the supposition that his mother was the daughter of the elder Praeiecta. P. J. Barnish suggested that his family was related in some way to that of the philosopher-senator Boëthius (qv *sub* Eusebia above). He was still alive in 619 and probably in 623. He escaped the depredations of **PHOCAS** through remaining in Egypt, although he would have retreated to Constantinople in 623 if he was then still living, as the Persians were then temporarily in control of Northern Egypt [PLRE III Apion 4; Barnish (1988) 150].

Flavius Georgius

An honorary consul by 587, he also held an estate at Oxyrhyncus in Egypt, but was dead by 590 [PLRE III Georgius 10]

Flavius Petrus Sabbatius Justinianus

See above **JUSTINIANUS I AUGUSTUS**

Flavius Strategius Apion Strategius Apion

Descended from a senator of Egyptian family called Apion, who was an honorary consul, or had been a suffect consul before 497, by which time it is thought he was fairly old. His career may have reached its apogee under **MARCIANUS** or **LEO I.** This man was his great-great-grandson and son of the patrician Strategius who had been *comes sacrae largitionum* (Keeper of the Privy Purse) 535-538. Fl. Apion was a *vir inlustris*, one of the last ever eastern ordinary consuls, holding the office in 539, being also in that year being appointed *comes domesticorum*. He was appointed patrician by 548 by which time he was also *dux* of the Thebaïd in his native Egypt. His links there were further strengthened by his appointment as *pagarchus* (governor) of Arsinoë with the rank of *magister militum* in 556. He died about 578 as pre-eminent amongst the senators of Constantinople [PLRE II Apion 1, Strategius 9, PLRE III Apion 3].

Germanus

A *vir magnificus* and *magister militum* in the East in 441 who was sent in command of a naval expedition to expel the Vandals from Sicily having probably also campaigned against the Blemmyes, a troublesome Nubian people. It is suggested that he may have been the grandfather of the Germanus who was the nephew of **JUSTIN I.** His origins are not known [PLRE II Germanus 3].

Germanus

He was *magister militum* (in Thrace) and a *vir inlustris* in 519, at which time he must have been quite young, establishing the fact that his anonymous father was probably from a grand family, hence the attribution of the other Germanus as his grandfather, although the accession of **JUSTIN I** the previous year must have aided his prospects no end. In 536 he was a patrician, bore the rank of an ex-consul (effectively equivalent of having been suffect consul in earlier times), in which year he was sent to Africa as C-in-C, where he defeated *STOTZAS I*, but failed to end the claimant's career completely. He served against the Persians in Antioch in 540 but the hostility of Theodora held his career back until her death in 548. The following year he married the Ostrogothic princess Matasuntha, possibly in connection with his ambitions to lead the completion of the re-conquest of Italy. In 550 he was appointed C-in-C Italy and his marriage to Matasuntha was used as a propaganda tool to seduce the allegiance of most Ostrogoths into supporting Roman re-establishment of control, but he died before the expedition could get under way. He is one of the few people of whom the hypercritical contemporary author Procopius really approved, by whom he was portrayed as a 'man of energy, and able general in war and a capable administrator in peace, upright and generous, a pleasant companion in private life and a man of dignity and presence in public and of devoted loyalty to the emperor' [PLRE II Germanus 4].

Johannes 576

Honorary consul in 576. He is conceivably a conflation with John the grandson of Theodora, on whom see **Table LXVIII(a) Brief Lives** above.

Johannes

See above **TABLE LXVIII(a)**

Juliana

See above **TABLE LXIII(b)**

Justinus

See above **IUSTINUS I AUGUSTUS**

Justinus

See below **IUSTINUS II AUGUSTUS**

[Justus]

The prevalence of this name and its variants amongst his posterity strongly suggest that this man was actually called Justus, but this is nowhere attested; only his lowly bucolic origins.

Justus

With his brother Boraïdes, he seized *HYPATIUS* in the Hippodrome during the *Nika* riot in 532 and dragged him before the emperor for judgement. A decade later and he *was magister militum*, probably serving against the Persians in the East. He fell ill and died whilst still *en post* and was succeeded by his nephew Marcellus, brother of **JUSTIN II** [PLRE III Justus 2].

Justus

He died in the lifetime of his parents, probably at no great age and was buried in the Sophianae Palace chapel in Constantinople [PLRE III Justus 3].

Marcellus

See above **Table LXIII(b) Brief Lives**

Marcianus

We only know of his relationship to **JUSTIN II** but not the names of his parents. Conant asserts that his mother was the sister of Germanus' wife Passara. Described as an experienced and brave soldier, he was appointed *dux* in Arcadia (Egypt) in 549/550, and later in 563 *magister militum,* suppressing a Moorish revolt in Africa, being made a patrician and styled *vir gloriosissimus* for his pains. In 572 he was sent to the eastern frontier as *magister militum*, gaining some minor successes before winning the Battle of Sargathon. He was later on the point of taking Nisibis after a long siege when he was replaced by the emperor who considered his efforts insufficiently vigorous. He was insultingly told of his dismissal by the emissary Acacius (no relation of the Empress Theodora) in front of the army, with whom he was popular, and as a result the troops refused to continue the siege. PLRE separates the Egyptian *dux* and the later Patrician, however [PLRE III Marcianus 6, 7, cf. Conant (2012) 221-222 & n. 110].

Matasuntha

An Ostrogothic princess, she was the daughter of the Eutharicus Cilliga, and Amalasuintha, the daughter of the King of Italy, Theodericus. She was also sister of the youthful King Athalaricus (526-534). She was born c. 520 and in 536 was obliged to marry her brother's successor, the non-Royal Vitiges (Witigis, reigned 536-538), by whom she had no issue. In 540 Belisarius (qv **Table LXIX(b) Brief Lives**) carried both of them off to Constantinople, but she was widowed two years later. Her marriage to Germanus was probably in 549. This alliance made her a *patricia*, very possibly in her own right, rather than as the wife of a patrician [PLRE III Matasuntha].

Passara

Died before 549 when Germanus re-married, and was said to have been a member of the Anicii. If the latter statement is true, then it is not clear how she was so related, but it would have been to the Pertronii rather than the surviving Anicii proper, for the former had relocated to Constantinople. Perhaps she was another descendant of **OLYBRIUS** [PLRE II Passara].

Praeiecta

She accompanied her husband Areobindus to Africa in 545, later as a widow, falling into the hands of *GUNTHARIS*, by whom she was well treated, but obliged to write to **JUSTINIAN** defending the imperial claimant's actions. Had he not been overthrown, she would have become his wife and indeed, the claimant's Armenian *nemesis*, Artabanes, also intended to marry her, but this was prevented by the emperor, who encouraged her subsequent marriage to Johannes, a prince of the house of **ANASTASIUS I** [PLRE III Praeiecta 1].

Sabbatius

He was living at a fortress called Bederiana (Bader) hard by Tauresium (Gradiste, Macedonia), in the 480s when **JUSTINIAN** was born, suggesting his father may have been an army officer but not necessarily a native of the area (i.e. Thracian). Nevertheless, the original form of his name Istok, certainly sounds ethnic. The transmission of his name to his son as second element, suggests that it was a surviving example of a *nomen* and if so, might suggest that Sabbatius came from a part of the empire where the older form of nomenclature was still in use, like Africa, Illyricum or Noricum. He is likely to have been dead before either his son or his brother-in-law became emperor [Fauber (1990) 9; PLRE III Sabbatius].

Sittas

See below **Table LXIX(b) Brief lives**

Sophia Aelia

Sophia was a *patricia* before 565. Apart from her two children, she had a niece, Helena, whose statue once adorned the capital. Unfortunately it is not clear whether this lady was related through her husband or her own family, so Helena is omitted from **TABLE LXIX(a)**. The name Aelia (sometimes shown borne before her given name of Sophia), was an imperial embellishment added after she became Augusta in 565. She was the first empress to have appeared on coins with the emperor. When the Emperor became mentally ill, she governed on his behalf with the future **TIBERIUS II,** whom she had recommended as successor, although once he had succeeded she refused to allow his wife and family into the palace out of jealousy. This resulted in her being given a household of her own, being permitted to retain the title of Augusta, and where she lived, under the arms-length control of a picked staff. Last heard of in 601, she may have perished in the massacres that followed the elevation of **PHOCAS** [PLRE II Helena I, Sophia 1]

Strategius

Made a patrician before 557 and died by 586. He was a *comes* and somewhat later a *vir gloriosissimus* and held high office in his family's native Egypt [PLRE III Strategius 3, 5, 7].

Strategius

Born between 594 and 598, and living in 603, being mentioned in a letter to his mother from Pope Gregory (himself a member of the Anicii). He had more than one sister [PLRE III Strategius 8].

Theodora

See above **IUSTINIANUS I AUGUSTUS**

Theodora

Believed (but not certainly proved) to have been Baduarius's daughter, she was joint owner with him of a town house in Constantinople, once in the family of the Areobindi. Alternatively, she could have been a second wife of Baduarius [PLRE III Theodora 2]

Theodorus *qui et* Tzirus

Son of an unidentified Justinianus and it is highly likely that this reference was to the future emperor of whom he would therefore have been a natural son. He was appointed *magister militum* in the east in 573 by **JUSTIN II** to replace his cousin Marcianus (qv) who was publicly sacked, but he is not heard of again [PLRE III Theodorus 31].

Tiberius Constantinus

See below **TIBERIUS II AUGUSTUS**

Vigilantia

She was still alive in 565 and able to advise her brother **JUSTINIAN I** to name **JUSTIN II** as his heir. She was apparently commemorated by a statue in Constantinople [PLRE II & III Vigilantia].

Vig[ilantius]

Although the name of the brother of **JUSTIN I** is nowhere recorded, the fragment datable to 511 and reading Vig[.......], a *vir gloriosissimus,* found at Apamea (Qalaat al-Madiq, Syria) may refer to him. The name, if expanded to Vigilantius, would be a highly probable one in the context. There is nothing against him having had a distinguished career by this date [PRE II Vig.....].

Vitiges

His name is thus spelt on his coins, although it is frequently rendered elsewhere as Vuitigis [= Witigis]. He rose to prominence as a soldier under Theodericus in 504. Under Athalaricus he became a *spatharius* (imperial bodyguard, the name derived from the longer, late Roman fighting sword, the *spatha*) after 526, and rose to become the commander of this élite group in 534. He was chosen as king on the deposition of Theodahad in 536, despite his non-Royal origins, and was married to Matasuntha to cement his position in December 536, or in January the year following. His defence of Italy against Belisarius ended in failure, partly through his inability to ally with any other Germanic peoples, like the Franks and Lombards. After the fall of Ravenna, he ended up in Constantinople with his wife, where **JUSTINIAN** treated him with honour making him a patrician. Many of his fellow Visigothic companions were sent to the east by the Emperor to fight the Persians in 541, but he did not join them and he died the following year; it may have been that he had some illness that prevented him from rejoining his troops [PLRE III Vitigis].

*

TABLE LXIX(b): THE CONNECTIONS OF THEODORA

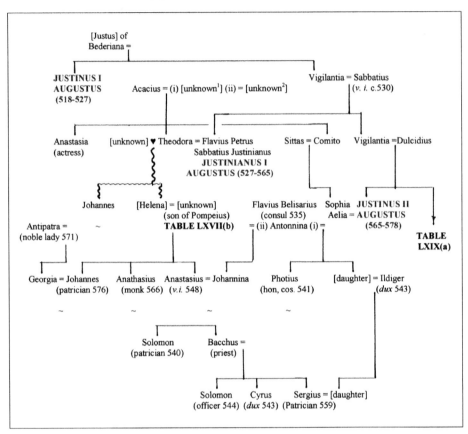

TABLE LXIX(b): BRIEF LIVES

Acacius

Keeper of the animals at the circus at Constantinople for the Green faction. His wife, whose name is not recorded, was a dancer and actress. He was possibly a native of Cyprus, and had another wife (presumably after having married the Empress's mother) dying in c. 516/518 [PLRE III *sub* Theodora 1].

Anastasia

A younger daughter, she is thought to have followed her mother onto the stage [PLRE III Anastasia 1].

Anastasius

He was certainly betrothed to the daughter of Belisarius, c 543; the marriage was celebrated in 548, the year of Theodora's death; possibly her passing facilitated it. Although a grandson of the empress, it is not wholly certain that he was a full blood brother of Athanasius and Johannes [PLRE III Anastasius 8].

Athanasius

Grandson of Theodora, presumably as set out in **Table LXIX (b)**. He was a Monophystie and by 566 was a monk, and in that year was hoping to be made Monophysite bishop of Alexandria.

Missing out, his heresy became more extreme and he resorted to using his personal wealth to bribe people into becoming his followers. His will left much of his property to **JUSTIN II** and the Empress Sophia, although he fell out with another legatee but died before he could alter his will [PLRE III Athanasius 5].

Comito

Eldest daughter, she was only seven years old when her father died. As a result she was swiftly put on the stage in order to keep the family finances topped up. She married in 528 so was probably born c. 509/511 [PLRE III Comito].

Dulcidius

See above, **Table LXIX(a) Brief Lives.**

Flavius Belisarius

See box above, *sub* **IUSTINIANUS I AUGUSTUS**

Flavius Petrus Sabbatius Justinianus

See above **IUSTINIANUS I AUGUSTUS**

[Helena]

Her name is not certain, nor her parentage, but some circumstantial evidence suggests that she was called Helena.

Johannes

See above **Table LXVIII(b) Brief Lives**

Justinus

See above **IUSTINUS I AUGUSTUS**

Sabbatius

See above **TABLE LXIX(a) Brief Lives.**

Sittas

He may have been of Gothic descent, and married Comito in 528 having met his wife when he was serving as a bodyguard under **JUSTINIAN I** when he was still *magister militum* and merely betrothed to his future sister-in-law. He then served successfully under Belisarius in Armenia and was later, in 528, made *magister militum* there serving until 539, scoring several victories against the Persians and securing a peace accord thereafter. He was made patrician by 535 and an honorary consul a year later. Although widely acknowledged as one of the best generals of his age and a fine warrior, he was killed in an ambush whilst fighting the Persians in 539 [PLRE III Sittas 1].

Sophia Aelia

See below *sub* **IUSTINUS II AUGUSTUS**

Theodora

See above **Theodora Augusta** *sub* **IUSTINIANUS I AUGUSTUS**

Vigilantia

Her name, locally, was rendered Bigleniza (= Vigilantia) [Fauber (1990) 8].

Vigilantia

See above **Table LXIX(a) Brief Lives.**

*

TABLE LXIX(c): THE POSTERITY OF GERMANUS

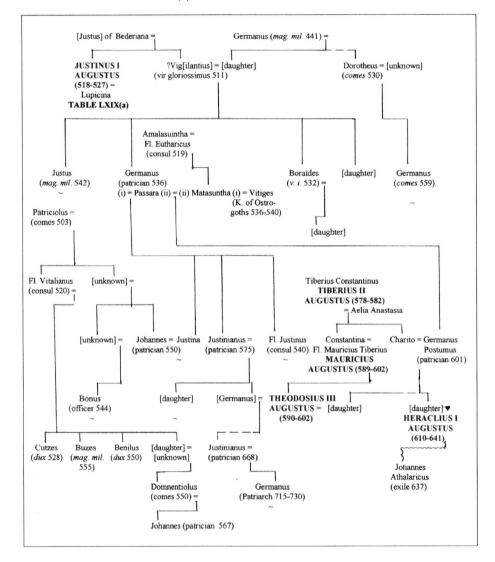

TABLE LXIX(c): BRIEF LIVES

Amalasuintha

Daughter of Theodericus, Ostrogothic King of Italy by his second marriage to Audefleda, sister of Clovis I, King of the Franks. She was well educated and fluent in Latin and Greek as well as pro-Roman. She acted as regent for her son Athalaricus until he died, leaving her as titular Queen, the power inherent in which style she devolved by nomination upon Theodahad, who at first neutralised her and on April 30th 535 had her strangled in her bath [PLRE II Amalasuintha; Moorhead (1992) 229].

Benilus

Attested as brother of Buzes and therefore also brother of Cutzes and by clear inference son of

Vitalianus. He first comes to notice as a commander of Roman forces in Lazica (Western Georgia) 550-551 but was unable or incapable of facing down a Persian force on the River Phasis and is not heard of again, so perhaps killed or ignominiously dismissed [PLRE III Benilus].

Bonus

He was Roman garrison commander in Genua (Genoa) in 544. His name was subsequently used falsely by Gothic spies in attempt to draw Belisarius from Pola (Pula) [PLRE III p, 212 and Bonus 2].

Boraïdes

See above, **Table LXIX(a) Brief Lives**

Buzes

Born about 497, *dux* at Palmyra in 528 when, with his brother Cutzes (*dux* in Damascus), he was sent with troops to re-inforce Belisarius in the East, where he served with some distinction until 531. He was sent to command a force against the Armenians in 539, but his efforts only managed to drive them into the arms of the Persians. *Magister militum* in the East 540-542, a command he shared with Belisarius. He was honorary consul in 542 when he was locked up at Constantinople for three years for having irked the Empress Theodora, which broke his health. Nevertheless, he had recovered enough to command a force in Italy in 549, before in 554 being again made *magister militum* in Lazica (Eastern Georgia) for two years. He was described as an experienced general but inclined to be headstrong [PLRE III Buzes].

Charito

She married Germanus in 582 [PLRE III Charito]

Constantina

Originally she bore the personal name of Augusta, but she was re-christened Constantina

by her father on her betrothal in August 582 to **MAURICIUS,** and the imperial *praenomen* Aelia was added when she became Augusta (by 585) in style rather than by name. Had she not done so, she would have become Augusta Augusta! After her husband's murder she was put under house arrest with her three daughters, moving after being involved in a failed *coup* to a convent. Further evidence construed by **PHOCAS** as plotting against him resulted in her murder, along with her daughters in 605 or 607 [PLRE III Constantina 1].

Cutzes

Presumed, through his relationship to Buzes and Benilus (qqv), to have been a third son of Vitalianus (the alternative is that he or one of the others might have been a distaff half-sibling). As a young officer in 528 he was appointed *dux,* based at Damascus, his brother Buzes holding a similar position at Palmyra. He later became a Persian Prisoner of War (PoW) and is not heard of again [PLRE III Cutzes].

Domnentiolus

His parents' names are unknown. He served as an junior officer under his uncle Buzes against the Persians but in 531 was captured and became a PoW. He returned after an exchange of prisoners and in 545 re-appears as a commander on the Eastern front, where he campaigned with notable success and returned with much plunder. He is last heard of defending Messana (Messina, Sicily) against the Gothic King Totila in 550 [PLRE III Domnentiolus].

Dorotheus

He came from Bederiana, so could well have been close kin (thus perhaps brother-in-law) to **JUSTIN I**. That his son was called Germanus greatly strengthens the suggestion. He appears to have been a cavalry commander under Belisarius at the battle of Dara in 530, probably as *comes*. He would thus have owed his position to his kinship with the emperor. He may also be identifiable with the man of this name who was made an honorary consul at some time in this era [PLE III Dorotheus 1, 5, 11].

Flavius Eutharicus Cilliga

An Ostrogothic prince, he was the grandson of Beremudus (a younger son of King Thorismudus) and son of Vetericus. He lived in Spain (where his grandfather had settled), from whence he was summoned by Theodericus to marry Amalasuintha in 515. He was Western consul in 519 with **JUSTIN I** (who apparently adopted him as his 'son in arms') as his eastern colleague, all clearly arranged to indicate that Eutharicus was Theodericus's designated successor. An Arian, he was an opponent of orthodox Christians but had died before 526 [PLRE II Beremudus, Eutharicus, Thorismudus, Vetericus; Moorhead (1992) 201]

Flavius Just[inus]

In full his name was Flavius Mar[cianus] Petr[us] Theodor[us] Valent[inus] Rust[ic(i)us] Boraïd[es] Germ[anus] Just[inus] (restored here from PLRE). It is not entirely certain that this is absolutely correct, thanks to its abbreviated state on his consular diptych. The second element might be Marcellus which also occurs in the Imperial family or the Christian name Marianus; Marcius is less likely at this date. Likewise, it is just possible the *Petr*[ ] could be Petronius, especially if his mother was indeed of Anician/Petronian stock. By the same token, if she was a descendant of the second marriage of **OLYBRIUS** the *Valent*[ ] element could represent Valentinianus. He was in 540 a youthful *vir inlustris*, (honorary) *comes domesticorum* and the penultimate ordinary consul. In 549 he was instrumental in foiling

a plot against the emperor and in the 550s he commanded armies against the Slavs and also against the Persian, ending up as *magister militum* in Armenia from 557. In 561 he held an important appointment on the Danube frontier, but after being appointed *dux et augustalis* (military commander and governor, a definite step down) of Alexandria by **JUSTIN II** in 566, he was assassinated in 568, allegedly for plotting against the emperor because his position in the family and respect in the empire had aroused the jealousy of the emperor [PLRE III Justinus 4].

Flavius Mauricius Tiberius
See below **MAURICIUS AUGUSTUS**

Flavius Vitalianus
Born in Zaldaba (Zaldapa) in Thrace, he was perhaps of ultimate Gothic descent and was in some manner related to a monk called Leontius and a senator called Stephanus. He was not very tall and stammered but was high spirited and a fine general. He served as his father's legate in Persia in 503 and was made *comes* in charge of barbarian allies in 512, after which the government's refusal to provide his federate troops with supplies incited his first rebellion against **ANASTASIUS I** in whose side he remained a thorn for the remainder of his reign. He batted away attempts at mediation, held *HYPATIUS* hostage and treated him badly, twice invested the capital before being bought off with a bribe and the post of *magister militum* in Thrace (514-515). **ANASTASIUS** had a habit of breaking his word in negotiations, prompting a third rebellion in 515 during which Vitalianus was finally defeated. In 518 **JUSTIN I** came to terms with his turbulent subject and in 518 he was made honorary consul, *comes* and *magister militum* (home HQ). Shortly afterwards he became patrician, was styled *vir magnificus* and was Eastern consul in 520, the

year he was liquidated (in July) probably by **JUSTINIAN** [PLRE II Leontius 26, Stephanus 22, Vitalianus 2]

Germanus 441
See above **Table LXIX(a) Brief Lives**

Germanus 536
See above **Table LXIX(a) Brief Lives**

Germanus 559
He was taken up by **JUSTINIAN I** as a young man, being a member of a family from the same home town, as the emperor; it is likely that they were related, too, as with Fl. Justinus (qv above). As a relatively young man he was appointed *comes rei militaris* in 559, stationed in the Thracian Chersonese (Crimea) where he defeated a determined attack by a force of Huns, but thereafter nothing is heard of him [P LRE III Germanus 4].

[Germanus]
We have the word of Gregory of Tours that the son of the patrician Justinianus married **TIBERIUS'S** daughter, but he does not actually name him. Nevertheless, the identification with Germanus seems unambiguous. He was possibly a victim of **PHOCAS** in 602 [Greg., *HF* v 30; PLRE III Germanus 5].

Germanus Postumus
Born after the death of his father (as his name implies) in winter 550/551. Intriguingly the Gothic historian Jordanes celebrates his birth as uniting the Anicii with the Gothic royal house of the Amali. Had he been a son of Passara he would, as we have seen, been an almost certain descendant of **OLYBRIUS** and thus an Anician, but unless his great-grandfather Germanus (*magister militum* in 441, see above **Table LXIX(a) Brief Lives**) was married to a member

of that illustrious family, the passage would have to be dismissed as rhetoric. As Jordanes is generally fairly reliable, this is unlikely. Settipani equates this man and the Caesar of 582, as the son of Germanus 559 and Matasuntha and the husband of Charito, as here. Thus in 582, when he married, he was already *magister miltum* and patrician. He was thereupon, on August 5th that year, along with **MAURICIUS** declared **nobilissimus Caesar.** He appears to have declined the honour for within a week he seems no longer to have been so described. He thereafter retired to a private station in life. It is probable, bearing in mind so distinguished an ancestry, that he was the patrician recorded as a leading member of the senate in the later years of **MAURICIUS** whose daughter married **THEODOSIUS III,** the Emperor's eldest son whom he rescued from an angry mob in February 602 (see also below, **MAURICIUS AUGUSTUS**). He was later accused by the emperor of having designs on the throne (hence the strong likelihood that he is one and the same with Germanus and Matasuntha's son) and when **MAURICIUS** was deposed, **PHOCAS** considered making him emperor, but in the end assumed the purple himself. He was later again suspected of aspiring to the purple and was forcibly tonsured. Sometime later he was discovered to have been exchanging secret messages with the empress Constantina and was executed in 605 or 607. [Jordanes, *Getica,* 314; PLRE III Germanus 3, 11; Settipani (2000) 429].

Germanus
Son of Justinianus the patrician; castrated as a child and tonsured, later Bishop of Cyzicus. Patriarch of Comstantinople as (St.) Germanus I 715-730; he resigned when the emperor adopted the Muslim inspired policy of iconoclasm, and died 732/740 at a great age.

Heraclius

Flavius Heraclius was the son of Heraclius a Georgian/Armenian and Exarch of Africa in the reign of **PHOCAS**. In 608 both men raised the standard of revolt against him and in 610 entered Constantinople deposed and executed him, the younger **HERACLIUS** assuming the purple. He was the first emperor to change the language of official business in the empire from Latin to Greek, although the Latin formula **D[ominus] N[oster Flavius] Heraclius Perpetuus Augustus** continued to appear on his coins. He finally defeated the Persian empire, restoring the True Cross to Jerusalem from whence King Chostroes had removed it, but whilst still reeling from the gruelling campaigns, was faced with having to counter the first *Jihad*. In a decade the empire lost Egypt, Palestine and Syria, leaving it permanently weakened. **HERACLIUS** married twice, first to Fabia Eudocia in 610 (died in childbirth 612) and then to his niece Martina, and had a large family by them [PLRE III Heraclius 3, 4, Eudocia, Martina]

Johannes

He was a famous and successful military man even in 537, when he was made *magister militum* at Home HQ and sent to Italy to re-inforce Belisarius. There followed twelve years of varying success and petty disagreements with colleagues as the war against the Goths fluctuated. At the end of that time he was transferred with the same rank to Illyricum where he served until 553. During that time he fought a successful sea battle against the Goths off Ancona. Later he was Narses' right hand man in his 552-553 campaign in Italy. We thereafter lose sight of him, but he may well have been the Johannes who as patrician, was *magister militum* in Italy in 599 or be identifiable with another man of this name then campaigning in Italy who was an honorary consul, a *vir gloriosus* and *magister militum* [PLRE III Johannes 46, 71,72].

Johannes

Sometimes called Johannes of Callinicum (Syria) which, however, was not his place of origin, but one in which he had notable discussions with Monophysites. In 562 he held a financial post in Constantinople, in which year he also revealed a plot against **JUSTINIAN I** in 562 which appears to have resulted in his being made patrician by 567 when he was sent as ambassador to the Persians. This seems to have gone badly as far as **JUSTIN II** was concerned and he was cashiered, dying the same year [PLRE III Johannes 81].

Johannes *qui et* Athalaricus

A son born to the future Emperor **HERACLIUS I** by a mistress who is not identified in the sources. From his name – suggesting a descent from Matasuntha (sister of the Gothic King Athalaric, successor of Theoderic,) and thus through Germanus Postumus, it suggests that this man's mother was either **THEODOSIUS III's** wife or a sister. He was exiled after becoming involved in a plot against **HERACLIUS** in 635/637, and nothing more is heard of him [PLRE III 260].

Justina

She was kept unmarried through the hostility of the empress to her father but in 545, despite Theodora, she was married to the patrician Johannes (qv). It is probable that the empress raised no serious objection as her husband was of inferior rank [PLRE III Justina1].

Justinianus

Born c. 525/530, he embarked on an unremarkable military career, commanding troops in Italy in 550-551 and in Illyricum in 552, going on to aid the Lombards in their effective ethnic cleansing of the Gepidae in the NE. In 572 he held the rank of patrician when appointed *magister militum* in Armenia, going on to hold the same appointment in the East generally to 577, where he followed some successes with two major defeats at the hands of the Persian King, Chosroes I, being dismissed for his pains. In 578 when **JUSTIN II** died, an attempt was made to put him on the throne, but which failed. A further attempted *coup* instigated by the dowager empress Sophia also ended in failure and on both occasions **TIBERIUS II** pardoned him [PLRE III Justinianus 3].

Justinianus

A patrician when executed in 668 in a plot against **CONSTANS III;** his son, significantly bearing the name Germanus, considered a threat to the dynasty of **HERACLIUS**, was castrated and put into a monastery, but later became Bishop of Cyzicus. His name strongly suggests his descent from the family of **JUSTINIAN** and hence merits inclusion on this table, as does that of his son, the Patriarch [Settipani (2000) 430].

Justinus

See above **IUSTINUS I AUGUSTUS**

[Justus]

See above **TABLE LXIX(a) Brief Lives**

Justus

With Boaraïdes, he seized H*YPATIUS* from his throne in the Hippodrome and dragged him before **JUSTINIAN I**, who, at the prompting of Theodora, condemned him to death. A decade

later Justus was made *magister militum* at court, being sent to the East to bolster resistance to the Persians, serving there until his death from disease in 544 [PLRE III Justus 2].

Matasuntha

See above **TABLE LXIX(a) Brief Lives**

Passara

See above **TABLE LXIX(a) Brief Lives**

Patriciolus

Possibly of Gothic descent, he was an officer in the wars against Persia in the reign of **ANASTASIUS I** where he gained some success; in the period following he seems to have been *comes* in charge of barbarian federate forces and to have joined his son's rebellion in 513 [PLRE II Patriciolus].

Theodosius

See below **THEODOSIUS III AUGUSTUS**

Tiberius Constantinus

See below **TIBERIUS II AUGUSTUS**

Vig[ilantius]

See above **TABLE LXIX(a) Brief Lives**

Vitiges

See above **TABLE LXIX(a) Brief Lives**

⋆

HYPATIUS
18th - 23rd January 532

Background

One of the three closest relations of **ANASTASIUS I** was Flavius *HYPATIUS*, son of the emperor's sister Caesaria and Secundinus. This familial proximity had two consequences: first, that he was destined for a brilliant career, and secondly that he was always going to be vulnerable during transitions of power. His brother Pompeius and cousin Probus were also in the same position, and enjoyed equally illustrious careers thanks to their proximity to the purple, although **ANASTASIUS** passed all three over for the succession as a result of all three failing a capricious exercise in sortition.

Hypatius (a Greek name, it means 'consul') was born c. 475 and served against the Isaurian rebels in the 490s before holding the eastern consulship for 500, serving unsuccessfully thereafter as *magister militum* in 503 as co-commander against Persia, where his failure was ascribed to inexperience. He was replaced in 505. In 513 he was re-appointed to the same post but in Thrace, where he provoked Vitalianus by insulting his wife, which resulted in Vitalianus's second revolt. He was re-appointed and sent against the rebel, but was defeated and taken prisoner by him, being held prisoner until 514. He was appointed *magister militum* in the east 516-518 and again from 520 to 525 (by which time he had been made patrician), but was relieved of office by **JUSTIN I**, probably on trumped-up grounds. He was made *magister militum* in the east a third time in 527, concluding a successful treaty and serving for nearly two years until the prospect of further conflict caused the emperor to replace the somewhat unmilitary prince with Belisarius. By the time the *Nika* Riot broke out, he was retired and living at his palace in Constantinople.

Reign

The *Nika* riot began on 13th January 532, and there is no suggestion that *HYPATIUS* was involved in it at that stage. However, as matters got increasingly desperate and it looked inevitable that **JUSTINIAN** would be deposed, the more influential senators and others, aided and abetted by the rioters, decided that **ANASTASIUS'S** nephew Probus would make an ideal candidate for the purple. He, however, was prudently absent, and the resentful mob burned his palace down in any case before moving on to acclaim his cousin *HYPATIUS,* another man who would made an ideal interim ruler with impeccable credentials. On the 18th he was tracked down, taken to the Forum of Constantine, gowned in purple and crowned with a gold diadem and duly acclaimed emperor; being accepted as such throughout most of the city. About four days later, with the riot brutally crushed, order was restored and *HYPATIUS* and his brother Pompeius were arrested and brought before the emperor, who was inclined to be merciful, being aware that his elevation had been *force majeur*. Unfortunately, Theodora was implacable, and he was condemned to death, facing his end with courage. His body was afterwards thrown into the sea. **JUSTINIAN** is said to have raised a cenotaph to commemorate him when his corpse was washed up later. No official style has survived and no coins were minted in those few chaotic days.

Family

The family of is set out in **Table LXVIII(a) & Brief Lives**. His grandson Johannes married the sister of **JUSTINIAN'S** successor **JUSTIN II**, thus binding the family firmly back into the Imperial circle: see also **TABLE LXIX**. Petrus, a patrician living in 578, was his great-grandson and, by another descent Strategius, a 'noble youth' living 603 was his last certain descendant.

*

MAXIMINUS III
539

Background

MAXIMINUS was an officer of the bodyguard of Theodorus, *magister militum* in Africa in 537. He planned a revolt, but the emperor's kinsman Germanus, in order to neutralise the threat he potentially posed and in some way to assuage his ambition, appointed him commander of his own bodyguard. He nevertheless persisted in his plans but, having made a *pronunciamento,* the mutiny was promptly put down and its leader, described by Procopius as a *tyrannus* and therefore an imperial claimant, was brought before Germanus, condemned and executed at Carthage in 539 [PLRE III Maximinus 1; Conant (2012) 216]

*

STOTZAS I
?536/541-October 545

Background

The *magister militum* Martinus was one of the leaders (in his case of the federate troops) of the expedition against the Vandals in Africa in 533 and the commander of his personal guard was **Stotzas**. Three years later, there was a mutiny in the army and the ringleaders chose **Stotzas** as their leader. They proposed to throw the remainder of the imperial contingent out of the province and seize control. He besieged Carthage at the head of more than 9,000 soldiers, but raised the siege on the appearance of Belisarius, who defeated him, causing him to withdraw into Numidia, where he started a rebellion amongst the troops there too. At one time almost two thirds of the Roman forces in North Africa had gone over to him, although significant numbers later deserted when the Prince Germanus arrived late in 536 and announced that there would be no reprisals for those prepared to return to the imperial cause.[910]

The following year **Stotzas**, supported by Moorish and Vandal allies, fought Germanus's forces at Cellas Veteres (Fedj-es-Siouda, Algeria) after which he took refuge in Mauretania, where he married the daughter of one of the Moorish princes there and settled.[911]

Reign

One chronicler specifically avers that in 541 he assumed the purple in his own name, and he is elsewhere referred to as a *tyrannus*, the normal term for an imperial claimant. It seems odd that he should have waited until five years after his (largely unsuccessful) revolt to so style himself, and it may be that he assumed the imperial style when he first was chosen as the leader of the uprising in 536. We have no record of the way he was styled, but it was presumably **Dominus Noster Stotzas Pater Patriae Augustus.** If there was a provincial *concilium* so soon after the *reconquista* of Africa, it may or may not have acknowledged him.

In 544 *STOTZAS* tried again to assert his control and defeated a Roman force, possibly that of the praetorian prefect of Africa Solomon, at the Battle of Cillium (Kassarine, Tunisia), after which he left Mauretania and plundered Byzacena, where he suborned more recruits from the regular forces there. He went on to plunder other cities in the Province of Africa itself, but he was killed in battle against the *magister militum* Johannes who was also killed in the engagement. Amazingly, this did not end the rebellion and he was succeeded by one Johannes, otherwise *STOTZAS II*. We know nothing of his family.

*

STOTZAS II
October 545-546

Johannes was a commander under *STOTZAS I* who was elected as his successor on the claimant's death in battle by a motley collection of 500 Romans, 80 Huns and over 400 Vandals. He was henceforth known as *STOTZAS II* or *STOTZAS JUNIOR*. Soon after his elevation his forces marched on Carthage along with Moorish allies and encouraged a second Roman revolt under *GUNTHARIS*, allowing him to take Carthage after a battle with the prince Areobindus (**TABLE LXIX(b) Brief Lives**), who was killed. Later, after the fall of *GUNTHARIS*, he was captured and sent in chains to Constantinople where he was crucified.[912]

---

910. At this juncture another officer of a gubanatorial bodyguard (that of Germanus and Theodorus the Cappadocian) called Maximinus attempted to establish himself as a breakaway imperial claimant through the medium of a mutiny but failing a placatory promotion, he was anticipated and executed: PLRE III Maximinus 1.
911. PLRE III Stotzas ; Conant (2012) 216, 301-302.
912. PLRE III Ioannes 35

GUNTHARIS
December 545-January 546

Background

GUNTHARIS was a Roman officer of Frankish descent, first coming to notice in 540 as a member of the personal guard of the patrician Solomon, commanding in Africa as Belisarius's successor. By his rapid action the proconsul was saved from certain defeat whilst leading a pre-emptive strike against rebellious Moors. Solomon was later killed at the Battle of Cillium (against STOTZAS I qv), due to the treacherous performance of GUNTHARIS who had fled at the crucial moment. Nevertheless, he was later in 545 made *magister militum* and *dux* of forces in Numidia under the patrician Sergius, who thereafter left Africa for the capital. Encouraged by STOTZAS II, GUNTHARIS therefore plotted rebellion, persuading the Moors to attack Carthage, which led to his being recalled from Numidia by the new Commander, Areobindus, to assist with the City's defence. He acted treacherously throughout, hoping his commander would be killed in battle allowing him to seize power opportunely, but this failed, so he finally allied with the Moors whom he allowed to over-run Carthage, defeating Areobindus, who was soon afterwards murdered at his instigation.[913]

Reign

He established himself in the Imperial palace at Carthage and planned to marry Praejecta, Areobindus's widow, sister of the future emperor **JUSTIN II** and niece of **JUSTINIAN** (see **Tables LXVIII(a) & LXIX(a) Brief Lives**) Whether his style as claimant was the expected **Dominus Noster Guntharis Pater Patriae Augustus** or not is unknown in the absence of coins. Procopius describes him as *basileus* and both he and STOTZAS II as *tyranni*, terms clearly indicating that they wore the purple. His first project was the reduction of the Moors in Byzacena in order to extend his rule over more of North Africa, and he despatched a force under the command of an Armenian, Artabanes but, after a perfunctory victory, Artabanes returned for re-inforcements, and contrived to assassinate the imperial claimant during the banquet held on the evening prior to the despatch of the re-inforced army. Although he subsequently gave a pledge of safety to STOTZAS II he soon afterwards had him sent to Constantinople where he was killed.[914]

*

---

913. Conant (2012) 223-2243
914. PLRE III Artabanes 2, Guntharis & Sergius 4.,

JUSTINUS II
(Known to history as Justin II)
14th November 565 – 5th October 578

Background

During the final years of the reign of **JUSTINIAN I**, his nephew, soon to succeed him, was said to have been the virtual ruler of the Empire. He had been born about 510, but his only known office was the largely honorific one of *cura palatii* (Head of the Imperial household), which he held from before 552, the year he was accorded the status of honorary consul. He spent the rest of the time trouble-shooting for the emperor: holding talks with Pope Vigilius, supervising the movement of peoples in the Balkans and twice supressing factional violence at Constantinople. He had long been a friend of his cousin Flavius Justinus, the Eastern consul in 540 (see above **TABLE LXIX(c) Brief Lives**) to the extent that an understanding existed between them that whichever of them succeeded to the purple would give the other second place in the empire. In the event, the new emperor felt too insecure to let this happen and had his kinsman demoted and then killed.[915]

Reign

The succession went very smoothly and **JUSTIN II** was crowned on the very day on which his uncle died. He was styled **Dominus Noster Justinus Pater Patriae Augustus** and acknowledged by the senate in the usual way. He held the ordinary consulship on his accession, and again the year following and for an unprecedented third time (for that period) in 568. He considered himself the embodiment of the old Roman virtues: courage, prudence, self-confidence and fortitude. He was confident (and naïve) enough to believe that these qualities could be applied to the governance of the empire, especially in his dealings with its enemies, and that he was the God-given instrument by which all might be achieved.

His first move therefore was to halt the payment of tribute to the various groups and polities which ringed the limits of the empire, the distribution of which **JUSTINIAN I** had used to channel the aggression of these peoples into defending the frontiers from yet more determined enemies swarming and mingling beyond. The policy had long proved successful, but **JUSTIN** was minded to halt payments. This had the unfortunate effect of re-igniting the Persian War and simultaneously turned the Tartarish Avars east of the Danube against the Empire as well, with the knock-on effect that in 568 the Lombards moved west and entered Italy, just after it had finally been re-conquered and before any serious reconstruction of its devastated infrastructure could begin.

At about the same time the emperor had appointed a formal governor of Italy, treating it more like one of the dioceses set up under the system initiated by **DIOCLETIAN**, and styling this new viceroy the exarch (*exarchus*), although the title was not recorded as such until 584. An official of similar rank also oversaw the control of Africa from that date.

---

915. PLRE III Justinus 5

Narses, who had taken over from Belisarius, was effectively the first Exarch of Italy, but his position was somewhat more anomalous in reality. He was succeeded by Longinus who served until 575.[916] The settlement left by Narses envisaged the separation of powers, in that the old civil and judicial system in Italy was restored and the military administration was in the hands of *duces*, answerable to the exarch. As the Lombards swarmed in and settled, their leaders were recruited as nominal Roman *duces*, and the duchies that were to dominate Italy for almost a millennium and a half began to evolve, some firmly under the control of Lombard freebooters and some under the direct control of the Exarch. The Lombard kingdom itself was finally contained within Northern and North West Italy and survived until absorbed into the restored Western Empire of Charlemagne. Nevertheless, it was under **JUSTIN II** that a large amount of southern Spain was re-conquered for the Empire.

In the aftermath, the death of the western provinces was to be slow, with their existence becoming increasingly notional; the exarchate itself survived until 751, after which the bulk of Eastern Imperial territory was given by Pippinus II, King of the Franks to Pope Stephen II who assumed the authority of the Exarch with it. The accession of the Eastern empress Irene in her own right (considered utterly *de trop* in the West), led directly to Charlemagne's restoration, with the connivance of the pope, of the Western Empire in 800. The remainder of Italy under imperial control in the north was annexed to Dalmatia and that in the south eventually became eastern imperial *themes* (military districts), snuffed out very gradually over more than three hundred years. The penumbra of the West was a long time fading.

Meanwhile in 571 came a turning point in the reign. On one hand **JUSTIN II** initiated a persecution against the Monophysites (amongst which he himself had been numbered in his younger days) which, although falling short of the creation of martyrs, led to a wholesale replacement of Monophysites in high office, a change which came about at a time when anything of the sort would have been best avoided. On the other hand, following the defeat of the Romans by the Persian army at Dara in November 573, the Emperor began to lose his sanity, suffering fits of child-like behaviour contrasting with attempts at self-defenestration and extreme violence. The empress therefore, took upon herself the day-to-day administration of the empire.

Finding this a severe burden, the Empress Sophia, in one of her husband's more lucid moments, persuaded him in 574 to adopt as heir the *magister militum* **Tiberius.** He was made **nobilissimus caesar** and at the end of September 578, promoted to the rank of co-Augustus as **TIBERIUS II**, about nine days before **JUSTIN** died on 5th October.

*

---

916. PLRE III Longinus 5.

TIBERIUS II
26th September 578 – 14th August 582

Background

Tiberius was a Thracian and was born c. 530, becoming a *notarius* (civil servant), soon entering the service of the future **JUSTIN II**. He was made *comes excubitorum* (commander of the guard) before the accession of his patron, a post he held until 574. Shortly after **JUSTIN'S** elevation, in 569, he was made *magister militum* (master of the soldiers, unattached) and the following year, after conducting negotiations with the Avars (which broke down due to the obduracy of the emperor), he soundly defeated them in Thrace, although the following year he suffered a defeat at their hands, but once again through adroit diplomacy and tactfulness managed to secure a satisfactory peace. After the end of 573, he assumed control of affairs at the behest of the Empress Sophia.

Reign

On 7th December 574 he was adopted as his son by **JUSTIN II,** proclaimed **nobilissimus caesar** and given the additional name of **Constantinus.** Nearly four years later, he was raised to the rank of co-Augustus on 26th September 578, and succeeded as sole ruler on 5th October. His style was **Dominus Noster Tiberius Constantinus Perpetuus Augustus**, although on some coin issues he is styled Constant[inus] Viv[at] Felix Au[gustus] ('Emperor Constantine, may you live in good fortune') which marked a radical change from the normal formula. More conventionally, another issue styles him D[ominus] N[oster] Tib[erius] Constan[tin]us P[er]p[etuus] Aug[ustus]. He held the ordinary consulship in 578 and again the following year. His accession was disputed by the patrician Justinianus, the great nephew of **JUSTIN I** (greatly encouraged by the dowager empress), but an assassination attempt organised by him right at the beginning of the sole reign failed miserably, although Justinianus was forgiven and his son (presumably Germanus, for no other son is known) was betrothed to the emperor's daughter Charito.[917]

One problem he faced in the east he had solved by making peace with the Persians, but at the expense of putting out of joint the nose of the Khan of the Turks, who enter history at this point. They had been promised an alliance by the Persians which promptly collapsed, leaving them exposed; they seized the Chersonese (Crimea) in revenge and proved difficult to dislodge.

TIBERIUS himself, however, provided a steady pair of hands, relatively popular and a pragmatist. His only Achilles heel was to overcompensate for the parsimony of his predecessor and indulge in an excess of liberality (which probably explained his popularity); his first act was to remit 25% of all taxes for a year, which was rash indeed. On the other hand, he ended to persecution of the Monophysites (although he remained antipathetic to the Arians, mainly because its adherents were mainly barbarian). He also cultivated the

---

917. Greg., *HF* v.30.

Greek speaking provinces, realising that the stability of the empire depended on this core element of which he himself, as a Thracian, was a representative. He also spent much of his reign strengthening the army, depleted by recruitment problems (a legacy of the plague of four decades before) and the thrifty inclinations of **JUSTIN.**

He died on 14th August 582, probably as a result of complications following food poisoning but, as with the demise of his more famous imperial namesake, it was rumoured that his repast of mulberries concealed a fatal potion. Perhaps the culprit was his *Comes Sacrarum Largitionum* (Keeper of the Privy Purse), desperate to stem losses to the treasury through the Emperor's ill-advised open handedness.[918]

Be that as it may, on his death-bed he adopted as his successor the successful *magister militum* **MAURICIUS,** who had returned not three days beforehand from the east, and whom he made **nobilissimus caesar** a mere eight days before expiring. There was, as a result, a smooth transition of power.[919]

Family

Quite early in his career the emperor had become betrothed to the daughter of an army adjutant called Johannes and of his wife, Ino, but both Johannes and the girl died, quite possibly of the plague, and he instead married the widow, Ino. When he became emperor she was given the name Aelia Anastasia instead.[920] She came originally from Daphnudium, probably an island off the Black Sea coast of modern Turkey.

The Empress Sophia was not struck on Ino and excluded her from the palace whilst **JUSTIN II** lived, but on his death she moved in with **TIBERIUS** and Sophia was set up in her own heavily protected household elsewhere. Ino was proclaimed Augusta by her husband in the wake of his sole accession and retained the style until her death in 593. One of their three children had died before **TIBERIUS** assumed the purple. The marriage of their daughter Constantina secured the succession, whilst that of his younger daughter Charito to Germanus incorporated the family of **TIBERIUS II** into that of **JUSTINIAN** and **ANASTASIUS.**

∗

---

918. We do not have the name of this official for 582 unfortunately.
919. PLRE III Tiberius 1
920. PLRE III Anastasia 2

MAURICIUS
(Known to history as Maurice)
13th August 582 – 27th November 602

Background

The new emperor was the son of Paulus and was born at Arabissus in Cappadocia (Afşin, formerly Yarpuzin, Turkey) in 539. It is said that Paulus, his father, was descended from a family originally from Rome itself. The source, Evagrius, does not claim that they were particularly aristocratic, and in view of the intensity of Roman settlement in the general area of Asia Minor over the previous 600 or so years the claim is entirely possible.[921] His mother's name is unknown, but one Damiana, daughter of Iannina, shared a niece with **MAURICE**, suggesting that she may have been herself a first cousin through the mother of the emperor.[922]

He embarked upon a bureaucratic career and was an *élève* of the Emperor **TIBERIUS** who made him commander of the *excubitores* (Imperial guard) with the rank of *comes*. He was still *en post* when he was appointed *magister militum* in the East, by which time he had been styled *vir illustris* and made a patrician. His task was to continue the war against Persia, which he did with considerable success, invading that empire twice, taking much booty and concluding in 581 with a favourable treaty. He returned in triumph to Constantinople in 582 and was probably named as **TIBERIUS'S** heir (as **nobilissimus Caesar**) on the strength of his success. The date was 5th August, and the Emperor was already dying. He was also betrothed to Constantina, the Emperor's daughter. He was proclaimed Augustus on the 13th August, the day before **TIBERIUS II** died, taking the additional name of Tiberius at the old emperor's request, and is sometimes consequently known as **MAURICE TIBERIUS**, but, as there was to be another two Emperors called Tiberius (one an imperial claimant in Sicily and another who reigned at Constantinople from 698-705), it is less confusing to prefer the style of **MAURICE** alone.[923]

Reign

MAURICE succeeded **TIBERIUS II** on 14th August, taking the style of **Dominus Noster Tiberius Perpetuus Augustus** and holding the ordinary consulship for 583.[924] The Empress, now called Constantina in lieu of Augusta, was duly appointed Augusta at some date before May 585.[925] In 587 he associated his eldest son with the purple by making him official heir with the title **nobilissimus caesar** before promoting him, aged about six, to co-Augustus. He was the first Emperor since **THEODOSIUS II** to have been born to a ruling emperor: he was thus *porphyrogenitus* – 'purple-born'.

---

921. Evagrius, Ecclesiastical History v. 19

922. She was the mother of Athenogenes, Bishop of Petra: PLRE III Damiane (*sic*).

923. Even so there was a claimant in Rome 643-644, *MAURICIUS II.*

924. PLRE III Mauricius 4.

925. PLRE III Constantina 1

The first success enjoyed by the new emperor was the ending of the very draining war with Persia. A civil war there enabled him to support one contender, Chosroes II and once established, the Great King agreed an extremely favourable settlement with the Empire in 591. **MAURICE** also formalised the exarchate of Ravenna to govern Italy, Sicily and other dependencies in the face of the Lombardic incursions there and established a second one at Carthage to control Africa in response to increasingly frequent Moorish attacks. These were essentially the old Praetorian Prefectures revived under a new name. He also re-ordered the provincial boundaries, taking into account more recent changes on the ground and making the empire somewhat easier to administer.

A serious problem was the fiscal profligacy of **TIBERIUS II,** which resulted in **MAURICE** being obliged to retrench, leading to pay reductions to the army, with the consequence of a mutiny having to be quelled in 588. Cuts were sought in all sorts of ways, one of which was the order to part of the army in the Balkans to over-winter on the inhospitable north bank of the Danube in 602, a decision which was to have dire consequences.

Indeed it was the incursions of the Avars in the Balkans which caused the biggest head-ache. Under **TIBERIUS,** Sirmium (Sremska Mitrovika, Serbia) had fallen and the immense agricultural and social disruption caused by the uncontrolled movement into settled communities of these barbarians had a deleterious effect on the economy of the Empire and tied down large military units which made heavy inroads upon the exchequer.

MAURICE also fell out with Pope Gregorius (Gregory the Great), who had objected to the Patriarch of Constantinople unilaterally adopting the title 'ecumenical'. Instead of placating the Pope as had happened on previous occasions, he supported his patriarch, thus causing a breach at a time when unity was of the essence. It was eventually patched up but was a straw in the wind in relation to events more than four centuries later.

Yet it was the emperor's attempts to replenish the treasury which led to his undoing. He refused to ransom some 12,000 prisoners taken by the Avars in 599, the result being that the barbarians called his bluff and slaughtered the lot. The decision to prevent part of the army on the Danube to remain beyond the river for the winter of 602-603 caused a mutiny, for the men, after a season's hard fighting had acquired much booty and without a return to base would have been unable to sell it in the city markets at home. Furthermore it would have deprived them of the comfort of their wives, families or mistresses. This placed the C-in-C Petrus, the emperor's brother, in a difficult situation, but he was firm and, as a result, a middle ranking officer with a previous record for general bolshiness called **PHOCAS**, was raised up as revolt-leader.

Petrus rushed back to Constantinople to warn his brother and to present the mutineers' demands, which included that **MAURICE** should abdicate in favour of **THEODOSIUS** or, failing him, his father-in-law, Germanus. The inevitable result was that both, who were away hunting, were recalled and accused of treason. This news leaked out and rioting instigated by the circus factions began, with the Greens baying for the emperor's blood. On 22nd November **MAURICE** and his family decided to leave the city, and **THEODOSIUS III** was sent on to obtain help from Chosroes II. Meanwhile, Germanus had been in sanctuary, and with the emperor gone, made a bid for the purple himself, but this failed for the same reason as the attempt by **MAURICE** to resist: the Greens refused to support him and instead opened the gate to armed military delegation led by **PHOCAS** which had just reached the vicinity of the capital. The following day he had himself crowned in a suburban church and on 24th November entered the City proper and obtained the recognition of the senate, made a donative to the army and raised his wife Leontia to the rank of Augusta.

The same day a detachment of the guard was sent to eliminate **MAURICE** and his family, prompted by shouts of 'Remember, Mauricius is not dead', during his inauguration. It was recorded that he died on 27th November, unresisting and with great dignity and, such was the detestable character of his successor, he was being widely mourned within weeks.

THEODOSIUS III
26th March 590 – 1st/2nd December 602

Eldest son of **MAURICE**, **THEODOSIUS** was born on 4th August either in 583 or 585 (the future Pope Gregory was his godfather), and was named after the last emperor to have been *porphyrogenitus*: **THEODOSIUS II**. He was proclaimed **nobilissimus caesar** sometime in 587 and raised to the purple on 26th March 590, taking the style **Dominus Noster Theodosius Perpetuus Augustus**. On 8th February 602 he married the Patrician Germanus's daughter, thus cementing his family to the dynasty of **JUSTINIAN** and to the family of **ANASTASIUS,** although it would seem that there was no move to make his wife, whose name is consequently unknown, Augusta. By the time of his death, there would appear to have been no issue.

When the revolt broke out in November 602, he was offered the chance to remain emperor if his father abdicated, but fled instead with his father, being sent on from Chalcedon where they landed, to liaise with Chosroes of Persia. Inexplicably, when arrested, his father recalled him, which sealed his death warrant, and he too was apparently killed at Calcedon on his return, accompanied by the patrician Constantinus Lardys, probably in the first few days of December. The words 'apparently' and 'probably' are used advisedly, as some accounts suggest that he did not obey his recall but made his way to Persia. More likely this story derived from the existence of an imposter sponsored by the general Narses, who soon afterwards rose against **PHOCAS** in Mesopotamia, exploiting these rumours. The false **THEODOSIUS** was then presented to Chosroes by Narses. The Great King claimed to have him with him and recognised him as rightful emperor, although the alleged pretender is subsequently said to have died in Lazica (Eastern Georgia). The Persian king, however, was only too keen to seize upon the chaos in the empire to regain territory lost in the 591 treaty and indeed, the war he waged over the following two decades was theoretically to right the wrongs meted out to the unfortunate **MAURICE**.[926]

---

926. PLRE III Narses 10, Theodosius 13

Either way, the dynastic succession which, by the interconnections of descent and marriage could plausibly be said to have originated with the rise of **PROBUS** in 274 came to an end with the destruction of the family of **MAURICE** and his son, leaving only a few fortunate survivors, like Germanus, to carry the line into the seventh century. If further posterity there still is, it must rest amongst the descendants of the Bagratids of what was later Georgia and that of the Visigothic princely houses that emerged in the aftermath of the Arab conquest of Spain.

*

TABLE LXX: THE FAMILY OF MAURICIUS

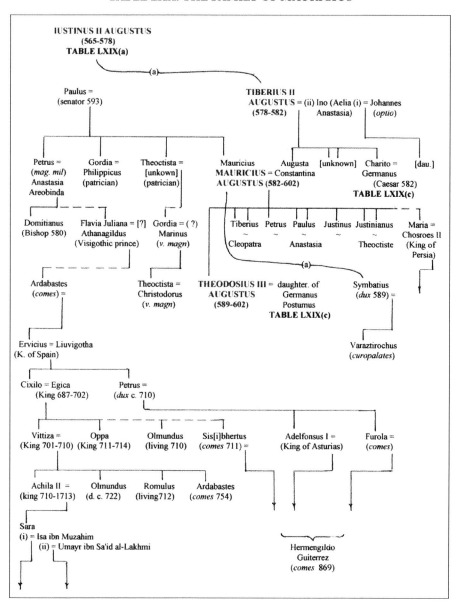

TABLE LXX: BRIEF LIVES

Abdu'r Rahman I ibn ºUmar ibn Said

By Sara he had a son, ancestor of Ibn al Qutiyya, who wrote a memoir of his family and who died in 989.

Achila II

King of the Visigoths in the North of Spain and later Narbo (Narbonne), Gerunda (Gerona) and Tarraco (Tarragona) 710-713, following the death of Vittiza. He was succeeded by a kinsman, Ardo, who lasted until 720.

Adelfonsus

As Alfonso I, he was King of the Asturias 739-757. He married Ermesinda, daughter of Pelagius, *comes et spatharius* of the last Visigothic King of all Spain, Rodericus (d. 711) and who became King of the Asturias in c. 720, dying in 737. His line died out with the death of his grandson Adelfonsus the Chaste (Alfonso II), King of the Asturias in 842.

Anastasia

Daughter of **MAURICE,** killed 605 or 607 [PLRE III Anastasia 2].

Anastasia Areobinda

For her family, see **Table LXIII(b) Brief Lives**; her name establishes her family, but her parentage is unclear. She may be identifiable with one or other of two *grandes dames* called Anastasia recorded with estates in Egypt at this period [PLRE III Anastasia 3, 4].

Andreas

A close connection of Theoctiste, **MAURICE'S** sister, possibly a second husband. He is mentioned in the letters of Pope Gregory, who styles him *vir illustris*. The family was then (597) at court in Constantinople. As the Emperor's sister, her title of *patricia* may not have been invalidated by marriage to a mere *illustris*, indeed, he may himself have been made a patrician before 602 [PLRE III Andreas 14].

Ardabastes

Comes, born c. 595 or c. 611, the name being a Latinisation of the aristocratic Persian/Armenian name Artavazd[es], suggesting Mamikonian ancestry; possibly he was descended from the Armenian *dux* Artabazes, killed in combat against the Goths outside Verona in 542. He was sent as *comes* by **HERACLIUS I** to imperial Spania (Southern Spain) with his wife (although possibly as exiles after the Emperor's death in 641) and remained there. A Spanish ninth century document of arguable authenticity, but thought to contain what is probably authentic genealogical information, tells us that he came 'from Greece' and purports to elaborate upon this man's kinship with **MAURICE** and his descent from Petrus, the Emperor's brother. The *Chronicle of Alfonso III*, also late, to some extent supports this. The name of his wife was said to have been Glasuintha, daughter of King Reccesuinthus, but the chronology is against this, and Reccared I (586-601) might be intended and which would make them close kin. Elsewhere she is stated to have been a niece of Chindasuinthus, who was King of the Visigoths 642-653 [PLRE III Artabazes, Reccaredus 1; Livermore (1971) 253; Barnwell (1997) 184].

Ardabastes

He was of Corduba (Cordova) and a *comes* in 754. His descent from Egica is reasonably certain [Livermore (1971) 253].

Athanagildus

Younger son of St. Hermenegildus, Visigothic King in Spain 581-584 (died 585) by Ingundis, daughter of Sigisbertus, Frankish King of Austrasia (Metz). He was named after his great-grandfather (*dux* and *comes* in Hispania Carthaginensis and later King of the Visigoths 551-568) whose daughter Bruneguilda (Brunnhilda) married King Sigisbertus. He was exiled, apparently, to Constantinople, or took Roman service. [PLRE Athanagildus 2]

Augusta Constantina

See above **MAURICIUS AUGUSTUS.**

Charito

See above **Table LXIX(c) Brief Lives**

Chosroes II

King of Persia 590-628, surnamed Parwez. Even if the marriage can be accepted, Chosroes had other wives (his chief wife was Shirin), so that his posterity may not have been of the blood of the Emperor **MAURICE.** The establishment of peace between the Emperor and King may be a reflection of the marriage alliance (if indeed fact); on the emperor's murder in 602, Chosroes declared war on the empire to avenge him, although he continued it into the reign of **HERACLIUS** which eventually led to his overthrow and death [PLRE III Chosroes II].

Cleopatra

Daughter of **MAURICE,** killed 605 or 607.

Domitianus

Bishop of Mytilene (Lesbos) 580-602, being appointed by his uncle, to whom he was a close confidant before he became emperor. He subsequently became a successful diplomat in the imperial service and was also a friend and correspondent of pope Gregorius. Luckily for him, he died at Constantinople of natural causes on 12th January 602 [PLRE III Domitianus, Petrus 55].

Egica

King of the Visigoths in succession to his father-in-law, 687-702 and previously by 683 a Roman *vir inlustris* and *dux* in Spania (Southern Spain).

Ervicius

The modern (Germanic) spelling is Erwig; he reigned as King of the Visigoths 680-687. His wife Liuvigotha is thought to have been descended from the house of King Liuvigildus (King of the Visigoths 572-586), the grandfather of Athanagildus (qv). Another daughter married Sunefredus, *comes* and *dux* in 683, King of the Visigoths at Toletum (Toledo) in 691.

Flavia Julia

This lady, whose second name could perhaps be more convincingly rendered Flavia Juliana, is not fully attested; indeed it is difficult to trace references to her back beyond the writings of Luis Salazar y Castro, the late 17th century genealogist. If accepted, she would have embodied the same resplendent genealogical ascendancy as the posterity of **ANASTASIUS'S** niece [?]Helena who married Gurgenes of the Georgian royal house (see Appendix III).If Anastasia Areobinda was her mother, however, it would explain her very Anician-sounding name, cf. **Table LXIX(a).** She is not in PLRE III, however.

Furola

Comes at Bartulio, and *dux* of Cantabria, his name may have been Furiolus. He was father of Aurelius, King of the Asturias (768-774) and Vermudus [Vermudo I] the Deacon, who succeeded to the Asturias in 788 for three years and was ancestor in the male line of the Kings of Léon and thus of the present Spanish Royal House.

Germanus

Appointed Caesar, see above **Table LXIX(b)**

Brief Lives

Gordia

She was living at Constantinople in 597 when in receipt of letter from Pope Gregory. The evidence for her relationship to **MAURICE** rests perhaps too heavily upon the naming sequence: Gordia/ Theoctista, although this recurrence is highly suggestive of a fairly close relationship, as suggested here [PLRE III Gordia 1].

Gordia

Living 602, having married Philippicus in 583. It has been suggested, mainly on the basis of naming patterns, that they must have had a daughter married to Artavasdes, a member of the Mamikonian dynasty of Armenia (cf. Ardabastes, above) and had descendants. This suggestion stems from Settipani and Doria to explain the occurrence of two subsequent men, the one descended from the other, called Ardabastes, but the descent suggested in the table above is perhaps more convincing, albeit no more supported by direct contemporary attestation [PLRE III Gordia 2]

Hermenegildo Guiterrez

Comes in Aeminium (Coimbra), 878. Allegedly a descendant of Ervicius or a putative brother. His posterity through Ramiro II of Leon would link to most modern Royal European houses.

Ino

See **Aelia Anastasia** *sub* **TIBERIUS II AUGUSTUS** above.

Isa ibn Muzahim

He was of Damascus and was a courtier; married in 740, settled in Seville and died in 755. He had two children, Ibrahim and Ishaq, of whom the elder left issue.

Johannes

See above *sub* **TIBERIUS II AUGUSTUS**

Justinianus

Son of **MAURICE,** killed 602 [PLRE II Justinianus 4].

Justinus

Son of **MAURICE,** killed 602 [PLRE III Justus 13].

Maria

Relationship attested, but known only from later Eastern sources as the daughter of **MAURICE**; the relationship, whilst perfectly plausible, has no contemporary Roman attestation. Mother of Cavades II of Persia who reigned briefly in 628 having murdered all 18 of his brothers and half-brothers [PLRE III Maria 6].

Marinus

Pope Gregory's letters seem to establish him as a son of Narses, *comes* (d. 597 or 598) whom the letters imply was a member of one of the senatorial families who fled Italy and settled in Constantinople. The same source strongly implies that if the identification is correct, his (first) wife was Hesychia (almost certainly also an ex-westerner) who also died by 597. By her, he seems also to have had two daughters, Eudochia (married to Alexander, a senator in 597, possibly to be identified with Alexander, son of Proclus, *magister militum* c. 600) and Dominica (married to Theodorus, also a senator in 597) [PLRE III Alexander 9 cf. 16, Dominica 2, Eudochia, Marinus 3 & 6, Theodorus 41].

Mauricius

See above **MAURICIUS AUGUSTUS**

Oppa

King of the Visigoths from the death of Rodericus in 711 until deposed at Caesaraugusta (Saragossa) in 714. [Collins (1989) 29-30, 147-149; Collins (2004) 133-134, 137-139].

Olmundus

Only known to have been alive in 710

Olmundus

No doubt named after his uncle (about whom little is known) he was based in Hispalis (Seville) and received some of his family's royal estates from the Muslims. He was alive in 756 and is known to have had three sons.

Paulus

Born c. 510/515, presumably in Arabissus, Cappadocia, and of an old family of Roman stock (see above). He was summoned to court in 582, adlected into the senate, presumably as a *vir illustris*, where he was aided in being able to live in the style expected through having had half the wealth of **JUSTIN II**'s brother Marcellus settled on him (the remainder went to his younger son Petrus). By 593 he had also been *caput senatus* (leader of the senate) with the style *protopatricius* (pre-eminent patrician). He was also referred to in one source as *vir gloriosus*. One of his diplomatic functions was to head a drive to improve relations with the Franks and as such was the recipient of a letter from King Childebert II. He died in 593 [PLRE III Paulus 23].

Paulus

Son of **MAURICE**, killed 602 [PLRE III Paulus 49].

Petrus

Presumably also born in Arabissa in Cappadocia, the younger brother of the Emperor, with his father Paulus, (qv) received half of the estates of the brother of **JUSTIN II**, Marcellus. In some later sources he is referred to as Petrus Augustus, with the second element as a name and not an indication of having held the purple, rather as **MAURICE'S** empress Constantia was formerly called Augusta (qv). He came to court with his father, and was likewise no doubt adlected into the senate as a *vir illustris*. In 593 he was appointed *magister militum* probably in Thrace, where he campaigned ineffectively against the Slavs and Bulgars, eventually suffering a defeat and dismissal in 594. By 600 he had been made *curoplalates* before being once again appointed *magister militum* in Thrace. In 602, part of his army was ordered by the Emperor to over-winter on the north bank of the Danube, but Petrus failed to communicate adequately with the officers involved, resulting in a mutiny which rapidly ran out of control, with the eventual result that the emperor was ousted by the middle-ranking officer **PHOCAS**, who seized power, killing Petrus, **MAURICE** and most of their families [PLRE III Petrus 55].

Petrus

Said to have been descended from 'the ancient line of Kings Reccaredus and Leovigildus'. He was *dux* in Cantabria in 710. He was also a descendant of Fonsus, a *comes* whose daughter Ibada married King Raccaredus.

Philippicus

A consummate survivor, Philippicus was made *comes exubitorum* (commander of the Imperial guard) by **MAURICE** in 582, and the following year married Gordia. He was long remembered as a successful general who intelligently applied the lesson to be learnt from successful commanders of the past to the situations in which he found himself; apparently he was a particular enthusiast of Scipio Africanus. He was also a friend of Pope Gregorius, and in particular urged him to accept appointment as Bishop of Rome. In 584 he was also made *magister militum* in the East in succession to Johannes Mystacon and acquitted himself well by successfully raiding deep into Persia and carrying off much booty. He continued with mixed success until 589 (being temporarily replaced during 588) when he was finally replaced after failing to re-take Martyropolis (Silvan). He later headed a diplomatic mission to Persia after the Persians had been defeated by his replacement. In 598 he was *magister militum* in Thrace. In 602, as a patrician, he was suspected of disloyalty after **MAURICE** had received a prophecy that his successor's name would begin with PH (Φ in Greek) but Philippicus, who had endured dealings with **PHOCAS** in Thrace five years before, exculpated himself by suggesting the rebellious officer, albeit to no avail. In 603, **PHOCAS** expelled him from court as untrustworthy and, feeling that discretion was the better part of valour, he took the tonsure. When **PHOCAS** was overthrown by **HERACLIUS I,** he was sent to negotiate with the late ruler's brother Comentiolus, by then in rebellion, and was nearly executed for his pains. He was thereafter made *magister militum* in the East, luring a victorious Persian army away from Chalcedon before dying *en post* in 614. It is believed that he had descendants but their details are lost to us. Possibly one was the (unknown) mother of Bardanes son of Nicephorus, who was briefly emperor (711-713) under the regnal name of **PHILIPPICUS** [PLRE III Philippicus 3].

Romulus

He was based in Toletum (Toledo) and like his brother received former royal estates from his new Muslim masters c. 712. He was said to have

been the ancestor of Paulus Alvarus of Corduba (Cordoba) a prominent Christian author and anti-Muslim polemicist.

Sara

In c. 739, she chartered a ship to travel to Damascus with the intention of pleading for the return of estates usurped by her uncle Ardabastes before Umayyad Caliph Hisham. He welcomed her, upheld her claim and instructed his governor to enforce it immediately. She then married a courtier 'Isa ibn Muzahim and they settled in Seville. They had two sons, Ibrahim and Ishaq. In 756 Sara married Umayr ibn Sa'id al-Lakhmi, whose family went back to the pre-Islamic Lakhmid kings of al-Hirah in Iraq. Sara bore a son to Umayr, the descendants being known as the Banu Hajjaj. Our knowledge stems from a memoir written by the great grandson of her son Ibrahim, Abu Bakr ibn al Qutiyah' (d. 978).

Sis[i]bertus

Named after his ancestor, the Frankish monarch whose daughter married St. Hermenegildus and was mother of Athanagildus (qv). He was made *comes* of the Christian community at Coimbra by the invading Arabs after the defeat of King Rodericus in 711. In this he was succeeded by his son Ataulfus (still living in the 770s), then by his grandson Athanaricus (living c. 800), and his great-grandson Theudis (Spanish Teudo) who succeeded as *comes* c. 805 – a classic example of the late Roman appointment of *comes* becoming an hereditary title. Theudis left a numerous posterity [Collins (1989) 29-30, 147-149; Collins (2004) 133-134, 137-139]

Symbatius

A member of the Bagratid dynasty, then of Armenia, cf. **Table LXVIII(b) Brief Lives. Symbatius** (Smbat IV Bagratuni, Prince of

Armenia) changed sides between the Empire and Persia more than once before being adopted as a son by **MAURICE** and being appointed *dux* 589. By 595 he was back on the side of the Persians and died in the service of Chosroes in 617. He had, with elder son Viraztirochus, a younger son, Garikhpetes [PLRE III Symbatius 1].

Theoctista

Husband's name not known, but as she was ranked as a *patricia*, he must have held that rank too, although he was dead by 582. It has been suggested (based on mention of names in the letters of Pope Gregorius I), that she may have married again, but there is no direct evidence that she had any issue, although such has been postulated, based on the recurrence of the names of Theoctista and Gordia [PLRE III Theoctista 2; kinship: *ibid*. IIIA p. 543].

Theoctista

Daughter of **MAURICE,** killed 605 or 607 [PLRE III Theoctista 3].

Theoctista

Named along with her husband by Pope Gregoius in correspondence [PLRE III Theoctista 1].

Theodosius

See above, **THEODOSIUS III AUGUSTUS**

Tiberius

See above **TIBERIUS II AUGUSTUS**

Tiberius

Son of **MAURICE,** killed 602.

Varaztirochus

Eldest son, with wife and family he was in 628 appointed by Persian king Cavades governor (*aspet*) of Armenia. He is usually listed as Varaztirots II, Prince of Armenia. He later fell out with a neighbouring governor and fled to **HERACLIUS I** by whom he was at first exalted and later exiled to Africa c. 635. He was recalled by **CONSTANS III** c. 646, appointed *curopalates* and returned to Armenia, but died soon afterwards, probably in 646. He left children, including a daughter, who married Mamikonian Prince Gregorius I, later also Prince of Armenia (686-690). The Princes Varaztiroch III and Ashot II of Armenia were probably grandsons [PLRE III Viraztiroch]..

Vittiza

King of the Visigoths as heir and colleague of his father 698-710. His anonymous wife was a relation of Ervicius (qv).

Further reading:

Haldon, J. F., *Byzantium in the Seventh Century: the Transformation of a Culture* (Cambridge 1990), Introduction and Chapter 1.

Norwich, J. J., 2nd Viscount, *Byzantium, the Early Centuries,* London 1988.

Shlosser, F. E., *The Reign of the Emperor Maurikios (582–602): a Reassessment,* Athens (1994)

Whitby, M., *The Emperor Maurice and His historian: Theophylact Simocatta on Persian and Balkan Wars* (Oxford 1998).

*

EPILOGUE

There are very many different opinions as to an acceptable date after which the East Roman Empire becomes the Byzantine Empire, ranging from the division between east and west in the wake of the death of **THEODOSIUS** the Great in 395 and the final end of Latin as an official language, for example on coin inscriptions in the early 8th century. To all intents and purposes the successful usurpation of **PHOCAS** marks the transition as well as any. His three predecessors were Greek speaking emperors, but the old Roman system as strengthened by **JUSTINIAN** continued, although the ordinary consulship effectively lapsed in 541 after a notional 1,050 years continuous existence (but probably nearer 908 years). With **PHOCAS,** unstable and insecure, the old ruling class were decimated, the governance of the empire largely neglected and the fisc allowed to be emptied. His successor **HERACLIUS I** took over a ruined polity, and although he was an active and effective commander and a sensible administrator, his ultimately successful war with Persia weakened the empire just as the rise of Islam - understood initially by the ecclesiastical authorities, still wrestling with the problems of Monphysitism, as just another irritating and transient heresy - threatened to overwhelm it. Yet the Avars were finally beaten off in 626 and **MAURICE'S** treaty with the Persians was re-instated two years later, bolstered by plans to evangelise the Persian Empire in its wake, although Spania (Southern Spain) was finally to all intents and purposes lost in 629, despite the arrival of the *comes* Ardabastes from Constantinople at about that time or shortly thereafter. The achievement of **HERACLIUS** by 630 had been truly remarkable, the tragedy being that the stability so dearly won lasted so short a time before the appalling depredations of the first *Jihad*.

After the death of **HERACLIUS** in 641, with the loss of Jerusalem and Antioch, came the loss of Carthage in 689, forcing the Empire's centre of gravity to shrink into a concentration on the capital, the provinces losing their vitality as alternative centres of Roman culture, learning and potency. Southern and eastern Italy and Sicily continued as part of the Empire in the west despite the ruin of the peninsula in the Gothic Wars and the Lombard incursions and settlements. Ravenna fell to the Lombards in 751 and Imperial control of the mainland effectively devolved upon the Pope as the only effective authority outside the Lombard sphere of influence, the later Papal states being the constitutional remnant of the Empire in Italy which indeed survived until 1870. Sicily was finally lost to the Arabs in 902 and much of Southern Italy under still under nominal Imperial control was gradually taken over by groups of Norman freebooters. This process was peppered with imperial claimants, most ephemeral. Despite a ceremonial visit to Rome by **CONSTANS III** in 663, he alienated hearts and minds of his western subjects by an extortionate demand for additional taxation.[927] The Imperial hold on Italy and other outposts was then long in terminal decline.

---

927. **CONSTANS** was the last person to hold an ordinary consulship, in 642.

All this in its turn changed the empire and finally confirmed its essential Greek rather than historic Roman nature in this new era. Yet, crisis or no crisis, its vitality, despite constant Moslem assaults, was to become resurgent and had a further 800 years before it before the Sons of the Prophet finally beat down its doors and extinguished the last embers of the historic empire in 1453, Morea in 1460 and Trebizond the year following.

*

APPENDIX I
CAESAR TO GORDIAN III

Although there is no continuous blood line from **JULIUS CAESAR** to **GORDIAN III**, such a connection can be constructed, as in the table opposite, using ties of kinship: marriage, descent from a common ancestor and so forth. This has areas of uncertainty, where kinship is suspected but not proven, as between Marcia Furnilla, the wife of **VESPASIAN** and Marcia who was mother of **TRAJAN**, although the Flavian family is connected with their Julio-Claudian predecessors and their Antonine successors through the marriage of **DOMITIAN** and Domitia Longina.

Likewise, the Severans are securely connected to the posterity of **MARCUS AURELIUS** through the marriage of **ELAGABALUS** to the daughter of the former's grandson Ti. Claudius Severus Proculus (consul 200). We only enter the realm of speculation when we use the largely unattested M. Velius Cornificius Gordianus as the key to joining the posterity of **MARCUS AURELIUS** with the Gordians. This has too much reliance on the HA to be anything like secure, but it was thought interesting to add.

Even more insecure - not because of reliance on the HA, but because of lack of additional attestation - is an attempt to add in **DECIUS, GALLUS** and **GALLIENUS**, as shown below. All one can say is that it is possible, although the ramifications of the Vibii may more extensive than appears here.

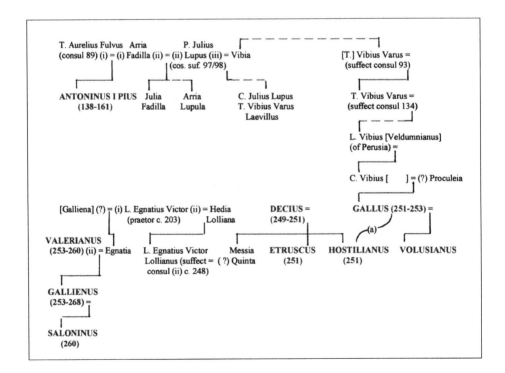

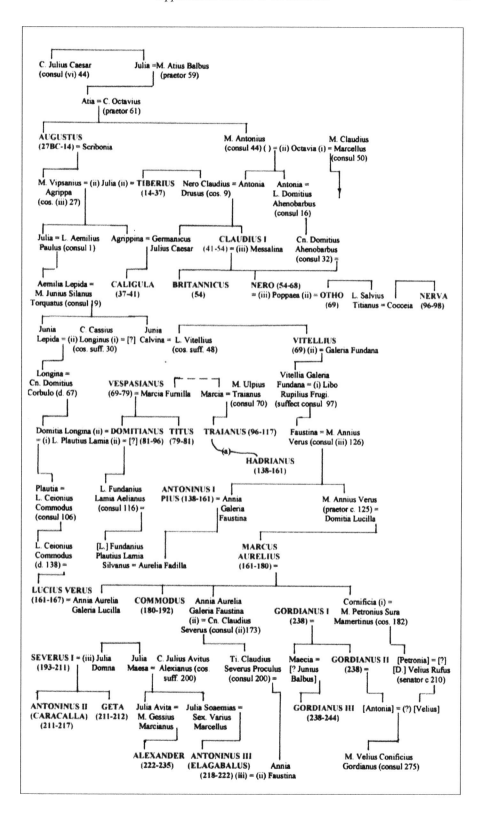

APPENDIX II
MAGNUS MAXIMUS IN BRITISH LEGEND

As was made clear in the main text, **MAGNUS MAXIMUS** has a parallel existence in British early history (as written down somewhat *post facto*) and Welsh legend. Here are entertained no doubts about his wife, and although one of the various sources endows him with his attested son, **VICTOR**, the remainder provide others which could, taken at face value, amount to as many as seven. Close analysis (as set out in the **Brief Lives**) enables us to reduce them to a more credible four. The only daughter, attested in one of the earliest sources, is Sevira/Severa, married to the *tyrannus* Gwrtheyrn/Vortigern who, in any other context than Britain, cut loose from Imperial control, would have been labelled an imperial claimant. Indeed, his situation is almost exactly analogous to that of *AEGIDIUS* and of *SYAGRIUS* (qv above **Table LXVI**), with only the difference that we have a more reliable near-contemporary account of the Gallic claimants.

It is very difficult to deny Sevira's husband's existence, since he appears in numerous sources. One, Gildas, is equivocal but respectably close to the time, two others not necessarily reliant on British sources but considered generally reliable: the *Anglo-Saxon Chronicle* and Bede, both written much later on. If one looks at the evidence provided by the British genealogies (and sets aside for the moment the inevitable doubts about their accuracy) one might get the impression that if **MAGNUS MAXIMUS** (hereafter Maxen) left behind four sons and a daughter, then rather young but, entrusted to a relative or trusted aide, they might well have grown up to take responsible positions under **CONSTANTINE III**. Sevira would have to have been born before 383, say in 380. This would make her marriageable from c. 396.

We could therefore speculate that she might have married Gwrtheyrn/Vortigern around 400, which would fit in with the birth of the well-attested Bishop Fautus of Riez, one of their alleged sons. Thus the sons of Maxen would all be in the prime of life just as **CONSTANTINE III** left the Diocese of Britain to try and stem the barbarian tide on the Continent, and the impression from the genealogies is that someone placed them all in quasi-military positions of trust to hold the line in Britain during his absence. Subsequently, in the absence of a resumption of imperial authority, whatever powers were being exercised in Britain at the time left them in place to keep the lid on things whilst the provinces of the island adjusted to a new reality. In such circumstances, one can imagine that they were able to remain *en post* for long enough for their positions to become at least quasi-hereditary, leading to the establishments of various shadowy dynasties, mainly in the North and West.[928] The chronicles' embellishment that Gwrtheyrn/Vortigern was essentially ruling Britain from before 425 until c. 455 might well lead us to suppose that he placed trusted kinsmen

---

928. As Whitaker (1994) 243-278 for this phenomenon elsewhere in the Empire, cf. (on Magnus Maximus doing the same thing), Jones & Mattingly (1990) 307.

to secure the troublesome periphery, whilst he concentrated on the problems of various Germanic invaders and barbarian coastal raiders in the South and East.

Sources

That this extraordinary and speculative saga is relegated to an appendix is because of the unreliable and generally late dates of the sources. All were written down well after the events they describe, in most cases much later, and are thus sensibly recognised as to a large extent legendary. It follows, then, that the degree of accuracy to be ascribed to them remains highly uncertain, a fact underlined by their internal inconsistencies. Nevertheless, the etymology of some of the names (given and indexed below as written) takes the date that some were first written down back much further, in some cases into the seventh century.[929] The traditional view is that these genealogies were at first transmitted orally by bards praising rulers, but that a much greater degree of literacy was enjoyed in Dark Age Britain has recently been accepted and the longer survival of Latin-based culture acknowledged.[930]

The MSS on which **Table LVIII(b)** has been based mainly derive from those collected in Bartrum (1966), and are here listed in approximate order of date of writing (abbreviations in brackets): Gildas, *De Exidio Britanniae* (DEB) of c. 540; Beda (Bede) *Historia Ecclesiastica Gentis Anglorum* (HE) of c. 680s; the inscription on the Pillar of Eliseg, Valle Crucis, near Llangollen, Powis (PE) of c. 820/830[931]; *Historia Britonum* (HB: History of the Britons), compiled c. 830; British Library Harleian MS 3859 (HG) of before 988; *Vita Beatissimi Cadoci* (VBC: Life of the Blessed (St.) Cadoc) written down c. 1100; Jesus College, Oxford MS 20 (JC) of c. 1370 but based on an earlier work of c. 1180; *Achau Brehinoedd a Thywysogion Cymru* (ABT: Pedigrees of the Kings and Princes of the Britons) compiled c. 1220; *Bonedd y Sant* (ByS: Lineages of the Saints) the earliest of several MSS of c. 1260; *Achau'r Sant* (AchS: Pedigrees of the Saints) compiled some time after ByS; *Bonedd Gŵr y Gogledd* (BGG: Lineages of the Men of the North) compiled .c 1280 but based on a compilation of the 12th century and *Bonedd yr Arwyr* (ByA) of uncertain date, but preserved in a late copy. Reference has also been made to the *Anglo-Saxon Chronicle* (ASC), a running compilation set down in the late ninth century and added to thereafter. Some of these descents were later 'improved' by elements found and vastly elaborated upon in Geoffrey of Monmouth's quasi-historical best seller *Historia Regum Britanniae* (HRB: History of the Kings of Britain) of c. 1136, some of the contents of which Dr. Russell has suggested we take more seriously.[932] Many of these are copies of copies of copies, and thus inevitably there are transcription errors which we have limited means of checking.

In the table that follows, the names are given as in the ancient sources with Latin equivalents in brackets, where applicable).

---

929. Koch (2013) 5 & n.12, 11-14, 16.
930. Charles-Edwards (2013) 625-650.
931. Charles-Edwards (2013) 416-417
932. Russell (2017) *passim*.

TABLE LVIII(b): MAXEN WLETIC

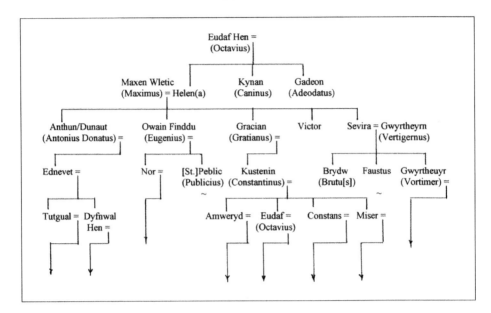

TABLE LVIII(b): BRIEF LIVES

Amweryd

Supposedly the founder of a line ultimately holding power in Demetia (Dyfed, South West Wales), but whose attested members have long thought to have been of Irish origin, albeit rapidly integrated into their British milieu. Their Irishness has been plausibly disputed by Dark. [ABT.18A; Dark (2000) 188-189; Koch (2013) 9-10].

Anthun (Antonius)

Named as a son of Maxen in the early source HG and as father of Ednivet, whereas JC names the father of Ednevet (*sic*) as Dunawt (Donatus). All the other genealogies describing the same lineage descending from Ednevet/Eidnivet have him as a son of Maxen. As both sources mentioned above are relatively early (JC, although written c. 1370, seems to have been copied from a compilation of c. 1180 but with orthographic evidence suggesting a still earlier origin) one is inclined to suspect that originally Ednevet was generally seen as a

grandson of the emperor. Furthermore, Anthun and Dunawt probably represent the same person, thus a hypothetical Antonius Donatus, a perfectly credible late imperial name, and one that actually occurs in the acknowledged family of **MAXIMUS**, in the person of Antonius Maximus, his *comes* in Spain (see **Table LVIII(a)**.) [HG.4; JC.19].

Brydw (Brut[ti]us)

Attested as a son of Gwrtheyrn/Vortigern on PE, although there seem to have been two stories about his origin, both early, hinging on whether he was the child of Vortigern and Sevira or Vortigern by incest. The Pillar at Valle Crucis tells us that Britu (*sic*) was the son 'that (St.) Germanus (not *necessarily* the Bishop of Auxerre) blessed', which effectively relegates the incest story to the realms of fantasy, possibly concocted because the shadowy British *tyrannus* seems either to have been admired or detested by his British chroniclers. Another source has Vortigern as the father of St. Faustus, Bishop of Riez (qv) which, like everything in the shadowy world of British legendary history, is perfectly possible but unattested elsewhere. It may be, as Charles-Edwards has suggested, that they are the same person. The name Brydw/Britu harks back either to an early (but clearly not pre-Roman) British foundation myth that the island was named by a Trojan refugee named Brutus, or to the Roman *nomen* Bruttius, which certainly survived into the fourth century, cf. **Table V** above [Charles-Edwards (2013) 449; Morris (1873) 63; Russell (2017) 58-79] .

Constans

He seems to exist solely as an ancestor of Emreis (Ambrosius Aurelianus), Uther Pendragon, Arthur and various characters found mainly in the untrustworthy pages of HRB and thus needs to be treated with more caution than most in these Brief Lives. He does, of course, bear the same name as the son of **CONSTANTINE III** and as his father is called Constantine, too, one may see hear an out-of-context implanted echo of reality. This is compounded by the insertion of *GRATIANUS II*. Whilst one might be able to accept that *GRATIAN* might have been a connection, even a son, of *MAXIMUS,* what follows seems just garbled history turned into genealogy [ABT.28]

Dunawt (Donatus)

A son of Maxen only in JC, and possibly to be identified with Anthun son of Maxen, see above.

Dyfnwal Hen

Most sources make Dyfnwal/Dumnual son of Ednevet, although the hagiography of St. Llawddog (the only MS being 16th century) has Dyfnwal as son of 'Ednyved ap Antoni ap

Maxen' which gives Anthun a second strand of support, but disagrees with all other accounts of Dyfnwal. Again, *hen* here means 'old'. He was apparently active possibly as far North as the Clyde c. 480/500, and was famous as a lawgiver. He retained sufficient *Romanitas*, according to Morris, to have conducted a census amongst his subjects and is attributed a son who bore the Roman name of Garmonyawn (Germanianus) named no doubt after the Gallic saint, and he was great-grandfather of Rhydderch Hael (*hael* = 'the generous'), King of Strathclyde c. 573. Most of his descendants were northern British notables with connections to Rheged (Cumbria) and the pre-Saxon Kingdom of York. [BGG.8,10, 11; ByS.18, 53 (Ms*G*); ByA 17, 20-22; Morris (1973) 123-124].

Ednevet

The name occurs in a variety of spellings, the earliest being Jesus College MS20: Eidinet, more modern spelling being Ednyvet/Ednyfet.[933] Only JC and HG have him as a grandson of Maxen; all others name him as a son. The *Buchedd Llawddog* (the Book of St. Llawddog) makes him son of Anthun, following the early *Annales Cambriae* in HG. His descendants comprise the distaff lineage of Rhodri Mawr, King of Gwynedd (c.820-878) 16th in descent from Ednevet (as JC), or 10th (as in ABT), potentially a 150 year difference! [ABT 6L; BGG.11; ByS.18, 76; HG.4; JC.19; Morris (1995a) 44]

Evdaf Hen (Octavius)

Given as the father of Helen[a] by ByS. The epithet *hen* also equates to Latin name 'Priscus', leading some to suppose that Helen's father was called Octavius Priscus, whereas most commentators consider that it was added by Welsh bards at a later date, along with his father and his

---

933. A mutation doubted by John Morris: Morris (1995a) 43 n.4.

mythical line of ancestry back to Brutus, founder of Britain. Evdaf is consequently described as *vrenin ynys Bridain* (King of the Island of Britain) .The implication might be that if one accepts his existence, he was *vicarius* of the British diocese or held some similarly paramount post in Britain in the fourth century. Apart from his daughter, the Mabinogion's *Dream of Macsen Wletig* (compiled from oral tradition by c. 1180 and known from a 14th century MS) gives him two sons, Kynan (Cunobelinus, the legendary Conan Meriadoc of HRB[934]) and [G]adeon (Adeodatus)[935], the former being the supposed founder of Brittany. Morris thought that the material ultimately went back to the 6th century. The earlier traditions stick with Kynan (JC, ByS, ByA) with only one MS recording Gadeon as a son (JC.7) and a further one adding another son, Morvawr (=Maximus: Mostyn MS.117) although closer inspection reveals that this is a case of a missed generation, with either Kynan or Gadeon omitted. To confuse matters further, Gadeon is given as the *son* of Kynan in all but JC.7, which provides Gadeon with a daughter, Gwreic who turns out to be the wife of Coel Hen. Eudaf's posterity also includes Custennin [*sic*] and Geraint, rulers of Dumnonia, suggesting possible lost genealogical links with **CONSTANTINE III** and his *magister militum* Gerontius (British, Geraint) [ABT.6; BGG.11; ByA.27A, 30B, 31; ByS.63, 76; JC.7, 11; Morris (1973) 419].

Eudaf ap Kustenin (Octavius son of Constantine)
He appears solely as the father of one Kynan [JC.4]

Faustus
A well-attested character, later a saint, known to have been born in Britain c. 400/410. He became a monk at the island monastery of Lérins, by 434, its abbot before being made Bishop of Alebaece Reiorum (Riez) in 462, dying c. 488. He is said in an early source (HB) to have been the son of Vortigern, not by Sevira, but by incest with the daughter of the *tyrannus*. Various parallels suggest that this was a later slur, and that he is possibly to be identified with the Britu of PE [Charles-Edwards (2013) 199-201, 449].

Gracian (Gratianus)
Also spelt Grasian/Cradian in other MSS, he occurs solely in ABT.28 as a son of Maxen, and as father of Kustenin. Whilst it might be objected that as **MAGNUS MAXIMUS** killed **GRATIAN,** he would be unlikely to have named a son after him, given the alleged kinship of **MAXIMUS** to **THEODOSIUS I** and the latter to **GRATIAN** (qv. above, **Table LIX(a)**), and the suggestion made above (under **MAGNUS MAXIMUS**) that he may have married Helena on a previous tour of duty in Britain, then it is quite a likely name. If, on the other hand, one was concocting a pedigree decades or centuries later, aware of the circumstances of **GRATIAN'S** demise (as HB and HG.4), one would be unlikely to attribute Maxen with a son of this name. That he might have been identifiable with the second *GRATIAN* is perhaps asking too much even of the most open minded [ABT.28].

Gwrtheyrn (Vertigernus)
Commonly called Vortigern, all his attestations are well *post facto*, but the consular dates in HB, putting the start of his period in control of Britain

---

934. In some cases deriving from the Latin Caninus, cf. Gildas's tyrant Aurelius Caninus:DEB. 27.
935. British/Welsh variations on this name are numerous: Gadeon/Cadfan/ Cadien/Cadwr/Cador, none certainly written down before c.1180.

as 425, are mildly convincing, although PLRE puts him in with a dubit. He was still going strong in 455 according to ASC, a very unreliable document at this date. Although his name means 'high king' = British *vor* (Welsh *vawr*) = 'great' + *tigern* = king and is so punned (without naming him) as *superbo tyranno* by Gildas, it is probable that it was a normal given name, possibly in conjunction with a more Roman one, for he was probably born in about the time of Maxen. Morris, on the other hand, suggested that the original MS from which the genealogies we have was copied may have read something like 'Vortigernus *qui et* Vitali[nu]s' which could have mutated through copyists' errors into a two generation descent as in HB where Vortigern is '…son of Vitalis and grandson of Vitalinus' and with familial ties to the *colonia* of Glevum (Gloucester), suggesting, albeit at a significant temporal remove, a Romano-Briton of distinguished family married to the daughter of an ex-emperor: just what one might expect from a *tyrannus* [ASC *sub* 449 & 455; DEB 23; HE i.14, 15, ii.5; HB 31, 49, 66; Dark (1994) 63; Morris (1973) 55; PLRE II *!Vortigern!*].

Gwyrtheuyr (Vortimer)

Vortimer Vendigaid (*Vendigaid* = 'blessed') first appears in the part of HB known as the *Kentish Chronicle*. With his alleged brother Categirn (not shown on **Table LVIII(b)** above), he was said to have led a series of campaigns counter-attacking and driving back the Saxons. In the third campaign, Categirnus was killed and Gwyrtheuyr himself died shortly after the fourth. The fighting appears to have taken place in Kent and the account shows congruence with the Anglo-Saxon Chronicle's entries for the period, although this source fails to mention the brothers and mentions Gwrtheyrn only twice, but in the same context, these events taking place on the ASC's shaky reckoning c 442-452. HRB adds an unlikely tale of

Gwyrtheuyr having been poisoned by his Saxon step-mother after having been elected king in place of his father, in order to allow Gwrtheyrn to take over once more. Gwyrtheuyr is called Vendigaid due to a much later tradition that St. Germanus blessed him for his efforts to drive out the Saxons; needless to say, this element is notably absent from the Gallic monk Contantius's *Life* of Germanus. In ABT he is supposed parent of Emreis (Ambrosius Aurelianus), grandfather of Uther and great-grandfather of King Arthur, no doubt written under the baleful influence of HRB [ABT.28; HB 31, 36-38, 44, cf. ASC in Morris (1973) 80-81].

Kustenin (Constantinus)

He appears twice in early pedigrees, once as son of Maxen in one part of ABT, and in another as grandson, Gracian being interposed between him and Maxen. One or other is probably closest to whatever reality we can claim, and it is here supposed that Gracian (Gratianus) was the son, and that Kustenin the grandson, as with Ednevet (qv). It is also possible that he represents the emperor **CONSTANTINE III** chronoclasmically given his predecessor *GRATIAN II* as father.(see **Table LX(a)** above), all grafted on by later speculation and confusion [ABT.18A & 28].

Helen (Helena)

See main text, on her authenticity. Roman sources nowhere name Maximus's Empress by name.

Maxen Wletic (Magnus Maximus)

He appears in numerous legendary British pedigrees, his name usually being spelt as above, except in HG, where he is more correctly Maxim[us]. Later, the name mutated into Macsen, as in the *Mabinogion*. In BGG & ByS he is correctly described as *amherawdyr Ruuein* (Emperor of the Romans). Only the former allows

him Helen[a] as wife, also adding her parentage. ByS in one version even endows him with
a father, Lly[wely]n (Leolinus), and Geoffrey of
Monmouth (HRB) goes one further in making
Llywelyn the brother of Coel Hen, ancestor,
according to the genealogical lists, of many of
the Northern bloodlines, the *Gŵr y Gogledd*.
As ByS, as we have it, post-dates HRB, Maxen's
father must be viewed with extreme suspicion,
whereas Coel ('Old King Cole' of nursery rhyme)
appears in a number of sources believed to pre-
date Geoffrey. Coel's name, of course, could also
be Roman (Coelius, as in HRB) and he has been
suggested by a number of writers to have been
C-in-C frontier troops in Britain at the time of
CONSTANTINE III. In fact, had he been uncle
to Helena, he should have been holding a British
command earlier, c. 365/75. The only early Welsh
pedigree to name Maxen's attested son, Victor,
is HB [BG.4; BGG.11; ByS.63 & Ms G; HB.29].

Miser (Mistor)

The name is puzzling; it appears also as Pincr-
Misser in HG (but as son of Constans) and as here
in JC.13, as son of Kustenin ap Maxen. In the *Life*
(*Vita*) of St. Petroc, he appears not only with a son
called Piner (tentatively Latinised as *pincerna* =
steward) but as the son himself of 'Constantini
imperatoris' (Emperor **CONSTANTINE**)! The
MS is late (14th century), although the content
is undoubtedly much earlier [HG.2; JC.13; *Vita
St. Petroci*: Bartram (1966) 29-30].

Nor

Legendary second ruler of Glywyssing (approximately Glamorganshire) and ancestor of St.
Cadoc [VBC 45]

Owain Finddu (Eugenius)

Son of Maxen (and father of St. Peblic and
Nor) in VBC & JC; *Finddu* = 'black lips'. The

popularity of the name in Dark Age Britain may
reflect a benevolent view having been taken of
the Imperial Claimant *EUGENIUS*. Yet it was a
relatively common Roman name in the 4th century, and Owain if not a fiction or misplaced,
was almost certainly born before the claimant's
elevation and (passing) fame. He was in later
legend also said to have been ruler of Glywyssing
(Glamorganshire). St. Cadoc, was a descendant,
being fifth in descent from Owain via Peblic's
supposed brother Nor. Cadoc was also said to
have been ruler of Glywyssing and, according to
legend, was killed (presumably by Saxons) whilst
building a church in *Calchvynydd*, c. 550/580. As
the latter name means 'chalk hills', this has been
supposed by some to have been in the Chilterns
but could just as well have been in Wiltshire or
Dorset, where British culture endured to this
period [JC.4; VBC.45; Bromwich (1961) no. 13;
Dark (2000) 109].

Peblic (Publicius)

St. Peblic was a son of Maxen, uniquely claimed in
ByS, although most sources suffix his name with
'ap Owain Finddu ap Maxen Gwletic'. Hence, as
with Anthun/Dunawt (qv) he is best regarded
as a grandson of Maxen. He is associated with
Segontium (Caernarvon) according to ByS, as of
course, is Helen, and the hamlet of Llanbeblig is a
suburb of the modern settlement. It includes the
ancient church of Llanbeblig, said to have been
founded by St. Peblic himself in 433 and built
within what is believed to have been the cemetery
of the Roman fort. By archaeological precedent
in Gaul, all very plausible [ByS63; Knight (2007)
82-83 & Fig. 21; VBC.45].

Tutgual (Tuduvallus)

Spelt alternatively Tutagual/Tutwawl, which name
occurs twice more amongst this man's posterity,
ancestors of Rhodri Mawr. He was one of the *Gŵr*

y Gogledd (Men of the North), one line of whose descendants ended up on Man and thence came to rule Gwynedd. He is also thought to be identifiable with the King Tuduvallus whom Alfred of Rievaulx claims was converted to Christianity by St. Ninian, which fits his Northern milieu, but the name is not uncommon at the period and in this lineage especially. Furthermore, since J. T. Koch convincingly broke the legendary link between the first house of Gwynedd (that of Maelgwyn) with the Men of the North, particularly Cunedda, ruler of the Votadini, this Tutgual should perhaps be located rather further south [ABT.6L; HG.4; JC.19; Koch (2014) 66-84]

Victor

See main text **Table LVIII(a)**. He occurs only once in British texts.

APPENDIX III
A POSSIBLE FIFTEEN HUNDRED YEAR BLOODLINE

In **Appendix I** an attempt was made to show genealogical links from **CAESAR** to **GORDIAN III** and even to **GALLIENUS**, thus spanning 288 (or 312) years, but without any possibility of any continuity of blood. Likewise it has been suggested above that there was indeed a blood line descending from **PROBUS** and **MAGNUS MAXIMUS** to **MAURICIUS** via **OLYBRIUS** and the family of **ANASTASIUS**. It it thus in theory possible to extend back from Anicia Faltonia Proba (No. 33 below) the grandmother of **PETRONIUS MAXIMUS**, through the Anician family. Although there was an Anicius as curule aedile in 304BC, it is unlikely in the extreme that the Anicii of the Imperial period were descended from him, as we know that although they probably originated in Praeneste, they latterly originated from outside Italy and rose to prominence under **MARCUS AURELIUS** and **SEPTIMIUS SEVERUS**. However, they were of Italian stock and could have been remotely connected with the republican senatorial Anicii back in Praeneste (Palestrina), where the name seems to have originated in the 4th century BC.

However, using female lines, one can trace back through the Asinii (making a few perfectly reasonable and credible assumptions along the way), believed to have been descended from the Asinii of the early empire. New man C. Asinius Pollio (consul in 40BC and later elevated to patrician status by **AUGUSTUS**) married a Quinctia (no. 16 below), who is the presumed daughter (or conceivably sister) of the L. Quinctius drowned in the wake of the Triumvirs' proscription of 43. He in turn, is thought to have been the son of a patrician Quinctius Crispinus, who served as a legate during the Social War in 82. His ascendance prior to that we owe to the reasoning of Münzer and Broughton.[936] The one problem is that Quinctia's father may alternatively have been an unrecorded son of the low-born L. Quinctius, a follower of Crassus who was praetor in 68.[937] If one can accept the connection with the Quinctii Crispini (giving a distant collateral relationship with the empress of **COMMODUS**) then a fifth century BC marriage enables us to take the line back to the earliest Valerii.[938]

Likewise, although we lose sight of the line within the empire in the early seventh century, the marriage of a princess of the House of **ANASTASIUS** (usually named as Helena, no. 39 below) to a prince of an Iberian dynasty enables us to go well beyond that: to 786 in the line of direct descent and to the present via a cadet branch, who became princes of Tao Klarjeti and later Kings of Georgia. The difficulty here is the links of the Tao Klarjeti line to the main Iberian line. These are generally accepted but for which chapter and verse are difficult to pin down.

---

936. Münzer (1999) 109-116 & n. 73; Broughton III (1986) *passim*.
937. Gruen (1995) 174 & n.
938. Münzer, *op.cit.*

The writer's late cousin by marriage, HSH Prince Michael Grousinski, a descendant, and an *élève* of Professor Prince Kyril Toumanoff, would have been gratified, one feels sure, by this connection to two imperial houses. His ancestors were far keener on an implausible descent from the Holy Family and King David (whose sling and harp appeared on their French-designed 18th century armorials, along with Christ's seamless robe) than the princes of the later Roman Empire.

1. **Volusus Valerius,** a descendant of M. Valerius (a fetialis c. 672-640 [FS p. 934]) without doubt in turn a descendant of Volusus Valerius, a leading advisor of Romulus [Dion. Halicarnassus, *Roman Antiquities* II. 46, 1-3]

2. **P. Valerius Volusi f. Publicola** (cos. 509, (ii) 508, (ii) 506 (iv) 504).

3. **Valeria** marr. A. Postumius [P.f.] Albus Regillensis (cos. 496) who had issue:

4. **Postumia** marr. T. Quinctius L. f. L. n. Cincinnatus Poenus (cos. 431 (ii) 428), son of L. Quinctius L. f. L. n. Cincinnatus (suf. 460, cos (ii) 457, dict. 458, (ii) 439 [ILS 9338] by Racilia, and had issue

5. **T. Qunictius T. f. L. n. Cincinnatus Capitolinus** (dict. 380) [FS2873] had issue a younger son:

6. **T. Quinctius T. f. T. n. Capitolinus** (cos. 354 (ii) 351, mag. equ. 367 (ii) 360, dict. 361 marr. Postumia , dau. of M. Postumius A. f. A. n. Albinus Regillensis (tr. mil. c. i., 426 (ii) 403), and had issue

7. **Cn. Quinctius T. f. T. n. Capitolinus** (aed. cur.366, dict. 331) had issue:

8. **L. Quinctius Cn. f.** (tr. mil. 326) had issue:

9. **K. Quinctius L. f. Cn. n. Claudus** (cos. 271BC)

10. **L. Quinctius K. f.** (inferred)

11. **T. Quinctius L. f. K. n. Crispinus** (cos. 208BC) [Munzer tab. 6]

12. **L. Quinctius T. f. Crispinus** (pr. 186BC) was father of:

13. **[L.] Quinctius Crispinus** (pr. 143BC) was father of:

14. **[?L.] Quinctius Crispinus** (legatus 82BC) probably father of:

15. **L. Quinctius [?Crispinus]** (senator proscribed in 43BC & died at sea) [Appian, BC iv. 12, 27] had issue:

16. **Qunictia L. f.** marr. C. Asinius Cn. f. Pollio (cos. 40BC, d. 5, patrician c. 23) [W50], son of Cn. Asinius, the equestrian son of the Italian leader in 85, Herius Asinius, and had issue:

17. **C. Asinius C. f. Cn. n. Gallus** (cos. 8, d. 30), [ILS 5923; FS741] marr. (ii) Vipsania, dau. of M. Vipsanius L. f. Agrippa, formerly wife of Ti. Cludius Nero/Ti. Julius Caesar otherwise **TIBERIUS I AUGUSTUS** (14-37) and had a third son:

18. **Q. Asinius Gallus** (pr. c/ 36, exiled 46) marr. (?) Claudia, sister of M. Claudius Marcellus Aeserninus (pr. 19) and had issue:

19. **M. Asinius Q. f. Tro. Marcellus** (suf. before 69) [PIR [2] A1234] marr. and had issue:

20. **Q. Asinius Q. f. Marcellus** (suf. 96, living 112) [PIR [2] A1235 FS745] marr. and had issue:

21. **Q. Asinius Marcellus** (senator d. 141) [PIR [2] A1236] marr. (?) Ummidia Quadratilla and had

22. **[Q.] Asinius [Quadratus]** (existence inferred; his sister was Asinia Quadratilla who marr. L Titius Plautius Aquilinus cos. 162). This Asinius may have married a Julia and had issue:

23. **C. Asinius Julianus** (senator living c. 200) marr. (?) Laberia Lepida and probably had issue:

24. **C. Asinius Quadratus** (suf. c. 229, author) marr. (?) Julia Protima and had issue:

25. **C. Asinius Nicomachus Julianus** (senator living c., 260) marr. (?) Junia and had issue:

26. **Asinia C. f. marr.** <u>Sex</u>. Cocceius <u>Anicius Faustus</u> Paulinus (suf. C. AD260, (ii) ord. 277 [PIR² A600/PLRE I Paulinus 16] (see no.10 above) and had issue:

27. **M.** Junius Caesonius Nicomachus **Anicius Faustus** Paulinus (suf. C. 275 (ii) ord. 298, PUR 299, VIIvir Epulonum) [PLRE I Faustus 6 & Paulinus 13], marr. (?) Julia and had issue

28. **Amnius Anicius Julianus** (cos. 322, PUR 326-329) [PLRE I Julianus 23] marr. Caesonia [M'f.] and had issue;

30. Amnius **M'.** Caesonius Nicomachus **Anicius Paulinus** *signo* Honorius (consul 334) [ILS1220 (filiation); PLRE I Paulinus] 14 marr. (?) Auchenia, perhaps dau. of an Auchenius Bassus, and had issue:

31. **Anicius Auchenius Bassus** (qu. & pr., [CIL.vi.1679], PUR 382-383, 'restitutor generis Aniciorum' [CIL.xiv.2197; IL 5702, 8984; PLRE I Bassus 11] marr. Tyrrenia Honorata [PLRE I Honorata 3] and had issue:

32. **Tyrrenia Anicia Juliana** [PLRE I Juliana 3] marr. Q. Clodius Hermogenianus Olybrius (cons. Tusc. et Umbr. 370, cos. 379) [PLRE I Olybrius 3], son of Clodius Celsinus *signo* Adelphius (PUR 351, brother of Clodia who marr. Petronius Probinus) by Faltonia Betitia Proba (see Table XLVII) also descended from M. Anicius Faustus, cos. 298), and had issue

33. **Anicia Faltonia Proba** (b. c. 350, d. betw. 410/432: ILS 1269) [PLRE I Proba 3]; marr. Sex.Claudius Petronius Probus (cos. 371), son of Sex. Caelius Petronius Probinus (cos. 341), whose mother, Anicia Demetrias was daughter of Sex. Anicius Faustus (cf. above) and had:

34. **Anicius Probinus** (cos. 395, procos. Africa 396-397 marr. (?) (grand-)daughter of **MAGNUS MAXIMUS** (Augustus 383-388) and (great-)grand-daughter M. Aurelius **PROBUS** (Augustus 276-282) [PLRE I Probus 1] and had issue:

35. **Petronius Maximus** (cos. 433, (ii) 443, **MAXIMUS V** Augustus 455) [PLRE II Maximus 22], marr. (i) [?Eparchia], daughter of Avitus (cos. 421) and sister of Eparchius **AVITUS AUGUSTUS** (455-457) and had issue:

36. **Anicius Olybrius** (cos. 464, **OLYBRIUS AUGUSTUS** 472) [PLRE II Olybrius 1, 6] marr. (ii) Placidia, dau. of **VALENTINIAN III AUGUSTUS** (425-455) and probably had:

37. **Magna** marr. Paullus (cos 496) [PLRE II Paullus 26], brother of **ANASTASIUS I** and had issue:

38. **Probus** (cos. 502) [PLRE II Probus 8] marr. (?) Helena and had, with other issue a daughter (described as the 'daughter of the Roman Emperor' in Georgian sources, but who could only be a niece):

39. **Helena** marr. (ii) Gurgenes, Iberian Prince [Toumanoff (1963) 368-369 and by her had issue:

40. **Leo** [PLRE III Leo 9] marr. and had issue:

41. **Gurgnenes I** King of Iberia 588 – 602 [PLRE III] who marr. and had issue:

42. **Demetrius,** *hypatos* (honorary consul) [PLRE III Demetrius 9] and had issue (or his el. brother Stephanus):

43. **[Anonymous]** father of:

44. **Gurgenes II** King of Iberia 684-c 693 and father or grandfather of

45. **Gurgenes III** King of Iberia c. 693 – c 748 who had issue:

46. **Gurgenes** marr. dau. of his kinsman Adarneses III of Iberia and had issue:

47. **Stephanus III** King of Iberia c. 779/780 – 786 *A descendant of one of these by another line was:*

48. **Adarneses,** Prince of Tao Klarjeti marr and had issue:

49. **Ashotes I The Great** King of Iberia & Prince of Khartl'i 813 – 830, *curopalates* had issue:

50. **Bagrates I** King of Iberia & Prince of Khartli 842/843 – 876 had issue:

51. **David I** King of Iberia, Prince of Khartli 876 – 881, curopalates, had issue:

52. **Adarneses IV** King of the Georgians, 888 – 923 had issue:

53. **Sumbatius I** King of the Georgians & Kartli 937-958 had issue:

54. **Bagrates II** King of the Georgians 950 – 994 & Khartli from 975 had issue:

55. **Gurgenes V** King of the Georgians & Khartli 994-1008 mar. Guranducht, dau. of Georgius II King of Abkhasia and had issue:

56. **Bagrates III** King of the Georgians, Abkhazia & Khartli 975-1014 had issue:

57. **Georgius I** King of the Georgians from whom many traceable descents.

*

ABBREVIATIONS

A. = Aulus

Aed. Cur. = curule aedile

Aed. Pl. = plebeian aedile

Ap.= Appius

b. = born

C.= Caius

Cn.= Gnaeus

Col. = Colina (tribe)

Cos. = consul

CQ = *Classical Quarterly*

d. = died

D.= Decimus

Dict. = dictator

f. = *filius, filia* [son, daughter of]

Fl.= Flavius

HA = *Historia Augusta*

HS = Sesterces/Sestertii

K.= Kaeso

KIA = killed in action

L.= Lucius

Leg. = legate

Leg. leg. = Legate (commander) of a legion.

M'.= Manius

M. = Marcus

marr. = married

n. = grandson/granddaughter of

N.= Numerius

P.= Publius

Pal. = Palatina (tribe)

PBSR = *Papers of the British School at Rome*

Pf. Aeg. = prefect of Egypt

Pf. pr. = praetorian prefect

Pol. = Pollia (tribe)

Pr. = Praetor

Procos. = proconsul

Propr. = propraetor

PUC = Prefect of the City of Constantinople

PUR = Prefect of the City of Rome

Q. = Quintus

Ser. = Servius

Sex.= Sextus

Sp.= Spurius

suff., = suffect consul

T.= Titus

Ti.= Tiberius

Trib. lat. = military tribune of senatorial rank

Trib. mil. = military tribune

Trib. Pot. = tribunician power

Tr. pl. = tribune of the People

V. = Vibius

vc. = vir clarissimus

vi. = vir illustrius or inlustris

BIBLIOGRAPHY

[Author, title, publishing history]   **[Abbreviation]**

1. Ancient Sources:

Anon., *Anglo Saxon Chronicle*, trans. Ingram, J. (London 1825)   [ASC]

Anon., *Scriptores Historiae Augustae,* 3 Vols., Trans. Magie, D.,   [HA]
   (Harvard & London 1954/1960)

Aurelius Victor, Sex., *De Caesaribus* trans. Bird, H. W. (Liverpool 1994).

Avitus of Vienne, *Letters*, ed. & trans. Shanzer, D & Wood, I. (Liverpool 2002)

Caesar, C. Julius, *The Civil War,* Trans. Mitchell, J. F., (London 1967)   [Caes. *BC*]

Caesarius of Arles, *Life, Testament, Letters,* Trans. Klingshirn, W. E., (Liverpool, 1994)

Cicero, M. Tullius, *Letters to Friends* 2 Vols.,   [Cic. *Ad. Fam.*]
   Ed. Shackleton-Bailey, D. R. (Cambridge 1977)

Cicero, M. Tullius, *Cicero's Letters to Atticus* 7 vols.,   [Cic. *Ad Att*]
   Ed. Shackleton-Bailey, D. R. (Cambridge 1965-1970)

Curtius Rufus, Q., *Historiae Alexandri Magni Macedonis,* Trans., Yardley, J. (London 2001)

Dio Cocceianus, M. Cassius, *Roman History,* 9 Vols., Trans. Cary, E., *et al.*   [Dio]
   (Harvard & London 2000)

Dionysius of Halicarnassus *Roman Antiquities,* trans. Cary, E., 7 Vols. (Harvard & London
   1937-1950)

Eusebius, *History of the Church,* Trans. Williamson G. A., (London 1965)

Eusebius, *Vita Constantini,* Trans. Cameron, A & Hall, S .G. (Oxford 1999)

Eutropius, *Breviarum ab Urbe Condita,* trans. Bird, H. W. (Liverpool 1993)

Evagrius, *Ecclesiastical History* (Amsterdam 1964)

Gregory of Tours, *Historiae Francorum* Trans. Thorpe, L. (London 1974)   [Greg. *HF*]

Gregory of Tours, *Life of the Fathers,* Trans. James, E., 2nd edn., (Liverpool 1991)

Herodian, *History of the Empire,* Trans. Whittaker, C. R., 2 Vols. (Harvard & London 1969)

Inscriptions:

Corpus Inscriptionem Latinarum, ed. Mommsen, T. *et al* (Berlin, from 1863)   [CIL]

Inscriptiones Latinae Selectae, ed. H. Dessau 5 Vols. (Chicago 1979-80)   [ILS]

Remains of Old Latin: Vol. IV Archaic Inscriptions, ed. E. H. Warmington (London &
   Cambridge, Mass. 1967)   [CIL I²]

Josephus, Flavius, *Antiquitates Judicae* Trans., Whiston, W., (Ware 2006)   [Jos. *AJ*]

Josephus, Flavius, *The Jewish War,* Trans. Thackeray, H. St. J., 3 Vols.   [Jos. *BJ*]
   (Harvard & London, 1997-2001)

Juvenalis, [Ju]nius, *Satires,* Trans. Green, P., (London 1967)   [Juv. *Sat.*]

Livius, T., *History of Rome from its Foundation books I-V,* Trans. De Sélincourt, A. (London
   1960)

Lucanus, M. Annaeus, *Pharsalia* Trans. Graves, R., (London 1956)

Plinius Caecilius Secundus, C., *Letters* Trans. Radice, B. (London 1963)   [Plin. *Ep.*]

Plinius Secundus, C., *Natural History* 10 Vols. (Loeb, Harvard)   [Plin. *NH.*]

Plutarchus, L. Mestrius, *Parallel Lives* 6ᵗʰ edn., 6 Vols., Trans. Langhorne, J & W., (London 1795)   [Plut.]

Procopius, *The History of the Wars,* 5 Vols. Trans. H. B. Dewing (Harvard & London, 1928)   [Proc. *HB*]

Procopius, *The Secret History* Trans. G. A. Williamson (London 1980)   [Proc. *SH*]

Procopius, *De Bello Vandalico* Trans. H B Dewing (LOondon 1916)   [Proc. *BV*]

Pseudo-Dionysius of Tel-Mehre, *Chronicle Part III* Trans. Witakowski, W. (Liverpool 1996)

Ruricius of Limoges *et aliis, Ruricius of Limoges and Friends: A Collection of Letters from Visigothic Gaul,* Trans. Mathisen, R. W. (Liverpool, 1999)

Sozomenus, Salminius Hermias, *Ecclesiastical History* (New York 1890)

Suetonius Tranquillus, C., *Duodecimi Caesares* Trans. Graves, R.,   [Suet. + *name*]
(London 1957)

Tacitus, Cornelius, *Annals of Imperial Rome* Trans. Grant, M.   [Tac. *Ann.*]
(London 1966)

Tacitus, Cornelius, *The Histories,* Trans. Wellesley, K. (London 1964)   [Tac. *Hist.*]

Valerius Maximus, *Memorable Doings & Sayings* 2 vols.,   [Val Max.]
Trans. Shackleton-Bailey, D. R. (Harvard & London, 2001)

Velleius Paterculus *Historiarum Libri Duo*, ed. W. S. Watt, 2nd edn. (Stuttgart 1978)

Zonaras, J., Trans. & ed. Bandich, T. M. & Lane, E. N., *Prologue and History from 222-395* (Abingdon 2009)

Zosimus. *Historia Nova,* Trans. Buchanan, J. & Davis, J. (San Antonio, 1967)

2. Secondary sources

General

Arnheim, M T W, *The Senatorial Aristocracy in the Later Roman Empire* (Oxford 1972)

Arnold, J. J., *Theoderic and the Roman Imperial Restoration* (Cambridge 2018)

Badian, E., *Notes on Roman Senators of the Republic* in *Historia* XII (1963)

Badian, E., *Cato and Cyprus* in *Journal of Roman Studies* LV (1965) 113-115

Badian, E., *The Consuls of 179-49BC* in *Chiron* 20 (1990)

Bagnall, R. S., Cameron, A., Schwartz, S. R., & Worp, K. A., *Consuls of the Later Roman Empire* (Atlanta, 1987)

Barbieri, G., *L'Albo senatorio da Settimio Severo a Carino, 193-285* (Rome, 1952)

Barnes , T. D., *Some Persons in the Historia Augusta* in *Phoenix* 26 (1972) 140-182

Barnes, T. D., *The Sources of the Historia Augusta* (Brussels 1978)

Barnish, P. J., *Transformation and Survival in the Western Aristocracy c AD400-700* in *Proceedings of the British School at Rome* LVI (1988) 120-155

Barnwell, P. S., *Emperor, Prefects and Kings: The Roman West, 395-565* (London 1992)

Bartrum, P. C. *Early Welsh Genealogical* Texts (Cardiff 1966)

Birley, A. R., *Two Names in the Historia Augusta* in *Historia* 15 (1966) 249f.

Birley, A. R., *The Fasti of Roman Britain* (Oxford, 1981)

Bowersock, G W., *Roman Arabia* (Cambridge, Mass. 1983)

Bowman, A. K., *Egypt after the Pharaohs 332BC-AD642* (London 1986)

Braund, D., *Georgia in Antiquity: A History of Colchis and Transcaucasian Iberia 550BC – AD562* (Oxford 1994)

Breed, B. W., Damon, C. & Rossi, A. (eds.), *Citizens of Discord: Rome and its Civil Wars* (Oxford 2010)

Bromwich, R., *Trioedd Ynys Prydein* (Cardiff 1961)

Brown, T. S., *Gentlemen and Officers: Imperial Administration & Aristocratic Power in Byzantine Italy* (Rome 1984)

Burgess, R. W., *Chronicles, Consuls and Coins: Historiography and History in the Later Roman Empire* (Farnham 2011)

Burnett, A., *The Coinage of Allectus* in *British Numismatic Journal* LIV (1984) 21-40.

Cameron, A. (ed.), *Fifty Years of Prosopography: The Later Roman Empire, Byzantium and Beyond,* (Oxford, 2003)

Cameron, A., *Gratian's Repudiation of the Pontifical Robe* in JRS LVII (1968) 97

Cancik, H. & Schneider, H., (eds.), *Der Neue Pauly: Enzyklopädie der Antike,* Vol. 11 (Stuttgart 2001)   [DNP]

Carroll, M. *Romans Celts & Germans: The German Provinces of Rome* (Stroud 2001)

Charles-Edwards, T. M., *Wales and the Britons 350-1064* (Oxford 2013)

Chausson, F., & Wolff, É, *Consuetudinis Amor:Fragments d'Histoire Romaine (IIe-VIe siècles) Offerts à Jean-Pierre Callu.* In *Saggi di Storia Antica,* 19 (Rome 2003)

Collins, R. *The Arab Conquest of Spain* (Oxford 1989)

Collins, R. *Visigothic Spain,* (Oxford 2004)

Collinson, R., & Breeze, D., Limitanei *and* Comitatenses: *Military Failure at the End of Roman Britain* in Haarer (2014) 61-72

Conant, J. *Staying Roman: Conquest and Identity in Africa and the Mediterranean, 439–700* (Cambridge 2012)

Cornell, T. J., *The Beginnings of Rome: Italy and Rome from the Bronze Age to the Punic Wars* (London 1995)

Dark, K. R., *Civitas to Kingdom: British Political Continuity 300-800* (Leicester 1994)

Dark, K. R., *Britain and the End of the Roman Empire* (Stroud 2000)

Dessau, H., Stein, A., Groag, E., *et. al., Prosopographia Imperii Romani*   [PIR²] 2nd Edn., (Berlin, from 1933-2006)

Di Giuseppe, H., *I Bruttii Praesentes, Proprietari e Produttori in Val D'Agri,* in Russo, A., et al., *Dalla villa dei Bruttii Praesentes alla Proprietà Imperiale. Il Complesso Archeologico di Marsicovetere* Siris 8 (2007) 105-114.

Dill, Sir S., *Roman Society in the Last Century of the Western Empire* (London 1921)

Dill, Sir S., *Roman Society in Gaul in the Merovingian Age* (London 1926)

Dodson, A. & Hilton, D, *The Complete Royal Families of Ancient Egypt* (London 2004)

Drinkwater, J. F., *The Gallic Empire; Separatism and Continuity in the North Western Provinces of the Roman Empire AD260-274* (Stuttgart 1987)

Drinkwater, J & Elton, H. (eds.) *Fifth-Century Gaul: A Crisis of Identity?* (Cambridge 1992)

Drinkwater, J. F., *The Alemanni and Rome 213-496: Caracalla to Clovis* (Oxford 2007)

Eherenberg, V. & Jones, A. H. M., *Documents Illustrating the Reigns of Augustus & Tiberius,* 2nd edn. (Oxford 1955)

Elton, H., *Defence in Fifth Century Gaul* in Drinkwater & Elton (qv., Cambridge 1992).

Everett, A., *Cicero: A Turbulent Life* (London 2001)

Fanning, S., *Emperors and Empires in Fifth Century Gaul,* in Drinkwater & Elton (qv; Cambridge 1992).

Fauber, L. H., *Narses, Hammer of the Goths* (Gloucester 1990)

Fink, R. O., *Lucius Seius Caesar, 'socer Augusti'* in *American Journal of Philology* LX (1939) 329

Freudenberg, K., *Recusatio as Political Theatre: Horace's Letter to Augustus* in *JRS* CIV (2014) 105-132

Gelzer, M. (ed. & trans. Seager, R.), *The Roman Nobility* (Oxford, 1969)

Grant, M., *The Roman Emperors,* (London 1985)

Grant, M., *The Climax of Rome* (London 1993)

Griffin, M. T, *Seneca: A Philosopher in Politics* (Oxford 1976)

Gruen, E. S., *The Last Generation of the Roman Republic* (Berkeley 1995)

Haarer, F. K. (ed.), *AD 410: The History and Archaeology of Late and Post-Roman Britain* (London 2014)

Haegemans, K., *Imperial Authority and Dissent: the Roman Empire in AD235-238* (Leuven 2010)

Haldon, J. F., *Byzantium in the Seventh Century* (Cambridge 1990)

Halswell, G., *Worlds of Arthur: Facts & Fictions of the Dark Ages* (Oxford 2013)

Handley, M. A., *Death, Society and Culture: Inscriptions and Epitaphs in Gaul and Spain,* BAR International 1135 (Oxford 2003)

Harlan, M., *Roman Republican Moneyers and Their Coins 63-49BC* (London 1995)

Harries, J., *Sidonius Apollinaris and the Fall of Rome AD407-485* (Oxford 1994)

Heather, P., *The Fall of the Roman Empire: A New History* (London 2005)

Hekster, O., *Emperors and Ancestors: Roman Rulers and the Constraints of Tradition* (Oxford 2015)

Henderson, J., *Figuring Out Roman Nobility – Juvenal's Eighth Satire* (Exeter, 1997)

Holloway, R. R., *The Archaeology of Early Rome and Latium* (London 1994)

James, E., *The Franks* (Oxford 1988)

Jaques, F., *L'Ordine Senatorio Attraverso la Crisi del III Secolo* , in *Societa Romana e Imperio Tardo-antico* , ed. Giardina, A., (Rome 1986) pp.81-225 & 650-664.

Jones, A. H. M., *The Later Roman Empire: A Social and Economic Survey* 3 Vols. (Oxford 1964).

Jones, A. H. M., Martindale, J R & Morris, J., *Prosopography of the Later Roman Empire*, 3 vols in 4, (Cambridge, 1971, 1980, 1992)   [PLRE]

Jones, B. & Mattingly, D., *An Atlas of Roman Britain* (London 1990)

Kaldellis, A., *The Byzantine Republic: People and Power in New Rome* (Cambridge, Mass. 2015)

Kelly, J. N. D., *The Oxford Dictionary of Popes* (Oxford 1986)

Kennedy, D., *C. Velius Rufus* in *Britannia* XIV (1983) 183-196

Kent, J. P. C., *The Revolt of Trier against Magnentius* in *Numismatic Chronicle* 9 (1959) 105-108

Kienast, D., W Eck & M Heil, *Römische Kaisertabelle. Grundzüge einer Romischen Kaiserchronologie* (Darmstadt 2017)

Kiilerich, B., *Visual Dynamics: Reflections on Late Antique Images* (Bergen 2015)

Kirk, M, with Kelley, D. H., Mommaerts, T. S. & Stone, D. *Reply to note by Settipani, C.,* (New Jersey 2001).

Knight, J .K., *The End of Antiquity: Archaeology, Society and Religion AD 235-700* (Stroud 2007)

Kulikowski, M., *The Career of the Comes Hispaniarum Asterius* in *Phoenix* 54 (2000) 123ff.

Lancon, B., *Rome in Late Antiquity* Trans. Antonia Nevill (Edinburgh 2000)

Lewis, M. W. H., *The Official Priests at Rome under the Julio-Claudians* Papers and Monographs of the American Academy in Rome XVI (Rome 1955)

Livermore, H. V., *The Origins of Spain and Portugal* (London 1971)

Llewellyn, P., *Rome in the Dark Ages* (London 1993)

MacGeorge, P., *Late Roman Warlords* (Oxford 2002)

MacKenzie, A., *Archaeology in Roumania: The Mystery of the Roman Occupation* (London, 1986)

Mabbott, T. O., *A newly found coin of Bonosus* in *The Numismatist* LXVIII (Oct. 1955).

Madsen, J. M., *Eager to be Greek: Response to Roman Rule in Pontus and Bithynia* (London & New York 2009)

Martin, Peter, *The Chrysanthemum Throne: A History of the Emperors of Japan* (Stroud 1997)

Mathisen, R. W., *Roman Aristocracies in Barbarian Gaul: Strategies for Survival in an Age of Transition* (Austin, Texas, 1993)

Mathisen, R. W. *Ruricius of Limoges and Friends: A Collection of Letters from Visigothic Gaul.* (Liverpool 1999)

Mathisen, R. W. & Shanzer, D., *Society and Culture in Late Roman Gaul: Revisiting the Sources* (Aldershot 2001)

Mathisen, R. W., *'Qui genus, unde patres?': The Case of Arcadius Placidus Magnus Felix* in *Medieval Prosopography* 24 (2003) 55-71.

Matthews, J., *Continuity in a Roman Family: The Rufii Festi of Volsinii* in *Historia* 16 (1967) 484-509

Matthews, J., *Western Aristocracies and the Imperial Court* (Oxford, 1975)

Mattingly H. & Sydenham, E. A., et al., *Roman Imperial Coinage* 10 vols. in 11 (London 1923-1933, reprinted 1965-1994)   [RIC]

McEvoy, M. A., *Child Emperor Rule in the late Roman West AD367-455* (Oxford 2013)

Mennen, I., *Power and Status in the Roman Empire AD193-294* (Leiden & Boston 2011)

Millar, F., *Paul of Samosata, Zenobia and Aurelian* in JRS LXI (1971) 16ff.

Mitchell, R. E., *Patricians and Plebeians: The Origin of the Roman State* (Ithaca 1990)

Moorhead, J., *Theoderic in Italy* (Oxford 1992)

Morris, J., *Munatius Plancus Paulinus* in *Bonner Jahrbucher* 165 (1965) 89-96.

Morris, J., *The Age of Arthur* (London 1973)

Morris, J., *Arthurian Period Sources* vol. V *Genealogies & Texts* (Chichester 1995a)

Morris, J., *Arthurian Period Sources* vol. VI, *Studies in Dark Age History* (Chichester 1995b)

Münzer, F., *Roman Aristocratic Parties and Families* (Stuttgart, 1920, new and rev. edn., trans. Ridley, T., Baltimore, 1999)

Musset, L., *The Germanic Invasions: The making of Europe 400-600AD* (New York 1965)

Norwich, J. J., Viscount, *Byzantium: The Early Centuries* (London 1989)

Novak, D., *Anicianae Domus Culmen Nobilitatis Culmen* in *Clio* 62 (1980) 473-494

Ooteghem, J. van, *Les Caecilii Metelli de la République* (Brussels 1967).

Patterson, J. R., *The City of Rome Revisited: from Mid-Republic to Mid-Empire* in JRS C (2010) 210-232.

Pearce, S., *The Kingdom of Dumnonia* (Padstow 1978)

Pettinger, A., *The Republic in Danger* (Oxford 2012)

Pflaum, H. G., *Deux Familles Sénatoriales des IIᵉ et IIIᵉ Siècles* in *Journal des Savants I (1962) 106-121*

Pomeroy, S. B., *The Murder of Regilla: A Case of Domestic Violence in Antiquity* (Cambridge, Mass. 2007)

Potter, D. S., *The Roman Empire at Bay AD180-395* (London 2004)

Rajak, T., *Josephus: the Historian and his Society* (London 1983)

Rohl, D. M., *The Lords of Avaris* (London 2007)

Roller, D. W., *The World of Juba II & Kleopatra Selene : Royal Scholarship on Rome's African Frontier* (London 2003)

Rufino, A. C., *Los Senadores Hispanorromanos y la Romanización de Hispania* 2 Vols. (Seville 1990)

Rüpke, J. & Glock, A., Trans. Richardson, D. M. B., *Fasti Sacerdotum*   [FS] (Oxford 2008)

Russell, M., *Arthur and the Kings of Britain* (Stroud 2017)

Salway, B., *What's in a Name? A Survey of Roman Onomastic Practice from c 700BC to AD700* in JRS LXXXIV (1994) 124-145.

Scott, R., *Byzantine Chronicles & the Sixth Century* (Farnham 2012)

Seaby, H. A. et al., *Roman Silver Coins, arranged according to Cohen,* 5 Vols (London 1952-1978)

Settipani, C., *Les Ancêtres de Charlemagne* (Paris 1989)

Settipani, C., *Les Ancêtres de Charlemagne : Addenda et Corrigenda* in *Histoire et Genealogie* 28, 19-36.

Settipani, C., *Continuité Gentilice et Continuité Senatoriale dans les Familles Senatoriales Romaines a L'époque Imperiale : Mythe et Réalité* (Oxford 2000)

Sherwin-White, A. N., *The Roman Citizenship* (Oxford 1973)

Shiel, N., *Carausius et Fratres Sui* in *British Numismatical Journal* XLVIII (1978) 7-11.

Sims-Williams, P., *The Submission of Irish Kings in Fact and Fiction: Henry II, Bendigeidfran, and the dating of the* Four Branches of the *Mabinogi,* in *Cambridge Medieval Celtic Studies,* 22 (12/1991) 31–61.

Spann, P. O., *Quintus Sertorius and the Legacy of Sulla* (Fayetteville, 1987)

Stech, B., *Senatores Romani qui Fuerint inde a Vespasiano usque ad Traiani Exitum* in *Klio* X (1912)

Swift, E., *The End of the Western Roman Empire: An Archaeological Investigation* (Stroud 2000)

Sydenham, E.A. *The Coinage of the Roman Republic* revised Haines, G. C., ed. Forrer, L. & Hersh, C. A. (London 1952)

Syme, Sir R., *The Roman Revolution* (Oxford 1939)   [Syme RR]

Syme. Sir R., *Personal Names in Annals I-VI* in *JRS* XXXIX (1949) 9

Syme, Sir R., *Marcus Lepidus: Capax Imperii* in JRS XLV (1955) 22-33

Syme, Sir R., *Antonine Relatives: Ceionii and Vettuleni* in *Athenaeum* 33 (1957) 306-315

Syme, Sir R., *Tacitus* 2 Vols., (Oxford 1958)

Syme, Sir R., *Ammianus and the Historia Augusta* (Oxford, 1968)

Syme, Sir R., *Ten Studies in Tacitus* (Oxford 1970)

Syme, Sir R., *Domitius Corbulo* in JRS LX (1970) 34-39

Syme, Sir R., *Emperors and Biography: Studies in the* Historia Augusta (Oxford 1971)

Syme, Sir R., *The Crisis of 2BC* (Munich 1974)

Syme, Sir R., *History in Ovid,*(Oxford 1978)

Syme, Sir R., *Roman Papers, III,* Ed. Birley, A. R. (Oxford 1984)   [Syme RP III]

Syme, Sir R., *Roman Papers IV,* Ed. Birley, A. R. (Oxford 1985)   [Syme RP IV]

Syme, Sir R., *Roman Papers, VI,* Ed. Birley, A. R. (Oxford 1991)   [Syme RP VI]

Syme, Sir R., *Roman Papers, VII,* Ed., Birley, A. R. (Oxford 1991)   [Syme RP VII]

Syme, Sir R., *The Augustan Aristocracy* (Oxford 1989)   [Syme AA]

Taylor, L. R., *The Voting Districts of the Roman Republic* Papers and Monographs of the American Academy in Rome XVI (Rome 1960).

Taylor, N. L., *Roman Genealogical Continuity and the 'Descents from Antiquity' Question* (review of Settipani (2000)) in *American Genealogist* 76 (April 2001) 129-136

Thomas, A. C., *And Shall these Mute Stones Speak?* (Cardiff 1994)

Thomas, B., *Laterculi Praesidum,* 3 Vols. (Gothenburg 1972-74)

Thompson, E. A., *The Visigoths in Spain* (Oxford 1969)

Thompson, E. A., *Romans and Barbarians: The Decline of the Western Empire.* (Madison, Wn 1982)

Toumanoff, Prince C. L. H., *Studies in Christian Caucasian History* (Georgetown 1963)

Townend, G., *Some Flavian Connections* in *Journal of Roman Studies* LI (1961)

Wagner, Sir A., *Pedigree and Progress* (London 1975)

Ward, J. H., *Vortigern and the end of Roman Britain* in *Britannia* 3 (1972) 277-289,

Webster, G., *The Roman Imperial Army* (London, 1969)

Webster, G., *The Cornovii* (rev. edn., Stroud 1991)

Weinand, J (ed.), *Contested Monarchy: Integrating the Roman Empire in the Fourth Century AD* (Oxford 2015)

Whitaker, C., *Frontiers of the Roman Empire: A Social and Economic Study* (Baltimore 1994)

Whitby, M., *The Emperor Maurice and his Historian: Theophylact Simocatta on Persian and Balkan Wars* (Oxford 1998)

Williams, S. & Friell, G., *The Rome that did not Fall: The Survival of the East in the Fifth Century* (London 1999)

Wiseman, T. P., *Some Republican Senators and Their Tribes* in *Classical Quarterly* (1964) 130-131.

Wiseman, T. P., *Pulcher Claudius* in HSCP (1970) 207-221.

Wiseman, T. P., *New Men in the Roman Senate* (London 1971)

Wiseman, T. P., *Cinna the Poet and other Roman Essays* (Leicester 1974)

Wiseman, T. P., *The Myths of Rome* (Exeter, 2004)

Wiseman, T. P., *Unwritten Rome* (Exeter 2008)

Wood, I., *The Merovingian Kingdoms* (London 1994)

Imperial Biographies

Alföldi, A., *The Conversion of Constantine and Pagan Rome* Trans. Mattingly, H. (Oxford 1948)

Arrizabalaga y Prado, L. de, *The Emperor Elagabalus: Fact or Fiction?* (Cambridge 2010)

Astarita. M. L., *Avidio Cassio* (Rome 1983)

Barrett, A. A., *Caligula: the Corruption of Power* (London 1989)

Birley, A. R., *Marcus Aurelius: A Biography* (London 1987)

Birley, A. R., *The African Emperor: Septimius Severus* (London 1988)

Birley, A. R., *Hadrian, The Restless Emperor* (London 1997)

Bishop, M. C., *Lucius Verus and the Roman Defence of the East* (Bradford 2018)

Cameron, A., *The House of Anastasius* in *Greek, Roman and Byzantine Studies* Vol. 19 (1978) 259-276.

Casey, P. J., *Carausius & Allectus: The British Usurpers* (London 1994)

Crawford, P., *Roman Emperor Zeno* (Barnsley 2019)

Drinkwater, J. F., *The Usurpers Constantine III (407-411) and Jovinus (411-413)* in *Britannia* 29 (1998) 269-298

Goldsworthy, A, *Caesar: The Life of a Colossus* (London 2006)

Grant, M., *The Antonines* (London 1994)

Hartley, E., Hawkes, J., Henig, M. & Mee, F., *Constantine the Great, York's Roman Emperor,* York Museum Exhibition Catalogue, (York, 2006)

Holland, R., *Nero, The Man Behind the Myth,* (Stroud 2000)

Jones, B. W., *The Emperor Titus* (London 1984)

Jones, B. W., *The Emperor Domitian* (London 1992)

Kokkinos, N., *Antonia Augusta* (London, 1992)

Körner, C., *Philippus Arabs* (Berlin 2001)

Leadbetter, W. L., *Galerius and the Will of Diocletian* (London 2009)

Levick, B., *Claudius* (London 1990)

Levick, B., *Vespasian* (London 1999).

McHugh, J. S., *Emperor Alexander Severus:Rome's Age of Insurrection AD222-235* (Barnsley 2017)

Morgan, G., *69AD: the Year of the Four Emperors* (Oxford 2006)

Murdoch, A., *The Last Pagan: Julian the Apostate and the Death of the Ancient World* (Stroud 2003)

Murdoch, A., *The Last Roman, Romulus Augustulus and the Decline of the West,* (Stroud, 2006)

Opper, T., *Hadrian, Empire and Conflict,* British Museum Exhibition Catalogue, (London 2008)

Peacock, P. B., *Usurpers under Elagabalus* (Washington 2000)

Pohlsander, H. A., *The Emperor Constantine* (London 1996)

Seager, R., *Tiberius* (London 1972)

Shiel, N., *The Episode of Carausius & Allectus* BAR 40 (Oxford 1977)

Shlosser, F. E., *The Reign of the Emperor Maurikios (582–602): a Reassessment,* Athens (1994)

Sivan, H., *Ausonius of Bordeaux: Genesis of a Gallic Aristocracy* (London 1993)

Southern, P., *Mark Antony* (Stroud 1998)

Southern, P., *Augustus* (London 1998)

Southern, P., *Empress Zenobia: Palmyra's Rebel Queen* (London 2008)

Syvänne, I., *The Reign of Emperor Gallienus: The Apogee of Roman Cavalry* (Barnsley 2019)

Turton, G., *The Syrian Princesses* (London 1974)

Weigel, R. D., *Lepidus, The Tarnished Triumvir* (London & New York, 1992)

White, J. F., *Restorer of the World: the Roman Emperor Aurelian* (Staplehurst 2005)

Williams, S. & Friell, G., *Theodosius, The Empire at Bay* (London 1994)

*